*The Home Front*

The Cresset Library

The Best Circles
*Leonore Davidoff*

Britain by Mass-Observation
*Arranged and written by Tom Harrisson and Charles Madge*

Byron: A Portrait
*Leslie A. Marchand*

China: A Short Cultural History
*C. P. Fitzgerald*

A Farmer's Year
*H. Rider Haggard*

The Home Front
*E. Sylvia Pankhurst*

Ishi in Two Worlds
*Theodora Kroeber*

Japan: A Short Cultural History
*G. B. Sansom*

From Ploughtail to Parliament: An autobiography
*Joseph Arch*

The Making of the Middle Ages
*R. W. Southern*

The Pub and the People
*Mass-Observation*

A Short History of Ireland
*J. C. Beckett*

It Takes a Thief: The life and times of Jonathan Wild
*Gerald Howson*

Wittgenstein
*W. W. Bartley III*

Cover: *The Food Queue* 1918 by Joseph Southall
Reproduced by courtesy of Oldham Art Gallery

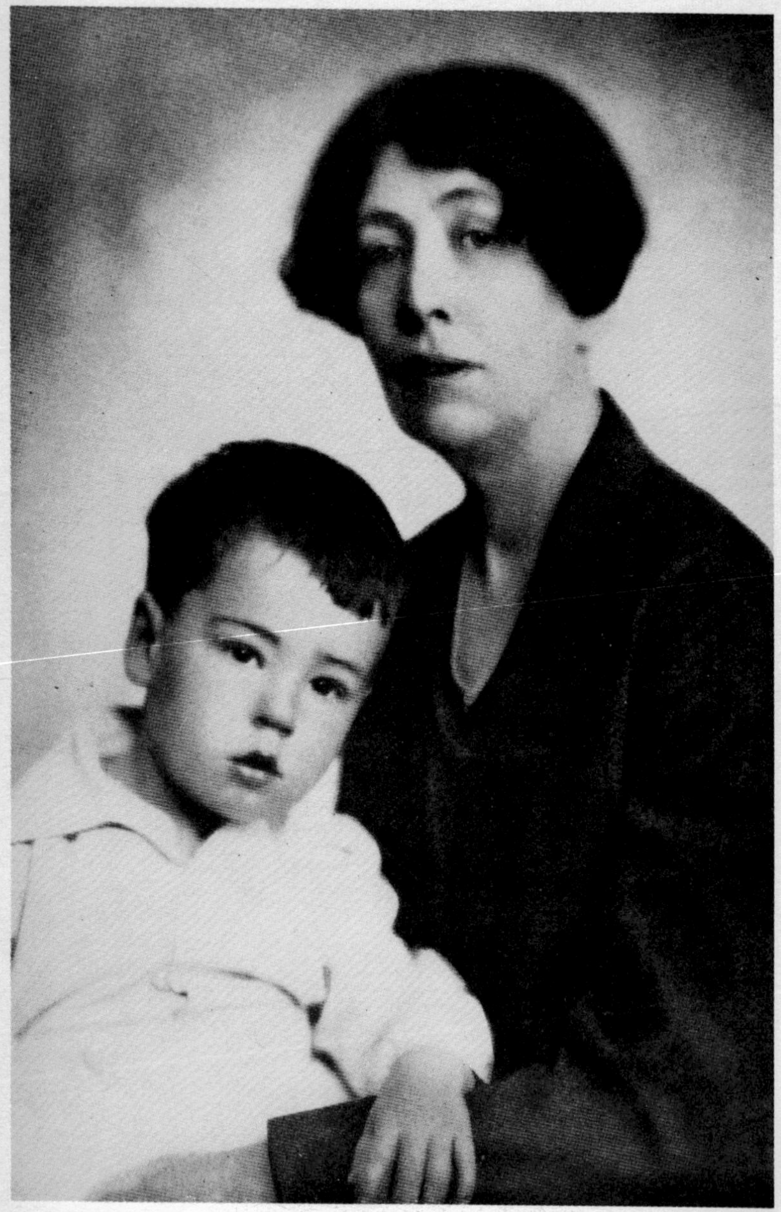

*Cigarini, London*

SYLVIA PANKHURST AND HER SON RICHARD

# THE HOME FRONT

## A MIRROR TO LIFE IN ENGLAND DURING THE FIRST WORLD WAR

*E. Sylvia Pankhurst*

Foreword by The Rt Hon. Mrs Shirley Williams
Introduction by Richard Pankhurst

THE CRESSET LIBRARY

London Melbourne Sydney Auckland Johannesburg

The Cresset Library

An imprint of Century Hutchinson Ltd

62–65 Chandos Place, London WC2N 4NW

Century Hutchinson Australia Pty Ltd
PO Box 496, 16–22 Church Street, Hawthorn,
Victoria 3122, Australia

Century Hutchinson New Zealand Ltd
PO Box 40–086, Glenfield, Auckland 10,
New Zealand

Century Hutchinson South Africa (Pty) Ltd
PO Box 337, Bergvlei 2012, South Africa

First published 1932



Made and printed in Great Britain by
Richard Clay, Bungay, Suffolk

ISBN 0 09 172911 4

TO

EMMELINE PETHICK LAWRENCE

WHOSE GENEROUS APPRECIATION ENCOURAGED
THE PENNING OF THIS RECORD

Herein is told the story of my life and time during the War years 1914, 1915, 1916.

# Contents

## CONTENTS

# *List of Illustrations*

## LIST OF ILLUSTRATIONS

# *Foreword to the Cresset Library edition*

There were two home fronts in First World War Britain, and they were very different. The home front of middle-class England suffered the worries and anxieties of all those whose husbands, brothers and sons were at the fighting front, though little information seeped back to them about the horrors of trench warfare until late in the war, by which time the early mood of idealism and excitement had soured. Their way of life, its luxuries and privileges, had changed little. Middle-class women complained about shortages and servants, and read with apprehension reports of Zeppelin raids on coastal towns. Those of their husbands who were too old to go to war, saw business activity surge and profits multiply, as home-produced goods replaced those from overseas. Only the drift of War Office telegrams, soon to become a blizzard, each one announcing a man dead or missing in action, recalled to them the holocaust of a generation across the narrow Channel.

The other home front ran through the dingy terraces of working-class Britain, where huge families of six or eight children lived in cramped houses with outside lavatories, gas lighting and a coldwater tap for washing everything from clothes to bodies. For them the war meant the loss of the breadwinners, long and often futile battles to get the pathetically small separation allowances for dependent wives and children, hunger and sometimes eviction for lack of money to pay the rent. As the war rolled on, devouring more and more soldiers, women's labour became indispensable. From this second home front, women in their thousands were recruited into munitions factories, to work for a pittance filling shells and fashioning bullets, often handling poisonous or dangerous chemicals. Sylvia Pankhurst's account of the second home front describes a society of such brutish class division, so callous in the administration of its own partial and biassed laws, that one is amazed not only that we today share with it the same country, but that we also share with it the same century. The 'sure advance of progress' to which Sylvia Pankhurst, the author of *The Home Front*, so passionately clung, has proved hollow. The destruction of Kampuchea or of Beirut match the destruction of Flanders. But at least in Western Europe, the grinding, terrible poverty of the First World War and its aftermath has disappeared, thanks to higher wages and the welfare state. Hardship and the misery of long-term unemployment remain, however, for men and women forget quickly the social evils they have overcome, and allow them to recur.

Sylvia Pankhurst was a remarkable woman, Suffragette, Pacifist and

Socialist, her fortitude and determination were formidable indeed. As a suffragette, she suffered repeated imprisonment, forcing the authorities to release her by hunger and thirst strikes or by walking around her cell until she fell to the floor from exhaustion. Attempts at forcible feeding were rendered useless when she learned how to make herself vomit up the food forced down her throat. From these ordeals she emerged strong enough to cope with hundreds of calls on her time and energy while simultaneously organizing a nursery, a toy factory, a nonprofit cheap restaurant and speaking for the many causes in which she believed. She led deputations to cabinet ministers, to Parliament, to anyone who might bring redress to the misery around her. She ate the sour bread of broken promises. She served on many committees, especially for the relief of poverty, and learned that men played political games even on the edge of the precipice. She was let down, betrayed, and not least saddened by the rift in her own family when her mother, Emmeline, and her sister, Christabel, once fellow warriors in the cause of women's suffrage, channelled their own passions into virulent and jingoistic support for the war. Yet nothing broke her. All through the war, the fire in her burned strongly. She was kept going by the hope of a better future, as well as by the devotion and loyalty of her friends and fellow-workers in the East End. Encountering their instinctive sympathy for 'gallant little Belgium', Sylvia Pankhurst longed to convey her own view that the war was the result of capitalist powers seeking advantage over one another, and finding new ones to exploit. It was not about principles at all. But she hesitated: 'to show them that the rivalry of the Governments to secure preferential opportunities for their Nationals was the vast master-cause of the war', she wrote, 'was to thrust on them a vision of human society, ruthless and without scruple as the grip of the boa-constrictor on the lamb'. She cherished a different vision: '. . . today's haphazard production of commodities, turned out without measure to compete for buyers in the world market, is destined to be outlived by advancing humanity; to become the horrified amazement of the historian, when a cooperative social system has made possible a general spirit of fraternity unknown today'. It is a sad irony that Sylvia Pankhurst, who acclaimed the Bolshevik revolution of 1917 as the harbinger of that new system, died in the very year that Khrushchev denounced the atrocities of his notorious predecessor, Stalin.

The painful breach with her family was buried in work to assuage the misery of her neighbours. Much of *The Home Front* is taken up with her account of their lives and deaths. On page after page we read of women trying to feed half a dozen children on a pound a week or less; children crying with hunger and suffering from the illnesses of malnutrition; women working at sewing shirts and uniforms until an hour or so before their confinement or their early death in dark little hovels without food or warmth. Her door reverberates with the knocking of desperate mothers trying to keep their last surviving son from the long reach of the recruiting officer, or pleading for a pension to keep a broken, mutilated ex-soldier husband. Their desperation matches the desolation of the trenches, the mud, the rats, the grim hopelessness that made men welcome the loss of a limb so they might decently escape.

Sylvia Pankhurst was not the kind of woman to bear all this with patience and resignation. Time and again she assaulted the citadels of the Establishment, which had its own grudging admiration for her. In the summer of 1915, she accompanied George Lansbury and Mrs Drake to the Home Secretary Mr McKenna to plead for price controls over necessities like flour and corn, and to tell him of the privations ordinary people were suffering as prices rose while wages were held down by regulation. 'The war must be paid for', he told them, but when they pressed for higher taxation on large incomes, McKenna responded: 'rich people have their commitments; they would be miserable if their incomes were greatly reduced'. They left empty-handed. Yet as they left, McKenna stretched out his hand to Sylvia Pankhurst. 'I must shake hands with you', he said, 'you are the pluckiest girl I ever knew.' McKenna did indeed know. He was, of course, author of the Cat and Mouse policy under which suffragettes were released from prison if they refused food, only to be rearrested as soon as their health recovered.

The heartlessness of the British governing classes, if the accounts in *The Home Front* are accurate, beggar belief. Separation allowances for soldiers' families went for months unpaid. Babies conceived out of wedlock, even if parents wed before they were born, were not entitled to any allowance at all. If men or women sought to supplement their wretched pensions or allowances with a few shillings from work, the pension was immediately stopped or reduced. Soldiers' letters sent in non-regulation envelopes were destroyed, although some regiments had not received the regulation envelopes. In some instances, these were the last letter written before the soldier's death on the battlefield.

Discipline was ruthlessly maintained. Under the Registration Act, everyone had to register. Civilians working on essential jobs like munitions or shipbuilding were tied to their jobs, and could not leave without their employer's permission. Wages were determined by the minister, and strikes were illegal. Those who did dare to strike often found themselves sent to the front as a penalty. Conditions were unspeakable. Men and women worked in factories for eighty or ninety hours a week. Minimum wages, especially for women were often disregarded, yet few employers were punished. Sylvia Pankhurst cites case after case: one that sticks in the mind was a woman who worked from 8 a.m. to 8 p.m. five days a week, from 8 a.m. to 5 p.m. on Saturdays and from 8 a.m. to 6 p.m. on Sundays. She spent two hours a day travelling, and earned 2¼ pence an hour. The First World War had brought back industrial serfdom.

Discipline was enforced with equal rigidity among the military. Soldiers and sailors were punished for minor misdemeanours, like being a few minutes late for roll call, by the most condign punishments. They were shackled for hours to guns or carts, sometimes while bombardments were going on. They were suspended on crucifixes or hung by the wrists, and, near death from exhaustion, flung into compounds surrounded by barbed wire to spend the night without bed or bedding. One young soldier, in between long stints of digging with pick and shovel, had to quick march carrying 95 pounds of stones around his camp. Conscientious objectors fared even worse, sometimes standing for days up to their waists in cold water and sewage, while being threatened with a firing squad next morning.

The rulers of Britain seemed to know little about what was being done, and to care less. Ministers would neither confirm nor deny allegations of brutality against soldiers at the front. Soldiers were under orders not to communicate with Members of Parliament. It is certain that thousands were tortured or shot for everything from desertion to minor breaches of orders. Parliament itself was ineffective, though the House of Lords showed a greater willingness to criticize and amend legislation than did the compliant House of Commons. The Defence of the Realm Acts, and their predecessor, the Official Secrets Act, massacred many rights and traditional liberties without objection from the representatives of the people.

After the obscene slaughter of the Somme, in which 600,000 Allied soldiers died, voices were raised for peace negotiations, including that of the Pope; a peace initiative was undertaken by Colonel House on behalf of the American President, Woodrow Wilson. Wilson expected the proposal to be rejected out of hand by the Central Powers, Austria and Germany. But in December 1916, they proposed a peace negotiation, and were supported by the President. It was the Entente of Britain, France and Russia that rejected any such idea. Lloyd George, after a visit to the front which he described as 'the door of hell', went on to say that the war was not nearing its end. Peace was being demanded by those who supported Germany. The war had to prosecuted to the end. That end was to be nearly two years and many hundreds of thousands of deaths away.

It is impossible to read *The Home Front* without being awed by the extraordinary patience and stoicism of the British people, and particularly of the English. The Clyde workers did, after all, organize and fight against the more extreme regulations of the Munitions Act. The Welsh miners on more than one occasion used the strike weapon to protect their fellows from victimization. Both realized the power their key industrial roles gave them. But the English working people rarely fought for their rights, or protested against the extreme injustices meted out to them. After the war, when revolution swept like a forest fire through the European continent, the English settled for an extension of the franchise and, in 1924, for a minority Labour government. The two decades between the wars brought little relief. Unemployment reached 25 per cent and more in the old industrial areas. The dole provided little enough to live on. In 1939, a new war claimed the sons of the First World War veterans. Many of the recruits sucked into the Second World War had to be rejected, so stunted were they physically by the privations they had suffered in their childhood.

In retrospect, the two World Wars of this bloodstained century look like two acts in a European civil war, a modern Thirty Years War. Certainly some lessons were learned. In the Second World War, soldiers' lives were not wasted so cavalierly. Generals sought to save their men from destruction. It was the civilians whose lives were cheap, and who died in their tens of thousands in fire raids and in the saturation bombing of cities. Air raids were not respecters of social classes. In the second war, most women, including those from the middle classes, were involved in some kind of war work. Evacuation of children and general mobilization broke down social barriers. Free milk and orange juice were provided for children and mothers, emergency food kitchens were organized, and rationing was introduced very early in the war. The coalition government made common cause in constructing an efficient and reasonably humane civil administration, in which Labour politicians, some of them powerful trade unionists like Ernest Bevin, were involved from 1940 on. The foundation of the postwar welfare state was laid down, and a consensus was established in the 1944 Education Act. As so often happens in English history, the rulers reformed themselves just in time.

But the seeds of bitterness had been sown. We in this generation know its sour harvest. After reading *The Home Front*, the persistence in Britain of class antagonism and suspicion in industrial relations become easier to understand. So does the hatred that feeds the IRA, for it was engendered by the 1916 Easter rising, when hundreds of innocent Irish men and boys were shot out of hand and Yeats's 'terrible beauty was born'.

*The Home Front* leaves me awed and appalled at the suffering my fellow citizens so uncomplainingly bore in the first half of this century, a suffering that constrained their expectations had crushed their aspirations. The burden of our history still weighs heavily upon us.

The Rt Hon. Mrs Shirley Williams
*1987*

# *Introduction to the Cresset Library edition*

My mother, Estelle Sylvia Pankhurst, was born in Manchester in 1882. Her father, and lifetime hero, Dr Richard Pankhurst, was a Radical lawyer and advocate of women's rights who joined the Independent Labour Party – the ILP – in 1894, and stood, unsuccessfully, as one of its parliamentary candidates. Her mother, Emmeline née Goulden, who also came from a Radical family, followed him into the ILP. After his death in 1898 she devoted herself to political and social affairs. She founded a Women's Labour Representation Committee in 1903, but, finding the name already appropriated, changed it to the Women's Social and Political Union, soon better known as the WSPU.

Sylvia, who was sixteen years old at the time of her father's death, attended Manchester High School, but, showing artistic interests at an early age, moved to the Manchester School of Art where she won a travelling scholarship, and chose to go to Venice to study its mosaics. On returning to England in 1903 she obtained a scholarship to attend the Royal College of Art in London.

Though passionately interested in art she was soon drawn into the struggle for Votes for Women. The WSPU, seeing almost three decades of constitutional effort to obtain women's enfranchisement had produced no tangible result, embarked in 1905 on a policy of greater militancy. My mother, still a student, that year had her first brush with Winston Churchill, then a Liberal candidate whom she heckled for opposing the extension of the franchise to women. Towards the end of the following year she was subjected to the first of her many spells of imprisonment – and drew a series of prison sketches which were published in the *Pall Mall Magazine* and the WSPU newspaper *Votes for Women*.

After assisting her mother in transferring the hitherto Manchester-based movement to London, she travelled to the north of England in 1907 to canvass for the women's movement, as well as to study the life of working people, then grievously exploited in industry and agriculture, and to record – and sketch – their lives and the grim surroundings in which they dwelt.

Her artistic activities were now increasingly devoted to the women's cause, and included the design of emblems for banners, membership cards, and calendars. She also produced the murals for the great Women's Exhibition of 1909.*

---

* Reproductions of her work appear in my book *Sylvia Pankhurst, Artist and Crusader*, New York and London, 1979.

Notwithstanding her active participation in the movement she was reluctant to subscribe to the use of violence – including arson – favoured by both her mother and her older sister Christabel, who to avoid arrest had fled to Paris to lead the movement from afar. Sylvia was not convinced that women's emancipation could be achieved by such means. She believed that the movement 'required, not more serious militancy by the few, but a stronger appeal to the great masses'. With this end in view she wrote her first book *The Suffragette: The History of the Women's Militant Suffragette Movement 1905–1910*, which she completed while on a lecture tour of the United States. It was published in 1911.

As a result of the upsurge of Suffragette activity she decided to devote herself entirely to the women's struggle, and, as she then thought, temporarily to abandon her art. Believing that the Suffragette movement, despite its Socialist origins, was then too 'middle class', she decided to extend it to the East End of London. She did this partly because she felt that the taunt that the Suffragettes wanted only a 'Vote for Ladies' was beginning to be accepted in working-class circles, but also because she believed that the birth of a militant movement among the under-privileged would help 'to fortify the position of the working women' when the vote was won. Elaborating on this she later wrote:

> I was looking to the future; I wanted to rouse these women of the submerged mass to be, not merely the argument of more fortunate people, but to be fighters on their own account, despising mere platitudes and catch-cries, revolting against the hideous conditions about them, and demanding for themselves and their families a full share in the benefits of civilisation and progress.

Filled with such aspirations she walked down the Bow Road in 1912 in search of offices. Finding an empty building she rented it, mounted a ladder and wrote in gilt letters the words 'VOTES FOR WOMEN'. The women of the East End soon flocked to her meetings, and on 14 January 1913 she took a delegation of working women to Whitehall to plead their case before two Liberal cabinet ministers, Sir Edward Grey and Lloyd George.

It was shortly after this that my mother was first forcibly fed. Arrested with five other women and incarcerated in Holloway prison she went immediately on a hunger and thirst strike. For the first two days, as she recalls in her semi-autobiographical work *The Suffragette Movement*, the prison authorities tried to tempt her by offering her food such as was never normally seen at Holloway. This stratagem failing, on the third day six wardresses flung her on her back, and held her firmly down. Her mouth was then forced open, a steel instrument thrust into it and a screw turned to prise open her jaws, whereupon a feeding tube was pushed down her throat. The operation failed, however, for she vomited as soon as the contraption was removed. She was left gasping for breath and sobbing convulsively.

This routine continued daily. Though suffering from almost continuous headache, she discovered that by putting her hand into her mouth that she could make herself vomit, and thus frustrate efforts to feed her. After some days the flesh around her eyes became increasingly painful. She shrunk from the light – and noticed that the prison officers began to stare at her.

Impatient at her continued detention she decided on an entirely new tactic: the sleep and rest strike. She began walking up and down her cell until she fell, and then got up and continued walking. After twenty-eight hours the Home Office doctor ordered her to be released.

Faced by such resistance on the part of many women of Britain the Liberal – but very illiberal – government introduced the Prisoners' Temporary Discharge for Ill Health Act, nicknamed by the Suffragettes the 'Cat and Mouse Act'. It gave the Home Secretary the power to release hunger strikers to allow them to recover, and then to take them again to prison. The legislation failed to crush the women's movement. My mother, for example, was on several occasions arrested at one public meeting, but able to gain her release in time to speak at the next. In the twelve months beginning June 1913 she carried out no fewer than ten hunger and thirst strikes, in some cases strengthened by sleep strikes.

Early in 1914, though subject to re-arrest under the 'Cat and Mouse' Act, she travelled to Paris to confer with her mother and sister. The latter declared the East End movement too working-class in composition and too democratic in organization to remain within the framework of the WSPU. Criticizing Sylvia, Christabel complained, 'You have your own ideas. We do not want that; we want all our women to take their instructions and walk in step like an army!' Their mother then ordered the East Enders to sever themselves from the WSPU and cease calling themselves Suffragettes. Sylvia and the East End movement refused, however, to abandon the cherished name, and decided to call themselves the East London Federation of the Suffragettes. Having thus gained their autonomy Sylvia founded her first newspaper, *The Woman's Dreadnought*, which appeared on the streets on 14 March 1914.

The Liberal Prime Minister, Herbert Asquith, had for years been arguing that the demand for suffrage reform came only from a handful of women, and not from the masses. Sylvia therefore determined to confront him with a delegation of working women elected at one of her East End rallies. She planned to accompany the deputation, which, she believed, he would almost certainly refuse to see. She was then liable to re-arrest under the 'Cat and Mouse' Act, but determined to continue a hunger and thirst strike, inside or outside prison, until the deputation was received. 'Asquith', she thought, 'might maintain his refusal to the bitter end; he had always been stubborn. In that case I must leave others to carry on the fight. I did not want to die and leave all we hope to do – yet I was willing to die if it might help to ensure the victory'.

She accordingly wrote to the Prime Minister asking him to receive the delegation. When this was, as she anticipated, refused, she replied, recalling that he had 'on many occasions stated that he was unaware of any popular demand for Votes for Women', and declared:

## INTRODUCTION

Do you realise that since I was arrested for a speech to the people who had come in procession from East London to Trafalgar Square, in which I asked them to go to your house in Downing Street to hoot you for your refusal to give votes to women, I have spoken at dozens of immense public meetings when liable to arrest by the police; and in each case the general public, who have come quite freely and without tickets or payment, into the largest halls in those districts, have rallied round me, to a man to a women, to protect me from the police, although they have incurred many hard blows and risked imprisonment in doing so?

Observing that 'a large proportion of the women' of the East End 'living under terrible conditions', were 'impatient to take part in the moulding of the conditions under which they have to live' she continued:

I regard this deputation as of such importance that I have determined, should you refuse to receive the deputation and I be snatched away from the people, as I probably shall be, and taken back to Holloway, my 'Cat and Mouse' licence having expired, I will not merely hunger strike in Holloway, as I have done eight times under this present sentence, but when I am released, I shall continue my strike at the door of the Strangers' Entrance to the House of Commons, and shall not take either food or water until you agree to receive this deputation. I know very well from what has happened in the past that I am risking my life in coming to this conclusion, because, so far, you have almost invariably refused the appeals which suffragists have made to you. At the same time I feel it is my duty to take this course, and I shall not give way, although it may end in my death.

On receipt of this letter Asquith again refused to see the deputation. When she announced this at her next meeting, on 10 June, women burst into tears. A clergyman, Reverend Wills, asked permission to pray. Already enfeebled by earlier hunger and thirst strikes she was carried in procession by a group of supporters, who included the journalist H. W. Nevinson. At a narrow point in the road the police broke into the crowd, and seized her. Once back in Holloway she began her hunger and thirst strike which she continued until 18 June when she was released and taken by the prison wardresses to her home in the Old Ford Road where a crowd of weeping women had already collected. She at once asked her friend Norah Smyth to drive her to the House of Commons. She then crawled to the Strangers' Entrance and lay near Oliver Cromwell's statue. Nevinson recalls:

I stood beside her, very helpless, while she lay on the steps, apparently dying, and the police, perhaps in pity, hesitated to drive her away. At last, to my infinite relief, Keir Hardie came out of the House, and on hearing from me what the situation was, stood with me. George Lansbury joined us and hastened to see Mr Asquith, who consented to receive six working women in two days time.

My mother agreed to accept Asquith's promise, and was lifted in a taxi to drive home – but stopped en route to take her first sip of water for a week.

The Prime Minister's surrender created great excitement. Many people in the crowd laughed with joy, and there were shouts of 'We are winning! We are winning!'

The outbreak of the First World War scarcely over a month later was a great turning point both for the women's movement and for the people of the East

End among whom my mother continued to live and work. She found much to do, for the war brought to the area immense hardship and sorrow. Factories closed down and prices soared. Fathers, husbands and sons, in many cases driven to fight by unemployment and later by conscription, went off to war, leaving their womenfolk with only the most meagre separation allowances which were slow to arrive – and often callously withheld for bureaucratic reasons. Mothers, she recalls, 'came to me with their wasted little ones, and I saw starvation look at me from patient eyes'.

Aided by her newspaper the *Dreadnought* in which she exposed injustices she was soon engaged in a ceaseless battle of wits with authority to wrest from it the social assistance to which she believed the under-privileged were entitled. This necessitated so much correspondence that she was soon employing four shorthand-typists in addition to many voluntary workers. Faced with the mounting distress she also founded cost-price restaurants, as well as a Montessori school and a toy factory to give work to the unemployed.

The conflict, she recalls, resulted in an unparalleled upsurge of war hysteria. There were anti-German riots – fuelled by the popular press – in the East End where even some non-Germans with foreign names were assaulted. Conscientious objectors were in many cases bullied and beaten, and those who hunger-struck were on occasion forcibly fed. The cases were brought to her of five East End Jews in the army who had been executed for cowardice. Intolerance of dissent reached such lengths that Bertrand Russell, because of his support for conscientious objection, was dismissed from Trinity College, Cambridge, and denied a passport to take up an alternative position at Harvard University.

No less serious to her mind was the erosion during the war of welfare legislation – for the protection of factory workers and the prohibition of child employment – for which social reformers had struggled for almost a century. The 'war to end wars', as it was then called, also witnessed the curtailment through the Defence of the Realm Act – the DORA – of some of the country's hitherto most cherished political rights, as exemplified by the suppression of the Clyde workers' newspaper *The Worker*.

In this atmosphere of repression – and intolerance – the government frustrated efforts by internationally-minded women to work for an end to the war, and rejected out of hand the German Peace offer of 1916. This intransigence led to the prolongation of hostilities – and hence to a mounting death toll which included well over half a million casualties in the battle of Passcendaele in 1917 and almost as many in the German spring offensive of 1918.

The war was accompanied by an unparalleled upsurge of chauvinism which to my mother's sorrow engulfed many Suffragettes. Though Emmeline Pankhurst had earlier been a pacifist, and had resigned from the Fabian Society on account of its refusal to oppose the Boer War she gave her full support to the war for 'gallant little Belgium'. The WSPU in 1914 suspended its agitation for Votes for Women, and became one of the most vociferous of the pro-war factions. Its members stuck white feathers in the button-holes of men reluctant to fight, while its leaders accepted government funds to stage rallies in support of the war, and its newspaper, named *Britannia*, attacked the idea of any compromise peace with a vehemence equal to that earlier reserved for Suffragette militancy.

My mother for her part remained a Socialist and a pacifist throughout the war. Keeping faith as she saw it with the ideals of her father – and indeed of her mother in earlier times – she opposed the war which she termed a 'war of iniquity falsely extolled as the war to end war'.* She continued to demand universal suffrage, and urged the trade unions to press for equal pay for women then replacing men in industry. At her war-time meetings she called for two basic resolutions:

I. This meeting calls on the Government to introduce a Bill to enfranchise every man and woman of adult age.
II. This meeting calls on the Government to stop the war.

Sylvia, as she recalls in this book, warmly welcomed the Bolshevik Revolution of 1917. She saw it as a much overdue rebellion against the seemingly interminable war as well as the first effective overthrow of capitalism, with all its evils, and a pioneer attempt at the Socialist transformation of society. Her reactions to the Russian Revolution, her participation in the Socialist – and Communist – movement and her opposition to Allied intervention against the Soviet state, are not, however, described in this volume. They are the subject of another book entitled *In the Red Twilight* which she had virtually completed in 1935 when as an ardent anti-fascist she stopped work on it to defend the cause of Ethiopia, then about to be attacked by Mussolini's Italy.† After her death in Addis Ababa in 1960 I deposited the unpublished manuscript with the International Institute for Social History, in Amsterdam.

*The Home Front*, like her earlier work *The Suffragette Movement*, is partly autobiographical and partly a wider history – in this case of British capitalist society in war-time. An essentially anti-war book – and thus free from the jingoistic propaganda of the time – it is a document of social history which attempts to portray the First World War as it affected the ordinary men and women of the East End whom its author had learnt to love and respect.

Richard Pankhurst
*1987*

---

*She was reinforced in her view of the war when the Soviet government in the aftermath of the Russian Revolution of 1917 published the text of the secret – and highly cynical – correspondence of the Great Powers in the period leading up to the conflict. This correspondence revealed for example how smaller countries such as Italy had been induced to enter 'the war to end war' by offers of territorial aggrandisement at other peoples' expense.

†Though a pacifist until the 1920s she felt that the evil fascism, which she analysed for many years successively in *The Workers' Dreadnaught* and *New Times and Ethiopia News*, could be defeated only by recourse to arms.

# THE HOME FRONT

## CHAPTER I

### GOING TO WAR

HOURLY the War drew nearer; threat followed threat; ultimatum, ultimatum. My mind shrank from the menace sweeping down on us, as children's do from belief in death and misfortune, vainly clinging to the fancy that great disasters only happen to other people. To the last I trusted that somehow the clash would be averted; the madness of world war, our own country drawn into the maelstrom, too hugely inconceivable.

Keir Hardie's heart-wrung warnings of the great catastrophe, his passionate pleading with the workers of all countries to rise up against it; even his talks with me when Haldane's Army Bill[1] was passing through the Commons, full and confidential as they were, had failed to rouse me to the imminence of the tragedy, despite my deep love and respect for him. I had heard him with a sympathy which lacked the acuteness of realisation. For me the strenuous social struggles in which we were engaged at home had obscured even the dim realisation I had of the foreign policies drawing us all into the world conflict. It could not be otherwise. Held as I was in the grip of the "Cat and Mouse Act,"[2] plunging repeatedly into new challenges to the Government, new contests between the police who came to re-arrest me, and the East End people, flocking in their thousands to my defence; repeatedly dragged back again to the prison cell, from which release came only by the painful miseries of the hunger and thirst strike; my horizon was narrowed to the fierce, immediate struggle. On account of that struggle I had seen, during the past twelve months, but little of Keir Hardie, with whom for the nine previous years I had ever been closely in touch.[3] Such knowledge as I had of economics and of politics,

[1] Hardie opposed this Bill stubbornly and bitterly, seeing in it a prelude to war and conscription.

[2] The Prisoners Temporary Discharge for Ill-health Act applied to Suffragette hunger-strikers, who were let out of prison on licence to recover from their privations, then taken back to prison to complete their sentences. (See *The Suffragette Movement*. Longmans Green.)

[3] Not yet had I read my father's speeches of 1870 revealing the huge ambitions and commitments which were now to play their part in making our country a principal in the appalling conflict he then foretold.

and my general attitude towards Life itself, made it impossible for me to regard the possibility of war as other than a supreme calamity. Yet so impervious was I even yet to belief that it might actually come to pass, that instead of rallying our people against the War I was leaving home to go to Ireland. Shocked by the news that a company of soldiers had fired on an unarmed crowd in Dublin,[1] I had decided upon a brief visit there, that I might investigate and publish the facts in my paper,[2] *The Women's Dreadnought*.

In my blind confidence I was not alone. No outcry against the coming war had yet been raised.

As I made my preparations for departure, the members of our Bow branch had gathered for a concert in the ramshackle little meeting hall at the rear of the house, 400 Old Ford Road, which served as a home for Norah Smyth and me and the Paynes, and as central office of the Federation.[3] Only when I came to make a little farewell speech from the platform I said, in a swift flash of intuition, which assailed me as though from an outside source : " Should war be declared I shall return at once."

. . . . . . . .

I passed to the grey city of Dublin, lately so melancholy in decay, now forbidding with hatred of England, displayed in its white heat at sound of every English voice—yet kindly towards me, when folk knew me as one of England's persecuted.

A little round shallow dent in the wall of a house by the Liffey, at Bachelor's Walk, a dent one could think had been scraped by a child with a rusty nail, a cross and the letters R.I.P., roughly drawn in straggling chalk lines, marked the spot where old Mrs. Duffy met her death, when the soldiers fired on a jeering crowd of children flinging bits of banana-peel. Tragic and wellnigh incredible in its cruelty, the event appeared to us then, before the War had dimmed our sense of the value of human life.

I visited the houses of sorrow and anxiety for the victims of that deed : a little boy shot in the back, a girl with her ankle shattered, a good father lying dead in the mortuary, three people killed and thirty wounded by a moment's firing.

" You killed my father ! " the frail girl cried, shaking her slender fist in sobbing anger, as the troops marched by, their flashing bayonets

[1] The Irish Unionists, backed by Conservative support in Britain, had established in Northern Ireland a rebel armed force to oppose the then Home Rule Bill. The supporters of Irish self-government had retaliated by setting up the " National Volunteers." The Ulster Volunteers had landed arms without hindrance. The National Volunteers landed arms at Howth on July 26th. They were intercepted by police and military. As the British soldiers were returning to barracks they fired on a jeering crowd, mainly composed of children, at Bachelor's Walk.

[2] Later *The Workers' Dreadnought*.

[3] The East London Federation of the Suffragettes, later Workers' Suffrage Federation, later Workers' Socialist Federation.

—great murderous ugly knives—gleaming at the end of their long guns; a strange and horrible menace to parade through the quiet streets of civilians on their peaceful rounds and children at their play. I shuddered at thought of those hideous weapons plunged in the shrinking human breast; but even yet I could not conceive of war.

On the morning of August 4th I was at the inquest on the three who were killed. Not half a dozen spectators were present. Public interest had turned from these sad proceedings to the European theatre, for already war had begun between Russia and Germany, Germany and France. In the half-light of the Court the young soldiers, whose guns had been fired, stood in the box to give testimony, their voices cowed to a whisper, weedy and undersized, mere pygmies beside the tall, athletic members of the Irish Constabulary, towering over them. The jury refused to place responsibility upon these lads, directing all blame to the Government, and asserting that the military were illegally on the streets. The verdict passed almost unnoticed—for when we awoke on August 5th we learnt that the great blow had fallen; Britain and Germany were at war!

Stunned by the news, I could not yet realise its full horror. I would take the boat home that night. In the meantime, almost automatically, I followed my previous plan, to attend the morning's sitting of the Dublin City Council. All was confusion there, the members streaming out from the Chamber, blocking the corridors in their talk. Miss Harrison, the one woman Councillor, complained that the roll-call had been taken eight minutes before the time, and the session adjourned for lack of a quorum, in order that resolutions censuring the Government might be shelved. A few of the members took up her protest, but the majority howled them down; three people dead and thirty wounded counted for nothing in the teeth of a great war—an unhappy augury of future ills.

Maud Joachim,[1] who had been my companion in Dublin, set out with me for the boat. The dark streets were densely thronged with people swarming toward the quay. Often our cab was jammed in the press, and before and behind us were many other vehicles thus stayed. On a jaunting car a woman clung to her man, weeping aloud in complete abandon. It was not a pleasant crowd, neither light-hearted, nor earnest with enthusiasm, but irritable and inclined to wrath. Curses flew freely and impatient altercations rose. Occasionally we heard a faint cheer on the outskirts, but sombre gloominess brooded over all. The dense, dark masses of people, surging about the station, seemed like a human sea, beating against our little vehicle. Suddenly, clinging to our cab door, as a drowning man to a spar, appeared a thick-set, strange old man, with weird, wild red-grey locks and spreading beard. Inaudible in the deafening din, by gestures he assumed control of me. I hastily parted from Maud Joachim, as he seized a bag of mine in either hand, and hurling himself among the people, attempted to force a passage for himself and me to the great closed door of the boat station.

[1] Niece of the great violinist and active as a Suffragette.

Thousands of people were struggling for the same objective: men, hideously intoxicated, shouting and cursing; women, stricken with grief, piteously weeping. Women strove with their frail arms to bar men's passage. "Don't let them through! Don't let them through!" they screamed despairing. "Johnny! Johnny! Johnny!" a sad voice wailed. Occasionally the great door was opened for a moment, and the fight around it grew fiercer. Here and there in the press a couple of men wrestled and kicked in vicious anger, flinging each other to the ground. A band of big policemen came hurling themselves upon us with heavy force. "Get back! Get back!" they roared at us. As one of them thrust me aside, I clung to his arm, begging him to let me through that I might reach the boat. He roared: "We cannot help ourselves! The boys are here!" It was a whirlpool of indescribable chaos.

Hours passed. At last, by the pressure of those behind, we were carried past the portal. Within was wild confusion. Dozens of young soldiers in khaki flung themselves, with excited cries, against the great door, to prevent the throng outside from forcing a way in. Hundreds of soldiers were massed about the booking counters. The majority had been drinking, many staggered about helpless. The steps leading to the quay were packed with men struggling upward, thrusting before them, with shouts and imprecations, the more grossly intoxicated; some wellnigh inert, incognisant as oxen; some wildly uproarious, vainly essaying to win downward, glassy-eyed, purple of face, foul-mouthed, with bibulous lips slobbering, hiccupping, vomiting, cursing, stupidly obstinate, viciously desperate—a writhing agglomeration of human folly, of shuddering, horrified reluctance, vainly striving to smother thought.

At the boat-side women gave vent to their sorrow, clinging with uncontrollable misery to departing men, stretching their yearning arms to receding forms. Beside me a young creature flung herself against the cold, grey wall, in a paroxysm of sobs. The decks were crowded; few women among the mass of men; young soldiers in khaki, older Reservists in civilian dress.

At last we were under way. I saw with surprise that the quays and the vessels moored alongside, to the furthest outskirts of the town, were thronged with people waving and cheering, waving and cheering, a very storm of it—a revelation this of the volatile spirit of Dublin, and of the long habit of regarding Ireland as part of Britain, Sinn Fein was striving to destroy.

Our ship's syren screamed and hooted monstrously, and every ship in sight raked the still air with strident echoes, like demon bellowing of the ghouls of war.

On board the men called up to fight maintained, the night through, a noisy revelry; yelling of tuneless choruses, shouting of mirthless laughter, hideous to the sensitive ear, poignantly sorrowful to deeper thought. Vainly I tried to shut out the noise of that sad wassailing, tormented by visions of the drunken faces at the station, seared by the thought that men were going thus to die, without heed to the beauty and purpose of Life, untouched by the cleansing fires of enthusiasm; going like cattle to be slaughtered, mere pawns in the hands of those whose very identity was unknown to them. I thought of the armies marching now along the great main thoroughfares of Europe, everywhere bringing destruction to peaceful homes; of all the multitude called up to fight, each one leaving behind him the desolate grief of women. I saw the countries I had passed through in the spring, Hungary, Austria, Germany, Belgium, France; the scenes, peoples, movements I had visited—bitterly would they suffer under the guns of contending armies! Women struggling for emancipation, Socialists, educationists, libertarians and reformers of every school, each and all had spoken of universal peace. The League of Youth, those gay and radiant beings, who had come to me in Vienna with words of international love and solidarity on their lips, now saw their dreams of freedom shattered and brought to nought. The lads would be pressed as slaves to the hideous work of carnage; the maidens, their fair eyes red with the scalding tears of new bereavement, left to the sad loneliness and loss of their unfruited love. Throughout Europe would be a vast widowhood, the cries of fatherless children, the groans of injured men; a gigantic arrest of human progress; a huge vanquishing of the higher life of culture, and the finer processes of thought; a triumph, sadly immense, of the annihilating power of violence, maintained by great stores of wealth, drawn up from any and every source, and ultimately from the hard toil and harsh privations of the people; beneath all a great hunger, till famine prove the victor. All this I realised in deep anguish, as I clung to my berth, beating the wings of my soul against the granite wall of inevitable fact, longing, with a fervour of torment and yearning inexpressible, that this thing had not been; that somehow I might awake from its intolerable reality, to find it only an evil dream.

The night long, as I grieved there in my solitude, the men called up to war yelled on, in quenchless mirth.

. . . . . . . .

Debarking in the grey dawn, weary and sad, I hastened to the dear, friendly hearts at Old Ford, as a storm-spent bird hies to its nest. Even their close, warm welcome could not assuage the numbed misery of those tragic days.

. . . . . . . .

I sat between Norah Smyth and good Mrs. Payne, the shoemaker, on the sofa in my workroom, repeating my thesis : " This war, like the Boer War and all the others we have known, is fought for material gains. It is not glorious and noble, but a hideous blot on the escutcheon of the European Governments, a huge and shameful loss to humanity."

Norah Smyth wrinkled a puzzled brow. She had taken on the look which always accompanied her oft-used phrase : " I have a dishevelled brain ! "

" If Mrs. Payne and I were France and Germany, and you were Belgium, would you think it right for us to fight out our quarrel on top of you ? " she queried.

" You must look deeper and further into it than that, Smyth, if you want to understand it," I told her.

Mrs. Payne, her work-seamed hand on my knee, affectionate, confiding, reached up her worn, pale face to me, appealing : " You see, Miss Pankhurst, it's like this . . ."

As children unable to comprehend the long words in the story-book, they stared at me, nonplussed ; their minds all dazed and glamoured by the torrents of Press rhetoric, and the atmosphere of excitement and rumour growing apace in every street. I saw in those two questioners the type of millions. How should one rend from their eyes the veil of illusion, how unravel for them the tangled and knotted skein ? Behind the miseries of " Little Belgium " torn by contending armies, unseen by these two beside me, so innocent and so ignorant, was the avid struggle of the governments of the Great Powers for dominance ; the fierce rivalries of their naval and military chiefs ; financiers, company promoters, civil engineers, greedy for concessions ; manufacturers and merchants demanding raw materials on favoured terms, and monopoly of closed markets for their wares ; armament makers eagerly seeking occasion for their hideous products. In the great chaos and tortuous convolutions of this unbodied thing we call Capitalism, wherein too often we are as corks, tossed on the ocean, all this was vague, amorphous. How could one make it plain to those whose untutored minds craved only for curt, net slogans ?

They plied me with simple, foolish questions :

" What would you do if you saw a great strong man killing a baby ? "

" Suppose I pointed a pistol at you ? "

" It was them as started it first : are we to let 'em go on till they've killed everyone ? "

To write on the tablets of their consciousness the truth as I saw it, seemed to exile them to some far-off purgatory, remote from the easy heaven of their desires. They flinched from the huge conception that a perpetual reaching out for new fields of exploitation was inherent to the Capitalist system. To show them that the rivalry of the Governments to secure preferential opportunities for their Nationals was the vast master-cause of the War, was to thrust on them a vision of human Society, ruthless and without scruple as the grip of the boa-constrictor upon the lamb. It was to tear from them the tinsel and the glory, to send their souls shivering and naked into a grey, cold world of disillusion, peopled by harsh and revolting truths. How could I give them back joy and confidence in the teeth of that shattering knowledge? How convey to them, as a living certainty, my own unfaltering belief in a Society, consciously and concertedly providing for the needs of the world's population, estimating it, catering for it, eliminating scarcity, and avoiding glut? How convince them that to-day's haphazard production of commodities, turned out without measure to compete for buyers in the world market, is destined to be outlived by advancing humanity; to become the horrified amazement of the historian, when a co-operative social system has made possible a general spirit of fraternity unknown to-day?

## CHAPTER II

### WAR HARDSHIP DESCENDS UPON THE POOR

A GREAT heaviness overwhelmed me. I saw our members and neighbours, women who loved and trusted me, grief-stricken that their husbands and sons had been torn away to the war, hungrily grasping at every shred of news and every breath of rumour, pathetic in their eagerness to believe the dictum, retailed with every news-sheet, that the war was needed and noble. Who, without quailing, could say to a mother: " Your son is dead; he was sacrificed in a struggle evil and worthless? "

Stout old Mrs. Savoy, the brushmaker, was on her doorstep, a throng of mothers around her. Despite her palpitations and her dropsy she was a leader amongst them, the cheeriest and jolliest woman in many a mile of streets. A young soldier, son of some friend or relative, had sent home his photograph in a daily newspaper, taken as he went riding on a pig, cheered by the laughing lads of his company. Excited, she hailed me, waving the journal with trumpetings of delighted pride, so confident in her pleasure that she did not observe my silence. I flinched from thrusting, so soon, the iron of resentment into the heart of this old friend and all her cronies.

Ruthless economic pressure supplied, with unpitying haste, the teaching my lips were loth to utter. Already before war had been declared, dealers had sent their emissaries to buy up commodities at the small shops, to make a corner in supplies. From day to day prices rose hugely. Reservists were called up, men enlisted, their families left without sustenance; for there were no separation allowances yet. Industry was dislocated, employers shut down their factories in panic, leaving their workers to starve, or enlist; to shift for themselves as best they could. Three hundred thousand people engaged in the manufacture and sale of goods imported by Germany were bereft of employment. The fishing industry was thrown into chaos. The weavers and spinners of Lancashire and Yorkshire were working short time. All sorts of clothing manufacture was brought to a standstill. The export of many foodstuffs was prohibited. The purchasing power of large sections of the people had dwindled to zero. To be workless then meant literal starvation. The small unemployment benefit obtainable under the National Insurance applied only to a few trades. It was an axiom of then Poor Law practice that relief, save the shelter of the Workhouse, must not be granted to the " able-bodied " and their dependants. Even to the impotent, Poor Law relief was then but a meagre supplement, mainly in kind. The " dole," as it developed after the War, was non-existent. Even had Poor Law procedure allowed it, the Guardians had not the funds to cope with this great wave of unemployment, though their expenditure actually rose to double its former rate.

. . . . . . . .

Up and down the Old Ford Road under my windows, women were wont to hurry past, pushing the battered old perambulators of children, or packing cases on wheels, laden with garments for the factories. Now, with their little conveyances all empty, they lingered hopeless. "Any work?" Always they asked each other that question; the answer, so obvious from the downcast face and the empty vehicle, was always: "No." I gazed on them mournfully, tenderly, feeling as though the wings of a great pity enfolded me. The absence of work, the cost of food—these were the burden of every talk, floating up to my window, passing me on the road.

Across a neighbouring street a rudely lettered calico banner hung:

> "Please, landlord, don't be offended,
> Don't come for the the rent till the War is ended."

Was it a product of our Suffragette call for a No Vote, No Rent strike?

Women gathered about our door asking for "Sylvia." They had followed and fought with her in the hectic Suffragette struggles; they turned to her now in these hours of desperate hardship; poor wan, white-faced mothers, clasping their wasted babies, whose pain-filled eyes seemed older than their own. Their breasts gone dry, they had no milk to give their infants, no food for the elder children, no money for the landlord.

Their faith in me seemed a sacred charge, their sorrows stirred me—I girded myself to fight for their interests. I had no thought, as yet, of collecting charitable donations for them. On the contrary, I wanted the need for such charity abolished, by the Community taking the responsibility for the well-being of its members; for the unemployed, not doles, but work at a living wage; for the men drafted away to fight, pay at least not worse than the best obtainable in industry; nationalisation of food to keep down prices and insure that the incidence of shortage should be equally shared; such measures as steps toward the goal of plenty for all by mutual aid.

In face of the hideous ugliness of war, good people of humanitarian aspirations yearned for compensation, weaving fond dreams of social regeneration. In the Press were fairy-tale stories of the great schemes afoot for manifesting national unity. Class distinctions were to be swept away. All the children of the nation were to stand as one, Austen Chamberlain[1] perorated, and Parliament cheered him. Sidney Webb

[1] "The common interest of all classes is much greater to every one than the separate individual interests of any one class. We all stand or fall together, to whatever class we belong."

produced a pamphlet, *The War and the Worker*, giving forth glowing impressions of what might happen. Socialism was to advance, war-time was to be a period of national re-building. Lloyd George declared the country would be made a nation worthy the prowess of heroes.

A Cabinet Committee for the prevention and relief of distress was formed. John Burns was made Chairman of the committee for London; a seat was found for Mrs. Sidney Webb. Both these appointments were calculated to appeal to progressive sentiment; for Burns had left the Government from opposition to the War, and Beatrice Webb had received more praise than any woman of her generation, for her authorship of the Minority Report to the Poor Law Commission of 1905–9. To many people the ideology of the Webbs was still the last word in Social regeneration. Of the first £100,000,000 which Parliament voted for the War a part was promised for civilian distress. Moreover, a National Relief Fund was inaugurated under the auspices of the Prince of Wales. It was to be administered by so-called Local Representative Committees convened by the mayor of each area. The Government promised £4,000,000 for the erection of working-class dwellings.

The machinery of succour might be preparing; but the people were hungry. I ran round to Lansbury's house in St. Stephen's Road, to ask what plans he and the local Labour Party were making to stem distress and keep down prices. On the way I met little Rose Pengelly, one of our junior Suffragettes—out of work, like the rest. "What are you doing in Ranwell Street?" I asked her, knowing the chronic poverty of that little alley.

"All out of work, all helping each other," she chirruped gaily, flashing a merry smile to me from her clear green eyes, her red plaits tossing. Yet I saw she was pale, and her gait not buoyant as usual.

Lansbury was hopeless of action, and advised me to get on to one of the relief committees which were being formed, "to show what women could do." He offered to nominate me. I told him women had always done that.

Already from Ireland, I had telegraphed Smyth to call our Federation Committee for August 6th. Its members were in a ferment. Mrs. Bird, the wife of a docker earning 22s. a week, and mother of six children, wanted the "No Rent" strike to begin at once, for the people could find no money for the rent with food at its present cost. We adopted a programme of immediate demands, including the nationalisation of the food supplies; and arranged to run a campaign of street corner meetings, as though an election were in progress. Many organisations, stunned by the War, were suspending activities; to us the need of propaganda was intensified.

That first week-end of the War I went lecturing in the provinces, as I did constantly, to build up new branches of the Federation and extend the circulation of the *Dreadnought*. As always, I hurried back to Old Ford by an early train on Monday. Mrs. Payne met me on the doorstep lamenting. A lady had telephoned that she was bringing milk from the country for distribution to the poor. Mrs. Payne had hied her into the by-streets to gather a score of the neediest mothers. The news of the promised windfall reverberated through the streets. Hundreds of women came rushing from every quarter. The road was thronged. The lady arrived in her car ; but, alas, she brought only a few pints of milk ! Sad were the tears of the disappointed mothers, seeing the dear illusion fade which was to have succoured their starving infants. The poor old Payne, whose heart was too tender to witness trouble, wept in recounting, striving in vain to thrust from her the memory of those poor ones. " Oh, Miss Pankhurst, don't let anyone bring them here like that again ! I can't bear it. Oh them poor little babies ! I can't lose the sight of 'em ! " She sobbed on my shoulder, then looked up, smiling through tears, a confident hope in her loving gaze : " Miss Pankhurst, couldn't you help 'em ? Couldn't you get milk for 'em ? Couldn't you do it ? "

I wrote to the *Times*, describing the incident, as she told it ; the misery of those hundreds turned empty away. I demanded attention for the distress. In immediate response came £10, to buy milk, from a Suffragette, Mrs. Forbes of Kensington. Other sums followed. 400 Old Ford Road became a milk centre. The old house had been used as a school. " There were cornfields around it when we were children," the son of the owner told me. At the rear of the house a queer flat-roofed building, which served as our general office, communicated with a small hall, a poor mean edifice, its interior walls of unplastered brick merely brightened with a rough colour-wash. At one end of the hall was a low platform ; at the other, a wooden archway, with niches holding plaster casts of Homer, the Venus of Milo and the Delphic Apollo. Here we held our meetings. Here, and in the passage through the house, the queue of distressed mothers extended : poor young mothers in their starving fortitude, with faces of ashen pallor, and sorrowful eyes, dark-ringed ; beautiful in their fading as pale lilies in the moonlight, to those who had eyes for their mournful loveliness ; divorced from the vigour of health, as is the night from day. Tidy, hard-working little women they were, even at the best of times daily accomplishing a miracle of endurance and devotion, clad in their poor, ill-shaped clothing, dingy and drab ; clean aprons over their shabby shirts, in respect for themselves and others. Some wore their hair closely braided, or screwed up in curling pins, to save spending time on it. Tragic mothers, anxious mothers, mothers with knotted, work-worn hands, and deep-lined faces, older in looks than women of their years in more fortunate circles ; grandmothers, sad and sorrowing, a world of unmerited suffering in their patient eyes and drawn, white faces.

Already the babies were ill from starving ; they could not digest the milk now we had got it for them. Moreover, the other members of destitute families all had their needs. A comprehensive organisation was necessary for dealing with hardship ; yet still I did not contemplate that our Federation should undertake this; it was the workers' mate, through which women submerged in poverty, and overburdened with toil were finding self-expression, and a medium through which they could force their needs and aspirations upon the attention of those in power. I feared that organised relief, even the kindliest and most understanding, might introduce some savour of patronage or condescension, and mar our affectionate comradeship, in which we were all equals, all members one of another.

Moreover, no private effort could cope with the great misery around us; it was the responsibility of the Community, of the State. In the *Dreadnought* of August 15th I published a paragraph headed, "Our Duty," urging our members to seek election to the Local Representative Committees for administering the National Relief Fund, and declaring that our main duty was to bring pressure to bear on the Government to secure the great needs of the people. I regarded our milk distribution as so temporary a stop-gap, that I made no mention of it in our paper then.

Yet public assistance tarried; the plight of the distressed weighed heavily on me. Under pressure of the need, daily confronting us, I announced an employment bureau, with Maud Joachim as secretary, and appealed for work for brushmakers, shoemakers and others. In the following issue I had thrown away reserves, and was pleading for funds to buy milk, for eggs to provide albumen water for infants too ill to digest milk, for other invalid necessities, and announcing that a nurse to advise mothers whose babies had fallen ill would attend every afternoon at the Women's Hall. Henceforth every week Dr. Lilian Simpson was in attendance, and a regular clinic was established in the Old Ford Road, and soon at five other centres.

How could one face a starving family with nothing to offer save milk for the baby? Orders for the various sorts of home work our distressed people could do, we gave out, as they came to us, through the employment bureau; but these were miserably few, as compared with our numbers. Expectant mothers were unable to provide for their confinements. We purchased material, cut out garments for mothers and babies, and older children, and paid our starving applicants for employment to make them up.

From the first we laid it down rigidly that we should pay no woman less than 5d. per hour, the district minimum wage of the unskilled labouring man. To pay a woman less, and call it charity, was to connive at sweating; and cost what it might, we were resolved not to depart from that standard.

We had now a systemised distress bureau. Already before the War we carried on a continuous house to house canvas of East End districts, to draw the women into our movement. Our canvassers returned to me now with piteous stories of misery accentuated, of hard lives rendered harder. I urged them to take notes of every case. From the canvassers' reports, and from the constant stream of distressed callers, who came at all hours to consult me in their despair, great shoals of misery were cast up to me, the very bowels of hardship were disclosed. To aid these unhappy souls one must deal with each case in detail, appealing, demanding, exhorting the Government Department, or the Board of Guardians, the landlord, the employer, the Trade Union appropriate to the case. Sometimes one must attend a police court to plead with the magistrate. Occasionally a lawyer's aid became necessary, and soon we had three firms of solicitors willing to act for us gratuitously.

People I knew as good comrades filed in with the rest to tell their troubles ; mothers and fathers, pale and spiritless, with wasted children. The cry : " Enlist or go ! " was already raised ; a knell of despair to many a father, cast on the streets with every door shut against him. Large families with eight and ten children were absolutely destitute, not a penny coming in from any source ; or, at best, a child or two earning a paltry wage, from three to five shillings a week, too little even to pay the rent. One of the young fellows who had fought beside me in many a Suffragette tussle had come in with his little family. He was white to the lips from privation. Edith Jones, dark-eyed and serious, a young Suffragette from Holloway, come here to help us, took down particulars.

" Why do you not enlist ? "

Her question to him stabbed my heart with a pang. This war virus was everywhere ! Tragic that even one of our own helpers should be urging these poor youths into the carnage toward which economic pressure was irresistibly driving them !

A member, whose husband was out of work, came with her four months baby in her arms ; a child of two and a half was ill at home, and she had eight of them under the age for leaving school. The wife of an unemployed stevedore, expecting another baby in three months time, fainted on our doorstep. She had an infant of twelve months in her arms, and another of three years clutching to her skirts. " Everything pawned and nothing coming in," was the common condition. Mrs. Walker, in her canvassing, called on a woman with six children under thirteen years. Her twins, only two months old, she was feeding on boiled bread, having no other food in the house, and but little of that. A mother came pleading for work, already worn down by toil for her eight children, whose ages ranged from four months to just under fourteen years. The wife of a ship's greaser told us the Government had taken over her husband's ship, since when she had had no money from him, nor any tidings of his whereabouts. She and her six children had gone four days without food. Starving householders, whose lodgers were thrown out of work and unable to pay any rent, forgave them this default in the large charity of the very poor. A girl of nineteen, the sole support of her mother and four little brothers and sisters, was unemployed. She was flagging from anæmia and debility ; if her plight were prolonged she might never be fit to work again. More fortunate than many, they got 8s. a week and four loaves from the Guardians, " and a job to get that ! " In a household of ten children, all the breadwinners, and the lodger also, had lost their work. A widow supporting three children by brushmaking was unemployed. Her fifteen-year-old daughter had been bedridden five months, as the result of a street accident, and was still incapacitated ; her action for compensation was suspended, as two of the witnesses had been called to the War.

The plight of soldiers' wives and mothers was appalling. Men were taken from their homes at a few hours' notice, and sent off without knowledge of their destination. " I had one letter," a poor wife told me. " He wrote that he was going in a boat, but didn't know any more. Only those who have anyone taken away understand what it means not to know whether you'll ever see them again, or whether you'll be left, a widow, with three or four children to rear ! "

A woman stopped me in the Old Ford Road to tell her trouble. Her man had been taken for the War, with only three hours' respite to say good-bye. He had served his time in the Army before she knew him, and until the calling-up notice came, she had never realised what his being a Reservist might some day mean. He had given her ten shillings when he went away, and told her to make it last as long as she could. It was all spent now ; no more money had come from any source, and she could get no work—her voice failed in a sob. As we spoke together her two little boys ran up to her. They had the wilted look I saw growing upon the children ; they seemed like fading flowers.

The War Office had issued notices stating the separation allowances to be paid to the men who had been called up or enlisted. They were paltry indeed ! 1s. 1d. a day for wives of privates, corporals and sergeants, the great majority ; 1s. 4d. a day for wives of colour-sergeants ; 2s. 2d. a day for wives of quartermaster-sergeants and equivalent ranks ; 2s. 3d. for wives of warrant officers. The children of all these ranks were put off with a mere twopence a day for the boys under fourteen years and the girls under sixteen years of age ! 3s. 6d. a week could be claimed by families living within the London area at the time of mobilisation, but not by those who moved in subsequently for any cause. The soldiers might further allot to their families, if they chose, up to half their pay, which ranged from a shilling a day for privates. To most of them it became a matter of routine to do so, for their families sorely needed this little subsidy. The allotment later became compulsory. Small as were the allowances, they were not always forthcoming and their issue was generally attended by most hideous delay. It was common for wives to be left waiting several months without receiving a penny. It was common also for men to be called up, and sent off to their regiments, without receiving the month's pay due, according to regulations, on mobilisation. They were thus unable to make such purchases as they required for themselves, and were obliged to leave their wives and children destitute.

Such separation allowances as came through during the first months of war were paid in part direct, in part through the Soldiers and Sailors Families Association, a semi-patronal, semi-charitable organisation, which had existed before the War. The Association was supposed to add something to the Government allowance, should this be considered necessary, in view of the special circumstances of the case. So far, however, from such additions being possible, it appeared that the Association generally failed to receive from the Government the sums necessary to make up the promised Government allowance.

After applying to the Association women were often kept waiting weeks without receiving a penny. Some received small doles and loans to tide them over till the separation allowances came through. The Prince of Wales's Fund (the National Relief Fund), ostensibly collected for civilian distress, was systematically milked to supply the deficiency in Army and Naval payments.

From all over the country, not least from my own district, came complaints that officials of the Soldiers and Sailors Families Association were telling the women whose men were at the War to move into one room, and to sell pianos, gramophones, even furniture, before applying anywhere for aid. The notion that the women were entitled to separation allowance as a right, not as a charitable act of grace, seemed difficult for the Association's officials to assimilate. In Newcastle soldiers' wives were given food tickets instead of the money due to them, and were permitted to obtain household commodities only from a prescribed list, which comprised the cheap, inferior qualities of food.

All day long, rain or fine, the soldiers' dependants stood in a queue outside the Bromley Public Hall in the Bow Road, where many a Suffragette skirmish had been fought in the days before the War. Day after day they stood ; for when closing time came, they were dismissed, to return again. All over the country they were standing thus ; and when at length they were registered, many of them were refused all aid.

A man living near us in Ford Road had the order from his firm : " Enlist or go ! " He joined the Territorials, and went into training at the barracks in Tredegar Road close by. His employers had promised him five shillings a week when he went to the Front, but during his training they gave him nothing. No money had come from the War Office. There were six little children between ten years and eight months, the youngest was wasting, another had abscesses in the head. The mother, after waiting two days in the queue, at length got her case registered, and was told to go home and wait till an official of the Society called upon her. When she came to us in despair on Monday, there was no food in the house. On Wednesday she came again ; still no money had come through for her. The visitor from the Association had called at last ; but had left without giving her anything, declaring that there might be " something " for her on Saturday.

A fragile little mother came to us with three toddling children under four years. She was expecting another very soon. The military authorities had sent her a month's money—10s. short of the promised allowance, small as it was. " They said it wasn't as much as I ought to have, but they were getting short of money," she said plaintively. She too had been told at the S.S.F.A. to wait till a visitor called on her ;

but none had come. Then she wept: "I have heard that a lot of Mr. Jackson's regiment have fallen down!" Poor brave little woman; the thought of his peril broke down her reserves.

Five sons had supported a father ill with Bright's disease, and a mother going blind and "worn out," at sixty-two years. The sons were all at the War, the parents starving. The Government had not yet decided whether to make any allowance to soldiers' parents! A mother of five young children had sent her marriage certificate to the War Office. It had not been returned. She was told that without it she would get no separation allowance, and even a loan from the Soldiers and Sailors Families Association had been refused. Mrs. Murray, one of our Canning Town members, was denied all aid for the same reason. She had sent her marriage certificate to the War Office by registered post, and had written begging for it to be returned to her. The officials had sent it instead to her husband in Devonshire. He, poor fellow, had received no pay and, lacking a penny, had to run about amongst the other men, who were mostly in like case, to borrow a stamp to return the certificate to his wife. Before it came she had spent the last money she had for food to procure another copy. Then the S.S.F.A. lent her 6s., and told her to make it last a fortnight. It went immediately in rent, for the landlord was threatening eviction. She wrote to me:

"I think it is a shame that the Government should be allowed to do such things just because you are poor. . . . When they take your man you might as well say they have took all you possess; and they don't care so long as they have him, what becomes of them left behind. . . . We have a right to have what our husbands slave for, and get treated like dogs to earn. It is enough to make one go mad to think what they go through!"

Another poor soul had both her husband and son at the Front, and no money on account of them yet. She had two little children under school age and no food for them. Though far advanced in consumption, she came to us pleading for work. The tragic annals of the poor—how they make the heart bleed when one comes to probe them!

A Reservist's wife came to us crying. Two of her children were ill with measles, and another with pneumonia. She was penniless, and had had no money since her husband was called to the War.

A soldier's mother wept with rage at being "pauperised," for she had gone to the Relieving Officer and had received some loaves of bread. Her husband was over military age and unemployed. Her son, "a good son," who largely supported the home, was at the Front, and no money had come in respect of him. She had five young children at home, and another was daily expected. The pauper disqualification was a boomerang to be dreaded; it could disqualify for the franchise and the Old Age Pension, worse still for school meal for the children!

There was terrible confusion. Masses of women did not know how, or where to apply for their allowances, and waited long and vainly for them to come through automatically. Some in their destitute condition had not money to purchase their marriage certificates and the birth certificates of their children, which were demanded as an essential preliminary to any allowance. The price even of the certificates had been raised, the children's from 3d. to 7d. each, a hardship indeed to people lacking pence to buy bread! There was doubt and confusion as to whether the certificates should be sent to the War Office or the Army Paymaster. Often the certificates were lost by the officials who handled them, and had to be supplied a second time.

Often for some reason the woman failed to discover, the money did not come through. Sometimes it was because the soldiers forgot to fill up the forms for separation allowance and allotment; or, as the men themselves insisted, the forms were not forthcoming. Entire companies of men had often to complain that no forms had been supplied. If, as often happened, men were late in responding to the summons to the colours, or tardy in returning from leave, or if they committed some other veniality—an offence[1] according to military standards, which might be no offence at all in civilian life—their families were punished by the stoppage of allotment and separation allowance for weeks or even months. Weeks of privation were frequently endured before the unfortunate wives learnt why they and their children had thus been plunged into destitution.

Daily I was striving to speed up the payment of separation allowances and to induce the Soldiers and Sailors Families Association to grant the women larger doles. In a typical case, a mother with a baby under two years old and shortly expecting another, after waiting without money till debts had accumulated about her, received from the military authorities a sum which was less than the money due to her for the month she was told to make it last. She was obliged at once to pay the greater part of it to the landlord and the shopkeepers who had trusted her with food. She applied to the S.S.F.A. for a dole. They promised her 4s. 6d. a week till her separation allowance came through. I pleaded with them to treat her more generously, in view of her imminent confinement, for which she had been unable to make preparation. They promised her 12s. 6d. the next week, but the promise was not kept. She came to me, sobbing and sighing in her heaviness, on the very eve of her delivery, to plead for aid.

A mother of five little children between two and eleven years, whose husband had gone to the Army and left her without a penny, was granted 5s. a week at the S.S.F.A., from which she had to pay out sevenpence for one of the children's birth certificates. Her rent was 6s. 6d. a week. Two of the children were at home from school ill, and a third was

[1] In December this rule was modified by an Army order providing that if a soldier were in hospital, in prison, or otherwise absent from his regiment, the wife would lose his allotment, but not her separation allowance, unless he were imprisoned for more than 28 days on home service, or six months abroad. If the imprisonment were for less than seven days the allotment would be paid to the wife, but the amount of it deducted from the soldier's subsequent pay.

refused school dinners, on the ground that she was too delicate to digest them!

Even the women who had received the full separation allowances promised, were in sad case. The wife of a Territorial, with two young children and expecting a third, got 1s. 5d. a day from the War Office. Having moved into London when her husband was called up she got no London allowance. Her rent was 6s. a week. She wept with despair at finding herself with only 3s. 11d. a week for food, fuel, light, and all the needs of her family! Another came crying that there must be some mistake. She had only 1s. 9d. a day, plus 3s. 6d. a week, to keep herself and her four little children. She could not do it, she could not possibly do it, she repeated in despair. Another had only 1s. 1d. a day—the childless wife's allowance—for herself and her baby, because her husband, in the turmoil of being called up, had forgotten to register the child's birth. She lamented that she had lost her milk through worry and privation, and now must bear the expense of cow's milk for the infant. Many a nursing mother, left without separation allowance, had the same complaint to make! "How can I keep my little boy on 2d. a day? How can I get him his milk, and his eggs, and the oranges, and cod liver oil the doctor said he was to have?" poor careful mothers wailed.

The high cost of food accentuated all hardship. Under the pressure of want, sickness went unattended. Many of the mothers who came to us had children due to attend some hospital as out-patients; but the mother could no longer afford either the fare to take them there, or the small charge for medicine. Widows assisted by meagre doles from the Poor Law Guardians, to eke out their scanty earnings at pinafore making, and other ill-paid work given out by the factories, suffered not only loss of employment, but a shrinkage appalling in the value of the Guardians' contribution. One poor soul, supporting a bedridden husband and five children, had 10s. weekly from the Guardians. Her rent was 7s. weekly and the Relieving Officer had forbidden her to take a lodger, on the ground that her rooms were only sufficient to accommodate her family. Her hungry little children were refused school meals because their mother was getting Poor Law relief.

. . . . . . . .

Our members were daily at the House of Commons demanding the nationalisation of the food supply; work for the unemployed; and adequate separation allowances for the dependants of the men who had gone to war, to be paid as a right, as wages which had been earned. Will Thorne, the stout Labour Member for West Ham, answered, jovial and complacent:

"I had a Bill before the House of Commons twelve months ago for municipal work for the unemployed, but they would not touch it with a barge-pole!"

"What it amounts to is that they are going to starve the men into joining the Army," said Mrs. Drake in her blunt, straight way.

Thorne shrugged his shoulders. A pupil of Eleanor Marx in the long ago, he was now one of the noisiest war men.

At our Federation Committee on August 6th Mary Philips had proposed that our members should go to the shops, offer to buy food at the old price, and take it forcibly if refused. I know that some women did this, in other districts as well as our own, and went out with the goods they had seized unmolested. The shopkeepers feared to provoke a riot by calling the police. Yet the effect of the War and its sorrows smothered rebellion even against the grossest extortion.

The little back street shopkeepers were wellnigh as sorely tried as their neighbours who dealt with them. Usually widows or industrial workers incapacitated by accident, they worked on narrow margins, and received no credit from the wholesalers; yet knowing their customers with friendly intimacy they found difficulty in refusing to starving people the credit they could not get. Good little Mrs. Wakefield in the Old Ford Road told me she was selling commodities for the price she had paid for them. To continue this would mean ruin for her, but she had not the heart to charge more. High Government purchases for the Army accelerated the rise in prices. Timothy Davies complained in the House of Commons that Government buyers had gone into the meat market and offered £80 per ton for meat which was selling at £65.

To allay discontent an Emergency Act was rushed through on August 10th, providing that where the Board of Trade was of opinion that foodstuffs were being unreasonably withheld from the market, the Board might be empowered by Royal proclamation to commandeer such foodstuffs, at prices agreed upon with the owner, or determined by the arbitration of a judge of the High Court. The Act was virtually a dead letter. Its procedure was at once too limited, and too cumbrous. An occasional seizure of goods in cases of peculiarly flagrant profiteering could not meet the need. Prices soared; discontent murmured.

Lloyd George called a number of the large retailers to advise him on prices. A recommended price list was adopted. Framed as it was by those whose interests it concerned, it was not surprising that it suggested advancing pre-War prices on almost all commodities. The wholesale prices for bacon were fixed at a higher rate than the former retail prices had touched. Margarine was raised from 5d. to 10d. per lb. Sugar, which had been 2d. and 2½d. per lb. before the War, was fixed at 4½d. and 5d. Many shops continued selling it at 6d.

After a fall from the first panic leap, prices continued rising steadily, though as yet there was no food scarcity. The Government on August 5th was able to state that there was wheat enough in the country to last four months, and that further large consignments were steadily coming in; that home-grown meat supplied us with 60 per cent. of our needs, that an exceptionally large supply of foreign meat was in cold storage, and heavy consignments on their way here.

No appeal to patriotism could stem the rush for profits. The price of coal and of flour to retail customers had gone up, before the cost of wheat or of wholesale flour from the corn millers had advanced. Canadian exporters professed their solidarity with the Empire, declaring the Overseas Dominions prepared to give their last man and their last shilling " to aid the mother country " ; yet when war conditions removed the competition of European supplies, they seized the opportunity to raise the price of their wheat to British consumers. It was vainly hoped that prices might fall when the expected record crop from the United States should appear, to compete with that of these fine Canadian loyalists. The lust of gain which swayed world markets, bringing starvation to millions, displayed itself in small matters and in great. The Shop-Assistants Union complained that certain London shops had put their employees on half pay and were working them full time " on account of the war," which had enabled the shopkeepers to raise their prices.

Lady Frances Balfour wrote to the *Daily Mail*:

" Let there be no complaining in our streets. . . . Women can save the situation by accepting it. We have heard of women giving tongue over the counter because the full tale of their goods could not be delivered at the usual price. Such people are as deserving of being treated as deserters as ever any soldier is who runs from the rifle fire of the entrenched position he has to take."

A callous saying this to mothers whose children were crying for food.

Though gambling in food prices continued apace, martial law was applied towards refractory workers. If dockers unloading the ships quibbled over their task, they were dismissed and soldiers were ordered to take their places.

# CHAPTER III

## MEETING THE GREAT EMERGENCY

INTERNATIONALISM seemed vanquished ; its most prominent sponsors turned war-mongers : Green, of the Peace and Arbitration Society, whom my father called " peace and arbitration Green " ; Hervé the French Anti-Patriot ; Norman Angel, who named war " the great illusion " ; H. G. Wells and a host of others ; my mother, though I did not know it yet, one of the fiercest jingoes ; even the sage, Peter Kropotkin, not untouched by the hypnotism of the great conflict.

During those brief days I had spent in Ireland the last vain, desperate efforts had been made to avert the impending tragedy. Lloyd George had deserted the peace party. Morley, Burns and Trevelyan had resigned from the Government rather than soil their conscience by participation in the War.

On July 29th the International Socialist Bureau, hastily convened in Brussels, had resolved on a special conference in Paris, on August 9th ; a conference which never met ; for war had sealed the frontiers, and the international Socialist movement had been rent in twain, its principles of fraternity vanquished by the trump of war. This debacle still unforeseen, on July 30th the Bureau participated in a great peace demonstration. Keir Hardie, Jaurés, Haase of Germany and the rest, marched under white banners, bearing the inscription : " Guerre à la Guerre ! " " War on War ! " Haase declared that Germany must not intervene even should Russia enter the conflict. He warned the Governments in the event of war :

" The peoples, tired out by such manifold misery and oppressions, may wake up and establish a Socialist society."

Jaurés, with his leonine head and impassioned oratory, in the last speech he was to make before his assassination, uttered a last prediction :

" . . . typhoid will finish the work of the shells ; and as death and misery aid in striking men down, so the masses, sobered and come to their senses, will turn towards the directing Germans, French, Russians, Italians ; and will ask what reasons they can give for all these corpses. Then revolution, freed from its chains, will say to them : ' Away and seek pardon from God and man ! ' "

On July 31st Keir Hardie as chairman, Arthur Henderson as secretary of the British section of the International Socialist Bureau, had issued an appeal to the workers against the War. It is said to have been drafted by the long-standing jingo, H. M. Hyndman. How lightly men draft manifestos they scarcely mean!

"... Stand together for peace! Combine and conquer the militarist enemy and the self-seeking imperialists, to-day, once and for all.... Proclaim that for you the days of plunder and butchery have gone by....

"Down with class rule! Down with brute force! Down with war! Up with the peaceful rule of the people!"

On August 2nd a Trafalgar Square anti-war demonstration was held by the Bureau, with as many speakers of prominence who could claim to speak for Labour and Socialism as the brief notice allowed. Keir Hardie was there and Arthur Henderson, H. M. Hyndman, Will Thorne, Ben Tillett and many others who presently were cheering for the War.

In every belligerent country such demonstrations were held, organised by the Socialists, responded to by the populace far beyond the Socialist ranks. The cry went forth: "War on War!" "Long live the International Brotherhood of the Peoples!" Greetings were sent from Britain to Germany; from Germany to France and Russia. Yet when the great conflict had actually been joined, only a small fraction of those who had cried for peace and brotherhood maintained their stand.

When Grey made known that Britain had declared war on Germany, Keir Hardie protested on behalf of the workers,

"Had they been consulted war would not have happened. Why were they not consulted?"

J. R. MacDonald said:

"I think Sir Edward Grey[1] is wrong. I think the Government which he represents, and for which he speaks, is wrong. I think the verdict of history will be that they are wrong.... Whatever may be said of us, whatever attacks may be made upon us, we will say this country ought to have remained neutral."

Keir Hardie being dead, those words of MacDonald assured him, when the conflict was over, the position of first Labour Prime Minister; when uttered they covered him with obloquy.

Hardie and MacDonald voiced their protest against the war to a House of bitter hostility, which in that hour amounted to a passionate hatred such as MacDonald had never faced. Even after that scene, the Labour Members of Parliament met and adopted a declaration:

"That the conflict between the nations of Europe, in which this country is involved, is owing to foreign ministers pursuing diplomatic policies for the purpose of maintaining a balance of power; that our own policy of understanding with France and Russia only was bound

[1] Afterwards Viscount Grey of Fallodon.

*Norah Smyth*

SELLING THE *WORKERS' DREADNOUGHT* AT AN EAST END MEETING

Mrs. Walker speaking.

*Norah Smyth*

HOUSES FOR HEROES

*General Photographic Agency*

"OVER THERE"

to increase the power of Russia, both in Europe and Asia, and to endanger good relations with Germany. . . .

"That the Labour movement reiterates the fact that it has opposed the policy which has produced the War. . . ."

The very night on which this manifesto was adopted, as the *Socialist Review* disclosed, the majority of the Labour Members refused to permit MacDonald to read its terms to the House. MacDonald resigned from the chairmanship of the Parliamentary Labour Party, which he had held since 1911. As the War advanced, he flinched somewhat from the courage of that first stand. There was a letter of his to the mayor of Leicester to be read at a recruiting meeting; there were speeches in the House of Commons, one of them stating: "We entered the War with a bright flag of ideals," which failed to support his first declaration. Yet he advocated peace by negotiation throughout, he gave his name for the collection of funds to aid Conscientious Objectors, he was vilified by the War Party—for these things he received admiration and loyalty without stint from those who hated war.

His place as chairman of the Labour Party was taken by Arthur Henderson, who had joined with Hardie in issuing the appeal to international brotherhood, in the name of the International Socialist Bureau. But recently a Liberal, opposed to the creation of an independent Labour Party, Henderson had been given the post of secretary to the British section, in the hope of drawing him unequivocally into the Socialist fold. A grievous mistake this, for the position required a Socialist of well-grounded theory and proven trust.

Before August was out, on the invitation of Asquith, the Labour Members agreed to co-operate with the Liberals and Tories in a joint recruiting campaign, wherein the war policy of the Government must be justified and extolled. The *Socialist Review* complained that thereafter, with the exception of four of the six I.L.P. Members of Parliament, Ramsay MacDonald, Keir Hardie, F. W. Jowett and Tom Richardson, all the Labour Members of Parliament "in a greater or less degree" identified themselves with the war policy of the Government and its so-called "non-political" recruiting campaign.

W. C. Anderson, who came in at a by-election, was not yet elected to Parliament. Philip Snowden was in America when war broke out. His I.L.P. colleagues were in doubt and anxiety as to the attitude he would take—but on his return he clove to the pacifist minority—a tiny minority indeed!

A handful of Liberals aided the I.L.P. pacifist group to defend, with such courage and faith as they could muster, the ideals of peace and human fraternity: Joseph King and R. L. Outhwaite, who are dead, Trevelyan and Ponsonby, and Lees Smith, who later went over to the Labour Party in the hope (alas! still unrealised) that it would open a new era in world affairs, D. M. Mason, Richard Lambert, J. H. Whitehouse, T. E. Harvey, Arnold Rowntree and a few others.

. . . . . . . . .

Keir Hardie had hastened to his constituency. In the London streets, and even in Nevill's Court where he lived, at the railway stations on his journey to Wales, he was hooted and hustled. Everyone knew him; war fury burst out upon him. His meeting in Aberdare was broken up by a determined crowd of jingoes who had come from the Liberal and Conservative clubs. His words were inaudible to the majority of those present; but Harry Morris told me that in reply to a taunt, "Where are your two boys?" Keir Hardie answered: "I would rather see my two boys put up against a wall and shot than see them go to the War." His voice broke; overwhelmed by his grief he could say no more. His friends would have it, even Morris who loved him dearly, that the meeting arranged for him in Merthyr should be abandoned—a false move, as such flinching always is. Only the fact that they saw him thus broken and bowed by the stroke of illness could excuse it. He spurred them to another meeting in Merthyr soon, and was received with cheers and affection as of old.

Already he was a broken man. The shock of the War had dealt him a mortal blow. Each time I saw him, I realised with increased uneasiness, that he was despondent and restless, as I had never known him. One night when I was speaking at the Poplar Town Hall a telegram from him was brought to me, telling me not to worry about a Press report concerning him. My anxiety aroused, I rushed off to Nevill's Court as soon as the meeting was over. He disclosed that he had had a seizure in the House of Commons. Dr. Addison had gone to his aid. It was the first sign of a grave condition.

. . . . . . . .

The Labour movement accepted the War quietly, as an accomplished fact. On August 6th, at a meeting in a House of Commons committee room, a War Emergency Workers' National Committee was formed, representing the great body of the working class political, industrial and co-operative organisations, to safeguard the interests of the workers in the great emergency. The Committee was largely without power, for the national officials of the organisations represented, had mostly entered into the war-time truce of solidarity with the Government and its policies; it lumbered somewhat slowly to its opinions, and was often late for the emergency in its decisions; it was purely a mouthpiece and lacked all machinery for action; yet it was the one collective means of expression which the Labour movement possessed. The movement would have acted wisely had it maintained such a committee as a permanent institution.

. . . . . . . .

Before the British Government could declare war it had parleyed with the great banking interests which control the financial machinery of the country, recognising them as its masters. These must be satisfied, though the little homes without financial reserves went over the rapids of war dislocation.

On August 2nd a proclamation had been issued postponing the payment of certain bills of exchange for a month beyond the original date of their maturity. Next day three successive Bank Holidays were announced, to prevent a run on the banks, and an emergency Moratorium Act was rushed through, giving the Government power to authorise by Royal proclamation the postponement, for any specified period, of all or any sort of payments. On August 6th and 12th the Bank Holidays which had ushered in the War, were followed up by proclamations, authorising the postponement of most payments over £5 for one month, subject to the payment of interest on the debt at the current Bank rate. Subsequent proclamations made further postponements.

Paper money was issued and lent to the banks up to 20 per cent. of their liabilities. Lloyd George, in negotiation with the Governor of the Bank of England, the bankers, the accepting houses and the great trading interests, agreed to place the credit of the Government behind the banks in discounting approved pre-moratorium bills of exchange, giving the acceptor the opportunity of postponing payment until one year after the close of the War, provided he paid interest at 2 per cent. above current Bank rate. Meanwhile the Government was to make good any loss to the banks.

It was instructive to notice how Acts of Parliament sped through both Houses in a single day, now that Party rivalries ceased to obstruct, and Parliamentary histrionics were no longer the main business of Ministerial life.

In November the Treasury appointed a committee representing the banks and the chambers of commerce to make advances to British traders in respect of debts outstanding in foreign countries. The traders were to pay the banks for the accommodation at 6½ per cent., the Government was to bear 75 per cent. of the eventual loss, if any. The Treasury also provided the finance to ensure that certain loans to members of the Stock Exchange need not be repaid until a year after the War.

In all this, and in many other directions, there were unwonted opportunities of enrichment for bankers and financiers, unwonted honours and emoluments for the persons who manned the numerous committees which were being set up to deal with every aspect of finance and trade. These transactions, as always, were mysterious to all save a few experts. A Mr. Crisp who had floated loans in China in opposition to the policy of the British Government and four other Powers, and who appeared to have ousted the Barings from the Russian Government's loan business, complained that he was denied the facilities granted to other banks. Lloyd George replied that the "trained sense of the financier indicates on the whole which is good business and which is bad business. That is the answer to a case like Crisp." He added that advances had been mainly made on the reputation of the name applying for them, security had been seldom asked for. The public could form no judgment on all this money mystery.

. . . . . . . .

Civil liberty is ever the first victim of war. On August 8th and 28th Defence of the Realm Acts were slipped through which nullified all existing constitutional safeguards for civil liberty. Anyone who contravened the regulations established under these Acts could be tried by court martial as though he had been a soldier on active service. One of the offences created by the Act of August 28th was the spreading of "reports likely to cause disaffection or alarm" among any of His Majesty's forces or among the civilian population. All opposition to the policy and action of the Government or the military and naval authorities could thus be stifled. Power was given to search and inspect premises at any time of the day or night, and to seize documents or "anything" which the competent naval or military authority had reason "to suspect" was "being used, or intended to be used for any such purpose." Suspects could be arrested without warrant, and detained in military custody or otherwise until such time as the offender could be dealt with "in the ordinary course of law." The competent naval or military authority was also given power to direct that persons who contravened or were suspected of contravening the regulations should be precluded from living in any specified area, and when thus driven from home, should be compelled to report the address to which they might afterwards go. This regulation was presently to be made use of to deport munition workers who were inconveniently agitating for improved conditions.

. . . . . . . .

A hurricane of war propaganda was sweeping the country, from Parliament, platform, Press and pulpit. Whilst war yet threatened, so early as July 27th, 1914, the War Office and Admiralty called together the Press committee, which had been formed in 1911, in preparation for this long anticipated great war, enjoining the strictest secrecy in relation to the movements of troops and battleships. On August 7th, the Press Bureau was set up under the militant Tory F. E. Smith, Carson's lieutenant: to censor telegrams and cablegrams, both internal and external, to issue secret instructions to editors on the attitude they should adopt towards questions of moment, the matters they should enlarge on, the matters they must suppress. Editors were invited to submit for censorship all doubtful matter, in order that unwelcome facts and opinions might be suppressed. The Censor's sanction afforded, however, no protection against a charge under the D.O.R.A. The Post Office and the War Office had also their censorships of telegrams, letters and parcels; the Home Office and the Foreign Office their news departments and their censorship policies, enforced by instructions to the Press Bureau and the police. The intelligence section of the War

Office, the official " eye witness " at the Front, authorised war correspondents ordered to avoid all matters of controversial interest, the War Propaganda Bureau, the Neutral Press Committee; all these disseminated the official war opinion. Even the clergy were circularised with advice as to the tenor of their sermons. A host of impecunious writers got jobs atrocity-mongering for home and foreign consumption. E. F. G. Masterman, a many times defeated Liberal ex-M.P., got £1,200 a year for supplying foreign Press clippings to the Government. No time like war-time for finding sinecures !

. . . . . . . .

What liveliness and vivacity in London! Beautiful women in long white coats, flawlessly tailored, already were taking the part of chauffeurs. How speedily they had learnt to drive! It was truly amazing! One scarcely saw women driving before the War. How important, how joyously important they were, their gait more triumphantly instinct with pleasure than ever it was in the ballroom. To serve, to be needed, to feel themselves part of this world-embracing Cause, with all the nation beside one! Every woman who put her hand to the wheel was releasing a man for the trenches. Even if she had still a chauffeur in the background, for certain occasions, she was making a gesture—striking the right note—giving the men the cue for the trenches!

Already skirts were becoming shorter, elegant feet and ankles twinkled smartly under the petticoats. "The women are wonderful!" It was Northcliffe, our old opponent, who said it, seeing their new emancipation—for war—for the slaughter.

As I saw them there was a cry within me: "Stop all this! Stop this breaking of homes, these sad privations, this mangling of men, this making of widows!"

For women of means, undreamt-of activities, opportunities, positions, opened on the horizon. The War brought a vast unlocking of their energies. They threw themselves into its work pell-mell, and more adventurously than had been conceived of in any previous war.

Mrs. Fawcett's N.U.W.S.S.[1] had suspended its suffrage work for the war period on August 3rd, and had dedicated its machinery to sustaining the nation. A Women's Emergency Corps had sprung into being under Lena Ashwell, Decima Moore and Evelina Haverfield, our W.S.F.[2] treasurer, to give service wherever it might be needed, to find employment for women, food for the hungry, comforts for the troops. Mrs. Haverfield was drifting away from us; ere long she was forming the Women's Volunteer Reserve, with the Marchioness of Londonderry as honorary Colonel; its members uniformed, drilled, saluting their officers, preparing to play their part at the Front. Its creator by then had departed from us, to be succeeded by Barbara Tchaykovsky, who had formed the Children's White Cross League to feed the children in the Dock Strike before the War.

Dr. Flora Murray and Dr. Louisa Garrett Anderson of the W.S.P.U.[3] and Elsie Inglis of the Scottish Federation of Women's Suffrage Societies were forming their women's hospital corps, declined till they had proved themselves by the British Army, but accepted by the French, the Belgian, the Serbian and the Russian.

War Societies of every sort sprang up, Tipperary Clubs for the soldiers' wives, Comforts Funds for the British, French, Belgians, for troops of every sort, Refugees' Funds, Bread Funds, Prisoners' Funds, Wounded Funds, war libraries, war economy leagues, ambulance corps, women police, women patrols.

[1] National Union of Women's Suffrage Societies.

[2] East London Federation of the Suffragettes, afterwards Workers' Suffrage Federation.

[3] Women's Social and Political Union led by Mrs. Pankhurst.

Patriotism flamed high ; the best and the worst of it ; service and sacrifice, love of excitement, desire for advertisement, fear and prejudice. The magnitude of the great struggle drew people from their grooves, and roused in them a sense, or at any rate a show of unity with Society, whether they stood for peace or war. All sorts of people one knew were rushing about on war work. Hector Munro, the little Socialist doctor from Bradford, running an ambulance corps, Mrs. Brown, Smith and Robinson serving as volunteers in some canteen ; all very busy and important, though in 1916 the Central Control Board dismissed the volunteer canteen workers from the factories, announcing that fifty part-time volunteers accomplished only the work of one full-time paid worker.

Special constables were being enrolled to keep the populace in order. As soon as the police enrolment began, Joseph Clayton, the old Socialist journalist, enlisted as a soldier. A friend of his quizzically told me Clayton feared he might be conscribed as a special constable, and compelled to arrest his old friends the militant Suffragettes. The Women's Freedom League, bitten by the war virus, like so many more, offered a corps of women constables to the Chief of Police. He replied his instructions were only to enrol men, but no such rebuff could daunt them, a corps they must have, be it authorised or no.

## CHAPTER IV

RELIEF DELAYED—" BOTTLING UP " THE PRINCE OF WALES'S FUND—" COST PRICE " RESTAURANTS—EVICTION OF WAR SUFFERERS

STILL there was no relief for distress from the great Prince of Wales's Fund, save in so far as it helped, and that most sparsely, to make good the deficiency in naval and military allowances. The Local Representative Committees, which were to administer the Fund, were slowly being formed under the chairmanship of the Mayors. Big committees they were, consisting of all the Aldermen and Councillors and Poor Law Guardians of the locality, with representatives of Trade Unions, employers of labour, the Soldiers and Sailors Families Association, charitable societies, religious denominations, women's organisations. The outside bodies came in more or less by favour of the political parties on the Council.

I was notified that I had been appointed to the Poplar Committee. Its first meeting was on August 17th. Already an age, it seemed, since the outbreak of war. We met in the Borough Council Chamber, a pompous-looking hall, its seats upholstered in scarlet plush and arranged in horse-shoe formation. The members grouped themselves with their parties, the majority business men and employers ; the Labour Party only numbered a third of the Council in those days. From the first I was looked on askance by the bourgeois majority, not merely as a Suffragette, who had been a thorn in the spiritual flesh of the Government and had brought the Suffragette turmoil into the locality—but still more, and increasingly, as a persistent hornet, stirring up the local populace to revolt against evil conditions, which long custom had sanctified.

" You are so delightfully noisy ! " Susan Lawrence once said to me, when she wanted our Federation to press for something she thought important. It was only by being noisy that we could make any impression against the accepted view that poor people must starve because their Government was at war. Susan Lawrence, like many other successful politicians, preferred to mount the political ladder by a reputation for being moderate, leaving the noisy work to other people.

For the most part it was a committee of thick-set middle-aged men, clad in broadcloth, with gold watch-chains and protuberant corporations, suffering, if at all, from over, rather than under-feeding. Amongst them—mainly silent, and if they spoke, scarcely audible—were a few women, accustomed to act a subdued, subordinate part where public affairs were concerned, as women mostly did in those days. The most self-reliant was Susan Lawrence, pleasant-looking and sensible, but devoid of charm and emotional fire. Julia Scurr,[1] her tragic destiny overhanging her—unknown to us—with her red cheeks and black eyes, and the strange immobility of her face, recalled the Dutch dolls of our childhood. With all her limitations—and they were many—there was a mother's kindliness about her not discernible in Susan Lawrence, the capable administrator. Mrs. Atlee (whose husband became Under-Secretary for War in the Labour Government of 1924), a tall fair young woman, had the appearance of an early garden suburbian. They are much like other people in these days, partly because their notions of dress and living have largely spread into ordinary life; but one used to know them by their sunburn and general air of sartorial emancipation, to which the body never seemed quite to have accustomed itself—and that was partly because our eyes were deceived by stiff conventional standards. One would have thought her a middle class fish out of water without any affinities here in Poplar; but probably she was shy.

Miss Wintour, sitting amongst the Liberals, pale and dreary—as well she might be, working in the wretched forlornness of the Isle of Dogs. No doubt she was essaying an excellent work there amongst the overburdened motherhood though handicapped by her conventions. She was painfully ladylike, and entirely inaudible to most of us, when she attempted, which was but seldom, to address some observation to the Chair.

Warren, the Mayor, presided over the throng, a small, pale, querulous old man, with a little crumpled-looking white face and twitching lips. He clung like a spoilt child to his own way of doing very little, and came near to tears when occasionally he was opposed. Everything was dominated by the city fathers; we others were but extras, imported to satisfy the Cabinet Committee's regulations, designed to please the public, by giving a suggestion of breadth and impartiality to the scheme. The Councillors quarrelled and wrangled over trivial matters of party prestige, and flew into a wordy combat of great noise over the representation of parties on the General Purposes Committee. George Lansbury roared out that the Labour Councillors had been insulted by a remark of one of the others, and a great shouting match ensued—a much-ado-about-nothing, which only the Councillors could understand. I soon learnt that on the larger questions, for which we were gathered together, the Councillors of all parties were inclined to leave everything to the paid officials at the Town Hall, and to the obstinate little Mayor, who considered it synonymous with patriotism to disburse as little as possible in relief.

When the Councillors had settled their differences as to their representation on the General Purposes Committee they were all anxious to get away. I raised an urgent, but, alas, isolated appeal on behalf of the starving people, and read from a painful list of typical cases of destitution,

[1] Wife of John Scurr, afterwards Labour M.P. for Mile End, E. She died insane.

collated from the stream of callers at our office. I was met with the general retort : " It is not so bad as it was in the Dock Strike ! " Even George Lansbury, to my dismay, contented himself with this saying, which was enlarged upon by one of the Labour members who had become officialised as a professional investigator under the Unemployed Workman Act. Only Susan Lawrence gave me a mild word of support.

My plea for action thrust aside, the Committee adjourned till August 24th. I was crestfallen and distressed. I had come there with schemes, already elaborated with our members, for giving work to the unemployed, for saving food, increasing the amenities of the district. The writings of Webb and the other scheme-makers had been canvassed, our knowledge of local conditions brought into play. The fruit was rotting in the country ; the East End preserving factories were closed, or working short time ; the clothing factories were at a standstill. We wanted the Committee to get busy and employ the workless people in these directions. A needed tramway running through the borough had been stopped ; the horses had been taken for the War ; let the Committee take steps to get it electrified. The dustbins, small open tins, were bulging with refuse in the fly-infested backyards of those serried ranks of too populous cottages, a source of contamination mortal to infant life ; let them be daily cleared, and so spare illness and employ additional labour. Our people were overcrowded ; let the hideous patches of vacant land, dusty and littered, be used, in part for building dwellings by aid of the Government's £4,000,000 housing allocation, in part for laying out as playgrounds for the toddlers playing in our dusty and dingy streets. Let cheap restaurants be opened to assist the women whom war would force out of their homes to take the place of men in the factories. Let day nurseries be opened for their children. Let the permissive Local Government Board scheme for maternity and child welfare be adopted in Poplar. The scheme had been issued, prophetically as it might have seemed, on July 30th. Actually it was one of the first of the war measures, a typical war-time gesture, for when the population is being reduced by war, appeals to " Save the Babies " find access to the patriotic heart.

It was for projects such as these I thought we had been called together ! I too had been gulled, in some measure, by the Press romancing of social regeneration, the scheme spinning of Webb, the Cabinet Ministers' perorations. One is easily gulled when appeal is made to one's heart's desire—and this was mine, to wipe out poverty, to transform the dreary wastes of the slums to a pleasance of happy well-being. I had grown up with the dream of it.

Vain was all hope of discussing such projects ; the committee-men had no intention of permitting themselves to be hustled into action ; they were waiting for instructions from the Cabinet Committee and by no means disposed to depart from the beaten track. They were steeped in the method of the Poor Law. To provide small doles mainly in kind, postponed as long as possible, was the sole thought in their mind.

. . . . . . . .

Starvation, that strange, dull gaze, daily stared in my face from the eyes of mothers and children. Their hunger stung me like a scourge; I could not rest for it. Some means of allaying it must be found. It could not wait the intolerable tardiness of relief committees. "Not as bad as the Dock Strike!" How could that aid the pregnant woman who swooned that morning on my doorstep?

"Cost Price Restaurants!" The phrase sprang into my mind. Cost price, or under cost price mattered not. The name should be a slogan against profiteering, and would carry no stigma of charity. We should serve in the Cost Price Restaurants two-penny two-course meals to adults, penny meals to children, at midday; and each evening a pint of hot soup and a chunk of bread for a penny; to be consumed on the premises or taken home. Tickets for the meal, or books of tickets to last the week, would be purchased at the door. To people wholly without means we should supply free tickets, and no one at the tables would be aware whether the tickets of people sitting beside them had been purchased or given free.

Communal restaurants, supplying first-rate food at cost price, were in line with our hope of emancipating the mother from the too multifarious and often hugely conflicting labours of the home. The hall at Old Ford must be turned into our first restaurant; others would follow.

A few days saw the project accomplished. Gas stoves and boilers were hired from the gas company. Willie, George Lansbury's eldest son—a good fellow, who took no part in politics, gave wood for the tables. They were made by the Rebels' Social and Political Union, a band of local men who before the War had aided our struggle for the vote. Somehow or other I pressed in Mrs. Ennis Richmond, a gaunt, grey-haired woman, the wife of a country clergyman, and her sister, Miss Morgan Brown, as managers of the restaurant. "Food reformers" and "experts" in food values, they called themselves. Their assistants we engaged from the numerous unemployed women who came to us. Crockery and utensils were given from near and far, but most of it from the homes of our working class members in the locality. An elderly Suffragette in the country brought us the carcases of the old hens she had not hitherto had the heart to kill, for boiling in the soup. Others sent the best of their chickens for our invalids, some gave the produce of their gardens and allotments, and pickles and jams of their own making. For many months twelve loaves of bread reached us daily; from whom we never knew. When they ceased there was a sense of loss—as though a friend had died—killed in the War, perhaps; we never knew. For a year or more a man called occasionally in the evening, laid down a bundle of money with a muffled word and hurried away. We never knew his name or what became of him. He disappeared as suddenly as he came.

Our Old Ford restaurant was opened on August 31st. There was at once a rush of customers—100 people at a meal, 120, 160, the numbers rose till the place was full. Many were destitute people with free tickets, but many came spontaneously for the cheap meal. Whilst we strove for relief from other sources, we now always provided poor families with a book of meal tickets; that eased a little their terrible situation.

We made quite a festival of the opening. Smyth[1] and I and all the organisers took a meal in the restaurant the first day. Smyth and I kept it up for some time, but I had to withdraw at last, for Mrs. Ennis Richmond's large use of dried beans was too much for my digestion, which still suffered the effects of the pre-War hunger and thirst strikes. I went about embracing a hot water bottle, to assauge my pains, till Mrs. Payne persuaded me to return to the individual catering from which we were endeavouring to emancipate her.

Zelie Emerson had scurried back to us from the United States, eager to be in the thick of it. She was stirring me up to do something for our old Bow Road district. Presently she was ladling out soup in Tryphena Place, Bow Common Lane, an unsavoury neighbourhood, her black eyes frowning intent, and her red lips pursed—her little plump figure hurrying, scurrying. Mrs. Bird, Mrs. Walker and others were doing the same in the East India Dock Road. These were cramped, unsuitable premises, both; I changed them shortly.

We opened another clinic and milk station at Crowder Hall, Bow Road, where we had hidden in a disused stable one night when I had been a fugitive under the "Cat and Mouse" Act. Mary Philips was pleading to start a clinic and milk centre in Canning Town. This too was done. Then Zelie Emerson persuaded us to let her organise another in Bethnal Green.

Amongst the Press people who came to us at that time almost daily in quest of copy was a woman who took some photographs in the restaurant. She induced two little boys to go out into the yard and pose for her, sitting on the doorstep, with their plates on their knees. About two months later the photograph appeared in a paper accompanied by a nasty little story warning the public against misplaced appeals to its sympathy. It was alleged that these little fellows, though not in want, were in the habit of begging, and had run round and begged "a plate of nice soup" from the Suffragettes, their mother being idle and careless. In actual fact the mother was a poor hard-working woman who took in sewing to eke out her husband's scanty earnings. Her baby was dying when she gave her boys the pennies to get a meal at our restaurant that she might give all her time to the infant. The mother came round to me indignant, complaining that the neighbours were sneering at her, and the boys and girls making game of her children. I assured her that we had no part in the article; and wrote at once to the editor, protesting that the libel had caused serious annoyance to

[1] I hoped that our "Cost Price" Restaurants, which the Press obligingly advertised, would be widely copied. This hope was not vain. Many voluntary agencies followed suit in other districts and at length the Ministry of Food opened restaurants not so cheap as ours, it is true, but less expensive than those supplied by private enterprise. It was hoped that they might remain as part of the new era which many people preached would follow the War, but they died away with the Food Ministry itself.

the mother and her children and was detrimental to our organisation and its work. I was astonished to learn that in response to my complaint the paper had sent an emissary post haste to the home of the little boys, and had given their parents £300 to say nothing more about the affair. Submerged in poverty, they were overjoyed to receive this amazing sum. I was told that the father would set himself up in business with it, as a vendor of hardware.

The management of our first restaurants did not proceed entirely without jars. Mrs. Richmond's views on food values were regarded by our Bow friends as outrageous, whilst to her the rigid application of her tenets was a matter of principle. She expatiated on the valuable properties of the potato skin, and insisted that the tubers must go unpeeled into the soup. Her East End assistants, one and all, objected. It was a shame, they declared, to give such " muck " to poor people ! Even the customers, hungry as they were, were seen surreptitiously to examine with pained and disappointed resignation the dark-hued tubers.

I reasoned with Mrs. Richmond ; she bristled with importance, prepared to do battle for her theories.

It happened that I saw Keir Hardie the same night. " What shall I do ? " I asked him. " Shall I permit the Expert to improve the people against their will ? "

To my surprise, he answered decisively : " I think so."

When I urged that the people associated potato skins with contempt he expressed impatience with those who murmured at wholesome food provided in friendly guise, and broke off : " Have we fallen so low that we must discuss potato skins ? "

I felt rebuked. In the struggle to provide for our people my mind was withdrawing itself from the thought of the great tragedy over there.

Dear Keir Hardie, how he was martyred by perpetual consciousness of that carnage ! I had been awed by his misery at a mine explosion years before. Now in his deep eyes was the restless agony of a man in torment.

. . . . . . . .

When the Mayor's Committee met again, all party acerbities had vanished; it was a body of mutual agreement that the present distress was of no importance at all; the real hardships of war were to come. It was a feature of war time that the popular mind assumed a craving for the fabulous and immense, refusing to concern itself with the common, everyday sorrows and needs.

No minutes were read, a genial familiarity pervaded the scene. A representative of the Board of Trade attended to inform the Committee on the state of unemployment amongst men. I asked him for information respecting women, but he admitted that he had none to offer. Women were always an afterthought, if they were thought of at all in those days!

The Committee now applied itself to the construction of its own machinery. A report from the General Purposes Committee was accepted, wherein it was laid down that four registration offices should be opened in the borough to receive applications for relief, and that after registration the applications should be transferred to fourteen ward committees, in order that the bona fides of applicants might be investigated, both by visiting them at home and by calling them up for examination by the ward committees. Applications would only be registered from those who before appealing to the Mayor's Committee had already registered both with the Distress Committees set up under the Unemployed Workman Act of 1905, and at the Labour Exchange. This entailed queueing up at three different offices. For poor women the War was indeed a very nightmare of queueing and registration! There was no Labour Exchange for women in the borough of Poplar. Penniless and hungry as many of them were, they must tramp into a neighbouring district, carrying, in many cases, a baby in arms with a toddler or two clinging to their skirts.

The Committee entered upon a long discussion as to whether applications for relief should be registered in duplicate or in triplicate, and, this decided, it was in haste to disband. Again I pleaded alone, and in vain, for relief for the starving people, reading out particulars of distressed cases, till I was stopped by the Mayor, who petulantly refused my request to name a date for the next meeting, declaring that nothing could be done until the Cabinet had issued its promised scheme for the distribution of relief.

Consumed by unhappiness at this further delay, I wrote to the Cabinet Committee and to the Local Government Board, asking whether it was contemplated by those responsible for convening the Local Representation Committees for the relief of distress that these Committees should remain inactive. The Cabinet Committee replied:

"... they contemplate that the Local Committees will survey the position and make suggestions to the Local Authorities to undertake or expedite schemes of work which would provide employment for men or women who have been displaced owing to the outbreak of hostilities."

Apparently the Fund was to remain in store whilst the committees appointed to administer it acted merely as powerless and irresponsible advisers to the Local Authorities. Pressed in Parliament for a statement as to when the promised White Paper giving instructions to the Local Committees would appear, McKenna, on September 14th, answered evasively :

" I do not think it advisable to lay down at this stage a set of regulations or conditions for the Local Committees."

A circular of the Local Government Board issued to Local Representative Committees a month previously provided the clue to these prevarications.

" Single men, who are physically fit and within the prescribed ages for enlistment in the Army, Navy, or Territorial forces, should not ordinarily receive assistance from the local committees until other applicants have been provided for."

The Government was leaving unemployment and hardship to do the work of raising a " volunteer " army. There was no relief yet even for women. Appeals were being made through the Press to individuals and philanthropic organisations, not to deal with distress on their own account, but to link up with the National Relief Fund—which was disbursing nothing ! The few voluntary organisations which started workrooms for unemployed women applied in vain for grants from the Fund.

A. J. Balfour, in the general share-out of complimentary office amongst the political leaders of all parties, had been made chairman of the National Relief Fund Executive. In reply to Parliamentary criticism he protested that there had been no " bottling up " of the Fund, and repudiated the suggestion that it was only to be used for the dependants of soldiers and sailors :

" It is the women thrown out of employment who seem to me to have the strongest claim on our sympathy, and so, I believe, think my colleagues on the Executive Committee."

Yet actually the Fund was mainly being used to make good the deficiency in Army and Navy allowances. Whilst the White Paper giving the Cabinet scheme for relief still failed to appear, the majority of the Mayors' Committees were marking time. In London no grants had been made to the Local Representative Committees for the relief of civilian distress. In Manchester food tickets, varying from 1s. to 6s. a week in value, were given out to distressed persons. The situation in Hackney was more typical ; on August 21st, at a meeting of the Local Representative Committee there, its chairman was asked whether a grant had been applied for from the National Fund. He replied that as a committee they had as yet no evidence of distress. He did not doubt its existence, but they had not yet set in motion the machinery to discover it.

In Southgate members of the Local Representative Committee were busily collecting for the National Relief Fund, but the Committee had never met to consider the distress in its own district.

On September 3rd, just a month after the declaration of war, the machinery of the Poplar committee for registering applications for relief was completed. It was mid-September before the names and addresses of distressed applicants had been sent to the secretaries of the ward committees for investigation. Investigated they were, and called up for further investigation by the ward committees, which had no aid to give them.

Everywhere shortage of food and clothing met me. The homes were bare—everything possible pawned or sold, the rent in arrears. A farrier with nine children had lost his work through the Government commandeering the horses, four of his children were too young even to get school dinners. A woman was weeping because she had notice to quit. She had a baby seven days old and five other little ones, only two of them old enough to get dinner at school. Her husband was a dock labourer unemployed.

A mother came to me with worried face. Her husband had lost his employment after working twenty-three years for the same firm. Seeking everywhere for a job, he was accosted by a man in the street who showed him a letter " from the Government," as he believed, asking him to get men to go down to work at putting up huts. The poor fellow accepted the work with alacrity, then discovered he must pay 10s. for his railway fare. His wife's sister pawned a ring to provide it. The husband's letters revealed very poignantly how he had fared:

LIZZIE—DEAR WIFE,

I hope you and the children are all right and well. I know it must be a hard struggle for you to keep the place a-going on your little bit what you earn. I was very sorry I could not send you any money on Saturday, as I could not get much, as they only pay out once a fortnight and I could only send a few shillings. We are not getting much money, so I cannot send you up a lot, but I will do my best for you on Thursday when we draw our money. When it rains we have to lose time. We are working out on the fields and sleeping under tents on boards, and the water comes up to them. We sleep in our clothes.

The food is so dear down here; bread 4d. per loaf, ½ oz. of cheese for 1d., 2d. for a bit of brawn. It is shocking down here! I will come home as soon as I can get enough money to ride home.

We are about ten miles from anywhere and have to walk thre emiles for each meal. We get up at 4.30 in the morning and wash ourselves as best we can, and go three miles for a cup of coffee or tea, and back to the job by six o'clock. Then it starts to rain and we have to leave off and stand about under sheds with no sides to them and the wind blowing all round you. . . . It is a hard life.

I am always thinking of you and the children. I do miss my bed.

Can't go anywhere; as soon as we are done three miles for tea and back to our tents. It is pitch-dark unless we buy candles; then the wind blows them out!

I shall be glad when I get home to see you, dear Liz. Remember me to Cassie and kiss the children for me. . . . Tell Mr. C., the landlord, I have not forgot him. I will send him up some soon and pay him up as soon as I can; he is very good to let me owe it.

Dear Lizzie,

There are hundreds of men keep coming and going down here. One of the tents is holding 500 men sleeping on canvas and one blanket they sent us to cover up our feet. On Saturday you know it rained all day, and when the men got their sub. they went up to the marquee and came back drunk and wet through to the skin with rain. It is pouring in torrents while I am writing this letter to you. When they go to rest they want to fight each other. One man who was drunk wanted to fight the 500 men, so they pushed him over to sleep, but he would not be quiet, so they threw two pails of piddle on him what the men piddled in their pails. It was an uproar, fighting and hollering all night, no sleep that night, and bread and jam for breakfast to make you strong, and tea with no milk in it!

Good-bye for the present. Please write if you have a letter from T—— F—— of Poplar about work, or anybody else who sends for me.

J. H——

your husband.

. . . . . . . .

Though the moratorium arranged between Lloyd George and the bankers in the first days of war had only applied to debts over £5, Judge Atherley Jones, in a gesture worthy of his Chartist father, adjourned all the judgment summonses for debts under £5 *sine die*, declaring that he would not make committal orders in such times. In other Courts many such orders were made; many evictions took place, and many more were threatened, sometimes because rent was in arrears, sometimes because a workman had gone to the War and his landlord-employer desired the house for another workman. In Glasgow evictions of soldiers' wives rapidly became a scandal. It was estimated that 500 summonses for eviction were being issued each week. In East London many women came to us in terror of being turned out. One of them, a poor trouser finisher, who maintained by her sweated labour two children at school, and a third thrown out of work by the War, had been given by the magistrate only a week's respite before eviction.

In face of the public outcry, a Courts Emergency Powers Act was passed on August 31st compelling landlords to go to the Court for a magistrate's Order, before evicting tenants, or distraining their goods; and providing, where the magistrates thought fit, for the postponement of proceedings against all debtors whose inability to pay was due to the

War. In spite of this Act, numbers of women came to me displaying notices to quit from their landlords. These were exceedingly interesting documents, for they contained printed reports of Police Court cases which had taken place before the passage of the new Act, and in which magistrates had expressly stated that it was " wholly unnecessary " for landlords to go to the trouble and expense of obtaining ejectment orders from the Police Court before thrusting their tenants into the street. The obvious intention of these notices, an intention undoubtedly successful in many cases, was to make the tenants believe that the law had not been changed.

Unhappily the Emergency Courts Act did not induce all magistrates to refuse ejectment orders,[1] even against unfortunate people whose breadwinners were at the War. A poor woman from Wyke Road came to me overwhelmed by misfortune. Her three married sons, and a young single one who gave her 12s. a week, had all gone to the War, and neither she nor her daughters-in-law had received a farthing on their account. Her blind husband, " always unlucky," had had no work since the previous Fèbruary. For a time she herself had also been unemployed. Then, agonised by the tears of her two little sons of nine and eleven, who were crying for food, she had accepted a small job in a button factory for her daughter who would not be fourteen till October. For this breach of the law her husband had been summoned to the Police Court and fined 13s. They could not pay ; indeed, they were almost starving ; for though she had now got work again, she was earning only from 7s. to 10s. a week, from which must be deducted 1s. 6d. a week for the hire of her sewing-machine, 8d. for cotton, and the cost of gas for her flat-iron. The police had now taken her husband to prison. The rent was in arrears, and the landlord had informed her that he was sending a bailiff with a warrant for distraint. The Education Authorities had informed her that she would be made to pay for the dinners her children had been given at school. To make matters worse, she had spent so much time queueing up in the hitherto fruitless effort to get separation allowances for herself and her daughters-in-law, that up to Wednesday evening of that week she had only earned 2s. 3d. at her sewing-machine. I succeeded in getting her husband released and the warrant for distraint refused.

[1] On October 8th, 1914, at Thames Police Court, Clark Hall, the magistrate, granted an ejectment order against an unemployed man with six children, although the landlord had already defied the Courts Emergency Act by selling up the tenants' goods without applying for an order of the Court.

# CHAPTER V

## WITH RUNCIMAN AT THE BOARD OF TRADE

I HAD written for deputations from our Federation to all the Government departments and committees concerned with the well-being of the people. Runciman, who was then President of the Board of Trade, consented to receive us on September 2nd.

I went with half a dozen of our most active members. I had aroused them from the voiceless millions of the submerged poor ; they were to me, in Gladstone's phrase, *vox populi, vox dei*, the touchstone of eternal verities ; my mothers, my sisters, my daughters. I had need of no other kin than they. Of our party that day were Charlotte Drake, a fair Saxon type, bleached by the hardships of an East End mother, clear-eyed in serene tenderness for her children, with a unique bluntness of racy utterance, always decisive ; Melvina Walker, a native of Jersey, steeped in the bohemianism of the London poor, with the nose and jaw of a famine victim, and elusive, Celtic black eyes, feline in their mysterious aloofness and uncertainty, blazing at times with a swift and sudden fire ; frail Mrs. Parsons, flushed and consumptive-looking, showing in every line of her the evidence of an ill-nourished childhood ; pretty Mrs. Farrell, with her loveliness of red-gold hair and roseate skin even the drabness of poor, East End clothing could not obliterate, retained by her easy-going Irish temperament, despite the toil of a woman who bears, and suckles, and works, as wage earner, and as home maker.

These, with the rest of my brood, wore an air of hostility to the sumptuous offices in Whitehall. The ire of mutual contempt flashed between them and the " flunkeys," as Melvina Walker scornfully dubbed the attendants who guided us to the spacious audience chamber. Here Runciman, with his pale countenance, received us stiffly, seated at an imposing table, flanked by an array of departmental officials. I was interested to observe how seriously Cabinet Ministers treated our little band in those days, how anxious they were to conciliate our storm centre in the East End. National unity was a necessity of war time.

Our case was a two-fold attack. We complained of the sweating and evil conditions of women engaged on Army contracts, already looming up as an important factor of war-time economics, and of the exorbitant food prices. We asked that the Government should take over the food supply, either—as we preferred—by nationalising it, and engaging the shopkeepers as managers at a definite salary, or at least by establishing fixed rates, at which the farmer, importer and manufacturer must sell commodities, the Government making up the deficit, should the profit fall below a certain fixed standard, and recouping itself from other sources. Our women showered protests and budgets on Runciman. Mrs. Farrell declared that every week she was more in debt to the shopkeepers, Mrs. Parsons that she and her children were short of food. Sugar, which used to cost her 1½d. per lb., was now 3½d., beans which had been 2½d. were 4d. One of the big multiple shop companies was allowing women who bought margarine to get their sugar for 2½d. per lb. ; but if they bought butter they must pay 3½d. " Why should they force poor people to give margarine to their children ; miserable stuff which would not nourish them ? " she asked, indignant, protesting that her children were delicate children ; they needed good feeding !

Mrs. Drake produced the weekly budget of a mother who had eleven children to cater for. Before the War she had purchased weekly 8 lbs. of sugar and 2½ lbs. of margarine in lieu of butter. She was now obliged to content her family with but 3½ lbs. of sugar and 1¾ lbs. of margarine. " Many people are considering raids on the warehouses," she bluntly concluded, and Runciman winced perceptibly.

Melvina Walker, her hat awry, her hands, in their old black gloves, folded genteelly, eyed him with the mocking nonchalance of one who has been a lady's-maid, and knows the foibles and peccadilloes of the highly placed. With the practised aplomb of a street corner orator, she expatiated on the cost of her every-Sunday knuckle bone of imported mutton, which had risen since the War from 4½d. to 8½d. per lb. It was useless to talk of a scarcity of sugar or of flour, she insisted sharply. " There are tons and tons of them stacked in the docks ! Our men go in and see them, and they know ! "

Again Runciman and his companions looked uncomfortable.

" Something must be done for us, or we shall have to take the food ! " she blazed at him, striking the table.

Mrs. Payne turned on him her gaze of sorrowing humility, pleading with him that if he could see the people with their pinched faces coming to our door at Old Ford, he must feel with her the necessity of our case.

He answered with expressions of sympathy for our demands and our arguments ; yet happily, he congratulated himself, the food had not yet reached " panic prices."

" Not at your salary, Mr. Runciman ! " Melvina Walker snapped at him, fierce as a tigress ; " but to people with 25s. a week, and four or five children to bring up, they *are* panic prices ! "

" It is not a question of salary," he retorted. She insisted : " It *is* a question of salary ! "

The Government could not nationalise every shop ; but it was doing, and would do, all it could, he urged, striving to be encouraging and conciliatory, assuring me that I would do the Board of Trade a service by notifying every case of sweating which came to my knowledge, protesting his own determination to provide redress.

## CHAPTER VI

### QUEEN MARY'S WORKROOMS—WITH JOHN BURNS AND THE CABINET COMMITTEE—MARY MACARTHUR

ON August 10th Queen Mary's Needlework Guild, to " organise a collection of garments " for war sufferers, was announced; a great unpaid volunteer garment-making was anticipated. The officials of the Women's Trade Union League and others raised a protest, on behalf of the masses of workless women ordinarily employed in the garment working trades. The protest was not ignored. Ten days later " The Queen's Work for Women Fund " was set up to provide employment for women thrown out of employment by the War. The Fund was to be administered by a Central Committee for the Employment of Women, controlled by the very officials of the Women's Trade Union League who had criticised the needlework scheme. Mary Macarthur was made the Hon. Secretary, Susan Lawrence, Margaret Bondfield, Dr. Marion Phillips of the Women's Labour League, and Mrs. Gasson of the Co-operative Union were members of the Committee. Their appointment received a wide and cordial welcome, in which I heartily joined. We hoped that these women would take the lead in protecting the status of women's labour. The first four had proved useless, if not hostile, to the Women's Suffrage cause; but it was believed they were staunch on the industrial side. Mary Macarthur had a great reputation as a pioneer organiser of trade unionism for women, and as a propagandist against sweating. Alas, the Committee speedily covered itself with ignominy by setting up the sweated wage of 10s. per week for adult women, to be paid in the workrooms established under its auspices. Local committees receiving grants from the fund might pay adult women less than 10s. a week—and in many cases did—but in no case would the committee sanction more. The wage was to be nominally 3d. an hour, but the hours must be limited, to prevent more than 10s. weekly being earned. Girls between 16 and 18 years were to get 2d. per hour, making a wage of 5s. a week, or 1s. per six hour day. These miserable rates were on no account to be exceeded, but they might be reduced at will. A circular of the Central Committee issued in November, stated " in some cases it may be desirable to keep the weekly wage below 10s." Clearly no risk must be run of producing a scarcity of women willing to work at a sweated wage for the ordinary employer. Many of the Queen Mary Workrooms paid as little as 6s. a week. A woman came to me from the

Hackney rooms bringing proof that she had only had 3s. during the week.

"Queen Mary's Sweat-shops!" was the slogan I coined to attack their parsimonious standard, the influence of which was to depress even the existing most beggarly economic status of the woman wage earner. Our members took up the phrase with avidity, and cried it in the ears alike of conventionally-minded patriots, and East End clothiers seeking cheap labour. How unnecessarily low was the standard fixed for the unemployed woman war worker by those who affected to be the unique custodians of her interests, may be gathered from the fact that 3d. per hour was below the minimum rate fixed by the Clothing Trade Board. Moreover, the Distress Committees operating under the Unemployed Workman Act were at the time actually paying to unemployed women in their workrooms 10s. a week, plus an allowance for each dependent child, and providing a free dinner valued at 6d. a day and the fares to and from the Workroom. A woman with five children would draw from the Distress Committee 16s. 6d. a week, fares and free dinners. In the Queen Mary Workrooms she would get a bare 10s. and have to find her own fares, and pay 3d. a day for her dinner and a penny or twopence for tea. Unhappily the Distress Committee work was largely a dead letter, so far as women were concerned.[1]

Even before war prices had raised the cost of living, the Distress Committee scale had been denounced by the Labour movement as parsimonious. The Labour War Emergency Committee was demanding that war relief should be at the rate of 12s. 6d. for one adult, 17s. 6d. for two, 20s. for two adults and a child, with 2s. 6d. for each additional child and 3s. 6d. extra in London. As members of the Labour War Emergency Committee, Mary Macarthur, Susan Lawrence and the others had joined in adopting this scale; then had thrown over their Labour colleagues by establishing the 10s. maximum for the Queen Mary workrooms. In my opinion it was a gross betrayal; in theirs it was "practical politics," I presume.

From their inauguration until February 1915, when war work had largely liquidated unemployment and relief work came to an end, only some 9,000[2] women passed through the Queen's workrooms. Yet they had set the common standard for women's war relief wages organised under other auspices, and they undoubtedly contributed towards riveting sweated wages on the women who were flocking into all branches of industry to replace men. This was the desire and intention of the employing interests, which blindly regarded cheap labour as the greatest of industrial boons. Again and again the ladies of the Trade Union

[1] Many women were refused relief work on the ground that their fathers or husbands should support them, although they were themselves unemployed and destitute. Out of 145 women who registered with the Distress Committee in Poplar within a period ending Nov. 7th, 1914, only 5 were recommended for work, and only one actually obtained it. In West Ham amongst 880 women who were registered only 17 got work.

[2] According to the *Encyclopædia Britannica*.

League, who were managing Trade Unionism for women, heedlessly sold the pass to the employing interests. Only women who were in regular employment before the War might be employed in Queen Mary's Rooms, yet a common excuse officially offered for the miserable payment was that the women were being "trained." Such experience as they got was mainly in garment making, in most cases not of a sort which would fit them for factory work. They were largely employed in repairing and converting old garments which had been given by charitable persons for distribution to the poor. Many of the workrooms were managed by amateurs with knowledge entirely restricted to home dressmaking.

It was promised that the ill-paid workers would in no case compete with women engaged in the ordinary labour market. The workrooms opened by the Lord Mayor's Committee in Manchester were refused a grant because the dolls and toys made there were offered for sale. Yet this pledge proved unreliable. The *Scotsman* announced that Colonel Cranston had ordered the shirts for his regiment from the Queen Mary Workrooms in Edinburgh; the *Morning Post*, that commercial orders for 1,000 dressmakers and others had been placed with Miss Macarthur's own Central Committee. Sir William Chance indignantly complained that the Central Committee had offered to supply socks at 2s. 9d. per dozen to a certain West Country industry, the proprietors of which had replied that they would not countenance such disgraceful sweating.

The New Constitutional Society for Women's Suffrage was refused a grant for its workroom because it paid more than 10s. a week, although the workers there were unemployed professional women who had been accustomed to substantial earnings. The organisers of the Queen Mary Workrooms in Southampton gave work to women in response to need, irrespective of red tape. After a fortnight the fact became known to the Central Committee that work had been given to women who had not been wage earners before the War, but who were now in urgent need, because their husbands were unemployed. Orders were given to turn these women away as ineligible. At bottom this ruling, whoever may have been responsible for it, sprang from the fear of providing a respite for men whom economic compulsion was driving into the Army.

The Trade Union ladies on the Central Committee for Women's Employment were among the notable early examples of the political truce which caused Trade Union officials to place what was regarded as National Unity before the wage standards of their members. They bent themselves to the task of supplying employers with labour—at almost any price. In this case the failing doubtless sprang from fallacious reasoning, based on the irrelevant premise that half a loaf is better than no bread.

. . . . . . . .

The Cabinet Committee arranged for John Burns to receive us on September 16th. In the centre of a long row of officials he greeted us with a grumpiness, which gradually melted to benevolent geniality. He called for each new point: " Next, Miss Sylvia, please."

We poured out to him the pitiful accounts of our poor: men and women thrown out of work at the commencement of war, who had not received a penny of relief from any source yet, despite the existence of the Cabinet Committee and the National Relief Fund, set up for the very purpose of aiding them; of families with little children, without income; people selling and pawning their clothes and furniture, terrorised with ejectment notices from their landlords. . . .

Burns interrupted; the Courts Emergency Act would prevent evictions.

We showed him the printed notices to quit, which landlords were still serving upon their tenants, claiming power to evict without orders from the Court. In the last two days five women had come to me with such notices. Our canvassers had found a poor mother in bed with a baby a few days old, weeping over one of them.

Burns insisted that the West London magistrates were refusing to sanction evictions. The Marylebone magistrate had in fact taken a strong line, telling the people threatened with eviction to lock their doors, and sending an officer of the Court to tell the landlord that if he attempted to eject his tenants he would be doing a very dangerous thing. Yet at Old Street ejectment orders were being issued, in some cases against the lowest paid women garment workers. One of these, the sole support of her family, had actually to complain that her sweated rate had been reduced since the War. By three days' work she had only contrived to earn 1s. 8d. I had protested against the sweated rate to the President of the Board of Trade, and against the magistrate's eviction order to the Home Secretary, who had replied that he could not interfere.

" I am sure you ought to know by now, Miss Pankhurst, that the Home Secretary never *can* interfere with a magistrate's decision," said Burns, with a sly grin, well knowing that I had many memories of such prevarication from the days of Suffragette strife.

" So it is said," I answered him dryly.

Again he insisted that no one would be evicted during the War; but next day the Old Street Court gave an order for a family to be evicted in three weeks' time.

We urged on him the need for raising the Poor Law scale of relief to keep pace with the mounting prices; and the cruel parsimony of refusing school meals to the children of parents receiving the meagre Poor Law doles. Poplar, even then, was considered a relatively generous Board of Guardians; yet how miserable was its scale! To a family where there were five children aged eleven to five years, the Guardians were allowing only 5s. worth of food and four pints of milk a week. An unemployed carter had offered himself for the Army, but was rejected as medically unfit. He had eight children between thirteen years and three months old. The Guardians were now allowing only 5s. 6d. worth of food, after an interval during which no relief of any kind had been given. Everything had been pawned, including the children's bed-clothes. A deserted wife with three children, having lost her work, applied to the Relieving Officer, when penniless, and without food, fuel or light. She was offered only the Workhouse. Refusing it, because this would mean separation from her children, she went empty away. What was to happen in such a case ?

Already women and children were being crowded out of the hospitals to make way for soldiers. We had to tell him of many such cases in our experience. A baby with a cleft palate could not be admitted to the London Hospital till after the War. A child critically ill with pneumonia was refused admission by the same hospital. Admitted to the Bethnal Green Workhouse Infirmary, he was so grossly neglected that his mother removed him and exposed his condition to the Guardians, who finally thanked her and remitted the fee. The poor mother excused the Infirmary nurses, pleading that they had more cases to attend to than they could possibly manage. A little girl of twelve disfigured by a hideous skin disease had been brought to us at the Old Ford clinic, having been turned out of the London Hospital to make room for soldiers.

We urged the scandalous treatment of soldiers' and sailors' families ; the hardships and humiliations they had suffered from the long failure to pay their allowances, the meagreness of the allowances when at last they came ; the disagreeable manner in which they were paid and made up by doles from the Soldiers and Sailors Families Association, to the accompaniment of fussy and impertinent interrogations—though already the women had been compelled to furnish their marriage and their children's birth certificates.

We demanded that the payment earned by the soldiers at the risk of their lives should be treated as wages, to which they and theirs had an inalienable right ; little enough as the price of a man's life ! The wage should be paid where a man had been maintaining a family as husband and father, whether the woman could show a marriage certificate or not and also where a son had been maintaining his parents or brothers and sisters.

We asked what share of the £4,000,000 housing grant was coming to the East End, and told him of women, with children starving, prohibited by the inspectors from taking in garment work from the factories because of the overcrowded condition of their homes.

We protested against the wretched maximum of 10s. a week to be paid in the Queen Mary Workrooms, when these workrooms should eventually appear—for none were opened yet—pointing out that this miserable rate would militate against women's wage standards in industry as a whole, and also against the wage standards of men. We demanded, at least, the minimum payable in most districts to the unskilled labouring man. We reminded him that the gross underpayment of women in all branches of industry had long been a blot on Society, and urged that if relief committees would set the example of paying a living wage, and the Government would oblige its contractors to do the same, private employers would be compelled to follow suit. Here Burns expressed most cordial sympathy with our view; and declared his eagerness to take the chair in a discussion between ourselves and Mary Macarthur.

We demanded that registration of distressed persons at one office should be sufficient for all purposes, and that the officials should send the particulars through to the body appropriate to the case. To stop unemployment we demanded the opening of factories for the work now at a standstill. The fruit crop had been lost; the Government might have saved it. We reminded him of the Maternity and Infant Welfare circular his Department had issued before he left office. Was that to remain a dead letter, or would the Government take steps to implement it? To do so without ensuring food for pregnant and nursing mothers would prove futile. A poor woman had come to me crying, because, for lack of pence, she had missed taking her wasting infant to the hospital, where they were giving it Scott's Emulsion. Ill and starving, she was trying to feed the child at her shrunken breasts, whilst it cried all day, unsatisfied. "It is *you* we must nourish first!" I told her, shocked by the cruel folly of this paradox. She went on to our list for free milk, barley water and dinners at the restaurant. At the end of a week we sent her to the hospital with the fourpenny fee, requesting that it be remitted in future. We received a reply thanking us for the wonderful improvement in the baby.

When we had done, Burns assured us that all we had said would be considered and dealt with. He added, with a paternal smile at me: "Miss Sylvia, I have been impressed, and I have been pleased."

His tone was sincere and generous. I respected him for his resignation from the Government on the War issue; yet I considered his imperative duty was to disclose to the people at large his reasons for his refusal to share responsibility for the War. I had long been prejudiced against him for his ill relations with Keir Hardie and with the Labour Party. Above all I condemned him that he was on the Cabinet Committee to relieve distress, and that the hungry people were unrelieved.

. . . . . . . .

Much later in the War he proved my most unexpected protector in Parliament Square. A little band of us were parading there with peace posters. A man assailed me with a wordy torrent of threats. Burns, who had come up behind me, suddenly sprang forward, with fists up ready for a fight, and ordered the abusive one to depart. Though I recognised his kindness, I was a trifle embarrassed by this championship by one who despite his resignation I still was inclined to regard as on the other side. It disconcerted me more than the assailant had done. I gave the word to my companions that we should roll up our posters, and go inside to interview Members. As we waited in the entrance hall for them to come to us, I unfurled my poster and spread it across my knees. A policeman warned me that it must not be displayed there. Again Burns was at my elbow. I heard him say to one of our women: "Persuade her to put it away. We don't want her thrown outside for that. We love her too well to let her do it." Again his solicitude worried me. I was prepared to face opposition and violence; sympathy from within the citadel could only be distressing. Already some of our women were taking their cue from him and beginning to plead with me. Such action would be ridiculous with one's own friends trying to stifle it. I folded up the poster, oppressed by the thought that our protests, which in other times might have reverberated through the country, could count no more to-day than the wings of a moth beating against a fortress outside in the darkness of the tempest.

. . . . . . . . .

Later still, when the War was wearing to its end, I met Burns in the cloisters of Westminster Abbey. He hailed me with friendly mien and we walked together among those ancient walls. He ruminated sadly on the dragging on of the War and its wrecking of many hopes. I told him that I was attending the Inter-Allied Labour and Socialist Congress, and expressed my sorrow at its dearth of international Socialism. "Yes," he assented, "they have forgotten all that."

"Why do you not speak? Why do you not expose the truth?" I urged him.

"My silence speaks louder than any words!" he answered; then added that after the War he would come out and astonish everyone. He would be "more revolutionary than anyone." I mentioned the word Russia—the revolution there was already in its spate. At once a wave of reserve and impatience seemed to pass over him. He indicated the door from those tranquil sun-kissed cloisters into the thronged passages of the dark and never restful church, telling me that my way lay in that direction; dismissing me with imperious, though not unfriendly haste.

. . . . . . . . .

In Poplar the Mayor's Committee still failed to meet. The people had registered and were registering their distress. The members of the ward committees had canvassed them separately and together, had laboriously discussed the canvass. Many poor applicants had been rejected for many reasons: that there was not sufficient proof that they were unemployed through the War, that their unemployment was chronic, that they were wives who should not require to be wage earners, and whose husbands were the persons who ought to register; that they were, or ought to be, recipients of Poor Law relief; that their income was a little too large for them to be classed as requiring aid.

For those who passed the ordeal still no relief appeared. The National Relief Fund had sent no grant to Poplar. The Fund had now reached £3,000,000, one-sixth of it advanced to soldiers' and sailors' families; to civilian distress still closed. Some Local Authorities, notably West Ham, had undertaken local improvements, the loans for this purpose were double those of the previous year. The Government had sanctioned small disbursements from the Housing grant, and the Road Fund.

A tiny proportion of the workless men were thus employed. The Army got more of them. That the boasted Volunteer Army was recruited by hunger was a fact it was bad form to mention.

The Queen's Fund, amounting to a mere £60,000, was assumed to be the only source available for relieving unemployed women, though their numbers were officially estimated at 60,000, and may have been much larger.[1] Their numbers could not then be ascertained by the unemployment registers, for few were thus insured.

The Local Representative Committees were now invited to form sub-committees, representing local organisations of women, to administer Queen Mary Workrooms. Our Poplar Mayor formed the sub-committee on his own initiative, selecting its members according to his own fancy. He included all the women members of the main committee excepting me—because all the others were warranted to make no protest against the beggarly 10s. rate—a sad proof of their subservience. Our Federation, though the only considerable organisation of women in the borough, was ignored for the same reason. The Labour movement had no women's organisation there then.

Some of the other Local Representative Committees, less habit-hardened to destitution than that of Poplar, were now protesting against the inactivity of the Cabinet Committee, which issued to them neither funds nor instructions. The Fulham Committee had published its intention to relieve distressed persons at the rate of 12s. 6d. in food tickets—always food tickets—for one adult, 7s. 6d. each for additional adults, with children's allowances of 3s. to 4s. up to a maximum of 25s. per family.

On September 28th the Poplar Committee was called for the third time. Two days before I had learnt that " a stout man in a motor car " had driven round doling out a few shilling food tickets, telling the distressed people, in the words of one poor woman, that " he was doing it out of his own pocket and I mustn't say nothing to no one." Actually the " stout man " was the Mayor who, having secured a preliminary grant from the National Relief Fund, had distributed such meagre assistance as he thought fit.

When the Committee met, it brushed aside the Mayor's irregularities, despite my protests, and decided to adopt for itself the Fulham scale, though according to the Mayor, there was not a penny in hand to disburse.

[1] The Central Committee for Women's Employment published a table indicating the proportion of unemployment and short time amongst women and girls in London as ascertained by the Committee's investigations. It was here shown that out of 66,000 women employed in dressmaking only 34 per cent. of those employed by large firms were working full time, only 31 per cent. of those working for small firms. In boot and shoe making only 13 per cent. of the women employed by large firms were working full time. In printing and books 26 per cent., in jams 39 per cent., in furnishing and upholstering 18½ per cent., amongst furriers and skinners 33 per cent.

At the beginning of October 36,000 unemployed women were on the Labour Exchange registers, estimated as less than half the number unemployed, and the Queen Mary Fund amounted to £68,000.

The Vacant Lots Society, a creation of Joseph Fels, the American soap boiler and Henry-Georgite, had sent through Lansbury an offer to supply land and the materials for cultivating it, if the Mayor's Committee would provide wages to set men to work. Fels was an old friend of Lansbury and well known in the borough for his charitable "back to the land" efforts. Without argument it was agreed that his offer be accepted; but nothing more was ever heard of the decision and even Lansbury never referred to it again.

As the Committee broke up and came together in greetings and conversation, Julia Scurr, a member of our Federation executive, though never an active one, came to me timidly, telling me that the Queen Mary Workroom in the Borough was very comfortable and the dinners very nice. I saw that her conscience pained her. "Sylvia does us good; she keeps us young," she said to Lansbury wistfully. I knew she regretted many a compromise, but could not stand out against the others. I wished I had by me on the committee women on the economic level of the poor employees in Queen Mary's Workrooms, to prick this bubble of complacency.

. . . . . . . .

Already I had written to the Queen, challenging her not to permit the 10s. wage to be established in the workrooms associated with her name. At her instance, Mary Macarthur received us at the magnificent residence placed at the disposal of her Central Committee for Women's Employment.

We waited long beyond the appointed time in a spacious, ornate chamber, with gilded chairs upholstered in crimson silk and deep-piled, crimson carpets; our women in their dark poor clothes eyeing this pomp indignantly.

At last a large lady entered elegantly arrayed in old gold silk, with a rustle of petticoats, and plump white forearms, advantageously displayed. A Botticelli Madonna, Dr. Mills of Kensington once called her, from her paleness and her slimness. The simile was poor; she had always the small, narrowly-set Scotch eyes, and the heavy, long, upper lip. To-day, portly as she was, he must rather have called her a Rubens matron! Despite her plain face and mouth-breathing voice, her energy and assurance lent her, at moments, the charm which often makes an ugly woman more attractive than a beautiful one.

She was cordial and pleasant with us. My companions accepted her proffered hand with reluctance. One and all they regarded her sternly.

Her friendliness smote me unpleasantly, for I could not respond to it. I warned her, as obviously was the case, that the standard set by her committee would react on the wages of women throughout the country. Had the standard been good, it would have helped women to refuse sweated conditions.

Charlotte Drake, white-faced and earnest, had brought with her the budget of a single woman actually existing on 10s. a week; revealing the meagre bareness of it; challenging Macarthur to explain how it could suffice further to meet the needs of a woman with children; passionately urging her to concede that mothers with little children dependent on them should be treated as men in the same position.

Melvina Walker flashed out, with angry eyes: "We have no need to tell *you*, Miss Macarthur, how working women live in the East End; no one knows better than *you*, with all *your* experience! You *know* that 10s. is not enough to live on!"

Walker also had budgets to confound her, showing what it costs "when mother has to go to work and have her children minded."

Mrs. Pascoe, cook at our E.L.F.S. restaurant in the Old Ford Road, fiercely independent, protested, as breadwinner, in place of an invalid husband, that she could not exist on the miserable pay at Queen Mary's Rooms.

Mrs. Parsons reminded her that a magistrate had just refused permission for a Russian girl to enter this country till her prospective employer would pledge himself to pay her not less than 17s. 6d. a week.

When they were done Macarthur turned to me, expostulating:

"Miss Pankhurst, you know the average wage of women is only about 7s. 6d. a week,[1] and we are paying 10s.! How can you expect us to pay more?"

She ran to a table, snatched up and held out to the women dramatically some babies' woollies, crying:

"See, they are making these lovely things in the workrooms! Some of them will find their way to the East End!"

"I would rather take poison than them!" Charlotte Drake exclaimed, with a gesture of anger. Even her lips had blanched.

Out we strode, with but stiff acknowledgment of Macarthur's leave-taking.

We followed up our visit by a memorial to the Queen, demanding a minimum wage of 5d. an hour or £1 a week for the women employed in her workrooms. Some suffrage societies and their leaders, and such notable people as Olive Schreiner, Margaret Macmillan, Hertha Ayrton, Lillah McCarthy, Beatrice Harraden, Laurence Housman and Henry Nevinson joined us in signing the memorial; but the brunt of the battle was left to us. Many rank and file women Trade Unionists and some who were organising under the very officials who had fixed the 10s. standard sent us their blessing. The Manchester and Salford Women's Trades Council, under the leadership of those active, devoted people, Eva Gore Booth, Sarah Dickinson and Esther Roper, placed on record its view that the wretched 10s. maximum of the Central Committee for Women's Employment was "an industrial disaster for women . . . bound to have its effect on the rates given by private employers."

I could not flag in determination to struggle for a higher standard. Poor little missives containing such budgets as this, of a widow

[1] It had been stated so, but sufficient statistical information to declare an average was not then available.

supporting two children by her sewing-machine, kept the hard facts of great poverty always before me :

| | |
|---|---|
| Wage weekly .. .. .. .. | 14s. od. |
| Rent one room .. .. .. .. | 3s. 6d. |
| Payment for having little girl minded .. .. | 2s. 6d. |
| ,, ,, ,, baby ,, .. .. | 2s. od. |
| Nestle's milk for baby .. .. .. .. | 1s. 4d. |
| Gas for boiling water for baby's bath and morning cup of tea .. .. .. .. | 3d. |
| Errands at work .. .. .. .. | 1d. |
| Insurance .. .. .. .. | 3d. |
| Cooking at work .. .. .. .. | 2d. |
| | 10s. 1d. |

Only 3s. 11d. left for food, fuel, clothes, etc !

She was up at six each morning to feed and dress her children and take them to be minded, before hurrying to the factory. On Saturday afternoons and Sundays she washed, cleaned, mended and cooked. The children had influenza. To pay for the doctor she cleaned door-steps in the evenings. All night she was kept awake tending her sick children. How would she exist were she to lose her work and be compelled to fall back on Queen Mary's Rooms ?

Eventually, under gradually marshalled public opinion, children's allowances were grudgingly sanctioned, and actually paid in the few districts where women war sufferers, who did no work for their dole, were getting from the National Relief Fund 10s., plus children's allowances. In April 1915 when the cost of living had greatly risen and many workrooms were closing down, the Central Committee for Women's Employment issued a belated permission for the maximum rate of 3d. per hour in the workrooms to be raised by not more than 10 per cent., and for the working hours to be increased to 46 per week. Girls between 16 and 18 years getting 1s. a day might now be paid 1s. 3d., and girls between 14 and 16 years getting 4s. a week might have 5s. !

# CHAPTER VII

## POOR OUTCAST PEACE

IN my big batch of letters I received an unusual one.

" After having protested against this inexpressibly sinful European War, within a few hours of its declaration, we women everywhere have appeared to accept it as a necessary evil. . . .

" It has not to follow its course like the measles. . . . It is man-made—it must be woman-undone ! . . .

" Let us start an international ' Every Woman's Movement ' to stop this War. . . ."

The missive brought a thrill of joy to me. An hour or two later appeared its author, Lucy Thoumaian, " your little bird," as she subscribed herself in some of her many letters, a Swiss of Armenian citizenship by marriage. Not the pale, tragic figure Romance had conjured for her mission, she entered, stout and matronly, her rosy flesh beaded with the heat, her tight dress redundant with passementerie. She summoned me to join a thousand women[1] whom she would muster to make their way to the Front and fling themselves between the contending armies.

Which Front, and how to reach it from this island closely guarded, were practical questions not yet considered. With that I did not quarrel, knowing that great ideas are not always born fully-fledged. My desire was to go with her, tour the country, labour to bring her idea to fecundity. Only the thought that our effort here in the East End was to build towards permanent well-being, not merely to assuage and strengthen for war-time, held me from leaving all to join her ; for the cessation of the European struggle would not cure the poverty of our mothers. I would not refuse to join her high mission ; I knew that by many she would be rebuffed. I promised to join her when she had gathered her company and made her plans. The brightness of the day was gone from me, so keenly I felt the truth of her indictment that all this labour for the pensions and allowances was a condonement of the War.

[1] In September the same idea was broached by Dorothea Hollins, a delicate woman of means and leisure who wrote from Swan Walk, Chelsea, to several newspapers under the pseudonym *X*, calling for " at least a thousand " women to go to the Front, as a Peace Expeditionary Force, to stop the War. Private meetings in support of this project continued for some time but no action was taken.

She wrote to me soon that she could not gather a company of women, and asked if I were ready to go with her—we two alone to the Front—to get there somehow. She had no plan. I foresaw much journeying, much difficulty, expenditure of immeasurable time and money, commitments unmet and colleagues anxious.

I replied that I could not leave my work till she had gathered at least a few to go with us, had made some plan. She upbraided me bitterly. Sadly I felt the virtue of her reproaches; and still more sadly believed her project vain.

. . . . . . . .

In September my sister, Christabel, returned from her self-imposed exile in Paris, by which, since March 1912, she had evaded imprisonment with Mrs. Pankhurst and the Pethick Lawrences on the Suffragette conspiracy charge. The Amnesty covered her now ; she could come and go as she chose. She was to speak in the London Opera House on September 8th. I had not heard from her since our Federation was severed from the W.S.P.U. at the beginning of the year.[1] I went to the meeting. The empty stage was hung with dark green velvet. She appeared there alone, lit by a shaft of lime-light, clad in her favourite pale green, graceful and slender. Her W.S.P.U. adorers filed up and presented her with wreaths. She laid them in a semicircle at her feet.

The tableau was charming ; but to me, imbued with the sorrow and suffering of war time, strangely incongruous and unreal. She vouchsafed not one of the militant suffrage points her audience desired to hear. Victor Duval, of the Men's Political Union for Women's Enfranchisement, interrupted with a cry of " Votes for Women." She checked him impatiently : " We cannot discuss that now." Her speech was wholly for the War ; light, dialectic, as though of some academic political contest ; no hint appeared of the appalling tragedy. I listened to her with grief, resolving to write and speak more urgently for peace.

When she had done, I made my way to the speakers' ante-room. Christabel was alone there, save for an occasional steward or secretary, coming and going for this or that. An impenetrable barrier lay between us. " Is Mother here ? " I asked her. She answered laconically that she would be coming soon ; and occupied herself over some papers, with unraised eyes. I waited, impatient, till Mrs. Pankhurst entered, surrounded by a group of women I may have known, but did not recognise. We exchanged a brief greeting, distant as through a veil.

As I left the hall alone, a little knot of East End women, with yellow-haired Mrs. Watkins and black-eyed Zelie Emerson in the van, raised vociferous cheers for me, which were cheerfully echoed from the outer fringes of the crowd gathered at the doors. Embarrassed, I pushed my way hastily through the press, and heard the shrill yelling of my name, in opposition to cries for Christabel and Mrs. Pankhurst, as they came out to a waiting car. I was irritated beyond measure, and hurried home without waiting for my henchwomen.

. . . . . . . .

Again Mrs. Pankhurst and Christabel were in Paris. Then, a little later, it was announced that they were coming back to England for a platform campaign to recruit men for the Army. Reading the Press announcement I wept under a surge of old memories and affections, which broke over me—I thought of my father's peace crusade of the 'seventies in which she had met him, the girl, Emmeline Goulden, in the ardour of her youth ; his unswerving life-long advocacy of Peace and Internationalism, in which, for nineteen years, she had supported

[1] See *The Suffragette Movement*, by Sylvia Pankhurst. Longmans Green.

him ; her stand with us, her children, against the Boer War—all this negated a vast rift lay between our past and her present intention !

I wrote to her on the impulse. She replied, very haughtily : " I am ashamed to know where you and Adela stand."

It was a shock to me when I read some speech of hers that she wished her boy had been marching with the armies. The vision of him came to my eyes, that gentle youth seeking amongst ancient philosophies the perfection of ethics. I knew that he must have loathed the War. A doubt sprang to my mind ; would he have been coerced into enlistment by his love for her ? Was it best that he had died ? The very thought seemed treason to him. Yet the doubt troubled me, as though he were here with the choice before him. Her words recurred to me horribly. She wished he had been marching with those poor lads driven out there to the carnage. I was anguished that she had said it ; that she could contemplate the thought of sending him to destruction. Had she forgotten him in his loveliness, that boy my heart would have burst to save ? Whenever the memory recurred, it stabbed me with a new wound. How could she think of sending her darling to be rent and mangled ? How could she know so little of him that she had failed to sense how alien, how hideous in its bestial hate and gross materialism, this butchery must have been to him ?

. . . . . . . .

" I don't agree," Lansbury said to me, " with the way the I.L.P. is doing—attacking the foreign policy of the Government ; I think they are spoiling the movement."

Constant struggle with the miseries of the great conflagration often made the causes which led to it seem tragically remote to me, in those days ; but I considered Lansbury conceded too much to the War Party.

A little later when Keir Hardie bitterly complained of the *Daily Citizen*, the Labour Party organ, calling it a " jingo rag " he was " ashamed " to open, I asked him : " Why don't you get Lansbury to make the *Daily Herald* a Pacifist paper and join forces with him ? "

He made no answer, only an impatient movement. A minute later I wondered that I could have thought it possible to combine, in a closely-knit venture, two men so different—the one tenacious as a rock, stirred by swift fire and passion, yet reserved, according to the old adage that still waters run deep ; the other volatile, voluble, changeable as the winds, working up to the popular thrills of the moment, and riding the storm of them with delighted zest. Yet though I saw their huge incompatibility, I could not wholly abandon the idea which would give Keir Hardie a voice in a daily paper. I mentioned it to Lansbury : " Why don't you make the *Herald* an out and out Pacifist paper and throw in your lot with Keir Hardie and the I.L.P. ? "

Lansbury stared at me. " I don't think you read the *Herald*. It *is* a Pacifist paper," he said reproachfully.

Alas, folk do not know their inconsistencies !

. . . . . . . .

Bernard Shaw's *Common Sense about the War*[1] was published that autumn. It was the naughtiest agglomeration of contradictions the great jester had ever perpetrated. In provocative mood he flung out :

" No doubt the heroic remedy for this tragic misunderstanding is that both armies should shoot their officers and go home to gather in their harvests in the villages and make a revolution in the towns."

And :

" There are only two flags in the world henceforth : the Red flag of democratic Socialism and the Black flag of Capitalism."

He insisted that British militarists, and not German, had begun the propaganda of an Anglo-German war ; that the Kaiser's assumption of God-given right to rule was outdone by that of the British ruling classes, and quoted Lord Roberts on " the will to conquer which has never failed us," and " the great task committed to us by Providence." He argued that the war guilt amounted to six of one and half a dozen of the other, so far as the rival groups of belligerent Powers were concerned ; and the Franco-Russian alliance just as much a menace to peace as the Austro-German one.

[1] Supplement to the *New Statesman*, November 14th, 1914.

Then he blew all this case to the winds, and announced that Britain "was compelled to enter the War" as "the responsible policeman of the West."

"Had the Foreign Office been the International Socialist Bureau . . . the result would still have been the same." "We are supporting the War as a war on war." "We must have the best army in Europe." "We in England are fighting to show the Prussians they shall not trample on us or our neighbours if we can help it, and that if they are fools enough to make fighting efficiency the test of civilisation we can play that game as destructively as they. That is the simple truth, and the jolliest and most inspiring ground to recruit on. It stirs the blood and stiffens the back."

Though this was his conclusion, and all his spicily-phrased "common sense" thus negatived, an avalanche of condemnation descended upon him; for a moment no man was more vilified by the jingoes, and notably by the Labour organ the *Daily Citizen*.

Keir Hardie, who in his work-driven existence had not time to wade through much verbiage, however witty, read Shaw's bold opening passages and wrote to him in an expansive moment, concluding:

"It is the expression of a heart which now throbs towards you with feelings almost of devotion."

After Keir Hardie's death Shaw disclosed the existence of the letter, and the fact that he had never answered it!

. . . . . . . .

The War and its measures proceeded, monstrous and ruthless. Only the rush of work and activity shaded our vision from its horror. I was reading, writing and speaking about diplomatic history and the international politics of war in the light of the great suffering I had seen arise from it. Morel's *Ten Years of Secret Diplomacy*, of which a second edition came out in December 1914, and a third in October 1915, Brailsford's *War of Steel and Gold*, Morel's *Truth and the War*, which was published later, provided masses of scathing facts. They were read by hundreds of people who would have laid them aside as too heavy and difficult at ordinary times. I had these and many more. Herbert Dunnico lent me books from the library of the Peace Society. The writings of Karl Marx, Kropotkin, William Godwin, William Morris—all those who attacked the ethics of present society at its base took on a deeper meaning.

The main facts of the dark history of fear, duplicity and greed which had led the belligerent nations to the brink of war were already known before the conflict. New details have since been supplied by those who wielded power and responsibility in making the tortuous mosaic of intrigue. In their own defence they have been unable to gloss over its sordid cruelty. Whether one reads it in the writings of the political leaders of the belligerent governments, of apologists for the permanent officials, like Harold Nicolson, or of their sternest critics, the story wounds. As I and others learnt it, under the influence of the mounting casualty lists, and the grim experiences of war, it aroused a deep and poignant horror.

## CHAPTER VIII

### BRITISH TOYS

GLUTTED with appeals for work, our employment bureau had little to supply save garment making for the destitute mothers and babies coming to our own clinics. " What hideous sewing ! " our helpers deplored when the work came home. One felt it a shame to give such cobbled work to anyone's tender little new-born baby. Yet till other work came we must employ the neediest. Poor destitute mothers, without food or fuel, they had no peace to work, with ailing, hungry little ones crying about them, no adequate light to sew when the children were in bed. Factory repetition work before marriage, and after marriage till a growing family, capped by some spell of unemployment, forced them to desist, had not prepared them for any sort of craft work.

We must husband our donations, to make the best use of them in this ocean of need ; better results could be obtained if the women could come to work in some warm, light place, and bring their babies. We had no space for this at 400 Old Ford ; the building was overcrowded. I rushed out one October afternoon to look for more premises and found an empty house, with a workshop in the garden, in a quiet street, just across " the Roman." Here we could organise a little factory and a day nursery.

It was all quickly done, as things were in those days. Crowds of people were eager to help, furniture, crockery, toys, pictures, babies' cots, clothing and perambulators were given without delay, in response to an appeal in the *Dreadnought*.

Revolting from the social round of Mayfair, and puppy shows, with her husband, something in Lloyds, and a very dull foil to her, lovely Lady Sybil Smith agreed to manage the nursery. On four days a week she left her seven children to " top and tail " East End babies, bringing with her a magnificent dolls' house, and a host of more useful trophies which could be abstracted unnoticed from her charming home at Rolls Park, Chigwell ; bringing also one of her ex-nurses, who was exceedingly doubtful as to the merits of East End women. Under Lady Sybil's gay auspices voluntary workers of all sorts and conditions worked merrily. She possessed a rare absence of class consciousness, a sensitive perception of the good qualities in other people and the precious ability to perceive that, at bottom, we most of us have the same needs. A Tolstoyan, secure from the grosser features of the economic struggle, she was probably more successful in the culture of her own soul than most of his followers.

For a time we continued making garments at the new factory, but I wanted also to start work of another sort; something which would take us out of the beaten track, give the workers scope for developing personal initiative and craft-skill.

Toy-making was my choice; it might be made to answer these requirements, and having trained as an artist, I should not find myself so wholly out of my depth in initiating this, as in many other industries. The stoppage of the large import of German toys had created a market. That did not influence me in choosing; but it helped our little industry to get a start. I engaged two art students from the Chelsea Polytechnic as designers. They fell into the work without difficulty. My old fellow-student at the R.C.A., Amy Browning, came down on Saturday afternoons to teach drawing and painting to any of the workers who cared to learn, both as a pleasure and to give them a chance to improve more quickly in the toy-making. The majority of the younger ones were glad to attend this class; the older workers were too hard-driven by home work. The factory was a place of happy activity, like an art school class of enthusiastic pupils. We encouraged the toy-makers to design, and if any of them produced a toy which was saleable, the factory purchased it and paid a royalty on the sales. One young mother of two toddlers, who had been employed filling sausages, developed so much skill, both as maker and designer, that when her husband was discharged from the Army medically unfit with a small gratuity, she took him down to the South of England and started a little factory of her own there. Another good worker had been a carriage cleaner. A girl from one of the poorest homes in Old Ford made a little figure of George Robey, as she had seen him on the variety stage, reproducing his attitude to the life; a remarkable achievement for an untaught girl.

Of course, as one of the beacons from which the fiery torch of better payment for women in the relief workrooms might be carried around the country, as a rod with which to belabour the wretched 10s. of the Queen Mary Rooms, we paid what was then the men's minimum wage of the district, £1 a week. Though this was important to our general struggle, to me the pleasantest feature of the factory was its happy cultural influence upon girls and women starved of beauty and opportunity.

Yet the factory was to our subscribers the ugly duckling amongst our activities. It was desperately hard to get money for it. Babies' milk and free meals made an instant appeal; the plea for aid in the cultural development of East End women fell on deaf ears. Subscribers were apt to consider that a factory, if efficient, should be self-supporting from the hour of its inception, forgetting that we were collecting our working capital, our industrial and business experience, training workers as we ourselves were learning the ropes.

There was no need to explain the point of it to Sybil Smith. She arranged many drawing-room meetings to collect funds in the houses of rich people, where I talked of the toy-making and the day nursery,

*Norah Smyth*

THE W.S.F. MOTHER AND INFANT CLINIC AT POPLAR

*Norah Smyth*

DAILY DISTRIBUTION OF MILK AT 20 RAILWAY STREET, POPLAR

Mrs. Schlette in charge.

*Norah Smyth*

THE FIRST "COST PRICE RESTAURANT" IN THE WOMEN'S HALL, 400 OLD FORD ROW, BOW
*From left:* third, the Author; fourth, Mrs. Payne; fifth, Mrs. Farrel; sixth, Mrs. Watkins.

and she sang delightful songs. We were together at Henry Holiday's beautiful Oak Tree House at Hendon, she like a lovely nymph from a Greek vase. " I have found you again, my angel ! " he cried, ecstatic, determined, no doubt, to put her in one of his pictures.

At the factory we commenced with soft toys and the flat wooden painted toys like those the Tyrolese peasants make. I had seen them in Parten Kirchen when I went there with Mrs. Pethick Lawrence, on our way from Innsbruck to Oberammergau, to visit the Passion Play. These toys were the easiest sort for a student fresh from a school of art. I set a designer to work on them and went round to St. Stephen's Road to buy three-ply wood from " Lansbury's Yard ", I. Brine and Company, as the firm was styled. Incidentally I told Willie Lansbury my purpose.

" Do you want a big fellow, a splendid chap who knows everything about woodwork ? " Willie asked me, explaining that the best worker in the yard was a German named Niederhofer, whom Lansbury senior feared to employ any longer, lest the works should be wrecked by jingo patriots. I asked to see Niederhofer, and found him all, and more than all, Willie Lansbury had said of him ; a great gentle fellow, unfortunately for these hard times, the father of seven little children. An orphan brought up in a German convent, he had been taught there to make just the very toys I intended. I engaged him at once to work for us at the same wage he was getting in the yard. He presently showed us that he could design as well as make the painted toys, and could also execute highly skilled cabinet work, inlay and upholstering. He was a patient teacher, and all our workers liked him ; not one murmured at learning from him on account of his nationality.

The flat painted toys proved too easy to make ; relief workrooms, like those of the Women's Emergency Corps, soon took up the work. Scores of commercial firms followed suit ; laying down power machines, and having no scruples about sweating, they could easily beat us in price.

The soft toys had a permanent market. I wanted a chubby cuddlesome baby doll, to replace the limp, flat-headed rag doll hitherto known. Amy Browning introduced me to a sculptor friend, Miss Acheson, who produced for us quite a new sort of rag doll of muslin and cotton wool. I sat up at night to draw out a pattern of it for factory use. We had blocks made from my drawings for dolls of three sizes, the largest three feet high. E. H. Williams, the *Dreadnought* printer, rolled them off on muslin, ready to be made up. Even with the printed pattern, the stuffing and painting of these dolls gave scope for a fair amount of skill. We added Negro and Japanese babies from similar patterns.

When the samples were complete I took them to Selfridges in a cab. An order was immediately given for them—our first commercial sale. Jessie Lansbury, Willie's wife, went off with her little girl to see them in the shop, and came back bubbling with the news that she had seen a number of them sold.

" The War did not exist for the average citizen," wrote Bernard Shaw in one of his prefaces.[1] This, though a quip, had a spice of truth

[1] *Heartbreak House,* page xxiii. Constable, 1919.

in it. Such social experiments as the toy factory might well have veiled from me its sorrows, but for the daily contact I had with the maimed and bereaved.

The new type of baby doll received instant popularity. The Women's Emergency Corps presently produced a rival to it, less artistic, more grotesque, but more quickly and easily made, and therefore cheaper. To fill these dolls was so simple that the Queen on a visit to the workroom was said to have stuffed one.

Hilda Jeffries, who came to us from the Chelsea Polytechnic, had remarkable aptitude for toy designing. She poured out monkeys, extraordinarily alive and knowing, playful lambs, saucy terriers, a stream of successes which took repeat orders for years. Factories of all sorts began making soft toys. The many varieties we know to-day were not seen before the War. The Teddy bear and the flat-faced rag doll practically monopolised the field.

Dolls with hard heads and limbs were more difficult. Edith Downing, a sculptor who had been a militant of the W.S.P.U., modelled for us one of the first of them with a pretty child's head, far removed from the conventional doll. I got it very efficiently reproduced by a manufacturer, somewhere in London, who before the War pretended his goods were French, because British dolls were regarded as mere imitations of no account. I essayed to get a china reproduction from the Potteries. After many enquiries a firm agreed to do it; but though the sample seemed just passable, the bulk delivery was exceedingly bad; the colour fugitive, the glaze uneven and sticky-looking. We did not adventure any further in the china dolls, but the firm which had sent us a barrel-load of failures and other potteries persevered in the quest.

We were able to watch the progress of other factories at the exhibitions of British toys which the Board of Trade organised periodically for the new toy industry.

The management of the factory was a source of anxiety. One morning in the early stages a Polish woman, perhaps thirty-five years of age, came to me with a letter from Keir Hardie, to whom she had gone with a letter from someone else. Pale and crushed-looking, she said she had come to London to organise an exhibition of Swiss products, which had been abandoned on account of the War. She pleaded that she was utterly stranded. She told me she had previously been employed in the management, though not the technical management, of a philanthropic training school for corset-making in Switzerland. Her English was broken and scanty; but I assumed she could add up a column of figures, and engaged her forthwith to keep the books at the factory, then just beginning. She knew nothing of commercial book-keeping, but I telephoned to my uncle, Herbert Goulden, who dealt in paper and book-cloth in the City, to come over and tutor her; which he did very kindly several times a week till she knew the ropes. Very soon she was manager of the factory; the self-effacing Joachim quickly slipped away, leaving her dominant. In those days the manageress professed for me unalterable devotion, flinging her arms around me with ecstatic cries: "Ah, Miss Pankhurst! Sweet! Sweet!" and declaring that flowers should spring from the ground where I trod. I pitied her as a woman alone and bereaved. Insistent in her demands for the factory she would conjure me, in the name of Karl Marx, whenever I cited finances as an obstacle to her wishes. As a "clerical worker" she must be employed shorter hours than the toy-makers, on no account beginning till 10 a.m. This was an established Trade Union principle.

I found myself under the constant necessity of inspecting the factory products. Many times in the early days I had to stop batches of dolls and toys going out, and Smyth and I had to put other things aside to work late at night, touching up painted toys, re-fastening dolls' wigs, renovating dolls' clothes. More than once I went to the factory early and discovered the young girls playing ball with the toys, which got thumbed and soiled in the process. When the enthusiasm of learning a new toy had evaporated and output failed to keep pace with anticipations, I suggested that piece rates might be a regrettable necessity to enable the toys to pay their way, but the tenets of Karl Marx were cited as an insurmountable barrier with so much vehemence that I capitulated.

Pricing, of which I had learnt the rule of thumb from my mother's Manchester adventure in shopkeeping, was Greek to the staff. The first toys despatched to Selfridges went out without a delivery note, and this big firm declared it contrary to their custom to pay unless delivery could be proved. All such failings I strove to remedy. Generous helpers responded to my appeals. Amongst others an I.L.P. traveller in fancy goods, Mr. Durant of Birmingham, gave coaching in business management. A Suffragette comrade, whose fine sewing was a marvel, taught our workers some of her craft and her pride in it. Little Agnes Kirner gazed at her with admiration, and wept with disappointment when her own sewing failed to reach the standard. Smyth poured some hundreds of her modest inheritance into the factory, others gave smaller sums.

One evening, long after war work had liquidated unemployment, and the Queen Mary Rooms were no more, and after many declarations that unless the factory could be made self-supporting it must close, Smyth and I went sadly thither, to say that the closing time had come. All responded with proposals to take reduced wages until they could pull up output. Karl Marx now was ousted in favour of "your great economists, Stuart Mill and Adam Smith." The manageress urged the piece rates she had denounced. Smyth provided a little more capital from her inheritance. Later, when the corner was turned successfully, Dr. Tchaykovsky deposited shares to guarantee the factory an overdraft in the slack summer season.

Our manageress blossomed into a capable saleswoman, a watchful manager, keen to reduce prices, demanding that the number of designs should be limited, and the style of the toys be altered, in order that the price might be brought down. Commercial necessity was crushing most of its virtue from the little venture. The names of " Your great economists " were often upon the lips of the manageress. She insisted that her remuneration must be increased, the wages of the toy makers reduced. Their needs, she told me, were less than hers, though she was alone and some of them had little children to support. Her spirit dismayed and saddened me, surrounded as I was by people who had gathered together from a sense of social solidarity: for woman's emancipation, for Socialism, for Peace; for some impersonal idea—all making some sacrifice, in time, money, and comfort. She seemed to me thirsty as a tigress for her prerogatives, yet hers was but the everyday habit of commerce, which enables the employer by drawing some mickle from each of the weak ones who toil for him, to make a pleasant muckle for himself, to provide him and his a more comfortable apartment, better food, better clothes, the hearing of good music and intellectual drama.

The factory continues still in the same small premises, in the same small way; yet not the same way. The expert has not rationalised nor the financier mechanised it. Had they done so, would they, could they have raised it above the level of the ill-paid industries? Could they have spared its workers the stultification of monotonous repetition work? The little factory taught me, in sharp experience, the difficulties which beset the hardy adventurer who essays to build an offshoot of Utopia in competitive trade, struggling with the iron fact that whoever attempts to pay a decent wage runs the risk of finding cheaper commodities sweeping his own from the market.

# CHAPTER IX

## RECRUITS ILL-SUPPLIED—
## SOLDIERS' WIVES AND MOTHERS AT THE WAR OFFICE

AUTUMN drew on; privations, confusion and heartbreaking delays continued still. Soldiers wrote from camp to their wives complaining that they were fighting for food and short of clothes.

"You have one basin between two and 1 lb. of bread to last you all day. . . . There was a man walking about the camp with a blanket round him because he had no trousers on, and more men nearly the same. . . . I have been waiting for a pair of boots for a week, and have not got them yet! My boots are nearly off my feet and I have not had a clean for two weeks. You have to take your shirt off and wash it out yourself. They are getting some more shirts now, but there are not enough to go round. There are hundreds of men waiting for them. . . . They told us Friday that if there is any man that can get a suit, a pair of boots, overcoat, cap, knife, fork and spoon they will give us ten shillings for the loan of them until they get others for us. Not one man has got his kit given him."

Asquith in his memoirs records that Kitchener admitted "the recruits had been badly treated in the way of clothing, boots and other necessaries." The poor fellows who had joined Haldane's vaunted Territorials were compelled to provide equipment costing £2 10s. or more. If, as in a large proportion of cases, a man lacked this sum, he must purchase at the regimental store, and have the charge docked from his pay—a bad arrangement for him, as the store charge was higher than outside. The contractor reaped the benefit.

A poor neighbour of ours, who got into debt to buy new underclothing for her husband when he went to camp, was surprised to find him come home, a runaway, ten days later. He had been sleeping on the floor without mattress in a harness room over a stable. The roof leaked, the blankets were verminous. He had but the one set of underclothing his wife had bought him; for the military authorities had supplied him only with outer garments. He had to buy soap and candles from his pay. For breakfast he and his mates had only a slice of dry bread with a little piece of butter unspread in the middle of it, which they threw away, because it was always rancid. On this fare they had to walk ten miles, carrying 56 lbs. on their backs, after which they received a bottle of soda water, and on returning, a pan-lid of broth.

Their evening meal was a slice of bread, and again the rancid butter, with a can of tea. Some jobbery doubtless accounted for this poor fare. He and three others had run home to get clean. Twenty men had decamped ten days before. On Monday he returned to camp with a heavy cold and looking, his wife said, very ill. She had heard nothing for many days since, and came to me, fearing he was in prison and that her own separation allowance would be stopped.

I was clamouring for an interview at the War Office. On October 2nd Lord Kitchener deputed Harold Baker to see us. I took with me Charlotte Drake, Edith Jones and nine soldiers' wives and mothers, sorrowful, anxious, their faces a very epitome of all the miseries women suffered in those dark days. At the sight of their poverty Baker, immaculately tailored, arrogant with class prejudice, was taken aback. He turned to me sharply :

" I only want to hear the officials ; I do not want to listen to the actual cases ! "

The " cases." Oh, wounding, misused term ! The poor beings thus designated quivered in dumb distress.

We jarred and jangled, I indignant :

" But surely you want to understand their point of view and to know what their actual experience is ! "

He, imperious : " This is not a Court of Enquiry . . . it is no use listening to them."

I, insistent : " This deputation is to represent the opinions and experiences of the women concerned."

He weakened a little, but, as I considered, with insolent unreason declared he would not allow more than five women at a time into the room. " This room is too small ! " he glared round the spacious chamber.

I complained of the terrible delays in paying separation allowance. Sir Charles Harris, a ruddy, bellicose man at Baker's elbow, who conducted the business for his stiff chief, denounced the ignorance of women : the cause, he was confident, of every trouble. Mrs. Drake tersely enquired whether particulars as to their families could not be obtained from recruits on enlistment, in order that their wives should not be left to discover the Army procedure for themselves. He replied that men sometimes " forgot " they had families and were " glad to bolt ! "

We pleaded that no woman could keep going the smallest home in any degree of decency, with less than £1 a week ; and that, given this nucleus, no child could be kept, even sparely, for less than 5s. a week. On leaving the elementary schools the children whose fathers had been killed should either be sent to secondary schools and supported by maintenance grants, or apprenticed to trades, as was done for orphans in pre-War Hungary. Harris eyed us satirically, convinced that some of us were fools and the others knaves. He refused to admit the inadequacy of the miserly pension, of 5s. a week for the wife, and

1s. 6d. per child, fixed in the Boer War, and still obtaining. " It all depends who has to live on it ! " he smiled scornfully.

Dumb thus far, the soldiers' wives spoke out their resentment. A mother of six had pawned, and sold, and gone days without food, whilst waiting her allowance. A mother of five had been told by the ladies of the S.S.F.A. that she ought to show her patriotism by selling her furniture and moving into a single room before coming to them for aid, when her allowance failed to appear. A poor woman, left with two infants by an absconding husband, had lived six years with a Reservist and borne him children. She complained of her destitution, the harsh denial of all allowance, and urged the claim of the soldier's unmarried wife to the pay her man had earned.

Baker interrupted her brusquely. " I will hear no more of the cases. I am going to make my reply."

He did so woodenly, without a gleam of understanding, conceding nothing, giving no hope of improvement. No trace of sympathy for these sore-tried women did I myself perceive.

. . . . . . . .

In my correspondence, just then, came a fitting reply to Sir Charles Harris. A Welsh soldier's wife sent me a letter from her husband :

" Dear, I hope this war won't last long, for I am quite sick of it. They don't do right by wives at all. It is the same with everyone up here. Dear, it is not my fault that your money is stopped, I can tell you, but I have wrote away about it for you, and the Sergeant Major is writing again to-night, so you see I am doing my very best about it, for it must be hard on you without any money, love, and I shall see you get it too, my love."

This woman had been left five weeks without separation allowance. The relief committee had suggested her husband was to blame.

The original separation allowance of 1s. 1d. a day for soldiers' wives and 2d. a day for their children had by this time been raised to 11s. 1d. a week for the wife, and 1s. 9d. for each of the first three children, 1s. 2d. for the fourth, a maximum of 17s. 6d., with no further increase, however large the family might be. These sums included a compulsory allotment of 3s. 6d. per week for the wife and 7d. per child up to a maximum of 5s. 3d. a week deducted from the soldier's pay.

In response to the stream of horrified protests against the grievous poverty of the soldiers' wives, Asquith announced another small increase, bringing the scale up to 12s. 6d. a week for the wife, 2s. 6d. for each of the first four children, and 2s. each for the rest. Great and general satisfaction welcomed the promise that henceforth the allowances should be paid through the Post Office, without the intervention of the impudent, charity-mongering S.S.F.A., upon which the popular mind heaped, not only its own shortcomings, but all those of the Government and the Army administration.

Sad was the consternation of the soldiers' wives to receive on October 12th, instead of the promised increase in the allowance, a reduction of at least 3s. 6d. Other influences had been at work; the vacillant Government had reversed its policy. The official explanation of the broken promise was the absurd pretence that the War Office had no power to pay the husband's allotment through the Post Office, and that the new method had necessitated stopping the small grants from the S.S.F.A. by which the former allowances had been made up.

Though the general outcry caused the restoration of the allotments, the promised increase proved a delusion. The hope deferred, which maketh the heart sick, was the common portion of the soldiers' and sailors' wives and relatives!

The parents and other dependants of unmarried soldiers had been promised allowances; none were as yet forthcoming. Some had received odd pittances from the S.S.F.A.; the majority got nothing. The Government still debated.

The scale of allowances for the wives of the sailors in Britain's famous Navy remained undecided till September 22nd. When some weeks later the women got knowledge of it they found, if married to Ordinary Seamen, Able Seamen, Leading Seamen and Second Class Petty Officers, they were to get a mere 6s. a week, with 2s. a week for their first and second children, and 1s. a week for the rest. To supplement these wretched sums the men could make a minimum allotment of £1 a month.

Many a woman, despite her own straitened circumstances, was sending money, food and clothing to her husband "roughing it" somewhere in camp or on ship; for the compulsory allotments made too large a drain on men's pay, and the pay itself often failed to appear.

Towards the end of October the War Office decided to relieve the soldier's hard-pressed condition at the expense of his wife. Should a husband "object" to making the full allotment to his family, the wife would be asked whether she would be content to accept less, and if not to state her means. Meanwhile enquiries would be made to ascertain whether her income, without the allotment, was up to the "standard scale." Should the woman fail to return the form, as many weary and anxious women did, not knowing how best to answer a communication, at once so poignant and so terrifying, the reduced allowance would be sent her. Without the consent or knowledge of the soldiers such letters as the following were sent to their wives:

"Madam—Your husband has represented that in view of his own expenses and requirements he finds himself unable to continue the allotment to you. . . . It is thought that you may find yourself sufficiently well off not to claim from your husband a share of his pay."

Many a wife who received such a missive was not yet getting the separation allowance due to her. Alderman J. R. Hurry, J.P., of West Ham, exceptionally well informed, because he was aiding the work of the local S.S.F.A., and also a member of the West Ham Mayor's Committee, told the Press early in November: "I don't suppose more than one woman in twenty is receiving the full amount she is entitled to from the War Office."

The wives of many Naval and Fleet Reservists whose allowances were due on October 1st in his experience had received nothing.

Whilst the wives were thus urged to forego their allotments of 3s. 6d. —half the soldiers' pay—it was at last announced that unmarried wives might have separation allowance, but only on condition that the soldier surrendered to them not less than 5s. 3d. a week, leaving only a meagre 3d. a day for his own needs—a harsh proviso, truly, when the payments of the legally married husband were actually being reduced. Official parsimony, in the guise of Mrs. Grundy, desired to put his loving faithfulness to an acid test. Even this was only conceded if the woman had been entirely supported by the soldier before enlistment, and would now be wholly destitute without his aid.

The War Office still refused allowances to children born less than nine months after their parents' marriage.

Already many thousands of women were widowed. On November 9th a new scale of pensions for widows of seamen and marines was issued: 7s. 6d. a week for the childless widow, 5s. a week for the first child, 2s. 6d. each for the second, third, and fourth, and 2s. for subsequent children—meagre allowances, which kept them pinched and needy.

At the same time it was at last conceded that some allowance should be made to the parents and little brothers and sisters who had been supported by unmarried soldiers before enlistment. At best the promised allowance was appallingly mean. The highest amount to which the Government would contribute was 12s. 6d. a week. To secure this sum the soldier must give 3s. 6d. a week from his pay. When he had done so he often found that his aged parents, or his widowed mother and young brothers and sisters failed to receive the promised dole, small as it was. Before any payment was made inquisitors called at the soldier's home, and closely questioned his mother as to how she had spent the money her son had brought home to her. The promised 12s. 6d. would only be paid if the inquisitor considered the mother had retained that sum as clear profit, beyond the amount she had expended on her son. The Government would only contribute towards the profit, frequently giving the mother no more than 5d. or 6d. a week.

No indication of this procedure was given in the memorandum promising dependants' allowances, issued by the War Office, nor in the posters put up to induce young men to enlist.

In fixing the allowances no account was taken of the rise in the cost of living, no latitude given in respect of death, unemployment, or any misfortune which had befallen the father, or other members of the family, since the son enlisted. "My son would have given me more had I been placed then as I am now; he would have given his last penny rather than see his little brothers and sisters go hungry," many a poor mother pleaded. One of them wrote to me from Edinburgh:

"I have a son in the 9th Royal Scots. My boy signed a paper allowing me 6d. a day, being told the Government would allow his mother up to 10s. . . . a Pension officer came down. I will not say what I suffered from that man; but I was insulted by our generous Government by the offer of fivepence a week for my son! It is a disgrace! My boy gave me 10s. a week; in a month or two he would have been getting 12s. and in the course of a year he would have been out of his time and getting 18s. to £1. The Pension officer said I was not any the loser, but suppose my son does not come back! Many a mother has had a hard struggle to bring her son up to be a man, and just as he has got to be a fine help he goes. My boy went away the very week the War broke out and offered to fight for his country—and I had taken rooms at a higher rent last May, because I thought his pay would be always increasing. I had to buy all his kit in the Territorials, and I did not get the £5 they speak of. Now I am unable to pay my rent next week, and I will be compelled to leave this house; I cannot keep it up on my husband's small pay. I have five other children, the oldest is 12 years of age. The one that is in the Army is the only boy I had working. It is very hard, and I will have to go and get work of some kind to do at home. I have a young infant I cannot leave, and my husband is not strong now. . . . When I had my boy giving me 10s. a week I put 8s. 7d. of it away for the rent, as it took all his father's pay, which is not big, to keep us in food and everything is so dear since the War."

Another wrote to me:

"My son says the 5s. 10d. a week I am getting is all from him. Is it a good principle to let a boy pay 10d. a day out of 1s. 2½d. to me and for the Government to pay nothing? Now I know I am taking nearly all my son's money it hurts me, and although I cannot make two ends meet with his 5s. 10d. I will save him some."

Jack Sutton, one of the Manchester Labour Members of Parliament whom I knew well, complained that in the Lancashire coalfields mothers with several sons, who had each given her £1 a week, were only able to get from the War Office a few shillings in respect of one of them. Thomas Richardson protested that the War Office and its investigators disregarded the recommendations of Pensions committees in respect of parents' allowances.

A poor old father appeared at Bow County Court to answer his landlord's application to evict him for non-payment of rent. In eight weeks he had had but 2½ days' work. His wife was ill and he had to support five grandchildren, whose father was in Australia, and of whom nothing had been heard since the outbreak of war. He had three sons at the War, and a fourth had been killed in action. He had received not a penny of separation allowance on account of any of them.

Eight soldiers wrote to the *Daily Citizen :*

" When we enlisted we little thought how those at home were going to fare ! We were given to understand that if we allotted a small portion of our pay the . . . Government would add to it. This we did, but . . . our people have failed to draw even our own allotments."

A soldier's mother brought me a letter from her son :

" . . . I was sorry to hear Dad is not doing much work. You ask me to send you 3s. through the paymaster. I am afraid you don't know how quick they work in the Pay Office. I applied for a form two weeks ago, and yesterday the Pay Sergeant sent for me and told me to go down the line as far as —— and find out how many men wanted forms. We had 70 in our company and I sent the numbers on to our Paymaster at ——. They have to wait now till all the companies send in their numbers and they will send off the forms. By the time they are filled in, and sent back, I expect it will take a month, and then they will be sent to the War Office for their examination. . . . In the meantime I will send you the 3s. because I know you will have to wait a long time before the War Office moves. The town is placarded in every street with the forms showing what you get[1] if you allow the Pay Sergeant to stop so much. Our boys are so disgusted continually asking for forms that they have thrown mud at the notices. . . ."

For some time we were alone in our demand for £1 a week for the soldiers' wives and dependent mothers, and 5s. a week for each child—little enough, and tolerable only because wage standards were so low. In November the Labour organ, the *Daily Citizen*, adopted the same cry, the Labour War Emergency Committee also took it up.

Crowds of women flocked to me in their troubles, clutching their sheaves of documents. Spurred by their need, I attacked the work with unresting energy, learning new ropes every day and dragging a band of willing helpers with me in the quest. I impressed on them that it was our mission to be the advocates of the people ; to get for them the highest possible terms we could ; they could never be too high ; nay, in this welter of meagre standards always immeasurably too low ! I had four shorthand-typists busy on the work and a number of voluntary aids.

Difficult cases, refused by all the authorities, began to reach to me from all parts of the country. Mrs. Drake and our other organisers and secretaries were dealing with similar problems. I dictated letters each day from 10 a.m. till 2 p.m., and often later, to demolish the piles of correspondence which rose about me, then turned to other work. Public meetings, branch meetings, committees, the *Dreadnought* to edit and largely to write, the newspapers and the Parliamentary reports—I read the whole of them—kept me at it from waking to sleeping. I was always up working two nights a week and went on next day without a

[1] As explained above, in most cases dependants did not get what the form appeared to indicate.

break. I often had to go back to the diets I had used when recovering from the hunger strike; days of hot water, days of white of egg and water, then gradually prune juice and dried biscuits, a teaspoonful of scraped raw beef, or an all-fruit diet, assisted at times by dried seaweed. With such expedients I kept on, unceasing.

Tracing the sums due to the women was a tedious business. Paymasters wrote in pencil, their writing often almost illegible. Army departments contradicted each other, failed to keep their own rules, and made unconscionable muddles.

The unmarried wife of a soldier came crying to me from Bethnal Green, bringing three little children between three years and three months. Her man, who was now wounded and in hospital, had allotted her 9s. a week, but neither the allotment nor any other money had reached her in the three months since he was called up, save small doles amounting to 39s. 9d. from the S.S.F.A. She had pawned all her furniture and was in desperate straits. Should her man die before the allotment question were settled, she would probably get no pension of any sort.

A woman whose separation allowance was 18s. 6d. a week, had 10s. a week deducted from it, to repay some doles she had had from the S.S.F.A., which amounted to 50s., and which she had not known to be loans. In dozens of cases I was pleading with the authorities that if they would insist upon recovering such doles, the repayments should be in very small sums.

A Bow Reservist, set to guard Wapping tunnel, came over to see me. Called up fourteen days before, he had had no pay, and had only managed to get a loan of five shillings from the colour-sergeant to bring home. He had Army rations, of course, but his wife had no money to feed his five little children. On their account he had hurried here. His baby was ill and his wife—little wonder—was far from well. I telephoned to the local S.S.F.A. The office was closed. The officials were not present on Wednesdays, a charwoman said. The soldier blasphemed when he heard it. Relieved when I told him Nurse Hebbes should go round to supply his family with their immediate needs, he talked of his own hardships. He and his mates were sleeping in their clothes on the floor of the ladies' waiting-room in the railway station. They got little rest, for they were forbidden even to take off their belts, and officers came round frequently to inspect them. Their uniform was arriving by instalments. He showed me some of the garments marked "made in Germany." "It's a fool's trick," he grumbled, "taking me from my work in Bow to guard that tunnel. There's men in Wapping out of work could do it, and sleep in their own beds!"

## CHAPTER X

### BEARDING HERBERT SAMUEL—THE BITTER BREAD OF CHARITY

APPEALS poured in on us:

" Will you open a workroom for the poor women in Hackney Road or Mansford Street? I am a poor mother with two sons at the War and I am nearly starving. If we ask for help we are told to sell our homes. We have plenty of people coming to enquire all our business, and then walking away."

" Chronic poverty"; thus lightly the Pharisees dismissed this lack which seared my heart. People in terrible need constantly appealed to us. Often I was constrained to take the food from our table to give to starving people, sometimes the blankets from our beds. Smyth had a board in her room covered with little bits of paper intended to record the repayments of unfortunate people to whom she had lent her money. Once, twice, thrice, even four times they might come with their pennies and shillings; then, almost invariably, they broke down. " Do not lend," I begged her; " they cannot repay except by starving their children. Give what you can afford and leave the rest."

An inquest on a Southwark baby revealed that a man working short time and his wife and six children had been struggling to exist on 12s. 6d. a week, out of which 6s. 6d. had to be paid in rent. The baby at fifteen months weighed only 7 lbs. 6 ozs., instead of the normal 18 to 20 lbs. They had had no relief from any source. The coroner's jury returned a verdict of " Death from natural causes." A poor charwoman went to the caretaker of a mission house in Notting Dale, crying: " I haven't had any food for three or four days, I have strangled my little boy!" She was tried for the murder of the two-year old boy and sentenced to ten years penal servitude. It was admitted that she was suffering from lack of food. Though sometimes relieved, we were informed in Poplar that charwomen were " casual " workers, ineligible for aid from the National Relief Fund; this being the opinion of a Local Government Board Inspector.

Beside the time-honoured Poor Law disability there were all sorts of foolish and cruel restrictions against granting these or those children the free school meals, which should have helped to protect the children from hardship—the children had been having the meals already a certain time (though the family income, so far from improving, had actually been reduced). The school meals were indeed nothing to boast of: meat pies one day, boiled rice and bread another. " They ask for more bread when they get home," a mother told me sadly. " Can you have a second helping?" I asked her little ones. " They'll give you more if they have any left, but generally they haven't," they answered wistfully.

It was a shock to learn that the children of British wives of Germans whose husbands were interned were refused school meals because of their fathers' nationality, though themselves legally British subjects, compelled to attend school, and liable to conscription when old enough.

At last the Cabinet Committee and the Central Committee for the National Relief Fund published a model scale of doles for civilian distress: 10s. a week for one adult, 4s. 6d. for each additional adult, 1s. 6d. a week for each child, up to a maximum of £1 a week for a family. The scale was hotly denounced in Labour circles as grossly inadequate. Lansbury fulminated against it in his *Herald*, but in Poplar, where he had been popularly elected to protect popular interests, the Mayor's much lower scale still prevailed—and only our Federation would protest. That is politics. With sorrow and bitterness I learnt it, and a disillusionment which often meant for me a lonely aloofness from all save the little band who struggled with me and the great mass of the poor. To them my heart clove; I was theirs, theirs with all my strength.

. . . . . . . .

The Poplar Local Representative Committee had not met for a month. Its adoption of the Fulham scale was a dead letter. The Ward committees had not been notified of it; the Mayor had ignored it. The food tickets he had doled out in person were now distributed by Borough officials according to his instructions, on a maximum scale of 4s. a week per adult and 1s. a week per child to the entirely destitute. At least a fortnight after registration must elapse before even these paltry doles could be received.[1] Meanwhile the applicant must pass the scrutiny of the registration clerks, the ward committees, the Borough treasurer, and finally the almoner appointed by the Mayor. To earn 2s. or to receive it from a wage-earning child, a lodger, or anywhere, was to reduce relief by 2s. To receive relief from the Poor Law meant complete disqualification. One poor fellow had almost passed the inquisition successfully, but spurred by hunger, he appealed to the Poor Law relieving officer for a loaf of bread. When the almoner enquired: "Have you had any Parish relief?" he answered truthfully, and was struck off the list. The Relieving Officer refused to assist him a second time, declaring his a case for the National Relief Fund. Men do not die of such iniquities—only lose health.

So cursory was the treatment of distressed people that no appointments were made for the disbursement of relief, and whoever chanced to be away from home when the distributor called was left without for that week.

When all the evidence of this procedure[2] was in my hands, I exposed the facts in the *Dreadnought*, demanded a meeting of the Local Representative Committee, and placarded the borough with the caption:

"THE MAYOR'S MEAN SCALE OF RELIEF."

I concluded my *Dreadnought* indictment with these words:

"When the Mayor's Local Representative Committee was called together, much time was spent in discussing the representation of the various interests in the Borough, and each and all were clamorous for their full share. I have been astonished to discover how unprotestingly these lately clamorous interests have allowed the functions and activities of the main committee to disappear. Unceasing was their vigilance when the measure of representation for their parties was in question, but they are slumbrous in matters which concern the measure of sustenance to be apportioned to the distressed."

The shot went home. The *Dreadnought* appeared on Friday and the Mayor and every member of the Local Representative Committee received a copy. By the last post on Saturday the Mayor summoned the Committee to meet on Wednesday, November 4th.

He faced us then, a poor feeble old man, protesting that he had had to plead "like a cripple at the gate" for the £374 which was all that

[1] In Camberwell applicants were relieved within three days.

[2] Emily Dyce-Sharp, my sub-editor, as Hon. Secretary of the Bow West Ward Committee assisted me materially in collecting the facts.

Poplar had received from the Fund since War began, though its neighbour West Ham had had £5,000.

The *Dreadnought* had done its work in making the whole council uncomfortable ; some were anxious to hush up the disagreeable matter ; others to dissociate themselves from the action of the Mayor. A certain clergyman, though popularly regarded as one of the greatest niggards in the borough, treated the Mayor with irony, asking whether it was outside the scope of the National Relief Fund to make grants to the Local Committees for the relief of distress. Another parsimonious reactionary accused the Mayor of " peddling with relief." Susan Lawrence, with a magisterial air, observed that nothing was worse than inadequate relief. She would have preferred that no relief at all should be given than on the Mayor's low scale.

The scale recommended by the Cabinet Committee was discussed. I pointed out that we on the Poplar committee had already resolved to relieve on the Fulham scale, which was a higher one. I moved that we should adhere to that decision. George Lansbury seconded in a bellicose speech. It was objected that the Central Committee might refuse its grants if our scale were higher than it proposed. I answered that even if it did so we should retort by collecting our own funds, as several other districts were doing.

George Lansbury seconded me with his usual torrents of excited oratory. I have often observed that the noisiest speakers are the first to compromise. St. John Hutchinson, a Liberal and the L.C.C. Member for the borough, an adept at drawing the teeth and claws of the lion rampant, moved an amendment that we adopt the Cabinet Committee scale but strongly urge that the family maximum be increased from £1 to 25s., and the children's allowances from 1s. 6d. to 2s.

Lansbury at once swung round to this proposal and urged me to do the same. When I refused he withdrew as seconder, and as no one else came forward in his place my motion fell to the ground.

Councillor Green, whose business was prospering most exceedingly through the War, now requested that the expression " strongly " be deleted from the resolution, in case the Government might be embarrassed thereby. The country, he said, was in " a very serious state " and " people must not be led to think they could have *anything* they wanted." Hutchinson at once agreed to the deletion of the offending word and the resolution was carried with almost unanimous satisfaction.

The rest of the business was scrambled through with unseemly haste, the bulk of it referred to the General Purposes Committee. As had happened each time we met, neither minutes nor correspondence were read. The latter omission was entirely comprehensible, since the ward committee had written angry complaints of the Mayor's autocratic mismanagement and parsimony, and the conscienceless inactivity of the main committee. I moved that the minutes and correspondence be read as a matter of course at each meeting, but again my motion failed, for lack of a seconder. This was an amazing revelation of the irregularities of local administration. The procedure was perhaps no less irregular in other districts. Even the Mayor's miserable scale was not the lowest! The Leyton Local Representative Committee had adopted a relief scale giving 3s. a week per adult with a maximum of 10s. per family—with prices at famine height! These people must subsist on bread alone and too little of that! The Reading Committee, on the other hand, denounced the Government scale as too low and refused to administer it.

Saddening as was contact with municipal politics, at least, I thought—too credulously—that we had done with the Mayor's mean scale. Poor folk who had starved on his miserly 4s. dole would welcome the Cabinet scale, unsatisfactory as it was. I had secured also the carrying of an instruction that the names of relief applicants rejected by the officials at the Town Hall must be sent to the ward committees for further investigation. This would be a check upon arbitrary rejection. We might hope at last for improved administration. Alas, in less than three weeks the Mayor informed the ward secretaries that the Cabinet Committee refused to permit the grant necessary to relieve the distressed applicants recommended by the ward committees, on the basis of the Government's own scale. Therefore he would revert to his original scale, unless the ward committees would drastically reduce the number of persons to be relieved. Already the officials at the Town Hall had struck off the list a large proportion of the people whose claims the ward committees had sanctioned.

Enraged at this new attack on those whose misery hourly concerned me, I wrote in hot haste to Herbert Samuel, the chairman of the Cabinet Committee, that I would come with a deputation to wait on him next day. I sent him a copy of the Mayor's scale, protesting "It is a national disgrace that such meanness should be allowed!"

Joined by the Rev. Henry Parrot, a member of the Bow West Ward committee, who, as indignant as we, asked leave to come with us, ten of us presented ourselves at the Local Government Board offices, and were received by Herbert Samuel and John Burns.

Samuel protested that the Committee disapproved the scale of the Mayor, but urged us to reduce the number of persons relieved. After seeing a list of our distressed people, and hearing some of them speak for themselves—they were starving, even on the present scale of relief—Burns asked me what I desired should be done. Of course I answered: "Find more work for the unemployed; give adequate allowances to the mothers, young children and all who cannot work." I reminded him that only 14½ per cent. of the men and 10 per cent. of the women who had appealed to the Central unemployed body for work had received it.

Burns promised to see what could be done—an inspector would be sent down to Poplar to talk to the Mayor. He was exceedingly friendly, treated me like a father, and assured us we had been "more frightened than hurt."

Yet despite his cordiality, and the promises of Samuel, the scale of relief was steadily decreased; in some cases even below the wretched scale of the Mayor. A husband and wife, who between them managed to earn 2s. 5d., were given only 4s. in food tickets. Another couple, wholly without income, got 5s. A husband and wife with two children, who had no income, got 10s. Two adults and three children were given 12s., and a man and wife with four children the same amount, though they, too, had no income. A woman with dependent children aged seven and ten had earned 1s., her only income, and got 3s. in tickets.

Whilst thus cruelly cutting down the doles, the Mayor again failed to summon the committee. I endeavoured to secure a Town's Meeting of protest ; the requisite number of ratepayers' signatures were sent up, but the Mayor and Council refused their sanction. All this I exposed in the *Dreadnought*. The Committee, on which so many important personages had seats, acquiesced in being totally ignored.

# CHAPTER XI

## WAR CONTRACTS AND WAR LOANS—BIG PROFITS FROM SWEATED LABOUR

WAR work was already growing up, to provide a rich harvest for contractors, served by a piteous army of sweated women, ill-clad, ill-fed, starved of sleep and rest. A mushroom-like growth of new clothiers and equipment-makers began to appear, dwelling houses were converted into factories, factories extended their premises.

With unemployment still rife, the working of excessive overtime—often unpaid for—was exacted, on the plea of " national necessity." Time was " cribbed " from the workers' dinner-hour, seven days' labour imposed, wages often reduced. Close by us clothiers on Army contracts were working till 8 p.m. and on Sundays ; at a well-known preserving factory women worked from 7.30 a.m. to 6 p.m. for 11s. a week, and on till 9.30 p.m. for 2¼d. per hour. At another East End factory women, standing in water at their work, were paid 8s. a week. A Poplar firm was giving out soldiers' shirts at 2s. 1d. per dozen, minus 2¼d. a reel for the cotton. The harsh, dark khaki material tried the women's eyes and made their fingers sore. They could not produce more than a dozen shirts a day, try as they might. Army vests were being made in Woolwich for 10¾d. a dozen. The Amalgamated Society of Tailors and Tailoresses complained that in Plymouth soldiers' breeches were being made throughout for 7½d., and khaki uniforms complete for 1s. 6d. The Stepney Public Health Committee declared that Army contracts were often four times sub-let, each sub-contractor making a profit at the expense of the sweated women doing the work, soldiers' trousers were being finished at 1¾d. per pair. H. D. Roberts, Chairman of the Liverpool Anti-Sweating League, complained that on kit-bags and military uniforms women were paid 25 per cent. less than the low minimum of 3½d. per hour prescribed by the Clothing Trade Board.

I had constantly availed myself of Runciman's invitation, of September 8th, to appeal to the Board of Trade for redress in cases of sweating, but with little result. On October 23rd, I received a somewhat amazing letter :

MADAM,

I am directed by the Board of Trade to acknowledge your letter of October 14th, with enclosure addressed to the President, on the subject of rates of wages paid by a sub-contractor for machining Army shirts, and in reply to say that no minimum rates having been fixed for the branch of trade in question, the Shirtmaking Trade Board (Great Britain) have given notice of certain minimum rates of wages which they propose to fix; but it is not known whether, after considering objections to the rates, they will adhere to the proposals, and at the present time no such rates are in operation.

I am, Madam, your obedient servant,

S. G. Barnes.

This was an utter denial of Runciman's own promise, and of the Fair Contracts Clause, which was supposed to protect all persons employed on Government work against unfair rates. I wrote to Runciman in a rage of indignation:

"In substance I take the letter to mean that you cannot, will not, and do not care to do anything to prevent the sweating of working women, who are executing orders for the Government, through the medium of contractors and sub-contractors. This being the case, to reply to us as you did, when we saw you, was dishonest in the extreme."

I sent the correspondence to the Press. *The Manchester Guardian* published it in full. To my astonishment, and still greater indignation, an official of the National Anti-Sweating League leapt into the lists to defend the Government and the sweating contractors. Replying to me through an interviewer sent to him by the *Manchester Guardian*, he declared: "As a matter of fact the prices being paid for Government work are in general good . . . any good worker used to the particular kind of work" should be able, he said, to earn £1 a week or more. He insisted that girls in well-equipped power-driven factories were earning 40s. a week and upwards. That was not my experience.

About that time a crowd of workers at Kent's big brush factory in Victoria Park Road, Bow, had come to me with their brushes and bristles, and their pay envelopes stamped with the broad arrow—to show they were doing Government work. Their fingers were cut and bleeding, bent and permanently deformed by the wire, their eyes red and sore from excessive labour. They were paid 1s. 2d. a dozen brushes, each having 163 holes to be filled. The quickest worker in the factory had managed to earn 11s. 1d., of which 3s. had been made by taking her work home at night, after toiling from 8 a.m. to 6 p.m. in the factory. Other workers had made only from 6s. to 8s., part of it also at home. Out-workers were paid a penny a dozen less than the factory hands, machine workers only 9d. a dozen, the quickest of them making but 12s. a week, the average 7s. or 8s.

I cited this case, in replying to the Anti-Sweating League, and quoted also the rates complained of by the Stepney Public Health Committee, and the Liverpool Anti-Sweating League.

The Anti-Sweating League official still, through the *Manchester Guardian*, defended the contractors, denying the charges from Stepney, and ignoring those from Liverpool, though the League was originally an offshoot of his own organisation. He observed sententiously that if the facts in regard to Kent's brushmakers were as serious as alleged, they should at once be communicated to the Director of Contracts at the War Office. This I had done, as a matter of routine, as soon as the case came to my notice. Moreover, the facts had already been communicated to Mr. J. J. Mallon, the Secretary of the National Anti-Sweating League, a member of the I.L.P. and an intimate friend of Mary Macarthur. Arthur Henderson, M.P., had sent the facts to the National Anti-Sweating League when I had appealed to him for aid. War time patriotism provided the Government with many strange defenders!

As usual, it was Keir Hardie who secured increased pay for Kent's brushmakers. The method I learnt from him then, and often employed thereafter, was simple, though tedious. It was to goad the Government into compelling the worst wage-payers among its contractors to conform to the rates of other firms of the same sort by appealing to the "Fair Contracts Clause." Yet alas, alas, even the best of the contractors paid grievously little to women workers.

Roberts, the chairman of the Liverpool Anti-Sweating League, refused to be ignored. He retorted that women who earned £1 a week on Army work usually accomplished it by the aid of overtime. He showed that employers paying women 2¼d. for soldiers' kit bags were selling them to the Government for 5s. He gave a list of authenticated cases of sweating, including that of a woman, after four years' experience on power machines, working from 8 a.m. to 8 p.m. and paid 6s. a week.

The Public Health officers of Bethnal Green, undismayed by the doubt the Anti-Sweating official had cast on their statements, continued publishing gross instances of sweating. The making of soldiers' flannel belts paid for at 8d. a dozen, cotton provided by worker, time to make, eight hours; khaki sleeve waistcoats at 3s. per dozen; a contractor paying 3½d. a dozen for soldiers' needle-cases to a woman farming them out at 2d. a dozen. The Workers' War Emergency Committee, to which Mallon, Mary Macarthur and their friends all owned allegiance, also rushed to the charge, reporting cases of women making soldiers' shirts in the West End at 2s. 6d. per dozen, women earning 1d. per hour on soldiers' pillows, and 1s. for a long day's work on soldiers' beds. The Paddington Local Distress Committee declared 1¼d. to 1½d. the district price for "finishing" soldiers' trousers; capable workers could do only one pair per hour.

Women complained to me daily. A mother supporting six children brought me her pay envelope. In four hours she could make seven soldiers' bags and received 5½d. The material was so thick and harsh that she sometimes broke many needles. A Bow contractor was paying 1d. a dozen less for brushes than Kent's before the increase; another paid 1s. 8d. for 400 eyelet holes on soldiers' kit bags; a woman earned 5s. 7d. at the work in 42 hours.

I complained to the War Office of the rates for soldiers' shirts paid by a Stepney firm; the employer transferred the shirts to outworkers, and kept the indoor workers to blouse-making. The rates for the shirts were not increased. A Government contractor of Bethnal Green, convicted of paying less than the low Trade Board Rate, was fined only 10s. for the first case, and 2s. each for seven others. In the same court a woman making soldiers' trousers at 3d. a pair was summoned for sending one of her children to school in a verminous condition. She pleaded that she was compelled to work so hard to pay her way that she was unable to do what she would wish for her family

Stories of jobbery and corruption in Army work, of laxity and overpayment by the War Office had become current talk. A case in Shoreditch County Court revealed that the Army Clothing Stores at Pimlico had sold 1,500,000 soldiers' body belts at 4s. a dozen, which were being bought up at 18s. a dozen, to be sold again at a still higher price for the use of the troops.

On November 18th, 1914, the Lord Chancellor promised that a flat rate would be established for the prices the Government would pay the contractors for Army clothing; eventually on February 18th, 1916—they took their time over such matters at the War Office—it was announced that in agreement with the Wholesale Clothiers' Association, certain rates had been fixed; 28s. for a greatcoat, 12s. 6d. for a jacket, 8s. 9d. for trousers and 18s. 6d. for pantaloons. It was shown that the combined labours of men fitters and pressers, and women machinists, finishers and buttonholers received on the average only 2s. 3½d. for a greatcoat, 2s. 1½d. for a jacket and 7½d. for trousers. Nevertheless the Government declined to fix any standard rate of payment for Army clothing workers. The request of the Workers' War Emergency Committee for a list of Army contractors, in order that the conditions of employment might be investigated, was also denied.

. . . . . . . .

According to long-established social usage, it is ever a crime to be poor, a merit to be rich. The Government War Loan provided the great reward for possessing superfluous cash. By an Act of August 28th, 1914, the Government, with the opulent autocracy approved in war time, took power to raise money for the slaughter " in such manner as the Treasury think fit." The first War Loan prospectus was issued in November. It bore interest at $3\frac{1}{2}$ per cent., with the added advantage that £100 of War Loan Stock could be purchased for £95. The Bank of England agreed to lend for three years, at 1 per cent. below Bank rate, sums equal to the value of the war loan stock deposited, which meant that for three years investors might patriotically lend to the nation, and be able to borrow an equivalent amount of capital, for disposal in other, yet more profitable war ventures. What a glorious game!

The terms were not yet good enough! Investors hung back, hoping for another loan at higher interest. The second War Loan (in March 1915) bore interest at $4\frac{1}{2}$ per cent. and exceedingly favourable facilities were given for exchanging for it the first war loan stock. Consols, bearing what now appeared by comparison the miserable interest of $2\frac{1}{2}$ per cent. and annuities with interest at $2\frac{1}{2}$ and $2\frac{3}{4}$ per cent. could also be exchanged for war loan on excellent terms. Thus the whole Government-lending fraternity moved up to a higher scale of interest on their capital, securing better terms than any previous British Government had ever given to investors.

Later in 1915 came another loan giving 5 per cent. interest at par, another in 1916 again giving 5 per cent. interest, and in this case £95 would buy £100 of stock. Then came 4 per cent. loans, tax free. Exchequer Bonds and Treasury Bonds bore corresponding interest, War Savings campaigns, " Tank " weeks, " Feed the Guns " weeks, kept the ball rolling when investment flagged.

Except where the loans have been repaid, the tribute of interest still continues; the country groans under it, little alleviated by conversion schemes; social amenities are stultified by it. An international holiday from the external War debt has been negotiated, but the internal War debt continues.

## CHAPTER XII

### POLICE SUPERVISION OF SOLDIERS' WIVES

WHENEVER I could snatch the time for it, I ran out on Saturdays in the noon hour to the crowded Roman Road, thronged by its market stalls, and the press of women, laden with bags bursting cabbages and overflowing carrots ; women in old worn garments, faded to the nameless greys all colours take at last, bearing the last vestiges of the dyed rabbit skin, the velvet and passementerie they bore in their brief, cheap prime ; full-bosomed matrons clasping their sticks of celery and rhubarb ; wispy hair, drawn faces, older far than their years, marked with the brand of poverty ; children bearing the stamp of it. " Buy ! buy ! buy ! " the butchers cried their wares ; the buyers answered with a caustic fun. Gay and rollicksome greetings passed. There was a friendliness and a jollity here in " the Roman " not found in smug suburbia. We bore our troubles cheerfully, having so many of them. Moreover, this was the great festival of the week, when such poor cash as we got was yet in its fullness—to spend on a good Sunday's feed—even if it were only relatively good, by comparison with the meagre scarceness of the week. Folk laughed with merriment ; but in the jolly cheeriness of the crowd passed many faces unrelieved in their ashen sorrow ; some bags remained slender ; the few scant buyings could not swell them. Some eyes were red with weeping ; tears coursed down.

I threaded my way among the people, a bundle of *Dreadnoughts* over my arm ; a passport to friendship, an introduction to talk with everyone. " Sylvia ! " " Sylvia ! " I heard my name around me. Anxious faces lighted ; woe-stricken faces crumpled to tears, and hands clutched mine, telling their misery in the dumb language known to grief. " See to it for me, Sylvia dear, see into it." Saddest the dull, despairing cry : " He's dead ! He's gone ! "

Returning by side streets, away from the crowd, I would hear the talk of women in front of me, ignorant of my nearness : " I bought one of them *Dreadnoughts*, I always read it. You get the truth in it ! "

I visited all the public houses on my round, swing doors opened to trapezoidal compartments converging to the bar where beer flowed incessantly. In each compartment men and women sat drinking. They all bought from me ; some jolly and joking ; others, the heavier drinkers, glassy-eyed, moist-lipped, offering their beer-wet pennies with slow, trembling fingers. Grievous it was to see them, thus reduced in their mental stature ; these sodden ones, but a tiny minority amongst the industrious masses. What sorrows, what weakness and incapacities lay at the root of their sad descent ! One such I remember in Fleet Street, a man with means sufficient to maintain him, a solitary misanthrope, crucified in his fall by an intelligence still rising in its tortured flight above the sordid level of his companions.

Here in our Bow comradeship was old Harriet Bennett, huge and big-booted as a grenadier, robust and neat in her plain blue serge. Jessie Payne, who had been her neighbour since their girlhood, always spoke severely of this fellow Salvationist. Poor Harriet ! Long ago in their youth she had gone to the docks to meet her sailor sweetheart, and learning on the gangway that he was dead and buried at sea, she had crushed down her sorrow in liquor, and had been subject to periodical drinking bouts ever since. More than once she was carried round to us, late at night, in a drunken stupor, by some kind-hearted constable, reluctant to take her to the cells, when she murmured, " 400 Old Ford Road," in her last half-consciousness. When first she was carried in thus, I was in terror lest her stupor might be due, not to excess of alcohol, but to some injury. She was always ashamed to meet me after one of her bouts and would hide away from me for days. Her breakdown usually occurred when she had worked herself up to a pitch of delight, because at some big meeting she had sold a record number of *Dreadnoughts*. " This little bit of truth ! " she called the paper, enlarging on the good things it contained, though she could not read a word of it, and was dependent on others to inform her of its contents. Yet according to herself it was not exhilaration but despondency which caused her outbreaks.

" What makes you do it, Miss Bennett ? " I once asked her, breaking an habitual silence on this topic.

" I come over so miserable; then I thinks: there's nothing for it but to bottle down ! "

At first she sold the paper for love alone, but after a time we prevailed on her to accept the newsagent's commission. She received a small pittance in Poor Law relief for incapacity to make full use of her hands, the tendons having been severed, in what manner I do not know, and the fingers stiff, with little power in them.

What an outcry she raised on my arrival at a meeting, waving her arms and capering in delight ! I wanted to dive underground to avoid it.

. . . . . . . .

The legend that the soldiers' wives had more money than they had ever had in their lives remained impregnable.

Occasionally some tragedy momentarily disturbed the complacency of the public. In the *Manchester Guardian* the inquest on the premature infant of a Rochdale private was reported. The child's grandmother and the midwife testified that the mother had been short of food in her pregnancy. Her separation allowance of 15s. weekly, being insufficient to maintain herself and two other young children, she had appealed to the local relief committee; but after giving her one dole of 5s. the committee had decided she had sufficient for her support.

. . . . . . . . .

The War had brought into poor slumdom an unusual influx of the leisured and prosperous, to whom the bedraggled meanness of aching poverty seemed mere sluttish absence of self-respect, the street life teeming from these crowded hovels wholly incomprehensible. To these remote ones, obtuse and obscurantist, the allowance anxious mothers craved for the nourishing of little bodies and the booting of little feet, appeared merely "money to spend in drink," which should be cut down to the sparsest limits, in the interests of sobriety and thrift. War-time hysterics gave currency to fabulous rumours. From Press and pulpit stories ran rampant of drunkenness and depravity amongst the women of the masses. Alarmist morality-mongers conceived most monstrous visions of girls and women, freed from the control of fathers and husbands who had hitherto compelled them to industry, chastity and sobriety, now neglecting their homes, plunging into excesses, and burdening the country with swarms of illegitimate infants.

Living amongst the poorest, and constantly journeying to the working class areas of provincial towns, I witnessed nothing of this alleged phenomenon. On the contrary, I saw a steady waning of drinking and drunkenness. On Saturday nights before the War, when the public house next door to us in Old Ford Road turned out its customers, the air had been rent by uproarious sounds of intoxication. Gradually during the War this nuisance abated until it altogether disappeared, and did not recur. I saw dwindling the crowds of women who of old stood drinking on the pavements outside the beer shops, clasping their puny infants the law forbade them to take inside. In the East End we have no nursemaids; our failings are open to all eyes. The great advance in sobriety in all classes, which had begun long before the War, was accelerated by the shortening of public house hours, the reduction in the strength of beer, and other factors.

Nevertheless, in the anticipation that soldiers' wives would indulge in excessive drinking, the public houses were closed to women during certain hours open to men, an impertinence towards the more temperate sex which aroused indignant sarcasm from the Suffrage societies, but was unnoticed by the average woman wholly oblivious of public house regulations.

Already in October Mrs. Creighton, Adeline Duchess of Bedford and other ladies, strongly convinced of the peccability of lower class womanhood, announced that with the Home Secretary's consent they were making arrangements " for influencing, and if need be restraining " the behaviour of women and girls in the neighbourhood of military camps. Under the ægis of these ladies, thousands of women patrols were introduced whose efforts to control the behaviour of their sex were not seldom the subject of irritation, and also of mirth.

The busybodies of Whitehall, Scotland Yard and Mayfair were determined to establish effective control over the conduct of soldiers' wives. On October 20th an Army Council Memorandum entitled " Cessation of Separation Allowances and Allotments to the Unworthy," and a Home Office letter to Chief Constables issued intructions for placing all women in receipt of separation allowances under police surveillance. Herein it was written :

" The police in each area can obtain full information as to the wives and dependants who are in receipt of Army Allowances from the above committees,[1] and though it is hoped there will not be many cases in which extreme measures will be necessary, the Secretary of State is confident that Local Committees may rely upon your co-operation in their endeavour to ensure that relief shall not be continued to persons who prove themselves unworthy to receive it."

Reports of alleged unworthiness, received from the relief committees, the soldiers or their commanding officers, or any other source, were to be investigated by the police, and if in their opinion proved, the separation allowance and the husband's allotment were to be discontinued, for unchastity, drunkenness, neglect of children or conviction on a criminal charge. Soldiers' wives and relatives were thus to be subject to a penalty in excess of that imposed by the ordinary law. They were placed at the mercy of secret reports, without any public or private trial or opportunity of vindication or reply.

Besides investigating reports of misconduct against them from other sources, the police were to keep the women under observation, reporting misbehaviour, and checking it by precept and warning.

The children's allowances were not to be withdrawn, though obviously with only their pittances to maintain them the mother could not protect them from a serious lack of necessaries. Were her own pay withdrawn, if the Army Council thought fit the children's allowances were to be issued at the motherless rate to some other person in trust ; apparently a euphemistic manner of stating that the children should be removed from their mother's custody.

The scheme was absurd as well as disgraceful. Its effrontery in view of the cruel parsimony and scandalous mismanagement, of which the soldiers' wives and relatives were victims, did not pass unperceived. In some quarters, at least, it was realised that the police were a body of men at least as fallible as the women whom it was proposed to place under their control. The long-confirmed tradition of the police force

[1] The S.S.F.A. or Local Relief Committee.

to shield the misdemeanours of its members had just been exemplified in an ugly case.

Of course there was a public outcry. McKenna, whom we had fought as " Prison Secretary," was still at the Home Office. In reply to Parliamentary protests, he declared the plan had been devised in the interests of the women themselves. His tone was apologetic, and the impression arose that the Government realised it had gone too far and that the whole business would be shelved. On the contrary the Home Office and the War Office still clung to their scheme. Early in December the police were notified that they should index the " records " of soldiers' wives and relatives, whilst Army paymasters were instructed to forward to the Chief Constable particulars of all persons receiving allotments and separation allowances within their area. It was not merely an affair of official communications ; the police in some districts began entering and inspecting the homes of soldiers' wives and mothers, inquiring of them, and also of their neighbours, whether they were in the habit of getting drunk and catechising them on the disposal of their bedrooms, and what visitors they admitted. A woman told me that the police inquisitor had informed her that one bedroom was sufficient for the use of her family, and that there was no good reason for another to be occupied. Women were even ordered to get themselves photographed to supply a means of identifying them to the police.

Again there was an outcry. In response to it, an alleged modified order was issued for London, under which soldiers' and sailors' wives were to be given a second chance, if arrested for drunkenness, and only to suffer withdrawal of allowance if actually convicted. The Government prevaricated through its Press Bureau : the action of the police would be limited to women who had rendered themselves liable to prosecution in the ordinary course ; no other surveillance was contemplated, and no lists were to be kept, except of cases in which " specific complaint " had been made to the Home Office. " Let us all assume in perfect good temper that the circular is dead, and that somebody who made a pardonable slip in doing a novel task, quite sees the point now." So said the *Manchester Guardian* ; but the same day it was disclosed that the War Office had supplied the Chief Constable of Manchester itself with a list of 20,000 soldiers' wives and dependants and full statement of their income !

The Manchester Local Representative Committee and the Lord Mayor expressed indignation. They, it seemed, had no complaint to make of the conduct of soldiers' wives. We reiterated in vain the simple demand we had made from the first—that the allowances would be regarded as wages, to which the soldiers' families should have inalienable claim. A soldier's wife wrote :

" The Government ought not to issue such an order unless the wives of all Government paid men are to come under the same rules. Why should it not be applied to the wives of postmen, why not the wives of the police themselves ? "

Where the Government led, Local Authorities followed. At Chesterfield notices were hung in the schools, in full view of the children, headed " Cessation of Separation Allowances to the Unworthy," urging school managers to report cases in which soldiers' and sailors' children came to school in a neglected condition. A monstrous thing this, that the children should see these notices in the midst of the privations imposed upon them by the meagre allowances !

At Preston the Mayor and members of the Local Representative Committee made speeches, declaring that soldiers' wives were " feeling a freedom which they ought not to treat as freedom," that " harsher measures " were needed to deal with them, and that their children must be taken away. At the next meeting of the Committee Mrs. Hunter, a soldier's wife, appeared to confront these accusers, all of whom meekly withdrew their utterances, declaring they had not intended them " in the sense in which they had been interpreted." In the meantime the National Society for the Prevention of Cruelty to Children in Preston announced that the Society had instructed its inspectors to report cases of women who had become addicted to drink since their husbands had enlisted ; but not a single case of the kind had they found. It now further transpired that since the War broke out the presiding magistrate at Preston Police Court had on two occasions been presented with a pair of white kid gloves because he had no cases to try. Never in the history of the town had two such unusual occasions been recorded within so short a period. The Chief Constable of Preston reported a great decrease in drunkenness since the War and the Chief of the Lancaster Constabulary made a similar report. It is true that for the country as a whole there was some increase in the convictions for drunkenness amongst women in 1914, as compared with 1913 ; the figures being 37,311 in 1914 ; 35,765 in 1913. It may be that this was mainly due to excessive zeal on the part of the police owing to the outcry which had been raised ; it is impossible to say. Thereafter the figures fell, year by year, to 7,222 in 1918. They rose again somewhat when the men came back from the War ; but not to the old standard. The convictions of men, though always much more numerous than those of women, followed a corresponding course.[1]

Though never definitely abolished, the police supervision of soldiers' wives gradually faded from public notice, because whenever it appeared publicly there was an outcry. Moreover the mass of the women were so orderly and inoffensive that the scare-mongering quickly gave place to some other war-time stunt.

[1] *Convictions for Drunkenness :*

| | Men | Women | | Men | Women |
|---|---|---|---|---|---|
| 1913 ... | 153,112 | 35,765 | 1917 ... | 34,103 | 12,307 |
| 1914 ... | 146,517 | 37,311 | 1918 ... | 21,853 | 7,222 |
| 1915 ... | 102,600 | 32,211 | 1919 ... | 46,767 | 11,180 |
| 1916 ... | 62,946 | 21,245 | | | |

# CHAPTER XIII

## ATTEMPT TO REVIVE THE STATE REGULATION OF VICE—PAUL PRY

ARMY Commanders who had gained their military experience in the Crown Colonies, where the State regulation of vice still existed, regarded the supply of undiseased prostitutes for their troops as a part of military routine. They were demanding the power to control and license women for this purpose by the revival of the Contagious Diseases Acts, the repeal of which Josephine Butler and her co-workers had secured after a heroic struggle of seventeen years.[1] Already in October (1914) the Plymouth Watch Committee had made a similar demand. The old Army attitude towards prostitution was being spread among the soldiers of Kitchener's New Armies. Young recruits came home telling their mothers and sisters that prophylactics for use when consorting with prostitutes were handed out to them as they went on leave, protestations that they had no use for them being contemptuously dismissed. Men came home with stories of arrangements made for the soldiers to queue up to visit prostitutes in France. The *Manual of Military Hygiene*, issued for the instruction of the troops, observed that " having regard to the method of transmission, thorough washing after connection may lessen the chances of infection."

Venereal disease was alleged to be causing tremendous havoc among the new soldiers. Sir Ivor Herbert declared, in the Commons on November 16th, that this infection, termed " avoidable disease " in military parlance, had incapacitated from 30 to 40 per cent. of the men in some units. Asquith refused to supply any figures ; and to this day, official statistics of venereal disease in the British Army during the War

[1] The C.D. Acts provided for the registration and police supervision of alleged prostitutes ; their periodic compulsory surgical examination to detect venereal disease—imprisonment to follow refusal ; their compulsory detention in " certified " hospitals if found diseased ; the arrest and compulsory examination of any woman alleged to be in any place for prostitution unless she could produce a certificate showing she had been examined and was free from disease.

Such provisions have everywhere proved worse than useless. Men have never been controlled or examined. They experience a false sense of security when consorting with registered prostitutes who often become infected between the periods of the compulsory examination. Many prostitutes evade registration and diseased women, from whatever cause infected, fear to seek medical treatment in dread of being placed on the police register. Women who have never been prostitutes are occasionally arrested and placed under police control, which makes it impossible for them to retain employment, or to continue peacefully in ordinary walks of life. Such regulations facilitate the hideous traffic in " White Slaves " bought and sold by procurers.

have not been published, though the Army figures for other years are available.[1]

Later came complaints of a great havoc from venereal disease amongst the Australian troops stationed in Egypt, and also amongst the Canadians. Though many reports were doubtless exaggerated, there was undoubtedly something behind all this rumour. I was surprised by a telephone call from Cheatle,[2] the surgeon, whom I had met once only, when he had come as consultant in the last vain efforts to save my brother's life. He was troubled ; men, and it seemed they were often of the prosperous classes, were coming home with venereal disease and infecting their wives and children. He wanted me to put him in touch with whoever was working to combat this evil. I did so, and he did his part in it very earnestly I believe ; but when I saw him in 1920, and asked him of his work in that direction, he said he was no longer concerned with it ; his main interest now was cancer. People of settled habit were deflected from their accustomed pursuits by the urgent problems of the War. More profound was the influence upon the young, who learnt with the swiftness of revelation how diametrically naval and military standards conflicted with the precepts taught at the mother's knee. The result, on the whole, I think, has been a groping towards the creation of a new morality, broader and more sincere than that of the old dual code and perhaps a good deal of cynicism in some cases.

Lord Claude Hamilton demanded power to commit prostitutes to hospitals and reformatories ; the Home Secretary replied that the existing law against soliciting must suffice ; but as soon as Parliament adjourned in December, Colonel East, who commanded the troops in the West of England, banned all women from the public houses of Cardiff between the hours of 7 p.m. and 6 a.m., and issued notices under the Defence of the Realm Act to certain women in the city, prohibiting them from being out of doors between 7 p.m. and 8 a.m. Five women who declared the notice seemed to them " like a dream," were arrested and committed by a military court-martial to 62 days' imprisonment. The military authorities were obviously in train to establish a form of surveillance not sanctioned by the ordinary law.

In the words of the Women's Manifesto of 1869, the new military regulations removed, so far as women were concerned :

> " every guarantee of personal security which the law had established and held sacred, and put their regulation, their freedom and their persons absolutely in the power of the police."

It was a parallel attack with that which had been made upon the soldiers' wives ; less serious, in a sense, because in practice likely to affect only a small number of women, yet having peculiarly hideous

[1] These show a fall from 422 cases per 1,000 soldiers in 1859, to 19 per 1,000 in 1928. These figures relate to the Army in the United Kingdom. The venereal disease rate is higher in the Navy : 45.76 per 1,000 in 1928 in U.K. stations. In the Air Force it is lower : 13.5 per 1,000 at home and 31.3 abroad in 1928.

[2] Sir Lenthal Cheatle, K.C.B., C.V.O., F.R.C.S.

features of its own. It was a gross defiance of the established law. It was felt that if protest were not made emphatically against such encroachments upon civil rights other encroachments would follow, and the Army might presently dominate the home populace, as an army of occupation dominates a conquered people.

The Press reported the Cardiff case on November 29th. I wrote immediately to the War Office announcing a deputation from our federation on Tuesday. We were joined by Mrs. Arncliffe Sennett of the Northern Men's Federation for Women's Suffrage.

Cubitt, who received us, had no official knowledge of the Cardiff case, but after all, Cardiff was " under martial law, you know." He was sure that " if there was a lady who was a notorious drunkard," we should not object to her being placed under restraint.

The interview unsatisfactory, I wrote to Lord Kitchener, urging that the military authorities should concern themselves only with the troops and leave civilians to the ordinary law. To keep prostitutes in their homes would not prevent soldiers from following them thither, nor prevent girls and women who had hitherto led normal lives being drawn into prostitution. The sweated pay of women in industry and in the Queen Mary Workrooms, and the large numbers of unemployed women not getting relief of any sort would bring recruits to the sad army of prostitutes.

At a further deputation to the War Office, in which we were joined by the United Suffragists and the Women's Freedom League, Nina Boyle, of the latter organisation, told a funny story, which seems almost too good to be true. She alleged that a General who had issued an Order that intoxicants should not be supplied to women after 6 p.m., had been hoist with his own petard when he gave a dinner to the officers of an American ship, and desired to waive his prohibition for this function. The Chief Constable had insisted that the Order, having been issued to him, must be strictly enforced, and that detectives would be present at the banquet to ensure that no intoxicants should be allowed to the ladies at the table. If any Chief Constable had the humour and independence to compel a general to obey his own Order he deserved hearty congratulations.

Before the end of the year the War Office assured us that the Cardiff Order had been withdrawn, but the same order was still placarded at Grantham.

. . . . . . . .

*Norah Smyth*

THE FIRST W.S.F. DAY NURSERY
Lady Sybil Smith on left.

*Norah Smyth*

DWELLERS IN PRINCE ARTHUR'S AVENUE, BOW

*Workers' Dreadnought*

OUR TOY FACTORY

Later in the War, when darkened streets lent colour to sombre stories, propaganda for the State Regulation of Vice became noisy. The Press gave place and space to professional sensationalists like Conan Doyle, who substituted detective romances by lurid appeals for the protection of young soldiers " preyed upon and ruined by harpies." The Waterloo Road was written of as the scene of scandalous misdoings unchecked by the police. On the other hand it was more quietly contended that police constables were so much harrassed by charges of alleged laxity in apprehending prostitutes that respectable women were in danger of arrest should they venture down that infamous road.

Conceiving it my duty to see for myself, I determined to investigate the road one Saturday night. Mrs. Drake pleaded to join me. It was a dreary night, biting cold, a light haze from the river hung upon the air. The chill pierced to one's very bones. The dingy obscurity of brick and pavement, scarce pierced by the glimmer of paint-smudged lamps, oppressed the soul. I turned to the river, craning on tip-toe to see it over the high, dark wall of the bridge as it flowed on, wonderful in its gleaming and its shadows, bearing what histories and what mysteries in its depths, lovely in its craft, with the tang of enchantment hanging about all which pertains to waterfaring, mournful with the poignancy of supreme beauty.

The spell of the river could not fall on the crowd passing over it, shut off as it was by the black high wall. Its loveliness lost to my gaze, the dreariness of the place closed down on me.

At the corner of the bridge a policeman stood watching. When women appeared through the haze he swayed towards them, alert in menace. They seemed to swerve from him with hurried gait.

In one of the alcoves of the bridge sat a merry party—two sailors and two women—opening packets of sandwiches and cake, with quip and joke. In another a man and woman were together silent, hand clasping hand, in the moveless throes of sorrow.

Over the bridge the people were denser; policeman and special constables met one almost at every step. Sometimes a woman stood by the curb, or hung back close to the wall. Just as one chose, one could deem her a " harpy," or merely a respectable woman waiting for a 'bus or a friend. Two soldiers went by us together, and behind them two girls, giggling noisily—to attract the attention of the men, one might judge if one pleased, or just with the jolly unconsciousness of youth, enjoying its night out.

A poor, battered creature, of sixty years or more, drunk or demented, railed dismally to the unheeding void: " You, you, you'll be getting me locked up! You'll be getting me locked up! "

A crowd had gathered, helmeted policemen in the centre, special constables on the outskirts, urging the people to move on. " Get away from me! Get away from me! " a man's voice shouted. " I've lost a leg at the Front, where *you* ought to be! " Women and girls were wringing their hands with cries of protest: " They are treading on him! He has got eight wounds and only one leg! Oh! Oh! They are treading on him ! " A one-legged soldier lay on the pavement. The police had taken his crutches; they lifted him to an ambulance, and wheeled him off. No one could tell us why.

A group of soldiers and women tumbled out of the public house at closing time. The men were rolling drunk ; the women approximately sober. " Good night ! See you to-morrow ! " they chorused cheerfully. A stout woman patted the cheek of one of the sailors with a loud guffaw. The men reeled off round the corner, shouting some ditty, the women went together by the main road, chatty and jovial.

A sample this of London night life, common enough, dismal and grey. As the War proceeded, all this dwindled. People grew anxious to be indoors, away from the blackness of the streets.

. . . . . . . .

I reached the Bow West Ward Committee a little late one December evening. The small and dingy schoolroom—a poor place in which to confine the spirits of growing children—was already filled with heavily coated people. A little woman was in the midst of them, flushed and tearful, at bay, in her threadbare black.

George Lansbury's big, sing-song voice, with its Bow accent, admonished her in his fatherly style; the rest of the committee sat stiff and silent.

"Now you go home and have a good try!"

She interrupted him, sobbing defiantly: "I have got some kind friends, I have!"

"What is the matter?" I queried in an undertone to the committee-men nearest me. No one answered.

"Now you try again!" Lansbury's voice persisted, striving to drown her protesting treble.

Her tones rose higher, swiftly outrunning him: "Of course there'd be *someone* to speak against me—and I know who it is!"

Clearly she was not disposed to be meek and contrite.

He broke off testily: "Well, if you don't we shall have to stop the tickets!"

She hurried out, weeping, angry, defiant.

"What is the matter?" I asked again, impatient to know the facts.

Parson Smith's small, pale face twisted a wry smile at me.

"I saw her the other night dancing a hornpipe in the Roman Road," he uttered perkily.

"That does not concern the committee!" I blazed at him, indignant.

He turned on me sharply: "She was drunk!"

I answered: "I understood you to mean that."

"We cannot allow her to get drunk on our money!" George Lansbury deprecated reproachfully; it was my turn to be admonished.

"We do not supply any money to her! She cannot get drunk on food tickets!" I retorted.

The committeemen eyed me coldly, resolved to dispense public assistance only to the virtuous and prudent.

I stated my case: "The woman is unemployed through the War; our duty is to relieve her on that account; nothing else concerns us."

"Persons having relief must behave themselves." It was the professional investigator who answered me, backed by an approving chorus from the rest: "We can't permit it!" "Relief cases must keep sober."

"If she had any intoxicant someone must have treated her; she has no scope for frivolity on what she gets from us! One glass would be enough to turn her head, I should think, considering how little food she gets! You all of you know she and her children are starving! It is disgusting that we should sit here playing Paul Pry to a woman in her condition." I challenged them fiercely, prepared to fight for her tickets with every weapon.

In truth they were all familiar with her circumstances. Living in a dilapidated hovel in a wretched court, absurdly named Prince Arthur's Avenue, she was the mother of six children, the youngest twelve months old. Two were at school and three young girls were at work, earning respectively 4s., 4s. 6d. and 6s. a week. Their father was in prison. One Saturday night before the War, he and some of his cronies had been enjoying themselves a trifle noisily in St. Stephen's Road, close to the parsonage. Parson Smith, annoyed by their din, had called the police to drive them away. The men resisted, a crowd gathered, a policeman and others were hurt. Arrests and sentences followed. This woman's husband got half a year in gaol ; she was left to maintain the children as best she might. The matchbox-making, by which she and her little ones earned a few shillings, was cut off, when such work was reduced at the outbreak of war. The almoner at Bow Baths had allotted her 5s. worth[1] of food tickets weekly on that account. We on the Ward Committee were merely the watch-dogs, to safeguard the proper employment of this relief.

"I move the matter be dropped," I said. "No doubt is raised that she is unemployed through the War ; beyond that we have no right to interfere."

"I can't accept that !" the Parson interjected, supported by approving groans.

The atmosphere hardened. My motion had no seconder. As the matter stood I seemed to be in a minority of one. The wrangle continued. In the thick of the struggle I uttered : "If the woman loses her tickets I shall expose it in the *Dreadnought*." The words seemed to fall like oil upon turgid waters. Angry voices subsided, benignity began to reign.

"She used to be a decent little girl." Lansbury appealed lachrymose : "Shall we give her another chance ? After all, we are giving the tickets to the children—and not to her."

"I won't have anything to do with it," the Parson protested, knowing himself defeated. He eyed me fiercely across the table. "Perhaps you'll take her on your list ; I don't want to visit her !" he snapped at me curtly.

"Certainly," I answered with equal curtness.

"You'll have to see she behaves herself," admonished Lansbury gruffly ; "we have only given her one more chance."

I saw the woman next morning and told her how matters stood. "I shall not bother you with visits. Come to me if you need me."

She pressed my hand. No one reported anything further against her.

Paul Pry was still at large.[2] Soon after the investigator, incoherent, mysterious, observed at the Ward Committee that the Relieving Officer had told him "that widow" had a man going round to her at night. That widow was painfully identified as a woman on my case list, a clean,

[1] His interpretation of what was due to her under the National Committee's scale.

[2] The Charity Organisation Society demanded that unmarried mothers and their children should not receive the full scale of relief, poor as it was, which was meted out to those bearing the hall-mark of legal wedlock.

well-spoken mother, whose son was learning to be a cabinet maker. She showed me a cupboard he made for her with maternal pride.

" Mrs. X is one of my cases ; I have nothing to report against her. The Relieving Officer is not entitled to make a report ! " I blustered.

The committee upheld me without dissent. Overridden by the Town Hall officials, it was unwilling to be superseded also by the Poor Law officers. " Tell the Relieving Officer to mind his own business," someone said, and all agreed.

Perhaps in this case also the *Dreadnought* had had its influence.

## CHAPTER XIV

### HOOVER AND THE BELGIAN RELIEF COMMISSION

ALL sorts of people came down to the East End in those days to visit us, amongst them Mary Boyle O'Reilly,[1] a fine vigorous creature, splendidly alive. We were friends at once. She had been adventuring on the Continent to see the War, had journeyed through Germany on a troop train, left it and walked into Holland, was arrested as a war correspondent in Maastricht, and released for lack of evidence; then travelled by river to Liége, where on the night of August 30th, she came upon a train-load of Belgian women deported from Louvain. She wrote the story of her adventures for the *Dreadnought*. She told me that the Belgians spoke bitterly of Britain and her broken pledge to protect them. "Where are the English?" was their cry when the Germans overwhelmed them. Especially did they complain of Winston Churchill, who when they felt compelled to retreat, had induced them to remain fighting in Antwerp on promise of reinforcements which never came. They spoke to her with pity of the English lads whom Churchill had sent into the Belgian trenches wholly unequipped, "without so much as an overcoat."

Such charges, made very widely, received confirmation when Asquith published his *Memoirs and Reflections* in 1928. His jottings of the period convey an appalling spectacle of confused impotence combined with a jovial and callous recklessness. "Indeed I had to remark," he wrote, "that we looked more like a gang of Elizabethan buccaneers, than a meek collection of black-coated Liberal Ministers." Churchill having induced the Belgians to remain in Antwerp, the Cabinet was, in Asquith's words, "trying hard to get in troops to raise the siege, by telegrams to the military commanders to send aid, if they thought fit." Having despatched some tentative messages, they were confident that, "in one way or another, a diversion was certain." To send Winston's little Army "would be idle butchery," Asquith had written in his diary; yet two days later he agreed that it should go. He presently recorded:

"Winston ought never to have sent the two Naval Brigades . . . only about one quarter were Reservists and the rest were a callow crowd of rawest recruits, most of whom had never fired off a rifle, whilst none of them had even handled an entrenching tool."

[1] Daughter of a well known Irish-American. In 1869 he had escaped to America from an Australian penal settlement to which he had been transported for his activity in Ireland as a Fenian. In America he achieved a reputation as poet and publicist.

A few days after the Antwerp sacrifice Asquith was writing that Winston " having tasted blood " was " beginning like a tiger to raven for more."

" His mouth waters at the sight and thought of Kitchener's new armies. Are these glittering commands to be entrusted to dug-out trash . . . mediocrities who have led a sheltered life mouldering in military routine ? "

To such as these had the peace of the world been confided !

On a second visit to England Mary O'Reilly took me to interview Herbert Clark Hoover, chairman of the American Relief Commission in Belgium, who was to become President of the United States. He received us in a dark little office in the City, very courteous, very informative. We exchanged expressions of horrified regret at the rapacious profiteering which did not scruple to make money out of the starvation of the people during the terrible World War. He seemed deeply impressed by the benefits to be derived from disinterested management of the food supply and the unwisdom of permitting it to be the sport of speculation. Yet, with a note of sadness, he observed that what might be accomplished in Belgium, prostrate under the foreign invader, might prove impossible of achievement elsewhere. How much of the humane and thoughtful spirit which appeared to dwell in the Herbert Hoover of those days remained when he ascended to the high office of President of the United States ? Ah world ! Ah time ! How little the successful politician remembers the truths which were clear to him when out of office !

Hoover described how the Relief Commission bought produce in the primary markets and chartered special ships to carry its purchases to Rotterdam, and later sent me a report containing further information. All the existing machinery of wholesale and retail trade had been set aside and a new system built. This extended from the ships at Rotterdam to the individual food-ticket holder. There were 156 provincial mills and district mills and warehouses, and 4,657 communal committees, presided over by the Burgomaster or Maire. Almost all the private mills had been taken over by the Relief Commission, which in each case had approached the miller and offered him a salary, usually about £40 per month, to manage his mill on the Commission's behalf. If he agreed, all charges were met by the Commission and the workers paid their usual wage. A reserve of wheat was maintained at Rotterdam, in case the delivery of overseas consignments should be interrupted. The mills kept reserves of flour to ensure regular supplies. The mills were in most cases situated on canals, of which there was a network, capable of serving as the distributive agency to the surrounding country. The communes were granted flour on a population basis. They conveyed the flour from the mills at their own expense. In the original scheme each baker supplied a list of his customers to the communal committee and the committee supplied him with 250 grammes of flour per customer, to be made into 330 grammes of bread. This proving unsatisfactory, the new method was for the committee to send flour to the baker to be made into bread under a contract providing that 1 kilo of flour should produce 1.35 kilos of good bread, and that the baker should receive 8d. per kilo for his work. The baker delivered the loaves to a depot, from which the people could obtain it in exchange for food tickets. The price of bread depended on the price of wheat and was periodically fixed by agreement. Home-grown wheat was controlled by a committee consisting of American, Belgian and German representatives. A proportion of each peasant's crop was set aside for next year's seed and for food for his household. The remainder was sold at a price equal to that of imported wheat. In spite of the special difficulties of Belgium, and the rise in world prices, the price of the 4 lb. loaf was 7½d. in Belgium when it had reached 10½d. in London.

In October 1915 rice cost 60 cents per kilo in Belgium, and the equivalent of 94 cents per kilo in London. Most commodities were in fact more costly here, where there was no genuine scarcity, than in invaded Belgium, where imports were only permitted through the Relief Commission and where the net import of human food in October 1915 had fallen from the normal 1,690,000 metric tons to 640,934. The import of animal food had fallen from 1,350,000 metric tons to 102,815. The live stock in Belgium itself had decreased from 40 to 60 per cent.

The money received by the Commission from the sale of commodities between November 1st, 1914, and October 31st, 1915, amounted to £15,197,000 1s. 1d. Of this sum £1,138,411 2s. 9d., about 7 %, was set aside as profit to be handed over to the benevolent department. What an enormous sum such a charge on the food supply of our own country would have yielded for social welfare! How magnificent had this co-operative effort in Belgium been tried out, not in scarcity but in abundance, for peace and not for war! The Dutch Government had aided to the value of 147,824 guilders in providing free transport and remitting harbour and port dues.

I seized on these facts from the Belgian Relief Commission as an argument in our campaign for the nationalisation of the food supply. Alas, the great forces of commerce went their way, crushing the people between the upper and the nether millstone!

To me the huge lack of equalitarian sensibility, the vast absence of solidarity with the masses who were toiling, the soldiers who had been maimed, which displayed itself in the Government and its officials, was a sad, and withal an amazing factor. I did not attempt to follow or criticise the war strategy, I framed no hope as to which country might win or lose. I was persuaded that the powerful capitalist interests in every country would continue to make profit for themselves, either in victory or defeat; that the masses in all countries must, in any event, be the sufferers from the burdens and losses of the War. I believed that an end to the War without victory for either side, would be best for the world and the people, and the sooner it came the better.

# CHAPTER XV

## CHRISTMAS 1914—SCARBOROUGH BOMBARDMENT—WAR HOSPITALS IN FRANCE

"ECONOMY in the National Interest" was one of the maxims at this time issued by the Government for the guidance of patriotic citizens. As Christmas approached the Lambeth Guardians responded by announcing that the little pauper children under their care must forego their Christmas Egg, the only egg they were privileged to taste in the whole year. An outcry was raised, questions were asked in Parliament, the Christmas egg was restored. Yet the very same people who rightly defended the Lambeth children were apt to forget that soldiers' and sailors' offspring could not possibly be supplied with eggs from a separation allowance of 2s. a week each. Some Boards of Guardians were urging the local Government Board to reduce the scale of pauper rations, then fixed at 7½d. per day. Lansbury told me a little later that the children at Shenfield Poor Law schools, of which he was so proud, had had their rations cut. The girls and infants from Shenfield had been distributed amongst other Poor Law institutions to make way for 700 officers, teachers and red-coated boys learning to drill from the Duke of York's School in Dover, rendered unsafe by war conditions.

Lloyd George had introduced his first war budget in November. He had doubled the income tax and taken tribute from the working classes in tea and beer. In the Cabinet he had talked of nationalising the drink traffic; but finding the Tories against him, he had treated the brewers very generously, arranging for them to make a profit from the tax, and giving them also a rebate as compensation for the earlier closing of public houses.

. . . . . . . .

It was on December 16th that German warships shelled West Hartlepool, Whitby and Scarborough, and departed unhindered. A storm of imprecations rose. Winston Churchill's denunciation of the German raiders as "baby killers" was widely echoed. Only a few of us found voice to answer: "This is war." Ignored was the fact that our British blockade would destroy vastly more children by starvation in neutral, as well as in enemy countries, than would be injured in all the bombardments.

In the brief Christmas days, when the slackening of propaganda gave me a respite, I went with Smyth to see the havoc wrought by the Scarborough bombardment. Travelling by night we arrived in a cheerless dawn. The sky and sea were a leaden grey. The big amusement "palaces" on the front were scarred and battered by shell-fire, iron columns twisted and broken, brickwork crumbling, windows gone. Yawning breaches disclosed the pictures and furnishings, riddled and rent by the firing, dimmed and discoloured by blustering winds and spray. The little steep streets, leading up from the foreshore, were barred by wire entanglements—the first I had ever seen—great stakes driven into the ground, with a mass of stout barbed wire threaded around and around them, and tangled about between. At many points were high barricades of sand-filled sacks, with a row of loopholes for the rifles.

We knocked at one of the sea-front boarding houses. The woman who opened to us was weary and dishevelled as though she had spent the night out in the storm. She gazed at us, startled and hostile, when we asked for a lodging. When we urged that we had come from London and understood she was accustomed to let, she hesitated suspiciously, then reluctantly explained that she had promised to hold herself in readiness to receive any shipwrecked seamen who might be saved from drowning. "I've been up with them all night—some of 'em's gone, some of 'em's still here. We have to put 'em in hot blankets as soon as they're carried in."

"But there won't be another wreck to-night!" we essayed, rather feebly, to rally her.

"There were three lots brought in here yesterday, and two the day before," she answered mournfully, and pointed to the many craft out in the bay, telling us they were all minesweepers engaged in the perilous work of clearing away explosive mines laid by the German warships and daily causing the loss of many vessels.

This was an aspect of the German visit not recorded in the Press. In our ignorance of war, we heard her with shocked surprise.

She agreed at last that we should stay with her, on condition that we would leave at once if another party of shipwrecked mariners were brought in. Barely an hour had passed when her daughter flung open our door:

"Another boat's blown up! You'll have to go!"

Out we went to the blast. Groups of shawl-wrapped women were gazing seaward. " They've landed some of them at that slip," a woman told us, and pointed to a small dingy brown steamer with a cluster of people looking down at her from the quay. " A motor-car's gone off with one of them—he was covered with a white sheet ! " a shrill voice cried ; and even as the words were uttered another car dashed away. A bent old crone ran by us wailing : " He was a young man with black hair ; with thick black hair ; his head was all smashed in ! "

Groups of people moved about us, awestruck, with a hand shading the eyes, gazing out to sea, or across to the little steamer at the end of the slip.

Someone advised us to enquire for lodgings at a near-by cottage, the front door of which opened directly on to the foreshore. A fisherman in his blue jersey was seated by the fire ; his wife was too much troubled by the peril of the men out there in the bay, to consider whether or not she would give us a bed. She talked to us a long time before she could bring her mind to it. She spoke of the bombardment ; it was terrible, the noise so loud, so fearfully loud, she thought she must go mad. Little children were killed ; many people were injured. " A lady who not five days before was singing in this Bethel " was helping a poor old woman down into her cellar, when she was struck dead by a piece of shell. No one knew when it might happen again ; people could not settle down to ordinary life ; all sense of security was destroyed. Her husband and the other fishermen were prohibited from following their calling because of the mines. Their means of support was stopped ; yet he was best at home ; yes, even if they should have to starve ! She had a son in the Navy and a son-in-law on a mine-sweeper ; that was enough !

It had been a hard year in Scarborough ; the holiday-makers had cancelled their bookings when war broke out. If they had only paid a little for the rooms it would have helped poor people. The big hotels had compelled their clients to pay in full, but little lodging-house keepers could not enforce their contracts. She could not understand the War. She could not understand why Scarborough had been left without protection—why there were no guns. " The War's nothing to us—we didn't want it ! Cleverer people than us know what it's for ! " So she ran on with bitterness, until at last, having grown used to us, she said that we might stay.

Later her daughter looked in to speak with us. She too must talk of the bombardment ; it had terrified her inexpressibly and had seemed to last for years. People could not sleep now ; many would not even go to bed. Everyone had a bundle made up in readiness for flight ; but how little one could carry in a bundle ! One could not afford to move one's home ; and one's living was here in Scarborough. A widow she knew had her boarding-house, her only means of livelihood, completely smashed and shattered. When would it be rebuilt ? She shook her head. I asked her what was being done to relieve distress. Not much, she thought, and laughed ironically. " They only think of asking women to knit socks for soldiers ! " A club had been started by philanthropic people for soldiers' wives. Some of her friends thought they would like to go there to see the War news ; they could not afford to buy newspapers out of their miserable separation allowances ; but when they read at the foot of the club's announcements : " To keep you out of the public houses," they would not go. She tossed her head. " They only get bits of rubbish there ! " Pleased to find listeners, she poured out her thoughts unprompted. " Oh, it was terrible when war began ; the streets full of soldiers jostling you, and trying to get you to speak to them—everyone could have got a young man ! And they were making the girls drunk. I never thought before that we had crowds of girls in Scarborough who would behave so ! But generally we have hardly any men here—they all have to go away to practise their trades. My brothers have gone—they all go. Perhaps it was because so many men wanted to make friends with them the girls' heads got turned—and so many of the girls were out of work ! As for the men, I suppose they thought when they came to the seaside they ought to have a good time ! They say there are 80 girls in the Workhouse maternity ward through it —and I know there are eleven from ——'s shop alone ! People talked about it a lot, and they started women patrols ; but it didn't do any good. As often as not the patrols scolded girls who were with their brothers or men they were engaged to. Some girls I know were waiting to meet their brothers at the Bar church. One of the patrols began to lecture them, and the clergyman joined in. The girls' soldier brothers and their friends arrived in the midst of it and made the clergyman and the patrol apologise. Interfering with the girls did no good, but now they don't seem to let the soldiers into the town after about nine at night ; and anyway things are quite different now ; the place is only too quiet. Nobody wants to come to the seaside any more ! "

. . . . . . . .

On Christmas morning, climbing by winding ways above the town, we saw the trenches recently dug by British soldiers along the cliffs ; and higher still, great heaps of stone which fell from the old castle when its walls were shelled by the German ships.

Lodging among the cottages of the fisherfolk in these terraced streets of the old town seven years before, I had wandered often beneath those ancient walls, regarding them curiously as a relic of an age of barbarism long dead, confident in my faith in the sure advance of progress. To-day, in face of the evidence of present barbarism, my thoughts were sad.

Vainly seeking my old landlady, for she had left the town, I was accosted by some neighbours of hers who remembered me. It was the anniversary of their wedding, and hospitably they would have us enter, to celebrate it with tea and plum cake, in their warm kitchen. It was a Yorkshire custom, they said, to exchange visits on Christmas morning. The wife was a very pretty woman, turned forty, with the bluest of blue eyes, a little shy and diffident and pleased to let the rest of us talk. The husband was black-eyed and swarthy as a Spaniard, with great gold rings in his ears. He told us, as others in the town had done, that the German battleships came so close to the shore that the people (believing them British) feared they would run aground. He was at the window when the firing began, and he called to his wife: "It's no good, lass, the Germans have come!"

Then he told her to go next door and help their neighbour to pacify her children. She was running to the back door, but he locked it and said: "I'm an Englishman and a Yorkshireman, and they'll not make us go the back way!" He walked to the end of the terrace and stood facing the battleships. He was not hit, but he showed us a big bit of shell which had fallen beside him. Believing, like everyone else, that the Germans intended landing, he looked around for our soldiers. They were nowhere to be seen. After the bombardment ceased they got into their trenches and sang a hymn. "They were no better than wooden soldiers!" he cried indignant. His wife reproved him, with a timid glance at us: "What use would it have been for our British soldiers to come out to be killed?"

Turning to the new town, we found much damage, and especially in the neighbourhood of the wireless station. A shell had fallen and burst before a lofty building, boring a great hole in the ground; and almost to the roof, the walls were splashed with mud thrown up by the impact and scarred by shrapnel. In a small house with a side wall down, and two great holes in front, a mother and all her children had been killed—only her husband was left to mourn them. Three out of four rooms had been wrecked in a house near by, and within a stone's-throw the shattering of a classic portico had killed the postman and the housemaid at the front door. No street here had escaped; in some streets house after house was conspicuously battered; in others it seemed that only the windows had been broken—till from another angle one saw roofs broken in and walls with gaping holes.

Returning to our lodging we learnt that yet another boat had been blown up. It was bitterly cold; the wind howled fiercely. We huddled by the fire, saddened and chilled. A girl ran past the window sobbing and wailing. A few minutes later she passed again. As I heard her coming a third time I went out to her, and saw that she was about sixteen years of age, hatless and poorly dressed. In abandonment of grief, she flung herself now against the wall, now leaned her head for a moment upon a window-sill, crying: "Dad! Dad! Oh, Dad!" As I came up with her two women met her. They knew her and understood what she muttered between her sobs better than I. They told me that her father was on one of the mine-sweepers out in the bay. She shrank into trembling reserve and, faltering nervously that she must go to her mother, fled from us in the dusk.

Next morning we called on our first landlady to learn the news of the night. As we came in sixteen lately shipwrecked mariners, who had recovered in her house, were leaving the door. She told us six others had been drowned, and a third vessel since our arrival blown up. Another, another, and yet another vessel was sacrified during the morning. Again we had notice to quit our lodging to make way for the sea-drenched men. Scarborough was too sad for me. "Let us get away to-night," I said to Smyth.

As we stood on the breakwater before leaving we saw the lifeboat set forth again to the rescue, over the cold grey waves in the gathering dusk.

I was unnerved ; the thought of death on the ocean—mankind in its courage, so small, so impotent on the vast waters—tugs at my heart more poignantly, I think, than death in any other guise. After the lapse of more than thirty years, I still can scarcely recall without tears the loss of the little Manx *Ben ma Chree* plying between Liverpool and Douglas, whose old hulk was lost in mid-winter storms, it was thought, by the sheer force of wild waters, battering on her hatches.

. . . . . . . .

As the train carried us Londonward, away from the grey, sad sea, a revulsion of feeling seized me. How should one give one's mind to anything save the War?

"Let us go over to France," I said to Smyth. "One ought to know what one can."

Passports and visas were obtained without difficulty. At Victoria Station we joined the long queue of people of many nationalities, lined up for examination in temporary wooden structures.

The formalities were brief: "Vous êtes British?" from an interrogator unmistakably English, and our assurance that we were carrying no letters: that was all. The train and boat were crowded; soldiers and civilians crushed in together.

Boulogne was transformed: Cockney porters more numerous than French, grey-bodied motor cars for the British Army stacked on the quay, British motor-buses, painted even to the windows a dull mud colour, waiting in the road for British soldiers, British soldiers in khaki thronging the platform, a buffet announcing: "Soldiers' Refreshments Here."

The train went slowly. At every station women came in with collecting boxes for the French wounded.

We found Paris less brilliantly lighted than of old, but not in the grim pitch-darkness then shrouding London. None of the recruiting posters, we had grown accustomed to, glared from her walls; having Conscription, the French Government needed no such appeals for obtaining men. The replacing of men by women's labour, though more extensive, was less ostentatious than it was already becoming in Britain. The War was too near a reality for Paris to make a show of it as they did over here. Some of the large shops had been turned into relief workrooms for unemployed women; one saw them in their dark clothes sewing behind the plate glass windows, for a wage, we were told, of only 5d. per day. Some of the finest hotels were converted to military hospitals.

Dr. Flora Murray and a staff of women were running a hospital under the French Government at Claridge's Hotel; for the British War Office was as yet unwilling to accept their aid.

We found Claridge's still as a sanctuary: in the entrance hall, no one; in the spacious inner hall, silence and lights shrouded in veils. A man in uniform sat at a high desk.

"Dr. Murray," we murmured.

He pointed beyond us and we saw her seated, far away and small, writing under a shaded lamp. She did not see us till we were close to her; and then she was so much the pitiful, small-voiced woman who had come to my bedside in the days of the Cat and Mouse Act that at first I did not notice she was in khaki, a dull subdued tone of it, with a narrow, dark red piping: the uniform she had chosen for "the women's hospital corps." Flat-chested, hipless, emaciated, one might have judged her devoid of stamina; yet she was tireless in efficient activity; a characteristic example of the intelligent middle class woman, whom an earlier generation would have dismissed as an "old maid." With her almost excessive quietude and gentleness, she had overborne many a seemingly cast-iron Army tradition. In defiance of all precedent, she gave equal treatment to officers and privates, placing them side by side in the same wards.

She led us into the great, brilliantly lighted wards. The soldiers had put up Christmas decorations: "A Merry Christmas to our Doctors, Sisters and Nurses!" in letters of cotton wool. The unfinished hotel had lacked its heating apparatus when war broke out; no such work, even for hospital use, was undertaken now. Huge open braziers of glowing coke had been brought in. "Highly unsatisfactory," Dr. Murray rightly called them, but to the casual observer cosy and picturesque. Convalescent soldiers gathered about them exchanging yarns. All turned in welcome to Dr. Murray and her women orderlies. There was an atmosphere of friendliness and peace, wherein life seemed ordered well.

When we had taken tea, and the typical thin bread and butter and toasted bun of a modest English household, with Dr. Murray and her orderlies, we returned to the wards, and were left alone to talk to the patients. They spoke of the hospital as the desert-worn traveller of the oasis; yet some murmured sadly: of what use to be healed thus speedily of one's wounds, to be sent back only the sooner, to death or worse? Dr. Murray had often complained in the days of the Cat and Mouse Act that her work of restoring Suffragette prisoners, discharged in a state of collapse from the hunger and thirst strike, was futile. More hopeless indeed was her task to-day! Some of the lads now due for return to the Front looked enviously at those who had lost a limb; the cripples congratulated themselves on their mutilation; and yet thought ruefully of the years to come.

A sad little Frenchman, his right arm gone, told us in hopeless grief that he did not know what had happened to his wife and children; the invading Germans had swept over the country where they lived. A giant from Normandy, handsome and fair, with a knee which would not mend, complained that his wife had only 25 sous a day and his children 10 sous each.[1] "It is not much!" he said. "My God! not much!" A Reservist from Sheffield, a serious fellow, older than most of them, with bitter complaint that he would never be well again, turned from us, resenting intrusion. Then he heard my name and eagerly begged for me to be brought to him, grasping at a talk with me as someone familiar, not merely one of the many sightseers, doing the round of the hospitals; for he had heard me speak at some time, and my sister Adela often when she was a Suffragette organiser in Sheffield. He unburdened himself: the horror of the War and its ugliness; the terrible misery of the first day under fire, the deafening noise of the shells bursting on all sides, and the dreadful sight of them flying overhead, the fear of being hit, the sight of other men killed, their bodies

[1] Approximately 1/0½d. a day for the wife and 5d. a day for each child.

hideously mangled. At last the pressure of routine work at the gun, the sheer physical strain of hard toil, dulled the senses. He had served with thirty others in relays of ten, carrying ammunition to the guns. As one man was killed, another stepped out to replace him. When off duty they slept in a pit roofed with branches, but when firing was brisk only short sleeps of one or two hours were allowed. Toiling in all weathers, pains shot through him when he stooped to lift the heavy shells. At last he fell to the ground and could not rise. He was bundled off to hospital with rheumatism and heart strain.

. . . . . . . .

Some convalescent soldiers were preparing to act a play. The stage was a large platform, with the bare white wall behind, and a little door in the centre, through which the players came and went. The drama was called " The Deserter " ; it was a grim satire on Army life, acted with ingenuous fidelity and received with the fervent sympathy of the ward. Deep-felt murmurs of assent and whispered reminiscences buzzed round us. We were shown first the recruiting office. In comes the new recruit, a gay and perky little fellow, ambitious to be in the Guards. Rejected as too short, he goes off in the sulks, refusing to join at all ; but in a moment is back again, all enthusiasm : " I say, Guv'nor, put me in one of them Specials ! " He spreads out his papers obligingly : " See, this is where I've worked." Friendly, confident, brotherly, he feels himself a fellow worth having and is anxious to assist the Army to put his services to good use.

We pass to the barrack yard ; a squad is being drilled by " Ser'nt Brown," a ridiculous elderly figure with a red nose and abnormally prominent chest. The new recruit plays the fool to relieve his boredom, raising his feet abnormally high in contorted grotesquery, and looking round with a grin to receive the encouragement of his fellows. A young officer enters and exchanges absurdly exaggerated salutes with Sergeant Brown. He eyes the men in the ranks and curtly criticises each one's appearance, the sergeant slavishly emphasising his derision. The new recruit, impishly resentful, feigns stupidity. Coarsely reprimanded, he retorts and argues, determined to give as vehemently as he gets.

The privates in the audience rejoiced bitterly at his quips, whispering poignant personal recollections to each other : " Aye, that's it ! Do you remember when old Choker ——"

" Is it like that in the Army ? " I asked a young convalescent beside me. He answered seriously : " Oh yes ; just like that."

The scenes move quickly ; the soldiers are discovered by officers playing cards in the barrack room. All scamper out save the new recruit, who remains, calmly shuffling the cards, and is arrested for " gambling," to the evident satisfaction of Sergeant Brown. . . .

The privates are scrubbing the floors of the barracks, slovenly, surly, rated and browbeaten by the officers. The new recruit declares he is

" fed up," and will run away. We see him next marched on to relieve a sentry, made to repeat in stereotyped form the length of his beat and the position of an imaginary enemy. Left alone, he props up his gun, hangs his hat and coat on it, and absconds. . . .

Two officers sit gravely examining documents. The deserter is brought before them. Witnesses reel off the evidence in a style reminiscent of police courts: " On the umph of the umph, umph, umph I arrested the prisoner on the steps of the umph, umph, umph. When I arrested 'im 'e became disord'ly and in the barrack room 'e struck Ser'nt Brown a blow on the right cheek and Pri't Jones a blow in the left eye. . . ."

The deserter is committed to the Divisional Court Martial. The officers there take oath " not to divulge anything which takes place within this Court until the sentence is promulgated." The deserter questions the witnesses. Why, if he were drunk, did Sergeant Brown allow him to pay for drinks all round? Sergeant Brown and the other officer reply with a firm denial. " Sergeant Brown never drinks! "

" Then why is his nose so red? "

The judges silence the prisoner with shouts of " liar! " Asked whether he has anything to say for himself, he pleads that he ran away because he was " fed up." " What is 'fed up'? " asks the senior among the judges. A young officer explains: " Sick and tired of the life of the Army altogether." The prisoner is condemned to death. He staggers a little and covers his eyes with his hand. They march him out.

" Are they sentenced to death for running away? " I asked the lad at my elbow.

" Oh yes, on active service; and then you have to dig your own grave."

" Have you ever seen a Court Martial? "

" Yes," he said gravely, and raked the red coals in the brazier uncomfortably with a bit of stick, hunching his shoulders away from me, to preclude further questions.

The stage is again a barrack room; the soldiers squat on the floor playing cards. They are surprised by Sergeant Brown and another officer, and attempt ineffectually to gather the cards under their coats. Affecting not to notice, Sergeant Brown orders them out on to the parade ground. The deserter is brought in and asked if he wishes to be tied up. He prefers to stand free. He asks Sergeant Brown if his conscience does not prick him. A firing party is called out. The deserter is shot. Sergeant Brown brings a squad of men to remove the body.

The soldiers in the audience had grown depressed and moody, the play was too real to them.

. . . . . . . .

Not far from Claridge's was the great Hotel Majestic, now a war hospital and, with two others, run at the cost of H. D. Harben, Fabian-Suffragist—*Daily Heraldite*. The smell of ether met us as we entered. The air of the corridors reeked with it from the operations constantly taking place. Lovely young women from London, with snow-white skin and rose-red cheeks, serving as orderlies, dashed about, working tremendously hard, motoring with Harben to the other hospitals, zealously demolishing French pastries, as restoratives.

Harben himself received us gaily, effervescent with enthusiasm : such wonderful cures they had, such marvellous operations ! A great taciturn French peasant had been brought in with a bullet imbedded in the nape of his neck, completely paralysed in all four limbs ; the bullet extracted, he could move again ; what an achievement ! Marvellous ! Harben enthused ; the lovely young orderlies beamed their pleasure.

There was a hopeless misery in the wards we had not felt at Claridge's. They were more crowded ; the cases were more serious. Bed after bed was occupied by poor fellows one could not venture to disturb ; figures heavily swathed in bandages, racked in their torment, stilled in unconsciousness ; Algerians, Moors, Tunisians unable to speak to nurse or doctor, ghastly in pallor ; an English boy of nineteen, incurably injured, bandaged from head to foot, his beautiful face half hidden by wrappings and his dark eyes drawn with pain.

A Yorkshire footballer had lost for ever the use of a foot and a hand.

" What will you do when you go home ? " one of the doctors asked him.

" I don't know," he answered, " unless the Government have some idea of setting me up in a little business."

He turned to me as though he thought I had some power to intercede for him, his eyes dumbly pleading for assurance that his case would not be overlooked. I could not meet his gaze.

A Lancashire man, terribly wounded, who had undergone three operations and was awaiting a fourth, spoke to us with resentful suffering in his voice and horror in his eyes.

Three young French officers in a private ward (there was no defiance of Army standards here, officers and men were rigidly separated) had been wounded together when experimenting with a hand grenade. One of them had lost the sight of an eye and the use of an ear, but he spoke lightly of returning to the War.

. . . . . . . .

I wanted to see my mother ; much as her war attitude grieved me, far apart as our views had grown, I could not be in Paris, where her home was then, without a visit to her.

We found her at her fireside with Sister Pine. She would speak of nothing but the War, talking fast and emphatically, obviously perceiving —though we did not gainsay her by a single word—the opposition in our hearts.

I listened unhappily, speechless, resolved to occasion no quarrel. When she demanded suddenly : " What are *you* doing ? " with a strain of contemptuous irony in her voice, which I well knew from childhood, I answered only : " In the East End."

When Norah Smyth added : " We have been to Scarborough," Mrs. Pankhurst turned on her a tirade, declaring it impossible to police a vast coast-line such as ours when every man and every ounce of ammunition was needed at the Front. Then she reverted to the bellicose thesis which Christabel, now her unchallenged mentor, was propounding at the time : The blockade ! A war of attrition ! Intern them all ! She seemed a very Maenad of the War with her flashing eyes.

We were distant from each other as though a thousand leagues had intervened ; an aching void, in truth ; for we were near, so poignantly near in the memory of old efforts and old loves. My senses were bruised by each familiar mannerism employed to accentuate these unfamiliar themes. A sad anti-climax to a life's struggle—the thought knelled like a death bell in my brain. I was glad to get away, exhausted by sorrow.

. . . . . . . .

At Senlis, we were told, we should most readily see the damage done by the German advance in the first weeks of the War. The destruction was more hideously complete than I had imagined possible. The buildings had been systematically demolished and reduced to mere heaps of debris. It was difficult to realise that these deserted ruins had so lately been inhabited. A solitary woman stood sorrowing beside the charred remains of her home.

. . . . . . . .

On Christmas Eve Lily Macdonnell and other friends had gone carolling through the night to gather pennies for our distress work. In Covent Garden soldiers went with them to aid in the collection. In Westminster some passing soldiers, taking their last meal before departure for the Front, begged them to come into their hut to sing to them and share their frugal fare.

In the New Year we held great parties for the children in Bow, in Poplar, in Canning Town. In Bow Baths more than 1,500 children assembled. We had asked for a present for every child. Gifts poured in so lavishly that every child had an armful of toys and comfortable garments. Mrs. Arncliffe Sennett provided an enormous Christmas tree magnificently decorated. Actresses, singers, musicians, provided entertainments for children and grown-ups with all the old brilliance of the Suffragette movement. Rosy-faced, smiling Mary Philips, wearing a red cap of liberty, came knitting to represent Madame Lafarge; a gesture intended to remind us that Suffragette militancy was not dead. We were swept along in a whirl of loving enthusiasm. To me our goal was the equalitarian society of mutual service—in each of our band, even the remotest, the most casually attached to us, some glamour stirred.

## CHAPTER XVI

### A DARK NEW YEAR—RAPACITY OF THE SHIPOWNERS—THE LEAGUE OF RIGHTS—ANOTHER D.O.R.A.

1915 came in grimly.

The Hon. Albinia Brodrick was complaining, through the Press, that though the British Red Cross Society had 1,500 fully trained nurses waiting to be called up, ladies with a month or three weeks' training were going out to mishandle the wounded. In the Commons, Tickler, a Liberal, protested that 2,600 men had volunteered for the dangerous work of mine-sweeping ; 100 of them had already lost their lives ; but the wives of these brave men had received neither separation allowances nor pensions.

Prices were rising. Best English wheat stood at 60s. a quarter, and best American at 61s., as compared with 36s. and 37s. in January 1914. Yet still there was no real shortage. More margarine, cheese, coffee, rice, raw sugar, tea, bacon and preserved meat were imported in January 1915 than in the January of the previous year, and in every case at greatly enhanced prices. The cost of imported wheat and wheat flour had been £3,467,211 in January 1914. In January 1915 it was £5,431,490. Had prices remained stationary, the cost would only have been £3,800,000. Of Indian corn, which people were being urged to use as a substitute for wheat flour, the import had increased 154.8 per cent. ; the cost, now it had entered the domestic larder, was greater by 226.9 per cent.

In freight charges profiteering was rampant. On American wheat the freight had risen from 15s. to 55s. The *Daily Chronicle* spoke of " fairy-tale profits " by shipowners ; the *Manchester Guardian* recorded increased charges of 400 per cent. on some routes. The *Daily News* reported freights having risen from 7s. 3d. to 37s. 6d. between Newcastle and Naples, from 3s. to 13s. 6d. between the Tyne and London. These enormous increases were by no means justified by the hazards of warfare ; for the owners were well secured against loss on this account. Eighty per cent. of the war risks had been taken over by the Government at the outbreak of war. The maximum insurance rate was only £5 5s. per cent., the minimum £1 1s. On the last day of 1914 the minimum was reached, and underwriters were willing to take even 5s. per cent. for ships travelling between this country and the United States. Indeed, for the time being, the risk of transport had been reduced practically to the peace standard. The *Review of Reviews* in September 1914 declared that in ten days from the outbreak of hostilities the British

Navy had made the ocean as safe for British trade as before the War, and had swept the German mercantile marine from the seas. *The Times History of the War* declared that in three weeks British commerce was not merely " fast returning to normal conditions," but was seeking to conquer realms left derelict by the annihilation of German trade. Exports from Germany valued at £400,000,000[1] a year had been stopped. The *Times* annual *Financial Review* gave, as one reason for increased prices, the fact that the German mercantile marine was no longer able to compete in the carrying trade of the world.[2] The sailors' wives, pinching on their meagre allowances, were thus, with the rest of the public, actually suffering, in increased prices, for the services to British commerce performed by their husbands at the risk of their lives !

Such revelations of the mercenary forces which held the peoples in their grip aroused in me an abiding horror. Though I had no illusions about the purposes of the War, this callous greed of money-making astounded me. The *Times* deprecated protest, assuring its readers that the shipowners, who were thus making capital from their country's need, were " neither thieves nor philanthropists, but men with passions like ourselves." To this anti-social condition had the competitive system carried the trading community !

Week by week women from many districts sent me their budgets, showing that prices had risen most in the poorest districts, and on the commodities most purchased by the poor. The budget of a Canning Town woman showed a total increase of 40 per cent. Bread, a disproportionately large item in working-class budgets, because so much else is lacking, had risen from 4½d. to 7d. per quartern. For sugar she paid 3¼d. instead of 1¾d. before the War, for barley 5d. instead of 2½d. per lb., for tinned milk 7d. instead of 3¾d. The price of meat for baking in her district had doubled in price, that of the cheapest cuts for boiling had trebled.

A typical letter and budget from a woman in Bromley-by-Bow showed how debt and privations were growing amongst the workers :

" My husband is a casual worker earning £1 2s. 6d., sometimes a little more. I hardly know how to make ends meet. I have five children, the eldest not yet twelve, the youngest one year and five months. I am expecting another in June. This is how I spent my money before the War, and how I manage with it now :

| *Before the War.* | s. | d. | *February* 1915. | s. | d. |
|---|---|---|---|---|---|
| Rent .. .. .. | 7 | 6 | .. .. | 7 | 6 |
| Coal, 1 cwt. .. .. | 1 | 2 | .. .. | 2 | 0 |
| Bread (3 loaves a day at 2½d.) | 4 | 4½ | .. .. | 7 | 0 |
| Flour (4 lbs.) .. .. | | 7 | (2 lbs.) .. | | 4 |

[1] *Vorwaerts*, August 24th, 1914.

[2] In November 1914, out of 20,500,000 tons of British shipping, 20,222,000 tons were plying ; out of 5,000,000 tons of German shipping only 459,000 were either plying or unaccounted for—statement by Board of Trade.

| | s. d. | | s. d. |
|---|---|---|---|
| Gas .. .. .. | 9 | .. .. | 9 |
| Insurance .. .. | 9 | .. .. | 9 |
| Milk (½ pint daily) .. | 7 | (tinned skim) | 3¾ |
| Potatoes (18 lbs.) .. | 6 | (12 lbs.) .. | 7½ |
| Margarine (1¼ lbs.) .. | 10 | (inferior .. quality) .. | 10 |
| Meat .. .. .. | 2 6 | .. .. | 3 6 |
| Tea .. .. .. | 6 | .. .. | 7½ |
| Sugar (4 lbs.) .. .. | 7 | (3 lbs.) .. | 10½ |
| Sundries .. .. | 2 0 | .. .. | 2 0 |
| | £1 2 7½ | | £1 7 1¼ |

"We are eating less, and have pawned many things to make up the difference, but that cannot go on."

The price of coal at the pit's mouth had fallen away owing to the loss of foreign markets, but freight charges had increased the cost of coal to the consumer; the rates from Durham to London by sea had risen from 3s. per ton to 13s. 6d. per ton.

The South Metropolitan Gas Company circularised its customers, urging them to press their Members of Parliament to demand Government action to reduce freight charges, and threatening to raise the cost of gas by 8d. or 9d. per cubic foot.

Under the blanket of acquiescence, which the truce of parties had cast over the political field, there were unrestful murmurs; a town's meeting in Liverpool, demonstrations here and there, a Labour Party resolution in Parliament calling for Government intervention to keep down prices. Asquith admitted to the Commons that the cost of living had risen 24 per cent. in London, 23 per cent. in the other large towns, that bread was 75 per cent. and sugar 72 per cent. above the pre-War prices (housewives' budgets showed a greater increase); yet he refused to intervene, and advised the public to "wait till June, when prices might be expected to fall."

The poor must starve, but the Government trimmed its sails to the powerful interests.

The railways were taken over by the Government, but the dividends and directors' salaries were assured. Jobbery was rife. It leaked out that a London firm had been appointed boot buyers to the Government, getting £1,000 for each million pairs of boots received by the Government and salaries of £600 a year each for two members of the firm. So bad were the boots supplied by these buyers, that a War Office official had to go over to France to investigate, and Barlow, M.P., was able to inform the Commons that boots passed by the "expert," for one of the battalions "over there," looked "charming," but when put on the men's feet refused to hold together. "After a good deal of struggle," as Barlow explained, the contractor was forced to take them back, but a month later the same boots were sold to the Army again by a new contractor, at an increase of 1s. 9d. a pair ![1] It was further disclosed that the Government was paying £60,000 a year to a gentleman who bought timber for them.

War provides the supreme temptations for venality, the unparalleled opportunities for getting rich quick by illicit and brazen methods.

School attendance had been relaxed to provide cheap labour, masses of children had been turned out of school to make way for the troops, and either left without education of any sort, or crowded in where space could be found. The Government admitted in February that for 13,000 children no alternative accommodation had been found. The pleasures of the rich remained sacrosanct. Davison Dalziel was complaining to the Commons that wounded soldiers, many of them so critically ill that removal would be dangerous, were being taken from Epsom on account of the Spring races, whereat leisured society, from Royalty downward, was accustomed to seek amusement. The Government had sounded the cry : " BUSINESS AS USUAL ! " This business of the stables and the bookmaker must by no means be hindered. To economise fuel, the London County Council patriotically decided to send the children home from school at 2.30, instead of at 4 p.m., and to set the dinner hour forward to 11 a.m. On the mother was cast the added burden of cost and inconvenience. If her man came home to his midday meal, she must give it him cold, or cook a second time.

. . . . . . . .

In order that all available capital might be diverted to War Loan, and all labour to war work, Lloyd George, on January 29th, 1915, caused it to be announced that Treasury approval must be obtained for all fresh issues of capital, whether on behalf of Government Departments, local authorities, or public or private companies. Whilst he was at the Treasury he desired the Treasury to control the nation ; when he moved to the Ministry of Munitions he had a similar ambition for that Department. He set up another committee to deal ostensibly with all fresh issues of capital, but actually the Local Authorities were the quarry at which he mainly aimed. They were instructed that all new works, unless of " pressing necessity " either for public health or, of course, for war requirements, must be avoided ; public works already begun should be reduced or postponed. Even expenditure already approved by the Local Government Board must be re-submitted, and if the cost were to be raised by stock, bonds or bills, Treasury sanction must also be obtained.

Whilst factories for war equipment shot up on every hand, normal increase and replacement of dwellings was stopped. A great shortage of housing consequently grew, with unhappy social consequences, and a lowering of the standard of health and happiness in individual homes, which continued for many a year after the War. Of such is the life of the people !

. . . . . . . .

[1] Official Parliamentary Report, March 3rd and 4th, 1915.

A sentence of four months' imprisonment (afterwards reduced to a month) was passed upon a Hornsey soldier's wife, who was alleged to have obtained £2 15s. od. on false pretences from the Soldiers and Sailors Families Association; yet no one was punished for the scandalous delays which caused misery and suffering to many thousands of soldiers' wives and their children.

Stoker Thompson, of H.M.S. *Challenger*, invalided home with paralysis, committed suicide from anxiety as to how he and his family were to exist on his pension.[1] Muriel Scott, the young wife of a soldier, committed suicide; she had been thrown out of work through her employer joining the Red Cross; she was refused separation allowance for the indefensible reason that her husband was stationed in Aden, which, for administrative purposes, was regarded as India, and therefore subject to the cruel pre-War regulations which provided separation allowance for only about 4 per cent. of the soldiers' wives.

Our work was increasing rapidly; the need for agitation growing. In February I decided that we must form a "League of Rights for Soldiers' and Sailors' Wives and Relatives," to spur the women on to stand up for themselves and each other, instead of remaining inarticulate, to be dealt with by others as mere "cases." I broached the subject to George Lansbury; he was ready for anything new which promised a rousing campaign. Since the outbreak of war our Federation had held more big meetings and demonstrations in London than all the other organisations put together. We were taking the lead, and Lansbury was always glad to speak for us. I told him that though with the aid of our Federation staff I was prepared to continue doing the routine work of the organisation I wanted to bring into it the Trade Union and Labour elements who ought to be enthused on this subject. Therefore I wanted to give the honours of office to people associated with those circles. I suggested that his wife should be called the honorary secretary. Lansbury was pleased with the proposal, and assented on her behalf. He also accepted a seat on the committee, and George Banks, the secretary of the Poplar Trades Council (a hardened reactionary, although a Labour man), became a sleeping partner, termed co-treasurer with Mrs. H. D. Harben. It was no surprise that Mrs. Lansbury never signed a letter or attended a committee; no one ever expected that she would. If ever she had taken any active part in the Labour movement it was before I went to the East End. In my knowledge of her she was far too much overwhelmed, depressed by her housework, her excessively large family, and the long-standing varicose ulcers, from which so many working mothers suffer a martyrdom, to the disgrace of our so-called civilised standards. Indeed she was one of the sort of women who made women of my sort Suffragettes; hers to stint, suffer, and work in silence, enduring all the hardships of participation in pioneer causes, without a breath of the exhilaration.

We thus formed our League of Rights with the most attractive figure-

[1] Official Parliamentary Report, February 8th, 1918.

heads we could procure, as enthusiasts do; and we at 400 Old Ford Road went on with the work. It was my great joy that we were stimulating working women to speak up for themselves and their sort, and to master, despite their busy lives, the intricacies of Royal warrants and Army regulations, so as to secure the promised allowances, such as they were, for themselves and their neighbours. The stubborn cases they could not solve they handed on to me. I found much solid satisfaction, and consolation for other disappointments, in overcoming the harsh decisions of the authorities concerned; thereby securing the means of life for many poor families. Appeals from poor people who had tried, in many cases, every avenue they could think of—from *John Bull* to the War Office—came to me daily. Some of my victories were achieved when a man or woman had been denied allowance or pension for a couple of years or more. In the case of discharged soldiers and sailors, there was, alas, no stability about those victories. Periodical attendances before the medical boards soon pulled down a full pension to the four-and-eight-penny standard, or even less, though the victims of official economies still suffered grievously from wounds, illness, and loss of limbs, due to war-service, and were unable to procure the work for which officialdom " deemed them fit."

The League of Rights was not accompanied by the roaring enthusiasm some of our friends had anticipated. The meetings, held in halls of moderate size, were often but moderately attended by quiet, earnest little women, who joined the organisation with some diffidence in modest numbers. The dark streets were a growing deterrent.

Spoiled by the packed throngs our platforms had offered in the pre-War days of the " Cat and Mouse Act,"[1] and by the great provincial demonstrations worked up by the local rank and file to greet London speakers coming to fulminate on questions of striking popular appeal, Lansbury protested that he could not give his time to these small gatherings, where real spade-work was being accomplished. " I do not believe in beating the air ! " he protested—a favourite phrase of his, as I had learnt to know. The committees he rarely attended, it being understood that he was too much occupied and merely gave his name. That is, of course, how committees are largely run. No one, least of all I, ever complained of it. Happily in after years Lansbury was pleased to recall his association with the League of Rights.[2]

It was a little later that I induced his son Edgar's wife, née Minnie Glassman, to leave her work as an elementary school teacher and help me as assistant honorary secretary of our Federation. She devoted herself mainly to our distress work, and to the League of Rights. She knew the district and people, and in accordance with the first principle of work in our Federation, she was prepared to make herself unreservedly the advocate of the people, and to get the best she could for them. So many would-be uplifters of the poor allow their critical faculties to run amuck, and begin to fancy that, after all, " poor people like that "

[1] See *The Suffragette Movement,* by E. Sylvia Pankhurst. Longmans Green.
[2] *My Life,* by George Lansbury. Constable.

can manage on very short commons. I always felt that I could trust Minnie to realise that under the veneer we humans are all very much alike ; and that the most we could get for our poor, was very much less than we all of us need—and a wretched makeshift, indeed, for the social equality and assurance we desire. I was more than glad of her aid. A dear girl I thought her, and think so still though I lost touch with her towards the close of her brief life.

When the League of Rights had been going some time I wanted to put it on a national basis. I called a joint conference of Labour organisations to elect a more widely representative committee. I was a little concerned lest the work might fall into the hands of the pompous sort of person I had encountered in pleading for my people before the local pensions committees. I saw Lansbury, and said that in view of the conference, I thought that if I were to continue doing the work, I had better stand for election as honorary secretary.

Daily the stories were coming in to me of men broken and disabled by military training, ruined for ordinary life, yet denied compensation. A man who had been a stoker earning 40s. to 45s. a week wrote to me from South Wales. A Reservist, he had rejoined his regiment in September 1914, a perfectly fit man, and was promoted to be drill sergeant. In January he was sent home dangerously ill with bronchitis and pneumonia and cardiac weakness, medically certified to have been brought on by exposure to damp and cold. Owing to some hitch, no pay came through ; his wife pawned her wedding ring to buy bread. Eventually the arrears were paid up ; but his illness had been complicated by privation. He failed to make a good recovery. When called up for medical examination, he was discharged as unfit, with nothing but a free railway pass for his return. He was penniless. Ill as he was, he travelled 7½ hours without food and arrived home to find not a morsel of food in the house. He fainted from exhaustion. The neighbours gave aid, and preserved the family from starvation. He was only thirty-five, a total abstainer from alcohol with " a good character."

Many from our immediate neighbourhood came to me in like case. After a long correspondence I only succeeded in getting an allowance of 1s. 6d. a day for one such broken man with five dependent children. In the case of a poor young fellow disabled for life, the authorities only agreed to pay for a truss !

In October 1914 the War Office had relaxed its original decision to make separation allowances only to legally wedded wives and their children born in lawful wedlock. A poor woman who, by an error of the authorities, had had the allowance for two months before it was officially granted, was now left for two months without money !

Because the authorities had forgotten their own regulations one woman had her allowance and allotment stopped for 28 days in March 1915 on the ground that her husband was undergoing 28 days' punishment at the Front. Only after two months' correspondence through the League of Rights were the authorities convinced that this bad rule had been changed and the money finally paid.

Another unfortunate soul was told that her husband's allotment would cease for a year, because he had been sentenced to a year's imprisonment for a breach of discipline. She wrote in desperate grief to know the reason ; but a few days later was informed, in the brief official parlance which opposes a blank wall to the aching heart pleading for knowledge, that her husband had been killed at the Front.

Red tape ! Red tape ! Refusal met even the simple plea of Tom Wing that separation allowance might date from the time the soldier made the allotment of pay to his family, not from the filling up of a form of which many soldiers did not even know the existence.

. . . . . . . .

That spring the Government brought in a third Defence of the Realm Act to provide itself with yet further powers. The first hypnotism of war-shock had now somewhat abated. The Lords, in their impregnable position of hereditary legislators, the historic drag on the wheels of reform, now came forward as the defenders of abandoned Liberty. They inserted into the Act provisions that all civilian British subjects charged under it should be entitled to be tried by a civil court, and to have the general nature of the charge against them communicated to them in writing, and that the sentence, if any, should be passed in public. Women who had married aliens, but had been British subjects before marriage, were to be regarded as British subjects for the purposes of this Act.

## CHAPTER XVII

CLOSING DOWN THE NATIONAL RELIEF FUND—HUNGER STIMULATES RECRUITING—UNEMPLOYMENT LIQUIDATED BY WAR WORK—BUSINESS AS USUAL!

IT was now disclosed that gifts sent from the Dominions to alleviate war distress, here in the Mother Country, had been diverted to the use of the Army. 80 per cent. of the cheeses, and 42½ per cent. of the flour had been handed over, and the War Office had applied for 40 per cent. of the tinned salmon. A large part of Canada's gift consisted of potatoes. 100 tons were bought by a salesman in the Borough market. He was allowed to pick out the better potatoes, which were emptied from the sacks marked " Canada's Gift " to his private sacks.

The National Relief Fund in January had reached £4,430,000, of which £1,104,000 had been spent by the Soldiers and Sailors Families Association, in relieving women who ought to have been provided with Naval and Military separation allowances or pensions. Only £186,000 had been disbursed to relieve the civilian distress, for which the fund had been subscribed. The Cabinet Committee was urging local committees to cut relief to the minimum, in order that the bulk of the Fund might be invested in Canada.

The Poplar committee had met in the seven months of war only four times. The Mayor and the officials under his jurisdiction were rigorously cutting down relief. In flat defiance of the main committee's decision, they continued suppressing many applications without passing them on to the ward committees for investigation.

The North Bow ward committee discovered that some of the potatoes in Canada's gift were being sold to salesmen in Poplar, though refused to the hungry people the ward committees had recommended for war relief. The ward committee passed a resolution of protest and sent it to me for publication in the *Dreadnought*.

Goaded by such exposures, Susan Lawrence at last bestirred herself, and induced St. John Hutchinson, " Alf Yeo," the Liberal Member of Parliament for Poplar, and George Lansbury, to join her in signing a declaration that the Local Representative Committee should meet.

The Mayor was thus compelled to summon the committee. It met on March 4th. For the first time the minutes of the previous meeting were read. The instruction carried at the previous meeting that lists of applicants which the Town Hall officials refused to register should be sent to the ward committees for further inquiries did not appear. I complained of the omission. Banks corroborated my statement that the instruction had been carried. Nevertheless the omission was left unrectified.

Susan Lawrence moved that the committee meet monthly. Banks seconded, complaining that gifts of food from the Dominions had been received and disposed of without reference to the committee. An extraordinary scene arose. The Mayor sprang to his feet, shaking his fist at me, and crying: " Now I am going to answer you ! " After long wrangling, the resolution was carried, in the teeth of bitter complaint by the Mayor, and the furious invective of his friends. The pale Miss Wintour and others appealed to the Mayor not to be " offended " because they felt compelled to vote for the resolution. He replied, with the pettish mannerisms of a fractious child, that he *was* offended, that he would not go on doing the work, and that he would have a Local Government Board inquiry. The committee then fell to soothing him, and passed a vote of thanks for his services. My resolution, asking the Cabinet Committee to raise the scale of relief in accordance with the increase in the cost of living, was carried without dissent, the majority of the committee being still engaged in a crossbench continuation of this storm in a teacup. Several councillors aroused themselves too late, with cries of " Oh ! eh ! I did not hear ! " I then moved the instruction omitted from the minutes that lists of applicants whom the Town Hall officials refused to register should be sent to the ward committees for further inquiries. The Mayor in a fury sprang up to object, whilst his friends jeered at me: " Go and consult the Cabinet Committee ! " All parties preferred to placate the Mayor, than to shoulder responsibility towards the distressed applicants. Therefore my resolution was voted down. I then moved that the names of women recommended by the ward committee for employment in the workrooms should be sent directly to the workroom secretary, instead of through the officials at the Town Hall. I instanced the case, just supplied to me by Emily Sharp, of two girls recommended by the West Ward committee for the workrooms, whose names she had sent to the Town Hall on January 20th. Notification to attend the workroom had not been despatched to the girls till February 25th, though in the interim Emily Sharp had twice written on their behalf to the Town Hall. In spite of such cruel delays, my resolution fell to the ground unseconded. To the committee, the old Mayor with his childish humours, was one of themselves; they did not wish to trouble him further. These unknown girls, who had waited and starved for thirty-six days, were to them merely " distress cases " devoid of personality.

. . . . . . . .

When the committee met a month later, in conformity with the new rule, few members appeared. It was brought to light that a hundred sacks of flour from the gift of the overseas Dominions had been granted for distress in the borough, but the poor had received not an ounce of it. The Mayor explained urbanely that a certain firm of biscuit makers had offered to keep it and exchange it for other flour in the autumn.

Since Asquith had given Parliament to understand that the price of flour would fall in June[1] the arrangement might be quite useful to this obliging firm! Moreover, poor people were starving now. Closely questioned, the Mayor admitted that 328 tins of Dominions gift salmon and 1,194 tins of beef were still in his custody. I asked him why the requests of the ward committees to have these provisions given to their poor had been denied. Owing to the meagre attendance of other parties the Labour members had a majority that evening. The Mayor therefore answered with unwonted blandness. He admitted that the refusal had been given on his orders, because he thought it would be " nicer " to keep the meat and the salmon till flour and potatoes could be distributed with it. The sale of a proportion of the potatoes had been recently unearthed; he had now admitted his disposal of the flour! O, hypocrisy, despicable are thy subterfuges!

A railway worker chimed in, with his eye-witness's knowledge, that the potatoes sent by the Dominions were rotting in store, whilst the poor, for whom they were intended, went hungry. " It's very hard for us chaps to see them lying by! " he complained plaintively.

Despite the decision to meet monthly, taken after so much disturbance, the committee was again left unsummoned for many months.

. . . . . . . .

In the great pressure of distress at the outbreak of war the National Relief Fund would have been all too small had it been expended so as to supply a tenth of the actual need. It had been husbanded by leaving the destitute to starve, a method regarded as desirable in the interests of recruiting, though disastrous to the health of the nation. " Why ever did you join the Army? " " Because we were starving! " were the commonest observations exchanged in the 17th Battalion East London Territorials, according to one of its members, who wrote to me from St. Albans. Women, children, cripples, and old grandfathers suffered in the interests of recruiting along with the men of military age.

Walter Long, chairman of the National Relief Fund executive, informed the Commons that his committee had taken the view that they ought " to be very careful that funds of this character are not used under the cover of alleviating distress alone."

Recruiting and war work were now steadily liquidating unemployment and reducing applications for relief.

The apparent speed of the process was ruthlessly accelerated. The demand that more men should be obtained for the Front by setting women to do their work was already heard; every woman to whom relief was denied would be a ready recruit for war service; no matter if some went hungry until the factories could employ them. All economists know that a pool of unemployed workers is the surest means of securing cheap labour. Then off with relief, and on with the war work!

In Poplar—and Poplar was no exception to the rule—the Mayor and his officials were rapidly annihilating the relief lists. When in October

[1] This prediction proved false.

the committee at last met again, only two persons were being relieved, a shopkeeper and a corset-maker, who were getting respectively 4s. and 2s. a week in food tickets. The Mayor blandly appealed for our decision whether to continue these doles or refer the recipients to the Poor Law Guardians. Since it had been decreed that only unemployment caused by the War might be relieved, old age pensioners, and other poor people crushed into deeper poverty by the high prices, could obtain no aid from the Fund. So ended the Mayor's committee! We were never formally disbanded. As local representatives we were mere ciphers, leaving all to the Mayor, without control over expenditure and administration.

. . . . . . . .

Mrs. Payne brought her up to see me, a little plain old maid, neat, spare, respectable. Her face flushed and hands trembled as she spoke. She gave her name and age, 57, with the formality acquired by painful visits to other offices. Her painful sense of indignity embarrassed me. I tried to reassure her, parrying her pride. Her tale gushed out; gentility, penury, courage. She earned her living for forty years by making men's ties and silk belts, had become a forewoman over twenty girls. Then her eyesight began to fail. "But for my eyes, I am as well able to work as any of the younger ones, in fact better. I often had bad health when I was young—I haven't now!" This failing of the eyes compelling her, she ventured, a year before the War, to try her fortune as a small confectioner, buying her business with the whole of the savings she had accumulated in forty years—just £40. She had succeeded; her shop was opposite a pleasure garden, and some of its visitors there came to her for refreshments. She made a profit of 18s. to £1 a week on the average and 30s. to 35s. in summer. It sufficed for her simple wants. She was proud of her modest achievement and the independence it had given her. "I had a splendid business in ice cream!" she said wistfully. The War came, just as the best of the ice cream season was beginning. The gardens were closed. Seven hundred railway men, "my best customers," left the district; they were told they must either enlist or be put on half time. For a week she could get no sugar. Prices rose monstrously; she was afraid to buy. Having no capital to fall back on, overwhelmed by the prospect of debt, and torn by the bitterest disappointment she decided to close her doors. She went to the library of a provident society, to which she had belonged in her youth, to search the newspaper advertisements for a situation. The clerk there advised her to apply to the Local Representative Committee. The committee could not give her work; it had only money to offer. "I wouldn't take it at first," she said. "I sold my tea urn and other things from the shop, and lived on that for a little while—but I had to come to it at last!" For the first month the committee allowed her 3s. a week. Then the Government scale was announced, and her dole was raised to 10s. She strove unceasingly to find work. "It's my age that's against me, though, but for my eyes, I can do as much work as any of the younger ones. I've been to hundreds of places, and as I can't afford to ride, I've had to tramp. . . . I would do any kind of work if I could get it." Her voice quavered. Last week the committee cut her allowance to 5s. "My rent is 3s. 6d., so you can see what it means!" Even the 5s. would soon be stopped they told her, for they were "closing down the Fund." They had spoken harshly. "As though they believed I had closed my shop to get myself on to the Fund" to live in one room on 10s. a week; to take relief after keeping myself for more than forty years!" She stifled a sob, assuring me that her little shop had not been the only one to shut; five others of the sort had closed in the same road. They could not help it; their trade was gone. One of them had kept open till Christmas; then the owners had closed their doors, owing £500! "I came out of it without owing a penny to anyone! I wouldn't keep on and involve other people!"

I showed her the Board of Trade form of registration for War Service. "I should be willing to work on the land if they would have me," she said wearily. "I would train for anything they liked, but I do not think they would take anyone of my age! I suppose I shall have to sell all I have; things I have had since I was about twenty!" She tried to shroud herself in her pride; the despair in her voice told me plainly she had nothing left to sell. I would lend my efforts to find work for her, but that would not atone to her for her little business; her own achievement. It was the loveless tragedy of a little old maid.

. . . . . . . .

Amid the misery and slaughter the Press Bureau sounded the cry "Business as usual!" It struck a note popular in the commercial world.

The most ghoulish side of the war business peeped out occasionally from the veils which shrouded it. On April 28th, 1915, Lord Charles Beresford reminded the House of Commons that for every fuse made in this country the Government paid 1s. to Krupps in Essen, in respect of a patent held by them, and asked how much money that German firm would make out of the Battle of Neuve Chapelle. Sir Arthur Markham inquired of the German royalties on British submarines. On May 5th Philip Snowden revealed the other side of the gruesome picture, complaining that the British Whitehead Torpedo Company had a branch at Fiume in Hungary, whereat torpedoes, submarines, destroyers, floating mines and other armament accessories were made for the Austrian Government, and were now being used against this country.

Life went its cruel way. Councillor Turner was complaining to the Glasgow Trades Council that soldiers' wives were being evicted, in some cases by the very employers who had gained approbation as patriots by public promises to restore the soldiers' work to them when they returned from the War. In one such case the local Territorial Association had been appealed to, and had replied that it had nothing whatever to do with safeguarding the interests of soldiers' wives. On March 10th Lord Charles Beresford complained that sailors' widows were left without payments for an average period of six weeks after their husbands had been killed. Asquith refused Parliamentary appeals to him to grant an extra 1s. a week to the Old Age Pensioners.

The cost of the War for the first eight months had been £362,000,000, little of it raised by taxation, the greater part being piled up in debts to burden the future. War profits were still untaxed. Occasionally the disclosure of some huge haul startled the public. Joseph Travers and Sons, the provision merchants, published a balance sheet showing a profit of £10,504 in 1912–13, and £101,098 in 1914–15. Spillers and Bakers, a Cardiff corn and milling firm, had made £367,865 in 1914–15, as compared with £83,889 in 1913–14. This firm had received War Office contracts for 1,600 tons of flour and 220 tons of biscuits. On the day the balance sheet was issued the price of bread was raised to 8½d. per loaf. The local Poor Law Guardians cried out against the starving of the people by monopolists.

In India the price of wheat was at famine height, because the dealers refused to sell it below the price obtainable in England. To prevent starvation in India, the Government issued an order prohibiting the export of wheat by private persons, and appointed the exporting firms its agents, taking for its own revenue the difference between the low price obtainable in India and the high price paid in London. Thus the wheat ring was able to keep up its prices against the British public. On April 22nd, it was disclosed that wheat purchases on the Government's behalf had been made for a time by a Committee representing the War Office, the Admiralty, the Board of Agriculture, and the Treasury, but these had ceased. To disclose the reason of this would not be " in the public interest," the usual phrase by which inquiry was silenced. In actual fact powerful private firms had resented Government intervention, and the Government had bowed to their wishes.

The Factory Acts were abrogated to remove all hindrances to profit-making and production. In a seaport three women were killed and six injured by the collapse of a wall twenty-four feet high, and only nine inches thick, built, in defiance of the Harbour Commissioners' veto, of old unclean bricks, and of mortar which lacked all trace of the cement the contractor had pledged himself to use. " Patriotism " excused all such makeshifts in war time. The Coroner's jury gave a verdict of " accidental death " and omitted all censure.

## CHAPTER XVIII

### PATRIOTISM IN HIGH PLACES

IN mid-March Sybil Smith arranged a drawing-room meeting on behalf of our toy factory, at the Waldorf Astors' big house at Maidenhead. To conclude the arrangement I had to interview Mrs. Astor, as she was then, in their London house. I saw her very formally for a few moments, in a great dark room, where she looked like a bit of Dresden china with her flaxen hair and pink and white skin.

Sybil Smith and I went down to Maidenhead together. Mrs. Astor met our train, and we were packed into a big motor car with other guests, including two smartly tailored young men in civilian dress. Our hostess discoursed volubly on the " slackers," who refused their share of war service ; duty to one's country was obviously a favourite theme with her. She had been reading a wonderful book, which had informed her that to indulge in luxury was to increase " the poor man's burden." " I am going to be austere ! " she shouted, eyeing us all with a glance of challenge. " I am not going to increase the poor man's burden ! "

She told us merrily she expected a considerable audience at our meeting, adding, with an abundance of American slang, which rendered some of her observations incomprehensible to me, that invitations had been extended to many persons of the neighbourhood, who had long been angling for a chance to visit her.

Mounting an incline, the motor overtook a young horseman. To my astonishment Mrs. Astor thrust her elegant head out of the window, and sang out in strident tones :

" Charlie McCartney, the pride of the nuts ! " Her voice rose to a fierce shriek : " Why aren't you in khaki ? "

Then she reseated herself with a triumphant smile which claimed our admiration ; and fired off some caustic epithets anent that young neighbour of hers, whom she desired might be driven to enlist. Her own husband, a major then, was by no means at the Front ; but habited in perfect khaki was keeping up appearances and setting a proper example to others.

The car was now taking us up the drive to the Astor mansion, where the servants assisted us to alight. As soon as we crossed the threshold of the great entrance hall where a roaring fire welcomed us, our hostess was hurried away in a stir of talk. A tragic telegram had arrived in her absence. The news flew around. An officer had been killed at the Front. One of Mrs. Astor's beautiful sisters had lost her friend. She was heartbroken. Ah ! Ah ! sighs and regrets. All the guests learnt. All the guests sympathised. How sad ! How sad, indeed !

Mrs. Astor could not attend our little function ; she was beside her bereaved sister. Regrettable, truly ; yet, save for the cause, I should have been glad of her absence. Already I began to feel a fish out of water in her environment and wished myself a thousand miles away from her hospitality. Yet one's crest was subdued ; one's heart tamed by that sorrow, that stricken love, now striving with the agony of its loss. Ah Life ! Ah Time ! We are all as one, at heart !

This was the levelling influence of war time. Keir Hardie told me that when he saw a man whom he regarded as " one of the worst Members of Parliament " bowed by the news that his only son had been killed at the Front, he wanted to fling his arms about his neck.

Sadly we set out our toys in the ornate drawing-room. Whilst we yet laboured with the ill depression of the blow, a motley of well-dressed women swept in on us. I spoke to them quietly of the hard, grey life in the East End ; of the women and girls making toys in our little factory ; drudges, errand girls, charwomen learning to paint, the sausage-filler turned designer. I strove to reveal to them within our poor ones the eternal psyche, striving for release from its dull prison. I was well received ; many people enjoy having their hearts touched—then pass to the next sensation, quite unchanged. The collection taken, the crowd swarmed to a buffet laden with glittering delicacies, consuming, or discarding with a nibble, over the teacups, heedless of that austerity our hostess preached.

Now to our rooms to dress ; great chilly spaces, but each with its own bathroom and fine marble bath. Poor Sybil had talked so devotedly to the visitors that she had had no tea. She peeped into my room. " I am so cold and I wanted a cup of tea. I wish I had brought Mrs. Bowdson with me. She would have fetched me one from the kitchen ! "

. . . . . . . . .

Of the feminine portion of the house-party I was first to appear, and sat aloof, fingering magazines on a divan. The men in their starched fronts gathered around the fire. Balfour,[1] in the centre of the throng, with his back to the blaze, talked with his flippant, senile elegance : " All Governments lie, you know, but *this* Government ! " " Ha-ha ! " an admiring chorus hung on his words.

At last came the ladies, amongst them Mrs. Astor and her sisters, all with their delicate, flaxen fairness, in black silk gowns with delightful white ruffles. The more intimate guests tendered condolences, the less intimate wore an air of solicitous sympathy.

At the dinner, noisy with talk and sumptuous with abundant meats, I heard the voice of my hostess above the clatter, declaring her intended austerity. I sat beside my host who told me importantly that he had received two remarkable letters from my sister Christabel—one of them he had sent to the War Office, the other to the Minister of Blockade.

[1] A. J., afterwards Lord Balfour.

I preferred to talk with him of his efforts to secure clean and pure milk for children. Sybil Smith had impressed on me his crystalline virtue. It was said that his wife, already notorious for her sauciness, had been lucky to secure so good a man.

It seemed to me strange in the midst of the Great War to be filing out with the women, while the men sat on chatting over their wine, as they did in the time of our grandfathers. In the rush of an agitator's life, I had forgotten that such foolish customs still obtained. I wondered at this huge company gathered here, this great extravagance and display, and thought of the poor little homes in Bow, and our own frugal household. Smyth, just then, had decided that to spare more of our cash for the movement, and to leave more food for others, we must substitute margarine for butter, and maize for wheat-flour, and make other such economies. How tiny appeared such little sacrifices as we could yet make, in face of these huge luxuries! How amazing the futility of this life, upborn by the underworld of toil and striving I knew so well. . . .

My Sybil had vanished. Bereft of her company, I ensconced myself lonely on an ottoman. A troupe of lovely beings bore down on me. "What are you doing in war work?" a clear voice asked me.

"Nothing!" I answered with passion. "I am not connected with the War!"

"Of course we are all connected with the War!" the beauty answered haughtily.

The lovely women turned their backs on me. I felt the icy atmosphere of their disdain. . . .

Sybil reappeared. The men began to straggle in. Tall Lord Eustace Percy, pallid and drooping, was one of the first. A sister of Mrs. Astor, a slender sylph, clearer of feature, fairer, more flaxen, was at the moment explaining to Sybil, politely interested and admiring, that the dress she was wearing, with an ingenious waist belt, was the creation of her "little maid"—doubtless a war economy!

"How would you like to have a dress like that, Lord Eustace?" said Sybil, smiling indulgently.

I had slipped into the corner of a sofa. Balfour came in with a crowd of admiring old fogies and seated himself beside me. He spoke of some non-political subject of current interest. The sylph of the waist belt took the vacant place on his other hand, and sang negro folk songs to her banjo; her voice was soft, her ditties plaintive. Balfour bent towards her, ogling foolishly, with compliments a trifle too fulsome, in the manner of a dying epoch, wherein women were merely toys. . . .

When the songster was tired, an American journalist declaimed in raucous tones on the march of the German armies into Belgium, endeavouring to make our flesh creep by his story. He had witnessed them passing through some hamlet where he was staying. "For forty hours, tramp! tramp! tramp! tramp! this machine went on!"

Topical

DURING THE ANTI-GERMAN RIOTS

*London News Agency*

WOMEN NAVVIES IN WESTMINSTER

Those Germans were so mechanised, he insisted, that they were performing feats of endurance never achieved by any other army, at any time, impossible feats, superhuman feats ; a veritable evidence of their iniquity. His story contradicted itself as he elaborated.

" Amazing ! Astonishing ! " old Balfour interjected, politely, pretending to be deeply impressed ; in fact merely endeavouring to be agreeable.

" I think that every German should commit hari-kari by falling on his own sword ! " shrieked Mrs. Astor, rising and strutting about on the carpet before the fire.

" I'm all for it, of course ; but I don't quite see the genesis of the idea," answered Balfour, charming as ever, but one felt that Mrs. Astor had jarred on him.

" For the good of his soul ! " she shrilled, to a chorus of laughter.

" Oh, that—ah yes—ah," he responded, and wandered away to the opposite end of the room where his admiring old fogies surrounded him.

I had had more of such talk than I could stand and was glad to get to bed.

It was difficult to rid oneself of the notion that one was staying in an hotel. Breakfast was in a vast room of many tables. People dawdled in and out without troubling to greet anyone. Food was lavishly provided ; fish and meats of many sorts, fruits and cakes, big bowls of cream. What a babel of high-pitched merriment ! So noisy a company I have seldom heard.

From the table where I sat great shrieks of laughter rose when an elegantly attired young lady asked : " Who is the hairy one ? " The object of her sally was J. J. Mallon, of the Anti-Sweating League, pale and shock-headed, with the air of one who has not slept. His flannel shirt was the subject of much mirth. He could scarcely miss hearing the fun, but made no sign of resentment at this hilarity.

When the church bells began to ring word was passed round that Mrs. Astor would accompany her guests to the service. I abstained from attendance, but found a seat in an angle of a close-clipped box hedge to write for the *Dreadnought*, snatching between the sentences a glance at the delicious sunshine on wide green lawns and gleaming river.

In the afternoon all were bidden to visit the hospital for wounded soldiers in the grounds. The way thither was enchanting, the broad slopes of short grass sprinkled with gay spring flowers, flanked by dark clumps of magnificent vegetation. I found myself between my hostess and the American, who expatiated glowingly upon the beauties of the scene, as though its possessors had been its meritorious creators. Mrs. Astor, in tones of high patronage, questioned me on my work in the East End.

" I hope you teach the women to be good ? " she queried.

" I do not consider that my province," I answered, " they know as much of goodness as I do. I try to spur them to revolt against the hideous conditions under which they live."

She uttered a deprecating snort, and spoke of their need of "higher things." The American, scenting the breath of conflict between us, tactfully interposed with questions of the neighbourhood and its history.

. . . . . . . .

The guests gathered at the door of the small hospital building, eager to enter; but the matron met them acidly; her patients were at rest; none might enter. Even Mrs. Astor could not question her decision.

There was still something to be seen, for some of the "Tommies," in the shapeless garments of the now familiar hospital blue, were sitting about in wheeled chairs and playing on the lawn. Some stopped to have a word with them; but the ladies found them less willing to be talked to than patients prostrate in bed. The gentlemen, in their well-cut clothes, adopted a humorous tone towards these curious working men, who had never been thought so interesting before the War. The soldiers were surly, and little disposed to respond to their banter. The guests wandered away.

A poor fellow, whose bed had been brought outside, had his wife and little children beside him. He knew me, and signalled me to come to them. He was trying to talk cheerfully; but a dull torpor overcame him; there were depths of misery in his eyes. His wife, distressed by his silence, could hardly restrain her tears, but bravely assured me he would soon be well. When she rose to fetch their toddling baby running far across the grass, the soldier told me both his legs had been amputated, but his wife did not know it yet. Shocked by this knowledge, I found difficulty in facing her unknowing eyes.

. . . . . . . .

Returning aloof from the house party, I was overtaken by the long strides of the American.

"It is glorious to come to your country at a time like this!" he broke in on me; "to see all this wonderful selflessness and unity amongst all classes. I tell you it's an inspiration to us Americans! We did not know the old country had it in her!"

Some hot words burst from me, of hatred for such canting untruth, and of sorrow for the poor fellows we had left down there in the vale.

He answered quietly: "I understand you." His talk seemed quenched.

The words of my old great-aunt: "A fat sorrow is better than a lean one," knelled in my mind.

I was glad I had refused to remain till Monday. The great car was waiting now to speed me to the nearest railway station.

£15 had been collected at the little meeting and Mrs. Astor herself gave Lady Sybil Smith a donation to swell the sum; but of that anon.

## CHAPTER XIX

### PEACE EFFORTS—THE WOMEN'S CONGRESS AT THE HAGUE

THE War grew daily more terrible. The miseries of a winter in the trenches were followed by frantic efforts to break through the opposing lines, in which thousands of lives were lost without result. On the shores of the Dardanelles poor fellows were dying in attempting the impossible, the blockade was tightened—submarine warfare intensified. Behind the great offensive, Peace efforts were feebly striving. News filtered through that there had been a Truce in the Trenches on Christmas Day, that British and German soldiers had thrown down their arms to fraternise, exchanging little keepsakes and comforts, rejoicing in the respite from slaughter their mutual confidence had won for them, finding themselves as brothers in their adversity. This brief manifestation of human solidarity, banned from official reports, was never permitted to recur.

. . . . . . . . .

Vain efforts were being made to resurrect the Socialist International. The Dutch Socialists had given hospitality to the Secretary of the International Socialist Bureau, Camille Huysmans, a Belgian. It was their hope that on neutral soil he would be able to perform the difficult task of resuscitation. The difficulties were great, and Huysmans unequal to the task. The officials of the Majority Socialist Parties in belligerent nations maintained, until the end of the War, their refusal to meet the Socialists of the countries with which the capitalist Governments of their countries were in conflict.

The Socialist Parties of the northern neutral countries had met at Copenhagen in January 1915 and had issued a manifesto denouncing the War as a product of Capitalist imperialism and its secret diplomacy, and calling on the Socialists of the belligerent nations to be active for peace, and to work with renewed energy to conquer political power. The leaders who controlled the Socialist parties of the belligerent nations were in no mood to second such a pronouncement. Under the auspices of the British Section of the International Socialist Bureau, a conference, which was supposed to represent the Socialist movements of Britain, France, Belgium and Russia, issued a declaration strongly supporting the cause of the Allied Governments, and declaring the Socialists of their countries "inflexibly resolved to fight until victory is achieved." When this manifesto was condemned at the I.L.P.

conference, J. R. MacDonald, who had been a party to it, characteristically replied that it was a compromise. He urged his critics to " be very careful to remember the date on which it was passed."

Across the ruins of the International came the voice of Karl Liebknecht, demanding on the floor of the Prussian Landtag the democratisation of the franchise and of foreign policy.

" Democratic control by the people would have prevented the War. . . . Away with the hypocrisy of civil peace ! On with the international class struggle for the emancipation of the working class and against the War ! "

His words thrilled round the world, evoking the heartbeat of a multitude. Brave Karl Liebknecht !

Already on December 2nd, 1914, he had voted against the War Credits in the German Reichstag. No British Socialist was ready to follow his example. On March 10th, 1915, Liebknecht repeated his negative. We learnt with joy that on March 18th several thousand women, who had organised secretly with this intent, had appeared before the Reichstag, shouting for peace. Karl Liebknecht from a window in the Reichstag had addressed them. As punishment he was ordered to the Front—to his death his friends feared. He had been joined by Ledebour, Ruhle, Mehring, Clara Zetkin and Rosa Luxemburg in a manifesto calling for an immediate peace, without annexations, which would secure political and economic independence to every nation, disarmament, and the compulsory arbitration of international disputes. At Christmas Liebknecht had conveyed a message to the I.L.P. in London appealing for a new Socialist International.

In March a conference of Socialist women, summoned by Clara Zetkin, the International Secretary of the Women's Socialist Organisation, and one of the leaders of the German Social Democratic Party, met secretly in Berne. It was attended by delegates from both factions of warring nations, who met in their old fraternity, to utter a call for the speedy ending of the War, and a peace which should impose no humiliating condition on any nation. Unheralded and unchronicled, little was heard of the event. Women Socialists of all countries had overcome the nationalist hysteria of war time, which held the male leaders of the International in its grip. Clara had planned this conference with Rosa Luxemburg. They intended to go together across the frontiers to visit the Socialists of the other nations. Then Rosa was arrested. Clara saw her in prison, then went to Holland, but was unable to pass the Belgian frontier. She sent couriers to Huysmans but he did not reply. Soon Clara was herself in prison for four months ; she was ill when she came out, but she persevered with the conference. The Social Democratic leaders declared it an offence against the discipline of the Party and forbade their members to distribute the conference manifestoes.

Amongst women of another milieu a movement for peace was also germinant. At Christmas Emily Hobhouse, Helen Bright Clark, Margaret Clark Gillett, Sophia and Lily Sturge, Isabella Ford, Lady Barlow and Lady Courtney of Penwith had addressed a letter to the women of Germany and Austria, urging them to join in calling for a truce. Through *Jus Suffragii*, the organ of the International Women's Suffrage Alliance, whose editor, Miss Sheepshanks, bravely upheld its internationalism, despite very great discouragement from the majority of the British Suffrage Societies, a response was received from prominent German and Austrian women.

Dr. Aletta Jacobs and other Dutch Suffragists now issued an appeal for a women's international congress at The Hague, to urge the belligerent governments to call a truce to define their peace terms ; and to demand the submission of international disputes to arbitration ; the democratic control of foreign policy ; that no territory should be transferred without the consent of its population ; the political enfranchisement of women ; and the inclusion of women delegates in the conference of Powers which would follow the War. The conference was to cost £1,000 ; the Dutch Suffragists offered a third of the sum ; the German Suffragists responded with a further third. The National Union of Women's Suffrage Societies under Mrs. Fawcett, which represented British women in the International Suffrage Alliance, repudiated the Congress ; but a group of seceders from that organisation met with other women's organisations, including our Federation, in conference at the Caxton Hall to answer the invitation from Holland. The delegates were enthusiastic. More than 200 of us volunteered to go to The Hague.

The Congress now began to receive tremendous publicity. The Press condemned it ; prominent women assailed it. We who had agreed to go were execrated. Mrs. Fawcett declared that to talk of peace while the German armies were in France and Belgium was " akin to treason." Mrs. Cecil Chapman, President of the New Constitutional Society for Women's Suffrage, considered the time " painfully inopportune " for members of the belligerent nations to confer. The W.S.P.U., which had been *hors de combat* and existing on occasional speeches by Christabel and Mrs. Pankhurst, now burst into life to oppose the Congress. The *Suffragette* reappeared on April 16th, 1915, after eight months' suspension, declaring in its leading article that it was a " thousand times more " the duty of militant Suffragettes to fight the Kaiser for the sake of liberty, than it had been to fight anti-Suffrage Governments. Nina Boyle, in the Women's Freedom League organ, *The Vote*, attacked *Jus Suffragii* for becoming " the mouthpiece " of the promoters of the Conference, and protested that the Women's Freedom League " refused to ask for more legislation—even reform legislation—until women could help to control and administer it." She marvelled that there should be Suffragists " who imagine it possible for them . . . to be an international power, and set in motion reforms vaster and more quixotic than any body of men with franchise, representatives, and Cabinet Ministers in their pocket, would venture to attack at the present moment."

With such chilling and bitter sarcasm the ardent idealism of the pioneer is ever met; yet the true pioneers fling out their golden conceptions on the world, recking not of obstacles, serene in their faith.

From French Suffragists came equally emphatic denunciations. An American woman who considered joining the Women's International Congress Movement sent a copy of its objects to ex-President Roosevelt: he condemned them as "silly and base."

Mrs. Astor wrote to me that she would never have invited me to her house, had she known I would offer to attend such a Congress. She added that she had learnt we were paying £1 a week in the toy factory, instead of the 10s. of the Queen Mary Rooms. Had she known it she would not have aided us. Many members of the Women's Social and Political Union, who during its inactivity had worked for our Federation, now sheered off and left us. Some even of those who had professed internationalist and pacifist views now rallied to their old allegiance to Mrs. Pankhurst and Christabel; some hesitated, uncertain what course to take. Many subscribers to our work for mothers and children withdrew. By every post came letters refusing further support. "Subscribers are falling off like dead leaves at the end of the season!" I said to Smyth, but we held on, redoubling our efforts, that those who depended on us might not suffer. Many times, before and since, the choice came to me, whether for the sake of the work I was doing, to stay my hand and remain silent, or to speak and do what I believed to be right, knowing that through me, all else that I was prominently engaged in would suffer attack and perhaps extinction. I was guided by the opinion that freedom of thought and speech is more important than any good which can ever come of concealing one's views, and by the knowledge that in the hour of its greatest unpopularity the pioneering cause needs one most. Yet it was often hard to choose thus sternly, flying in the face of what seemed prudent, casting to the winds the result of laborious effort; hard, not on my own account; for I had shed all personal aims when I gave up painting in the years of the Suffragette struggle before the War; hard only on account of the work I was striving to do, and the people who looked to me for aid. On this occasion we weathered the storm. Smyth came forward as usual with donations and loans, writing off most of the latter, too, as donations, when she found, as financial secretary, they were too hard to repay. New workers and subscribers came gradually in to replace the departed.

The women of Russia, Germany, Austria, France and Belgium were permitted to proceed to the Congress; but the British Government, having directed the Press abuse of our mission, refused to let British women go. McKenna, at one point, conceded to Miss Courtney and Miss Marshall, who were conducting the negotiations, that passports should be issued to twenty women of discretion, whom he selected from the two hundred. Some of the chosen were quite flattered by his choice: such phrases as: "They don't mind when they feel they can really trust you" fell from their lips. It is impossible to describe the atmosphere of repression which overhung the movement. Vain efforts at diplomacy attempted to parry opposition. In the *Dreadnought* I had written of the Women's Peace Conference at The Hague. I received a letter of protest from Miss Crystal MacMillan of the British Committee for the Congress :

" British Committee of the
International Women's Congress.

" DEAR MISS PANKHURST,

" It has been pointed out to us that in the *Woman's Dreadnought* you speak of this International Congress as a ' Peace Congress.' This is giving rise to a good deal of misunderstanding, as the Congress cannot fairly be so described. The definition of the terms of peace is the only point in connection with peace on which it expresses an opinion or makes a demand. To call it a ' Peace Conference ' gives the impression that its object is to demand peace at any price. We shall be very glad, therefore, if you will do what you can to remove the false impression which has been created.

" C. MACMILLAN."

Alas, for the caution and confidence of the chosen ladies ; McKenna, for all his promises, did not permit them to sail. Miss Courtney, it is true, had been too sharp for him. When he assured her : " Of course I should have no objection to issue permits to you and Miss Marshall," she answered : " I will take mine now," and was allowed to proceed. The others were kept waiting expectant, until the eleventh hour. On one occasion McKenna assured them that he would have issued the necessary permits to them there and then ; but the official whose duty it was to affix his signature to the documents had left the office for the night. It would be quite out of order for himself, or anyone save that particular official to sign. On their final visit he assured the chosen ladies that he would assuredly have let them travel at last ; but, to his great regret, " the boats had stopped running " on account of a great event of which they would certainly read in the Press. No notice of the event ever appeared. The ladies declared they had been tricked. The rest of us were curtly and frankly informed that no permits to attend the Congress were being issued.

Having no illusion that I might receive a permit, I had drafted a series of resolutions to be sent to the Congress. These covered the abolition of secret and sectional treaties and alliances and the creation of a permanent peace treaty uniting all nations ; the abolition of national armies and navies ; the democratisation of the international Court of Arbitration and the extension of its scope. I showed the resolutions to Keir Hardie ; he took the sheets from me eagerly. " This is important," he said, in his forceful way, and urged me to propose that a committee be appointed by the Congress to consider such proposals. " Then something may come of it," he said. We did not know that the American delegates to the Congress, amongst whom was Emmeline Pethick Lawrence, had held a preliminary conference on their voyage from New York and had worked out a similar programme.

I saw little of Keir Hardie in those days, so burdened I was by the volume and stress of our work. He had sunk into a great sadness. Whenever we met I found him ill and suffering. I left him heavy with anxiety. As I waited in Bishopsgate for the Old Ford 'bus, a thought, tragic and luminant, seized me—not my thought it seemed, but one from without, which assailed me. In a flash I realised the long struggle sustained in the advanced countries, through many generations, to waken the masses that they might gain control of their national Parliaments : I saw them at last make entry into the citadel, only to find it empty, the power gone—removed to an international Government, wherein the dead-weight of backward peoples would strangle all progress for generations to come. Was this the truthful augur of Internationalism ? Was it thus that privilege and poverty would be buttressed in their ancient reign ? Profound melancholy closed down on me. How static was this poverty, cruel and stultifying, with which we warred !

All schemes for international arbitration and agreement seemed empirical. The belief flared up insistent that only from a society re-created from the root, replacing the universal conflict of to-day by universal co-operation, could permanent peace arise. Yearning for the golden age of the coming equalitarian society, I passed, in thought, to the extremist pole, whereat all save a world-embracing social rebirth and reconstruction seemed mere trumpery. Then the daily fight with misery and hardship recalled me to do what I could for each of these poor ones.

. . . . . . . .

The Women's Congress met in due course. Jane Addams, whom John Burns had described as America's finest citizen, presided over the gathering. She declared it the most deeply moving she had ever known. Historically it is to be regretted that the net demand for a truce made in the original appeal from Dutch women did not find a place in the final verdict of the Congress. Yet the belligerent governments were asked " to put an end to this bloodshed and begin peace negotiations." The neutral governments were urged to form a council offering continuous mediation, which should invite suggestions for a settlement of the conflict from each of the belligerent nations and should itself submit to them reasonable proposals for peace. Envoys were appointed to urge these demands. Jane Addams, Dr. Aletta Jacobs, and Rosa Genoni of Italy, for her country had not yet entered the War, went as neutrals to the belligerent Governments. Rosika Schwimmer of Hungary, and others of the belligerent countries, visited the neutrals. It was probably the unique position of Jane Addams in American regard which induced Asquith and Grey to receive the envoys of this Congress which British women had not been permitted to attend.

In France the envoys had audience of Delcassé and Viviani, and of Davignon, on behalf of the Belgian Government at Havre ; in Italy of Sonnino, Salandra and the Pope, in Berlin of von Bethmann

Hollweg, in Vienna of Count Stürgkh, in Budapest of Count Tiza and Baron Burian. Everywhere they received fair words of encouragement to no purpose. The European neutrals would gladly have undertaken the proposed mediation ; they were suffering too much from the British blockade to be other than anxious to take every step which might bring the War to a close ; but all neutral effort was rendered ineffective by the refusal to participate of America, the only powerful neutral. President Wilson referred the envoys to his special factotum, Colonel House, and to Robert Lansing, Counsellor of the Department of State, then assistant to W. J. Bryan in United States foreign affairs. House, who regarded peace negotiations on America's behalf as his own particular province, dismissed the appeal of the Women's Congress for neutral mediation as " utterly impracticable." Mediation by a group of neutral nations did not appeal to him ; he desired mediation by Wilson and America, to their everlasting glory, and to ensure an adequate share for American interests in exploiting the undeveloped territories of the world. He was by no means a pacifist of Jane Addams's gentle type.

. . . . . . . .

From the Women's Congress at The Hague arose a permanent organisation. A British Section, termed the Women's International League, was formed in the autumn. As at the preliminary Conference, all the women's organisations working for Peace were invited to send delegates : Suffragists, Socialists, Labourists and Quakers being thus represented. I was elected to the Executive. The majority of its London members were seceders from Mrs. Fawcett's National Union of Suffrage Societies. The work, therefore, assumed a cautious and moderate tone. Our Federation delegates were out-voted, when we proposed that the title should be the Women's International Peace League, and that women of foreign citizenship, resident in Britain, should be admitted to membership of the British Section. Mrs. Swanwick opposed the proposition on the ground that " a great deal of mud " would be cast at the organisation. Even the British wives of aliens were excluded.

The non-militant Suffragists felt the fierce opposition to our Peace efforts more sharply than Suffragettes and Socialists, who had already borne the brunt of championing unpopular causes.

The organisation was from the first overshadowed by the tremendous magnitude of its task. It worked many degrees below the high-keyed enthusiasm of the Hague Conference. It carried no fiery cross ; but tried, in a quiet way, sincerely, if at times haltingly, to understand the causes of war, and to advance the causes of Peace by negotiation, and the enfranchisement of women. From time to time it expressed itself by resolution in careful phrases ; from time to time it held a public meeting, from which notorious people were, as a rule, prudently excluded. All Peace work laboured under the weight of harsh adversity. The less could be accomplished, alas, the more lengthy, were the sittings of the Committee. They lasted from 10 a.m. to 6 p.m. It seemed almost like undertaking the labours of Penelope, when I essayed to induce the Executive to call a week's Conference to debate such international questions, then to the fore, as the Freedom of the Seas, Disarmament, the Self-Determination of Oppressed Nationalities and so on! Protracted as the task was, it was accomplished at length! When I returned to the East End after these lengthy sittings, to find myself obliged to cut out sleep, and work forty-eight hours, with scarcely a break, to cope with the arrears which had accumulated during my absence, I often told my East End colleagues I should prefer to resign from the W.I.L. "Oh, do stay there and leaven them!" Norah Smyth and others urged me: but I did so reluctantly. In the East End we were equally powerless to stay the hideous progress of the War; but we could alleviate some of its miseries. To me it was essential to be able to voice my opinions spontaneously, and without fear or favour. To trim one's statements, in order to conciliate influential opinion, oppressed me with a sense of insincerity.

# CHAPTER XX

## THE MUNITION WORKERS—SHORTAGE OF MUNITIONS—GOVERNMENT APPEAL TO WOMEN

THE hardships and dangers of munition work began to appear. On March 15th W. C. Anderson complained in the House of Commons that at Armstrong Whitworth's Elswick factory women were employed seven days a week for upwards of twelve hours a day. They got from 8s. to 11s. a week with a bonus forfeited for failure to work Sundays. Some of the girls had worked 20 hours at a stretch and 95 hours a week. Two girls had died of dope poisoning at the Army aeroplane works at Crayford, and when the first death occurred, 43 others were found to be seriously affected by the fumes.

News was coming through that the failure of the British attempt to drive back the German lines at Neuve Chapelle had been due to shortage of munitions. To the jingo super-patriot, failure to excel must needs be criminal: Asquith, the War Office, Kitchener, each and all had a share of execration from the extreme jingoes. Nowadays, military experts write dispassionately that the British military authorities were unversed in trench warfare, and slower than the Germans to appreciate the huge scale of the ammunition required and that British weapons were crudely inferior to the German. From the national arsenal at Woolwich came complaints that the men and machines there were, even then, not fully employed, and that before the War and since, the national armament factories had gone short of work in order that more orders might be given to the private armament firms. It was alleged that private firms had been subsidised to keep up equipment in case of war, but had not fulfilled their contracts in this respect.

Undoubtedly the munitions were inadequate to the vast scale of hostilities. The Government was abused for lack of forethought, for sloth and inefficiency. The attack was hastily diverted from the Government and the armament firms, to the munition workers overwhelmed by excessive toil. A twelve hour day and seven day week had become usual and was often exceeded in the munition factories. Nevertheless, Lloyd George received a deputation of employers who declared that drunkenness, and bad time-keeping in the factories were hindering the supply of munitions to the trenches. Under his sponsorship their charges were given wide currency as incontrovertible fact. Keir Hardie, acutely ill, flashed out a protest:[1]

[1] At a demonstration held in connection with the I.L.P. Annual Conference at Norwich.

" In time of war one would have thought the rich classes would grovel on their knees before the working classes who are doing so much to pile up their wealth. Instead, the men who are working eighty-four hours a week are being libelled, maligned and insulted ; and on the authority of their employers, the lying word, accepted without inquiry by Lloyd George, went round the world that the working-class were a set of drunken hooligans. That is the reward they got. The truth is that the shifts could be arranged to overtake all the work. Mr. John Hill of the boilermakers, has shown that if the shipbuilders would reduce their contracts 10 per cent., the Government would get all their work done, but the shipbuilders will not do it because their ships are being sold at two and three times their pre-War value."

Lloyd George squirmed at the attack and protested by telegram that he was misrepresented. Keir Hardie replied doggedly :

" I pointed out that the employers, when before you, had put the whole blame on the drinking habits of the workers, and you, by accepting their statement without challenge, had given world currency to the fiction that the workers were drunken wasters."

Lloyd George continued protesting : " Wild accusations . . . mischievous statements . . . excited prejudice," explaining that his own strictures had only intended to apply to a " small section " of the workers. The matter did not end there ; a Government White Paper was issued to drive home the charges of intemperance and absenteeism. James O'Grady, M.P., and other officials of approved societies under the National Insurance Act vainly replied that their books were flooded with cases of men who were ill from over-work.

Attacks were launched against Trade Unionism. Its practices were denounced as limiting the output per man and preventing the influx of new workers into the munition factories, although the men then employed, and all the members of the Unions concerned, were insufficient to supply the overwhelming stream of Government orders.

It is true that the Trade Unions were holding tenaciously to the system of demarkation between the processes allocated to various classes of workers. Above all, they clung to the sharp line drawn between the occupations of the skilled workmen who had served an apprenticeship to the trade, and the tasks which might be performed by the workers outside this relatively fortunate class. Yet such self-protective measures by no means justified or explained the excessive overtime employers were exacting in all classes of war work, whilst hundreds of unemployed people were clamouring at their gates.

That the employers were slow in adapting themselves to the vastness of war output need not be accounted to them as malice. Undoubtedly profits were the primary concern with the average of them, and the exhaustion of the workers counted little against the cost of additional plant or any difficulties and expenses of management which working three shifts might entail.

In March the Board of Trade issued an appeal to women to register at the Labour Exchanges for war service in industry, agriculture and munition making. 57,000 women who had hitherto been wage earners were still workless, according to official estimates, and there was no definite plan for the employment of the new recruits: but the enrolment of the women would help to keep patriotic fervour at boiling point: it would maintain a pool of surplus labour and the volunteers would be needed later on. Registration forms were sent out broadcast to the plethora of women's organisations which had grown up in pre-War years: Liberal, Conservative, Temperance, Religious, Philanthropic, and, above all, Suffragist, the most active by far.

It was grimly humorous that this appeal should come to us from the very Government which had so long and stubbornly opposed itself to our struggle for the vote, as those of us who had maintained our demand during the War were not slow to observe. Our Federation, the Women's Freedom League, the United Suffragists and the Irish Women's Franchise League immediately issued manifestoes demanding the vote, and insisting that a woman who did a man's work should get a man's pay. Even Mrs. Fawcett's N.U.W.S.S., though it kept silence as to the vote, rose to the point of asking "equal pay for equal work."

I at once issued an appeal to women's organisations to unite in demanding for women equal pay and representation on the tribunals which were being set up to deal with wages and conditions. I urged the calling of a joint conference of women's organisations and Labour organisations. I made it my business to ensure that the conference should be held and that the Labour organisations should be its conveners. I wanted the women pledged to demand equal pay, and to get them into the Trade Unions, as well as to ensure that the woman who needed her wage for sustenance should not be crushed out by the well-to-do volunteer working for patriotism and pocket money. I wanted the Labour organisations to take the lead in working-class interests, and also to commit them to the demand for equal pay, towards which they were apathetic. I called at the Labour Party office, then so small and sparcely staffed, despite its large membership. J. S. Middleton, the model official, with his air of being bled by too much desk work, met me with earnest agreement. I saw Mary Macarthur, and urged her that the Women's Trade Unions should not abandon the lead to non-representative bodies, formed in other than working-class interests. It was essential for their welfare that the wage earners—men and women—should be kept together as a united force, and that the Trade Unions should shoulder practical responsibility towards the women. Surprised, perhaps, that I should come to her thus after our acute differences over underpayment of women in the Queen's Workrooms, Mary Macarthur was genial enough. "What do you want us to do?" she asked me, and with a good deal of cordiality agreed to my suggestions.

A preliminary conference of women's organisations was accordingly summoned, and at its request, the Workers' War Emergency Committee called a National Conference for April 16th. Before even the preliminary conference had met Lloyd George had entered into an agreement with the leaders of the Men's Trade Unions at the Treasury, and Runciman had met representatives of the women's organisations at the Board of Trade.

The Treasury Agreement had a manifold purpose. Its first aim was to prevent the workers taking advantage of the law of supply and demand to force up wages when war conditions produced a shortage of labour. In the Food Prices Debate in February Runciman had said that rising prices could best be met by increased wages,[1] but within a week the Government had issued a statement, through the Press Bureau, that strikes for higher wages must be prevented, and disputes referred to compulsory arbitration by a tribunal composed of three Government officials.

On March 4th, Lloyd George had introduced a third Defence of the Realm Act to give the Government greater power to regulate the manufacture of war material. The Treasury Agreement was designed to secure the assent of the Trade Union leaders to this and still more drastic measures, which would sweep away the entire fabric of Trade Union conditions, make strikes illegal and secure a discipline over the industrial workers as strict as that applied to soldiers in the trenches. Compulsory arbitration, disciplinary tribunals, and the waiving of Trade Union rules and customs were agreed to without demur. A promise to limit the profits of munition manufacturers was given as a sop to Labour opinion. It proved largely a sham and even the form of it was withdrawn within a year. To induce the Labour world to accept compulsion, it had even been suggested that industrious workpeople would be given a share in the profits of munition work. Before the Treasury Agreement Lord Kitchener had said: "We hope that workmen who work regularly by keeping good time, shall reap some of the benefits that war automatically confers on these great companies." When Runciman was questioned on this statement two months later he declared that Lord Kitchener had given no promise of profit-sharing. On the contrary, his words were "not unconnected" with the war medals it was intended to issue on the successful termination of the War!

The profits of the munition firms were immense. There was much talk of the munition workers' big shilling, and the high wages of war workers, but even according to official estimates, which consistently underrated the increase in prices, as was proved by comparison with house-keepers' budgets, wages, throughout the War, lagged far behind

[1] When the Post Office employees retorted with demands for a War Bonus, Hobhouse, the Postmaster-General, refused their plea, though 59,000 of the postal employees were actually getting less than £1 a week. When a strike was threatened, he agreed to submit the dispute to arbitration, but declared the Government would sustain before the arbiters that the increased cost of living did not justify a demand for increased wages, and that if concessions were made to postal employees, they would be demanded in other Departments.

the cost of living.[1] Prices were already excessively high when war broke out. For ten years they had been rising, and under their pressure industrial unrest had been rife. The elimination of unemployment and short time added more to the income of the workers than increases in actual wages. Large families living together, with everyone working, earned fairly substantially in the aggregate, but often at the expense of health. The old hands in the munition shops, irreplaceable by new dilutees at lower rates, by dint of working at high pressure for excessively long hours, in some cases took home money which would have surprised them before the War; but their gains were hugely exaggerated; the have-nots remained the have-nots as before.

A memorandum embodying the Treasury Agreement was issued on March 15th, 1915, in which it was promised that the men who were coming in to replace the original skilled workers should get "the usual rate of the district for that class of work." The position of women was not made clear.

I wrote immediately to the Prime Minister, Lloyd George, and the President of the Board of Trade, asking an explanation, and urging that a woman should get the pay for the job given to the man who preceded her, with any increase or war bonus which might accrue. Lloyd George replied:

"March 26th, 1916.

"DEAR MISS PANKHURST,

"The words which you quote would guarantee that women undertaking the work of men would get the same piece rates as men were receiving before the date of this agreement. That of course means that if the women turn out the same quantity of work as men employed on the same job they will receive exactly the same pay.

"Yours sincerely,

"D. LLOYD GEORGE."

I answered that he had not dealt with my point respecting increases and war bonus, and that unless the rate of the men they replaced were assured to women for time rates, as well as for piece rates, the employers would simply resort to paying women by time.

A National Labour Advisory Committee was appointed to assist in carrying out the Treasury Agreement. We were indignant that it

[1] The general average of wages in the United Kingdom amongst bricklayers, printers (compositors), railwaymen, dock labourers, cotton operatives, woollen and worsted operatives, engineering artisans and labourers, coal mining, agriculture (England and Wales) and cost of living as given by the Ministry of Labour in July of each year.

| | 1914 | 1915 | 1916 | 1917 | 1918 |
|---|---|---|---|---|---|
| Wages index number: | 100 | 105 to 110 | 115 to 120 | 135 | 175 |
| Cost of living index number: ... | 100 | 125 | 147 | 180 | 205 |
| Food prices index number: ... | 100 | 132 | 161 | 204 | 210 |

contained not a single woman member, but the Committee long led a shadowy existence and when eventually it began to function the duties assigned it were rather to assist in imposing discipline than to protect the interests of the workers.

The Conference of Women's Organisations called by Runciman at the Board of Trade on April 13th, was crowded with well-to-do people: barely half a dozen of those present had the least claim to represent the working women who formed the majority of those it was intended to recruit.[1] Mary Macarthur complained that neither the women of the Labour Party nor the registered Trade Unions of Women had been invited with the sole exception of the Federation of Women's Trade Unions she represented.

Runciman told us that 33,000 women had already registered for war service, 6,000 of them for munitions. He hurried nervously over the wage question; it had been decided, he said, that on Government contracts the same piece rates should be given to women as to men but in regard to time rates "no special conditions had been laid down." I saw that, as I had feared, there was to be no real safeguard for equal pay. As everyone knew, all the work was to be reorganised. Only if it were decided that all the men and women, once trained, must have the same pay, would the sweating of women be checked.

Having surmounted the thorny question of wages, Runciman grew more urbane. He urged that the ladies before him could assist the good work by finding lodgings for the new women workers, and by keeping an eye on them to see that they came to no moral harm. "We know that this can be better done by your organisations than by any Government department." Smiles greeted his words. He passed on to the question of training: the Board of Agriculture had arranged to give women a fortnight's instruction in farm work: if they were active and intelligent they could learn enough in that time to make themselves useful. He ceased abruptly.

"Can anyone speak? Can I speak?" A clear voice cut the air; Mrs. Charlotte Drake from the East End, with her humble black clothes and her anxious face, was the questioner. She urged in her blunt, brief way that the men's Trade Unions should be asked to take in women members and the women be paid just as if they were men, whether on piece rates or time rates. Then there would be no reason to talk of the undercutting of men by "women blacklegs." The phrase

[1] The increase in the number of women employed in industry during the War, though large, was not so great as Press propaganda might have led one to suppose, as is indicated by the following table taken from the *Encyclopædia Britannica*.

Average Figures for men and women in industrial employment (Manufacturing):

| | July, 1913 | July 1918 | July 1924 |
|---|---|---|---|
| Men ... ... | 6,301,000 | 5,058,000 | 6,016,000 |
| Women ... | 2,178,600 | 2,970,600 | 1,987,990 |

angered her hearers, women cast indignant looks at her. Runciman shifted uncomfortably. Following her, I insisted on the uselessness of the promise he and Lloyd George had given. When I reminded him that the women whose service the Government required were still disfranchised Runciman interrupted. He would not have that question mentioned, he said irascibly. I was surprised to observe that not one woman infringed his prohibition.

Lady Aberconway, the doyen of an old Liberal Women's Suffragist family, spoke as representative of the Women's Liberal Federation:

" It is our earnest desire to co-operate with the Government." But was the Government employing as many women clerks and typists as it might? Runciman said the substitution of women for men was proceeding rapidly; but the lady was not satisfied; she wanted the economic screw pressed harder to assist recruiting, and to prove, since she was a Suffragist and ardent for the War, that women could serve it well. Mrs. Rackham, of the National Union of Women's Suffrage Societies, took up the tale, gruesome indeed to the few who could see in the War a gigantic slaughter. Margaret Llewellyn Davies, that notable builder of the Women's Co-operative Guild, tender in her broad humanity, protested against the cruelly long hours women and girls, the potential mothers of the race, were working in the munition factories. It was surprising that the Government should sanction this economic waste, she said, for it had long been proved that the greatest production was secured by shifts of workers employed for not more than seven hours a day. Mary Macarthur had just returned from Elswick, where women munitioners were working 84 hours a week, though crowds of other women were clamouring there for work. The employers preferred to occupy their machines on two shifts of twelve hours than on three shifts of eight hours, therefore this cruel absurdity continued. Mrs. Reed and Lady Samuels, representing Liberal and Conservative women, attempted to combat her protests, till Runciman interposed to check the wrangle. The anti-Suffragist representative declared: " We hope to co-operate with the Government without imposing any terms." The Girls' Friendly Society, the Y.W.C.A. and others pledged enthusiastic aid. Then Eleanor Rathbone of Liverpool (afterwards M.P.), plump, ruddy and complacent, intervened. She had been " disgusted," she said, by the poor response of women to the appeal for war service; but she thought it had not been sufficiently striking and direct. It was too refined; it should be more like the appeals for the Army. There should be recruiting posters and recruiting stations. To get middle-class women there should be " comrades brigades." The middle-class woman would not migrate for war work alone, or if she did, she would not stick to her job. To get her to persevere she must go with her own class and her own set. Women should be put through military drill and given a retaining fee " of even a shilling a week," and when they had " taken the King's shilling " they should be subject to penalties " if they backed out." If the Government wanted to get women to replace men on really skilled and hard work, she declared, they must get women of the upper classes. Working women were " too worn out, poorly nourished, starved and sweated." She spoke this, wholly oblivious, it appeared, of the tragic significance for woman, and for the race, if her words were true in literal fact.

Runciman promised that some of the suggestions, " notably those of Miss Rathbone," should be carried out.

" Will the Government stop the sweating of women ? " asked Charlotte Drake. There was no reply. Hers was the voice of the woman who toils : the others held aloof from her scornfully.

It was obvious now that the crux of the equal pay question lay in the Government's quite definite refusal to lay down any conditions for the wages of women employed at time rates. It was not desired to affront the great women's organisations by permitting it to be said that women who had volunteered to replace men were to get less money than the men had had for precisely the same job, but by his evasion the way was left open to pay women any wage the employer might choose. Despite this obvious fact it proved impossible to induce the conference called by the Workers' War Emergency Committee to demand equal pay for women and men, " whether employed by time or by piece." Our amendments to that effect were resisted by Mary Macarthur, Margaret Bondfield and their colleagues on the platform and defeated. It was a fact that not merely the Government and the employers, but also the leaders of Trade Unionism for women, regarded equal pay as an impossible demand. To many it seemed an outrageously extravagant demand, above all during the War, that single women should be paid the wage that a man with a family might exact. Our hard, vain efforts for equal pay brought home to me, as so often before, the supreme difficulty of securing under the wage system a decent subsistence for the woman who is the bread-winner of a family. In the great average she is crushed down to the wage level on which the single woman finds it just possible to subsist.

John Turner, of the Shop Assistants' Union, came to me on the floor of the conference, and openly said his Union could not claim a man's pay for its women members : there was no possibility of getting it. We succeeded in carrying a stipulation that maintenance allowances to women war workers in training should in no case be less than £1 a week. This, in effect, was a vote of censure against the officials on the platform who had adopted the miserable 10s. dole of the Queen Mary Workrooms.

. . . . . . . .

Events soon proved, as I had predicted, that women were generally employed on time rates to evade demands for the piece rates of the men they replaced. A bonus was used to supply the spur which piece rates provide. Their wage averaged from 8s. to 16s. a week, and even with overtime and bonus, did not amount to half the wage of the men. Councillor Barton of the Sheffield Trades Council complained that the great firm of Vickers had opened munition shops at Hillsborough, where women were paid 8s. a week. The same firm at Holm Lane, Sheffield, was paying women who filled shells and worked lathes 8s. to 14s. per week, and 1s. a week war bonus if full time were kept. The working day was from 6.30 a.m. to 5.30 p.m. The munition factories were no exception: in every sort of work women were engaged to replace men at a lower wage. The Trade Board for the sugar confectionery and preserving industries followed the usual custom, just then, in fixing minimum rates of 13s. a week for women, 26s. a week for men. Many patriotic people congratulated the women who took their fares on the 'buses and trams. The wages of 14s. a week they got in South End, and 16s. in Sheffield were typical.

In face of a pitiless sweating of women stubbornly continued, Press stories soon began to appear about the affluence of the women munition workers, and in particular of the fur coats they were said to be buying. If dependent on their own earnings, the vast majority of them had a miserable struggle to keep body and soul together. If they lived at home with their parents, and gave, as is customary, but a meagre pittance to their worried mother to pay for their keep, and if they fed cheaply and sparely at the canteen, they could save a surplus. Working seven days a week, they had no leisure to spend it, and by saving, or buying through clubs or otherwise on the hire system they might acquire some few articles of clothing or furniture, which might on occasion be rejected as too costly by the poorer middle class housewife, living up to her income in a degree of comfort and elegance unknown to the factory girl. Alas for the notorious fur coats of the munition girls: most of them never existed; those which had tangible form in munition girls' wardrobes were mostly the wretchedest imitation palmed off by war-time profiteers and not worth a quarter of the money saved to pay for them, not good enough even to pawn when the long day of adversity followed the War.

Excessive hours and the new discipline imposed under the D.O.R.A. were no less serious than underpayment. At Greenwood and Batley's armament factory in Leeds, a girl, only sixteen years of age, was injured at her machine. She had been kept at work for twenty-five and a half hours. She had started at 6 a.m. Friday, and with intervals totalling two hours for meals on Friday, and half an hour for breakfast on Saturday, she had kept on till the accident occurred at 7.30 a.m. The women beside her worked on for 31 hours. On the firm being prosecuted, the manager stated, by way of defence, that women subjected to this tremendous strain would earn from £1 to £2 per week. The magistrate, Horace Marshall, dismissed the case, with the observation that "the most important thing in the world to-day is that ammunition shall be made." The senseless folly of this overwork was revealed when, on May 21st, it was announced that 65,700 women had registered for war service, but only 1,250 of them had received employment.

Meanwhile the Clyde Armaments Committee of Employers' and Trade Union representatives established under the Treasury Agreement, had decided that workpeople keeping bad time should be fined £1 for the first offence, £2 for the second, £3 with immediate dismissal for the third. These conditions promoted the growth of the Workshop Committee Movement which presently was to make itself felt. Two men employed at the shipbuilding works, Cammell Laird's, after working sixteen hours a day for seven days, got drunk, and were charged under the Defence of the Realm Act :

> "With unlawfully doing an act of such a nature as to be calculated to be prejudicial to the defence of the Realm, with the intention, or the purpose of assisting the enemy."

True, indeed, the rulers of the people lose their sense of proportion in war time ! Clyde workers were fined 5s. for the loss of War Service badges valued at sixpence. The penalties for this offence were soon greatly increased. The new discipline prohibited women employed on night shift from leaving the machine room, even for meals, and made compulsory any overtime, however excessive, the employer might direct.

. . . . . . . .

I was up in Jarrow-on-Tyne for a meeting, and asked my way of a middle-aged woman in the street. She offered to accompany me, and in a moment she was telling me her great loneliness. Her husband was working in the Government Dockyard at Devonport ; one son was in the Royal Flying Corps, the other had been killed. She had nothing to do alone here in Jarrow, and would like to get a job in a munition factory to help the poor men who were forced to toil so hard there. "I see them almost falling as they go home from work !" she said ; but other women were pleading in vain for employment. There were crowds of them struggling at the gates, to get a word with the manager. Her husband's wages were good ; it would be unfair for her to take the work from others who sorely needed it. Her brow was puzzled ; the thought stirred in her strongly that some were fainting from too much work, whilst others starved for lack of it.

. . . . . . . .

An inquest was held at Brotherhood's Munition Works at Peterborough on a man who died of heart failure at his machine. He had complained of pain in his side during the past weeks, and had been paid for 109 hours the week before his death. A woman wrote to me then to tell me that her husband had been employed at the same factory, and had died from overwork. When leaving his home one morning, he had asked his fourteen-year-old son to meet him that night at the top of the street and bring a truck. The boy met him as he had asked. The father got into the truck ; his son wheeled him home. "I am dead-beat !" he said to his wife as he staggered in. Next morning he was too weak even to wash himself as he lay in bed. He died two days later. The boy went to Brotherhood's in his father's stead, and worked from 6 a.m. to 7 p.m. His mother trembled with grief and fear when she saw him falling asleep over his evening meal.

Munition work was rapidly extending in certain areas, into which masses of workers were being herded. Charles Duncan in the House of Commons revealed that the very beds in which they slept were often serving double shifts ; as one set of workers arose from their sleep, they had to clear out of the bedrooms, that they might be put in order for the next shift.

. . . . . . . .

To show how soldiers' clothes were made, our Federation held a Sweated Industries Exhibition in the Caxton Hall in May. For their fares and the few pence they estimated they could have made at home, the khaki workers were glad, nay eager, to work in the Exhibition, hoping, as the simple and unsophisticated do so readily, that the manifestation of their hardship would speedily bring reform. Poor jaded women, they had been toiling at war work, of necessity, before the high-flown calls to womanly patriotism had been sounded. One of them had a puny two months' baby in a box at her side; four other little ones had been left in a neighbour's care. Her eyes were red and sore. She thought the "funny" colours of the khaki were the cause of it; but her mother told her the trouble was due to working too soon after her confinement and with her baby to suckle.

A widow had a little boy going to school to support, two married sons in the Navy, and an unmarried son in the Army, on whose account she got a tiny pittance. She was "finishing" soldiers' trousers at 2s. per dozen pairs. After deducting the cost of the soap, cotton and thread she had to provide for the work, she was able, by rising at 5 a.m. and working far into the night, to make about 7s. 6d. a week. Her little son did the shopping, helped with the housework and prepared the meals when he came home from school, that his mother's needle might not pause.

The mother of seven children, with a husband earning a poor wage, was working from 5.30 a.m. to 10 p.m. to add 6s. to her weekly income. The mother of six children, with a face of martyrdom, worked from 6 a.m. to 11 p.m. to earn 10s. or 11s. a week on sailors' trousers, being better paid than the khaki workers.

A young married woman sewing buttons on soldiers' bandoliers at the rate of 2½d. for sixty buttons gave up work when her baby was born, but when her husband's employer took 2s. a week off his wage her husband said she must share the loss with him and docked 1s. a week from her housekeeping money. With rising prices she could not make ends meet, so she got her mother to mind the baby, and took in khaki work to sew.

Stout old Mrs. Savoy, the brushmaker, everybody's friend, who had been on many a deputation with us, had helped to gather these poor workers. She went about amongst the others in her homely, motherly style, getting them tea and introducing them to all and sundry: "This is our Sylvia! This is Miss Smyth, she's a good 'un! This is Nurse Hebbes; she'll look after you!"

Margaretta Hicks of the British Socialist Party had arranged a food prices exhibition, which showed in actual commodities the dwindling value of the wages earned by these exploited beings. All the Suffrage Societies which had maintained their Suffrage work sent speakers, glad to find a haven where all interests were not subordinated to the great slaughter.

## CHAPTER XXI

### LOSS OF THE "LUSITANIA"—ANTI-GERMAN RIOTS

DIMLY through the smoke screen of the Censorship we knew that the blockade was tightening. Since the outbreak of war there had been outcries that supplies were reaching Germany through neutral countries, that food was getting in to relieve her hunger, and above all gun cotton! Our Government's adhesion to the Declaration of London—another "scrap of paper"—was hotly denounced; its alleged subservience to American Big Business, execrated. "If cotton—let America say what she would—had been made contraband, not a shot could have been fired from a German gun!" amateur war strategists shrieked from Press and platform. That the Declaration of London was being steadily nullified, by modification, after modification, till it was finally swept away in July 1916; that the North Sea had been closed to commerce by the order of the British Navy escaped the notice of these patriots. That the European neutral countries were suffering hunger from the blockade was indifferent to them: to be neutral was to be ignoble in their opinion.

Britain and Germany were torpedoing each other's battleships; but the British public could think of the submarine only as an instrument of "German frightfulness." That it was the invention of an Englishman, and had been used so long ago as the American Civil War was unthinkable in those days. Still more was it incredible that Britain had begun the Great War with fifty-six of these death-dealing engines, whilst Germany had only twenty-eight, but nine of them capable of voyaging to the British Isles! The British Navy could employ both its submarines and its battleships to destroy its enemies; its battleships were able to hold up neutral merchantmen suspected of carrying goods for German use. The Germans, with their smaller navy largely bottled up in port by its big adversary, resorted to the submarine, which could creep out to sea unobserved.

Hitherto the submarine had been officially used on both sides against warships, military works and vessels conveying troops and military stores. The ruthless school in Germany was urging its use against British merchantmen as the only means of applying to her the hunger blockade she had cast about Germany. On January 30th, 1915, a warning was issued that merchantmen approaching France would be torpedoed if they appeared British regardless of their flag, on the ground that British merchantmen had adopted the ruse of flying neutral ensigns. When three ships had been sunk the British Foreign Office retorted with the announcement that any vessel carrying corn or flour to Germany would be seized ; though already it seems this was being done. The Germans then declared a submarine blockade of Britain from February 18th, and a barred zone around her coasts, wherein vessels would be sunk without warning or attempt to save life. The Germans excused these measures on the pleas that the blockade precluded Germany from feeding the prisoners, that the German people themselves were starving and that if warning to sink a ship were given, merchantmen made use of it to ram or otherwise destroy the submarine.[1] Such reasoning can only be admitted by those who justify the ethics of war.

The announcement of ruthless submarine warfare awoke the spectre of food scarcity in this country. It created wrath and consternation amongst American exporters who had profited exceedingly by the War. The American Government protested to the British against the unauthorised use of the American flag, and more severely, to the Germans against the submarine threat to American life and property.

Colonel House traversed the Atlantic to carry the President's confidential plea to the belligerents to avert the new menace. He sailed in the British ship *Lusitania*, and saw her hoist the United States flag on approaching the danger zone. He found Sir Edward Grey, as always, cordial, encouraging, raising his hopes to the pinnacle ; but, as ever, evading a definite issue, and ending by frigid withdrawal from negotiations. House proposed that if Germany would abandon the submarine blockade, Britain should relieve the food blockade of Germany. Grey replied by expressing his devotion to the principle termed the " Freedom of the Seas," the arrangement that all merchant shipping should be exempt from interference in time of war. When the Germans acclaimed this proposal as their own, Grey told House he would only assent to it if aggressive warfare on land were guaranteed impossible, and averred that even in this, he was speaking only for himself, and could not commit his Government. Actually, neither belligerent government was willing to make concessions. The ruthless school had its way. The submarine blockade was unstayed and both neutral and belligerent vessels were soon its victims.

The British Government issued an order in Council, the Reprisals Order, as it was called, declaring that henceforth its forces would stop all ships and cargoes with a German origin or destination ; contraband found in them would be condemned, non-contraband requisitioned or returned to the owner.

. . . . . . . .

The loss of the great Cunard liner, the *Lusitania*, was a shock to the

[1] Captain Oswald T. Tuck, head of the Historical Section of the British Admiralty, has since informed the world that it was the leisurely procedure of a German U-boat Commander in torpedoing a couple of merchant ships bound for Havre, which induced the British Admiralty to test the notion that a merchantman carrying hidden guns would have a " good chance of destroying a submarine." At the end of November 1915, the first of the many vessels so fitted, known as Q-boats, set sail on her first voyage.

world. The German Consul in New York had issued a declaration that as the ship was carrying munitions of war and a general cargo, she would not be permitted the immunity of a passenger liner, and would be sunk at sight. The threat appeared in the American press, but was discounted as bluff. In New York the War was remote as events in a history book; its naked cruelties were not realised. The Germans would not dare such a thing, it was said; the great British Navy would surely prevent it. America would not allow such an outrage with her citizens aboard. National pride was aroused: the threat seemed absurd. Eleven hundred and twenty-eight persons took passage with the ill-fated liner, bringing with them in their confidence, ninety children and thirty-nine infants in arms. With laughter the ship set sail for her doom. She was torpedoed in the early afternoon, in a smooth sea, but ten to fifteen miles from land, off the Old Head of Kinsale in Ireland. Many of her boats were broken and overturned; her crew and passengers struggled in the sea; of her company of 1,959 passengers and crew, eleven hundred and nineteen were drowned. Two-thirds of the children lost their lives, and of the babies only four were saved.

Great cries of wrath went up against the Germans, not least in America. Of one hundred and fifty-nine Americans on board, all but fifteen had been drowned. There were murmurs, too, against the Cunard Company and the Admiralty. Why was there no escort for the *Lusitania* it was demanded. It was admitted that she carried five thousand cases of cartridges; it was rumoured, though all this was denied, that she carried other ammunition, that she was transporting Canadian troops, and was equipped with trained gunners and masked guns.

Questioned in the Commons as to what the Admiralty had done to protect the liner, Winston Churchill admitted that vessels carrying horses, troops, munitions and "cargoes" vitally needed by the Government, had been met on the South coast of Ireland by destroyers, and convoyed into port; but naval resources could not supply escorts for merchant or passenger ships, he declared:

"Our principle is that the merchant traffic must look after itself, subject to the general arrangements that are made."[1]

La Follette and others in the United States Congress demanded that American citizens should not sail on belligerent ships; but Wilson, with his clear intention—since revealed—to assist the victory of the Allies and to assert the preponderance of America, declared that American rights must not be thus abridged, and demanded an apology and assurance that ships should not be sunk without warning being given and measures taken to assure the safety of lives on board.

W. J. Bryan, the old democratic leader, at this point resigned his position in Wilson's Cabinet, on the ground that the President was not strictly neutral and would end by drawing his country into the War.

[1] Official Parliamentary Report, May 10th, 1915.

The event created little impression in this country; even to the Pacifists it was obscured by the abuse showered upon Wilson for not having entered the War, and for his statement that a nation might be "too proud to fight."

It was not until September that Wilson received a qualified pledge not to sink without warning or life-saving. After the *Sussex* was torpedoed in the following March his ultimatum threatening to break diplomatic relations secured a more definite pledge in May 1916. This was acclaimed as a signal victory for his methods.

Twelve hundred men had lost their lives when the battle-cruisers *Cressy*, *Aboukir* and *Hogue* were torpedoed in September 1914. We scarcely heard of it till their poor widows came pleading to us for pension; but those were sailors, wedded to the calling of death. The loss of the *Lusitania* touched us nearer; her passengers were harmless and helpless travellers, not soldiers and sailors who had gone out to kill. Important people had gone down with the ship. Lord Rhondda and his daughter had been passengers; they had been hours in the sea; and she was on the W.S.P.U. platform, in the heart of London, telling her experiences. The Press teemed with accounts by the survivors. Britain was thrilled.

There was a fierce clamour for reprisals. The meanest elements among the jingoes worked up the first of the anti-German riots. These were deliberately organised, in no sense a spontaneous popular outburst; but the prospect of looting without fear of punishment made its appeal to certain sections of the poor and ignorant. Many a home was wrecked; many a peaceable working family lost its all. Stones were flung, children injured. Doris Lester of Kingsley Hall, Bow, was hurt in defending some of the poor families.

Mrs. Nuess, one of our Poplar members, an English woman, married to a German, a good voluntary worker for our Federation who had made innumerable little sacrifices to aid those poorer than herself, saw her home utterly dismantled, even to the tools, so costly and so essential, by which her industrious husband and son earned their living as cabinet-makers. She saw her husband, her son and daughter, dragged out of the house by the mob. What had become of them? Were they killed or imprisoned? A day of agonised suspense elapsed before they were able to rejoin her.

A neighbour, English as herself, and like herself, married to a German, passed through the same terrible experience; and in fear and grief was prematurely confined, alone in the empty house, with only the bare boards on which to lay herself. I was shocked, as one is by tragedies near to one. How cruel that such a thing could happen in a city where not a shot of the War had been heard! Ah, poor humanity, how far you must travel yet to become civilised!

We knew that in all the belligerent countries the same cruel hardships were falling upon people equally defenceless, equally innocent of their cause. It was officially stated in the House of Commons that 237 persons had been injured in the riots, but women like this poor friend of mine made no report of their suffering.

The saddest feature of all was that the disturbance, though its onset was organised from without, was largely a hunger riot ; the women and children who snatched bread and meat from the aliens, snatched it, not from hatred of Germany, but because they were hungry.

On May 13th orders were given for the arrest of all alien enemies of military age. The ostensible object of the rioting had been achieved. Niederhofer, our big, kind fellow at the factory, had never been molested, not a window of his was broken. He too was arrested and sent to Knockeloe internment camp in the Isle of Man. He wrote to me, begging my aid to release him, that he might return to his family. He offered even to assist in the making of shells ; for in his youth he had learnt this, too, in a German munition factory. I pleaded that he was essential for the training of our toy makers. Nothing availed. He was held till the close of the War. His wife and six children were repatriated long before him. They and he later returned to a Germany of acute poverty, and he wrote to me telling me of their straits and imploring me to find friends who would buy from him the beautiful Christmas toys he had made.

On May 8th, 1915, Lord Robert Cecil read to the Commons a letter from one of the poo English lads held as prisoners of war in Germany :

" We are locked up separately in small cells from 12 feet long to 6 feet broad, and not allowed to speak to anybody. A bowl with a little coffee in it forms our breakfast, and a mixture of potatoes and meat our lunch. At about 2.45 we walk in a tiny little yard about 20 yards long for about three-quarters of an hour, still not allowed to speak, and then back to the cell for the rest of the day. We are allowed to write as much as we like, and receive parcels and letters, but no smoking at any time. This life will become a nightmare."

Asquith commented, with the Pecksniffian hypocrisy frequent amongst politicians, and widely accounted as a virtue in war time :

" The maltreatment of prisoners is a form of cruelty which was not even common in the Dark Ages, and it appears to have been left, as so many other fiendish devices in this Great War, to one of the Christian nations to invent and elaborate."

The conditions of imprisonment the soldier's letter had described, were identical with those of the ordinary prisoner in this country, save that the ordinary prisoner is very much worse off since he may only receive and write one letter a month, on the one sheet of paper provided by the authorities ; for the rest, he has only a slate to write on, no paper, pen or pencil being permitted in his cell. As Suffragettes, some thousands of us had endured this sort of imprisonment at the hands of Asquith's Government before the War. Even whilst he spoke, women war prisoners, interned without any charge being formulated against them, were in Holloway under the same conditions. Many times these women asked me to visit them ; but as an ex-prisoner I was black-listed.

Internment was a weary agony, but the plight of those not interned was often more grievous ; not one per cent. of them could get work. As "enemies" they were outside the scope of the War relief funds, and even the Poor Law was closed to them. Only the internment of the husband brought some small relief to the wives and children. German wives of interned men got 10s. a week and 3s. for each child. The allowance to the British born wife was more meagre still, only 8s. for herself and 1s. 6d. for each child ! To this grievous penury now was added the risk and suffering of the "reprisals" pogrom.

## CHAPTER XXII

### WAR BABIES—THE "MOTHERS' ARMS"—AND THE "GUNMAKERS' ARMS"

SUDDENLY I noticed that the London Small Arms Factory in the Old Ford Road had added a huge new building. Great streams of workers poured out from it in the dinner hour.

High prices were driving the mothers into the munition factories. Our day nursery was full and applicants were daily turned away.

One April morning I woke with the thought that the mother and infant clinic and the day nursery must be brought together, extended and better housed. As soon as I had attacked the correspondence I ran out on my quest. In less than five minutes my eye lighted on a large empty building, only thirty-eight numbers further down the Old Ford Road, a public house, closed because its license had been withdrawn. It had been styled the "Gunmakers' Arms," and was in fact nearly opposite the gun factory. The public houses are with few exceptions the best built and most efficiently preserved premises in the East End. Structurally this building was no exception to the rule, but it was filthy in the extreme. The light filtered feebly through the grime of its windows. On great tables of unpolished deal, blackened by dirt, to the darkness of the floors, were heaps of fishbones, as though people had eaten there without plates. Yet they were spacious premises. I eagerly planned how to use them. A fortnight later we reopened the place as the "Mothers' Arms," brilliant with sunshine and white paint, pictures from Walter Crane's toy books on the walls, the brightest of chintzes at the windows. On the outer walls were painted red Caps of Liberty, surrounded by our initials, E.L.F.S., in gold letters. Within, the main bar, the appurtenances of beer selling torn out of it, was the reception and lecture room of the clinic. From a shop-breaker's in the Hackney Road, I had furnished it with great cupboards with sliding doors for the medicines and baby foods, and huge drawers for the layettes and maternity outfits. Opening from it was the doctor's consultation room, across the passage the bath-room and dressing-room, the kitchen and scullery, upstairs the babies' day nursery with sun pouring into it from windows on three sides, and opening on to a flat roof, where the babies might be out all day in fine weather, upstairs again a room for sick children, and two others, soon thrown into one, to make another nursery. It was a pretty sight in the Roman Road, thenceforward, to see the gay little cots and the babes on the roof of the "Mothers' Arms," an awning erected to shield them, when the sun was fierce, or the wind boisterous. The shabby old clothes, the broken boots and much darned stockings were doffed when the children arrived each morning. They were bathed and prettily dressed in the nursery garments, provided by friendly donors, and kept in careful order by Lucy Burgis, whom I had first met during my first term at the Manchester High School for Girls; a great girl in a sailor suit, she was then, with flaxen hair turned to pepper and salt now.

Opposite, just down the short Gunmakers' Lane, was the big Victoria Park. The toddlers went thither daily, each with a tiny hand grasping a rope, held also by nurses and teachers, to keep the group together.

We could take forty children into the day nursery now, but ten times that number of places were applied for.

Sybil Smith gathered more voluntary helpers for the bigger family in the new premises. Lady Emily Lutyens sent a daughter to develop a social consciousness. The Press made a stunt of the "Mothers' Arms." The City Corporation of London, the Ministry of Health and the Ministry of Education gave grants to it. Charles Gulliver of the Holborn Empire arranged Sunday League benefits for it. All sorts of people came down to see it. This great publicity gave the spur to start similar institutions both near and far.

. . . . . . . .

Eight months after the War began, arose a great talk of War Babies. Dear! dear! one might almost have thought that the business of the Army was to propagate infants! Ronald McNeill, a Tory M.P., had set the ball rolling by a letter to the *Morning Post*, wherein he had appealed to the religious leaders of the nation to come forward:

"With an honest and courageous pronouncement that under existing circumstances the mothers of our soldiers' children are to be treated with no scorn or dishonour, and that the infants themselves should receive a loyal and unashamed welcome."

He suggested a drastic reformation of the Bastardy laws "if only as a temporary measure." Since the mothers would have no separation allowances and no means of support, he urged that the infants should be "boldly adopted as the children of the State."

Separation allowances for these girls and their infants would have provided a more acceptable solution; but so far from any legislative aid being given to them, it remained the rule that even the paltry affiliation orders might not be applied for in respect of soldiers under orders for abroad.[1] Cathcart Wason reminded the Commons that a man whom the Court had ordered to pay towards the support of his illegitimate child could escape his responsibility by joining the Navy, but even this striking injustice the Government refused to rectify. Moreover, however much a man might be desirous of doing the right thing by his natural child and its mother, he could not get separation allowance for them, unless he had wholly supported the mother before the War. Many a youth would have married his sweetheart, when he found a baby was on the way, had he been able to do it. If he were killed before he could get home to marry, the girl must bear her burden alone.

The Government took no action. The Bastardy laws remained in their ancient iniquity. Public opinion was little changed. A committee of inquiry presided over by Mrs. Creighton decided that the war baby problem had been exaggerated. The W.S.P.U. with much advertisement had announced its intention "to deal with the problem of the war babies" by adopting as many illegitimate girl war babies as possible, but its effort stopped short at five infants. The question proved an unpopular one; people felt that to advertise the existence of such infants was a reflection upon the conduct of the troops. Mrs. Pankhurst found it necessary to observe that there had always been illegitimate

[1] The Naval Discipline (No. 2) Act 1915, declared sailors liable to support their wives and children though execution might not be taken against their person or pay in respect of maintenance orders. If the Admiralty thought fit, and if it were satisfied that the defaulter had not been prevented by naval service from attendance at the hearing of the claim against him, the Admiralty would deduct a portion of his daily pay not exceeding, "in respect of a wife or children sixpence, and in respect of a bastard child fourpence." No action for maintenance could be taken against a sailor under orders for abroad, nor unless a sum sufficient to pay his expenses in attending the case were deposited with his commanding officer.

children and that the number would not be greatly increased by the War; but such explanations could not render the fund popular. Mrs. Grundy objected to any relaxation of the social reproof and ignominy it was customary to visit upon the unmarried mother.

Happily for the girls they had guarded their maidenhood more efficiently than was anticipated; in spite of the war fever, the rise in the illegitimate birth rate was not great.[1] Yet rise it did somewhat, and war babies there were in this and all other belligerent countries.

. . . . . . . .

[1] Illegitimate births per 1,000 of all births.

| | 1911–14 | 1915–18 | 1919–22 | 1923 | 1924 |
|---|---|---|---|---|---|
| England and Wales ... | 43 | 52 | 49 | 42 | 42 |
| Scotland ... ... | 73 | 73 | 73 | 67 | 66 |

It was Saturday afternoon. I was alone in the house; someone was banging impatiently at the door.

"My sister!" a white-faced woman gasped as I opened, "the doctor says she's having a baby! I sent for him for her pains! I didn't know nothing about a baby. She's lame and she never goes out! We've got nothing ready for it . . . !" She trailed off plaintively with a sob.

It was poor Mrs. Harter;[1] we knew her well at the clinic, with a baby at the breast and two others under four, and a husband depending on casual odd jobs. I promised to bring her what would be needed for her sister and the baby. She ran off weeping and thanking. The "Mothers' Arms" would be closed now; but I had the keys. I fetched the outfit and took it to Mrs. Harter's. Her door was opened to me by the doctor, a young man in his 'thirties, coarsely exuberant, pink-faced and red-haired. "The first war-baby!" he exulted; "you'll have to help me deliver it." "I cannot. I am not trained." "Oh, nonsense," he said roughly, "there's nobody else; her sister's hysterical."

"You need an efficient person." "You can do as you are told I suppose! There's no time to get anyone else. I'm entitled to compel you!"

"Very well," I assented, and followed him upstairs to the bedroom, scantily furnished: not a drawer, not a cupboard or shelf. On the old, soiled coverings of the bed a dark-haired woman lay on her side with knees drawn up, fully dressed to the waist, and with boots and stockings, but with naked buttocks and thighs exposed. Her skin had the sallow look of neglected poverty. One foot was deformed and twisted; if she put it to the ground she must stand on the ankle.

"It's not a baby!" she whimpered peevishly, continuing an argument which had gone before.

"What is it then—a tumour?" the doctor gibed unpleasantly, seating himself on the bed at her back.

"Yes, it is a tumour; it must be—I ain't done nothing!" her voice rose to a wail.

She was holding the ends of a dirty towel, tied to the foot of the bed. The doctor had given it her to pull at, but her grasp was limp. He was working at the vagina with his hands. "Push up against me!" he ordered, but she shrank away from him.

"Don't hold your breath when the pains come! . . . Don't hold your breath! . . . Damn it, you've got to work!" he shouted impatiently. "Push up against me. Push! Push! I tell you. Push!"

The more he urged, the more she shrank from him, whining, obstinate as a mule: "It ain't a baby; it ain't! It ain't!"

He swore and shook her; then turned to me with a growl: "Can't you speak to her?"

"May I sit by her? Perhaps she would be less afraid of me," I suggested, anxious to be of service. He made way for me and I took

[1] In this case I have substituted another name to avoid disclosing the identity of the persons concerned.

his place at her back. She pushed against me instantly, obedient to the directions I gave from him. He worked at her still with his hands; with his tongue still gibing:

"How old are you?"

"Twenty-one," she snapped, resentful.

"Not you! Thirty if you're a minute! She's old and tough!" he turned to grin at me, then jeered again: "Come on! Let's get at your tumour!"

She whimpered occasionally and groaned . . . so it went on. . . .

At last he ordered me: "Get away; I can manage. Fetch a kettle of boiling water from that woman downstairs, and wash the basin. You'll have to sterilise those things I've put out there, and you'll need some soap."

I obeyed his directions as he gave them, gazing with anxiety which bordered on horror at the birth thus sordidly enacted. . . . The head was out. . . . There was a struggle. It seemed the infant would be strangled. . . . I turned away in dread. . . .

"That was a nasty one—got twisted somehow!" The doctor spoke cheerily. I turned and saw him holding a baby at arm's-length. He slapped it sharply across the back. It cried out, a marvel of shapely being, incredibly alive and vigorous.

He passed it to me: "Wash it well; use plenty of soap, but don't get anything into its eyes,"—he squirted some liquid into them—"That's for—you know!" he said and leapt back to attend to the mother.

The child was covered with a thick grey slime, almost like india-rubber, only removable by the use of abundant soap. I was consumed by anxiety, lest through my inexperienced handling, a mischance might happen to its eyes. The tiny creature clutched me with its fingers, amazingly strong! There seemed in it, indeed, a fierce, invincible vitality.

At last, when mother and child were tucked down in clean sheets, I could go—my mind in a turmoil, terrible and strange. . . . For many nights I dreamt of that birth.

. . . . . . . .

I returned several times to see the infant—feeling the curious bond of having assisted at its entry into life. The singular vitality of its first hour had passed from it, as it seemed. "A fine boy," it was called, fat and fair; it throve exceedingly, yet to me it seemed always less vigorous than when first I saw it.

I entered the mother for daily nursing and food from the "Mothers' Arms," for obviously Mrs. Harter was unable to provide what was needed. "If you can find out who the father is we may get some sort of allowance for her," I told Nurse Hebbes, but she rejoined: "You'd better talk to her. She simply doesn't answer me!"

. . . . . . . .

The mother lay silent, her mouth sullen, her eyes unlit by any gleam. I sat by her with the child in my arms, and after a silence casually observed: "If you were a soldier's wife you could get the allowance."

Gradually a light crept into her face: "I used to see a chap passing the door of an evening," she muttered sheepishly, then relapsed into her torpor.

We sat silent long. At last, seeing that she eyed me furtively, I prompted: "Did you never go out with him? Did he never come in to see you?"

She started slightly. After a pause she whispered: "Only once, the night they was called up. . . . He said, 'Have a glass of beer.'" I pressed for his name. She persisted she did not know.

. . . . . . . .

I was going out. A man in khaki stood on the doorstep:

"I'd marry her if I had the money!" he said, and smiled at me weakly, his long, crooked yellow teeth showing like fangs.

"Oh, it's you! Come inside," I invited, guessing him to be the father whose name I had not discovered. He told me he was guarding a tunnel somewhere near London, babbling on incoherently, boasting, complaining; familiar, as though he had known me all his life. He seemed to forget his errand till I drew him back to it. I offered to arrange the expenses if he desired to marry. He asserted his readiness to do it on his next leave.

. . . . . . . .

I went round to the vicarage in St. Stephen's Road. Parson Smith eyed me curiously as I outlined the story. "Will you marry them for nothing if I provide the ring?" His wry smile twitched; he agreed, small-voiced, laconic.

. . . . . . . .

The sight of glistening waves in a dazzle of sunshine danced before my eyes. Waiting a connection, I had spent half an hour by the sea at Swansea that morning, before I returned after a week-end of meetings in South Wales. Even here in these dismal East End streets the sun shone brilliant, lighting the new green leaves of rare, unexpected trees.

Suddenly Mrs. Harter's white face confronted me: "He's been back, and he's run away, and never done it!" she wailed. "He said he wouldn't get married with only cold potatoes for his dinner. I've done all I could. I give her my bedroom, and she's had what we haven't been able to have ourselves!" She wept. "It isn't my fault there was only cold potatoes for him. I hadn't any money to buy better!"

"Never mind; he will soon be back," I soothed her.

Had he funked it, I wondered, planning as I went. I fancied he would come back, or he would not have come at all.

At the " Mothers' Arms " Nurse Hebbes was weighing grey powders. She beamed on me with her happy smile. What an air of radiance that girl had! " We shall have to give Mrs. Harter's sister a job here," I told her. " She can bring the baby with her. It is the only thing to be done with them for the present." She smiled at me under drooped lashes: " All right! " she said, replacing her stock. " Shall I go and tell her at once? "

. . . . . . . .

Mrs. Payne opened the door to me, plaintive:

" That chap's gone away and never married that young woman—Ain't it all right? Mrs. Harter's been here crying for you."

" I know. Don't worry, he will come back again. Get Miss Cohen for me, please, Mrs. Payne."

My secretary came in, grave-browed, rosy lips pursed, notebook and pencil ready.

" Bodger;[1] you know his number? "

She nodded, and I began:

" Dear Mr. Bodger,

" I hope you will let us arrange a little wedding breakfast for you at the Women's Hall. Please let me have the date of your marriage when it is fixed. . . ."

. . . . . . . .

Smyth and I went shares in the cost. The nursery helpers did the rest. It was all very gay; Nurse Hebbes with the baby, little Mrs. Fern presenting flowers to the bride. Bodger appeared as a model bridegroom, painfully inarticulate; but managing to stammer some sentences in reply to a toast—a poor specimen, weak and garrulous, yet with something keen and ferrety about the nose and eyes which made one think of a sharp fox-terrier dog. The bride, with her heavy face, dull-eyed and indifferent, staggered out on her crutch.

" It is doubtful whether I have committed a mortal sin in helping to tie those two together permanently," I said to Hebbes and Smyth. " She will get her separation allowance now, but they will produce more children! "

. . . . . . . .

In a week Bodger appeared again: " It is cruel; they've took out all my teeth! "

. . . . . . . .

Four years had passed. I hurried through the cheerless purlieus of

[1] This name is fictitious.

the New North Road in the grey winter afternoon. A knot of people had gathered. A speaker shouted hoarsely fom the soap-box. At sight of me he leapt down, leaving another to take his place, and came to me at a run. It was Bodger: " They've only given me 11s. 6d. pension. They took out all my teeth and never give me any more! Can't you see into it. . . ."

A girl came to me with her trouble. Her child's father would have no more to do with her. I wrote to him. Shamed into promising a pittance, he answered callously:

"I met her in the latter end of January and kept company with her for about six weeks. . . . She is not the class of girl for me. . . . I am shortly leaving for the Front, and I am putting the affair in my mother's hands. She is in possession of all the dates, and should they tally with the birth of the child, I have instructed her to make a small allowance for the maintenance of the child."

. . . . . . . .

A gay fellow of the Scots Guards wrote a hundred and fifty letters to a servant girl, married her and lived with her for a month. At the end of that time he was charged with bigamy, the fact being disclosed when his new wife applied for separation allowance. The case was briefly disposed of. The magistrate merely asked him: "Do you plead guilty?" and when he answered in the affirmative, awarded him a day's imprisonment, which meant that he left the Court a free man. He left without a word to the girl he had injured, calling to a woman he knew: "I told you I'd get off. Now I'm going to have a drink. Come along!"

. . . . . . . .

About this time a woman came to me with her fifteen-year old daughter, pregnant by a soldier. The girl's employer had turned her out, her father refused to let her cross his threshold, or to help her in any way, and ordered her mother to hold no communication with her. Vulnerable through desire to cherish her other children, by reason of her economic dependence, her affection for her tyrant and long habit of servitude to his will, the mother bowed to this brutal inhibition. Secretly she managed to spare some shillings to provide her daughter with a cheap lodging; secretly she had come to implore assistance.

France and Austria legalised marriage by proxy from the trenches, but the old conventions were rigidly observed here.

Many war mothers came to me. For some I found work with their babies, for others foster-parents. Many were adopted by childless people and much beloved.

Mrs. Creighton's committee had dismissed the problem as negligible. In October 1916 an obscure little paragraph in the *News of the World*, which advised a correspondent seeking a home for a "war baby" to apply either to Dr. Barnado's Homes, to me, or to the Mission of Hope near London Bridge, produced a huge batch of letters appealing for aid. Forty-eight of them came by the first post Monday, and the stream continued steadily. Three of the applicants in the first batch were soldiers' wives unable to live on their allowances. The rest were unmarried mothers. The grandmother of one of the babies wrote piteously, revealing all the hardships inherent in these cases, not least the cruel and common fact that the girl would lose her situation should her employers discover what had happened:

"My daughter, a girl of nineteen years, gave birth to a female child, illegitimate, on September 21st. I cannot possibly have the child here, because her work is being kept open for her, and if it were known she had a child, she would, of course, lose her living.

"We are working people. My husband's wages are £1 a week and my daughter is the eldest of six. My youngest child is two years.

"My daughter has always been a great help to me till this downfall. She will willingly pay to help support the child if only she can get it into a good home. The father of the child is a soldier and under the circumstances we cannot make him pay. . . ."

## CHAPTER XXIII

### ASQUITH'S COALITION GOVERNMENT—MORE COMPULSION—THE NATIONAL REGISTER AND THE MUNITIONS ACT—THE WOMAN'S SHARE

THE Treasury Agreement and the power to discipline workers by penalties under the Defence of the Realm Act, had not ended the shortage of munitions, for despite the false reports published at the time, and the false history written since,[1] the whole munitions organisation was deficient, plant and equipment, inspection, storage, transport.

The Government which had led the country to Armageddon unprepared, and was " muddling through," was a vulnerable subject of attack, and though Asquith kept a stiff face against his accusers, and made speeches minimising the shortage of munitions, he admitted it privately in his own jottings. Lord Fisher refused to remain First Sea Lord under the headstrong and reckless Winston Churchill, whose Dardanelles venture was proving as ghastly a failure as that of Antwerp and presently concluded with the monstrous toll of 130,000 casualties incurred in eight months. The political truce, for some time past, had been honoured more commonly in the breach than in the observance. Bonar Law and Lansdowne had announced that they would take no further responsibility for the Government's prosecution of the War. The Tory Press belaboured the Government with a will.

Whilst the outcry of the Tories was for a more ruthless prosecution of the War, economic considerations played a larger part in their revolt from the truce than was permitted to appear. Lloyd George's statement to a deputation of shipowners : " We are fighting Germany, Austria and drink, and as far as I can see the greatest of these is drink," was made with a twofold object : to secure the industrial compulsion of the workers, and to pave the way for controlling the liquor traffic, as a measure of temperance and economy, for the saving of grain and the transport required for it, and also as a means of raising revenue. His penchant for large dramatic schemes had led him to desire nationalisation, but he discarded this project, when he found the opposition to it on the part of his own colleagues not disarmed by his rhetoric, or by

[1] The following statement of Earl Buckle, M.A., Hon. LL.D., scholar of New College, Fellow of All Souls College, Oxford, and 28 years editor of the *Times*, is a typical instance :

" . . . the insufficient supply of munitions of war due mainly to strikes, to trade union practices favouring slow output, and to drink——"

*Encyclopædia Britannica*, 12th Edition, Vol. 30, p. 1,008.

the King's declaration that intoxicants were to be abolished from the Royal Household. High liquor taxes were his alternative; but these, too, were abandoned without a struggle. Temperantia had to console herself with liquor control boards, which limited public house hours, and with beer of reduced strength. As Lloyd George himself pointed out, the brewer could compensate himself for reduced consumption by supplying, at the same price as formerly, a commodity more largely composed of water.

Asquith, in his since published diary, wrote of these incidents with frivolous indifference:

"As usual he (Lloyd George) launched out into irrelevant topics, amongst others an interview he had with Bonar Law on the subject of drink taxes. Bonar Law seems to have told him frankly that the Tory party was so much in the hands of the trade that they must oppose these root and branch. Lloyd George replied that, if so, he could not persist with them, and he would throw the whole responsibility for doing nothing in that direction on the Tories."

That even so arid a professional politician as Asquith could regard such a communication from his Chancellor of the Exchequer as an "irrelevant topic" is amazing. As usual the Tories were proving themselves the only Marxists on the political stage. To them the economic class war was an ever-present reality. They were striving whole-heartedly to maintain the advantage for their class. Lloyd George's first War budget had doubled the income tax and the surtax and secured a contribution from the workers by taxes on beer and tea; but had raised only an estimated sixty-five millions to meet an anticipated deficit of three hundred millions. The difference, which would have to be paid some day, had been produced in the meantime by piling up debt and interest charges. Baulked of his liquor taxes, with a Tory opposition daily growing more restive, Lloyd George's second War budget made no substantial new proposals for raising revenue, though the estimated deficit for the ensuing six months now exceeded five hundred millions.

On May 12th, Asquith was denying the rumours that he had been forced to invite the Tories to enter the Government. A week later, in the stir caused by Fisher's resignation, he had capitulated. In the new Coalition Cabinet were all the foremost Tory leaders whom Asquith had been opposing all his political life. Arthur Henderson was made President of the Board of Education—a thankless position, since education was at a discount, with all else pertaining to human welfare. His appointment did not prevent the children from being deprived of their education to supply cheap labour for the farms and factories. The Black Country glass trade secured permission for boys of thirteen and fourteen years to be employed at night, though upwards of 60,000 workless women were on the war service registers. Children of eleven years and upwards were released from school to work on farms, sometimes for food only, or for wages ranging from 1s. to 4s. per week.[1] It was made clear that Henderson's main business in the Government was to advise on Labour questions. By his inside knowledge of the Labour movement, he was to prove the most dangerous enemy of the rank and file movement growing in the workshops against the employers, the Government and the Trade Union leaders, who were all by this time united in imposing industrial compulsion upon the workers.

The Tories had demanded a business government; it was now in being. Lloyd George left the Treasury to create a Ministry of Munitions, controlled by directors of the great armament firms, railway magnates and shipowners. Sir Percy Girouard of Armstrongs, the armament makers, was made Director-General of munitions supply, Eric Geddes, of the North-Eastern Railway Company, became Deputy Director. The country was divided into ten munitions areas managed by business men whose interests were concerned in the work. The armament firms at first endeavoured to keep munitions as their own preserve and the Government bowed to them, but the orders were too vast for them to execute and eventually this great harvest for manufacturers was thrown open to all and sundry.

The National Register Act and the Munitions Act were now rushed through.

The first provided that all persons between 15 and 65 years of age must supply detailed particulars of nationality and residence, condition as to marriage, their dependants; their trade or profession, name and business address of employer, and to state whether they were willing to undertake war work. Certificates of Registration were to be supplied to persons who had registered. The penalty for refusal was £5 and £1 a day thereafter, and anyone falsely claiming to have been registered was liable to three months' imprisonment with hard labour, and to a fine of £20. Changes of address must be notified, and whoever arrived in the United Kingdom must register within twenty-eight days.

I saw that all this was the prelude to conscription, which would set the seal of compulsion on the best of our youth, the most humane and intelligent, who would never give themselves willingly to the War. Immediately I began to work against the Register Bill; but only the few, as yet, could believe that such a great innovation would actually come to pass. Scarcely a protest either in Parliament or from the outside could be obtained. The strange, dull apathy which had seized so many who cared for freedom left it to a handful of us to raise our voices in the wilderness.[2]

[1] On March 2nd, 1916, Yoxall, the teachers' representative, complained that 8,000 children under 14 had been released from school for farm and other work. Sir R. Winfrey stated that the Board of Education had permitted the local authorities to exempt children of 11 years in districts where not a single farmer had accepted the Government offer of soldiers to work on the land at 4/– a day.

[2] The Society of Friends is traditionally opposed to war: it advised its members to work in the relief of war suffering at the outbreak of war. Its Service Committee advised signing the National Register with a declaration of conscientious objection to military service and munition work.

The Munitions Act tightened up the compulsion envisaged by the Treasury Agreement, setting up Arbitration Tribunals, Munitions Tribunals, and Boards of Referees; making provision for paying them; and for punishing those who failed to comply with the awards by fines up to £5 per day, so long as disobedience to the award were continued.

It was provided that trade disputes should be settled by the Board of Trade or the Arbitration Tribunals. Strikes and lock-outs were made punishable by fines of £5 per day per man in all work connected with the manufacture and repair of war material, ships, vehicles, aircraft or the metals, machines and tools required for them, or in "any other work of any description" to which the Act might be applied by Proclamation.

If the Minister of Munitions considered expedient, he might make an order declaring any munition factory a "controlled establishment." In that case profits were to be controlled and wages might not be raised without the consent of the Minister of Munitions. If the Minister withheld consent the matter might be referred to the Arbitration Tribunal. Philip Snowden's amendment that the Tribunal should take the cost of living into account was defeated in the Commons by an enormous majority, only fourteen Members voting for it, though Labour held more than forty parliamentary seats; for many Labour Members backed the Government. All Trade Union conditions, regarded by the Board of Trade, or the Arbiters appointed by it, as tending to restrict employment or production, were to be suspended.

The control of profits was largely illusory, and it was promised that it would not be too strictly adhered to. The provisions governing it were vague and involved. Profits in excess of those made in the two years before the War, plus an increase of one-fifth, were to be paid to the Treasury; but if the manufacturer objected to the two years' standard, or the method of computation, it might be otherwise determined by agreement with the Minister, or by a Board of Referees. In any case consideration was to be given to increase of output, and provision of new machinery, plant or capital, and "other matters." Under these heads, loopholes for evasion were provided, and were seized with avidity. "We put up big buildings and laid down new plant to evade paying the excess profits tax," a manufacturer told me frankly. This was the common practice, winked at by the Ministry, which cared only to get the munitions made at any price, and by its local representatives who were often the heads of great munition-making establishments.

Workers in controlled establishments were under obligation to comply with "all" regulations of the Ministry of Munitions for the ordering of the work; employers with all "reasonable" requirements. It was obligatory for employers to post rules for "Order, Discipline, Time-keeping and Efficiency" which the workers must obey, under threat of punishment for disobedience by fines up to £3 by the Local Munitions Tribunal, and the possibility of further penalties being imposed by other Courts. Punishment was imposed for lateness, absence, talking at work, idling, producing too little, drinking too much.

Any man or woman who undertook to work at any controlled factory to which he or she might be assigned by the Minister of Munitions, was liable to a fine of £3 for failure to fulfil this agreement. Employers attempting to dissuade workers from entering into such undertakings or employing workers who had undertaken to work elsewhere, were also liable under the Act.

Workers in controlled establishments might not leave the service of their employer without permission. It was illegal to employ a worker within six weeks after he had left a controlled factory unless he could present a certificate from his employer that he had left with his consent, or a certificate of release granted by a Munitions Tribunal, which would only be vouchsafed if the Tribunal considered the employer had unreasonably withheld his consent. Employers were instructed not to return the unemployment insurance book to a worker who left without a certificate of release, but to send the book to the employment exchange in order that the defaulter might be deprived of unemployment benefit during the six weeks of unemployment he must suffer. Though the worker might not leave his or her employment without permission, and could be punished for so doing by fine or imprisonment, there was no appeal against dismissal.

Though the Government was making advances of capital, sometimes amounting to £50,000, to assist private firms in developing munition work, Government control of the factories mainly amounted to enforcing the employers' control over their workers.

The Minister was empowered to compel the wearing of war service badges by persons engaged on war work, to make rules concerning the issue and return of such badges, and forbidding their use by persons not so engaged. Fines up to £50 were authorised for breach of these regulations. The badges were issued through the employer, and must be returned to the employer on leaving his service. To lose or dispose of one of these badges, to wear or sell any badge similar in form was to incur a serious penalty.

The Munitions Tribunals consisted of a judge appointed by the Minister of Munitions, and Assessors drawn from panels of persons ostensibly representing employers and workers; but actually appointed to the panel by the Minister of Munitions. As may be expected, the men and women in the workshops often bitterly repudiated the Minister's choice. Even when the Assessors appointed to represent workers were persons they would themselves have chosen, these Assessors were hopelessly outclassed in defending the worker against too harsh a discipline, by having to contend with an equal number of Assessors defending the interests of the employers; and, as judge, a local magistrate, or naval or military officer, acting for the Ministry to secure increased output.

Munitions Tribunals were of two sorts: General Munitions Tribunals might try any offences under the Act and might impose imprisonment for non-payment of fines and costs. Local Munitions Tribunals could deal only with the smaller offences, and could not impose imprisonment; but could order that fines and the costs of the proceedings be deducted from wages.

No one proceeded against by a Munitions Tribunal could be represented by counsel or solicitor, in many cases a serious hardship. Appeals from the decisions of Local Tribunals might be referred to a General Tribunal, and if a fine of £20 or more had been imposed, from thence to a Court of Quarter Sessions.

Punishment by a Munitions Tribunal did not preclude additional punishment by the ordinary Courts, and power to impose heavier penalties, including imprisonment, was retained under the Defence of the Realm Act, the Minister of Munitions being given equal power with the naval and military authorities under that Act.

The promise that women munitioners would be paid like men, still persistently repeated, although it was clearly proved to be moonshine, found no place in the Act. The second schedule provided:

"4. Where the custom of a shop is changed during the War by the introduction of semi-skilled men to perform work hitherto performed by a class of workmen of higher skill, the time and piece rates paid shall be the usual rates of the district for that class of work.

"5. The relaxation of existing demarcation restrictions or admission of semi-skilled or female labour shall not affect adversely the rates customarily paid for the job. In cases where men who ordinarily do the work are adversely affected thereby, the necessary readjustments shall be made so that they can maintain their previous earnings."

Clearly such protection as was promised was for men and not for women, who were only mentioned to give assurance that their wretched pay should not bring down the wage of men.

One saw the impish diplomacy of the little Welshman peeping through these phrases. The words "Time and Piece rates," the very words I had endeavoured to press upon him on behalf of women, were inserted on the motion of Wilson, a Labour man, but that clause only applied to men. F. W. Jowett moved to substitute persons for men in order that women might be included in the protection conferred by the clause. He withdrew his motion when Arthur Henderson,[1] apparelled in his new dignity as Minister of Education, pleaded that the clause had been carefully constructed, after a three days' conference at the Treasury, to enable women to be brought into munition work. W. C. Anderson,

[1] Henderson's attitude, largely shared by his colleagues, is best expressed in his own words:

"During the War, on the plea of national necessity, some of the powerful men's Unions have so far relaxed their rules as to permit the employment of women, but not without rigid guarantees that the women shall leave the industry when the War ends. . . . The A.S.E., for example, decided at an early stage in the War to allow the introduction of women into the engineering trade; but the Union did not admit these women to membership, preferring rather to support the efforts of the National Federation of Women Workers to organise these women."—Supplement to *Ladies' Field*, February 1918.

who had brought many cases of gross sweating to the notice of Parliament, expressed the pious hope that women would not be sweated; "something like a decent minimum" should be given to them. The case for equal pay went by default.

The fact was as clearly apparent as need be: Big Business said "We are not going to pay men's wages to women; we are not going to have these women buying fur coats and pianos at our expense!" The Government was of the same mind. The women were left to the tea-and-bread and fried-chips-in-a-paper status which they had always occupied.

At the Women's War Service meetings representatives of the Board of Trade continued protesting that women would get equal pay with men for equal results. "The intention was not," oh no, assuredly not "to engage a cheap substitute for men's labour."[1]

On July 4th, 1915, Herbert Broome, who was said to have secured fifty recruits for the Navy, was asked, when speaking at a recruiting meeting, whether soldiers returning from the War would be sure of getting their jobs back. He replied that if women had taken their work at lower wages, he feared not, and deplored the fact that railwaymen, earning 27s., had been replaced by girls at 12s. 6d. An officer in the crowd protested: "You are doing more harm than good." As he stepped from the platform Broome was arrested for "using words prejudicial to recruiting" and got twenty-one days in jail, without the option of a fine!

. . . . . . . .

Whilst the ruthless school were thus gaining a firmer hold in the Government here, Italy was brought into the War. How French influences worked to that achievement, and the part played in the work by Mussolini, who, by aid of the pistol and bludgeon, was to become the Dictator of Italy, must be told in another volume. The Italian Socialist Party took no part in the War, and firmly adhered to its pre-War declarations of international solidarity.

[1] Captain Williams, Board of Trade representative at Manchester.

## CHAPTER XXIV

### THE FIRST AIR RAID[1]

I WAS writing at home one evening. On the silence arose an ominous grinding . . . growing in volume . . . throbbing, pulsating . . . filling the air with its sound. . . .

Then huge reports smote the ear, shattering, deafening, and the roar of falling masonry. . . . An air raid !

Mrs. Payne was on my threshold, her face ineffably tender. " Miss Pankhurst, come down to us ! " Half smiling, she reached out her arms to me : " Let us keep together ! "

I went to her from my little table in the corner. She clung to me trembling. The angry grinding still pulsated above us. Again that terrific burst of noise ; those awful bangs, the roar of the falling buildings, the rattle of shrapnel on the roof close above our heads.

" No use to worry ; only a few houses will be struck among the thousands," I rallied her gently, feeling detached from it all—and far away. The thought of the bombs crashing down on the densely populated city was appalling—yet for our household I had no least shade of apprehension—and for myself Life had no great claim. I was only a member of the salvage corps, saving and succouring as I might amid this wreckage, happy if I might aid in laying some stones to build the city of the future.

" Come down," she pleaded, in the next quiet interval. Up or down was the same in a two-storied dwelling, aged and gimcrack ; but to please her I went where she would, supporting her, for she almost failed at the stairs. Jim Payne was waiting for us below. . . . Again the huge reports, louder, yet louder ; the roar more monstrous. . . .

" Jim, go and find Miss Smyth," Mrs. Payne murmured, her voice breaking. Obediently he fetched Smyth. She had been out on the flat roof, trying to see the aeroplanes, and was eager to return. " Nonsense ! " I ordered, " do not be foolhardy ! " " This roof cannot save us if the house is struck," she protested. " I know, but you need not get shrapnel in your eyes," I answered her sharply. " Can you not hear it on the roof ? "

[1] British air raids on German towns began in September 1914. The first attempted German air raids on Britain were in December 1914. The first air raid on London was on May 31st, 1915. On October 1st, 1914, the Home Secretary had prohibited illuminated signs and directed the partial obscuring of street and shop lights. In December the lights were further dimmed, street lamps more heavily smeared with black paint, 'buses and trams lit only enough to collect fares. Street markets closed at dusk. Black curtains became the rule.

More crashes silenced us. . . . More crashes! . . . More crashes! . . . Again more crashes . . . and each more monstrous. . . . What a burst of sound, tremendous; the very earth shook with it! . . . More crashes . . . again . . . again, again. . . .

At last it was over. . . .

. . . . . . . .

Next morning there were pieces of shell on our flat roof. Swarms of children were out in the road picking up shrapnel, prizing up with impromptu tools the bits of metal which had imbedded themselves in the road.

. . . . . . . .

Anti-German rioting broke out again. Panic ran rampant. A lighted cigarette-end was enough at times to gain a man a blow. Little Minnie O'Brien, with her bent little legs and pinched face showing childhood's rickets, came crying to me to tell me her father had smacked her face when she sat playing the piano after dusk, the gas lit and the dark curtains not drawn.

. . . . . . . .

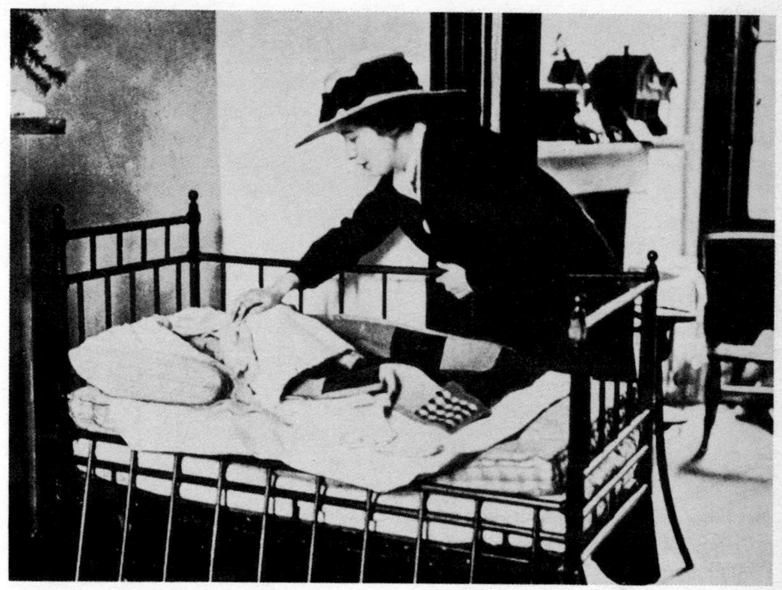

*Workers' Dreadnought*

THE OLD "GUNMAKERS' ARMS," BOW, BECOMES THE "MOTHERS' ARMS"

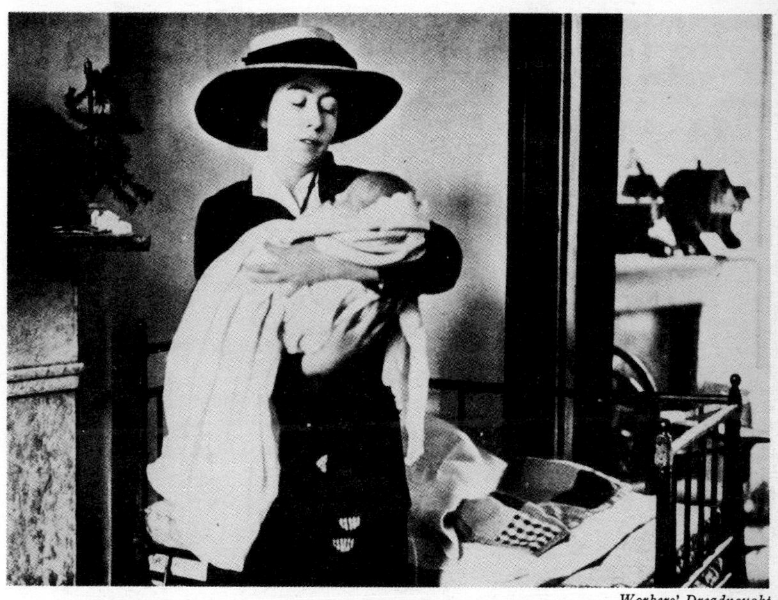

*Workers' Dreadnought*

THE AUTHOR AND ONE OF HER CHARGES

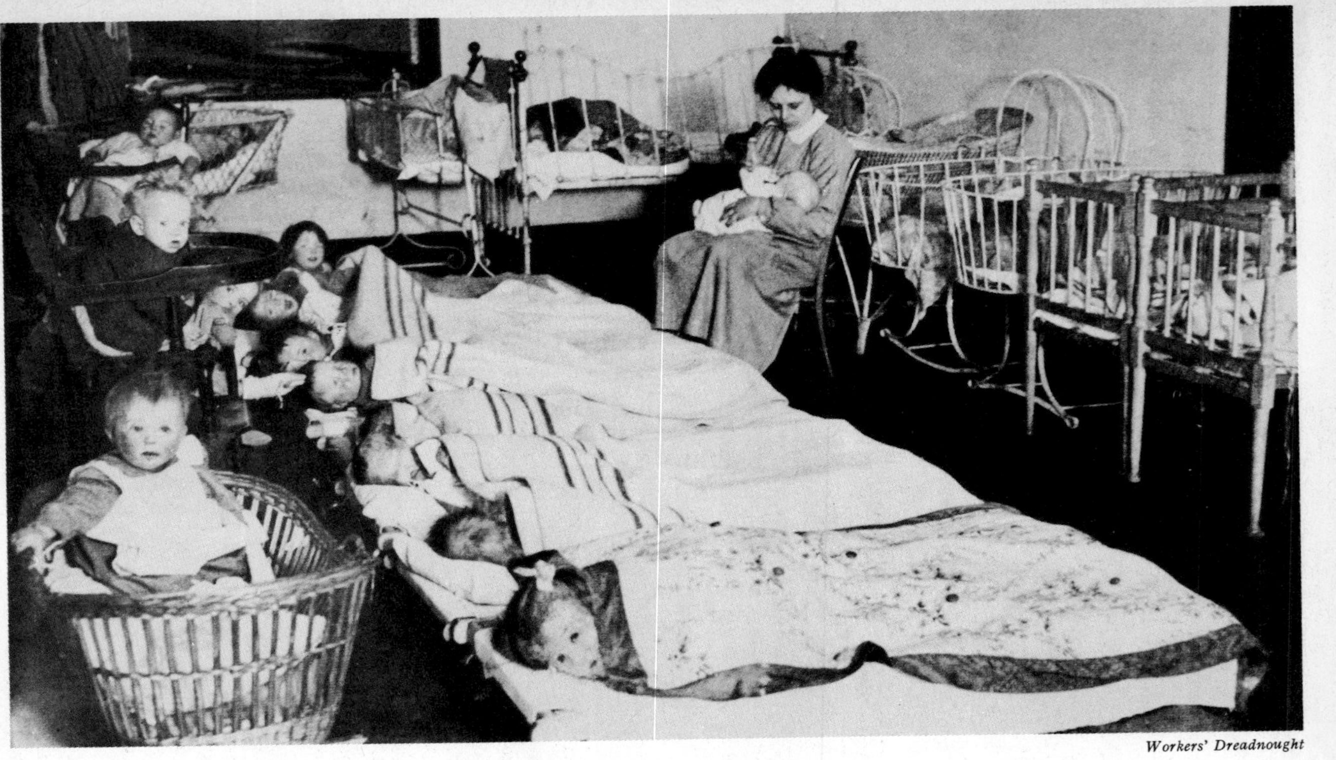

*Workers' Dreadnought*

REST HOUR AT THE "MOTHER'S ARMS"

Nurse Hebbes on duty.

To see the devastation wrought by last night's air raid unaccustomed visitors came flocking to the East End--well-dressed people in motors, journalists, photographers, high military officials, Red Cross nurses, policewomen, travellers from all over the world.

Impatient passengers on the tops of 'buses were asking before they had yet passed Bishopsgate: "Is this the East End?" Sightseers paused at Shoreditch Church because rumour declared it had been injured, though not a sign of damage was to be seen. Crowds stood with chins uncomfortably upstretched arguing whether the thin shadow cast by the lightning conductor might really be a crack. For hours a constant stream of people was passing through the churchyard, a cluster always gathering round the ancient stocks, because some lingered to looked at them from interest, and others craned over their shoulders, to see if those who paused were looking at a bomb.

Many West End folk gave up their search here and went home disappointed, yet only a stone's-throw further, in the poor alleys branching off from Hoxton Street, abundance of wreckage might be seen.

Every East End district has its own character. Bow always seemed to me the gayest, friendliest, and most colourful, Hoxton amongst the dreariest. In Hoxton Street I have more than once seen women fighting—a thing I have never witnessed in any other part of the East End.

To-day these mean streets were thronged and seething. Poor people in frowsy garments crowded the roadways and squeezed past each other in the narrow alleys. What sights for the pretty ladies in dainty dresses, craning their slender white throats from taxicab windows! What sights for the rather too generously fed business men and well-groomed officers: miserable dwellings, far from fit for human families, poorly-dressed women of working sort, with sad, worn faces; and others, sunk lower, just covered, no more, in horrid rags, hopeless, unhappy beings; half-clad, neglected little children—sadder these even than the havoc wrought by German bombs!

Streams of people led the way to the damaged buildings, a babble of talk rising incessantly: "We poor people are being made to pay for it!" . . . "Why is everything so dear?" "Potatoes . . . not fit for pigs, and such a price!" . . . "Conscription?" "What! They don't need it. They can get all the poor fellows they want without!" . . . "They put off men as always worked hard and tell 'em to give their lives!"

Crowds mostly made up of women gathered before each ruined home. One, where a child had been killed, was still inhabited. A soldier in khaki stood at the door striving in vain to keep back the press of human bodies surging against it. The people who lived there were scarcely able to force a way to their own door. A bomb had descended upon a brewery; from the roof to the cellar all had fallen, only the outer walls remained, and a mass of charred wood in the basement. Many dwellings were thus completely gutted. In the ashes left by the fires which had ravaged them nothing save the twisted ironwork of the bedsteads could be identified. A chorus of wailing stirred amongst the women: "Oh, my God! Look at the home! Oh, my God!"

Rumour raced hot-foot: "There were little lights signalling: telling them where to drop the bombs!" . . . "Germans!" . . . "Beasts." "Germans!" . . . "I saw taxi-cabs driving up and down signalling!" . . . "Germans!" . . .

"They should all have been cleared out at the beginning of the War!" . . . "The Government has nowhere to put them!" . . . "They go and give themselves up to the police and they tell them to go home. . . . Everywhere a bomb is dropped you'll find one of their shops was wrecked near!"

Alas, where in the East End would one fail to find a German shop which had been wrecked in the anti-German riots? Near to the brewery was a baker's shop with a German name on the fascia; the door, the shutters, the very window-frames had been torn off. It was boarded up now with new, unpainted wood. The crowds as they passed it growled imprecations; wild stories grew there. . . .

In Hoxton Street was a rush of excitement. A German baker's, one of the few still remaining, had just been raided. "They were serving bread there an hour ago!" a surprised voice uttered. "They go in to buy bread from them, and then they wreck the shop," another answered. The windows were smashed, only a few jagged bits of glass still attached to the framework. The pavement was littered with glass and flour. The shop had been cleared of everything portable. A policeman stood at the door. Two soldiers came out laughing. "There is plenty of new bread downstairs if you want it; it will only be wasted there!" they called as they went off seeking new quarry.

Down the street police whistles sounded vociferously: a babel of shouting, tremendous outcry. A crowd was advancing at a run, a couple of lads on bicycles leading, a swarm of children on the fringes, screaming like gulls. Missiles were flying. In the centre of the turmoil men dragged a big, stout man, stumbling and resisting in their grasp, his clothes whitened by flour, his mouth dripping blood. They rushed him on. New throngs closed round him. . . .

From another direction arose more shouting. A woman's scream. The tail of the crowd dashed off towards the sound. Crowds raced to it from all directions. . . . fierce, angry shouts and yells. . . . A woman was in the midst of a struggling mob; her blouse half torn off, her fair hair fallen, her face contorted with pain and terror, blood running down her bare white arm. A big drunken man flung her to the ground. She was lost to sight. . . . "Oh, my God! Oh! They are kicking her!" a woman screamed.

"Do help her!" I pleaded with a soldier who stood watching. He shrugged his shoulders. "I can't do anything." "You are a soldier; they will respect you!" "Why should I?" he asked with a curl of the lip. "Look, there's another soldier: can't you get on to *him*?"

" She is covered with blood ! " a woman's voice cried again. I struggled to reach her, but the closely-packed onlookers would not make way for me. An Army motor drove up and was halted by the press. An officer, hawk-eyed, aquiline, sat in the front ; there were vacant seats behind. I sprang to the step : " A woman is being hurt here. Will you take her away from the crowd ? " " I don't think we can ; we are on military business," he answered curtly. The horn was sounded, the people made way, the car drove on. . . .

The woman on the ground was unconscious. Those who a moment before had shrieked imprecations, were seized with pity. The nearest raised her and rested her on a fruiterer's upturned barrel. A couple of women supported her with their arms ; another was fastening up her hair. She drooped, still nerveless, her colour gone, her eyes closed. They chafed her hands, the crowd about them silent and awed. Passion was spent. " I believe in all things being done in a proper manner." " Killing the woman won't do any good ! " Two voices were heard. . . .

" Make a way there ! Make a way there ! Move on ! Move on ! " the police came shouting and pushing through the throng, hustling away with equal roughness the onlookers, the fainting woman and those who bore her.

Another mob swept round the corner, hot in fury, baiting a man in flour-covered clothing, wrenched and jerked by the collar, thumped on the back, kicked from the rear. " All right, Gov'ner ; all right," he articulated between the blows, in humble and reasoning Cockney-tones fully typic as that of his assailants. Alas, poor Patriotism, what foolish cruelties are committed in thy name !

. . . . . . . .

That night as I sat writing a shrieking crowd ran by in the dark under my window. "We want more bread! We want more bread!" a menacing cry. I looked out on a mass of hurrying figures. Amongst them a face turned toward me uplit by the light of my window, convulsed with rage, the face of a poor little dwarf woman, feeble, misshapen, who had come to us for relief. . . .

At the door below came an urgent knocking, knock! knock! knock! without pause, in desperate haste. I rushed to open. A man in his shirt sleeves, white and haggard, fell in, a small man with one leg deformed, so that he limped badly. He blurted a plea to telephone, and as I took him upstairs, told me he was from the baker's shop a few doors away, and born in London, though his old parents had come from Germany half a century before. A mob had come to raid them, and he wanted to telephone to the police to protect the old people. I helped him to find the number and left him, but presently I heard him cry out: "They only laugh at me!"

I rang through to the Bow police again; and giving my name, asked for the chief. When I reproached him, he offered excuses: "I am unable to do anything. Our men are absolutely powerless." "You did not say that when you were trying to catch me under the Cat and Mouse Act," I answered. "I was king in my own country then. Now I have to follow instructions." A strange reply. Finally he promised a couple of plain clothes officers on bicycles, and asked me to come out to speak to them to avert the resentment of the people. Whilst we debated, the lame man had slipped out again, and now returned in grievous despair, for the people were sacking his home, and his parents had disappeared. He limped away in the darkness to seek them. The plain clothes policemen arrived, but immediately mounted their cycles and rode away.

I went into the road to speak to the people, but my words died on my lips. I had no heart to plead with these poor mad creatures, seized with this scarcity-born rage of loot. It seemed as though Poverty itself were personified and were rushing to plunder—unheeding as the sea.

The air was filled by the babble of voices, and the noise of knocking and splintering wood. Men were lowering a piano through the window. The dwarf woman ran by, dragging a polished table. She rammed it against the pavement in her haste—a leg of the table was smashed, the top was split. Discarding the broken trophy she ran back to secure another. A woman and her children raced off with an easy-chair, rushing it along on its castors before them. "I shall sit, and sit, and sit on this chair all day," the mother yelled. "I never had an arm-chair to sit in before!"

"Bread!" "Bread!" "Bread!" the shrieks rang out. Women and children rushed by, their arms and aprons laden with loaves.

When the premises had been cleared, the mounted police rode up—to protect the property of the landlord. They galloped around in the dark and silent street.

. . . . . . . .

Looting continued with impunity for days, incited and organised by certain jingo factions. Men unknown in the district, with hatchets on their shoulders, marched through Bethnal Green Road, Green Street, the Roman Road to the very end. Wherever a shop had a German name over it they stopped and hacked down the shutters and broke the glass. Then crowds of children rushed in and looted. When darkness fell and the police made no sign, men and women joined in the sack.

Only when English shopkeepers contiguous to the Germans began to suffer, did the police begin to interfere. Mainwaring's boot shop in the Roman Road got its window broken through proximity to a German's, and a swarm of children made off with the stock. A boy employed in our toy factory boasted there that he had taken some of the boots. On learning of it, I sent for him, and told him that if I heard such a thing of him again I would send him away. Before leaving me he appeared to agree that it was cowardly to rob defenceless people who were persecuted for no fault of their own. An hour or two later his mother came to me, a fiery-faced termagant, denouncing me as a German, and threatening to scratch my face.

Still the rioting continued, first the German bakers, then any shop of any sort with a foreign name.

" Intern them all ! " " Intern them all ! " the cry was not abated. The looting continued. " They are going to do in the German public houses next ! " One heard the talk of it in the streets spreading from mouth to mouth, none could tell the originator. In this way the news of the previous riots had been conveyed. The men with the hatchets would come again. " To-night they are coming ! " everyone said.

This must not be, I thought; it was bad enough when they were sober; it will be hideous when they are drunk. I telephoned to the local police: had they been warned? Were they preparing? They averred they were powerless. I telephoned to Scotland Yard, was referred from one department to another, met by this official with jocularity, by that with bored indifference. I telephoned to the House of Commons, met tedious delays: Member after Member unobtainable. At last, W. C. Anderson came to my call. He was impressed and serious: he would go immediately to Scotland Yard and do whatever might be required. That night the mounted police were cantering about the district. The crowds were out, but nothing of moment happened. The men with hatchets did not come. The rioting was put an end to for a space.

. . . . . . . . .

The West Ham Guardians reported that rioting in their area had been so serious that a rate of 3s. in the £ would be needed to meet the damage. There were demands that the estates of those who had incited the outbreak should be attacked. Everyone knew that nothing would come of that. Almost all the rioters went scot-free; but a few of the people who had taken part in the looting were charged with theft. In one case five policemen were implicated.

## CHAPTER XXV

### WOMEN'S WAR SERVICE—RIVAL DEMANDS—LLOYD GEORGE AND MRS. PANKHURST—THE EAST END PROTEST—THE MUNITIONS ACT AT WORK

THE Coalition Government had started off ostensibly with the support and good will of all parties; but this was by no means the case. Many were determined to be rid of Asquith, and his nearest colleagues. The surrender of Haldane, who had been awarded the Order of Merit on his retirement, had by no means placated them. Agitations blustered against the Government, demanding increased stringency of the blockade, and especially that cotton should be declared contraband, let the United States say what it would; the banishment of all persons of German birth or descent from the Government service; above all, Conscription—military and industrial.

Out of 27,241 women who had by this time registered for War service, only 2,332 had been given work. Propaganda was insistent to get women into the munition factories, and every sort of work ordinarily performed by men. The sections clamouring for the military conscription of men saw in the industrial service of women a means to their end. Feminists who were advocates of Conscription for men believed themselves adding to the importance of women by demanding that women also should be conscripts.

The reawakened W.S.P.U. was loudest in the demand for "compulsory national service for men and women alike"; "Women demand the right to help in saving the country!" Lloyd George now possessed the implicit confidence of his old enemies Christabel and Mrs. Pankhurst; he was cheerfully disposed to accept their services. He agreed to receive a women's War Service deputation, to be organised by them on Saturday, July 17th; and to review a great procession which was to march with it. He promised finance for the show out of Government funds, and placed the official War Service registers at the disposal of the W.S.P.U. The Press boomed the function as a national event. Women with handbills advertising it were rushing round the East End. A letter signed E. Pankhurst, calling women to the War Service demonstration, was mistaken by some in our district as an appeal from me. That cut me to the quick; for my struggle was to prevent the exploitation of the people in the interests of the War.

Old militants of the W.S.P.U., who had suffered the hunger strike and been forcibly fed, were now interrupting its meetings with cries of "Votes for Women." Members of our Federation joined in the heckling. I did not want that; I desired our women to employ themselves in constructive effort, not in the fruitless decrying of those once our comrades, who had departed, as we considered, from progressive paths. If we must attack, let us attack the Government which held the power. At our members' general meeting I got a resolution passed that it was no part of our policy to interrupt the meetings of other Suffrage Societies.

Yet I could not rest content that this jingo demonstration, with its demand for compulsory War service, should stand forth unchallenged as representing the womanhood of the nation. Still less could I let pass, without protest, the new legislation which was so adversely determining the industrial position of women in war time. Our Federation also demanded an interview with Lloyd George and arranged a procession to Parliament for the night of Tuesday, July 20th. "*No National Service under Makers of Private Profit!*" "*Down with sweating!*" "*A Man's Wage for a Man's Job!*" "*Down with High Prices and Big Profits!*" Such were our slogans.

Lloyd George refused to receive us, but many both Labour and Liberal Members of Parliament urged us to persevere, including J. R. Clynes, though he was one of the greatest jingoes in the Labour Party, and Philip Snowden, who wrote:

"The fight is awfully hard, I know; but you are doing magnificent work."

How greatly subsequent events were to alter his political attitude!

The big W.S.P.U. procession was produced according to promise. Boomed as it was, it could not have been otherwise. There were two miles of closely massed ranks, a pageant of the nations, led by Belgium with bare feet in sandals bearing a tattered flag. There were representations of the trades and professions in which women were called upon to serve. Women who had registered for War work and could not get it, munition workers and trainees released from the grind of their seven days' work that they might march, warmongers, war workers and sightseers, office and shop girls who had stayed in town to see the fun, soldiers' wives out for a jaunt, women of all sorts and conditions fell in behind the banners and bands, and sang the popular war-songs, "Tipperary" and all the rest. The procession was lauded as a magnificent achievement, and a proof of the enthusiasm of women for the National Cause.

The significant fact remained that the organisation of this demonstration had been paid for by the Government; whereas in the pre-War struggle of the Suffragettes larger and more elaborate demonstrations had been financed by the enthusiasts of the movement itself. Where were those enthusiasts now? Scattered in a hundred directions. Even in the thinned ranks of those who remained supporters of the W.S.P.U. in its changed policy, there was not the disposition to sacrifice all for the Union, which had made it a power in its Votes for Women fight.

Lloyd George received the deputation in the wooden buildings erected for the Ministry of Munitions in the Embankment Gardens, and he and Mrs. Pankhurst went together on to the balcony to speak to the women outside. There was mutual praise and laudation. Mrs. Pankhurst said that the women munitioners should have equal pay with men. Cases of sweating had been brought to her notice and she knew that Mr. Lloyd George did not want that. Having just put through the Munitions Act from which equal pay for women had been deliberately excluded, he repeated to her the pledge he had made to me, and assured her that the munition factories would be controlled and the Government would see that there was no sweated labour.

The *Suffragette*, the lynx-eyed organ of the W.S.P.U., which prided itself on its ability to discern and unmask the subterfuges of politicians, received the evasion complacently :

"Our opinion is that we must see how these assurances work out in practice, and any complaint or criticism made before that would be unreasonable, destructive and injurious."

Yet the sweating was flagrantly obvious to all who cared to look for it ! It was all for the War, and the War before all with the W.S.P.U. !

I wrote immediately to Lloyd George :

"SIR,

"Your reply to the W.S.P.U. deputation is highly unsatisfactory, because, on the Government's behalf, you still refuse to women the same pay as the men whom they replace, except where the women are employed on piecework rates. The women are *not* being employed on piece rates, but on time rates. Therefore safeguards in regard to piece rates do not apply to them. In the case of the unskilled man provision is made that he shall receive the same rates, whether by time or piece, as the skilled man whom he may replace.

"You say that the women are not yet trained, but you do not give any promise that they are to be put on piece-work rates after a definite period has elapsed.

"You say that the Government will see to it that there shall be 'no sweating,' and that the wages paid to women in munitions factories shall be fair. (I see that you say nothing about a fair minimum wage on other Government work where gross sweating prevails.)

"But what do you mean by fair wages ? Do you mean the 3½d. and 2½d. per hour, which the Wages Boards have fixed, in order slightly to improve conditions in the notoriously sweated trades ?

"The work the women are asked to do in the munition factories has been one of the better paid trades for men. Are women to receive only the sweated Wages Board rates for it ?

"At Vickers in Sheffield, the women are paid from 8s. to 14s. a week. At Vickers in Erith the middle-class women who are being trained there are to receive 15s. 6d. for a 54 hour week.

"The Government has refused to interfere with the law of supply and demand where the buying and selling of food is concerned. Under that law, cruel and hard as it is, the high cost of living would be neutralised to a certain extent by rising wages, procured through the efforts of the workers to save themselves from starvation, and by the tendency toward a shortage of labour which the War will create.

" The Government refuses to interfere with the law of supply and demand in keeping down high prices; but, by compulsory arbitration and forced labour, it nullifies the law of supply and demand where wages are concerned. To starve the people is a short-sighted policy!

" I again call on you to receive the deputation which will march to see you on Tuesday night. . . ."

I received a reply that Lloyd George had left for Wales. I urged that he should appoint another Minister to receive us in his stead, but received no answer.

Opposing the great engines of war propaganda, as we were, with only the contributions of a small knot of enthusiasts to assist us in printing handbills to make our procession known, we could not hope that night to rival the great sightseers' carnival of the Saturday afternoon. With the factories working overtime, the home workers held more rigidly than ever to their sweated toil by the rising cost of living, the procession surprised me by its size and stirred my heart by its earnestness. The Old Ford Road was alive with the hurrying people. The workers were hastening straight from the factories to march in the ranks, or if they could not march, at least to give the marchers a cheer.

" We would come with you if we could!" many women called to us. " I wish I could come, but I am too old, too tired, too worn out with standing all day—my feet are too sore!—I am almost dropping with coming this far to see you!" " I must run home to the children; they have missed me all day; but I came to see you start. I wish I could come!" " Good luck!" " Good luck!" " Bravo!" and " Bless you all!"

Yet thousands came with us, facing the long march to Westminster after their twelve-hour working day without even staying to get a bite. Some joined our six-deep ranks; some went beside us on the pavement, " Because my boots are so bad, and the sets in the road hurt my feet." Folk thronged the roadway from kerb to kerb, because the police charges of recent, pre-war remembrance, made our East End crowds prefer to mass together in a swarm. Many of the women were carrying babies, some pushing a child or two in a perambulator. The colour-bearer took us along so fast that many could not keep up, and were left behind. Yet more held on, swollen feet, varicose ulcers, prolapses and poor health notwithstanding. They were marching for vital needs, and their hearts were full. They carried the banners bravely, though the strong wind tugged at them. A woman told me that she had gone to join the Saturday procession; but she had bought our *Dreadnought* from a paper seller on the Embankment; and on reading it, had left those ranks, convinced that her place was with the workers' procession on Tuesday night. She was making packing cases at Dingwall's from 8.30 a.m. to 7 p.m. for 12s. a week. The man she had replaced got 35s. Home workers spoke of the poor price they got for making and finishing soldiers' garments; a mother with little children to maintain got only 3d. for stitching 54 buttons on soldiers' trousers. These women were not urging a point of which they had read in books or heard on platforms; they were the sweated workers come to plead their own cause.

The Bethnal Green contingent awaited us with a big crowd assembled to wish them luck, and the faithful "Cowboys" band, with their fifes and drums, who had rallied to us in many a Suffragette display. It was dark when we met the Poplar procession at Gardiner's corner. Girls from the biscuit and provision factories, dockers and gas workers with the red regalia of their Union, members of the League of Rights for Soldiers' and Sailors' Wives and Relatives, known by their regalia, "Suffragette Crusaders" from South-East London, militants who had broken away from the war party, with their gold and purple banners. Masses of people cheered and waved to us. Mounted police galloped around us, their horses rearing.

We might not approach within a mile of Parliament during its session, and therefore broke our ranks at the Gaiety Theatre. It was now half-past ten, but many pressed on still to the Central Hall, Westminster, and filled it to overflowing.

A deputation had hurried forward to the House of Commons. It was met by friendly Members of Parliament, who, against the adverse tide of jingoism and war fever, were clinging to the principles they had cherished during peace. They brought out Gulland, the Government's Chief Whip, to speak to our women, and some of the Members came round to the Central Hall to urge us to persevere.

We were a large company walking home through the dark streets to the East End that night; with all the power in the land against us, high-hearted in our crusade.

I wrote next day that our elected deputation of nine women would wait on Lloyd George at the Ministry of Munitions the following Tuesday morning. On the appointed day nine of us arrived. We were flouted by the porters and ignored by the Ministry. We spent the greater part of the day in the entrance hall, alternately sending up notes to the secretary, and being ordered away by a factotum in uniform who frequently threatened to call the police. We were undismayed and were all in the greatest good-humour. Mrs. Cressall of Poplar—she became a Borough Councillor after the War—had brought her baby Charlie, who gurgled and laughed at us.

Finally a promise was verbally conveyed by one of his secretaries that Lloyd George would see us the following week.

Accepting the promise as *bona fide*, we were preparing to leave, when the secretary came after us saying that he had arranged for tea to be made for us. Not wishing to rebuff a kind impulse, I thanked him and accepted his offer on the others' behalf. "We have a room here," said the secretary, opening a door. We entered, descending a step or two. To my surprise we found ourselves in a bare little kitchen where some men-servants were at tea. "So this is the hospitality thought proper for a deputation of working women!" I thought with amusement. "I suppose they have abolished the drawing-room as a war economy!" I said to my companions, and they and the servants all laughed merrily.

The promise that Lloyd George would see us the following week was not kept. August passed, September wore on; still, though we pressed him continually, he procrastinated.

Mary Macarthur, as Hon. Secretary of the Central Committee for Women's Employment, had repudiated our demand for £1 a week minimum for women in the relief workrooms. As leader of the National Federation of Women Workers, she and her colleagues had opposed the handful of us who had striven in vain to commit the trade union movement to a clear-cut insistence upon equal payment of the worker, irrespective of sex. She was now constantly giving publicity to hideous exploitation of women and girls: women working 83 hours a week for 2¼d. per hour, girls of thirteen years working from 7 a.m. to 9 p.m. for a mere pittance.

Now that the value of the £ was admittedly less than the pre-war 14s., she and other Trade Union officials, who were received by Dr. Addison on September 8th, proposed £1 a week as a minimum wage for women, not in the relief workrooms, but in the hard and dangerous toil of the munition factory. Only now, at long last, had they come to the point of naming a minimum, and even now they could not bring themselves to demand for women the minimum which was being paid in the munition factories to men.

Again we presented ourselves at the Munitions Office, and received there a telegram from Lloyd George that he had been called to the country. Two days later we were there again, and at length received a definite appointment.

When the day came we found, not Lloyd George, but Dr. Addison and a number of "experts." We had already twice refused to meet Dr. Addison as Lloyd George's deputy, but now it was urgent to state our case. My mind, moreover, revolted at the thought of wasting any more time in chasing the prevaricating Lloyd George. Anticipating that he might again default, I had drawn up a statement covering the points we desired to raise. Herein was quoted the statement of Sir William Beardmore that the work of the women in his munition factory was "just as good and just as speedy as that of men."

From all over the country we cited authentic wages scales: Waring & Gillow paying 3½d. an hour to women, 9d. to men for military tent making; the Hendon aeroplane works paying women 3d. per hour, at work for which men got 10d. per hour; women booking clerks at Victoria Station getting 15s. a week, though the men they replaced got 35s.; and so on, in district after district, trade after trade. The majority of the women war workers on time rates were getting from 6s. to 18s. per week, a relatively small number on piece rates making from 6s. to 7s. a week to £1 or £1 5s. 0d. Firms like Bryant and May's, the match makers, were now making munitions. Accustomed to employ large numbers of women and girls at ill-paid work, they knew by long experience that piece rates would secure them a higher production than could be induced by a bonus. Without a care for pre-war standards, in a trade new to their factory, they had fixed for munition work, often perilous and heavy, similar sweated piece rates to those paid for matches.

I told Dr. Addison that when I had published, under the heading, "Records of Disgraceful Sweating," the fact that Maconochies in their East End works were employing women at 13s. 9d. for a 55 hour week, pushing trucks weighing 50 to 75 lbs., the firm had protested that 13s. 9d. was "the recognised Government rate of pay for a 55 hour week." A copy of that letter I left for Lloyd George to study for himself.

Mrs. Cressall said that her husband had worked in a white lead works for seventeen years—a dangerous trade in which the workers ran the risk of a serious form of industrial poisoning. His wage was 26s. for a 60 hour week; a starvation wage. This firm was now gradually discharging men and replacing them by boys at 17s. a week. Other such firms were employing women at a still lower wage.

We left reminders that women and girls were still working both by night and day on 12 hour shifts, and that many girls fell asleep on the night shift. Mrs. Leigh Rothwell of the National Federation of Women Workers, who was with us, cited instances of women at that time working from 7.30 a.m. to 11 p.m.[1] and of women standing at work all day on floors covered with water, for lack of the little care which would have provided a grating to raise them above the wet.

We complained of the injurious working of the Munitions Tribunals. Men employed under the Trade Union rate of pay were appealing to the tribunals for leave to go where they would get the standard rate of wages and were meeting with refusals, workers were appealing in vain for leaving certificates, though the firms for which they were nominally working had nothing for them to do.

Dr. Addison told us that the Munitions Department had all the problems we had mentioned "acutely in mind"; and as soon as it had time to do so, it would set up excellent conditions for the workers. His promise carried no conviction; we knew that the war machine would grind on without heed, and that only by strenuous agitation would the smallest ameliorations be secured for the poor drudges who served it.

. . . . . . . .

[1] It was disclosed in the House of Commons that thousands of boys from 14 to 16 years were working from 8 p.m. to 8 a.m. on night duty at Woolwich Arsenal. Many of them lived long distances from their work.

The National Register was in being. Clearly I could not sign it. For me that would be an act of treachery to conviction. I could not give my name to aid the slaughter in this war, fought on both sides for grossly material ends, which did not justify the sacrifice of a single mother's son. Clearly I must continue to oppose it, and expose it, to all whom I could reach with voice or pen. Clearly I must declare that the "National Service" in industry the Government was proposing, was not the collective action of a free people agreeing on equal terms to subordinate their individual ends for the common weal, but the enslavement of the many for the profit of the few.

Yet I was surrounded by masses of poor women who had taken war work, soldiers' clothes and equipment, munitions, whatever came, as the sole means of keeping them and theirs from starvation. Inevitably they passed to war work as peace employment failed. For these women the fight against sweating must be maintained. I announced my own refusal to sign the Register and urged all who had decided to take war work under the Register to stipulate for the standard rate of wages hitherto paid for the job, with the war increases or bonuses paid in the case of men.

Smyth and I and some others of our Federation in the East End who refused registration went scot-free in respect of penalties. We were told that the officials at the Town Hall had filled up the forms for us to avoid trouble. That may have been so, and I can believe that some of the Councillors helped to supply the particulars; but naturally we had no certificates of registration, and when, later in the War, certain articles of food were rationed, we received no ration tickets. We counted it a little price to pay for our convictions. Some registration resisters up and down the country were left unmolested, but some were fined and had their goods distrained. Some were sent to gaol, though the Act made no mention of imprisonment. One of these was James Sellar, who had come from Australia as a boy to escape compulsory military training on concientious grounds. Mrs. Girdlestone, the wife of a Bristol clergyman, was sent to prison for fourteen days. She hunger-struck and forcible feeding was decided on, though her heart and lungs were defective. Her doctor, however, paid her fine. Mrs. Garner, one of our members, was ordered five weeks' imprisonment. Alice Heale, an old member of the W.S.P.U., on refusal to sign the register, was discharged by the magistrate as a "pauper lunatic" and committed to the care of her sister. Miss K. A. Raleigh, another Suffragette, was fined because she had entered "Members of Parliament" as persons partially dependent on her, had stated she would only undertake war work if paid a man's wage for it, and that she considered women ought to have the vote.

Already young men who opposed the War were banding themselves together to oppose conscription. Stanley Rogers, the secretary of the Letchworth Anti-Conscription League, was imprisoned for refusing to register.

Conscription was drawing near; and the meaning of the National Register was made clear by Lord Kitchener:[1]

"When this registration is completed we shall be able to note the men between the ages of 19 and 40 not required for munition work; and therefore available, if physically fit, for the fighting line."

The Registrar-General had issued instructions that the forms for men between the ages of 18 and 41 should be copied on special pink forms, for the use of the officer commanding the regimental depot of the district.

. . . . . . . .

The Munitions Act was being rigorously applied. A fitter was fined £3 and costs at Wood Green Police Court for leaving his employment. In Glasgow, where industrial rebels were supposed to be plentiful as gooseberries, the Central Munitions Tribunal fined 17 workmen, who dared to strike, £10 each with the alternative of 30 days' imprisonment. An apprentice plater failed to obtain from the Munitions Tribunal permission to transfer to new employment, though his previous employers, James Fullerton & Co., of Paisley, had refused to restart him. He had left them and obtained work elsewhere because they were paying him less than the standard rate, but they had followed him up and procured his dismissal by another firm because he had left them without permission. Though Fullerton's would not take him back, the Munitions Act enabled them to punish the apprentice by keeping him unemployed for six weeks. It was all for the War, of course; but the interests of the employing class were by no means forgotten! At Armstrong Whitworth's in Manchester 151 men were discharged from the armour plate department, whilst the leaving certificates enabling them to accept work offered to them elsewhere were withheld. They appealed to the Munitions Tribunal for certificates permitting them to work elsewhere, but their case was shelved, lest the employer might possibly require them later.

At Cammell Laird's in Liverpool excessively long hours were being worked. It was common for a man to begin at 6 or 8 a.m. on Saturday, work through the day and after a couple of hours off go on night duty. Then after another short rest he would be expected to go on day duty till 8 p.m. on Sunday. If these exhausted workers were late on Monday morning, they were "docked a quarter," and reported for loss of time. The firm complained to the Munitions Tribunal that their 10,000 men had lost 1,500,000 hours in twenty weeks. The offenders were permitted not a word in their defence, but fined from 5s. to 60s. each. They cried out in their indignation that there would be a revolution in the country, and were ordered to leave the court; they went with defiant cheers.

The Munitions Act was being used to prevent workers from changing

[1] Speech at Guildhall, London, July 9th, 1915.

their employment in order to secure higher wages, or positions of greater responsibility, or to obtain work nearer home, or in another district in view of family responsibilities. Leaving certificates were refused when the work was proving prejudicial to the health of the worker and where the character of the work had been changed and the worker found the new machinery unmanageable or injurious.

. . . . . . . .

Shell-making had become the latest Society craze ; a ghastly sport indeed ! The Hillman Motor Company opened a factory for teaching "ladies with a few hours leisure." One hundred and twenty of them were to be accommodated, and it was hoped by their united efforts the weekly output would reach one shell per lady !

A band of leisured women were being trained at Erith to give week-end relief to the ordinary workers at Vickers who were toiling away continuously for 8s. to 14s. a week. For the well-to-do trainees a charming house had been lent by war enthusiasts, where board and service were provided for 15s. 6d. a week, their stipend during training being 15s. 6d. to 19s. 6d. Presently such well-to-do women were put in as overlookers at superior wages to supervise the ordinary worker.

The *Manchester Guardian* recorded the story of a lady of title who, having become a munitionette, gave a dinner-party to celebrate her first month of productive work. The guests were a duchess, the wife of a Cabinet Minister, and a working woman, introduced as "Mabel, my mate in the shop." The hostess and her "mate" wore print dresses with handkerchiefs swathed about their heads, their working uniform. The table was covered with oilcloth. The dinner was brought in by a maid, the hostess carved, the guests helped themselves to the vegetables. "The simple life," said the hostess. "Mabel and I only get fifteen bob a week and it won't run to more." The butler, as she gaily explained later, had been sent to the theatre "to get him out of the way." What fun indeed for the titled few—and behind it the trenches. What ghoulish sport !

. . . . . . . .

In the cotton trade the employers had refused the workers a 5 per cent. increase in wages, to aid them in meeting the enhanced cost of living. Yet Lloyd George was appealing to the cotton operatives to agree to come under the compulsion of the Munitions Act on account of the huge quantities of cotton goods the Government was requiring for the War. The great majority of the operatives had always been women ; the withdrawal of men for the Army thus affected the cotton industry less than others. To secure more cheap labour, the employers were demanding that children should begin work as half-timers at eleven years, instead of at twelve ; and as full-timers at twelve years, instead of at thirteen.

. . . . . . . .

As the War progressed trade after trade was put under the Munitions Act. Employers were eager to seize the powers it gave them. In 1916 a woman came to me who had been making military tents at Groom's, in Limehouse, and earned 23s. to 24s. a week. She was transferred to the making of garments for men civilians, on which she could earn only 11s. or 12s. Unwilling to accept such a pittance, she left the factory and applied for work to the Government-appointed Metropolitan Munitions Committee at Park Royal, Acton, set up to facilitate the recruitment of women for munition work. There she was told that she could not be given employment unless her late employer would release her. Groom's refused to consent. There seemed no alternative for the woman, save to return to Groom's, or remain unemployed for six weeks. She came to me for advice. I telephoned to the Munitions Office, giving all particulars and urging that discharge certificates were not required by women employed in the clothing trade. The official to whom I spoke, admitted that Groom's was not a controlled factory, but declared the question of discharge certificates so complicated that no opinion could be expressed in this case. By dint of persistence, I secured an interview between the officials at the Munitions Office and the woman concerned. They sent her back to me, with an involved communication, stating that if the woman found it difficult to get work without a discharge certificate, she might apply to a Tribunal; but that it was doubtful whether a Tribunal had jurisdiction "in cases where the applicant is not employed in an establishment falling within the Minister's orders." The Minister's own headquarters, the Munitions Office, was not prepared to say. A memorandum enumerating the classes of work in which leaving certificates were required was enclosed, in order that I might decide for myself whether the applicant belonged to any such class. The Munitions Office refused to take the responsibility of deciding. If the woman found further difficulty in getting employment, however, permission was given for her to show this most evasive communication to any prospective employer. For that purpose it might be regarded as an official letter.

Thus they were winning the war to end war!

## CHAPTER XXVI

### "EAT LESS MEAT"

MCKENNA, the new Chancellor of the Exchequer, announced that the War was costing more than £3,000,000 a day, which must be met by " our own domestic economies." War propaganda increased and grew more costly. Ladies of title took pledges to abstain from luxuries, " as far as possible." Rich men were tempted to patriotism by expensive dinners with which war loan vouchers were given away. Even in the East End, patriotic meetings were held to urge the working classes to self-denial.

The Board of Trade called on the public to eat less meat. Runciman circularised the secretaries of women's societies, asking us to impress this appeal upon our members, and offering to pay the cost of summoning meetings for this purpose. A general meeting of our East End members replied to him that the average working woman house-keeper could not introduce further economies without injury to the physique of her family, and that the majority of our members were only able to purchase meat for their families once a week.

The Coal Committee appointed by the Government declared that the price of coal was unjustifiably high. We demanded the national control of coal under the supervision of a committee, composed in one third of working women housewives, one third experts, and one third organised workers in the trade, and the establishment of similar committees to safeguard the supplies of food and milk.

The Parliamentary reports made sordid reading, crammed as they were with stories of hardship and corruption brought to light by the questions of Members, who told of soldiers' camps understocked, of other camps overstocked ; of bread, biscuits and bully beef thrown into the sea, used for kindling fires and mending roads, sold by pilfering officials ; of boots and clothing stolen and thrown away, and rifles burnt for firewood ; of fuses costing 15s. each, though French fuses of superior pattern cost only 7s. 6d. Members declared that the business men of the country were " sick " of the laxity and incompetence of War Office methods. A Member reported the lordly insistence of some official upon paying an account " in gross," though the manufacturer had sent in a reduced account giving credit for returned empties. One Member even went so far as to declare it necessary that two or three of the principal War Office incompetents should be hung in Whitehall as a warning to the rest.

Revelations in regard to meat, wheat, freight and munitions constantly appeared. We called for people's auditors, to investigate Government war expenditure, popularly elected, like the citizens' auditors of some of the great towns. At all times such auditors would exercise a valuable check on official probity.

The rise in prices was accelerated by huge Government purchases for the Army and Navy. On the fact being disclosed, the Government admitted that it had bought thousands of tons of Australian corned beef at 8¼d. per lb., though the average price in the London meat market per dozen 6-lb. tins was only 5¾d. per lb. Dr. Macnamara, however, declared the price paid by the Government " not unreasonable." Government buyers expected to pay high prices, and patriotic vendors were eager that they should. Patriotic farmers, foreseeing a shortage of low-priced labour, reduced their crops. Patriotic stock raisers, seeing the cost of fodder rise and anxious to profit to-day by the boom in the price of meat, killed off their stock, not scrupling to slaughter large numbers of cows in calf. It was reported that many poor beasts gave birth in the slaughter-house and that calves were taken alive from their mothers just killed.

Immediately after the declaration of war, Acts designed to safeguard the purity of the milk supply were passed into law. On June 22nd, 1915, an Act was passed postponing these safeguards. A committee of enquiry under Lord Milner and Lord Inchcape was now appointed to safeguard home food production. It contained but one representative of Labour and not a single woman.

Runciman told the Commons that he had made a very hard bargain for the carriage of frozen meat from the Argentine, and expressed the hope that he might be " exculpated from any moral guilt " since he had acted in the public interest. It transpired that the rates secured by Runciman under this " hard bargain " were actually higher than the contract prices private firms were arranging for themselves. A committee, mainly composed of shipowners, with Lord Inchcape, the chairman of the P. and O. Shipping Company, had been appointed to advise the Government what compensation it should pay to the owners whose ships were taken over by the Government. With Runciman of the great shipping family as President of the Board of Trade, their interests were in safe custody !

Dr. Macnamara told a meeting of East End munition workers that there was " no room for the man who desires more to make his bit than to do his bit ! " Yet that very week the *Manchester Guardian* published the fact that whilst the freight charge for wheat across the Atlantic was 1d. per bushel before the War, it was now 1s. 8d. The cost of carrying wheat from the Argentine had risen 500 per cent.

In the early months of the War the Government had given financial aid to assist in promoting British dyes ; it later acquired the greater part of the indigo crop to aid this venture ; yet it refused to take adequate steps to protect the people against extortionate charges for food and fuel.

Whenever one touched war work Scandal poked out her ugly head ;

there was abundant food for her, but she was swiftly thrust back into her kennel. Whilst compulsion was applied to spur exhausted workers in the privately owned munition factories, the thirty and forty ton hammers were idle at Woolwich Arsenal. The 4,000 ton press had only been worked on odd jobs since war began. On June 14th, 1915, the men working on it were told there would be no more work for them unless unexpected orders came in. The new field-gun annexe was only half used and work on 18-pounder field guns—the very guns which were supposed to be lacking at the Front—had entirely ceased. The total orders for these large guns since the beginning of the War had amounted to but 12 to 14 weeks' work. On July 1st Members complained that 97 per cent. of the large work was given out to contractors and only 3 per cent. to the Arsenal. Will Crooks, the Labour M.P. for Woolwich, declared that steel and other material bought for the Arsenal had been sent by the Arsenal for use by private firms. In the huge inability to see the truth affecting every belligerent nation men cried out for life to be saved by sending more munitions to the trenches. Even those who believed themselves Pacifists, like Lansbury, were of this mind. He wrote:

"The women of East London have sent their men to fight. Those of us who hate and detest war know that these men must be armed and fed, and while the War lasts we shall all do our best to see that this is done."[1]

Poor women, they did not so; I never knew one of them who did not see her man go with weeping and bitter regret, who did not strive and hope for him to remain at home.

Strikes began to break out. The L.C.C. tramway men struck for a war bonus, which was denied them, although receipts had risen by £8,500 a week, and owing to enlistments, 2,000 fewer men were handling the increased traffic. The strike caused tremendous excitement in London and an outcrop of volunteer strike breakers. When the men returned on promise of arbitration, they found that no men between 21 and 40 were to be reinstated. That was the war-time way of dealing with strikers; an effective means of procuring the docility of Labour.

In the burst of artificial war prosperity, in which anything would sell, scamping, adulteration and profiteering ran rife. A young Jew, dodging war service, who used to hang about our offices, disclosed to me casually that he was using our telephone to discover where certain commodities could be bought, then offering them for sale at an increased figure, and if his offer were accepted, instructing the vendor to deliver the goods to his customer. Thus without risk or expenditure, he was making a profit from the prevailing eagerness to obtain materials. On every hand one saw small firms becoming large ones; their owners moving from mean little houses into spacious ones, discarding omnibuses and buying motors, their way of life expanding in all directions into luxury.

[1] Article by George Lansbury in *Women's Dreadnought*, August 21st, 1915.

Patriotism was fashionable, and patriotism at other people's expense most fashionable of all. A poor woman whose husband had just been killed at the Front was informed that the Royal Patriotic Fund had granted her £7, and that she must apply for it to the local S.S.F.A. Then a certain lady called from the Association and told the widow that she had put the money in the bank for her and that if she wanted "to hear any more about it" she must call on this lady next week. Crushed by her grief, the widow heard of this "blood money," as poor women called it, scarcely caring what might happen to it; but a week later her two-year-old child was taken seriously ill, and the doctor ordered special nourishment which she could not afford to buy. She hastened to the S.S.F.A. and pleaded for the money due to her; for some of it; even for 10s. The lady she had previously seen refused to hand over one penny, insisting that £5 of it must be put into War Loan, and the rest held in the bank. A woman brought the poor widow to me. I put the case in the hands of one of our solicitors, who eventually secured the widow her money.

Poverty and overstrain were evidenced by the increase in the death rate of women from consumption, which had been falling steadily during the preceding ten years, and which mounted higher with every year of war. The general death rate for civilians, which had been falling, also rose.

The Minister of Education now gave instructions that the school feeding of necessitous children must cease. From one school near us nearly fifty children, whose need had been recognised by the School Managers, were thus left to go hungry. The number of children attending our "Penny Carltons," as the Press termed what we had named "Cost Price Restaurants," leapt up by 100 per cent. Though on the part of voluntary enthusiasts there was a concentration of effort to save the babies never previously made, the then appallingly high infant death rate rose, especially in London, where from 103 per 1,000 births in 1914, it became 112 per 1,000 births in 1915.

As the summer advanced diarrhœa and enteritis attacked huge numbers of tiny victims. Poor mothers came flocking to our clinics with their wasting infants, wizened and fleshless from wasting, twisted and misshapen by rickets. Rickets, impetigo, scabies—which the soldiers brought home with them—poverty diseases; I learnt to know them sorely.

We made no pretence of confining ourselves to preventive medicine, as the Minister of Health now advises. We did what we could for the sufferers, only referring them elsewhere for treatment we were unable to give. To have done otherwise would greatly have limited our usefulness; indeed the majority of our patients would have gone untreated. The hospitals were too much taken up with soldiers to give adequate attention to ailing babies. Our patients were generally too poor to pay for attention from the local private practitioners, who in any case were less able to advise in relation to pregnancy and infant nurture than our own doctors, who specialised in such work.

I believe that if professional interests were put on one side it would be found best for the present maternity and infant welfare centres to treat the bulk of the ailments they now refer to private general practitioners.

A lady came to me from the Beit clinic for sea water plasma injections, urging me to use this treatment for infantile diarrhœa. In a few days we had it working, and obtained from it remarkable results under Dr. Alice Johnson, who attended our cases at the Mothers' Arms. Numbers of infants brought to us in a state of collapse, despaired of by the general practitioners, were restored. I realised how handicapped is the doctor attending poor people when circumstances permit him to order nothing for his patients beyond a bottle of medicine. Many sick babies we took into the nursery by night, as well as by day. They were the special charge of Nurse Hebbes, who nursed them with patient tenderness, spending herself unsparingly. "I believe you love them better than the healthy babies," I said to her, watching her fondling a piteous little morsel, who crinkled his shrivelled face to smile as her finger gently stroked his cheek. She answered with wan brightness: "I think I do."

It seemed a miracle to witness the tiny creatures recovered from the collapse of imminent death, the listless, flaccid limbs gradually regaining vigour. Yet the process of recovery was slow indeed as compared with their swift failing. Several times it happened that after a baby had been nursed patiently to apparent health, and had been sent away to the country to assure its stability, it would return home, catch a chill or some childish ailment, collapse and die, quite suddenly, as though the physical well-being we had built for the little body had been merely a house of cards. It was the sad loss of infants for whom she had laboured with beautiful devotion, and the tragic state of overburdened mothers in crowded homes, which sent Nurse Hebbes to be the first nurse in the birth control clinic of Dr. Marie Stopes.

## CHAPTER XXVII

### REGISTRATION SUNDAY—WITH MCKENNA AT THE TREASURY

FOR Registration Sunday, August 15th, we were preparing a joint demonstration against Conscription, then obviously approaching, and to put forward a series of demands, including the National control of the food supplies, the mineral and other resources of the country, to bring down the cost of living and reduce the burden of taxation upon the people ; equal pay and votes for women. We were joined by the United Suffragists, the Welsh Suffragists, the Women Writers' Suffrage League, Lansbury's Herald League, the British Socialist Party, the Dockers' Union, and several branches of the I.L.P., the Amalgamated Toolmakers, Engineers and Machinists, the Electrical Trade Union, the National Union of Railwaymen and many others. Processions were to march to a Queen's Hall meeting from East and South London. To work up this demonstration we held in the ten preceding days a hundred open-air meetings in the East End alone. I was speaking at four meetings a night towards the end.

Four days before the meeting, Boosey wrote, on the proprietors' behalf, to cancel our engagement of the hall, on the ground that our advertisements were " objectionable," and the words, " Votes for Women," and " No Compulsion," likely to cause a disturbance. Lansbury, who was to speak at the meeting, promised financial aid to overcome all objections, by insuring the hall against damage, or by depositing a sum of money which the proprietors might claim if their lawyer and ours should agree that any loss or damage had been incurred. The truculent Boosey rejected these offers. Lansbury and I rushed to the hall to confront him, whereupon he declared the root of his objection : the meeting was to be free, people were to march there from the East End. This would be highly derogatory to the status of the hall, in the eyes of well-to-do concert-goers. Lansbury stormed, threatened an action for damages, and rushed me off in a taxi to his solicitors, Lewis and Lewis. Legally, however, we had not a leg to stand upon, because in a mass of small print on the back of the contract, which few people ever took the trouble to read, it was stated that a charge must be made for all meetings in the Queen's Hall. The rule was more honoured in the breach than the observance ; for years the Suffragettes had held Monday afternoon meetings there without making a charge ; yet there was the rule in print, on the contract form Smyth had signed !

The *Herald* headlined : " Boosey ! " declaring the East End workers insulted. Dyson produced one of his characteristic cartoons.

I should have turned to the open air then: Trafalgar Square, Hyde Park or Tower Hill; but Lansbury insisted we must find a hall; he positively refused to speak outside. To go on without him would offend him. He was touchy in those days, and apt to lose all his fight when rebuffed. He would have given up the whole attempt had it been left to him. Some of the halls were engaged, for others one had to apply to the L.C.C. or the Lord Chamberlain for a licence; finally we secured the Portman Rooms, Baker Street; too small for the occasion, but it must serve.

The day proved showery and thundery. Lansbury turned up at the pitch in a nervous, querulous state, which probably arose both from too much speaking, and anxiety about the *Herald's* finances. He was certain we should not march, and had only come to get confirmation of his opinion. Only a score or more of stalwarts had emerged after the last downpour; but Smyth brushed away his complaints. "Of course we shall march!" she said, and bustled about fitting up banners, impetuously lifting and wrenching; doing more than any half-dozen men in the crowd. She was seeking to thrust vitality into the hesitant with every impatient wrench at the loops and poles. In grey-black costume, short-skirted for those days, a small, black shovel hat surmounting her long pale face and tight-drawn hair, she dashed about; a slight, thick-shouldered, thin-legged figure, with a trace of elegance. She shouted to the bearers and stewards brief, sharp directions in a voice low-pitched for talking, but high, with a break in it, when she tried to raise it.

The banners were up. We were ready for starting, Lansbury smiling ruefully, inclined to turn back even now. Mrs. Crabbe, red-cheeked and cheerful, despite that poor heart of hers, her bright little Ruby beside her, frail little Minnie O'Brien with her mop of red hair, her thin hand outstretched with the *Dreadnought*, rosy-cheeked Katie Manicom, dark-eyed Patricia Lynch, the Irish girl who wrote poetry, the Carrs and Pengellys from Ranwell Street, Mrs. Payne and her Jim, sturdy Mrs. Bouvier the Russian, big old Harriet Bennett crying the *Dreadnought*, "this little bit of truth!"—a growing crowd of men and women, their names known and unknown to me; on we went under the banners.

A thousand people or more were pressed into the Portman Rooms, sitting or standing. Large crowds were turned away. All the rebels of those days in London were with us: Socialists, Anarchists, Individualists, Trade Unionists, Left Wing Industrialists, Pacifists—those who hated capitalism and compulsion—those who opposed the War—feeling was stirred into ferment by the jingo agitation for Conscription and industrial compulsion. The rank and file were feeling the actual compulsion of the Munitions Tribunals; the leaders were more incensed by a deputation of bankers who, just then, had waited on McKenna, the new Chancellor of the Exchequer, demanding a tax on wages, and the reduction of the Old Age Pension and the Social services. The redoubtable Harold Cox, that bellicose though mild-looking old gentleman, always the champion of forlorn bad causes, was declaring that we must follow the example of Prussia, by levying income tax on all workers earning more than £45 a year, and by having the tax deducted from their wages by the employer, and paid for in stamps.

The speakers were in a ferment of enthusiasm, the audience tense and earnest. Lansbury was more excited than any. He averred that Conscription would mean soldiers at ½d. a day, no allotments, no separation allowances, no pensions. The compulsionists wanted to cheapen the cost of the War, he declared, and to have the workers shot or imprisoned if they demanded higher wages. He (Lansbury) insisted that the Government, Parliament, the judges, and all the possessing classes were feathering their own nests. A deputation was elected to lay the resolutions before McKenna: Mrs. Despard, Evelyn Sharp, Lansbury, John Scurr, then prominent amongst Poplar dockers though out of the docks already, E. C. Fairchild of the B.S.P., Robert Williams, then the big noise of the Transport Workers' Federation, T. E. Naylor of the Compositors' Union, myself and half a dozen more. McKenna refused to receive the deputation; but after some parleying volunteered to see Lansbury and me. I took Mrs. Drake with me, in order that the voice of an East End mother might make itself heard.

When we were ushered into his room at the Treasury McKenna, in his black frock-coat, came striding towards us cordially, and gripped Lansbury by the hand. Mrs. Drake and I swept past him icily; but Lansbury, who at the meeting had been so combative, was entirely disarmed. He radiated geniality and confidence. "We think if you could—we don't know if you could——" couched his mild appeal that the Government should take control of flour and coal, as it had taken control of sugar. Almost apologetically, he urged that the rising industrial unrest was due to the high price of food. Even in his own home great economy had to be practised. He had never seen so many children in the streets without shoes and stockings as now. McKenna expressed his sympathy; he knew, he knew; but this was war! Lansbury sadly assented, as though he felt he was bothering a busy man unduly by coming here at all.

I resented this friendly confabulation with a member of the Government. I followed Lansbury brusquely, holding to the full terms of the mandate given us by the meeting, expressing with a singleness of conviction—which doubtless seemed Utopian to the two men—my detestation of the social inequalities which the War daily accentuated. With a bitterness, which I saw went home to McKenna, I described the miserable privations I daily witnessed. He assented to my reminder that only a small minority of workers had received either wage increases or war bonus, and that in no case were these equivalent to the increase in the cost of living. He assented, too, when I urged that though in some trades overtime was being worked, those who were toiling for long hours needed more nourishment to keep them going, and that wives and mothers reported as much, or more, than the increase derived from overtime, had often to be spent upon extra food. He winced a little when I gave him the budget of a widowed mother with ten children,

*Topical Press Agency*

DURING A DAYLIGHT AIR RAID

Some people spent considerable sums on such shelters.

*Alfieri*

AFTER AN AIR RAID

three of them working for a paltry wage. Though she was now buying only 7½ quarterns of bread instead of 16, and 3½ lbs. of sugar instead of 8 lbs., she was spending £1 11s. 10¾d. as compared with £1 0s. 4¾d. before the War. She could not keep that up. She was already in debt. The children must eat still less. The thin flank and scraps of beef bought by the poor had doubled in price, the scraps of mutton trebled. I confronted him with proof of the low wages of men, the hideous sweating of women, even on war work, and recalled the long struggle I had made to induce the Board of Trade to secure a better standard in respect of Government contracts. One result of the pressure on poor families was the increase in the infant death rate. Even in our own district it was increasing, despite the work of the mother and infant clinics we and others had opened there since the War. No private effort could cope with the devastating effect of rising prices. McKenna admitted the truth of all I said; but with grim cynicism asserted: " The rise in the infant death rate is appalling; but it cannot be stopped, for that is war! "

Bitterly I retorted with a protest against the heavy interest payable on War Loan, reminding him that for every £100 lent by the patriots with money to spare, the nation would have to pay £235 in the course of thirty years. He smiled the cold smile of a man without illusions, and asked how otherwise the money could be raised.

I blazed hotly: " Why does not the Government take by forced loan the superfluous money owned by the rich? "

" I do not know that a government could do anything so drastic," he answered. " But war profits will be taxed."

" Why has the Government waited more than a year to do it? " I demanded.

He began to be nettled, and protested that he had not been Chancellor of the Exchequer very long.

I questioned him on the method of taxation; would he take all profits beyond those made before the War?

He would not disclose his budget; but on this he was emphatic: " Manufacturers must have some incentive to increase production."

" People whose wages range from £2 to 7s. or 8s. a week ought not to be made to pay for that incentive! "

" The War must be paid for," he was impatient. " Its cost has been greatly underestimated."

" Why do you not nationalise the coal mines? They have been giving you a great deal of trouble lately."

" What! In a war! " he protested.

" Why do you not take all income above what is required for simple comfort—say £500 a year, or £2 a week for an adult and £1 or 10s. for each child? "

He smiled indulgently. " Rich people would not submit."

" Would they prefer to submit, or to give up the War? "

Lansbury was fidgeting; the cordial harmony of our entry had been jarred upon.

McKenna protested the impossibility of my demands, the public opinion, the powerful interests which constrained him. I answered coldly, unmollified. Lansbury supported him gently against my truculence. " They can't, all at once—in a war, you know, Sylvia ! "

McKenna proceeded urbanely : " Rich people have their commitments ; they would be miserable if their incomes were greatly reduced."

" Is it better that the poorer people should starve ? " I persisted.

" I haven't so much faith in the power of governments as some people," McKenna evaded. " I don't know how people could be forced to give up their money."

" You have managed to get the people registered."

" That is only putting names on paper."

" You have found it easy to punish the poor mothers of soldiers who, to get a shilling or two more on their allowances, have pretended they had a shilling or two more from their sons than was actually the case ! "[1]

He shielded himself behind a mask of sternness : " Do you approve of their making false representations ? "

The acid retort was obvious : " Their excuse is that the Government promised if a son would allot his mother 3s. 6d. a week, the Government would make it up to 12s. 6d. ; the Government has not kept its promise."

Mrs. Drake intervened in her quiet, blunt way ; but McKenna was growing restive. He suggested, with a trace of sarcasm, that perhaps the deputation would like to hear *him* talk for a little while. He summed up the position with the air of the Strong Man brushing aside sentiment ; imports must be paid for by exports. As productive work was now reduced by the urgency of war " the Chancellor of the Exchequer, by taxation, must make it impossible for the mass of people to buy clothes, or even some kinds of food."

" Under-nourished workers are not productive ; it is a short-sighted policy to starve the people ! " I answered, surprised that he should express himself with this brutal cynicism.

" I will not tax milk and bread," he conceded.

" The price of milk and bread has been raised ! "

War profits, he declared, were as nothing to the millions daily spent on the War.

" If a man made more than a certain amount of profit I would have him hung ! " cried Mrs. Drake ; her voice had the sound of tears in it. As keenly as I, she felt we were come to voice the claims of the exploited poor against the representative of the possessing classes who were profiting by the War.

[1] In one case W. G. Edrupt, a driver in the City of London R.F.A., was bound over to come up for judgment if called upon and his stepmother fined £2 and £2 10s. costs because they had represented that before enlistment he earned £1 a week and gave his stepmother 15/–, whereas he had earned 15/– and given her 10/–. On one day 14 summonses for separation allowance frauds were heard at Woolwich Police Court ; fines up to £5 were imposed.

Our visit was fruitless—obviously and entirely. Had the workers of Britain, solidly organised to enforce our mandate, been behind us, it had been otherwise.

We rose to leave. McKenna, exuberant, approached me. " I must shake hands with you. You are the pluckiest girl I ever knew."[1]

Impetuously I rejected him ; never would I surmount the barrier between the people and the governing classes whilst the masses starved on the other side !

. . . . . . . .

[1] McKenna was Home Secretary when, after a month's hunger and thirst strike and forcible feeding, I tramped up and down my cell for 28 hours to secure release. It was to this he referred, I thought. (See *The Suffragette Movement*, Longmans Green.)

McKenna introduced his first Budget in September. The cost of the War was now estimated at four and a half million pounds a day and at five millions a day in the following month. He added 40 per cent. to the income tax, and lowered the exemption limit to £130 a year. The super-tax was raised to 2s. 8d. on incomes over £8,000 a year, graduated up to 3s. 6d. on incomes over £10,000. The promised 50 per cent. tax on war profits was brought in. It was hedged around with provisions leaving many loopholes for evasion ; but even where it was not evaded, the profiteers went merrily on, scooping what remained into their coffers, and stoutly determining that their profits should be greater, and greater yet. No extra tax was put upon intoxicating liquors, the powerful interests would not permit it ; but the housewife was again heavily taxed. The duty on sugar, already so costly, was increased from 1s. 10d. to 9s. 4d. per cwt. The duties on tea, cocoa, coffee, chicory, dried fruits and tobacco were increased by 50 per cent. The Tories were cheered by this handsome instalment of Protection.

To cheat the tax collector there was extensive doctoring of balance sheets. One Colliery Company, for instance, reduced a profit of £21,700 to one of £4,700 by setting aside £17,000 for improvements in the collieries. The little manufacturers followed the great in expedients to evade the tax. I remember an eager young man, with the flowing locks and spreading collar of a musician, and the wide blue eyes of an idealist, who started up in business as a patent food manufacturer in some dilapidated cottages in a squalid quarter of London, surrounded by a bevy of charming girls, who were packing up the stuff in gay comradery. He was dispersing his excess profits in advertisements, paid with abundant generosity, in certain propaganda journals with which he sympathised. I remember a lady running a smart West End business who confidentially told a friend that she only entered in her ledger the cheques she received from her customers ; the cash she spent unbanked and unaccounted.

## CHAPTER XXVIII

### UNREST IN THE MINES

AT the week-ends I was often speaking in the South Wales coal-fields. Great bundles of *Dreadnoughts* and pamphlets heaped about me, I wrote my copy for the paper as the train sped on through the deep and narrow valleys, where sombre mountains frown through the heavy smoke of the colliery chimneys upon the workers' little homes. The dull-hued grass grows scantily on the black soil of the sheer hillside. The swift, torrential streams show black as ebony. Great dismal heaps of coal-mixed refuse from the collieries rival in size the mountain heights themselves; and sometimes one of them slides down, a devastating avalanche, burying the houses which stand before it. Valleys are filled with the refuse, dust blows about from it. The stark mine chimneys, a few dilapidated sheds and some gaunt ironwork, the battered iron " trams " in which the coal is carried, are all one sees of the mines. The numerous colliery villages, row upon row of tiny cottages clustered together, seem built for mankind in miniature. Wretched housing there is in the older villages and towns like Dowlais of the steel works. Back to back houses, anathematised by John Burns, are often the rule. Worse still are the " top and bottom " houses, the bottom houses built up against the oozing earth of the rising hillside; damp in the finest weather, they stream with water in heavy rains. Many an accident, above all to children, and much rheumatism there is in such perilous places.

In the newer villages are many improvements, yet ugliness prevails. The houses are small and cramped. In the one main street are a few poor shops, a cinema, perhaps a theatre of the meanest sort, the workmen's institute, maintained by the colliers themselves, with a lecture hall and maybe a swimming bath. Life is narrowed and restricted in the valleys, where the works of man have been built to minister to the business of getting coal. Yet the miners then were thrilling with a strong, warm sense of solidarity and power. In their great numbers, they felt themselves irrevocably pitted against the little coterie of colliery directors and managers guarding the interests of the coal-owners. The few struggling shopkeepers, ill-paid clerks and miscellaneous tradesman in the valleys, they regarded with a good-humoured tolerant contempt, which at times also characterised their attitude to the industrial workers of other areas. As the coal-getters for the Navy, their rank and file leaders believed they held the fortunes of the British

Empire in their hands. These leaders were omniverous readers of Blue Books, company prospectuses, and theoretical works on Economics. Marxist devotees of the Central Labour College in London and its classes throughout the valleys, they had nevertheless a special South Wales cult of their own, and some of them even talked of " marching on London," to take it for the proletariat when the hour of social revolution struck.

Nothing had been conceded to them save by the strike. By its stern means they had forced their way up from the lowest depths of exploitation. To-day the earnings of a hewer on piece rates in the favourable working place might be £2 10s. to £3 a week. If there were wage-earning sons to add to their father's takings, one found an abundance of well-cooked food on their table, a bright homely kitchen, with devotedly polished brass about the hearth and chimney; perhaps also a sitting-room; and sometimes a bath with hot and cold water attached had been fitted at the family's own expense. A son or daughter might be at college, at Cardiff or in England; but this was only done by the willing co-operation of their brothers, at the cost of many a minor or major sacrifice.

Ninety per cent. of the South Wales miners were in the Miners' Federation; the remainder were mainly rolling stones, moving from district to district. The Federation exercised a rigid discipline, by the will of its active members, who exulted in its power. As wages were drawn each week, the Federation dues were handed to its officials, stationed at the pit-head. Every two months, the officials appeared at the pit for a show of members' cards. Any member in arrears with his contributions, was turned back, and ordered home for the day. Should he rebel against this punishment, all the other workers would refuse to descend, and work would be suspended for the day.

The Departmental Committee on Coal had reported in June that though the war expenses of owners and merchants entitled them to an increased profit of 3s. per ton, they had taken 9s. to 11s. per ton. The war bonus of the miners amounted to only 9d. per ton. The Government had sent commissions to America, Newfoundland and Canada, to secure inexpensive pit-props for the coal owners; and had even induced the French Government to withdraw soldiers from the Front, that they might go to Bordeaux to fell trees for the British mines. There were trees which might have been used in this country, Runciman told the House of Commons, but the cost of conveying them by British railways was higher than the mine owners were willing to pay. Whilst miners who struck work for a day had been sent to prison under the Defence of the Realm Act, their employers were charging prices which Runciman admitted to be " far in excess of what the expense justifies." He hoped soon to announce that the prices had come " a little nearer to what was expected of them," but in the meantime nothing was done.

Robert Smillie, the President of the Miners' Federation of Great Britain, was a big Scotsman, handsome and venerable, grown grey in popular agitation, an early I.L.P.er and old friend of Keir Hardie. Many times he had been a Parliamentary candidate, many times defeated. He endeavoured to lead the miners in a lofty crusade to prevent the exploitation of the poor by high prices.

The five years' agreement, under which the South Wales miners were working, was due to expire in June 1915. Under the award of Lord St. Aldwyn, who acted as arbiter in 1910, the men would now be entitled to demand a wages advance in conformity with the increase in the selling price of coal. At the outbreak of war the miners' representatives gave notice that if the owners would not raise the price of coal any further, the men would forego the increase due to them. The owners merely offered a bonus of 10 per cent., if the miners would work under the old agreement till the close of the War, and continued raising the price of coal. The miners rejected this offer, and in March 1915 their representatives proposed negotiations for the new agreement. They suggested a wage which was less than the strict enforcement of the 1910 award would have given them. The owners were making an enhanced profit of 6s. 1d. per ton; the miners' representatives asked that they might share the profit to the extent of 4½d. per ton, a modest request indeed. The owners refused the advance and even to meet the miners' representatives to negotiate a new agreement. The miners announced that they would strike if the new agreement were not completed at the expiry of the old. The Government threatened punishment with a stern hand, should a strike take place. The miners laughed at the threat. Well knowing that their labour could not be substituted, they struck work as they had declared.

To placate public opinion, which already was irritated by revelations of profiteering, an Act was hurried through to limit the price of coal to 4s. a ton above the price charged in 1914 for coal of the same quality, sold under the same conditions at the same period of the year. This limitation was not to apply to coal for export or for use on ships, and its provisions were whittled away by other exceptions, the main sources of profit being allowed to escape its operations. Moreover, in all cases its provisions were practically illusory; for complaint against the coal owners who evaded the Act was left to the wholesale customer, who must appeal to the Board of Trade to take up his case. War conditions had produced so keen a competition to secure the output of the mines that merchants preferred to avoid litigation or offence, and to get what coal they could at any price, passing the enhanced cost to the consumer. Sir A. Markham, a coal owner, and Sir E. Cornwall, a coal merchant, strove in vain to induce the Government to take more genuine measures against profiteering. Every amendment they moved in the interests of the people was rejected. It was ever thus; the War enthusiasm of the great interests was perpetually stoked by war profits.

The miners being obdurate, Lloyd George, amid a chorus of Press eulogy, "settled" the coal strike. The men went back, but the trouble remained obstinately unsettled. With another flourish, Runciman re-settled it—all was peace, the newspapers averred. Then, as an item of stop-press news, came some words of Vernon Hartshorn, a South Wales miners' leader:

"The Runciman settlement is impossible . . . if leaders accepted it . . . workmen would reject it . . . they can stop the coal field. . . ."

Lloyd George, Runciman and Henderson were brought in together as arbiters, and in conforming to the law, found themselves obliged to decide the two main points in favour of the men. Some minor questions were left to be abitrated later by an independent chairman. The miners' representatives accepted Runciman as arbiter, believing, from the talk they had had with him, that he agreed to the justice of their claim. On the contrary, he decided every point referred to him against them. He even permitted the two points he had joined in deciding in their favour to be brought up again, and reversed the decision in favour of the employers.

"If a man fools you once, shame on him—if he fools you twice, shame on you!"

This dictum of witty Noah Ablett rang through the valleys.

The negotiators in London refused to sign the agreement because Runciman had withdrawn from the original award. Mass meetings were called in the coalfield. I chanced to be there in those days of excitement. I saw the colliers of Tonypandy, packed standing into a great dim-lit rink, and heard them give their decision, despite all threats of the D.O.R.A. and the Munitions Act, firmly, unanimously, for a strike, if the original award were not immediately restored.

On Tuesday delegates went from all the miners' lodges to the Cory Hall, Cardiff. I met the representatives of the 10,000 Cambrian Combine men, who had already downed tools to give the Conference a lead. Their faces were glowing, they seemed to walk on air. They felt themselves the advance guard of the workers. The Press denounced them: "Remember the soldiers in the trenches!" The reproach did not dismay them, for they regarded the men in the trenches as their brothers, whose interests they were defending by this fight at home. They responded eagerly to the cry of their Left Wing enthusiasts: "The War is being used for the exploitation of the workers; to force us back in the battle we are waging for the emancipation of our class and the brotherhood of man."

The struggle of the miners was stirring the hearts of the organised workers throughout the country. The South Wales rebels were regarded as the flower of the working class, the standard bearers of the workers against compulsion and profiteering. Wherever I went to speak on these things, I found great audiences thronging the largest halls and gathering in the open air in numbers beyond the reach of a single speaker. When I had spoken, I would jump down from the platform, and thread my way amongst the audience selling our literature. Pennies were eagerly reached out to me; great piles of *Dreadnoughts* and pamphlets disappeared. I returned to Bow laden with heavy bags of copper.

# CHAPTER XXIX

## KEIR HARDIE

KEIR HARDIE had been ill all that summer. We met seldom, we were both so busy ; but each time I saw him I knew that he was tortured by bodily pain and mental anguish. Sometimes he would be at peace for a time, and thrusting the cruel realities of those days aside, would read aloud to me as of old. More often he was obviously suffering without cease, and even his iron self-command could with difficulty maintain control. The War had shattered him. Rightly indeed John Morley had said to him : " You have been ill ; what was the matter ? Was it the War which so weighed upon your spirit that it made your body sick ? "

He complained of the old abdominal pain, and of loss of power in his right arm. So disturbed I was for him, knowing him there alone at Nevill's Court, with none to care for his bodily needs, despite the many who loved him, that during one of his frequent absences I advertised for a woman, used to attending on invalids, to come to him daily, to massage his arm if he wished and attend to his food and comfort. Applications I got for the post, but he would have none of them.

That Easter the Annual Conference of the I.L.P.[1] had met in Norwich. The hall taken for the Conference was cancelled, but the Primitive Methodists placed their hall at its disposal. The I.L.P. was facing an uphill struggle, so hard that it was found necessary for its National Administrative Council to move an emergency resolution that " the Party throughout the country should resume its educational propaganda." Resolutions were carried for international arbitration, democratic control of foreign policy and the right of Parliament to declare war. The British Government was called on to disclose its terms of peace, the I.L.P. to take action with the Socialists of other countries to bring the War to a close. The recruiting campaign of the Labour Party was condemned. The previous question was nevertheless carried when Dr. Salter of Bermondsey and Clifford Allen[2] moved a resolution that Socialist Parties of all nations should henceforth refuse to support every war, whatever its ostensible objects.

Keir Hardie, so ill and exhausted that at times the delegates thought him sleeping, made but one speech : a protest against the heavy sentences passed by the Russian Government on 53 members of the Russian Seamen's Union and five Socialist members of the Duma. The Secretary

[1] Independent Labour Party. [2] Now Lord Allen of Hurtwood.

of the Russian Seamen's Union had been illegally arrested in Egypt, and taken to Russia for trial and sentence, a violation of the right of asylum. Keir Hardie had vainly tried to induce Sir Edward Grey to intervene. Keir Hardie's last words to the conference were a denunciation of the alliance with the government of the Tsars, against which he had fought since its inception : " The alliance with Russia is not to help Belgium ; it is to open up fresh fields for Capitalist exploitation."

. . . . . . . .

I saw Keir Hardie at Nevill's Court when he returned from Norwich. He looked aged and broken. Deeply dejected, he told me he could not endure to be alone there any longer, and had made arrangements to go for treatment to a hydro at Caterham. Never before in all the years I had known him had he spoken thus. Often had I pleaded with him that he should abandon his solitary life, and urged on him his need of warmth and cheer, on returning from late sittings in Parliament and from journeys about the country. At all hours of the night and small hours he came back to the solitude of dark and fireless rooms ; where, save for the old woman who came in to clean, he had all to do for himself. Always until now he had declared his contentment.

Deeply concerned, I wrote to him at Caterham. In answer I received a letter written by another hand :

May 27th, 1915.

DEAR SYLVIA,

I wish I could respond worthily to your letter of the other day. That is out of the question.

I may be at Nevill's Court on Monday for about two hours—12 noon till 2 o'clock, and if you could make it convenient to come and see me then I shall be delighted.

I have given up Nevill's Court, and intend to gift and sell a lot of the stuff that is there. You have, I think, two products of your genius there, one hangs over the fireplace and the other on the left-hand side of the room as you go in. The one over the fireplace I have so closely associated with you that I should not like to part with it, and if you can see your way to allow my nominal ownership to continue, I shall regard that with pleasure.

I have a great many letters of yours, especially those from America, and a good many others. They are well worth preserving, and I should like to return these to you. I could let you have the whole of those now at Nevill's Court, and you could use your discretion as to which are most worthy of being kept and published. But I must leave the matter entirely in your hands. I have not *now* the capacity for dealing with such a matter.

There is much in what you say about the War and the state of my health.

As aye,

Frank Smith had been his scribe; only the concluding words, "As aye, K." were added in his own hand, shaky and trembling, which was of old so firm.

I read again the sad epistle. Not lightly was this decision taken. No hope deluded me that his intention was to move, as I had urged him, to more comfortable surroundings, or to share a home with others. Too well I knew him, thus to mistake his meaning. His words knelled on my heart with finality and farewell. For all that he was and stood for, grief surged within me. I saw that the word "now" had been inserted by his own hand. So that was his thought: to give permanency to those letters I had written to him in the unconscious communion of friendship.

. . . . . . . .

Anxiously I hastened to him at the time he had appointed. I found him alone in the old rooms. With a voice low and muffled, he confirmed the purport of his letter. I understood that he was announcing to me the final close of his working life, his imminent death, that he admitted no hope of recovery, expected never to return. My heart revolted against this decision, which he conveyed as an irrevocable decree; yet I could not argue or gainsay him. The surging of great sorrow, pent tears and cries suppressed, stifled all utterance.

Now he would even return to me the picture he had written his desire for, the child I had painted at Penshurst, which, he would have it, resembled me. That decision wounded me as a stroke of doom. I had clung to the thought that his wish to keep it meant he had hold on life still. Yet my lips could form no plea, no protest. . . . He wanted to give me some keepsake from his books or furniture; urged me to choose; tried, despite my silence, to enlist my interest in this or that.

"I don't want to be given anything!" at last I blurted. Only the poor little pang that he should seek by small things to divert me, overcame, for an instant, the anguish of the great loss.

We were tongue-tied as never before, I struggling dumbly, desperately, to maintain my slender self-control, that I might not distress him, might not add to the suffering obviously consuming him.

Frank Smith came in, talking disjointedly, moving awkwardly, in his kind clumsiness, cut to the heart like me, so well I knew. Grief held me speechless. They exchanged some words on indifferent matters, both constrained, laconic, heavy with the sorrow oppressing the three of us. Keir in his agony, mysterious, unkenned, seemed to loom over us like some great, tragic ruin.

At last in a transient moment, when Frank Smith was away on some errand, I summoned courage to take leave. Grieving too much to feel clearly aught else save grieving, I felt him near me, heard for the last time his voice: "You have been very brave!"

Torn with the hopeless misery one feels at death, I went from those old rooms.

His kind looks hung in my eyes, his accents in my ears. . . . Visions of youth and childhood mingled with the thought of him . . . happy scenes . . . high faiths and hopes . . . great imaginings. . . .

I would not surrender hope of him. No, no, despite the parting.

. . . . . . . .

On July 28th came a postcard from him, the postal stamp " Caterham Valley," the writing trembling, irregular.

" DEAR SYLPHIA,

" In about a week I expect to be gone from here with no more mind control than when I came.

Love."

Alas ! he had forgotten even the spelling of my so familiar name !

Yet, yet would I not surrender hope of him.

I dreamt in waking dreams of his return, rested, revivified, as he came back from that voyage round the world in 1908, after we all had thought him dying. I spoke of my hopes and fears for him to Frank Smith. Yes ; he too believed, so he reassured me, that Keir would return with his old fire.

Zelie Emerson put into my hands a copy of the *Suffragette*, displaying a vile cartoon from *Punch*, portraying the Kaiser giving a grossly vulgarised Keir Hardie a bag of money !

" Also the Nobel prize (though tardy)
I now confer on Keir von Hardie."

Greatly pained, I wrote to Mrs. Pankhurst that I had seen it, telling her : " He is dying." I believed that her old love for him must flame out against further insults, did she know his state. She did not answer me.

I learnt later that the W.S.P.U. had sent Flora Drummond into his constituency, the Merthyr Boroughs, to work for the Labour renegade, who hoped to succeed him, the jingo Stanton, who joined with the notorious Captain Tupper and others of the sort in smashing peace meetings.

Memories weighed on me. Flora Drummond and he and I, speaking together at the demonstration in the Merthyr drill hall after the first Suffragette conspiracy trial, when Mrs. Pankhurst and the Pethick Lawrences had stood in the dock together ; Flora Drummond squatting familiarly on the hearthrug beside Keir Hardie's chair in his old home at 14 Nevill's Court ; Flora Drummond, who had named her son, Keir, after him, and had been wont to run to him with confident importunity when any trouble threatened. I thought of his visits to our home in Manchester, so long ago ; my father's great love for him ; how staunch a friend Keir Hardie was to us in the after years !

I had written : " He is dying," yet I would not accept that thought ; there must still be hope. He was at Cumnock, with his family. I had no direct word of him.

. . . . . . . .

I woke early one Sunday morning with a dream of him fondling some little puppy, as he often did. There was always a strong attraction between the dogs and him ; not one of them approached him but he must have to do with it. I heard again the gentle regret in his " My old dog," spoken of one who had died, as of a well-loved friend. The thought came to me that a soft-furred, shaggy puppy, of some big dog sort, now humorous and rollicking, now snuggling to him appealing for sympathy and warmth, would soothe and divert him. Many times, in the years when I had lived alone, he had urged me to get myself a dog ; and had told me he would have one with him at Nevill's Court, save for his frequent absences.

I set my steps to the dog market held on Sunday mornings in the Bethnal Green Road. I would look for a grey old English sheep-dog, the most human of dogs, so far as I know them. As always, the market was thronged with shabby black-coated men, but the dogs were few. There was only one litter of big dog puppies of any sort—retrievers, six weeks old, the vendor told me ; fat little fellows they were, as round as barrels, with long, black, silky fur. I gathered up one and enjoyed the feel of it, warm and confiding, as it lay on my knees in the 'bus. Almost happy I felt, notwithstanding the sad occasion of it, to have thought of this little means to please and serve Keir Hardie. I could see his amused surprise at this new arrival—imagined his way with it.

At home the puppy presented well ; everyone liked him and laughed at him. " He is only here for a little while," I told Mrs. Payne.

But now I had bought the puppy, how could it reach him ? Was anyone going North who could take it ? I wrote to Frank Smith. He advised me against sending it, for the present, at least. Keir Hardie was much too ill to care for it ; indeed they had been obliged to send away a dog because it distressed him. Ill news indeed—to one who knew him.

I kept the dog—I hoped for only a little. Donald, I called him, after the best-loved of the many pit ponies Keir Hardie befriended in his boyhood ; but in the office, the kitchen, the restaurant, they called him Jimmie—Keir Hardie's familiar nickname when a lad, which he had from many an old friend still. After a week's attempt to keep him Donald, I accepted " Jim " for him, as though Fate had had a voice in it.

. . . . . . . .

We were preparing for a joint demonstration in Trafalgar Square against Conscription, now obviously at hand. All the active movements for Socialism, Social Reform and free institutions were rallying to us. Among the speakers nominated by the Socialist, Labour, Suffrage and

Trade Union organisations which joined us were H. M. Hyndman, the old Social Democrat, who had never shed the ethics of jingo imperialism, and for that reason was fighting a losing battle to maintain his hold on the Socialist organisation he had created, E. C. Fairchild, who was to succeed him in its leadership, W. C. Anderson, M.P., of the I.L.P., John Hill and Fred Bramley, the leaders of the Boilermakers' Union and Furnishing Trades Union, Outhwaite, the Single Tax M.P., Mrs. Despard, Emmeline Pethick Lawrence, and many more.

It was a great gathering, ordered, united. My part of the speaking was over, an effort not small in so large a crowd. Newsboys with posters of a special edition came running to the meeting, a sight unusual on a Sunday. Strange words glared at me:

"DEATH OF KEIR HARDIE."

The world seemed rocking.

"Is it true?" I turned to W. C. Anderson, standing beside me.

"It must be," he answered gently; then, practical and alert: "I'll draft a resolution; he was *our* man."

. . . . . . . .

Around me seemed a strange dullness. . . . "You feel faint?" Barbara Tchaykovsky eyed me, doctoral. "Sit down and put your head between your knees," she ordered, enforcing her words with kind constraint.

I was not faint, but stunned and stricken. Yet I let her have her way with me, not caring. The world was dreary and grey, and Life too pitilessly cruel. . . .

I felt as they who had lost their dearest in the War; for the War had killed him, as surely as it had killed the men who went to the trenches and were shot. The struggle we were waging to improve material conditions, though for the very poorest, suddenly appeared sordid, the fight against Conscription mere paltering. I wished, with an intensity which seemed to burn up all other feeling, that while there was yet time, I had gone with him as a missioner through the country denouncing the War. Ruthlessly I examined myself, deciding that though I had spoken against the War, the greater part of my struggle had been waged for economic conditions. "Oh yes, I know this is a capitalist war; if capitalism were ended, wars would be no more; yet the politics of this War, in their callous wickedness; these you have not sufficiently exposed. . . . You have attacked the effects of war and of capitalism more often than those two great causes from which they spring."

Through the speeches, the greetings, the leave-takings, reproaches stormed within me. In the silent night they bore on me with torment; too sharp, too sharp, it seemed, to be endured—and yet beyond was a great absence, an abyss profound, limitless, terrifying . . . oh, to return!

Feverishly the mind sought to transform what might have been to what was, nay is, is, is . . . bringing the dead to life, renewing again the dear old comradeship, making it dearer yet and more complete. Scenes of make-believe, more vivid than memories, raced through my brain—phantoms, delusions, mocking dreams, folly, folly . . . always again that drear abyss, silent, grey, fathomless. . . . Oh no! Oh no, no, no! Let this hour pass! Let this hour never be!

To have stood beside him; travelled with him; laid aside all else to support and cherish him. Not one had borne that part towards him fully. All had their work, their families, their health, their incapacities —not one had said: "I will give my all to serve with him, and to serve him." Lesser men and women have known such serviceable companionship. Not you, O you tower of strength! In the lonely heights of your isolation, this was denied to you!

The great regrets surged over me—for words unsaid and things undone, for hours unlived . . . ah, to have seen the last of him! Within me rose the great rebellion against the cruelties of our life, and its denials . . . its foolish, vain denials. . . .

In the exhaustion of early morning some calmness came to me. I thought of him mantled in his great reserve, impregnable.

I felt the charge laid on me to make a more pointed and urgent struggle against the War and the influences which gave it birth.

. . . . . . . .

I spent the day putting down for the *Dreadnought* some of the thoughts I had of him, and with conviction wrote:

"Keir Hardie has been the greatest human being of our time: when the dust raised by opposition to the pioneer has settled, this will be known by all."

. . . . . . . .

A letter came to me from Frank Smith, written at the office of Robert Williams, the architect, in Cliffords Inn, lent from love of Keir Hardie for the unemployed and other agitations.

"September 26th, 1915.

"DEAR SYLVIA PANKHURST,

"I feel I must send you a line, but I hardly seem able to do it. What a loss is ours. I don't think anyone, among the many thousands who mourn for him, knew, understood or loved him better than you and I —and *now!*

"I only had a note from his brother George written on Saturday afternoon saying he had left him sleeping at the nursing home in Glasgow—and then to see it in the papers!

"Dear old Keir—how true a friend he was. I know how deeply and sincerely he ever held you in his mind and heart—

"I cannot write any more beyond saying again how great a loss is ours.

"Ever yours sincerely,

"FRANK SMITH."

I saw Frank Smith later in the dark little office in Cliffords Inn and put to him a question, restless in my mind :

" He wrote to me that he had not ' mind control.' What did he mean ? "

" He had delusions."

" What sort of delusions ? "

" With Lloyd George riding in a motor car," Frank Smith answered, with a gesture of misery.

. . . . . . . .

A meeting to honour Keir Hardie was held in the Memorial Hall. I remember the hoarse, deep roar of applause which greeted J. R. MacDonald when he rose. Men sprang to their feet and cheered him, and cheered again because he was the target on whom the attack of the conscriptionists and the jingoes mainly centred. He spoke tenderly of Keir Hardie, as did all that night. The spirit loomed over us of our leader and friend, who had loved humanity as others love their immediate families, and, feeling more deeply than the many can, had been stricken unto death by the Great War, in which he had neither kith nor kin of his blood, but the shattered brotherhood of the world whereon his hopes were set.

Among the leaders of the Socialist International none had foreseen so urgently and painfully as he, the approaching menace of the World War ; none more clearly conceived its prevention by a general refusal of the workers in all countries to assist in the conflict.

The proposal for the international general strike of the workers against war had been pioneered in the international Socialist congresses by the Dutchman, Domela Nieuwenhuis, since 1891 and by Hervé, the French "anti-patriot," as he called himself. Bebel, the German Socialist leader, and the majority of his party had opposed it as "impossible and beyond discussion." Hervé's propaganda had found large support in the French Socialist Party. Jaurès, its leader, at the Stuttgart International Socialist Congress had given his assent to a resolution of the French party in which the general strike and insurrection was mentioned as one of the means by which the workers might oppose war. That this assent, though sincere, was mainly academic later events were to indicate. The Stuttgart Conference eventually adopted a formula in which direct endorsement of the general strike against war was avoided and the differences in the opposing policies glossed over. At the Copenhagen Conference in 1910 Keir Hardie and Edouard Vaillant of France moved an amendment, drafted by Hardie himself, declaring for the general strike against war, "especially in the industries which supply war with its implements (arms and ammunition, transport, etc.)." Vandervelde of Belgium, the skilful diplomatist, who was to find a seat in the Belgian Coalition War Cabinet, persuaded Hardie and Vaillant to accept the reference of their proposal to the International Socialist Bureau, for study and report to the next conference. The report should have been presented at the Conference which never was held, for the World War had come and found the Socialists unprepared. Like Hervé, the "anti-patriot," who at the first trump of war had become patriot of the patriots, jingo of the jingoes, the battalions of the International had turned to rend each other.

To Keir Hardie the International general strike against war was an article of profound faith. Once he had accepted it, in his clear-minded definite way, it became one of the great objects of his life to work for it steadily, persistently. Advocating it and defending it through Press and platform in this country, again and again he tore himself from the pressure of home politics, to pioneer for it abroad—in France, Belgium,

Hungary, Scandinavia, above all in Germany. He wrote to me from Copenhagen during the Socialist International Congress of 1910:

"We have been having the usual trouble with the S.D.F.,[1] but have now got them finally in hand and have turned Hyndman off the Bureau.[2] I have accepted invitations to speak at two meetings in Sweden next week, and from there I go on to Frankfort-on-Main for a demonstration. . . ."

H. M. Hyndman, as is well known, had long predicted war with Germany, demanding Conscription, to raise what he termed "a citizen army," and advocating naval and military preparedness for the approaching war. He had bitterly attacked Keir Hardie's propaganda of international working class solidarity.

In August 1912 Keir Hardie and Arthur Henderson, on behalf of the British Section of the International Socialist Bureau, had addressed a letter to the Trade Unions of this country, urging an "anti-war strike," as "supplementary" to political action, and to be used "where political action is not yet sufficiently developed to prevent" war.

In the Morocco crisis of 1911 Keir Hardie had called on British workers to hold themselves prepared, so that in the event of war, not a soldier or a cannon should be transported by ship or train.[3] Ten months before the World War he was at the German Socialist Congress in Jena, pleading for the establishment of the United States of Europe. Eight months before the War he was speaking for peace with Jaurès, Adler and Vandervelde in London. On the very eve of the conflict he was with the International Socialist Bureau in Brussels, striving to avert the War.

. . . . . . . . .

[1] The party of H. M. Hyndman. Hardie here used the old initials of this organisation, the "Social Democratic Federation," though it had become the British Socialist Party.

[2] The International Socialist Bureau, of which Hyndman had been an original member.

[3] Speech at International Peace Demonstration, London, August 17th, 1911.

May O'Callaghan, my sub-editor, who prided herself upon her compatriotism with Bernard Shaw, regarding him in some subtle fashion as a piece of her own property, urged that she should write him asking for an article on Keir Hardie for the *Dreadnought* of the following week. Having kissed the blarney-stone, like all the Irish, and sharing their gift of humour, she was much more likely than I to succeed immediately in such a task. She obtained at once the promise of a Shaw article which was to appear simultaneously in the *Merthyr Pioneer*. She received also one of Shaw's characteristic letters wherein, most unexpectedly, he observed that his article was "not nearly so good as Sylvia's." He added graciously: "Will you undertake to send me the *Dreadnought* every week during my life (I am now in my 59th year) if I pay you a ten years' subscription? Anticipating a favourable reply, I enclose a cheque for £2 3s. 4d."

It was a thrifty bargain, for though the *Dreadnought* lasted only nine years more, its price rose perforce, with the rising cost of paper and printing, and from a halfpenny became twopence before the War ended.

Shaw's article proved typically Shavian, with a bitterness, to me, almost too acid:

"There is, I feel sure, a very general feeling of relief in the House of Commons and the Labour Party that Keir Hardie's body lies mouldering in the grave. . . . I really do not see what Hardie could do but die. Could we expect him to hang on and sit there among the poor slaves who imagined themselves Socialists until the touchstone of war found them out and exposed them for what they are? . . . That the workers themselves—the Labour Party he had so painfully dragged into existence—should snatch still more eagerly at the War to surrender those liberties and escape back into servility, crying: 'You may trust your masters: they will treat you well.' . . . This was what broke the will to live in Keir Hardie."

. . . . . . . .

And there was Jim, poor fellow, who looked up at me with his eyes of love. He had proved to be no retriever, but a cross-bred old English sheep-dog. His black coat had turned iron-grey ; his black eyes golden-brown like the eyes of him I bought him for. " A funny old thing with a noble head," people called him. Hard driven as I was with work, I had no time for him, but I kept him with me, and fondled him more than I would have done under other circumstances. He responded generously, as a good dog will, repaying our poor care of them, in affection, a thousand-fold. He was given to pranks. The habit of poking shoes and slippers into convenient corners, into which some of the office workers had fallen, was quickly cured ; for towards shoes of all sorts he was ruthless. Hats, too, on many occasions he demolished. His period of destructiveness quickly passed, but never his playfulness. He had a great way of dancing before one on his hind legs, and gently dabbing at one with his fore-paws, his mouth open as though he were smiling and pleading for a game. " Dear Jim, you are the pet of us all ! " Mrs. Snedden, the cook in the restaurant, responded to his appeal ; a quiet little widow with grown-up daughters, she treated him as affectionately as though he had been a child, and so did all the workers about the place. Yet he was always my dog, though I never fed him and on the whole had little time to notice him. When I was away in the provinces speaking, he kept to my rooms, and if driven out would lay himself at my bedroom door in the little dark passage, where whoever came by was apt to tread on him. If he could elude the vigilance of Mrs. Payne, he would crouch on my bed and remain there, caring nothing for food or drink, his long hair in wet weather making a hideous mess of it, till Mrs. Payne rushed in to change the coverings with excited outcries. When I was at home Jim never once played that trick on us !

He knew my step and sprang always swift to the door to give me a greeting. Dear Jim, dear dogs, so faithful in your ungrudging love which satisfies us not.

. . . . . . . .

At one of the Labour conferences held about then to discuss the emergencies of the time, I met Katharine Bruce Glasier; I had not come across her for many a year. She seemed not a day older, the same emotional, impulsive Katharine as when I first saw her in Manchester twenty-three years before. Her daughter, the Jeannie I knew as a chubby baby, and a toddler of two or three, was beside her. I could not discern in the girl's pretty pale face and soft-voiced smoothness a hint of her mother's rebellious emotions, or her father's romantic vision. "She is Margaret Bondfield's secretary!" her mother told me with evident pride; but Katharine would have been secretary to none; she was ever for a way of her own. Malcolm, her son, came to greet her in the dinner hour; fair and flaxen, his curly hair growing far back from the forehead, like his father's, his blue eyes cold and prominent; they seemed without feeling—a lad who had not found himself, one would say. It was a shock to see his mother's son in a brass-buttoned Naval uniform; I felt a pang of sorrowful pity for her; but she seemed both happy and proud of him, and gleefully told me he had run away to sea. Yet despite her bubbling exterior cheerfulness, at heart, I felt, she must be stricken with grief, disappointment and apprehension. She talked with her old helter-skelter enthusiasm of her endless campaigning: "I told them that war is murder. . . . I gave them it straight from the heart! John So-and-so told me he didn't know which to admire most—the woman or her audience!"

Yes, she was the old Kate Conway of her early Socialist days, not one whit changed; but the Socialism had become Pacifism, and the Atheism, Christian Science.

In one of the conference intervals a crowd of us went to tea somewhere—perhaps the International Women's Suffrage Club in Grafton Street. Mrs. Glasier and I were alone together. She spoke of Keir Hardie, "Keir," as she always called him, his greatness, his wisdom, the early days of the I.L.P. She was one of the little band of its first speakers.

"We all recognised Keir as our leader. I obeyed him more than my husband—more than Bruce," she said; and babbled on in her incoherent fashion: "Hardie wasn't his name, you know. Hardie was only his stepfather. . . . . . . . . . . . . . . . . that's why he was so absolutely different from the rest of them. . . . His mother recognised it. 'Keir's father was a very different man from this!' she told me herself, the old lady; oh, lassie, a dear old lady, and a very fine woman . . . . of course it was a love match. She's said to me, the old lady: 'You love your man?' Oh lassie, she knew I did; that is why she could talk to me. 'And wouldn't you go to your man?' she asked me. 'Ah, that I would, my dearie, against the world!' I answered her; you may believe me! . . . Those three! Those three! . . . Ah, lassie, there is nothing like a love match! Love is the crown of life! You know about Bruce, of course. I must have told you the story. His mother's father wouldn't give his consent; Bruce's father rode away with her on a great black horse at midnight. . . . Her father sent a company of horsemen after them to catch them, but they got away clear. . . .

"Keir . . . poor Keir! . . . Ah yes, dearie, didn't you know? His mother, she thought the world of him but she wouldn't. . . . We all knew it, but . . . His beautiful silence."

Waves of thought were rending me, grief for the sadness of life, amaze at its poignant drama. Novels, romances, what is the need of them? Not one is so strange, so poignant as the true romance of Life.

In her talk Katharine Glasier had mentioned that the proof of the first chapter of Keir Hardie's autobiography had been found since his death. He had told me that the loss, at the *Labour Leader* office, of this first chapter had deterred him from continuing the book; he could not bring himself to begin it again. I begged that I might see it, and presently it was lent to me—two brief, pregnant galleys of print. A part of Mrs. Glasier's strange story it confirmed; for he told there that his birth was branded with "the bar sinister." He spoke of his mother, Mary Keir; but of his father not. A moving record of the childhood, both hard and tragic, of the man who was to build the Labour Party, it has been re-told in part by others; it should be published in his own burning words.

. . . . . . . .

Later that year I was speaking in Glasgow and met, for the first time, his sister Agnes Aiton, the only one of his mother's children I had seen who had some hint of a look of him in her tender face. Only some brief words we had together, but I felt a bond between us. Later I received a letter from her:

"You will be thinking I have forgotten you, but you are ever in my mind since I saw you in Glasgow. I had often heard of you, but never seen you until I met you in Mrs. Crawford's, and my heart went out to you for the sake of one I knew thought the world of you. . . ."

When next in Glasgow I stayed with her at Cambuslang. She told me things of him which brought both sorrow and wonder to my heart.

. . . . . . . .

It was under the spell of his eulogy of Keir Hardie that I asked Bernard Shaw to speak for us in aid of the Mothers' Arms. He consented very amiably. The demand for tickets was great ; we made a much needed profit of £75 for the fund.

Shaw's speech was to me intensely disappointing. In a being less wayward one would have said it was deliberately intended to efface the impression of his *Common Sense about the War*. Indeed in some of its passages it was decidedly jingo. I felt really ashamed to be his chairman and dissociated myself and our organisation from his remarks with as little offence as I could—I believe with success, for he told me I had " the family charm." Afterwards I wrote to him expressing regret, which I knew to be shared by many to whom his name was a household word, that he had not taken a definite stand against the War, and urging him to do so. He answered that in helping to save the babies I was accomplishing something effective ; to oppose the War was hopeless. " How can you hope to convert the public," he asked, " when you cannot even convert your mother and Christabel ? "

Later I read, with regret, and also with wrath, his flippant account of how he had been, as he termed it, " joy-riding at the Front." The article was in praise of the British military machine and its fighting qualities.

His *O'Leary, V.C.*, I considered an inexcusable production. His early attitude towards the Russian Revolution and his whitewashing of Mussolini enraged me ; but for much that he has written one must be grateful. I believe that in sum his influence has been of great value in our public life. I sympathise with the view of some witty person who observed, " Shaw is a good man fallen among Fabians." Had he imbibed the doctrines of Marx, as he would have us believe,[1] and turned thence to the genial influences of Peter Kropotkin and William Morris, the rapier of his wit might have been more penetrating.

[1] Vide *The Intelligent Woman's Guide to Socialism* (Constable) and many prefaces.

# CHAPTER XXX

## PENSIONS FOR BROKEN MEN—THE WOMAN'S TRENCH

DAILY I was confronted by the army of broken men discharged from the Army and Navy, penniless, pensionless, turned adrift without a word of information or advice as to how a pension, or sustenance of any sort, might be obtained. By February, 1915, £1,500,000 had been spent on pensions to the disabled. Had all the poor victims who were too far disabled to serve in the War again been pensioned on similar scale the cost would have been £2,250,000.[1] Thus a third of the great army broken in the War had been left to fend for themselves unaided. Not a man but had suffered the anxious bitterness of uncertainty and delay.

Lord Newton estimated that to pension all disabled men, should the War last till March 31st, 1917, would cost £11,360,000. The Government repudiated this as an unthinkable extravagance; yet the cost of the War was rising to £5,000,000 a day and the price of the slaughter was not grudged. Ministers often declared, with Bonar Law, that the soldiers must have "the first claim on the resources of the country"; but to implement such declarations would have entailed greater sacrifice than others were prepared to make, though the prompt payment of the most ample pension could not compensate these poor fellows for broken health and loss of limbs.

Even the cost of the separation allowances was jealously regarded. It was officially stated in the Commons, on January 15th, 1916, that the separation allowances to dependants of unmarried soldiers averaged only 5s. 4d. per week per soldier, and to wives and children of married soldiers no more than 17s. a week. Yet Lord Devonport[2] urged the Government to save £30,000,000 a year by re-casting the separation allowances so as to provide that no family should receive a larger income than before the War. The notion that no soldier's family should find its income reduced was outside his conception.

Unhappy women mourned the loss of sons and husbands, their separation allowances cut off, no pensions as yet forthcoming. Again and again the promise was made that there should be no hiatus; that the allowances should continue until the pension was assured; but repeatedly the promise was broken; delays, red-tape, confusion and chaos left many a family to starve when its breadwinner was killed, as it had starved when he first enlisted, because the separation allowance failed to come.

[1] Statement by Lord Newton, Postmaster-General, House of Lords, February 20th, 1915.

[2] House of Lords Official Report, November 19th, 1915.

In November 1914 the Government had announced that the old Boer War scale of pensions[1] would be replaced by a new and better plan; but the promised new scheme was shelved. The recommendations of a Select Committee, though ostensibly approved, failed to come into force. At last, on May 15th, 1915, a Royal Warrant raising the old scale was issued, to take effect from March 1st. Under this Warrant, discharged soldiers, sailors and marines were to receive 25s. a week for total disablement, with children's allowances of 2s. 6d. a week each. Few indeed were the men who received a pension on this scale! The partially disabled man—and the vast majority of cripples were so considered—was to get such allowance as "with the wages he is deemed capable of earning," would amount to 25s. a week. Children's allowances not exceeding 2s. 6d. a week each might be awarded in addition—but usually they were not.

"I know what it will mean," George Lansbury said to me, when the scheme was announced. "I have seen how it operates in the Workmen's Compensation cases, with people like Sir John Colley measuring the losses to men's limbs by inches!"

Actually the pensions administration proved harsher than that of workmen's compensation; for in the latter case there was trial by judge and jury and appeal from Court to Court. From the Naval and Military Departments there was no appeal save to themselves.[2] There was no compensation for pain and suffering. The actual earnings of the disabled man were not taken into account, unless by doing so a reduction or stoppage of pension could be achieved. The unwillingness, nay, the inability of employers to provide an unfailing stream of "light work" for cripples was ignored. No appeal that the man could not obtain work secured an increase of pension; but if he got a job, he must notify the authorities immediately, and his pension was cut at once.

Widows under the new scale got 10s. a week if under 35 years, rising to 15s. if over 45, with 5s. a week for the first child, 3s. 6d. for the second and 2s. 6d. each for the rest.

In any case no pensions, whether to widows and orphans or to disabled men, were granted, unless the cause of death (or disablement) was deemed to be "wholly and directly due to war service."[3] A man in the Royal

[1] The old scale of pension for soldiers, sailors and marines was 10/6 a week for total disablement, increased by children's allowances to a maximum of 17/6; for partial disablement 3/6 to 10/6. Widows got their separation allowances and allotments for a month after their man had been killed; then, if pensions were awarded, 5/- a week, and 1/6 a week for each child, pensions being closely restricted to legally married wives, and the legitimate children of the soldier; adopted children and step-children being barred.

[2] A Pensions Appeal Tribunal was set up in 1917.

[3] In February 1916 Will Thorne moved an amendment to the Address, expressing regret that the Government had not seen fit to pension all men discharged from the Army or Navy on account of diseases contracted or developed during service. The Government resisted this view, but when the Labour Party again pressed it by resolution, it was conceded that where a man's disease had been *aggravated*, though not *wholly and directly caused*, by war service, a pension might be granted on a lower scale.

Field Artillery fell off the tail-board of an Army wagon and was run over and killed. His widow was denied a pension. Under the Workmen's Compensation Act she could have secured compensation from an ordinary employer; but the Workmen's Compensation Act, the Employers' Liability Act, and any power to recover damages at Common Law were inapplicable to soldiers and sailors.

An Act to prevent such compensation being obtained by any others employed by the Army and Navy in warlike operations, was actually rushed through in the first month of War.[1]

The grant of Naval and Military pensions, pay and separation allowances remained legally an act of grace. In vain the plea went up that the men should be protected by the legal right for themselves and their families to their wages—both pay and separation allowance—whilst serving, and to their pensions on discharge, as well as by the power to sue for wages and pensions in the Courts.[2] Men who for thirty years had shown no signs of illness, were refused pensions, on the ground that their disease had not originated in the War. A man between 40 and 50 years of age, whilst at the Front, became afflicted with delusional insanity, never before apparent. In the effort to discover another cause than war for his malady, his wife was questioned as to whether he had been born at full term, whether instruments were used at his birth, and at what age he cut his teeth!

Lord Newton observed to the House of Lords, in February 1916, that appeals from the decisions of Chelsea Hospital in respect of pensions, were almost invariably made; and that increased payments were "frequently" granted as a result—an admission, certainly, that the "almost invariable" appeals were not made without warrant! Whilst the original decision of a man's pension by Chelsea Hospital was often hideously retarded, appeals, whether successful or not, entailed many further months of delay. A typical case was that of J— S—, an old soldier, who had fought through the Boer War, had re-enlisted and, like a substantial proportion of the older men, proved unfit to withstand the hardships previously endured. He was discharged in December 1914, suffering from rheumatoid arthritis, having lost the use of both hands through damp and exposure. There were five dependent children, the youngest six months old. Separation allowance ceased; no pension came. Until March 22nd, 1915, when the wife came to me, only a few small doles from the Soldiers and Sailors Families Association had been received. I applied to Chelsea Hospital the same day, and on

[1] Injuries of War (Compensation) Act, 1914.

[2] A Royal Warrant issued by Lord Kitchener on February 19th, 1916, in respect of dependants, expressed with frank brutality a ruling which applied to all Naval and Military pensions and allowances: "A pension or gratuity for the dependants of a deceased soldier shall not be granted as a right. It shall not be granted or continued when the applicant is proved to be unworthy, in the opinion of our Army Council, of the award, or unless the soldier's services were in their judgment such as to justify the grant. . . . Our Army Council shall have power to vary or revoke any grant, and their decision in any case shall be final."

April 9th was informed that a pension of 1s. 6d. a day had been granted for nine months " conditional "—which meant that if the man showed any signs of recovery during that time, the payments would be reduced or withdrawn. I protested that as the man was wholly incapable of work, he was entitled under the Select Committee's recommendations to 25s. a week and 10s. on his children's account. Recruits were being asked to enlist on the basis of the Select Committee's scheme; but Chelsea Hospital replied that the recommendations were not yet in force. When the Royal Warrant of the following May announced new regulations, I pressed again for a higher pension. On July 15th, 1915, Chelsea Hospital informed me that the pension would be increased to 18s. 9d. a week and 10s. for the five children—this after eight months' waiting! I continued writing, urging the grant of full pension.

This was but one of thousands of similar cases; if someone had not taken it up, the man would have gone without pension altogether. Men continued appealing to me from all parts of the country who had waited sometimes a year, or even two years, for settlement. No case was finally settled. After months of correspondence to get a pension for them, in a short time the men would return again; their pension had been cut off or reduced. The same old fight had to be made time and again for the same man. The same under-estimate of his injuries, the same over-estimate of his powers must be combated; the same mistakes and muddles; the same delays would be met again and again. Each case for its original, so fugitive settlement entailed a great pile of correspondence. New cases overwhelmed us daily; every few days I had out the old files and pegged away at the old stubborn cases. Nellie Cohen, and the others who helped me, habitually worked overtime doing it.

On July 15th, 1915, a poor fellow staggered into my room, begging with trembling lips to know whether I had news for him. Discharged very ill on April 30th, he had received not a penny of pay or pension since that day, though I had sent a doctor's certificate, giving a grave report of him, to Chelsea Hospital, and had many times written to the authorities on his behalf. He had scarcely left me before a distracted wife collapsed on my threshold. When I had restored her, she told me that her husband had been sent home wounded and paralysed in both arms. He was utterly helpless, unable even to feed himself, and in such terribly acute agony that she could scarcely stir from his bedside. It was quite impossible for her to attempt to earn their living. He had received no money from any source since his discharge, nor any advice. Her separation allowance had ceased on June 14th—an awful month ago! I protested vehemently by telephone and letters and presently secured for the man a pension of 25s. a week, arrears to date from June 15th. To me it was always an astonishment that no arrangements were made to provide for a man's pension at the time of his discharge, and that there were no official arrangements for after-care.

An East London youth who had lost one arm and received an injury to the other, and had several unhealed wounds in the legs, was awarded a pension of only 4s. 8d. a week, with the callous order to "go out and earn the rest!" A motor driver with shattered nerves was denied pension altogether. His late employer would have taken him back but he could not drive. I got for him 12s. 6d. a week pension, and after further protest and agitation 1s. 3d. a week for his child.

A lance-corporal became seriously ill through exposure. After delays, which occasioned untold hardship, and the report of his doctor that he was incurable, he was awarded a pension of 14s. a week for himself, his wife and child. He needed constant attention both night and day. His wife was therefore unable to earn anything. Nourishment and medicines were ordered to alleviate his suffering, for which the little dole he was receiving by no means sufficed. In her desperate fight to ease his pain, bit by bit, his wife sold their furniture, whilst she and the child went so short of food, that the little one became ill, and had to be taken to hospital. I learnt the unhappy story on July 17th, and at once applied for the full pension, making it clear that the man was dying. On July 21st Chelsea Hospital informed me that the pension would be increased to 20s. a week, with arrears dating from March 1st. Moreover the Commissioners promised to have the man medically re-examined, to ascertain whether the full pension should be granted. Glad to give the unfortunate wife this comfort, I immediately wrote her this news. The promised examination was made, and on August 8th Chelsea Hospital notified me that the pension would be increased to 25s. a week, dating from September 8th; and that an allowance of 2s. 6d. a week would be made for the child, dating from March 1st.

Alas, for so much precision, such futile calculation of dates! Again I wrote the poor woman, telling her what had been written to me, and expressing the hope that the new allowance came regularly each week, and that the due arrears had been paid. Alas, indeed, for her patience! On September 3rd she came, blanched and haggard, to tell me her husband was dead. She had sold by this time everything save his bed and a single chair. Only now did I learn that the miserable allowance of 14s. weekly had never been increased! In vain she had waited for the fulfilment of a single one of the promises I had transmitted to her! My heart smote me. If only I had known!

I wrote in the *Dreadnought*, begging our League of Rights members to form visiting committees, to keep in touch with poor pensioners in distress.

W. C. Anderson told the House of Commons of a soldier, discharged on medical grounds, who was taken by the military to Maybole Workhouse. Indignantly he refused to enter, and asked to be taken to his home in Sheffield. The military escort disclaimed further responsibility and left him in the street! He had but 2s. 6d. in his possession!

Laurence Ginnell, the frail old Sinn Feiner of caustic rhetoric, cried out in the House[1] that Patrick Sullivan of the Royal Irish Fusiliers had died of neglect in the Weymouth Workhouse and had been buried in a pauper's grave. How many unhappy cases went undisclosed?

[1] February 24th, 1916.

In the summer of 1915 the Government introduced a Naval and Military Pensions Bill, to remove the pensions administration from Government jurisdiction, and place it under a non-Parliamentary Statutory Committee. This move had a twofold purpose; firstly, it was desired to prevent Members of Parliament from continuing to expose, in the form of questions to Ministers, the hardships and grievances of the disabled, and of the widows and orphans of the slain. Secondly, it was hoped that, by this means, the Government might evade all responsibility for pensioning the parents and other dependants of unmarried soldiers, the unmarried wives and natural children. As first introduced, the Bill provided for the payment of such pensions from the National Relief Fund. It also provided for supplementary grants from the same Fund to persons who, having enjoyed a more prosperous status, would now greatly resent subsistence upon the ordinary war pensions scale; and to certain hardly-used people to whom pension had been refused. Curiously, the Bill contained no provision for monetary payments of any sort save salaries to the chairman and secretary of the Committee. Therefore, though the intention was not disclosed, it was probably hoped, after a time, to disburden the Government also of responsibility for the pensions to disabled men and to widows and orphans, and to transfer these also from the Government Exchequer to the National Relief Fund. The scale of these pensions had been fixed by Royal Warrant; by Royal Warrant it might at any time be varied or extinguished. Parliament was to have nothing to say in the matter. Such pensions as had been granted under the Royal Warrant had been granted, as yet, only for "twelve months conditional." For the dependants of unmarried soldiers, who were to be dealt with by the Statutory Committee, no pensions had as yet been fixed.

An obstacle to the Government plan to draw on the National Relief Fund[1] for the war pensions was raised up by the powerfully-placed committee men appointed to administer the Fund at the outbreak of war. Under the chairmanship of A. J. Balfour, they refused to permit any other committee to disburse any part of the Fund, which was now lying idle. Bowing to their political and social influence, McKenna, the Home Secretary, explained that he did not think it would be fair "to press" these gentlemen against their will. Ignominiously the Bill was withdrawn, but the Government still continued vaguely assuming that the funds for the Statutory Committee would be raised by charitable donations.

As usual, a complacent majority in the Commons accepted the Government's proposals; but once more a majority in the hereditary House of reaction came forward in defence of popular interests. The

[1] The Fund now amounted to upwards of £5,000,000. Only £364,645 from it had been dispensed for the civilian distress for which it was subscribed. Donations from the well-to-do and all independent gifts to it had now practically ceased, but the regular dues deducted by the employers from the wages of workpeople and Civil Service employees continued as before.

Lords had no incentive to assist a government of elected representatives to evade inconvenient responsibilities. Moreover they had in their midst some, like John Morley, Leonard Courtney, Parmoor and Russell, who, openly or privately, hated the War and its works. They inserted amendments into the Pensions Bill, firstly to make the Government financially responsible for all Naval and Military pensions and grants ; secondly, to make the Statutory Committee, which would administer the pensions, responsible to the House of Commons. The Government rejected the Lords' amendments, but agreed to make a grant of £1,000,000 to the funds of the Statutory Committee.[1] This very ineffective compromise was accepted by the Lords ; they had done more for poor pensioners than one has a right to expect from a House of Peers, when the Commons have lacked either the heart or the spirit to do anything.

One very dark spot in this Pensions Act was the gift to the irresponsible Statutory Committee of power :

" To decide whether any pension, grant, or separation allowance to wife, widow, child or other dependant, has under the regulations subject to which it was granted, become forfeit."

From the Committee's decision to declare a pension forfeit there was no appeal. Almost alone, save for humble, obscure women, who knew how hardly it might be used towards them, I protested against this iniquitous clause.

While the Act was still pending, one irresponsible seaside committee, to which had been entrusted the distribution of the additional rent allowances, often necessary in watering places, provided an example of the victimisation which could be practised upon soldiers' dependants. Mrs. Fiddes, whose husband and two sons were at the Front, who had one delicate child at home, and paid 12s. 6d. a week in rent, had her rent allowance withdrawn, on the report of an Alderman on the relief committee that she was " not temperate." Other members of the committee and the local Trades Council defended her. The charge was fully disproved ; but the allowance was not restored, for to have done so would have been to censure the Alderman !

It had been promised that the dependants of unmarried soldiers should not suffer from the delay in producing a scale of pensions for them. Yet many a widowed mother received the following letter when her son had been killed and her allowance ceased :

" SIR—

" With reference to your letter of —— I am directed to inform you that any claim you may wish to make to a dependant's pension or other

[1] It was presently disclosed that the supplementary allowances already made by the National Relief Committee, which were mainly rent allowances to soldiers' dependants, amounted to about a million pounds a year, and that this burden was to be passed on to the new Statutory Committee.

grant should be put forward when the Statutory Committee, which is being considered by Parliament, has been appointed.

"I am, Sir,

"Your obedient servant,

"J. G. Ashley.

"For the Assistant Financial Secretary."

On a great volume of protest against this breach of promise being raised throughout the country, the allowances were generally restored; but, as always, many for whom there was no influential intercession were left without.

When at last the pensions for soldiers' parents were announced, they were fixed at a maximum of 10s. a week, to continue only so long as the recipient was incapacitated and possessed no other means of support. The Old Age Pension and disablement benefit under the National Insurance were to be reckoned in diminution of the pension. Other dependants were to get a maximum of 5s. a week. The unmarried wife, if childless, was to be cut off with a year's separation allowance; but if physically incapable of working, she might possibly get from 5s. to 10s. a week, so long as her incapacity continued. If children of the dead soldier or sailor were in her care, they might get the usual children's allowances, and she might possibly have 10s. a week till the last of them reached the age limit. Then she would get a terminal gratuity of £13. All this was wholly at the discretion of the irresponsible committees, who might always refuse or reduce the official scale.

Whilst all the hideous errors and cruelties of the pension system poured in on us at Old Ford, and on whoever in all the country would bestir himself or herself to aid the unfortunate victims of war's iniquity, still the separation allowance problems were not yet settled, would never be settled, were always displaying new facets of misery and wrong. Again and again it had been promised that, in suitable cases, one parent of a soldier should receive the same allowance as a wife, and the other parent and younger brothers and sisters the allowances payable to soldiers' children. Though I constantly urged it in cases where families were plunged into destitution by the removal of the son who had been their support and mainstay, the promise was never honoured. Even where several sons by their joint earnings had kept their parents in comfort; even where the father had been suddenly stricken down after the son's enlistment, the rigid maximum of 12s. was adhered to.

A sailor's mother wrote to me from Manchester. Her son allotted her 4s. a week from his pay. The Admiralty added only 6d. The lad had given his mother £1 a week till just before his enlistment, when, being on half time, he was only able to give her 10s. There were four little brothers and sisters at home, whose ages ranged from 15 months to 11 years. The father had long been an invalid, and the mother had earned 9s. a week on her own account, but now the father had become acutely ill, and she had to give up her work to nurse him. The lad appealed to his paymaster on his mother's behalf, and was rebuffed by the answer that, since he had a father living, no allowance was due to his mother from Government funds! After many letters I secured 12s. a week for the mother.

Wherever this wretched maximum of 12s. dependant's allowance was granted, it was reduced to 10s. or less when the dear son was killed!

"I lost my dear lad in the *Bulwark*," a mother wrote to me. "My mother is 88 and I am nearly 60, and he helped to keep the home. . . . You speak so truly of what we poor mothers are feeling, *do keep at them!* An oldish mother needs it even more than a young childless wife—for the young have consolations that we have not. . . . My boy was just making life easier!

"Dear lady, thank you for your kind advocacy. . . ."

Whilst the people so often knew nothing of what might be due to them, the Army officials themselves were frequently ignorant of the regulations. When the War broke out it was the rule that no separation allowance was payable in respect of a marriage which took place after enlistment. Some officials failed to observe when this rule was changed. A soldier in the R.F.A. who married on January 10th, 1915, was still appealing in vain for his wife's allowance when he came to me on April 21st. I was happy, and much surprised, in this case to secure the allowance within three days. More often one had a month or two of correspondence to force the facts home, then after redress was promised, a month or more of waiting before the money came.

Sailors were obliged to buy for themselves many garments not supplied by the Admiralty, especially when serving in the cold North seas. Sailors' wives made many sacrifices to buy what their men needed out of their separation allowances. One poor woman, who had done so with loving generosity out of her weekly 29s. 6d., was soon obliged to repeat her effort, because her husband's boat was blown up, and he lost all save the clothes he was wearing. The men on that ship had received no pay for several months, and were thus compelled to rely entirely on their wives to make good their loss. This woman was struggling to buy what her husband needed when the paymaster wrote that her allowance would be reduced, for the amazing reason that she was "in debt to the Crown." She enquired how this could be, and was informed that her husband had reduced his allotment from 11s. to 6s. a week some time before. The devoted fellow had done no such thing. All he knew of the business was that he had received not a penny of pay for six months!

In face of the grievous delays to which the men and their families were victims, the War Office had the amazing effrontery to set a time limit to applications for pensions and separation allowances. A woman who had lived as the wife of a soldier for eleven years, and had borne him children, ignorant that changed regulations now entitled her to an allowance, had gone into the Workhouse, destitute. On June 29th, 1915, the very last day for her to make a claim under the new regulations, her plight came to my knowledge. Since it was too late to notify the

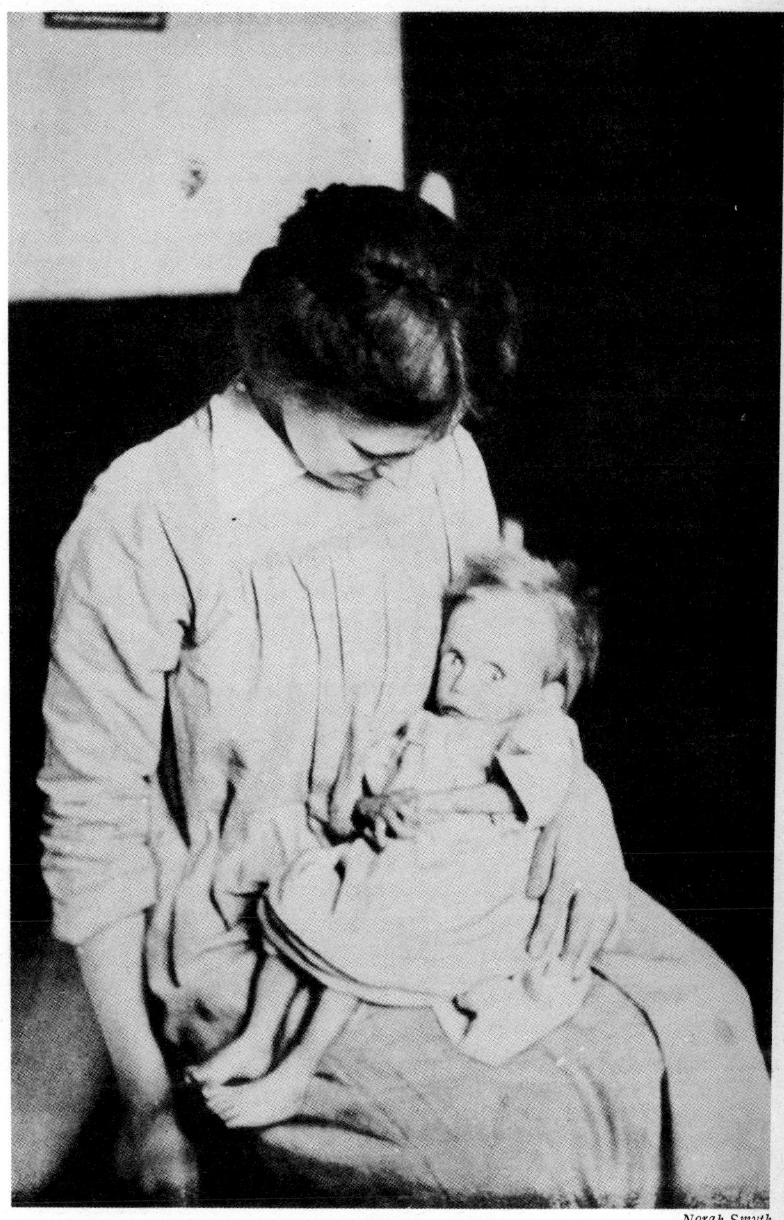

*Norah Smyth*

AS THEY CAME TO US

Nurse Hebbes and one of the war sufferers brought to the "Mothers' Arms."

*Reproduced from the "Workers' Dreadnought"*

PEACE OR FAMINE—WHICH?
Drawing by Joseph Southall
(1917)

woman and the soldier to apply in time, I wrote to the Paymaster and the War Office explaining the circumstances. Some sympathetic official in the War Office gave kindly attention to my plea. By this time I had made some headway within those stony portals, and I have been told that it used to be said in there: "Another letter from Sylvia; what have we got to do for her this time?" I was advised, to my great satisfaction, that my letter would be taken as "an application within the meaning of the Army Order." My pleasure gave way to dismay when I presently received a curt note from the Territorial Force Association that the soldier had "no wish to make an allotment." How could I meet my poor suppliant with such heart-grieving ill-news? Better a thousand times that she had suffered from ignorance of the regulations, than through the callousness of her man!

Whilst I cogitated anxiously as to how this obstacle might be overcome, the woman came out of the Workhouse to see me. Very bitterly she wept when she heard my news. She was unable to write so much as her name, but I got her to dictate to me a letter to her soldier, and to take the pathetic epistle herself to the Territorial Headquarters in the hope of seeing him. I never knew whether the man had changed his mind, or whether the report of his refusal was erroneous, as so many such reports were. I learnt only that the allotment was made in due course and heard from the woman herself that she had received her allowance.

Another unmarried wife got no separation allowance from May 19th to July 24th, when she came to me. By frantic efforts I secured her money on July 27th, only just in time to prevent her eviction for non-payment of rent!

The unwieldy machinery of militarism creaked and jolted miserably; red-tape strangled natural human feeling.

A new sort of envelope was issued for soldiers' letters from the Front. As usual, some regiments received no supplies, and the soldiers perforce continued using the old ones. The censors at the Front destroyed the letters and sent home the envelopes, inscribed: "Letter destroyed. This pattern obsolete."[1] Many a woman lost thus the last letter of her beloved son or husband, dead on the field!

Despite many official pledges and much agitation, wives were still suffering in loss of separation allowance for husbands' failings, due in many cases to illness and hardship. An unfortunate private in the Cameron Highlanders, sent home for seven days' leave, was so ill with rheumatism, that he was obliged to go into a local hospital. His leave expired, and 24 days later, a military escort took him out of bed under arrest. He was kept under punishment till he went to the Front. The wife's separation allowance was stopped.

Another soldier, who had overstayed his leave, wrote to me pleading:

[1] Mr. Neild protested against this practice in the House of Commons, November 18th, 1915.

" My poor wife and children are starving. . . . They have stopped my wife's allowance this three weeks. . . . If they don't soon send her some money God knows what she will do ! "

Private M'Adams, a poor fellow in the Poplar and Stepney Rifles, was torn from his sick wife's bedside as an absentee. The police magistrate, in pity, allowed him to return to her, but he found her dead. " Can a man soldier with a wife and children starving at home ? " pleaded Samuel Brook, a gunner in the Royal Garrison Artillery, when charged at Marylebone Police Court as an absentee. He had gone home in Christmas week, because his wife's allowance had stopped unaccountably, and she had neither food nor fuel in the house. He was handed over to an escort and taken back, a prisoner, to his regiment.

Serving soldiers sometimes applied to me to defend them. An Army driver was told off to arrest a drunken recruit, who flung a tumbler in his face, and thus deprived him of an eye. For eight months the driver was under treatment for this injury. Whilst still an out-patient at the London Hospital, he was mistakenly arrested as a deserter. His pay was also stopped in error. I had just succeeded in getting him most of the arrears due, when he wrote appealing to me to do my best " for an innocent chap." Again he had been arrested as a deserter, and on an easily disproved charge of obtaining 10s. on false pretences from the S.S.F.A. I appealed to the War Office and the commanding officer, and obtained the intercession of a Member of Parliament ; but no explanation of the case ever reached either the Member of Parliament or myself.

Shortly afterwards I approached the War Office and the Paymaster, on behalf of a soldier in the 10th Norfolk Regiment, who was informed that he had been overpaid, but declared he had only had his due. The Paymaster answered me curtly, with a threat of punishment for the soldier :

" I beg to acknowledge letter signed E. Sylvia Pankhurst, dated 23/9/15, re Pte. F. A. Prior, 10th Norfolk Regiment. Will you kindly inform the writer that her letter has been forwarded to his commanding officer, who will probably take disciplinary measures against the man for making frivolous complaints ? A statement of accounts has been sent to his C.O. " Yours faithfully,

" B. E. Winter, Lt.-Col.,

" For Regimental Paymaster."

Anxious on the soldier's account, I forwarded the letter to the War Office, pointing out that I had often intervened in such cases. In reply I was informed by C. W. Cooper, " for the Assistant Financial Secretary," that the man being a serving soldier, should address any complaint to his regimental officers. " Any other method of preferring complaints, such as approach to outside societies, etc., is expressly forbidden by the King's regulations."

I was not prepared to accept that dictum; I knew too well that many a case of hardship and victimisation would go unredressed if there were no outside appeal. I reminded the War Office that I had frequently induced it to alter military decisions. I agitated both publicly and privately, and presently received another letter from the same C. W. Cooper, virtually reversing his previous statement.

"I am directed to acquaint you that you will be quite in order in referring to this department any complaints from serving soldiers who have failed to obtain redress on application to their regimental officers.

"Your obedient servant,

"C. W. Cooper,

"For the Assistant Financial Secretary."

I felt I had scored a point in defence of the soldiers and their families. The reply was not wholly satisfactory, for many soldiers were afraid to make any complaints on their own account, either to their regimental officers or anyone else. However, that part of the letter I was disposed to regard as padding. Certainly I should continue to deal with the soldiers' complaints without formalities, as and when they came to me. Ah yes, indeed, as the poor mothers implored me, I would "keep at them!"

Again a poor widow came crying to me from the amazing lady official. An official communication had informed the widow that £7 2s. 7d. was due to her on her husband's account, that the money had been placed in a bank, and she might withdraw it, as she wished, on application to the local S.S.F.A. Desiring black garments for herself and children, in mourning for her dead, she applied for £2 of the money due to her, a very modest sum for such a purpose. The irrepressible official, whom I had already brought to book in a similar case, refused the money. Perhaps she considered the observance of mourning an unwarrantable extravagance on the part of a soldier's widow. Be that as it may, she impertinently told the widow that 10s. would be enough, and when the poor woman persisted in asking for £2 she was thrust outside the office and got nothing at all.

A sailor's wife had loans from the same local branch of the S.S.F.A. amounting to £3 5s. od., whilst awaiting her separation allowance. The allowance, when it came, was much less than her husband used to give her for housekeeping. She had to buy a part of his equipment, to pay his fare when he came home to see her once a week, and purchase little extras for the days he came, which all too soon would cease! She could not make ends meet; much less repay the S.S.F.A. loan. She went out to work, but the pay was small, and before she had time to benefit from her little wage, she received a threatening letter:

"Mrs. S——,

"Unless your debt to the S.S.F.A. of £3 5s. od. is repaid in full on

Tuesday morning, November 23rd, at the above address, the affair will be put into the hands of the police for prosecution.

"Yours truly,
"C. HALL."

It was impossible for her to pay at such short notice. A solicitor's letter promptly followed. The poor creature was in despair. A neighbour brought her round to me. Of course I reassured her and I succeeded in securing more time for her to pay. In the meantime her husband wrote to me from the Crystal Palace Sea Draft, begging me to "stop these people suing her. She has had enough to knock her over just lately. If I were at home it would be a trifling matter to pay £3 5s od., but as I am now it appears a gigantic amount." His pay, when 5s. had been deducted from it for his wife's allotment, was only 3s. 3d. a week.

Do I weary you, reader, with these accounts of poverty and humiliation? I urge them, I add case after case from the thousands I could cite; for these hardships are the rule, and not the exception, amongst the masses who go to fight. War is the great harvest of the financier and the trader; the great victimisation of the soldiers and sailors.

At the Hoxton coroner's court an inquest was held on an infant who had wasted and died of malnutrition. Its father, an engraver, had lost his work through the War and gone to sea. Nothing was heard of him for many months. Then news came that he had been shipwrecked and badly burnt. His wife, in the meantime, had parted with her home, and she and her three children had tasted the very dregs of misery and want. She had obtained work as a waitress, but earned only 9s. a week. The coroner gave her £1 from the poor box to ease her pressing need.

. . . . . . . .

A poor women, Mrs. B——, came to me crying, with a letter from Miss Hall and Miss O'Clay, of the local S.S.F.A. She had eight children under fifteen years and the school nurse had found some nits on the hair of one of her little girls. The mother had been ordered to take the child to the borough cleansing station, and had refused; to go there was regarded as a terrible disgrace, of which all the children were ashamed. Their hair was cut off there and their clothes baked. The garments often fell to pieces after being treated there. The letter ran:

"If we do not shortly hear that A—— is in a thoroughly clean state we shall write to the War Office, telling them that you are neglecting your children. . . . This will affect your separation allowance, no doubt. . . ."

Nits on the hair! Alas, they were all as common as flies in August among the elementary school children of crowded districts in those days. I am told that bobbed hair and other amenities have largely ameliorated that condition now. The Borough Sanitary Inspector was instructed to call on the woman and reported that there was no fault to find with the children's clothes or bedding. I went myself to her home, desiring to be armed with knowledge, in order that I might help her. I found her a hard-working nervous sort, living under most miserable conditions, in one of a group of cottages built close up against a towering factory belching forth smoke. All these dwellings were bug-ridden; indeed, their tenants were waging a hopeless struggle with vermin. One woman, who had come to the district owing to the War, had put her best feather bed in a cupboard, in the hope of protecting it from being infested, till she could find rooms elsewhere; but when she unfolded it to show me, we saw the insects running over it. She wailed in distress. The house of poor Mrs. B—— was infested like the others. She kept down the pests as best she could, and her home was as clean and well kept as it could be under her hard circumstances. I saw the little girl on account of whom complaint had been made; she had a mass of crinkly red-brown hair. I was able to get her mother exonerated and saved from victimisation. Many months later I happened to be passing that way and stopped to say a word to Mrs. B——. I was horrified to learn from the neighbours that she had lately committed suicide. Her struggle had proved too hard for her.

. . . . . . . .

She was a bent old woman of seventy-two years. Her wrinkled face was surmounted by one of those heavily jet-trimmed bonnets old grannies then affected; her withered hands emerged, demurely folded, from one of those sack-like mantles the grannies wore.

Forty-two years before—in 1873, to be precise—her husband had left his home one morning, to go to his work as usual. He had never been seen or heard of since. After a period of dwindling hope she took to calling herself a widow. She had a hard struggle to maintain her three little children, but the slow years passed; they all grew able to fend for themselves. Two of them married and went away; the youngest remained to support his mother. When war broke out he enlisted; but a good son, he applied for her allowance, kept her going from his savings till it came, and wrote to her constantly.

Suddenly, to her dismay, his letters ceased. She went many times to the War Office to inquire for him. He was among the missing; that was all they knew.

Once in conversation with an official she bemoaned her lot, telling how her husband too had disappeared—so long ago! "My fate! My fate!" she wailed. The official broke harshly upon her lamentations, and accused her of falsely representing herself to be a widow.

When her son's dead body was found, at last, she was informed that she might neither have his badge, his belt and the little things which belonged to him, nor his arrears of pay. These, declared the War Office, must be kept for his father, who had disappeared when the dear dead son was a baby at the breast. With difficulty, the old mother was made to understand that the law refused to regard her as the parent of the son she had born and reared—she the only parent he had known! Neither the evidence of people who had known the old woman living husbandless for forty years, nor any appeal to justice or common-sense availed.

At last, after much correspondence, I brought the authorities to accept the view that they could agree to hand over the son's effects to his mother if his father should still fail to appear when they had advertised for him for a year.

When that had been conceded, I suggested that the effects could be transferred to the mother immediately, if I were to enter into a guarantee with her to return them to the father should he come back to claim them within the year. The War Office agreed to accept the guarantee; but a new obstacle was discovered! As the law stood the father, should he appear, would inherit the entire estate of his dead son, who had made no will; but the old mother would only be entitled to one-third of her son's pay; the rest must go to his brother and sister. I wrote to them asking that they would transfer to their mother their shares in the few pounds due to the dead, and advising them to make the same guarantee of restoration, should the father appear, which she and I had made. Of course they agreed.

The old woman received her son's effects. In the meantime her separation allowance had ceased, and no pension was in sight. Her case was still on my hands !

. . . . . . . .

A soldier's mother, toiling to maintain her little ones, was told when her son was killed that the £20 due on his account could not be paid to her. It must go to her husband, who had left her many years before. I made in her case the same proposal, but the War Office rejected it on the ground that the woman and the other proposed guarantors could not prove their ability to refund the £20.

# CHAPTER XXXI

## LLOYD GEORGE AT TRADE UNION CONGRESS—LORD DERBY'S VOLUNTEERS

THE great delusion which kept the belligerent nations at each other's throats was sweeping us onward towards Conscription. The National Register was barely taken when Lord Derby publicly declared[1] that it was " only a question of the date " on which the Government would introduce " the new system." Lord Northcliffe and his Press and the more extreme Conservative politicians and war enthusiasts persistently demanded it. The active rank and file of the organised Labour movement, the people who keep it going, day in day out, opposed Conscription to a man, and to a woman. Week-end by week-end I saw great crowds of excited people filling large halls and cinemas to listen to speeches denouncing compulsion both military and industrial ; willing, with scarcely a dozen dissentients, to applaud appeals for peace.

The Trade Union Congress, held that year in Bristol, was moved by a different spirit. The war men controlled it still. For Ben Tillett, who was touring the country, making recruiting speeches at variety theatres, brandishing a German helmet, and who had lately returned from an officially conducted inspection of the Front, there was an expectant hush. He gave the delegates their fill of horrors, and told sensational stories about the shortage of munitions.

The majority of the Labour leaders were denouncing Conscription as a Northcliffe scheme, wholly unnecessary and harmful, perniciously urged upon an unwilling Government. The official resolution embodied this view, promising " hearty support " to the Government in securing the men " necessary to prosecute the War to a successful issue by voluntary means." Harry Dubery,[2] of the postal workers, spoke to an impatiently hostile audience when he pleaded that whilst secret diplomacy in the interests of rival alliances continued, Europe would never be safe from war ; and if this country were determined to secure a victory of the knock-out blow it must commit itself to the provision of a huge army, which could only be raised by Conscription.

J. R. Clynes, representing a great union of ill-paid men and women, came fresh from the Government recruiting platforms, a thick-set,

[1] Manchester, August 21st.

[2] Dubery, who was for a time the London organiser of the I.L.P., was then an exceedingly active propagandist. A few years later he left the movement, disgruntled and disappointed, and became the zealous servant of an employers' federation.

pugnacious-looking little man, much changed from the pale, frail, studious-looking workman he appeared when first he entered Parliament. Full-throated cheers from a mass of the elder delegates spurred his attack on Dubery and all Pacifists. There was silence when he asked curtly what the Parliamentary Committee of the Trade Union Congress proposed to do if Conscription were introduced. It was evident that he would support Conscription or any other Government war measure. Will Thorne proposed that if the Government introduced any Conscription project a special conference should be called to find ways and means to oppose it. Shaw, the stout weavers' representative of Colne, protested that he would not oppose any recommendation of the Government.

That was the case of the Trade Union leaders. They opposed Conscription as the plan of "the coroneted creator of Carmelite House," in the words of Sedden, the President of the Congress; but if the Government wanted it they would swallow it—on terms. Havelock Wilson, then a hale-looking, ruddy fellow, not yet the cadaverous prophet of woe and notoriously open employers' man he afterwards became, was to-day a bellicose opponent of compulsion. He spoke of hanging the proprietors of certain newspapers to the nearest lamp-posts, and declared that if the Government should show any signs of introducing any sort of Conscription it would be necessary to let them know that "we do not mean to have it." Probably no one took Wilson very seriously. It was big, popular Bob Smillie, of the great Miners' Federation, who swept the Congress to its feet. He declared that if that day's decision were against Conscription, it would be "the duty of organised labour to prevent it." The hall was filled with cheers at that saying, an incitement to direct strike action if it had any meaning at all. In fact it was mere fireworks. Neither Smillie nor the Congress was prepared to do anything save talk to further its decision. Even Will Thorne's modest proposal to call a conference should the Government actually introduce a Conscription Bill was quietly withdrawn.

To display its power the Government had put a Press censorship over the Congress until the Conscription discussion was at an end. When it was clear there was to be no serious opposition, Lloyd George telegraphed an appeal for a greater output of munitions, falsely declaring that as the bulk of the munition factories were now controlled, the benefit of increased output would "ensue to the State, not to the employers. No profitmongering," he said, "is possible."

As had been prearranged, Sedden asked leave to invite Lloyd George to address the Congress, and leave being granted he appeared without delay. As ever alert and facile, he delivered a stinging attack on the workers in the factories; but succeeded in producing the impression that he cherished the friendliest feeling towards the Congress. The delegates, of whom the majority were Union officials, thus disarmed, no jarring note was heard, no awkward questions raised.

Next day, when the words of the Munitions Minister had been read in cold print, there was a general realisation by the delegates that they had made a mistake in permitting their Congress to be used as a platform from which to justify industrial compulsion. Belated resolutions of protest failed to satisfy delegates with their own strategy; still less could they allay the bitter resentment of the rank and file workers in the munition shops that their Union officials had given Lloyd George, their oppressor, this amazing opportunity to attack them from the very platform of their own Trade Union Congress.

The machinery of Conscription was quietly being prepared whilst jingoes, in Parliament and out, were clamouring for this thing which was so obviously at hand. Captain Guest insisted that 25,000 soldiers must be recruited weekly, as the wastage by death and disablement at the Front amounted to from 120 to 150 per cent. Asquith was steadily conceding the demands of the compulsionists, who nevertheless were ruthlessly determined to oust him from the Premiership. Lord Derby had been appointed Director of Military Recruiting, ostensibly to safeguard the voluntary system by a great patriotic recruiting campaign, which should obviate all need for compulsion. Meanwhile, without any reference to Parliament, the voluntary system was superseded, not in the more or less haphazard fashion seen at the outbreak of war, but officially and systematically. No man was now permitted to leave the country without a passport, and passports for men of military age were refused. Shipping companies refused to carry them.[1]

By means of the National Register everyone could be tracked. If in State employ, all men, unless specially exempted, were ordered, on pain of dismissal, to enlist, or as it was termed, " attest " their readiness to join the Army when called upon—a legally binding engagement which could not be evaded. Employers of labour were asked to insist that their employees of every grade should attest, and to dismiss the recalcitrant. They were warned not to take unattested men of military age into their service. Brace, the miners' Trade Union official, now Under-Secretary of State for Home Affairs, issued a notice that young men attempting to enter the mining industry as newcomers would be prevented. The railways were under national control; to attest was now a condition of railway service.

All this economic compulsion by the employers, and every other possible means of appeal and warning, lay behind the hectic oratory of recruiting speeches, delivered by Ben Tillett, J. R. Clynes, Horatio Bottomley, Mrs. Pankhurst, Asquith, Carson, and a host of others; even Ramsay MacDonald sent the Mayor of Leicester a letter to be read at a meeting to recruit young men for the War.

Philip Snowden complained in the House of Commons that Lord Derby's letter was being sent out to boys under seventeen, and that

[1] The stokers of the Cunard steamer, *Saxonia,* struck work at Liverpool because 600 Irishmen were about to set sail for America. Thereat the Cunard Company cancelled the Irishmen's passages and issued a notice that it would not accept the bookings of British subjects of military age. The White Star, the Anchor and other Transatlantic companies issued similar notices.

lads of tender years were being canvassed to enlist under threat of being summoned before the local tribunal. From the first it had been difficult to secure the return to their homes of boys under age who enlisted without knowledge of their parents and soon most bitterly repented. It was not uncommon for boys of fifteen and sixteen to be brought into court as deserters.[1]

Recruits secured by economic compulsion, under the so-called voluntary system, hoped against hope that their enlistment might prove merely formal, and clung to every pretext of escape, or delay. Since entire staffs of men in essential services were enrolled, it was obvious that all the attested men could not be taken. Central and Local Appeal Tribunals, district Military Experts, and Advisory Committees were appointed to consider appeals by the men and their employers that the call to the colours might be postponed, and the reluctant victim transferred to a later group, if, by good fortune, he should be adjudged essential to important work. Such appeals for delay might be made repeatedly in respect of the same employee.

Amongst the unwilling pressed men who were fathers of little families, the cry that the single men should be the first to go was apt to receive a fervent welcome. Economists liked it; the single man was cheaper. Mothers and wives of men who were at the Front were incited to violence against those who stayed at home. Bonar Law recited with approval the tale of some mothers who broke the windows of a shopkeeper, because their sons were at the Front, and his refused to go. Law declared that if such feeling amongst the working class were given "fair play" there would be general consent to any plan necessary to end the War. It was the old ruse: divide and conquer. Conscription, as an ordered method, by which the men with least responsibilities should be the first to go, was made by skilful propagandists to appear beneficent beside the pell-mell compulsion of attestation.

To the Government, seeking to introduce Conscription without raising a storm of protest, the value of the slogan "Single men first" was most obvious. Asquith, the shrewd lawyer, was not slow to seize it. On November 2nd, he indicated that compulsion might presently be introduced on this ground, though Lord Derby's voluntary campaign had still nearly a month to run. Asquith admitted there had been differences of opinion in the Cabinet. He had himself "no objection of any sort to compulsion in time of war;" but if it were introduced, it must be by general assent. Wrapped up in the mass of verbiage with which politicians in office obscure intention, his statement was invested nine days later with the trenchancy it had lacked in his utterance.

[1] Frederick Stock, aged 15, of Major Road, Stratford, was charged in the Children's Court with being an absentee from the 18th London Rifles. The recruiting officer had known his age when he signed. The lad was remanded and the boy's mother given an opportunity to see the Clerk.

In October 1915, Sir A. Markham called the attention of the Under-Secretary of State for War to the enlistment of Private G. Jones on his fourteenth birthday, and the arrest of John Meakin aged 15, Alexander Guntripp aged 16, and William Haslewood aged 17 as deserters.

Lord Derby announced[1] himself authorised by the Prime Minister to express surprise that the Prime Minister's remarks had been considered ambiguous; and to state that if young men, medically fit, and not indispensable to any business of national importance, did not come forward voluntarily before November 30th "other and compulsory means" would be taken to enlist them, before calling upon the married men who had attested to fulfil their promise to serve. No marriage contracted after Registration Day, August 15th, would secure a place in the married groups. Whether a man were indispensable or not would be decided by the competent authorities and tribunals. Asquith still evaded Parliamentary questions as to whether the single men would be conscribed before the attested married men were compelled to go. Meanwhile the net of compulsion tightened. The position of the attested men who had been scheduled as engaged in vital services and supplied with badges on that account was now reviewed. Few men could consider themselves safe.

The No Conscription Fellowship of men of military age with a conscientious objection to serving in the War had begun forming before the passing of the National Register Act. In the autumn of 1914 Fenner Brockway, the editor of the I.L.P.'s *Labour Leader*, proposed in a letter to that paper the enrolment of a fellowship of men who would refuse Conscription should it come. Names rolled up, and Mrs. Brockway acted as honorary secretary. From early in 1915 unostentatious little advertisements were inserted week by week in the *Labour Leader* by Mrs. Clara Cole, of the Dial, Kemsing, who had formed a "League Against War and Conscription," and appealed for names of persons who would join a "united protest in case Conscription is thrust upon us." When Conscription drew near Brockway's organisation was formally inaugurated in London as the "No Conscription Fellowship," for men of military age. Mrs. Cole added 500 names she had collected to those Mrs. Brockway had been enrolling. The fellowship decided to do no public propaganda against Conscription, but to resist it, if and when it came.

[1] Press Bureau, November 11th.

# CHAPTER XXXII

## THE RENT STRIKE VICTORY—JOHN MACLEAN

RENTS were rising. Evictions were rife despite the Emergency Courts Act.[1] Rent strikes developed. At Wellington, Somerset, a soldier's wife had notice to quit and could find no home for her children. The owner began to demolish the house. The woman ran out and threw herself into a stream, where she was found in a fit. At Godalming an ejectment order was granted against Mrs. Gunter, the wife of a soldier imprisoned in Germany. The soldiers at Whitley Camp raised a subscription for her.

There were rent strikes round us in the East End. Appeals from the strikers came to us daily. In all cases we succeeded in preventing evictions, and in getting the demands for increased rent withdrawn. In munition areas, where the drafting in of workers from other districts had created great shortage of housing, the strife was greatest. On Tyneside the *Daily Chronicle* reported that men were paying 18s. a week each for the half-share of a bed, which as soon as they rose from it, was occupied by two further tenants, employed on another shift.

From the wretched one- and two-roomed " houses " in the great jerry-built barracks of Partick and other Glasgow districts, 15,000 people marched to the City Hall with banners, demanding municipal housing and complaining of rent increases of 20 per cent. Glasgow's disgraceful housing conditions had long been notorious. The entire Labour Movement, Left, Right and Centre, supported the procession. Despite the protests of the Labour councillors, the majority of the City Fathers refused the processionists a hearing.

A few days later the landlords applied for twelve eviction warrants against the rent strikers. Three warrants were granted, but the remainder were adjourned for a week, on representations being made that rioting would ensue if soldiers' wives or munition workers were turned out.

Protests were made in Parliament. Dr. Addison, the assistant and constant apologist of Lloyd George, repeated his oft-made, oft-broken promise, that the Ministry of Munitions would ease the rent situation by giving financial aid to the municipal authorities to erect additional

[1] On June 16th, 1915, in the House of Commons, W. C. Anderson drew attention to the case of a soldier's wife, Mrs. McHugh of Shettleston, whose husband lay wounded in Rouen Hospital, whose son was home on sick leave, and two of whose five younger children were suffering from pneumonia. This woman had got into arrears with her rent owing to her husband's illness. A warrant for her ejectment within 48 hours had been granted.

housing accommodation for the munition workers drafted into overcrowded areas. The old adage " Soft words butter no parsnips " was never more clearly exemplified. Even whilst the debate was going forward at Westminster, an official communication from the Local Government Board was being read at the Glasgow City Council, stating that the Government had decided to introduce still further large numbers of munition workers into Glasgow, but the existing housing accommodation must suffice. Popular indignation flared up. 15,000 householders signed a declaration of refusal to pay increased rent, and intention to resist eviction. Indignant rent-strikers made a bonfire of ejectment notices in the road before the City Hall. Two Labour Councillors, George Smith and George Kerr, were among the rent strikers. In Glasgow, Govan, and surrounding districts, pickets were set, and great throngs of people gathered to prevent the threatened evictions. Numbers flocked into the Women's Housing Association, formed by the Socialists to focus agitation. Sustained by appeals to sisterly kindness and mutual aid, and by visions of a better future for working people, to be won by present effort and solidarity, women kept watch all night on the common stair of the barrack dwellings, their neighbours heartening them with tea in their cold vigil. The men who came to serve the ejectment orders were greeted with volleys of flour.

The organisers of the agitation telegraphed to Lloyd George urging his intervention. He declared himself powerless. Warning was sent to him that the workers from the munitional factories and the shipyards would defy the Munitions Act, and march in their thousands to the Court where the rent-strike cases were being heard. At this threat to the execution of war contracts, his indifference was shed; he begged that all would continue at work, insisting that even the tenants concerned might safely refrain from attendance in Court, for he would " settle " the case in their interests.

His answer was received with suspicion, disgust and hatred, engendered by the prosecutions under the Munitions Act, and inflamed by his earlier refusals to intervene. Workers flocked in their thousands to the Court, and thronging the neighbouring thoroughfares, where impassioned speeches were delivered. In Hutcheson Street the police charged the crowd, and a sharp struggle ensued. Meanwhile within the Court the cases against the rent strikers were being withdrawn at the request of the Munitions Board.

To allay the agitation the Government promised legislation to protect Scottish tenants against rent increase; the appearance of similar agitations in other parts produced a Rent Act applicable to the British Isles. Originally the Act could only be specially extended to each district by Order in Council, which would only be issued as a result of agitation. It contained numerous other defects, many of which were gradually eradicated—but only by agitation.

A mass of prejudice opposed this measure of relief against a tragic evil. In reading the official Parliamentary reports—as I did without fail—I was amazed to read these words of Sir John Rolleston:

" I can only submit that the saving and the thrifty man or woman who has taken that increased rent has a right to do so. It would be wrong to leave that money in the pocket of the well-paid working man, to spend on his numerous and, in many cases, unwholesome pleasures."

During the height of the rent agitation in Glasgow, John MacLean, M.A., an elementary school teacher in the city, had been arrested and imprisoned for five days under the Defence of the Realm Act, for some of his fiery utterances during the campaign. At the same time a resolution for his dismissal was moved on the Govan School Board. MacLean was then widely regarded as the most revolutionary propagandist in Glasgow. Thick-set, and swarthy as a Neapolitan, he recalled to me irresistibly the thought of a great brown bear. His small eyes, dark and twinkling, his mouth, opening unusually wide, seemed to show, as he talked, his entire set of gleaming white teeth, like a dog, at times playfully opening his mouth in a game, at others drawing his lips back with a snarl. Both expressions were common in him. A kindly fellow, gentle and probably incapable of belligerent action, his mind leapt ever to theoretical extremes. His economics class, inaugurated ten years before, was spoken of as a dynamic focus of discontent in Glasgow, and he, with bated breath, as a " wild man." It was strange to hear him protesting against the police version of the remarks which had secured his imprisonment, and attempting to prove that his utterance had been entirely constitutional ; for I had just listened to him uttering a direct incitement to armed rebellion. To make a grievance of imprisonment under such circumstances had been foreign to the Suffragettes ; we had courted and expected it. Obviously earnest in devotion to his principles, he seemed, in this and many things, wholly lacking in the perception of realities, and almost devoid of executive capacity. Yet he had caused many young men to think and read for themselves, and many spoke of him with gratitude, almost with reverence. The iconoclast of inconoclasts, I have heard him in his hoarse voice, with delighted smiles, expounding to his class the Marxian theory of Labour values, and repeating the parable of the three coats, as though the very hearing of it were the universal cure-all, the true wine of life.

His dismissal from his school post took place in due course ; he found himself expelled from the teaching profession, never to return. I remember him, after he had suffered further imprisonment, separated from his family by reason of their hardships, living alone and precariously on such poor stipend as collections from extremist Left Wing propaganda and its adherents might afford him. His meals were of " pease brose " of his own making ; very good and sufficient for his need, he averred. Yet already he was a doomed man ; privations carried to a sharp pass, and constant open-air speaking in all weathers, had set their irrevocable seal on him.

Elated by the success of the rent strike the Glasgow Left Wing was seething with triumph and enthusiasm. McGill, a fiery old Anarchist-Atheist, who sponsored the *Daily Herald* League, without any great partiality for George Lansbury and his " Churchianity," had taken the City Hall for a meeting against Conscription and a welcome to MacLean on his release, and had invited the Free Speech Defence Committee to co-operate. Lansbury and I were asked to speak, and went up to Glasgow together, with Harford, the advertisement manager of the *Herald*. The paper was probably on the crest of its wave then ; at any rate the two were buoyant with hope for it. Its posters were placarded lavishly along the Clyde, and its editor cheered by the Left Wing movement as their doughty protagonist. As soon as we reached Glasgow we learnt that the Lord Provost had cancelled the letting of the City Hall. McGill threatened an action for damages. Labour Councillors raised a protest at the Council meeting, but were informed that McGill's threat of legal proceedings precluded discussion. George Kerr and P. J. Dollan[1] continued protesting till expelled from the Council for the day. Lansbury and I were taken by Baillie Stewart to interview the Lord Provost ; but he was not to be found at the municipal offices. We saw the Town Clerk, but he told us he had no power to revoke the Lord Provost's decision to refuse the Hall. On being informed that the munition workers were coming from the Clyde to attend the meeting, and since it was hinted by Lansbury and the others that they might prove riotous if flouted, the Town Clerk and the Chief Constable agreed that an open-air meeting might be held in Albion Street, a narrow thoroughfare near, but not too near, the City Hall. To hold the meeting in the big square in front of the Town Hall, they said, would seem like " defiance " of the Lord Provost's orders. The meeting in Albion Street was agreed to by Lansbury and the local men.[2] The night proved so wet that it was a marvel to get any audience at all. Yet in the almost pitch-darkness of war-time nights, thousands of men and women stood in the drenching downpour and puddles ankle-deep, to cheer defiant words.

Lansbury was elated. On the way home he talked of running a woman's paper in addition to his *Herald* and asked me to co-operate. I asked him : " Who would edit it ? " He answered : " Of course *you* would edit it ! " He was appealing then for a strike against Conscription. A little later when a strike broke out in the munition factories, he wrote in the *Herald* protesting that it was " murder " not to send guns to the trenches. The zealous Glasgow Herald League packed up and returned to him all the copies of that week's issue. Like many more, Lansbury was at the cross roads, his policy torn to tatters by inconsistencies.

[1] Afterwards M.P.

[2] Lansbury has since written (*My Life* by George Lansbury. Constable) that he spent the afternoon trying to persuade John MacLean and me not to lead a mob of munition workers to break down the doors of the Town Hall. As to what passed between himself and MacLean I do not know. I was not a party to any such discussion ; actually I spent the afternoon with women members of our Federation, calling on some prospective members and discussing our future work. I left the local people to make such arrangements as they thought fit.

# CHAPTER XXXIII

## EDITH CAVELL—PROSECUTIONS UNDER D.O.R.A.—SNOWDEN AND THE CAPITAL LEVY

THE air raids recurred with increasing frequency, now in the North, now in the Midlands. London was often revisited by the scourge. Her brilliant shop lights dimmed, her gay night-life ended, she was a city of murk and gloom. Street lamps heavily smeared with black paint cast feeble rays.

When air raids threatened men rushed about the streets shouting "Zeps! Zeps! Put out your lights!" furiously banging at the doors of houses where even the faintest glimmer was discerned. People rushed into whatever door opened for shelter; others rushed out to scan the sky; 'buses were at a standstill, vehicles deserted, confusion everywhere. Gigantic searchlights swept the heavens. The dreaded Zeppelin, carrying a heavier cargo of ammunition than several mere aeroplanes, was seen, like a fish-shaped cloud, picked up by the searchlights. From its tail bright lights flashed down, followed by a succession of huge reports, and the dread roar of falling buildings. The angry glare of conflagration rose from the devastated scene where the bombs had fallen.

As time passed and the people murmured, warnings were given as soon as enemy craft were sighted. Then police and special constables went through the streets telling the people to hide all lights and betake themselves to the cellars. When the police gave the official warning, not otherwise, the underground railways and cellars were open to the people. Great crowds flocked thither, often half-dressed, carrying their children, and laden with rugs and pillows and things most precious to them. As the terror grew, families ceased to wait for the warning, and camped out nightly on the pavements outside the closed doors of the tubes, their little ones huddled on the damp, cold stones. A panic took place on one occasion, and people were killed by the press of others crowding behind them.

"Why have the Zeppelins come so often to London, though the Allied aircraft never reach Berlin?" the terror-stricken populace complained. In the shops, on the 'buses and by the roadside the rumour spread that London had no protecting aircraft until September 8th, 1915, when, after a raid more terrible than its predecessors, some fighting planes were withdrawn from France. When Parliament reassembled, six days later, Members asked why the defence of London had not yet been considered.

The Government instituted an insurance against the air raids, but obviously poor people, struggling for the bare necessities of existence, did not insure. At the last meeting of the Poplar Mayor's Committee I appealed in vain for relief for the poorest sufferers in our own district. One of them, a widow with three children, her weekly income only 7s., had her bed, her clock and other essentials destroyed.

. . . . . . . .

One October morning a group of unhappy women came to me. They were workers at a food-preserving company in Limehouse. They complained that their wages were only 10s. with 2d. per hour overtime; that the basement where they worked was wet and steaming, and the food with which they had to deal, often vile-smelling and decomposing. That very morning twenty-four women had had to pluck five hundred fowls, some of them alive with maggots. It was said in the factory that these fowls were destined for the troops at the Front.

The *Dreadnought* was going to press. I wrote out their story in a brief paragraph, intending to take up the case with the Government Departments concerned as soon as the paper was off my hands. I was called out on the morning after publication, and returned to find Smyth in a state of excitement. Two women factory inspectors had called, much perturbed, as the firm were purveyors of turtle soup "to the Royal Household!" It would certainly never do to have scandals about the firm! The factory inspectors had urged that instead of publishing such cases, I should always notify the Home Office. I knew the value of publicity too well to agree to that; but thereafter I had the paper sent regularly to the factory inspectors' department. The workers of this firm presently received an increase of 1s. a week. I commented: "A paltry increase; we look for more!"

. . . . . . . .

That month came news of the execution of Nurse Cavell; her last words made one's heart thrill: "I realise that patriotism is not enough. I must have no hatred or bitterness towards anyone."

She had grasped a tremendous truth, and had risen nobly above resentment for her execution. Could her words have reached the Higher Command responsible for her death, one felt that her life must have been spared; yet maybe the notion was moonshine, for war is ruthless. The war-mongers here acclaimed her as a heroine, but spurned the truth she voiced in her last message. In the flood-tide of their lust for victory, they used her martyrdom to fan the flames of the hatred she had overcome.

The pacifists praised her in lower key; some even refused to admit her worth, hearing her so lauded by the war party.

In the future her story will become a great source of legend, because it typifies an important passage in social evolution. Herself of the fairest flower of patriotism, she understood that it had had its day, and must give place to its loftier successor—Internationalism.

Bernard Shaw wrote:

"What we can do is very simple. We can enfranchise her sex in recognition of her proof of its valour. The Bill might gracefully be introduced by McKenna in the Commons and Viscount Gladstone in the Lords.[1] If this proposal is received in dead silence, I shall know that Edith Cavell's sacrifice has been rejected by her country."

Shaw's comment was apt. I had it printed with Nurse Cavell's message on cards for those who cared to hang upon their walls.

. . . . . . . .

[1] Lord Gladstone, when Home Secretary, had introduced the forcible feeding of Suffragettes. McKenna, when occupying that office, had introduced the "Cat and Mouse" Act.

KEIR HARDIE

*Alfieri*

DOING THEIR SON'S JOB

Attacked from the Left and Right, the Government struck out at its less powerful opponents on either side. The Independent Labour Party's head office was raided in London and its printing works, the National Labour Press, in Manchester. The cases were heard in camera. Seven thousand pamphlets were destroyed by order of the Court,[1] and some which the Manchester magistrate had ordered to be returned were nevertheless destroyed by the police.

An International Conference was held at Zimmerwald in September, on the initiative of the Italian and Swiss Socialist Parties. F. W. Jowett, M.P., and Bruce Glasier of the I.L.P., and E. C. Fairchild of the B.S.P., were appointed as delegates, but the Government refused their passports.

The conference, which became a name to conjure with in the Socialist Movement, strongly condemned the War and repudiated all Socialists who had supported it. Lenin, who was one of the promoters of the conference there, upheld the doctrine that Socialists must not content themselves with pacifism, but must oppose the capitalist war with sabotage and insurrection, calling into being the Social Revolution to establish the Socialist era of international fraternity. These views were steadily gaining ground, but only amongst a minority of Socialists.

A representative delegated from the conference to confer with Socialists in this country was refused permission to land.

. . . . . . . . .

In an Abertillery lodging house a man peered over the shoulder of another who was writing, and read a denunciation of war based on a published article of Keir Hardie. The writer, a poor labourer named John Bennetts Bailey, was informed against and arrested. In his pocket was found another anti-war essay, recording a dream of his own. Neither document was intended for publication ; but Justice Bailhache at the Monmouthshire Assizes sent Bailey to prison for three months, declaring that had the prisoner been charged with the intention of doing harm the maximum penalty would have been death.

The *Globe*, a Tory newspaper, for extreme militarist attacks on the Cabinet was suspended for a day or so. Sir John Simon, the Home Secretary, said of it in the Commons : " So perish all who such crimes commit." Yet though he stigmatised the attacks on the Government made by the *Times* and the *Daily Mail* as prejudicial to British interests abroad, no action was taken against the organs of Northcliffe ; the powerful foe who had made, and was preparing to unmake, the Asquith Coalition Government, could publish what he chose.

. . . . . . . . .

" Votes for the soldiers in the trenches " was now one of the slogans of the extreme war party. All the advocates of Votes for Women who had maintained their Suffrage propaganda during the War, and many

[1] One of the documents destroyed was a leaflet by Clara Gilbert Cole, *To the Women of the World,* appealing to them to use their efforts to end the War.

who had abandoned it, saw in this cry an opportunity to assert the women's claim. Christabel and Mrs. Pankhurst fiercely opposed all attempt to drag women's suffrage forward until after the War. Their W.S.P.U. was now advertising a so-called " loyal and patriotic meeting " in the Albert Hall, the scene of its old Suffragette triumphs. The object was to demand a more vigorous prosecution of the War. Lord Willoughby de Broke, who had championed the most extreme suffragette militancy in pre-war days, and Annan Bryce, a pre-war anti-suffragist and a leader of extreme militarists, were among the speakers. The *Times* puffed the meeting hugely. Christabel, impetuous as ever, issued a circular bluntly declaring: " The Prime Minister and Sir Edward Grey are unfit for the responsible positions they hold."

Two days before the meeting Sir John Simon replied to a Parliamentary question that the proprietors of the Albert Hall would doubtless " consider the propriety of permitting their building to be used for such a purpose at such a time." Already that morning the proprietors had cancelled the letting of the Hall, no doubt on a hint from the Home Office. The *Times* made no protest. The names of Lord Willoughby de Broke and Mr. Annan Bryce were mentioned no more in connection with the meeting. The W.S.P.U. was abandoned to be the scapegoat. The London Pavilion, where the Union had been holding regular weekly meetings, was now also closed to it. Unable to procure any large halls in Central London, it was compelled to fall back on small meetings in its own offices in Great Portland Street.[1]

The Archdeacon of Westminster declared Mrs. Pankhurst's attack on Asquith and Grey prompted by their long refusal of Votes for Women in pre-war days, but this she indignantly denied. She and Christabel continued their campaign for the dismissal of Asquith, whom Christabel described as " the best friend of the Austro-Germans," and of Lord Robert Cecil and Sir Eyre Crowe, a permanent official at the Foreign Office, who was vilified for having a German wife and as being himself half German and the nephew of Admiral von Holtzendorff, chief of the German naval staff. The demand for the dismissal of General Sir William Robertson was presently added to the rest.

The W.S.P.U. organ, the *Suffragette*, had now changed its name to *Britannia*. In November it was raided. Its printing was transferred from Spottiswoode's to the Utopia Press of the *Clarion* people, who had come to its aid during the old Suffragette militancy, and who were themselves pro-war. In December *Britannia* was driven by police action from the Utopia Press. Thereafter it came out for some months in all sorts of types and sizes—sometimes a mere single foolscap sheet produced on a hand-worked duplicating machine and scarcely legible. The W.S.P.U. women were printing it on the roofs of houses, someone told me.

All this seemed to me unutterably remote from human realities.

[1] The great building, Lincoln's Inn House, Kingsway, the W.S.P.U. had occupied before the War had already been given up.

The War was being prosecuted to its bitter end whether one would or no. The W.S.P.U. with its women sticking white feathers into the buttonholes of reluctant men, and brandishing little placards with the slogan: "Intern them all!" was only the noisiest of the extreme war factions; its policy was the policy of Sir Edward Carson, who resigned from the Cabinet on the score that the Government had not sent the requisite troops to Serbia, of Gibson Bowles, of L. S. Amery, Captain Guest, Annan Bryce and a crowd of Tory hot-bloods, and of Northcliffe the "Cabinet Maker," who, driven by the Gargantuan hates of war, ended in megalomania and loss of reason.

Few who bore the hardships of the trenches suffered thus violently from the war spirit. I found the soldiers generally of my own way of thinking. As a rule, nothing I could say was too strong for them.

I remember one of our meetings at the Brotherhood Church, Southgate Road, maintained by the efforts of F. R. Swan as a centre of informal Christian Socialist propaganda and an open platform for many sorts of reformers. It was a pitch-dark night and snowing hard. Having gone there previously with others, I had not noticed the way to the church. As I stepped from our door an Army van driver pulled up to attend to his car. He recognised me with enthusiasm and offered to give me a lift. I accepted the offer. With the best possible intentions, he put me down far out of my course. Thus I got to the meeting late. Mrs. Swanwick was on the platform, entirely nonplussed by a crowd of uproarious youths in khaki, who crowded the front seats, and shouted hilarious nonsense in chorus, to the prompting of an officer. "Let us talk it out, boys," she vainly appealed, peering at them through her spectacles; then turned and hurried from the platform, shaking her head. She had seen me coming and left the task to me.

I did not doubt I could win the lads. In the surprise which followed her disappearance, I sped round to the platform and forged ahead on the subject of their conditions as soldiers, and the treatment of their families. At once a number of the disturbers began to listen. When those nearest the officer interrupted me at his signal, others called for order. Failing to secure it, a third of them walked out protesting, and telling our stewards at the door that they agreed with every word I said. A discharged soldier rose to appeal for silence. The officer, anxious to prevent the discussion of the soldiers' own grievances, called his squad to join him in a dirge-like droning: "Why don't you talk about the War?" I offered to explain my opposition to it in ten minutes, and to give any one of them ten minutes to reply. The lads enthusiastically accepted the challenge, and the officer was put up to reply. When he had had his turn, I replied to him, then he to me, and so we continued. There were only two slight breaches of the undertaking to keep order, and presently the lads had become my open supporters, and were shouting: "Good kid!" and clapping with animation, when I scored a point at the expense of their officer. Unaccustomed to platform ruses, he made no effort to disguise his lack of democratic opinion, which the soldiers were quick to perceive. Afterwards they listened to a broad, sentimental Cockney appeal from the mother of two soldier sons, old Mrs. Boyce of the Social Democratic Federation. It was an artistic triumph, in its own Albert Chevalieresque vein, and " brought down the house " as completely as any performance of the old London comedian. We parted from the soldier lads on the best of terms.

. . . . . . . .

In looking through the *Dreadnought* of that period, I find a witty little letter from Rose Rosenberg of Bethnal Green, who was afterwards made an O.B.E. for her services as Private Secretary to Ramsay MacDonald whilst Prime Minister. She suggested:

" Women should in future refuse to take over men's work, unless and until an undertaking is made by those who administer the law, that Members of Parliament who are of military age, be released, and enabled to join the colours with their pals, and women asked to fill *their* places. This proposition seems to me very pertinent and consistent."

. . . . . . . .

Snowden was advocating in the Commons a tax on capital, rising from 1 per cent. on fortunes over £1,000 capital value, to 10 per cent. on those over £1,000,000. A tax so graded would bring in a revenue of £500,000,000. How much better this, he declared, than to starve the poor! He asked how it was possible that in war time handkerchiefs were on sale in Bond Street at £20 the half-dozen, and that a portrait had been sold for £35,000. McKenna had said that the rich had obligations, but Snowden replied that " the country would suffer far less by the rich being compelled to break their obligations than by the poor being compelled to break theirs." Alas, how readily men forget such utterances.[1] The Capital Levy suggested by Snowden was originally proposed by F. W. Pethick Lawrence. Later on the Labour Party sponsored it for a while, then dropped it completely.

The Trades Councils summoned a conference to discuss the extortionate cost of food. W. C. Anderson called Runciman's attention to freight charges which had risen from £60 to £600. Runciman kept a stiff lip. His family and associates were profiting exceedingly by such charges. His wife, addressing the Yorkshire Council of Women's Liberal Associations, complained that " men seemed to regard food as a fundamental right." In her opinion it was not. She urged that people must not only economise, but stint themselves in war time.

On December 2nd Asquith and McKenna addressed a conference of organised workers urging economy. Asquith was obliged to hurry away to the much advertised costly wedding festivities of his daughter, which, unfortunately for his economy text, were held that day. Before leaving, he admitted a rise of 30 per cent. in the cost of living and that

[1] Alas, when Snowden, as Chancellor of the Exchequer in 1931, found himself faced with unusual difficulties he too protected the rich at the expense of the poor.

roughly one-third of the workers had received an average increase in wages of 3s. a week. A resolution to commend the speeches of Ministers to the " earnest and favourable consideration of Trade Unionists " was received with derisive laughter; but Fred Bramley's amendment, pledging Trade Union assistance in placing the financial situation on a legislative basis of " equal sacrifice for all," received only 40 votes amongst more than 1,000 delegates, because bellicose Colonel John Ward denounced it as a " pacifist " proposal, which would mean " the loss of 50,000 British lives."

Peace talk was growing. Ponsonby, Trevelyan and others were asking Parliamentary questions about the Government war aims. There were many rumours that peace terms had been received from Germany. Mrs. Payne wrote to the Press, offering two-thirds of her capital towards an indemnity to Belgium, to be provided by peace lovers, in the hope that on this basis the warring nations would open peace negotiations. She begged other women to join her in establishing this fund. Her offer and plea were ignored by all save the I.L.P. and the other small groups of pacifists; her offer of capital remained unseconded. She asked me to meet her at the Savoy Hotel. I found her a pretty young woman, fair-haired and rosy, spontaneous and unsophisticated, grieving that her husband was at the Front, and anxious to bring him home with the husbands of all other wives.

Shortly afterwards Henry Ford, the American motor manufacturer, offered his entire fortune to facilitate the calling of a conference of neutral Powers to mediate between the belligerents. He urged President Wilson to initiate this action. In the new year Ford chartered what was called his *Peace Ship* from U.S.A. to Stockholm, where an unofficial conference was held, calling on the neutral nations to mediate and the belligerents to state their terms of peace. Such efforts were as mere straws in the tempest. Not one whit did any belligerent government heed them. Wilson ignored them. Colonel House dismissed Ford's peace hopes as " crude," and respected him only as a manufacturer.

. . . . . . . .

Keir Hardie's Merthyr seat had been won by the war party. " The old Adam in most of us unaffectedly rejoices," observed the *Glasgow Herald*, announcing the victory of Stanton, the Labour renegade who had sounded the depths of jingoism. The expression was apt. It was a victory of primitive passion. James Winston, the Labour Party candidate, was by no means a strong fighter; he could neither take up the challenge of the War Party and express a firmly reasoned opposition to the War, nor make a vigorous offensive from the workers' standpoint against the Government and the profiteers.

. . . . . . . .

## CHAPTER XXXIV

### ANOTHER WAR CHRISTMAS

IT was the second Christmas of the War. I had a longing to go to Merthyr Tydfil, to renew myself in the communion of memory with him who had made the name of that place a household word. Smyth and I and Jim went down there together, enjoying long walks over the mountains, and pleasant meetings with comrades, gathered together as a little company of believers, working and hoping for the dawn of Peace to break, in a world distraught by war. Harry Morris, a frail, small man, rejoicing in regular practice with the Dowlais Male Voice Choir, and toiling with devoted zeal in the business management of the I.L.P., showed us his cherished collection of Keir Hardie letters. Originally a miner, Morris had been victimised for his Socialist activities, and was now an insurance agent. Obliged by this business to take long tramps over the mountains in all weathers, he often arrived home in a state of exhaustion which aroused the concern of his sharp-tongued, warm-hearted sister, who was always tender and considerate towards him. Their brother Tom, a clever fellow, who had gained his position by evening study, was manager of a mine at Troedyrhiw. In the hard days of unemployment and reaction after the War, he too was victimised, on his brother's account.

We helped the I.L.P. women members to dress the tree for a children's party, and later heard the children sing the verses Keir Hardie had written for the melody of the Welsh anthem. A vision of him crossed my eyes, as he came from the station that Easter I was in Merthyr, a scurry of children to meet him, his firm steps brought to a standstill by the clasp of a toddler's arms about his leg.

. . . . . . . .

Back again at Old Ford, our New Year opened with children's parties in Bow, Poplar, and Canning Town. Children are only children once ; we wanted to compensate them as far as we could for the dark days of war. In Bow Baths were gathered more than 900 children of our members, and two nights later a crowd of the members themselves. Smyth's whimsical cousin Georgie Mackey gave a huge Christmas tree, and Smyth, disguised as Father Christmas, presented the gifts. George Lansbury and his friend Hobday provided a marionette show. Dr. Harry Schütze of the Lister Institute, and his wife who writes stories as Henrietta Leslie, had arranged a spring pageant. Its flowers were our East End blooms : dark Mary Carr from poor little Ranwell Street, where people all helped each other, the two pretty Cohens, one as slender as the lily she represented and the other, Nellie, my secretary, glowing as a ripe peach; fair, straight Violet Lansbury, garlanded with primroses, "the Spirit of the Spring." Pale Lily Gatward, with our own purple, white, and green flag, was "the Spirit of Liberty," and beside her Joan Beauchamp, a stern, stiff young "Spirit of Peace," who afterwards became the editor of the Conscientious Objectors' *Tribunal*, and went to gaol for it. They were led by a quartet of merry three-year-olds, with red caps of liberty, and the mottoes: "Peace" and "Plenty," emblematic, indeed, of the urgent needs of our human case.

To me the central loveliness of it all was sixteen-year-old Rose Pengelly, "the Spirit of the Woods." A charming elf-like figure, with red-gold hair and skin rosy as a flower. Playing upon Pan's reeds, she danced with unimagined grace, artless, untaught—a vision of youth's loveliness, the denizen of a slum! Delicious little creature, I had loved her since that day, just before the War, when she led the strikers from Back's asbestos factory into our "Women's Hall," telling us they had nicknamed her "Sylvia," and that it was her business to pack the heavy "saggers" of ware and carry them to the furnace, to run errands for the housekeeper, to peel potatoes, to wash the "governor's" shirts and sheets.

On Thursday I saw her at the children's party dancing before the rest, a glimpse of moving ecstasy, which made my heart tremble with its beauty. On Saturday she should have danced again—but the knife of the machine she was working descended on her pretty right hand, rending and mangling the thumb and a couple of fingers. She fainted, poor child, and lay unconscious whilst someone was sent to seek a policeman and ask his permission to procure a small quantity of brandy to revive her. (Except by such sanction, war-time regulations permitted the sale of brandy only by the quart.) Her new employer making no offer to pay a cab fare, she walked to the station, took the train to the London Hospital, and there sat in the Out-Patients Department till late in the evening, when her crushed thumb and two fingers were amputated. Poor stoic maid of the working class!

. . . . . . .

A prize was offered to the child who wrote the best account of our Poplar party. I asked Bernard Shaw to judge the essays. He did so in amusing fashion:

"MISS MOLLY BEER,
9 Brabazon Street, Upper North Street, Poplar
*in account with* G. Bernard Shaw.

| | |
|---|---|
| Correcting two mistakes in grammar . . . . | 1d. |
| Striking out two apostrophes put before "s," when there was nothing belonging . . . . . . | ½d. |
| Completing the word "affectionately" as it was written "affec." . . . . . . . . . | 1d. |
| Counting 22 kisses for Miss Pankhurst . . . | 1½d. |
| | 4d. |

"I award Miss Beer a special prize of 3d. for laziness. She was in such a hurry to get into bed that she wrote the shortest essay and signed herself 'yours affec' to save herself the trouble of writing 'tionately.' So she has only 1d. to pay.

"G. BERNARD SHAW."

For each child was some quip. "Mr. Hornibrook" got a special prize of 4d. "for putting all the go he had into the songs," a penny was charged for "soap to clean up after reading Mr. Drake's essay." In each case there was a penny to pay, but a special prize of 1s. 6d. was finally awarded to every one.

. . . . . . .

Another year had begun, with food prices estimated by the Board of Trade at 47 per cent. above the pre-War level for the country as a whole, and 49 per cent. in the large towns. Housewives' budgets showed a steeper increase. Official estimates invariably under-estimate the true cost to small buyers. In West Ham, a typical working-class near London area, where prices were apt to be lower than in the provinces, the general staples of family catering amongst the poor had increased as follows:

| | *Pre-War.* | *January* 1916. |
|---|---|---|
| White granulated sugar | 1¾d. per lb. | 4½d. per lb. |
| Loose jam | 2½d. ,, | 6d. ,, |
| Treacle | 2½d. ,, | 4d. ,, |
| Bread | 5d. per qtn. | 9½d. per qtn. |
| Pieces of meat for stewing | 3½d. per lb. | 7d. per lb. |
| Kippers | 1½d. per pair | 5d. per pair |
| Haricot beans | 2½d. per quart | 6d. and 8d. per qt. |
| Rice | 1½d. per lb. | 3d. per lb. |
| Currants | 2½d. ,, | 5d. ,, |

Struggles with rent-raising landlords continued in spite of the Rent Act.

The Chancellor of the Exchequer addressed a plea for economy to the poor woman who, as he said, had "never before been able to clothe her children properly or to furnish her home." He urged her to postpone all purchases of clothing and furniture until after the War, and lend her money to the nation now, under the new War Loan scheme by which the poor might lend 15s. 6d. to the Government by instalments, and get £1 for it in five years' time. Such a scheme for arousing popular enthusiasm for high rates of interest had never previously been known! Surely it was a unique method of making the little investor protect the great against the discontent of the poor which might arise when the full burden of War Loan was loaded on the nation's neck in the lean years after the War!

Expenditure on Education was heavily cut. Children under six years were refused admission to school, though the rush of mothers into the munition factories and shortage of fuel in the homes rendered their exclusion highly undesirable. The Worcester Education Committee ordered head teachers to release children of eleven years from school on the application of any farmer. The Herefordshire Education Authority instructed school managers that boys under twelve might go to work. In Bradford the factory inspector proposed the earlier release of school children for full-time employment.

Qualified teachers were replaced by unqualified ; charwomen and ex-shop-assistants were rushed in to teach young children. Margaret Macmillan, the pioneer of open-air nursery schools and many other beneficent institutions for children, deplored the grievous impairment of an already greatly under-efficient system, and protested that the educational economies of the London County Council, though highly injurious, would not pay for two hours of the War.

Even the flowers and branches supplied for nature study were cut off ; a cruelly mean economy, the cost so small, the loss so great to town-bred children. The thought of it stirred me sorely. I wrote to the Press, begging country dwellers to send contributions from field and garden for use in the city schools, and offering to arrange the distribution to East End schools from our office. As usual, many warm-hearted people responded. We were able to supply about a dozen schools. Yet how small were such efforts ! Strive as we might in every direction, we could touch merely the fringe of the need. Oh, for a great united effort for happiness, for culture, for plenty for all—not, oh not for destruction and carnage !

Should we ever see the great awakening to love of one's fellow-creatures, to human solidarity and mutual aid ? Would the great forces of knowledge and energy acquired by the human race in its long progress ever be used for the collective well-being, that there might no longer be poverty and lack, no longer the ill-educated and ill-housed ?

Yes, yes, it would come ! Life would be intolerable without that hope.

Oh, that it might happen in our time, that we who have striven and suffered, here and now, might see it in our life !

## CHAPTER XXXV

### THE TURBULENT CLYDE

ON the morrow of Christmas we knew that there had been trouble on the Clyde. The advocates of compulsion and economy complained that both soldiers and munition workers were too independent and too highly paid. *The Times* said :

" We must deal as harshly with strikers who throw down their tools as with soldiers who desert in the field."

The great curtailment of profits which it was promised the Munitions Act would effect was already proving an illusion. In the case of one great manufacturing company, the balance sheet of which showed a net profit of £103,822 against £65,096 the previous year, the *Manchester Guardian* declared that matters had been so arranged that the Chancellor of the Exchequer would get none of the increased profit.

A Health of Munition Workers Committee had been appointed by the Government. It issued grievous reports of weary workers, spent by excessive toil, struggling for a place in overcrowded trains and trams, spending long hours in journeying to their homes. It stated :

" Family life is impossible. Mothers and grown children make munitions, younger ones suffer neglect at home. In the lodgings of munition workers beds are never empty, rooms are never aired, as day and night shifts prevent this."

Sometimes a woman wrote to me, broken down in health by overwork, complaining of long walks over sodden, impromptu tracks, ankle-deep in mud, to newly-erected factories ; of night shifts spent without even the possibility of getting a drink of water ; of workers obliged to take their meals amid the dust and fumes of the workshop.

By the end of the year there were three women to one man in the munition factories and *The Times* announced that the proportion of women would presently be doubled. Despite all promises their wages still averaged from 8s. to 14s. At a controlled factory in Croydon, women got 8s. a week, forewomen in charge of 50 or 60 others, 12s. 6d. Women replacing men who had earned £2 to £3, got 12s. 6d. The workers complained to me that some well-to-do ladies were paid up to 35s.

As to the men whom women were steadily replacing, their wages were variously estimated. Lord Charlemont, who had gone into a munition factory as a munition worker, said he earned from £1 15s. to £3 10s. on piece rates—scarcely an extravagant sum. The *New Statesman* reported that the wages of semi-skilled men on the Clyde averaged 39s. per week and of the women 15s. These rates were in fact common.

The promise that the men dilutees should be paid the standard rate of the skilled men who had previously done the work was soon broken, although the pledge had been embodied in the Treasury Agreement and the Munitions Act itself. Workers complained that the new-comers were getting 15s. a week less than their predecessors, and that whoever objected was dismissed. Some of the skilled men who had been replaced by the new dilutees were obliged to take work as unskilled labourers in other factories.

The Clyde Workers' Committee had sprung into being on the passage of the Munitions Act. It rapidly gained many thousands of supporters. Its object was to build up in the factories and shipyards a system of workers' committees, linked together by their chosen representatives or stewards. It was an essential principle that the organisation should be built "from the bottom up," each workshop sending its delegate to the committee for the factory, each factory to the committee for the area. The shop stewards were already established, the employers and trade unions alike recognising them as their medium of contact with the workers. Each factory had its convener of shop stewards, and so far as they could be brought into line, it was these conveners who formed the Clyde Workers' Committee.

In the height of its strength the Committee had supporters in all the local sections of the working-class movement in Glasgow. Its originators, and most active spirits, were members of the Socialist Labour Party, a small body founded in 1905 by James Connolly, the Irish Socialist and industrial unionist, on the model of the organisation of the same name created by Daniel De Leon in the United States. The De Leonite theory differed widely from the ideas entertained by the average I.L.P. and B.S.P. Socialist of the time, whose notions of the desired future Socialist community centred around Parliament and the City Council, and whose thoughts turned to the Post Office and the municipal tram service when occasionally they considered the management of industry in the Socialist State. The De Leonites assigned to industry the primary place in the Socialist community, conceiving it as managed by industrial unions built on the basis of the workshop. "Socialism must proceed from the bottom upwards," wrote Connolly, "whereas capitalist political society is organised from above downwards." The central administration of the country was to be entrusted to representatives elected by the various departments of industry. In Connolly's words: "Socialism will be administered by a committee of experts elected from the industries and professions of the land; capitalist society is governed by representatives elected from districts, and is based upon territorial divisions."[1] It was the guiding axiom of the S.L.P. that, as an essential prelude to the Socialist era, the workers should be fully organised on the basis of industry, and the industrial unions linked together to form an industrial republic within the shell of the old political state. When the workers, thus practically organised for the management of the Community, and consciously desirous of power, should appear on the political battle-ground, no power could

[1] *Socialism Made Easy,* by James Connolly. 1905.

withstand them; the invincible industrial republic would "crack the shell" of the old political State and "step into its place in the scheme of the universe."

The S.L.P. propaganda for industrial unions found a ready ground in the metal factories and shipyards, because the struggle of the workers therein was handicapped by a multiplicity of craft unions. The workers engaged in the manufacture of a single article were often divided into numerous unions, pursuing conflicting policies; many of them autocratic in constitution, and manned by permanent officials unresponsive to the new ideas permeating the workshops. The task of replacing or amalgamating these organisations must be a long and difficult one. The Socialist industrialists in the S.L.P. and elsewhere did not shirk the task, despite the difficulty of the meddlesome law which prevented any amalgamation of registered unions except by a two-thirds majority of the entire membership.[1] When, however, the war-time abdication of their Trade Union functions by officials, in conformity with the political truce and the Treasury Agreement, had rallied the workers behind the shop stewards for mutual protection, the most active S.L.P.ers turned with disgust from official unions of any sort, even industrial. They now set their hopes on the unofficial organisation of the rank and file workers. That the organisation should have no paid officials, that it should be managed wholly by volunteers, earning their living as wage earners in the shops, and responsible to their work-mates, was held to be essential. It was anticipated that the Workers' Committees would entirely supersede the old Trade Unions as the fighting organisations of the working class. To the Trade Unions, which were held to be dwindling products of the Capitalist era, would be left merely the administration of the sickness and other friendly benefits.

It was confidently believed that the social revolution, which was to emancipate the workers and establish the classless order of Socialism, was at hand. The unrest among the workers, which united them staunchly and defiantly behind their shop stewards, and sent them flocking in droves to the great meetings, was seen, not as the result of war conditions, but as a token that the hour of the decisive struggle with Capitalism was approaching; and that the control of the great contest would be in the hands of those who were leading the workers within the fabric of industry. In the meantime their struggle was to unite the workers against the oppression of the Government and the employers, and in revolt against official Trade Unionism, on account of its faulty structure, its restricted objectives, and because it had in some measure allied itself with the interests oppressing the workers.

The Clyde Workers' Committee demanded that the Government take over all industries and give the workers an equal share in the management. Despite this far-reaching demand, and the revolutionary doctrines which stirred the imagination of its S.L.P. leaders, the objectives for which the Committee actually took action were piecemeal ameliorations of hard

[1] In 1917 an Amending Act substituted a 50 per cent. poll and 20 per cent. majority.

conditions in defence of fellow-workers, which made no attack upon the Capitalist foundations of industry. The methods of the Committee were solidarity and the sympathetic strike. It adopted the slogan of the American Industrial Workers of the World: " An Injury to One is an Injury to All ! " Its declared policy was that if a worker were charged under the Munitions Act, and his work-mates struck work in his defence, the strike should be extended, if possible, to all the yards and factories in the area.

Having a similar conception of the co-operative social order which would some day replace this sad era of conflict, I was eager to come in contact with the pioneers who were leading this workshop movement. If I found them sometimes both truculent and exclusive, I was not disposed to complain, regarding such peculiarities as excrescences born of their struggle, and the natural defects of the aggressive qualities necessary to overcome the obstacles with which they had to contend.

Of the Clyde shop stewards the three who received most prominence were David Kirkwood, Willie Gallacher, and Arthur MacManus. Kirkwood, the convener of the Parkhead shop stewards, was in those days a fair, well-knit man, in appearance more like an Army officer than a factory worker. An I.L.P.er and later a Labour Member of Parliament, he was singularly unlike the typical members of the Left Wing industrial movement, with which, as it proved, his connection was brief. He knew little, if anything, of the doctrines of Marx and De Leon ; his opinions were often utterly illogical and inconsistent ; but he was the sort of good-natured, impulsive, emotional person who can rise to the occasion when indignation and enthusiasm need a leader, and a spice of daring is required to take the lead. So he shot to the fore, past men who may have been abler, and since he had a touch of pity and chivalry in his nature, he took up the case of the women, as will presently appear.

Gallacher was a jolly and volatile fellow, more Irish than Scotch in blood and temperament. He had a fund of genuine kindliness, was ready to help any work-mate in trouble. Genial and brotherly, almost paternal in manner, though he had barely reached his forties, he seemed impelled by a readiness not to climb out of the workshop on the backs of his mates, but to struggle for the betterment of his class. This trait endeared him to men who were smarting under the desertion of their Trade Union officials.

McManus was also a Scots-Irishman, several years younger than Gallacher but of a very different type. Exceedingly small, almost a dwarf in stature, his ambitions were great. His reputation as a daring and dangerous revolutionary was for a time extensive. An S.L.P.er of several years standing, he had nevertheless supported the War during the first eight months of its duration.

In his lighter moments Gallacher prided himself as a rhymster ; his particular *penchant* was for humorous songs. He told me with child-like pleasure of his great success in a ditty he had written for a variety theatre artiste of local repute with the refrain : " Oh Cavannah, Give me a sweet Havanna ! "

McManus poured scorn on such efforts, and once, as Gallacher told me plaintively, he had even destroyed the manuscript of some of his most cherished jingles. In the view of McManus, it was Gallacher's duty not to act the irresponsible comedian but to add dignity and popularity to the Clyde Workers' Committee.

A great source of discontent on the Clyde was the appointment, as the representative of the Minister of Munitions for the area, of a prominent employer of munition workers, William Weir, the managing director of C. J. Weir, Ltd., the Holm Foundry, Cathcart. Such a choice, for a position of such power over munition workers, was a glaring injustice no worker could fail to discern. It is amazing that Henderson—who was in the Government, we must remember, as its Labour Adviser—should have consented to it. Weir, acting both as Minister of Munitions for the area, and as managing director of his firm, was employing women on big shells at 15s. a week, and was resisting the Trade Union demand of £1 a week for women which Lloyd George had recommended, and now, under pressure—for we and others were still pressing him—had promised to make compulsory in Government factories.

On November 30th, in the Central Hall, Westminster, Lloyd George addressed representatives of the Trade Unions concerned in munition making, telling them that workers should no more be permitted to appeal against the refusal of discharge certificates by their employers, than soldiers in the trenches against the orders of their officers. During war, he averred, the State could not permit advances in wages in accord with the law of supply and demand. In the House of Commons on December 20th, he urged the employers to press forward with the dilution of labour, undeterred by any fear of trouble with the skilled operatives, for the Munitions Act would be enforced in support of any employer who put unskilled men and women to the lathes.

It was decreed that the munition factories and shipyards should work through Christmas. Lloyd George determined to address the stubborn recalcitrant workers of the Clyde on Christmas Day. Opposition to his purpose was immediately manifest. Arthur Henderson, with two Goverment officials, rushed up to Glasgow, and with Lord Murray of Elibank, addressed the Trade Union officials, in the vain hope of securing a friendly atmosphere. The Christmas morning meeting in the St. Andrew's Hall was fairly well attended, but violently hostile. Lloyd George was greeted by a storm of hooting, followed by the singing of "The Red Flag." He was unable to get a hearing till David Kirkwood, the Parkhead shop steward, called for order. The meeting ended in uproar when John Muir of the Clyde Workers' Committee claimed to be heard in defence of the workers, and was refused. Lloyd George then visited Parkhead Forge. The workers there had been called together before his arrival. When he entered with Henderson, Murray of Elibank, and the manager, the workers paid no attention, but continued debating some business of their own, so fearless was their defiance! Again it was only by Kirkwood's intervention that Lloyd George obtained a hearing. George conveyed, through the manager, a desire to be introduced to Kirkwood, and a request to him to act as chairman. Kirkwood agreed, announcing the Minister in truculent style :

"This is Mr. Lloyd George . . . we regard him with suspicion, because every Act with which he is associated has the taint of slavery about it."[1]

He demanded for the workers a share in the management of the works. Unless this were granted they would fight the Munitions Act "to the death."

Logan, one of the Parkhead shop stewards, was dismissed for an altercation with the manager arising out of Lloyd George's visit. A stay-in strike was organised in Logan's defence, and 28 men were fined £5 each in consequence. Hundreds of munitioners left work to attend the trial, and the strike continued for some time.

Lloyd George had warned every Glasgow newspaper, save one, to publish no unauthorised account of his Christmas Day visit ; to every paper, with one exception, a report of his doings, edited by himself, was circulated by the Press Association. The one exception was the *Glasgow Forward*, a Socialist weekly edited by a clever good-looking young Scotsman, Tom L. Johnston, who later got a place in the Labour Government of 1929. He edited the *Forward* with a scathing pen throughout the War, and gained for it a wide popularity in the Labour Movement so far afield as London, which it lost when he left the editorial chair.

The *Forward*, as might have been expected, published a detailed and graphic report of Lloyd George's visit. At Lloyd George's direct instance[2] the paper was promptly suppressed by the military authorities under the D.O.R.A. Eventually the *Forward* was permitted to reappear, on promising to submit all doubtful matter to the Government Press Bureau. In the meantime the Clyde Workers' Committee had begun to issue a weekly publication of its own called *The Worker*. Its pages were illuminated with a racy and acid humour, which emanated from its editor, John S. Clarke, a genuine original, an odd figure, Atheist, Republican, and rebel Socialist. His caustic verse on topical subjects was much admired by a wide working-class following ; his vitriolic epithets, which in some quarters might have been dubbed at times both blasphemous and obscene, were quoted with awe and delight as gems of priceless and daring wit. Clarke's biting propaganda rhymes, which added prestige and circulation to their paper, and were beyond their power to emulate, were regarded by McManus and his colleagues with a respect denied to Gallacher's guileless and unpurposed songs.

About this time Lord Balfour of Burleigh, that hugely built old Conservative, a most hardened reactionary in theory, who yet not infrequently proved more liberal in judgment than those who accounted themselves Liberals, was appointed, with Lynden Macassy, K.C., to enquire into the unrest on the Clyde. Their report in many matters justified the workers' most bitter complaints. They recommended the easing of

[1] Reported in the *Glasgow Forward*.

[2] This was stated in the House of Commons, January 4th, 1916, by J. H. Tennant.

the pressure imposed by the Munitions Act, notably in the refusal to permit workers to change their employment for legitimate reasons. The main outcome of the enquiry was that Munitions Tribunals were deprived of the power to impose imprisonment, but given authority to make orders for fines to be deducted by instalments from wages. To counteract any easement of compulsion which this might effect, came an announcement by the Law Officers of the Crown threatening legal proceedings by the Attorney-General against the trustees of any Trade Union issuing strike pay to workers controlled by the Munitions Act. The Government Committee on Production issued to certain Trade Unions a statement enjoining them not to press for further advances in wages.

Government Commissioners were appointed for further enquiry into the unrest on the Clyde and Tyne; for strikes were unpleasantly frequent, and the inflow of new workers, the dilution of labour, as it was termed, was not proceeding at the pace which the Ministry desired. The shop stewards of the Amalgamated Society of Engineers now mutually agreed to insist that the basis of any arrangement for dilution must be the payment of the old rates to all new-comers to the work, whether men or women. Further strikes were called in support of this principle. Again David Kirkwood came to the front, leading the men and women at Beardmore's Parkhead Forge so successfully, that this principle was accepted for that factory by the Government officials and by Sir William Beardmore. Whilst this agreement was operating at Parkhead 150 skilled men earning 8d. per hour were dismissed from another Clyde area factory and replaced by women paid from 12s. to 14s. a week.

## CHAPTER XXXVI

### CONSCRIPTION—CLYDE WORKERS ARRESTED—MILITARY SERVICE TRIBUNALS

CONSCRIPTION was swiftly advancing. The Lords were forcing the Government to the plunge, by threatening to reject the Bill for staving off a General Election. In the Commons the Liberal, Labour and Irish Members who had declared for the maintenance of the Voluntary System still held the majority, but little reliance could be placed on the stability of their convictions.

In the last week of the old year it was announced that the Cabinet had decided on the immediate redemption of Asquith's so-called " pledge to the married men," that before they were called on to fulfil their undertaking to serve, compulsion should be applied to the unmarried.

A special Conference was hastily convened by the Labour Party and Trade Union Congress, for January 6th. It was a great gathering; it seemed that everyone was there who cared for Labour. The delegates rejected the official resolution to leave the Labour Members free to vote as they thought fit; and by a huge majority of 1,998,000 to 873,000, declared against Conscription, urging the Labour Members to vote against the measure at every stage.

A Liberal, Sir John Simon, left the Cabinet, but Henderson and his Labour colleagues held to their posts, through those days of thunderous suspense, when all awaited the next event, wondering if any power or influence in the country could impede the introduction of a Conscription Bill.

Actually a meeting of the Labour Party Executive and the Labour Members of Parliament had instructed Henderson, Brace, and Roberts to withdraw from the Government. Their resignations were therefore tendered; but a meeting took place between Asquith, the Parliamentary Labour Party, and the Labour Party Executive. The resignations were withdrawn, pending the Labour Party Conference, which was to meet at the end of January. Conscription would be established before that date, if the Government had its way.

A little conference[1] was called in the Fabian Rooms in Tothill Street, by the No Conscription Fellowship, the Society of Friends, and the Fellowship of Reconciliation, a pacifist group of war-time growth. From this conference emerged a deputation to the House of Commons, and a body called the National Council against Conscription. I was elected to both. We passed, a little irregular stream of us, along the pavement to the House; mainly bourgeois, middle-aged, and elderly, black lace mantles and black

[1] January 10th, 1916.

silk skirts trailing and rustling: Arnold Lupton, emaciated, ascetic; Theodora Wilson Wilson, calmly ecstatic, mainly known for her children's tales from the Bible; A. J. Hobson, another spare intellectual; F. W. Pethick Lawrence, Margaret Bondfield, Catharine Marshall, old Lady Courtney of Penwith, and many more. I went with the rest through the familiar portals of St. Stephen's, expecting every policeman we encountered to turn me back; for still I was on the Speaker's black list for the stone I had hurled at the picture of Speaker Finch in the Suffragette days,[1] but I passed in with the throng umolested.

We pleaded to no avail.

Robert Smillie was made president of the new Council against Conscription, F. W. Pethick Lawrence, hon. treasurer, Langdon Davies, whom I saw then for the first time, secretary. We met in a bare little office in Bride Lane. Catharine Marshall, as usual, had been to the House of Commons, and could report the rumours flying about the lobbies, and in particular the opinion of Sir John Simon, whose recent resignation from the Government had invested him with a romantic halo. Someone suggested Lobbying. "Oh, Lobbying at this stage would do harm!" Margaret Bondfield deprecated severely. "I thought Mr. Hobson," interposed Catharine Marshall, smiling. "Oh, that of course would be different; if Mr. Hobson would, that would be excellent," Margaret Bondfield rejoined. Impatience flamed within me. If only all Britain might have rushed to the Lobby! Our Federation members were there each day pleading with the Labour men to stand to their pledges. If only they might have been joined in their effort by all who cared!

The No Conscription Fellowship issued an appeal:

"Freedom of conscience must not be sacrificed to military necessity. . . . Men's deepest religious and moral convictions must not be swept aside.

We believe in human brotherhood. We will not kill. We will accept no military duties. While the soul of Britain lives, our witness cannot be in vain! . . ."

In vain! In vain! Events raced on. When the Council against Conscription met again, the Bill had been introduced. Pethick Lawrence resigned the treasureship; we could not prevent conscription and he had agreed to be treasurer of another society (the U.D.C.). The Council decided to meet at ten o'clock each morning for the melancholy edification of receiving a réchauffé of the news as the Bill went through. I resigned when I heard it. I felt myself in an atmosphere stifling to me. In the East End one could act and help.

The Opposition crumbled and fell away. The Parliamentary Committee, formed the previous October to oppose Conscription, with three Liberals, C. E. Hobhouse, Percy Alden, and J. Howard Whitehouse, as its officers, had decided—so Outhwaite later revealed—to offer "as little opposition as possible, because they were afraid of stimulating opposition to the coming law in the country"—to my way of thinking a strange

[1] See *The Suffragette Movement*, by E. Sylvia Pankhurst. (Longmans Green.) This picture has been removed from its old place.

manner of fulfilling their trust. The Irish withdrew their objection after the first reading of the Bill, having secured the exclusion of Ireland. " We must be careful that in Ireland we do not force the pace," the Chief Secretary warned. R. L. Outhwaite declared that the exclusion of Ireland conveyed a message to British workers : " Resist ! Show that we shall have to send the military to your district ; then you will be excluded ! "

The Labour representatives now openly refused to leave their Government posts ; they remained to support Conscription. They had obtained assurances that the Trade Union and Labour Party officials would obtain exemption from military service. Their work would be declared of national importance ; their persons and the machinery of their movement would remain above the battle. They would face neither persecution nor the trenches. It was a wise precaution from their own standpoint. Henderson defended their refusal to obey the congress mandate, saying that Lord Kitchener had personally assured him that Conscription was essential to win the war : " I do not see how any man can set his opinion on a military question against the conclusion of Lord Kitchener and the General Staff."

About half the Labour Members voted for the Military Service Bill at every stage. Only 39 votes were recorded against its second reading ; only 33 against its most cruel clause, to include young lads of eighteen years—mere children still. Asquith gave a definite pledge not to conscribe the widow's only son : " When there is a single unmarried son left behind it would of course be a monstrous thing if the State were to call for military service from a man in that position." He quoted the instruction of Shakepeare's Henry V to the then Lord Derby in the French wars :

> " Go 'cruit me Cheshire and Lancashire
> And Derby hills that are so free.
> No married man or widow's son,
> No widow's curse shall go with me."

Asquith ignored the fact that the essence of the Shakespearean eulogy of martial chivalry and courage was free service :

> " We few, we happy few . . .
> He which hath no stomach for this fight
> Let him depart ; his passport shall be made
> And crowns for convoy put into his purse."

The married men were soon conscribed like the rest. The Military Service Tribunals gave no quarter to the widow's only son.[1] Amongst the earliest to be denied was a clerk, the only son of a mother in ill-health. He said it would kill her if he were taken. The chairman of the Tribunal replied : " We are at war and cannot take such cases into account." This

[1] W. C. Anderson, M.P., complained that at Bermondsey Tribunal the military representative opposed the exemption of a man who held three medical certificates of unfitness, who had four brothers in the Army, and was the support of his widowed mother and his wife and children. The Mayor had protested that the Tribunal was powerless and had better disband.

Official Report, November 7th, 1916.

was the general verdict of the Tribunals. Asquith refused to receive a deputation from widowed mothers of only sons.

The safeguards against using the Act as an indirect method of industrial compulsion were valueless. On the contrary, it supplied the final links in the chain of compulsion already forged.

As time went on, promises, not always kept, were made that employers getting soldiers lent to them at Army rates of pay should hand the difference between such rates and the usual wage to the Government. Employers often found boys more profitable than soldiers and in the general relaxation of principle and practice, J. H. Thomas, the railwayman's M.P., was heard mildly complaining that "boys of tender age" were doing the arduous work of firemen on goods trains. On September 11th, 1916,[1] an accident took place on the Glasgow and Paisley Railway in which 28 persons were injured. The fireman, who is the driver's only assistant, was only 15 years of age.

The desire to avoid serious agitation through the impassioned resistance of determined men, who might possibly receive a backing both widespread and influential, and the representations of influential Quakers and others opposed to compulsion, produced the semblance of a Conscience Clause, exempting from military service men whose convictions were opposed to the War. It would have been simpler, and more sincere, to decree that all men declaring a conscientious objection to military service should be imprisoned, or drafted to special service for the duration of the War; for this, with exceptions so rare as to be negligible, was in fact the final result of establishing a conscientious objection. Yet, as matters stood, a painful struggle, sometimes accompanied by most brutal torture, had first to be endured.

The Act left to the Military Service Tribunals the decision as to whether a man's objection to serve was in fact conscientious or not, no definition of the term being provided. Exemption on conscientious grounds might be absolute, conditional or temporary. In most cases the Tribunals refused any form of exemption, and handed the objector to the military authorities to be dealt with as they saw fit. The provision protecting the Conscientious Objector from the death penalty covered only "failure to obey an order calling him up from the Reserve for permanent service." Yet resistance to this order was but the opening of a long-drawn persecution, during which there loomed up before the objecting men and their relatives the dread probability of the death penalty.

Before the promise of exemption for conscientious objection had been put to the proof, it had helped to undermine agitation against the Bill. Immediately after Conscription became law, the Labour Party Conference met at Bristol, and whilst declaring its opposition to the Act, rejected a resolution to agitate for its repeal.

The falsity of the pretence that Conscription of the unmarried would permit the attested married men to remain at home, was exposed as soon as the Military Service Act passed into law. Four days later the first

[1] House of Commons Official Report, November 16th, 1916.

"HANDS OFF THE RING"
*Principal Scene in the* GRAND CHRISTMAS PANTOMIME ~ *European Theatre*
*Continuous performance ~ Prices as usual*

A drawing by the late Herbert Cole, reproduced from the *Workers' Dreadnought*.

COMPULSION BILL

"GOT HIM"

*Reproduced from the "Workers' Dreadnought"*

groups of married men were called up. "Married shirkers next!" shrieked *The Regiment*, a bellicose little paper which presumed to express the Army point of view. *The Times* observed that the Act, though better than it had expected, did not yet go far enough to suit its policy. The attested married men were already being urged to demand the conscription of married men who were unattested.

On March 14th J. H. Tennant, the Under-Secretary for War, cynically admitted as an argument for compulsion:

"By means of grading and putting them into categories, the men have been tricked and cajoled to get them into the Army."

The Derby Tribunals were the nucleus of those which were to operate Conscription, additional representatives being added by the municipal councils.

Without my consent, the Poplar Labour Party nominated me for the Local Tribunal; the Borough Council rejected me. By no means would I have served. I would not share part or lot in the odious work of Conscription.

Often after meeting or conference, as I rode home through the sad darkness of the East End in the crowded Old Ford 'bus, I looked up at some young soldier lad, who had given up his seat to me or another woman, and stood there, steadying himself by the hanging strap, his slim wrist and hand unfit, as yet, for heavy labour, his throat still childish-looking and smooth, his head a little drooping, fatigued, it seemed, by the weight of his knapsack and greatcoat. Anguish, almost unendurable, would seize me that this slender boy, here within touch, should be going out to the slaughter—and that all we adults should slavishly allow it. Memories of my brother Harry, gentle and sensitive, surged upon me. In all these soldier boys I saw him. I recalled him as he came to me, a child, white-faced with horror at sight of a cat some ruffians had hung. I heard him, a youth, discoursing on Internationalism, with clear, unprejudiced mind friendly and brotherly to all peoples. On boys of his sort Conscription would rivet the chains of militarism.

A group of young *Herald* Leaguers, all awaiting the calling-up notices which should be the cue for each one's individual struggle against the War, were holding meetings in Finsbury Park each week, their audiences growing in size and sympathy. There was always organised opposition. The platform had to be overturned, as a matter of course, by a rush of opponents; but this rite of patriotism performed, one could speak from the ground, and be patiently heard, while the literature sellers disposed of their wares, unhindered. It was later in the year that the L.C.C., fearing all we anti-war agitators were making too much headway, prohibited the sale of literature in the parks.

I went north for a demonstration on Glasgow Green, organised by the Trades Council, to demand the repeal of Conscription. The resolution was carried unanimously, but the crowd was listless and inert. Here on the Clyde they had hoped for action; the speakers had nothing save talk to offer. Uneasy foreboding, weary depression marked the faces before me ; the audience shifted and fluctuated ; the speakers had lost their grip.

The No Conscription Fellowship[1] had officially decided to organise no resistance, and to submit to the ordeal of the Tribunals, but many of its members were not of this mind. The Glasgow branch declared its refusal to appear before the Tribunals.

Whilst the Tribunals were still forming, the *Worker*, the newly-published organ of the Clyde Workers' Committee, was suppressed. Gallacher, Muir, and Bell were arrested under the D.O.R.A. and charged with attempting, through its pages, to cause mutiny and disaffection, and to impede the production of war material. The *Worker* had called for common action between munition workers and miners, to compel the withdrawal of Conscription, and had named Robert Smillie as the man who could secure unity in the effort. The Clyde workers were advised to "approach Robert Smillie, and offer him their assistance and co-operation in any measures he may take to make Conscription ineffective."

Robert Smillie did not respond to this appeal. His speeches, whether he meant them fully or not, were incitements to industrial action against the Government and its policies. They created a ferment in the minds of others ; but he took no steps to implement them.

Now that Conscription was in force notices were sent by the military authorities to unmarried men, ordering them to present themselves for service, and threatening them with arrest as deserters should they fail. These notices made no mention that exemption could be obtained for any cause, or of the Tribunals to which appeal might be made. Even *The Times*, which had vehemently and persistently demanded the Act, complained that men previously rejected as medically unfit were receiving these notices, and that when they displayed exemption certificates these were often taken away and destroyed. An atmosphere of terror was created to prevent resistance. At Lancaster, on February 22nd, a poor mother was sent to prison for "harbouring" her son, who was found crouching between the rafters and the ceiling of their home.

A special Non-Combatant Corps was formed exclusively for Conscientious Objectors. Their duties would be to dig trenches, erect barbed-wire entanglements, assist the lines of communication, sweep up mines, and any other work of danger which might not compel them to take part in actual fighting. A military representative rightly observed that the members of this corps would not have a very happy time ! Prominent Conscientious Objectors at once announced their determination not to undertake war work, of this or any other sort. The vast majority of the C.O.'s refused to take service in the Non-Combatant Corps.

The public were admitted to the Tribunals. I attended a sitting at Bethnal Green, as soon as the Tribunal there was formed. The appeals of four Conscientious Objectors were heard and wholly rejected, though all

[1] It had counselled signing the National Register, adding a refusal to undertake military service or munition work.

could prove they had long held anti-militarist views, and one was a widow's only son. A fifth C.O. was a local propagandist of some prominence, well known to the members of the Tribunal. They cleared the court to hear his case, and awarded him service in the Non-Combatant Corps, which he promptly rejected.

Amongst the other appellants was a small greengrocer and furniture remover, who pleaded for total exemption to carry on his business, as the sole support of his aged father, and of his two widowed sisters and their children. He was brusquely allowed a month's exemption to wind up his affairs before joining his regiment. Jews were treated even more relentlessly than other applicants ; the destruction of their small businesses seemed to give real satisfaction to the Tribunal.

A large proportion of the cases rejected by the Local Tribunals passed on to the Appeal Tribunals, but usually received from them no kindlier treatment.

Numbers of physically defective men were passed into the Army, despite their appeals. When they broke down, pension was refused on the ground that their disabilities did not originate through service.

Philip Snowden[1] cited the case of a Conscript whose eyesight was so defective that when he laid his spectacles on the table he could only find them by groping. The Under-Secretary for War had written to say that if the poor fellow had *three pairs of spectacles*, to change as the lenses became dimmed in battle, he would be fit for active service. Another Conscript was so far advanced in consumption that he died three weeks after enlistment, another was a physical wreck with a crippled hand, whilst one was vomiting blood and when taken for service, could only digest Benger's Food.

. . . . . . .

Asquith had said that agitation for the repeal of the Military Service Act was legal, and would not be prosecuted ; yet the police were confiscating anti-Conscription literature, and police and military were breaking up meetings against the Act. When Members of Parliament complained that soldiers broke up meetings Tennant replied: "I must defend my military." When it was shown that Tribunals denied to Conscientious Objectors the protection accorded to them by the law, Walter Long protested he must " defend and maintain " the Tribunals. The Home Secretary admitted that the Press Bureau had prohibited the printing of a record of the decisions of Military Service Tribunals for the information of Members of Parliament.[2]

Nellie Best, a frail white-faced woman I had never seen before, was tried under the D.O.R.A. and imprisoned for six months. She had republished as a leaflet an appeal on behalf of starving and broken men discharged from the War, which had appeared in *Ainslee's Advertiser* in America, over the signatures of some of the richest and most prominent leaders of United States Society. She headed the leaflet: "*A Warning to those*

[1] House of Commons Official Report, August 23rd, 1916.

[2] Official Parliamentary Report. May 18th, 1916.

*about to be Conscripted! This is how your King and country are treating the lads who voluntarily enlisted!*"

. . . . . . .

The day Mrs. Best went to prison a letter from Sir Frederick Milner (who was working to ameliorate the lot of disabled soldiers, and to provide hostels, clubs, and aural instruction for the deaf) appeared in *The Times*. He complained that the "cruel treatment of many discharged soldiers" was "enough to break one's heart." In September he had prepared a statement giving proof of "the callous and capricious way in which the men had been treated." The principal London papers had agreed to publish simultaneously, but the Censor had suppressed it. "Now that voluntary recruiting is over," he said, "I hope to be able to state the case for these gallant men." Sir Frederick Milner was too influential to be prosecuted.

. . . . . . .

Our East London Federation organised a procession from Tower Hill to Holloway to protest against the sentence on Nellie Best. We invited the Women's International League to co-operate. I was present on the League executive when our invitation was read.

To my surprise the chairman, Mrs. Swanwick, opposed acceptance. "I do not think the sentence is severe—when her country is at war—I should have thought it might have been death," she objected. Thus heavily did the hypnotism of war overhang even pacifist circles.

"It is merely a reprint of an appeal for funds in an American magazine with her own comment at the head," I urged, handing the leaflet.

"I see on it the names of several American millionaires!" Mrs. Swanwick answered acidly, as though the document were suspect on that account.

It was decided that the League could not officially support our protest; its members could follow the banners unofficially, if they chose.

. . . . . . .

All the well-known Conscientious Objectors were refused exemption[1]: Clifford Allen, chairman of the No Conscription Fellowship, Scott Duckers and C. H. Norman who had started a "Stop the War" Committee soon after hostilities began, Fenner Brockway, editor of the *Labour Leader*, and many more. Peculiarly unjust was the rejection of the claim to a conscientious objection of Reginald Roper, M.A., M.Ed., the brother of Esther Roper, secretary of the Suffrage Society in Manchester. Roper was an anti-militarist of long standing. As a headmaster he had substituted

[1] Since the vast majority of the Tribunals refused complete exemption, and the wording of the Conscience Clause was ambiguous, its meaning was tested by Appeal to the Court, on April 18th, 1916. The case was tried by Justices Darling, Lawrence, and Avory. Darling and Lawrence declared that exemption could be granted to C.O.'s from Combatant Service only; but Avory refused to agree. The Government thereupon passed an Amending Act directing that exemption on conscientious, as on other grounds, might be absolute, conditional, or temporary. The Tribunals still refused to grant absolute exemption to C.O.s.

scientific physical training for military drill, and for years had been working to introduce this change into all schools.

Daily came news of the cruelties heaped upon the Objectors. Their judges on the Tribunals greeted them with insult and abuse. A scientist employed by the Manchester Corporation was accused of "exploiting God" to save his own skin, and of being "a deliberate and rank blasphemer," a "coward," a "cad," and "nothing but an unwholesome mass of stinking fat." Another was told: "You are only fit to be on the point of a German bayonet." "A great many people have an objection to joining the 'no-courage corps.'" "I have had enough of these Conscientious Objectors; serve them all alike!" "If you insist on making a statement I shall send for the police."[1]

The Pelham Committee was appointed to advise Tribunals to what service of national importance a Conscientious Objector might be relegated; but the advice was ignored. Tribunals continued either to refuse all exemption, or to offer the N.C.C., in which the Objectors declined to serve. When a Conscientious Objector who was a teacher urged that educational work was of national importance, the chairman of the Tribunal replied: "Only for attested men." To be a Conscientious Objector was to be thrust into the Army though physically unfit in a most excessive degree, and even if doing work of essential importance for which soldiers were being brought back from the Army.

Philip Snowden protested:

"Never since the days of Judge Jeffreys and the Bloody Assize has such a travesty of justice been seen. . . . The Appeal Courts have acted even more illegally than the Local Tribunals."[2]

Whilst yet we waited anxiously for news of the Objectors whose appeals had been denied, J. H. Tennant in the House of Commons declared, on behalf of the Government, that protection from the death penalty for refusal to obey military orders, could only apply to men whom the Tribunals admitted to be conscientious. The majority of the Conscientious Objectors, since the Tribunals had dismissed their appeals, would receive no further protection from the conscience clause and would be subject to the Army Act.[3] Tennant appeared to imply that even if a man's conscientious objection were accepted by the Tribunal, refusal to enter the N.C.C. might be punished with death. I have no doubt that these threats would have been carried out, and many C.O.'s would have been executed, save for the shield of a considerable public opinion in their defence. Undoubtedly many Objectors, especially the earlier groups to brave the ordeal, looked death very squarely in the face.

[1] House of Commons Official Report, March 22nd, 1916.

[2] Speech at the N.C.F. Conference, Devonshire House, Bishopsgate, April 8th, 1916.

[3] The Army Act Section 9 (1) provides:

"Every person subject to military law who disobeys in such manner as to show a wilful defiance of authority any lawful demand given personally by his superior officer, shall on conviction by court martial be liable to suffer death or such punishment as in this Act mentioned."

For men who were not C.O.'s, exemption could often be obtained by influence, though simple justice was denied. Indignation was expressed when exemption was granted to the Amalgamated Press for 21 employees working on *Forget-me-not* and *Comic Cuts*. The cases most obviously modified by influence seldom received publicity.

. . . . . . .

Lansbury was fighting zealously for the young men of his circle. He had arranged that his brother-in-law, Artie Brine, a tall, consumptive-looking youth, and his friend Whitelock, a young workman of Bow, should employ themselves on a piece of land somewhere in the country, if the Tribunal would permit. Thus dimly the plan was outlined to me by little Minnie O'Brien, friendly in her solicitude. Whitelock, who was essentially one of Lansbury's supporters, had also been active in the Rebels' Social and Political Union, which some of the Bow men had formed to help us in the Suffragette struggle before the War. When Whitelock made his plea for exemption before the London Appeal Tribunal, at the Guildhall, Major Rothschild would have rejected him, saying that he could understand a religious objection to warfare but not this plea. George Lansbury roared out at him: "Shame on you, Rothschild! Herbert Samuel has said that a moral objection is as good as a religious objection! You ought to be ashamed of yourself!"

This outburst did its work; exemption was granted and Whitelock slipped through to land work with his friend Artie.

. . . . . . .

A young preacher in a South Wales Wesleyan chapel told his congregation that he had considered enlistment, but had gone for guidance to Christ's teaching and had decided to follow the commandment: "Thou shalt not kill." "Get out of the pulpit, you kid!" shouted a prominent member of the chapel. The preacher was hustled outside, while the prominent member led prayers for his soul.

. . . . . . .

The boy was nearing his eighteenth birthday. I wanted his mother to meet George Lansbury. I thought if he saw her misery he might help to find a way out for her boy. I thought there must be loopholes of escape. I did not know. I only knew the way of hard fighting, and that, it seemed, was not possible in his case. He had no practise in expressing convictions against the War, only an instinctive horror of it. His mother was against it, deeply and profoundly. The habit of relying on her, deferring to her, avoiding distress for her, because of her sorrows and her maladies, was strong in him; but she had talked to him little of politics. Her personal life had been too full of misery and hardship, she was so frail, so chronically suffering, so frequently prostrated.

Her struggle to rear her children, and especially this youngest, her only boy, had been tremendous. She had given her life for them, throb by throb; she was drained and spent. After that struggle, desperate, heroic, she would not give her darling to be a soldier, would not permit that he should be mangled in this hateful war; yet she could not face that he should be an Objector, the butt of cruelty and violence, a prisoner with his health destroyed, a fugitive always fearing capture. He was "only a country boy," she pleaded—they had come to London on his account—he could not face it; some way of escape for him must be found.

Lansbury said he would see her with me at one of the big railway termini; he was catching a train there. She was white and tragic, well-nigh speechless in her agony, ill and shivering in the bleak wind. Lansbury could not help her; he murmured that the R.F.A. was said to be safer than the infantry. . . .

The lad was working in Bow—he had a rough labouring job in Lansbury's yard. Good-natured Willie Lansbury had taken him on at my pleading; for it was an essential trade; but he plainly told me he could not make the boy one of his reserved men; his old hands had the right to be safeguarded first. I hoped, nevertheless, that the boy might somehow slip through; that we should somehow find a way out for him; but he was not happy in the yard; he suffered from the cold. His mother was anxious for his health.

His uncle promised to get him into an engineering shop, and from there into a mechanics' corps; he would not have to fight. The boy went up to enlist in the mechanics' corps, as his uncle told him. He came back a private in the infantry. How it happened he could not say.

He was swiftly trained, swiftly indeed, indeed! The last time he was home on leave before going to France there was an air raid. He went out into the road. His mother cried to him: "Come in! You will be killed!"

"I would rather be killed here, Mother, than out there!" he answered her, sadly.

In a few weeks he was "reported missing." Eventually he was "presumed dead."

His mother took to Spiritualistic séances, in the hope of finding him, and sought to obtain messages from him by a board the Spiritualists supplied. "Some have their boys; —— has her board!" her sister said.

. . . . . . .

The No Conscription Fellowship held a great convention of two thousand objectors of military age and many hundred sympathisers at Devonshire House, Bishopsgate, the headquarters of the Society of Friends. There had recently been rowdy scenes there during lectures by Roden Buxton. To provide against disorder only ticket-holders were admitted. The shouts of the would-be disturbers were heard outside. After the first great burst of applause, when the pledge not to undertake war service was adopted, it was decided not to provoke the opponents by further applause. The waving of handkerchiefs was substituted. Three sailors climbed over the barriers and were met in the passages of the building by stewards who induced them to depart quietly with friendly handshakes.

The atmosphere was very tense. Clifford Allen, the chairman of the N.C.F., a frail young man afflicted with curvature of the spine, was then regarded almost as a saint by thousands of followers. One could hardly realise that he had been satisfied to work as business manager of the jingo *Daily Citizen* until it ceased publication.

. . . . . . .

In December 1915[1] the German Social Democrats had made a plea in the Reichstag for peace negotiations. The Chancellor had replied that his government would welcome negotiations ; but the peace must guarantee security and freedom of development to Germany. General Hindenburg, however, announced in the Press that the time for peace was not yet. Asquith and the French and Russian Ministers made bellicose statements. In the New Year it had been reported here that crowds demanding peace had assembled at the opening of the Reichstag, that the military had fired on the people and four hundred men and women had been killed.

When our Parliament reassembled in the New Year F. W. Jowett had tabled an I.L.P. Amendment to the Address, urging that the British Government and its Allies should disavow aims of conquest, and intimate willingness to accept the mediation of neutral nations to conclude the War, on a basis providing for the evacuation of Belgium, Northern France, and all invaded territories. The Government refused to allow time for this Amendment to be debated. Its terms were undoubtedly inconvenient in view of the agreements for annexation the Allies had already made. Instead a general peace discussion, opened by Snowden, had been permitted on February 23rd. Asquith then scouted Snowden's suggestion that the Germans were willing to open peace negotiations, and repeated his old declamation that this country would " never sheathe the sword " until Belgium and Serbia had recovered " all, and more than all " they had sacrificed, until France was adequately secured against aggression, the rights of the smaller nationalities of Europe established, and the military domination of Prussia " wholly and finally destroyed." At the

[1] On June 23rd, 1915, *Vorwaerts*, the Majority Social Democratic newspaper, had published an appeal for peace negotiations. On June 26th it had been suppressed.

same time threats of a Trade War against Germany, during and after the War, were uttered from Government and other circles, and the Allies prepared to confer in Paris with this aim.

On April 11th Bethmann Hollweg again spoke of peace in the Reichstag, declaring he had already expressed his willingness to enter peace negotiations; but the Allies had refused to consider the proposal, and had threatened the complete destruction of Germany. Asquith retorted that the destruction of Prussia's military domination would not mean that Germany would be wiped off the map of Europe, or her national life destroyed or mutilated.

Behind the scenes Colonel House was vainly offering the mediation of President Wilson, and promising to bring the United States into the War on the side of the Allies should Germany refuse to enter a peace conference on terms acceptable to the Allies. America would add the proviso that the conference must be pledged to make warfare on sea and land more humane towards neutrals, and to bind the signatory Powers to unite against any Power refusing other methods of arbitrament than warfare. Sir Edward Grey, the recipient of these offers, had rejected them, though for many months he had led the gullible House to believe he was working with him precisely to this end. House animadverted in his diary on "the selfishness of Governments."

How the virus of militarist nationalism had gripped the belligerent peoples may be gathered from the fact that when Haase, a German Socialist of the Minority but by no means an extremist, suggested in the Reichstag that the War might end without victors or vanquished, the majority of the Socialist Members, of late the apostles of international fraternity, declared by 58 votes to 33 that he had violated the discipline and good faith of the Party!

## CHAPTER XXXVII

ONE OF THE VOLUNTEERS—CLYDE DEPORTATIONS—WITH THE COLONIAL SOLDIERS IN TRAFALGAR SQUARE

MY cousin, Bertie Goulden, had come back from the Dardanelles that winter. He was one of the Australian soldiers; for he was away in the Antipodes when war broke out. He enlisted the day after the declaration, believing it his duty to help the old country, the Dad, and the girls. I had spurred him to emigrate, seeing no scope for him here. He had gone almost without money, and had suffered manifold hardships. He was just beginning to succeed by great exertions, had bought himself a piece of land, and some horses, when he left all he had achieved.

He was one of those good, silent fellows who leave most of the thinking to other people, accepting what they see in the newspapers as literal truth, and assuming, in all sincerity, that the Government is sure to be right. "Bertie is just like the British public," I used to say in the old days at home, when his interests mainly centred in football and cricket.

Now that he was in the War I expected from him no criticism of its aims, no questioning of its authority. Knowing him in the maelstrom, I would not bother him with argument. Yet he looked at me now with a meaning kindness in his face, which made me feel that, in part at least, he agreed with me. When he assured me very earnestly: "The Turk is a gentleman," I knew that he had begun to realise the cruel iniquity of the War. He had been ill with enteric whilst his regiment was in Egypt, after the withdrawal from the Dardanelles, and was still the worse for it.

He insisted that Smyth and I should go to some show with him. We saw Pavlova on the films. I had always been too busy to manage to see her in the flesh. Dancing on the seashore, she was lovely, despite the limitations of the film. The drama she appeared in was of revolution, but where and when I have forgotten, if I ever knew. I was thinking of the War and the young man beside me, poignantly realising what a sterling sort he was. He was going now to France.

He was finally undone there. An injury to his knee, which never righted itself, would have been sufficient to disable him from working his land in Australia. Worse still, he had returned with consumption. It took ten years to kill him, the last five of them dragged out in suffering so acute that he sometimes rolled on the floor in agony extreme. The military authorities were all the time "curing" him; and at times his faith seemed implicit that they would accomplish it. I was eager for him to go to Switzerland, and would have set myself to accomplish it; but he would not entertain the proposal. He was afraid that by making any suggestion about his treatment to the authorities who were "curing" him, he might lose his pension. It was more liberal than if he had enlisted here. He discounted my anxiety, assuring me that the doctors were using every possible method.

Minnie O'Brien recounted to me what she had heard of the onset of his illness; I would not talk of it to himself. In hospital with pleurisy, over there in France, he had got out of bed and run out to follow his regiment in delirium. He had received a military distinction, for what I never knew; to me all that was as dust and ashes. No bravery, no unselfishness of his —and both I knew he had—could wipe out for me the sorrow that he had been drawn into the great massacre, one of the millions of pawns, duped and betrayed.

. . . . . . .

In March W. C. Anderson booked a committee room in the House of Commons that we might take soldiers' wives and widows there to talk to Members of Parliament. We had the same hard facts of misery and neglect to disclose to them which we had been fighting all through the War. The old soldier had the grievances still he had suffered in other wars. We had to tell of a gunner in the R.F.A. discharged pensionless with a shattered leg on which three operations had been performed, the painful wounds still suppurating. After a month of agitation we got him 25s. a week, but only for one month "conditional." The struggle for him must continue. Another private had served twelve years with "exemplary" character and received the Indian and South African medals. He had re-enlisted in 1914. Discharged with an incurable complaint, too ill to work and suffering grievously, he had received only 10s. a week sick benefit, which would soon be exhausted, and he had a wife and five children, the youngest five months old. After two months' correspondence I had received a promise of 4s. 8d. a week for him for 33 weeks "final." Poor fellows, they were but cannon-fodder still.

Despite the new stores of men opened to it by Conscription, the Army still kept its grip on the heedless boys who enlisted under age and then bitterly repented, begging to be sent back to their parents. A widowed mother who was with us wept for her sixteen-year old son. Always delicate, he had four brothers at the Front, and had offered himself to the recruiting sergeant from anxiety on their account. His mother and sisters had pleaded for his discharge from the day of his enlistment. I had summoned all the influence I could muster to their aid, but his release was not sanctioned till he had been sent back from France incurably paralysed. A gratuity was refused on the ground that his relatives had claimed him as under age.

At Old Street Police Court in October 1916 a lad of 14 was charged with being a deserter, and handed over to a military escort. His mother pleaded that he had joined the Army a fortnight before, and was in a draft warned for the Front.

. . . . . . .

Arrests under the D.O.R.A. became more frequent. Finlay Chisholm, a ploughman, and Kelman, a cattle driver, were imprisoned for an argument with a recruiting sergeant. Miss Howsin, for some time mysteriously referred to as a " country squire's daughter," was taken from her home by police in motor-cars and imprisoned in Holloway, her friends being left 17 days without knowledge of her whereabouts. Her offence, unconnected with the War, was her friendship with an Indian reformer regarded as troublesome. W. Iredale, a foreman warehouseman of Bradford, was imprisoned for two months because he said :

" The very people who want us to fight in their interests are the people who looked upon the Army as the scum of the earth in time of peace."

Alan Kaye, a young Oxford undergraduate, received two months' imprisonment for distributing the N.C.F. manifesto, " Shall Britons Be Conscripted ? " though he promised not to do it again.

Old Laurence Ginnell sneered bitterly at the quiescent Members of Parliament, declaring that the Government regarded them as " automats," the mere " filling-stuff " of the House.

Peter Petroff, a brown-faced Russian, whose whimsical smiles had drawn long crow's-feet from the corners of his eyes, a revolutionary of revolutionaries, had sometimes spoken for us at the Women's hall, accompanied by his German wife, a serious intellectual young woman. For Socialist speeches against the War he was sentenced to two months' imprisonment on the pretence that he had failed to comply with the Aliens' regulations. On appeal, his sentence had been quashed. The Government retaliated by interning him. When complaint was made, McKinnon Wood, the Secretary for Scotland, retorted that Petroff was a political refugee and his wife " a believer in neither government nor God."

. . . . . . .

There was trouble again on the Clyde. The agreement made at the Parkhead Forge to pay women the same rates as men had not been implemented. The management was even refusing the bare £1 a week which Lloyd George had promised to enforce in Government factories.

David Kirkwood, as convener of shop stewards, had hitherto been permitted to pass freely about the works for the settlement of small questions, as was customary in other factories. He was now ordered not to leave his vice without permission. Thus prevented from performing his duties as convener, he resigned the position. His work-mates thereupon informed the management that if Kirkwood's freedom of movement were not restored they would cease work at noon that day. The management remained obdurate, the strike took place. In the small hours of the next morning[1] Kirkwood and four other shop stewards, Messer, MacManus, Shields, and Haggarty, only two of whom worked at Parkhead, were deported to Edinburgh, because they were members of the Clyde Workers' Committee, which was regarded as the source of all the trouble in the area. Wainwright, another Parkhead shop steward, and four men from other factories, were later deported to Aberdeen. The 1,600 people who had downed tools at

[1] March 25th, 1916.

Parkhead remained on strike, and as news of the deportations spread, the strike extended. Twenty thousand munitioners left their work to attend a protest meeting on Glasgow Green, and a large proportion of them did not return. Some of the strikers were brought before the Munitions Tribunal and fined £5 each; but the strike continued, nevertheless.

Henderson, to whom loyal Labourists would imagine they might have looked for support, or at least for mediation, denounced the strikers without a word on their behalf. The Press vilified them.

The officials of the Amalgamated Society of Engineers, to which a large proportion of the strikers belonged, was bitterly implacable towards the Workers' Committee movement. They attacked the strikers in their journal, refused all strike pay, and posted a notice in their offices, informing the strikers that if they failed to return to work immediately the Government would take "drastic action," information as to the nature of which the Amalgamated Society was "not allowed to give publicity." This attack by the A.S.E. was more damaging to the strike than anything the Government could do.

In the atmosphere of doubt and terror created, persuasion prevailed; the strikers returned to work, on receiving a vague pledge from the Government that all their grievances, including the deportations, should be inquired into and redressed.

The pledge was wholly broken. Gallacher and Muir, with several Members of Parliament, had interviewed Dr. Addison in London and a further conference had been arranged; but Lloyd George was then in Paris. On his return negotiations were cut off. The deported men, from whom permission to return to their homes was still withheld, found themselves boycotted by employers in every locality, and unable to earn a living. On pleas being made for them in Parliament, the Government eventually offered to grant relief of 10s. to 15s. a week to their families. Many and deep were the imprecations uttered by Trade Unionists against Arthur Henderson, who though a Labour representative and a Trade Unionist, had shared the responsibility for the deportations.

Thus, assisted by the Government, the employers continued paying women such pittances as they chose. Their power was great, for, as the Board of Trade *Labour Gazette* reported, there were still more than 160 women applicants for every hundred jobs. The President of the Local Government Board proudly declared[1] that all the factory inspectors were engaged in "combing" the factories of men, and urging the employment of women in their stead. Thus men were driven to the Front, and employers supplied with cheap labour.

. . . . . . .

Whilst the Clyde struggle was at its height the Press reported an action for £20,000 commission on a £2,000,000 contract for supplying horses to the French Army. The Runciman company was concerned in it, and Philip Runciman admitted that his associates hoped to make £100,000 profit out of 40,000 horses sold to the French. Complaints were heard

[1] March 29th, 1916.

that the relatives of the President of the Board of Trade should be so heavily involved in war contracts, as well as in the shipping companies, which had driven up food prices.

Another Budget was introduced in April, with the taxes on cocoa, coffee, and chicory raised to 6d. per lb. " to bring them to the level of tea," and a further tax on sugar. White granulated sugar used ordinarily by the poorer families had cost 1½d. per lb. before the War ; it rose now to 5d. and 6d. per lb. The income tax was graduated up to 5s. in the £, and the excess profits tax to 60 per cent. Railway and entertainment tickets were taxed. Yet the deficit was greater than ever and must be met by a further borrowing of £1,323,000,000.

. . . . . . .

To spare tonnage for war material certain imports had now been prohibited, including fruit, an important food. The import of sugar, already so costly, was limited. People now stood in queues for it, and many shopkeepers would sell it only to purchasers of other commodities.

The import of paper was limited, and that of wood pulp and grass for making it prohibited. This struck a serious blow at education and propaganda. Newspapers became excessively costly and difficult to obtain. Williams, our East End printer, bought where he could and gave us paper, now pink, now grey, now yellow. We feared that a week might come when he would not be able to produce the *Dreadnought* at all. May O'Callaghan urged me to move the printing to the National Labour Press. The charge was much higher, but Moss, the manager, declared he could guarantee us paper, and the *Dreadnought* could be more expeditiously despatched from the press in Swinton Street to the wholesale agents and railway termini. Our provincial circulation was mounting.

Further economies were demanded. Public museums and galleries were closed, another blow at culture in the interests of war. Yet nearly £6,000 was spent on re-lighting a single room used by the Members of the House of Commons.

. . . . . . .

The militarists continued their agitation for "National Service" for all men and women "from 16 to 60 years of age," and a "Service Franchise" giving a vote to every soldier, sailor and munition worker, and disfranchising conscientious objectors. The women were to remain voteless till after the war.

Another and more drastic Conscription Act was obviously impending. On April 8th we were to march from the East End to Trafalgar Square, to raise our opposing slogans: "Complete democratic control of National and International affairs!" "Human Suffrage and no infringement of popular liberties." The *Daily Express*, the *Globe*, and other newspapers, wherein appeared frequent incitements to violence against "peace talk," directed their battalions of invective against our meeting, denouncing it as "open sedition." We knew that the professional disturbers, who were then systematically breaking up the meetings of the Society of Friends, the I.L.P., the U.D.C., and all Pacifists and Socialists, were organising against us; but we left fortune to deal with us as it would, and made no preparation to resist attack.

As usual, friends saluted us on our march through the East End, crowds gathered to speed us; they had struggled with us for a decade; they supported us still, though our standard seemed now more Utopian, more elusively remote.

At Charing Cross we came into a great concourse of people, clapping and cheering (*The Times* estimated the crowd at 20,000). They welcomed our slender ranks as an expression of the old, old cry: "Not might, but right!" a symbol of the triumph of the spirit over sordid materialism, and of their own often frustrated hopes and long unsatisfied desires. To them we were protestants against their sorrows, and true believers in the living possibility of a world of happiness. I knew the dear London crowd loved me, for having given it sometimes the thrill which frees men and women from the consciousness of economic necessity and its enslaving limitations, and transports their emotional being to rarified altitudes of hope and courage. In their jolly kindness some shouted: "Good old Sylvia!" I gave my hands to many a rough grip. They pressed round me, ardent and gay, sorrowful, hopeful, earnest. Many a woman's eyes brimmed with tears as she met mine; I knew, by a sure instinct, that she had come across London, overweighted with grief, to ease her burden by some words with me.

The people pressed closer. A man whispered in my ear: "There has been trouble already!" It was true; a troop of Colonial soldiers had been shepherded into the Square, and certain civilians—well known as provokers of discord—had addressed them, urging that we, whom they termed "the pro-Germans," should not be given a hearing.

As we entered the Square a rush of friends, with a roar of cheers and a swiftness which forestalled any hostile approach, bore us forward, and hoisted a group of us on to the east plinth, facing the Strand, whilst the banner-bearers marched on westward, leading the procession round the back of the plinth, to finish on its north side opposite the National Gallery, as had been arranged. There the banners were to be handed up; but the

*Daily Mail*

RED OCHRE THROWN AT THE AUTHOR BLINDS MRS. DRAKE AND HER DAUGHTER RUBY

Trafalgar Square, April 1916.

*Daily Mail*

COLONIAL SOLDIERS PULL THE WOMEN DOWN AND STORM THE PLINTH

Trafalgar Square, April 1916.

*Photopress*

YOUNG GIRLS AT A BALLOON FACTORY

north side was packed with soldiers who fell upon the approaching banners and tore them to shreds. The law offered no protection ; so few policemen had never been seen in the Square at any demonstration. Instead of the hundreds usually present at our meetings, a bare six of them were to be seen. Far from assisting us to maintain order, they prevented our men speakers, and numbers of our members who wished to support us, from mounting the plinth, though we urged that they should come. We were left, a little group of women and a child or two, to deal with what might arise. The Government had obviously given orders to leave us to the violence of the mob. We were not afraid.

To speak from the north was impossible for the din the soldiers were making. I opened proceedings from the east, where the crowd appl uded me. A small, hostile group had established itself by the plinth, prompted by the organisers of the disturbance, whom I recognised as old hands at such work ; poor, shabby public-house loafers, they shouted without pausing for breath till their red faces were purple. I continued in spite of them. By taking pains to speak clearly and not too fast, one can make oneself heard a certain distance, even through such a noise. From the north the disturbers hurled at me roughly-screwed balls of paper, filled with red and yellow ochre, which came flying across the lions' backs, and broke with a shower of colour on anyone they chanced to hit. The reporters on the plinth had drawn near me to listen ; thus, inadvertently, they intercepted the missiles aimed at me ; and were covered with red and yellow. They sprang back to avoid a further volley, and Mrs. Drake's twelve-year-old daughter, Ruby, received a deluge of red full in her eyes. Crying, she buried her face in her mother's dress, while the "patriots" raised a cheer.

A man who had climbed the plinth from the west, came stealthily round, and dusted red and yellow ochre on the little group of women behind me. He was removed by a policeman ; then a tall man wearing a khaki armlet was led from the Square by two other policemen. Only three guardians of the law remained in that vast concourse of people.

The soldiers from the north were now forcing their way towards us, resisted by the crowd on the east. After a brief tussle the soldiers prevailed, and came surging forward to storm the plinth. As the head of one of them topped it, Norah Smyth lunged at him vigorously and thrust him down. The other women sprang to help her ; but two of them were dragged to the ground, and dozens of soldiers swarmed up. They crowded round me.

"Why are you doing this ?" I asked.

"They say you are paid by the Germans," one of them blurted, shamefaced.

"Don't listen to her ! Don't listen to her !" cried the organisers of the disturbance.

Yet listen they did, and many already had apologised ; when two blustering civilians pushed past them, shouting : "You are women ; go away ! Go away before you are hurt !"

Two burly police inspectors then seized me, and forced me from the plinth; the other women were hustled after me by the men who had organised the trouble. The disturbers in possession raised cheers for their victory.

People pressed round me speaking their sympathy, thrusting opponents aside.

The flower girls in the gutter at Charing Cross greeted me affectionately, shouting opprobrious epithets at the soldiers, and refusing their wares to a couple of young officers who stopped to buy from them.

. . . . . . .

The *Evening Standard* called for the suppression of meetings such as ours, declaring that the movement we stood for had attained "far more formidable dimensions than would have been the case had the Government crushed it decisively at its first appearance." The *Christian Commonwealth* deplored that Colonial soldiers were wholly uninstructed in English politics, and could thus be procured for reactionary ends, which the home-bred soldiers refused to serve.

As always after such incidents, our mother and infant clinics, the day nursery, the restaurants, the factory, all our work for ameliorating distress, suffered immediately from loss of many donations. A cable repudiating me from Mrs. Pankhurst, who had read a Press account in America of the Trafalgar Square meeting, was published broadcast, and helped to detach some of the old W.S.P.U. members who still supported us, among them old Lady Lely, who had held to us throughout and had been an enthusiastic upholder of our struggle against the sweated payment in the Queen's Workrooms.

Some who had been Pacifists at the outbreak of war abandoned their position in the long, sad period when the armies were at a deadlock. The fear that their country might suffer defeat undermined the convictions of many who had counted themselves internationalists.

With sorrow I received a letter from Sybil Smith, telling me that she, a Tolstoyan of long standing, was a supporter of the War and desired, not a mutually negotiated peace, but an Allied victory at arms. She had withdrawn from active participation in our work for family reasons. Her letter indicated a division of conviction to me very saddening. She wrote that she regarded the contest as "a war of systems"; the German system typifying the autocratic and the military, ours the democratic. "And so my boy goes to the War," she added. Alas poor mother!

Many soldiers wrote to me their regret at the treatment we had received at the hands of soldiers, and some sent little donations to our funds.

. . . . . . .

On reaching home from Trafalgar Square I was called to deal with the tragically urgent case of a motor driver in the R.F.A. discharged with shattered nerves rendered worse by anxiety and poverty. Brought by the air raids to a state bordering on mania, he had completely lost control of himself, and reduced his wife and family to a state of terror. His two children had been removed to hospital, where the baby had died. The inspector of the Society for Prevention of Cruelty to Children alleged his conduct responsible, and threatened to prosecute him. He could not retain any employment. For a year he had been refused all pension. After two months' correspondence I had got him 12s. a week, but only for six months. My plea for allowances for the two children was refused, because one had been born two months after the father's discharge, the other was a step-child.

## CHAPTER XXXVIII

### THE EXECUTION OF AN EAST LONDON BOY

ONE of those zealous young Jews to be found in all movements for popular advancement came to me with the heavy sadness men wear in announcing ill-news. Five East End families, he told me, had received official notification that a son of the household had been executed at the Front. He wanted me to see the bereaved parents. I went with him at once to the Whitechapel Road, where another youth was awaiting us. They debated between themselves for a few moments. It seemed there was some difficulty about interviewing the people concerned. Then they led the way to a small, mean house in a side street.

A middle-aged man, humble and sad, father to one of the lads who had been shot, led us to an upper room and silently motioned us within. The boy's mother lay on a bed there, too miserable to care for life, moving her head from side to side in the restless way of one who is ill with grief.

The man and a young woman, who seemed his daughter, with hushed voices, now in English, now in Yiddish, told the story. The mother moaned, and turned in her bed, as though each phase of it were a stab to her.

The dead boy was an only son, and had joined the Army in September 1914, aged 18 years and three months. He had enlisted without his parents' consent or knowledge. They were bowed down with sorrow when he disclosed it; for to old-fashioned Jewish families it was an honour to have a son who was a scholar or a priest, a disgrace for him to be a soldier.

The daughter brought out from the press a pile of the boy's letters; dozens of crumpled letters, written mostly in pencil on small sheets of irregular size. In almost every one of them the lad expressed regret for the grief and anxiety he had caused his parents, and concern for their happiness—a good son and kindly. I picked out those which were salient; written after leaving home for training at Aldershot, on going to the Front, after experience in the trenches:

" DEAR MOTHER,

" I arrived safe and everything is all right. I was very sorry to leave you, and very sorry to see you cry so much as you did, but never mind, I will come back one day, so be happy at home. Dear Mother, do not forget my nineteenth birthday on Saturday 1st of May. I want you to enjoy yourself on Saturday. Dear Mother, I did not like to leave you on Tuesday. I was very sorry to see you cry. Tell Father and Kate to be happy . . . from your loving son Aby. Dear Mother, I would like your photo to hold on me."

"My dear Mother, Father, and Kate,

"I am going to the Front to-day. We go to Folkestone, and from there on ship to France. As soon as I get there I will send you a letter. Dear Mother, I am very sorry I could not see you all before I go away, but be happy all the time I am out. If I have luck I will come home. Dear Mother, as I am writing this letter to you I am trying to be happy myself. Tell Nick I am going to the Front. Give my best love to all the people in the street. Always think of me, Mother, and I will think of you, but don't cry, be happy. Good-bye, Father and Kate—your loving brother,

"Aby."

"Dear Mother,

"I received your letter on Friday night. I have been in the trenches four times and come out safe. We are going in again this week. Dear Mother, we go in the trenches six days, and then we get relieved for six days' rest. We get 4s. 2d. every two weeks. When I get my money I buy bread and other things. They are very dear and the money does not last very long. . . . It seems very funny to think it is Sunday in the trenches. Dear Mother, I do not like the trenches. I think you know I would like to ask you to send me some money to buy things if you can. You write you was nearly going mad waiting for my letter. You know it takes two days to get to London or more. . . ."

". . . You want to know why you don't receive any money. It is because I never signed a paper saying that I want to allow you sixpence a day—it is too late now. . . . Dear Mother, I know it is very hard for you to miss me from home, but still never mind be happy and don't cry. I think you know I am sorry I done that, but if I have luck I will come home. . . . When we come out of the trenches we stay in the people's houses. When the parcel came and I opened it they cried and said: 'What a good Mother!' They looked at your photo. 'Poor Mother!' they said. . . . You don't know how they like English people. What they have to eat they give you—don't matter how poor they are. . . ."

". . . I might be home for the Jewish holidays . . ."

". . . . Yes, dear Mother, it is a very long time since we have seen each other. For the New Year I think you will go to the Synagogue and pray for me to see you very soon . . ."

In January the parents received a terrifying yellow document.

"Sir, "Infantry Office, Hounslow. 15/1/1916.

"I regret to inform you that ——, 11th Battn. Middlesex Regt., G.S., is ill at 38th Field Ambulance, France, suffering from wounds and shock (mine explosion)."

The wife of the commanding officer wrote telling them their son was wounded, but that she did not know whether he would be sent to hospital in England or retained in France.

A letter from the boy himself reassured them :

"*1st January*, 1916.

"Dear Mother,

"I am very sorry I did not write before now, but we were in the trenches on Christmas Day and we had a lot to do. Also I was sent to the hospital. I am feeling a little better, so don't get upset. Don't send any letters to the company, because I won't get them. Also you cannot send any letters to the hospital, as I won't get them. Dear Mother, do not worry, I will be all right. Hoping all of you are getting on well. I was only hurt in the back. I will try to send you letters every few days, to let you know how I am getting on. We get plenty of food in the hospital. Dear Mother, I know it will break your heart this, but don't get upset about it. I will be all right, but I would very much like to see you . . ."

"*6th January*, 1916.

". . . I have been in hospital nine days, lying in bed all the time, and now I have a sore heel. . . . I had it cut and it is getting on better. . . ."

There were many letters from the hospital. Then he announced his discharge therefrom :

"*20th January*, 1916.

"Dear Mother,

"I am quite well and I came out of hospital on Wednesday (19th)."

His writings seemed to indicate that the boy had no recollection of the mine explosion ; he did not refer to it, and even asked the official explanation of his illness. Yet it may be that he wished to spare his mother from painful knowledge.

"*24th January*, 1916.

". . . Dear Mother, you don't know how I was longing for a letter from you ! I would like to know what the War Office said was the matter with me."

"*26th January*, 1916.

". . . I am sending this photo of one of the officers who was killed. . . . He was very good to us. . . . Please frame it for a keepsake. . . ."

Less than a month later he wrote that he was in trouble :

"*23rd February*, 1916.

"Dear Mother,

"I have sent you a letter that I have received the parcel. I am well, hoping all of you are quite well.

"Dear Mother, we were in the trenches and I was ill, so I went out and they took me to the prison, and I am in a bit of trouble now, and won't get any money for a long time. I will have to go in front of a Court. I will try my best to get out of it, so don't worry. But, dear Mother, try to send some money, not very much, but try your best. I will let you know in my next how I get on. Give my best love to Mother, Father, and Kate.

"From your loving son,

"Aby."

From the boy there were no more letters. In April came a curt official document:

"Sir,

"I am directed to inform you that a report has been received from the War Office to the effect that No. —, 11th Battn. Middlesex Regiment, G.S., was sentenced after trial by court martial to suffer death by being shot for desertion, and the sentence was duly executed on 20th March, 1916.

"I am, Sir, your obedient servant,

"P. G. Hendley,

"2nd Lieut.-Colonel I.C. Infantry Records.

"Hounslow, *8th April*, 1916."

That was the end. The cold brutality of it struck me like a blow.

Oppressed by the grief I had witnessed, I accepted the decision of my guides to visit the families of the others who had been executed another day. They did not return. I concluded that those concerned were afraid agitation would cause them to be victimised in some way. I knew the great fear of victimisation overhanging the foreign quarter.

I published in the *Dreadnought* the letters of poor Aby, and wrote to the War Office, protesting against the cruel injustice of executing a young lad who had endured nearly eight months in the trenches, and so recently had lain three weeks or more in hospital for injuries and shock.

Though nothing could compensate them, I claimed compensation for the parents, in the form of a pension allowance, as a matter of principle. This was refused. Outhwaite asked a Parliamentary question, but obtained no satisfaction.

Henceforward when a soldier was executed the fact, instead of being disclosed to his family, was covered by an official report that he had "died of wounds."

F. W. Jowett, then chairman of the I.L.P., pleaded in vain for exemption from the death penalty for lads under twenty-one years and for all soldiers who had been wounded in the War.

Reports of large numbers of executions at the Front came to us constantly. Men often told us sadly that they had been in firing parties which had been ordered out at dawn to shoot six or seven poor fellows. Such reports were so general, that on April 28th, 1920, the Under-Secretary of State for War was put up in the House of Lords to contradict them. He declared, as I still believe most falsely, though whether by misinformation, or deliberate intent on his part, I cannot tell, that the total number of officers and men sentenced to death, from August 4th, 1914, to December 31st, 1919, was 3,076, and that the total death sentences actually carried out numbered only 343.

On reading this statement H. V. Clarke, who had been employed at the British Headquarters in France, wrote indignantly to several newspapers, declaring that, to his knowledge, no fewer than 37,900 soldiers had been executed in France, i.e. 528 in 1914; 10,488 in 1915; 12,689 in 1916; 13,165 in 1917; 1,035 in 1918. Having access to the documents in the course of his work he had, in his own time, as he declared, copied the records of executions from the General Army Routine Orders, and so on. He had done so, he said, purely on account of the mournful interest he had in this matter. The records, so far as I was able to gather, were not the complete records of the Army, even in France.

None of the newspapers to which Clarke sent his letter were willing to publish it. Eventually he came with it to me. I considered his statement worthy of publicity. It accorded with those made to me by other men who told me thay had been employed on Army records. Clarke told me I might see his copy of the records. The *Dreadnought* was already in the machine, but I made a paragraph embodying the figures, and had another lifted to make room for it. I soon greatly regretted my precipitancy, since it deprived me of a sight of Clarke's evidence. When the *Dreadnought* was published, detectives called at his house, and finding him away from home, left word they would return next day. Clarke, much dismayed, hurried off to the *Dreadnought* office, which had been moved to Fleet Street, arriving at 9 a.m. The office did not open till 10, and in panic he rushed home, and destroyed the greater part of his records, retaining only the first page to show me. Then he came back to Fleet Street to look for me. I happened to be out. He left a note for me and returned home. The detectives had called again and had asked for his records. Still more terrified, he destroyed the only remaining page. On receiving his note I at once sent a messenger for the records. She arrived to find they had been burnt. Clarke came again: he was greatly distressed that his statement had not received the publicity he hoped. He had rushed to buy the *Dreadnought* at his newsagents and discovered it was not known there. On June 7th detectives from Scotland Yard called on me and insisted that I should publish "an apology and withdrawal," drawn up as they informed me by the Director of Public Prosecutions. It was here stated that the 343 executions mentioned in the House of Lords included all executions carried out among the Imperial troops, Colonial forces, overseas contingents and Native Colour corps; in short, the entire Army and its camp followers. The detectives told me that if I refused to publish the apology a prosecution would follow. At the time I thought it best to lay the whole matter before our readers, informing them that the detectives had brought me the document and that the Director of Public Prosecutions had fabricated it. I put it between inverted commas and in smaller type, in order that it might be perfectly clear to all that the document had been written by the Director of Public Prosecutions, not by me. I added that H. V. Clarke[1] told me it had taken him five months to copy the records at the British Headquarters on which he had based his

[1] According to the *Encyclopædia Britannica* the total British killed during the War were: officers 42,348, other ranks 724,500.

figures. I did not think my method of publishing his document would satisfy the Director of Public Prosecutions ; but I heard no further of the incident, and concluded the authorities did not desire to give further publicity to the matter. Clarke was undoubtedly a sincere man, passionately in earnest. If his figures were incorrect, then he was suffering from delusions.

# CHAPTER XXXIX

## CONSCIENTIOUS OBJECTORS

NEWS of the Conscientious Objectors—the C.O.'s, as they were called—began to filter out to us from the prisons and the barracks. They had refused to don the khaki and accept military training. To break down their determination, they were bullied and terrorised, kicked and beaten, kept in handcuffs, tried by court martial, and put in prison. Many were thrust into dark punishment cells and kept on bread and water. Some of them hunger-struck and were forcibly fed. D. S. Parkes of Camberwell at Winchester Prison was told he must be shot at dawn, and when dawn came a gun was loaded and pointed at him. The order to fire was given. Finally he was " pardoned " with brutal insults. R. W. Forrester was told he was to be certified insane. At Reading Barracks the food of the C.O.'s was given to them in pails. They were treated with such violence that one of them, Huxstep, wrote : " Only those prepared for death could face it." Some West Houghton C.O.'s, being handcuffed and marched to Kinmel, were waylaid by a company of regulars who pelted them with sods and stones. At Dover C.O.'s who refused pack drill were dragged along the floor and beaten about the face and head ; then chained to a wall with their hands above their heads. At Bettisfield Park Camp the Objectors were stripped, beaten with sticks, kicked and indecently assaulted.

The parents of C.O.'s were frequently misinformed, or refused information as to the whereabouts of their sons. Parents were many times told by the military who had their sons in custody that the lads were liable to be shot.

T. T. Hall wrote from Fovant Camp, Wiltshire :

" My life has been a perfect torture. . . . They take us into huts . . . bolt the door, knock us about shockingly, pour water over us, hit us in the face. One hit me in the stomach so that I could not breathe. I fainted, but two held me up, while others poured water over me. I feel very downhearted and queer."

At Wandsworth Barracks C. H. Norman was forced into a strait-jacket which was too small for him and caused great suffering. He hunger-struck and was forcibly fed with a tube too large. Frank Ward was bound with ropes and dragged along the ground till blood flowed. P. H. Larkman and R. Miller received blows on the head and face and were handcuffed for 28 hours with hands fastened to an iron bar over their heads, so that they were compelled to stand on tiptoe, and with a weight of 20 lbs.

attached to them. Sydney Cooper was frog-marched till blood gushed from his mouth. R. Palme Dutt, an Oxford senior classical scholar, suffering from a feverish chill, was put into a hut with Army convicts suffering from venereal disease, very inadequate precautions being taken against contagion.[1] Frederick Crowsley had a walking-stick pushed up his nose. He had gone to prison with Tom Mann in 1912 for urging the soldiers not to fire on the workers during the great strike of that year. Josiah Wedgwood, who knew him then, now protested on his behalf; but Wedgwood, alas, had been an advocate of conscription!

. . . . . . .

[1] In Parliament, on October 17th, Forster for the War Office, admitted that C.O.'s suffering from organic diseases of heart, lungs, kidney, etc., had been housed in Hut 16x, Royal Herbert Hospital, Woolwich, with men suffering from venereal diseases, sanitation being defective, and affording no protection against infection.

Mrs. Payne brought up all the newspapers as usual that morning.[1] One of them fell from the rest. I stooped to get it and saw on the front page—Eric Chappelow! Eric Chappelow in a barrack yard, standing on the concrete with stockinged feet, a blanket fastened round him with a leather belt which strapped his arms tightly to his sides. A couple of soldiers stood on guard beside him. The yard bordered on the public street, separated from it only by an iron railing, open to the gaze of every passer-by. Some pressman had snapped him for the *Daily Sketch.*

Chappelow and his cousin, Miss Helsby, had often sung at our concerts. Both were ardent Pacifists. A Civil Servant by necessity, a poet by choice, he had lately presented me with a slender volume of his verse. The Barnes Local Tribunal had given him absolute exemption as a Conscientious Objector—a marvel indeed! Most probably the members knew him as a talented, agreeable young fellow in private life. The military representative had appealed against the exemption, and had secured its reversal. The case was taken to Court, but Justices Ridley, Bray, and Avory upheld the decision of the Appeal Tribunal. Chappelow then wrote to the military authorities in regard to his case. A policeman requested him to go with him to the military authorities to discuss his letter. Chappelow agreed, and found himself under military arrest, thus missing the opportunity even to say good-bye to his mother, who was seriously ill. Poor fellow, his sweetheart had broken with him for his Pacifist opinions; his parents disapproved. Only his cousin stood by him.

It was easy to guess what had caused him to be photographed in this plight. Undoubtedly he had refused to wear the khaki, and this was his punishment—to stand out there in a blanket, to be ridiculed, the target of whoever cared to throw at him an epithet or a missile!

Indignation welled up in me. I rushed to the telephone and asked for Lloyd George. (I knew that the name only and no number was required to call a Cabinet Minister.) Lloyd George was out; his daughter, Megan, answered me. I poured out my wrath. She promised to convey my expressions to her father.

I wrote to Bernard Shaw, calling on him to protest, in the name of literature and humanity, on this ill-used poet's behalf. He responded dramatically, as I had hoped he would.

This sensational episode actually stood young Chappelow in good stead, for thereafter his lot was easier than that of many other C.O.'s.

He wrote a long poem on his prison experiences, "E Carcere," wherein he ejaculated:

> "So soul of mine, so heart of mine, wayfarer,
> Rise up, praise God, and get thee to thy furrow.
> Straight lies the road ahead, there's no returning.
> On! on! what if another hand than thine
> Shall hold thy ploughshare at the journey's end?
> God's splendid dawn shall somewhere break at last."

[1] April 14th, 1916.

Unfortunately he did not retain the exalted resignation here enunciated. On the contrary, he was the only C.O. I knew to express regret for the stand he had taken. When he was free again he reproached his devoted cousin, Miss Helsby, for having led him into extreme courses, which he complained had so greatly depressed him as to retard the flow of his creative muse. On learning her distress on this account, I wrote complimenting him on the improvement which adversity had wrought in his work. He replied morosely. He did not feel, I gathered, any regret that he had not been sent to the Front. His thought seemed rather that by diplomacy he might have escaped into some convenient " funk hole." He was restored at last to the good graces of the girl who had broken with him when he became a C.O. For the rest of his life he was disposed to be entirely orthodox. Yet before this time came he had many a weary month of imprisonment to endure.

. . . . . . .

John MacLean, who had been held in custody since February, was brought to trial in April, 1916, and sentenced to three years' penal servitude for advising the soldiers to lay down their arms, and the workers to down tools against Conscription and the Munitions Acts. Gallacher, Muir, and Bell were tried, at last, for publishing the suppressed *Worker*, Gallacher and Muir getting twelve months' imprisonment, and Bell three.

. . . . . . .

The I.L.P. was meeting in Newcastle that Easter. Mrs. Boyce was organising there for our Federation. I went up with Smyth for a meeting Boyce had arranged, and to attend the conference. I had not been to an I.L.P. conference for many a year; but in those days there was a drawing together of all who worked for peace. The Union of Democratic Control and numbers of Pacifist societies, old and new, gathered round the I.L.P., with its long established branches, its touch with the masses these others desired to influence.

I had pleasure and sorrow in meeting old friends I had known in childhood. The absence of Keir Hardie loomed over us.

Katherine Bruce Glasier, Katherine O'Bruce, as she liked to call herself, spoke at out meeting, talking in her effusive way of the "noble and true work" of our Federation, which seemed to her to typify the "working woman's soul"; calling up images of "the good grey poet," Walt Whitman; of Keir Hardie, William Morris, Edward Carpenter; denouncing with fervour the "hideous blasphemy of war."

At the reunion before the conference the great attraction was the caustic Irish fiddler, Casey, striding the platform like a quizzical satyr, lean and fit for leaping as a goat; his hard legs tightly cased in knee breeches; his goat's face, handsome in its odd way, more than half covered by a short, stubbly black beard. All the wild things of the woods seemed to gambol round him when his fiddle sounded, and his sprite of an accompanist, Dolly, played like a creature enchanted by his spell. She had the gift of perennial childhood; for they had been travelling about the country together, playing to working-class audiences, more years than I cared to remember, and one might have taken her for a school-child still. It was Keir Hardie who had discovered and employed on the *Labour Leader* Casey's mordant irony. Subsequent editors of that paper had found his plebeian jests too inelegant for publication; Casey was driven back upon his fiddling, but he still yearned to express himself by the pen. He told me he had a notion that he ought to abandon music to write on the War, and "just satirise the whole thing."

"Dolly manages her harmonics very cleverly; what a child she looks!" Katherine O'Bruce cooed at my elbow.

R. C. Wallhead,[1] whom I first knew as a working decorator in Manchester, gave humorous improvisations in Lancashire dialect. He had grown to be a prominent man in the I.L.P. I wondered what had really drawn him into the movement. Was it the contact he had with the I.L.P. when Henry Cadness, the teacher of design at the Manchester

[1] Later M.P. for Merthyr Tydfil.

School of Art, introduced him to me as a manual assistant to aid in carrying out of the decorations for the Pankhurst Hall, Hightown, I had designed?

"That is a pathetic story on your front page," W. C. Anderson said to me. He was referring to the execution of the East London boy I had recounted in the *Dreadnought* that week. All the delegates were talking of it. Fenner Brockway reproduced it in the *Labour Leader*. A reader of that paper paid for the I.L.P. to reprint it as a free leaflet.

Snowden, with cold, keen eye, nut-cracker jaw and bulging forehead, hobbled in on his stick. His narrowness and acidity had long repelled me; but in those days he appeared to have shed the raucous uncouthness of his earlier period. True, he never seemed a Socialist in theory; but one fancied him mellowing and broadening to the type of an upright, incorruptible Quaker, frail of physique, sturdy of purpose, as though he were qualifying to wear the mantle of John Bright in his great attack on the Crimean War. Snowden never rose to that height, though the time was more hugely tragic than that which had inspired John Bright's lamentation: "The angel of death has been abroad through the land. You may almost hear the beating of his wings."[1]

Ethel Snowden, who once had seemed like a caged bird in her marriage, chafing under her husband's infirmities and his brusquerie, now fair, plump and forty, had discovered his merit since the War. Wearing him, as it seemed, like a choice orchid, she declared herself "aided by a noble husband," and perorated: "I pray from the bottom of my heart that the War will soon be over." She came nearer to popularity with the rank and file Labour folk than she had ever been, though one of the zealous I.L.P.-ers grumbled: "When she is speaking in public she is like a cat walking on hot bricks—always afraid of offending the other class." She spoke to me affably: "You must have very able helpers, dear. Philip says your paper is about the best on our side."

I knew that the *Dreadnought* had one virtue: it was in touch with life—not made up in an office from Press cuttings, like most of the propaganda sheets.

MacDonald was there, erect and debonair, a drawing-room favourite rather than a Labour leader, he would seem to the passing observer; talking elegantly, with his Scots accent many people found charming; speaking so eloquently, as many considered, and at such length. He was really in the heyday of his popularity, had he but known it; for never again would comrades so zealously cheer him. Yet, even now, his temporising struck a chill to the heart of their warmth. I was anxious to think well of him. Despite his political gyrations and very obvious weakness, I appreciated the stand against the War he had taken, however imperfectly; I desired very heartily to unite in solidarity and comradeship in those ranks so hardly pressed; yet I could never overcome my distrust of him; he woke it within me perpetually by his tortuous strategy. To go by the straight road to a clear-cut objective seemed impossible to him. He must always be travelling roundabout, with so much concession to the

[1] House of Commons, 23rd February, 1855.

opposite pole, that unless rudely thrust on by a strong force behind him, he was apt to end to the rear of the point from which he started. The Conference began on the morrow, very tense, very earnest. MacDonald was temporising as ever. He said that the men who were responsible for the recruiting campaign were responsible for the imposition of Conscription, for the recruiting campaign had encouraged the Government to undertake policies which could not be carried through except by Conscription. The delegates knew that he himself had sent a letter to the Mayor of Leicester to be read in furtherance of the recruiting campaign.

Many of the delegates were Conscientious Objectors, at large for a brief space pending their appeals for exemption. James Maxton and others sent greetings from prison, others from barracks.

The much talked-of Bermondsey resolution, sponsored by Dr. Salter, that Socialists should refuse support to every war, had been shelved by a majority of one vote the year before. It was now adopted with but three dissentients. Henceforth it represented the policy of the I.L.P.[1] Yet C. H. Norman was induced to withdraw a proposal to give immediate practical application to it, by instructing I.L.P. Members of Parliament to vote against any further increase in the British Army.

Margaret Bondfield's suggestion that the Munitions Act should be amended rather than repealed, was swept aside.

A rift displayed itself in relation to Conscription and the Conscientious Objectors. Clement Bundock and Morgan Jones complained that the members of the I.L.P. executive had flinched from their original position. Before Conscription was enacted they had pledged themselves to resist it, and had called on the members of the party to do likewise. They had also expressed the hope that the I.L.P. might provide financial support for Objectors and their families. Later they had decided it would be inadvisable to establish a fund for this purpose, and when the Military Service Act became law, they had warned members and branches that any expressions or acts on their part which could be construed as an incitement to disobey the order for military service, might render those concerned, and the Party itself, liable under the Military Service Act and the D.O.R.A.

Such divisions and failings notwithstanding, the spirit of the gathering was that of a band of comrades facing great odds. " One half the manhood of the I.L.P. will be in prison before we meet again. We shall require to stand very near one another," Bruce Glasier said, in closing the conference.

[1] At Leeds, a year later, Dr. Salter moved a similar resolution in the form of a proposition to be laid before the Socialist International. Though Ramsay MacDonald opposed it with all his strategy, it was carried by 226 votes. Again practical application was rejected, by the shelving, by 178 votes to 62, of a resolution of the City of London branch that the I.L.P. members should henceforth vote against the war credits, as had been done by the German Minority Socialists. I had moved this resolution in the City of London branch of the I.L.P., which I had rejoined that year, having drifted away from it in the Suffragette struggles.

# CHAPTER XL

## EASTER WEEK, 1916

WHILST still we were in Newcastle we opened the newspapers, and learnt that the Irish rebellion had taken place. The hopeless bravery of it, the coercion and the executions which followed, to me were a grief cutting deep as a personal sorrow. Connolly on the Albert Hall platform, in the days of the Dublin lock-out of 1913, quiet-mannered and serious, came back to my eyes ; his voice, restrained and deep, with its undercurrent of strong emotion, rang in my ears. I mourned him as one who had lived laborious days in the service of human welfare ; a man of pity and tenderness, driven to violent means, from belief that they alone would serve to win through to a better life for the people.

Tied up in my mind with Eva Gore Booth, her pacifist sister, strove thoughts of Constance Markiewicz, the brilliant dilettante ; dabbling in art with her Polish count ; driving a four-in-hand at Winston Churchill's Manchester bye-election in defence of the barmaids' right to serve behind the bar ; ladling out soup to the starving poor in the Dublin lock-out ; drilling her company of Boy Scouts.

Day by day came news of amazing doings : the little Republic of a week, established by a tiny majority, with promises of " equal rights and opportunities " for all citizens ; the suppression of the rebels, with their " job lot " of old arms, by machine-guns, bombs, bayonets, and poison gas, massacres, imprisonments, executions.

Amid the destruction and the carnage shone the pure fire of idealism and bravery ; Connolly, mortally wounded, carried out on a stretcher and strapped in position to be shot ; the young lovers, beautiful Grace Gifford, art student, painted by Orpen as " Young Ireland," married in the prison to her poet, Joseph Plunkett,[1] on the morning of his execution.

Grave P. H. Pearse, the scholar and teacher of St. Enda's, Thomas MacDonagh, Tom Clark, Con Colbert,—fifteen of the company of young poets, glorious and radiant in their fervour for the renaissance of their national literature, of the old lovers of Ireland and the lads who burned to die for her were executed. Save Constance Markiewicz, all the signatories to the Republican Proclamation were gone to the death they had chosen, embracing her as a bride.

Their flame of romance extinguished, the world seemed darker, more sordidly ruthless in materialism and the rule of might. I felt it as a wound in the great comity of life, a dishonouring blot on our human escutcheon

[1] Son of Count George Plunkett.

that this had been. All that had happened in Ireland was but the logical issue of the great war-time propaganda that the small nations should take up the sword against their oppressors, and of the postponement of the Home Rule Act, which had been fairly won according to the Parliamentary constitution of our land.

Cutting across the tragic scene, with a fantastic recklessness which seemed to belong to another age, came the adventure of Roger Casement, landing from a German submarine off the Kerry coast, being captured, tried in London for high treason, and hung, on August 3rd. It was a strange fate for one who had been British Consul in Portuguese West Africa and the Congo Free State, and British Consul-General at Rio de Janeiro, who had been sent by the Government to investigate the atrocities practised upon the Indian labourers in the rubber forests of Peru, and who had been made a knight, G.C.M.G., for his services. Yet this was not stranger than that Carson, whom Casement had imitated in treasonable dealings with Germany, should have been made a British peer.

To me the death of James Connolly was more grevious than any, because his rebellion struck deeper than mere nationalism. It is a truism that countries held under an alien dominance remain politically stagnant, and to a large extent are culturally repressed. Recognition of this made me a supporter of Irish nationalism. Yet after national self-government had been attained, the social problems, with which we in England were wrestling, would still be present in Ireland. Some of the Irish deceived themselves with dreams that their compatriots had a keener sense of human solidarity, a greater esteem for liberty than other peoples, that the possessing classes were more altruistic, the workers more courageous and intelligent in their green isle of the west, than in any other part of the world. Were English rule but removed—they asserted—happy fraternity, without social strife, would readily establish itself. I was under no such illusions. I saw Ireland as she was; backward, politically, industrially, culturally. Connolly was of another order than these dreamers. He had engaged in the hard effort to organise Irish workers, whose status in most of the essential things of life was beneath that of the workers in this country. He was fully aware that the large conditions governing the position of the working class on both sides of the Irish Channel were of world extent. He had learnt this under the sharp tooth of experience, as a worker here and in the United States. He had buttressed experience by economic study. Though he had thrown in his lot with the Sinn Fein patriots, he remained an internationalist. By far the ablest personality in the Irish Labour movement, he was fitted to take a substantial share in developing Ireland's part in the world-wide social changes which slowly, and at times imperceptibly, are advancing to transform the face of human society. I knew that the Easter Monday rebellion was the first blow in an intensified struggle, which would end in Irish self-government, a necessary step in Irish evolution. I knew that the execution of the rebels had irrevocably ensured the ultimate success of their uprising. Yet Connolly was needed so seriously for the after-building; him at least, it seemed, Fate should have spared.

The sense of grief for it all, the passionate longing that this thing had not been, that the executions had been averted, were overwhelming. I wanted a gesture of love and solidarity, an act of humility under a common sorrow, from those of us, citizens of the more powerful nation, who felt shame that it should dominate. I thought of the joining by British lovers of Irish freedom with Irish, to raise a memorial, a fund to be settled upon the children of the dead. I broached the idea to Eva Gore Booth; she replied that the Irish would spurn such charity from British hands. Sadly I accepted her dictum.

Beside the central fact of the officially determined executions were the hideous by-products of the struggle: the suffering of helpless non-combatants, the sinister figure of Bowen Colthurst, the murder of Sheehy Skeffington and others in Portobello Barracks.

"Skeffy" as he was called, half in affection, half in derision, a little man in sandals, with a red beard, had been outstanding before the War and since, more outstanding in Dublin than he would have been in London, though he must have been essentially a minority man here too; a Socialist, an Internationalist, a Pacifist, an active upholder of women's right to equality, political, social, economic. His organ, the *Irish Citizen*, was the only women's suffrage paper in Ireland. He had opposed the War from its inception, and Conscription since first it was mooted. He had been sent to prison under the D.O.R.A., and had secured release by the hunger strike. A month before the rebellion he had written a pregnant letter to the English Press, predicting a rebellion by the Irish Nationalists should the oppressive attitude of the Dublin Castle administration be maintained, declaring that the militarists were goading the Irish Volunteers and Citizen Army to resistance, and preparing for a pogrom. This warning was not published in any English paper save the *New Statesman*. Skeffington had no part in the Easter rebellion, and was not in the confidence of the rebels. When the fighting broke out swarms of children and irresponsibles arose from deeply submerged poverty, to loot deserted buildings, broken open by shell fire. To check this, Skeffington invited men and women who would volunteer to prevent looting, to meet at the office of the Women's Franchise League, and posted a notice to this effect outside. Before his arrest he had actually saved several shops from being robbed, and had enlisted the help of many volunteers. His arrest was deliberate; for his description as a wanted man had been circulated at the bridge-heads he must pass on his way home. That he was accused of no illegal action, was proved at the subsequent official inquiry, for the charge sheet was produced, showing the words: "No charge" against his name; but he had already been imprisoned during the War for pacifist propaganda; he was regarded as a dangerous man, best under lock and key. What followed, as revealed at the subsequent trial and Royal Commission, and pieced together painfully by his widow from the evidence brought to her, seems a nightmare. He was taken out by Colthurst and some of his subordinates, and marched through the city as a hostage, with hands bound. A youth named Coade and another lad were coming out of church; Colthurst accosted them, telling them that martial law had been proclaimed and he could shoot them like dogs. As Coade turned away Colthurst cried: "Bash him!" A subordinate officer felled the youth by a blow on the jaw with the butt end of his rifle. Then Colthurst shot him with his revolver as he lay. Skeffington, bound and helpless, older, braver, more human than his captors, protested with grief and horror at sight of this awful deed. Colthurst retorted ominously, with a warning to say his prayers, as he would probably be the next to die. Coade was left lying in his blood, and later was removed by ambulance to the barracks, where he died that night, without regaining consciousness. Further on the march another murder was committed by the war-maddened Colthurst. Again the pinioned hostage, whose hands had never been used for violence, voiced in impotent sorrow his agony and wrath. Poor Skeffington, the kindly lover of freedom, in his sandals and his knee-breeches, with his dialectic enthusiasms; he was not made for hideous scenes like this!

When, at the order of Colthurst, Skeffington and two other men were taken from their cells to be executed, the firing party shot him in the back without warning. He did not die then; but when later he was found to be alive, he was shot and killed by Colthurst's order.

Dickson and McIntyre, who were shot with him, were editors of loyalist papers, but they had been found on the premises of Alderman James Kelly, whom Colthurst mistook for Alderman Tom Kelly, a Sinn Feiner. Rough justice—it is all one may expect under martial law!

Major Sir Francis Vane, whose boast that he was creating a revolutionary "People's Army" before the War might have led one to anticipate otherwise, was one of the commanders of the British Army engaged in quelling the rebellion. He had forgotten his revolutionary sentiments when war broke out, and was prepared to serve the Army obediently, either in France or Ireland, as his superiors might direct. When apprised of the murders, he went to the officer commanding the barracks and demanded Colthurst's arrest. Instead he was presently directed to hand over his command to Colthurst. Rebuffed at Dublin Castle, he went to London and reported the matter to Kitchener. Kitchener telegraphed to General Maxwell, who refused to act. Vane was dismissed from service.[1]

Under pressure of public opinion and the brave persistence of the widow, Hannah Sheehy Skeffington, whose courage was proof against raids and firing into her home, the imprisonment of her servant, and countless attempts to terrorise her, Colthurst was brought to trial and found guilty but insane.

In the meantime other murders had been disclosed. Men who had taken no part in the rebellion were murdered in their homes, or led out by soldiers, and shot before their doors. A poor old father died of grief when his son, innocent of all offence, was shot with a companion, their bodies

[1] On August 1st, 1916, King, Lynch, and O'Donnell alleged in Parliament that Sir J. Maxwell had discontinued the services of Sir Francis Vane, because he had reported the murders in Portobello Barracks, though General Maconochie reported he had rendered valuable service, and should be permitted to return to the Front.

*By kind permission of Mrs. Sheehy Skeffington*

FRANCIS SHEEHY SKEFFINGTON

JAMES CONNOLLY

*Reproduced from the "Workers' Dreadnought"*

A DRAWING BY JOSEPH SOUTHALL

bundled into a hole in the ground with their heads and feet jammed together. In the house of Mrs. Lawless four equally innocent men were shot and buried in the cellar. One hundred and fifty men were said to have been shot without trial, carted to Glasnevin Cemetery, and buried in a pit, unidentified.

The military authorities had thought so little of the murder of Skeffington and the others that a week later they had promoted Colthurst to the defences of Portobello Barracks, and dismissed Vane, his senior officer, for reporting the occurrence. At the subsequent trial, they provided an excuse for Colthurst, by asserting that it had been necessary to remove him from his command in France, owing to his nervous, or mental, condition. Yet they had sent him to take command in Ireland. In the course of the trial and enquiry, it was made clear that under Army discipline, a soldier must obey the order of his superior officer, even though he knows it to be illegal and wrong. In this case Colthurst told a certain Lieutenant Dobbin that he was going to have the prisoners taken out of the guard-room and shot. Dobbin sent word to the adjutant that Colthurst was going to do this, but what the adjutant answered and whether the answer had arrived when the first shooting took place, so far from being made clear at the Royal Commission, was enveloped in obscurity. There was no doubt that Dobbin had received the answer when he obeyed Colthurst's order for the second shooting.

The Royal Commission appointed to enquire into the murder declared insanity the only palliation of Bowen Colthurst's conduct "from first to last." Colthurst was sent to Broadmoor Criminal Lunatic Asylum, and released, ostensibly "cured," after eleven months.[1]

Whilst all this was pending, *The Times* was demanding that "the men who sat and looked on while armed potential rebels were being trained in Dublin" should be removed from office. Yet, as everyone knew, it was the Ulster Unionists, encouraged by *The Times* and the English Conservative leaders, who had begun the arming and drilling in Ireland. They had even refused to hand over their arms for use against Germany when the War broke out and the Home Rule Act was suspended to placate them, declaring they would need their arms to resist Home Rule later on.

Bernard Shaw wrote:

"I used all my influence and literary power to discredit the Sinn Fein ideal; but I remain an Irishman, and am bound to contradict any implication that I can regard as a traitor any Irishman taken in a fight for Irish independence, which was a fair fight in everything except the tremendous odds my countrymen had to face."

Terrorism continued with unabated violence. Sir Robert Chalmers, notorious as Governor-General when the then recent Ceylon riots were

[1] He lived some time in England but returned to Ireland after the Treaty which established the Free State. His family received compensation for houses burnt in Cork during the civil war. They were of "Planter" stock, having been given estates near Blarney in Cromwell's time. The hereditary bitterness of racial strife flowed in his veins.

suppressed, was appointed Under-Secretary for Ireland. 3,430 persons were arrested, most of them without warning or notice to their friends. They were crowded under hideous conditions into prisons not equipped to accommodate such numbers. Many had no connection with the rebellion. 1,424 men and 73 women were finally released without formal trial, and 1,841 removed to England for internment. 170 people were tried by court martial, of whom 160 were convicted. 75 people received sentences of imprisonment, ranging from life to three years. Dillon bitterly complained that the work of the constitutional Home Rulers had been wiped out in a sea of blood. In the middle of July there were still more than eighteen hundred interned Irish prisoners, whose ages ranged from fifteen to seventy years. Three months after the rising a lad of sixteen was sent to twelve months' imprisonment, merely for having been a member of the Irish Volunteers. Old Ginnell, the only Member of Parliament who by his sympathies could claim to represent the prisoners, was denied access to them, and when he attempted to visit some of them in Knutsford Barracks, by using the Irish form of his name, he was fined £100.

Ireland had entered upon dark and stormy days. Asquith went to Dublin, and returning, announced the breakdown of Irish government. A Government-appointed Commission declared the existing rule of Ireland anomalous in peace time, impossible in war. Proposals were made for a settlement. Lloyd George, as so often before, was appointed by Asquith as negotiator. Under his auspices, it was proposed that the Home Rule Act should come into force at once, the disputed Ulster counties and many other matters remaining under British control until after the War, when their permanent status would be determined by an Imperial Conference, called to deal also with other questions concerning the British Empire as a whole. Redmond, the Nationalist, agreed to these terms as he understood them. Carson, the Unionist, would have it that the offer made to him included the permanent exclusion of the disputed counties. The Tories supported Carson. Asquith capitulated to them, as he had done sooner or later in everything else throughout the War. The olive branch of conciliation vanished. The amnesty of prisoners was refused. Coercion was maintained. The hated "Dublin Castle" system, so lately condemned by the Commission, continued as before. Duke, a Conservative K.C., was appointed Chief Secretary, to rule with a firm hand. The extreme Tory Lord Lieutenant, Lord Wimborne, who had resigned, was reappointed with stronger powers.

Ginnell, feeble and old, proud and uncompromising of heart, was suspended from the sittings of the Commons for demanding that his countrymen be awarded the honours of war prisoners, as citizens of a nation in arms, not victimised with ignominy as felons.

. . . . . . . .

Returning one summer evening, a little earlier than usual, after sending the *Dreadnought* to press, relieved in an editor's way that the task was done, I paused on the bridge in the Old Ford Road, to see the last glow of the departing sun, to rest my city-wearied eyes on a glimpse of trees and waters, mellow, soft and mysterious in those enchanting rays. Even among those dreary streets some few oases of beauty still remained to us.

A man I had not noticed, leaning on the bridge, turned suddenly and spoke to me. It was Francis Vane. I had not seen him since our Suffragette struggles, when he came to us, offering to create for us the "People's Army." His dandy buoyancy and self-importance were gone; his long oval face, sallow and grave. His mood was melancholy, and no wonder; for the militarists he had proved too democratic, for the democrats, too militarist. Having promised to create a rebel army to fight for popular rights on both sides of the Irish Channel, he had been found fighting with the Government against the rebels when the rebellion came. He spoke wistfully of old times, and asked me to publish an article from him on the Irish situation. I felt severe towards him for the part he had played; yet in some measure he had atoned by denouncing the Portobello murders. For that service to justice he had been deprived of his command. I agreed to publish his article; it might throw some further light on the dark, sad doings in which he had been concerned.

On getting my assent, at once he said "Good-bye," and wandered off westward, with the air of a man who knew not whither to go, or what to do. The promised article disclosed that he had learnt of the murders through an old woman calling him "murderer." He had gone to the commanding officer of the barracks, and had, he averred, "said some very straight words to him." This officer he believed to be as much distressed as himself; but, added Vane:

"He made a fatal mistake by not at once placing the officer under arrest. Yet I do not believe the blame rests on him, for I am fairly certain he had his orders. . . . Finding that they intended to hush up the matter, I had, as soon as the rebellion had been quelled, gone myself to London and reported the matter to Lord Kitchener."

Vane had afterwards visited Mrs. Skeffington, whom he regarded as "a very noble and grievously injured woman," and offered to lend her every possible assistance in his power.

As to his part in quelling the rebellion he had helped to foment, his only explanation was that "the time chosen was a bad one." He observed, which was true enough, that only a small minority of the populace then supported the rebellion, but that English soldiers sent over to suppress it were largely ignorant of this fact, and regarded all the Irish as rebels. He asserted that "quite a number of senior officers, who were old enough to know better, lost their heads or their morality, or both," and that a clique of men "clearly encouraged indiscriminate shooting."

Few of us realised then, as we were forced to understand later, that atrocities are the commonplace of warfare, whether of nations or of classes. The Great War, which set internal warfare going in many nations, revealed this truth with bitter clarity.

## CHAPTER XLI

### CONSCRIPTION OF MARRIED MEN—N.C.F. PROSECUTED—BODKIN—PEACE PILGRIMS

PEACE talk was growing. The Pope had appealed to the warring nations to end the War. The speeches of Karl Liebknecht, widely published by our jingo Press for their denunciations of the German Government, encouraged in our Pacifists the hopeful belief that the peace movement was strong in Germany. A Peace Negotiations Committee was formed, on the initiative of Herbert Dunnico of the Peace Society. The I.L.P., the Society of Friends, the Union of Democratic Control, our Workers Suffrage Federation, the Women's International League, and other societies were represented. A Peace Memorial was circulated:

"We, the undersigned, urge H.M. Government to seek the earliest opportunity of promoting negotiations with the object of securing a just and lasting peace."

763,000 signatures were obtained to this memorial, not without some attempts at intimidation. My old friend Mrs. Brimley and Ethel Tollemache, both ex-members of the W.S.P.U. who had joined our Federation because of their opposition to the War, pluckily started out in Leytonstone on a house-to-house canvass for signatures. They were soon placed under arrest and taken to the police station, where after six hours' detention, they were released, with a warning that the powers of the D.O.R.A. would be used against them should they continue.

Secret Sessions of both Lords and Commons were held, that the Government might advance more pointed arguments for extending Conscription than it was considered politic to publish abroad. On May 2nd Asquith announced that compulsion would be extended to the married men, to rope in 200,000 more of them than could be obtained by voluntary means.

The committeemen of the No Conscription Fellowship, most of whom have since been elected to Parliament, were arrested, and tried at the Mansion House for a leaflet urging the repeal of Conscription. Bodkin, the unconscious comedian, who had become notorious for his absurdities in suffragette trials, declared in prosecuting them that "war would be impossible if the view that war is wrong, and that it is wrong to support the carrying on of war, were generally held." Edward Fuller, a young journalist, who often spoke at our meetings, printed Bodkin's *bon mot* in poster form, as an argument against war. He gave an order for its display to a Stratford billposter, who prudently dispatched a copy to the War Office to ascertain if its publication would be permitted. Fuller was thereupon charged with doing "an act preparatory to the commission of an act" prohibited by the D.O.R.A. He was fined £100 and £25 costs, or 91 days' imprisonment, but owing to Parliamentary protests on his behalf, he was released before the sentence was fully served.

Fines totalling £800 were ordered against eight members of the N.C.F. committee. It was agreed that five of them should refuse to pay the fine and suffer imprisonment. They were Fenner Brockway, W. J. Chamberlain, Walter Ayles, a Bristol Town Councillor and afterwards Labour M.P., A. Barratt Brown, afterwards Vice-Principal of Ruskin College, Oxford, and John P. Fletcher.

Conscription was being used as a means of industrial compulsion, to an extent which would have raised an outcry in peace time. When the Dundee jute workers struck work, men who had been exempted from military service, as essential to the industry, were called to the Army at the instance of their employers, as soon as they went on strike.

When the Military Service Act was extended to married men the Lords inserted, and the Government accepted, an amendment permitting the military authorities to claim exempted men a fortnight after ceasing to be employed as munitioners, though six weeks must elapse before they could obtain new employment unless the late employer would grant a leaving certificate. Philip Snowden complained to Parliament, on May 18th, that 300 men of the Labour Company Reserve Battalion Border Regiment were replacing navvies at Morecambe and getting only Army pay for their work. There were many such cases.

From the introduction of compulsory military service, there was a growing demand for the conscription of wealth. George Wardle, a Labour Member of Parliament, declared that the income tax ought to have been raised to at least 7s. 6d. or 10s. in the £; he would cheerfully have paid it, he said, to secure the equality of sacrifice of which so much had been said.

The Press declared that Germany was offering peace terms. In due course the British Press reproduced, from the *Chicago Daily News*, a reply from Sir Edward Grey: "The Allies can tolerate no peace which leaves the wrongs of this war unredressed." So public opinion fed on rumour and rhetoric.

. . . . . . . . .

Clara Cole and Rosa Hobhouse set out on a peace pilgrimage, walking through the country to distribute literature against war, including the Pope's appeal for peace. After five days they were arrested at Kettering and sent to prison for five months. Great rage was manifested by her accusers when there was found in Clara's pocket an "Anathema." She had written: "Is there no strength in your cold madhouse to cry halt, cowards, cowards, and again grey-bearded cowards!" Even Rosa was struck with consternation at the production of this denunciation!

Rosa Hobhouse was a Quaker with the mystic's temperament. She and her husband, Stephen, were living in a barrack dwelling in Hoxton, to aid and learn from their poor neighbours. She came to me offering £1 a week to pay the rent of a centre for our Federation in Hoxton. Her husband, Stephen Hobhouse, was soon in prison as a Conscientious Objector, though he was physically unfit and might readily have secured exemption on that ground. In 1913 he had worked amongst the refugees in Constantinople and Bulgaria. In August 1914 he formed an emergency committee of members of the Society of Friends, to assist poor foreigners of every nationality in the grievous troubles which overwhelmed them stranded here in war time. When tried by Court Martial for refusal to put on military uniform, he declared himself an international Socialist.

Clara Gilbert Cole was the daughter of a boot manufacturer who many years before had suffered business misfortunes through unwillingness to adapt himself to the harsh conditions of modern commerce, and from refusal to produce anything save honest, hand-made all-leather wares. Left an orphan without means, she had become a postal servant in Manchester and met there Herbert Cole. He was a student of the Manchester Municipal School of Art, then, as always, a cheerful centre of the cult of beauty in the dark ugliness of Cottonopolis. Like many other students of his day, Cole was deeply influenced by Walter Crane, then Principal of the Manchester School, as well as by the other Pre-Raphaelites, William Morris, Rossetti, Holman Hunt, and Frederick Shields, the Manchester artist, then in the height of their artistic power. The two young people drank inspiration from the same fount. Clara Gilbert, with her unusual slender loveliness, her deft fingers and vivid imagination, was like a caged bird in the post office. Herbert Cole had been taken up by a Manchester builder, and was painting saints and angels on church walls and making cartoons for stained glass, but his ambition was to illustrate books.

Clara and Herbert were soon married, and bearded Fortune together in London. Success came immediately. He was at once employed on the *Pall Mall Magazine*, and after, in steady succession on illustrations which became famous, for *Gulliver's Travels*, *The Ingoldsby Legends*, *The Ancient Mariner*, *Froissart's Chronicles*, *Fairy Gold*, and a host of others. These brought great profit to his publishers, but to himself only a modest outright payment for each set of drawings, and no further benefit from the huge circulations his work achieved. He remained the most unassuming and kindly of the devotees of art, eking out the modest sums made by his rapid craftsmanship in teaching at the Camberwell School of Art, where he gathered round him an ever-growing band of affectionate students ; whilst Clara still did the work of their simple household, wrote poems, and filled her mind with social causes. They had a talented son, Philip, with a passion for architecture.

When the War came they were stunned and shocked by it. Soldiers on their way to the Front marched through the village of Kemsing where they lived, camped in the fields, and dug trenches on the downs. A war hospital was opened. Clara helped to nurse the wounded. Then one day she protested : " I will nurse men for life, but not to send them back to the trenches ! " She wrote and got printed a pamphlet: "War won't pay!" and distributed it broadcast amongst soldiers and civilians. The Police went round and collected the copies of it from all who had them. They took no proceedings against her. "Poor lady!" They thought her driven crazy by the sight of wounded men.

Clara had persevered with her new hard task. She started a League against War and Conscription, and through it got in touch with the "Stop the War" Committee C. H. Norman and Scott Duckers had founded, and with Mrs. A. Cunningham in her "Women's Union for Peace." When Conscription came Clara stood in Trafalgar Square with a badge "Stop the War," and a banner against Conscription. She was arrested and brought into Court; but the charge was dropped, though she many times repeated the demonstration. She and Herbert had seen my articles in the *Clarion* years before, and now were reading the *Dreadnought*. He had heard my father in the old Manchester days. Herbert came over to see me and brought me a sheaf of her poems, and so our friendship began. Before the War was over Philip reached military age, and served imprisonment as a Conscientious Objector. From his cell he sent delicate pen drawings to his parents on the blue official sheet of paper, his sole monthly communication with the outer world.

. . . . . . . .

Tragedy followed tragedy. In May the Battle of Jutland, around which raged so many controversies in high places, sounded its knell of mourning to wives and mothers. 5,769 British men and 328 officers were killed in it. Of the Germans 2,385 men and 160 officers. In June the mysterious exit of Kitchener in the *Hampshire*, unchronicled as the humblest Tommy reported missing, conveyed with an impression of terrific menace the ruthlessness of Fate. Often the vision flashed to my eyes of him, a lonely figure, glimpsed in the lightnings of tempestuous night, drenched by the spray of gigantic waves crashing into the vortex, buffeted by the howling violence of the hurricane, fronting the wrack, with arms folded on his breast, erect and stern. Rumour grew fertile: German spies had compassed his destruction; he had been removed by order of the Government for his incompetence; he had withdrawn himself, and was still alive.

## CHAPTER XLII

### SOMEWHERE IN FRANCE—CRUCIFIXION—C.O.'S SENTENCED TO DEATH

FOR some time news had been leaking through of brutal punishments to soldiers at the Front. It was alleged that for trivial offences they were kept in handcuffs and fetters, and for hours were chained, roped, or strapped to a fixed object; fastened to the wheels of a gun or a cart with feet and arms extended; or "crucified," with the arms stretched out, and the feet raised above the ground.[1]

Questions were asked in Parliament. Tennant replied: "The rules do not contemplate such procedure"; but he could not say whether such punishments actually occurred. A soldier who had witnessed these punishments wrote to me from France:

"Either Mr. Tennant is a liar or else he shows absolute ignorance of questions affecting his position as Under-Secretary for War."

The soldier bravely told me I might publish his name; but I would nor risk getting him into trouble by doing so. An Order of Kitchener had been published instructing officers to prohibit soldiers from communicating their grievances either to Members of Parliament or others outside the Army.

A soldier wrote to me describing No. 1 field punishment, as he had endured it at 5th Base Remounts, Calais. His offence was being twenty minutes late from the evening roll call. During his fourteen days' punishment he passed the night, with others thus victimised, in a barbed wire-enclosed compound, having no bed, and only a couple of blankets in which to wrap himself. From 5.30 a.m. to 5 p.m. he was sent out to dig with pick and shovel. During this time only brief meal times were permitted. There were two intervals of half an hour, in which he was compelled to carry a bag containing 95 lbs. of stones, on one shoulder, round

[1] On August 8th, 1916, Forster admitted that an Army driver had been awarded 90 days' field punishment, part of which consisted in strapping the man to a wagon for two hours a day, and the stoppage of the wife's allotment.

Robert Blatchford alleged in the *Sunday Chronicle* that a soldier had died during "field punishment," which consisted of being tied by the neck, waist, arms, and legs. In the House of Commons Lloyd George was invited, either to admit the truth of the statement, or to prosecute Blatchford. He answered: "I am not quite sure."

Official Parliamentary Report, November 7th, 1916.

George Barnes complained that Private —— had been punished by 56 days' crucifixion for being late after the first leave home for 20 months.

Official Parliamentary Report, November 9th, 1916.

and round the camp. At 6 p.m. he was marched into a place which gave him the impression of a butcher's slaughter house, wherein were iron rings, straps, handcuffs and ropes, a crucifix and stocks for the torturing of unfortunate men. One of his eight companions in this agony was strapped to the crucifix. He was himself strapped into the stocks. The others were tied up to beams, their feet flung far apart, attached to iron rings in the floor, their hands fastened above their heads. So they remained for two hours, and thereafter were turned back into the comfortless compound, to weary the night through, without bed or bedding, as best they could. The soldier continued:

"I have seen men who have had to be taken out of these torturing stocks and carried into hospital. At No. 16 Veterinary Base, Calais, the soldiers doing No. 1 field punishment are strapped on to the crucifix in the main road (regardless of the weather) and they are compelled to hang there in this degrading manner in full view of the French people for two hours a day. . . .

"Men who have forfeited good positions, home, and practically everything they possess, for such paltry offences as I have described, are treated in this shameful manner."

I published this soldier's letter in full, thus giving opportunity for the authorities to proceed against me if they chose; but no action was taken, though the *Dreadnought* was regularly sent to many Members of Parliament and several Government Departments.

. . . . . . . .

J. W. Graham has recounted that early in May Professor Gilbert Murray received a telegram from the parents of Rendel Wyatt, a Cambridge C.O., telling him that a group of Objectors had been sent to France to be shot. Murray rushed off to Parliament. He got speech with Lord Derby, who replied that no doubt the men would be shot, "and quite right too!" then obtained an interview with Asquith, who promised to write the Commander-in-Chief, telling him that the executions must not be carried out without the knowledge of the Cabinet—a promise of rather doubtful value.[1]

On May 27th an Army Order was issued, declaring that where an offence against military discipline had been committed, and the accused "soldier" represented that the offence was the result of conscientious objection to military service, he would not be retained in military custody, but *committed to the nearest civil prison*. The order clearly condoned the violation of the pledge contained in the Military Service Act, and given by the Government, both then and later, to exempt Conscientious Objectors from Military Service. Nevertheless it was seized upon as a blessed respite, since it promised the great boon of releasing the Conscientious Objector from the Army.

[1] *Conscription and Conscience*, by J. W. Graham, M.A. (George Allen and Unwin, Ltd.).

The hopes which the Order had raised were soon rudely shattered. Three days later sixteen Conscientious Objectors were seen by some of their relatives on their way to the Front, whilst eight others were being dispatched there from another camp. On June 4th Stuart Bevis of Lower Edmonton, who had been taken in handcuffs to France, wrote to his parents :

" Just a line. We have been warned to-day that we are now within the war zone. The military authorities have absolute power, and disobedience may be followed by very severe penalties, and possibly the death penalty, so I have dropped you a line in case they do not allow me to write after to-morrow. Do not be downhearted ; if the worst comes to the worst, many have died cheerfully for a worse cause."[1]

The news thus cheerfully conveyed by this brave youth was transmitted to the parents of the other Objectors in France. Nine of the mothers came to me, asking that I would go with them to the War Office to plead for their sons. Of course I agreed and of course we were despised and rejected. Of course we persisted in spite of threats to order our removal by the Police. At last a message came that Brigadier-General Childs, the Director of Personal Services, was willing to receive me, but not the mothers. I was inclined to reject this offer, to insist that the mothers should be heard ; but they begged me to go up, and plead the case without further delay.

I found General Childs to be the most extraordinarily cadaverous-looking man I had ever beheld, his shaven head fleshless as a skull. He spoke kindly, assuring me that our fears for the Conscientious Objectors were groundless ; they would not be executed. He insisted that he was able to say this positively, because he was the head of the disciplinary department of the Army. I answered that until the men were back again in England, and released from military custody, we could feel no confidence in their safety. I expressed the fear that they might already have been shot without his knowledge. He declared that without his sanction no military execution could take place. To me that seemed incredible. I said so. He averred it was the fact. I mentioned the execution of the East London boy, whose parents I had visited. " Did you sanction that ? " I asked him, searching his face to know if truly he could be so callous. He affected not to remember the case. I described it more fully. " You must have had an *ex-parte* account of it," he told me. " If you will give me a day's notice, I will have all the papers in the case got out for you, and let you see them. Just telephone when you are coming. You shall go into it fully." Again he reassured me impressively. " Now go and tell those poor bodies they have nothing to fear ; not one hair of their sons' heads shall be hurt." He repeatedly expressed his sympathy with my views.

A few days later I telephoned that I was coming to see the papers concerning the execution of the East London boy, as General Childs had

[1] On July 17th Runham Brown was ordered £50 fine or two months' imprisonment for distributing a leaflet containing this letter.

suggested; but next morning I received a letter stating that as the case had been the subject of a Parliamentary question, the papers could not be shown to me. The Parliamentary question had already been asked and answered when Childs had made his offer.

Meanwhile thirty-four Conscientious Objectors were in France and had been court-martialled and sentenced to death there, as Tennant the Under-Secretary for War, admitted on June 26th. When this ordeal failed to break their determination, the sentence was commuted to penal servitude for ten years.

According to N.C.F. records sixty C.O.'s were sent to France, including nineteen New Zealanders. The death sentence was passed on the majority of them. Twenty-five Canadian C.O.'s were also sent. One of the New Zealanders, Mark Briggs, after long imprisonment on low diet was stripped, and by a cable wire round his chest was dragged on his back for a mile, along a footpath of planks with battens nailed across at short intervals. The result was a great flesh wound which became filled with dirt. He recovered after prolonged hospital treatment. Stanton, Bromberger, Brewster, and many others suffered the field punishment meted out to the soldiers. W. G. Tyrrell was sent to France in March 1917 and suffered field punishment at Bapaume. He declared that the post to which he was tied for two hours at a time was nearly always within range of shell fire. James Baldry Saunders was sent with the Army both to Egypt and France. He was crucified to a tree in the broiling Egyptian sun. A. P. Catheral, after serving three sentences of imprisonment, was sent to France. There, after twenty-one days' close confinement in a narrow cell, handcuffed, leg-ironed, and fed on biscuits and water, he was sentenced to be shot at dawn. An N.C.O. came to him that night and told him he could still escape if he would obey military orders. After being court-martialled six times he was sent to Shrewsbury Prison, where he was still confined in 1919.

The wife of James Blackman, who was sent to France on March 29th, 1917, was told that if her husband refused to obey orders, he would be tied to a wagon, and "the men allowed to do as they liked with him." If he still held out he would be shot.

On June 29th Asquith announced that the War Office would now sift the cases of all C.O.'s, to decide whether there was *prima facie* evidence of conscientious objection. If the War Office decided that there was such evidence the case would be sent to the Appeal Tribunal; and if the Tribunal thought fit the Objector might be released from prison for work of national importance, under direction of the Home Office. Thus recognised both by the War Office and the Appeal Tribunal as genuinely conscientious he would no longer be subject to military discipline, so long as he carried out the duties imposed on him under what was henceforth known as the Home Office scheme.

Objectors who were not thus recognised by the War Office and the Appeal Tribunal as conscientious, would be treated, said Asquith, "with the utmost rigour." In practice most of the C.O.'s were refused this recognition; but after they had endured the rigorous punishment threatened, they were frequently offered employment of various sorts under the Home Office scheme. Many C.O.'s refused to accept, considering that to do so was to condone and to submit to Conscription. These men became known as "Absolutists." On them was visited the most vindictive punishment. On August 16th they were officially threatened with execution. Forster announced, on the Government's behalf, that Objectors who had served their original sentence of imprisonment, and refused the "alternative service" offered under the Home Office scheme, would become subject to the ordinary provisions of the Army Act, under which refusal to obey orders would mean death. Many Objectors refused the scheme nevertheless; but the Government did not carry out the threat. Instead the men were in most cases sent to further terms of imprisonment.

A common form of alternative service was road-making, paid for at soldiers' rates, without separation allowance to the dependants. The family, if destitute, might apply, like other destitute people, to the Poor Law for relief; but unlike other destitute unfortunates, the families of the C.O.'s received such poor doles as the Guardians might choose to vouchsafe through the hands of the police.

# CHAPTER XLIII

## OLD AGE PENSIONERS PLEAD FOR MORE—THE CHILDREN'S FESTIVAL

THE sad plight of the old people starving on their meagre pensions of 5s. a week was sometimes raised in Parliament. Food prices in the summer of 1916 had risen to 65 per cent. above the pre-war level, according to official estimates; according to poor housekeepers' budgets, much more. The Government would vouchsafe no increase in the old age pension. Economists, like Lord Midleton, were even demanding that the pension should be reduced, or suspended altogether. The old age pension of 5s. a week of those days was only given to those whose income, including the pension, did not exceed 12s. 6d. a week. If the old man or woman already had 10s. or 11s. the pension would be 2s. 6d. or 1s. as the case might be. The earnings of the old people themselves, and the pensions and allowances on behalf of soldiers, still counted in reduction of the old age pension. The aged were being driven into the Workhouse from inability to exist on the pension outside. In Edinburgh alone 152 old pensioners sadly entered the Workhouse in the year ending May 1916.

One terribly hot day in August Miriam Price and I took twenty old pensioners from the East End to the House of Commons, to lay their case before the legislators. It was hard work getting them to Mile End Station, so feeble, aged, and starved as they were, and the day so sultry. Indeed, the party was larger when we started, but some of them could not hobble thus far with us, and were left behind. Looking back on it now, it seems strange we should have been so cruelly spartan as not to charter a brake for them; but conveyances were limited by war-time exigencies and difficult to obtain; even the 'bus services were drastically reduced. One aged creature nearly ninety, partially paralysed, and able only to totter, very bravely held on with tremendous effort. Many of these ancients had never visited the centre of London before; not one had been to Parliament. They were eager as children in their fresh interest in these new sights, and as trustful in their hope. "The deputation will be an education to Members of Parliament," said one old fellow confidently.

J. M. Hogge invited the party to tea on the Terrace; for them a truly entrancing experience! They admired the pigeons, the water, the architecture, the little tables with snow-white cloths, the waiters resplendent; their eyes sparkled at sight of butter, real butter, plastered thick on dainty thin slices of bread, and cubes of sparkling white sugar supplied without stint—amazing indeed; for already they stood in queues for the black manilla sort in the East End.

They tried with their poor little budgets to initiate well-fed legislators into the mysteries of their poverty. That afternoon Asquith made the first forecast of a concession to them; the Government was satisfied, he said, that amongst the old age pensioners there were "cases of hardship which called for relief, and for which provision must be made." Had their presence caused this softening in his harsh front? These poor old people thought so. Their hopes ran high; their triumph effervesced! Shortly afterwards it was announced that grants up to a maximum of 2s. 6d. a week would be made to the pensioners suffering special hardship, a meagre, unsatisfactory proposal; but months passed wherein no more was heard even of this poor pledge.

. . . . . . . .

Lloyd George was now promising that after the War there would be "a new heaven and a new earth for us all!"

. . . . . . . .

Visitors from far and near gravitated to us at Old Ford. Mrs. Black, wife of the Chief Secretary for New South Wales, came down to look at us, and was shocked by the sordid poverty and wretched housing of the East End.

Professor Masaryk, afterwards first President of the newly-created realm of Czechoslovakia, came up with Mrs. Hercbergova to take tea with me on the flat roof at 400, excessively nervous and irritable, his head close-shaven, hunched awkwardly in his chair, grimacing and knitting his brows. Mrs. Hercbergova had told me he was a Socialist, which was quite a mistake. I began to talk with him on that footing, but found him stuck full of prejudices and illusions, from which Socialists are supposed to be exempt. Rabid in his fury against Austria, he kicked his legs impatiently and snarled with rage, when I told him the belligerent governments were all alike to me, and that my anxiety was to end the War as soon as possible, and push on to establish a better social order, in which both war and the stultifying poverty we could see revealed in the street below us should be no more. Next day Mrs. Hercbergova told me he had expressed a poor opinion of me, and preferred my sister Christabel whom he had met in Paris. I laughed when I heard it. I regarded his opinions on the world situation as hopelessly unsound. Despite our brusque passages at arms, he was lecturing on "Tolstoy's Philosophy of Religion" in our little Women's Hall at the back of the house a few months later. Mrs. Bouvier had arranged it. Had I been consulted, I should probably have vetoed him. Our meetings secretary was often more catholic in her choice than I. She brought down, at some time or other, most of the active and prominent people in London sponsoring what were regarded as advanced causes.

. . . . . . . .

My cousin, Sylvia Bailey, had come to work with us. We called her by her second name, Joan, to avoid confusion. Her mother, who had saved my life when I was a toddler, had written me from the Isle of Man: "What shall I do with my daughters?" I answered: "Send the elder one." She came, a shy, slight girl in her twenties, with the dark Celtic eyes of Manx forebears and a lilt of Manx in her speech, devoted to music and dancing, and with dreaming aspirations towards casting her life in those ways. I had no touch with openings in either direction. Impressed from experience by the hard precariousness of life outside the beaten track, and believing, perhaps very wrongly, that unless she were firm in refusal of all other callings, she could scarcely have the determination to force a way through for herself as musician or as dancer—she seemed indeed too timid to surmount adversity or endure rebuff—I put her to work in the office. She was pliant, and at my direction attended an evening class for shorthand.

Striving, as I was through all that dark time, to rend from the wreck of things some brightness and joy for the beauty-starved people about us, and to satisfy, too, what I could of the fantasy and the yearning of a fay-out-of-fairyland in her eyes, I set her to arrange a festival in Victoria Park for the children. We sounded the call to them: "Come to learn dancing!" They flocked in, a crowd of them, far more than the "Women's Hall" could find space for, allowing them only to practise in relays. Such a mob; but she rose to it, guiding by gentleness and soft speech, finding amongst them one with the gift of rhythm, who by her own faithful persistence was enabled to follow the career she had dreamed for herself. Sixty of the youngsters were chosen to dance at the festival. What a work to make them dresses! Red-haired little Minnie O'Brien became Joan's satellite, helping, shrill-voiced, to galvanise some of them into order, whilst the others were receiving their lesson, or being measured for their costume. Joan had chosen for them white muslin, the thinnest and frailest, with garlands of flowers, willing workers had spent long in making, with paper and wire, very cunningly. Alas, for her choice! How it looked, that white muslin, transparent and flimsy, over the children's poor underclothes, made up of old garments cut down for them, all colours and patterns, hastily washed, hastily patched and darned by work-driven fingers! The shoes of so many were broken and shapeless. How ill they accorded with flimsy white muslin!

As I saw the long bedraggled train of them, hasting along the Old Ford Road to the Park, my eyes filled with tears for them. My dear little darlings, your poverty—oh, your appalling poverty!

"Where is my Mary?" a mother cried out, as she passed me, running to catch the tail of them. "Where is my Mary? I want to put a flower in 'er bloody 'air!"

Harshly, the ugly word smote me; yet it fell from her lips unconsciously, as she ran in her happy excitement to bedeck her little one.

# CHAPTER XLIV

## DOPE AND T.N.T.

OCCASIONALLY in some obscure news paragraph the death of a worker or two from the poisonous dust and gases in the munition factories was recorded. When a poor unknown fellow, James Steele, died of poisoning by the dope used for aeroplane wings, Brace, the Labour Under-Secretary at the Home Office, excused the use of the poisonous type of dope, by the plea that one of the essential ingredients of the non-poisonous sort was not produced in this country.[1] When Ellen Jane Clarke died at Silvertown, and it was complained that she had been employed with the poisonous stuff for twelve hours a day, Brace promised that in future no girl should work at doping for more than two half-days a week; a frivolous promise, made to be broken, like so many more![2] When more deaths occurred, and Members of Parliament urged that there were non-poisonous dopes which could be used, Brace answered that this was a matter which must be decided by the Admiralty. On June 21st Captain Bennett Goldney complained that the War Office was actually compelling contractors to use a highly poisonous dope, D.94. When the deaths of two more women dope varnishers were mentioned, Brace declared that the War Office and Admiralty were "developing as fast as they could," a non-poisonous dope. Despite such prevarications, written out by the permanent officials for Ministerial mouthpieces, the evil continued.[3] To the war mentality it appeared clear that the needs of the War must be paramount; whilst thousands of lives were being sacrificed at the Front, one must not be squeamish about illness or death amongst munition workers. The workers themselves, above all the women, had men at the Front whom they loved, and, womanlike, were willing to endure for their sake.

In July I was approached by women working at a London aircraft works. They were painting aeroplane wings with dope varnish at a wage of 15s. a week, for which they had to work from 8 a.m. to 6.30 p.m. They were frequently expected to work on till 8 p.m. and were paid only bare time rates for this overtime. There was no mess-room, and meals were often taken in the horrid atmosphere of the workshop. It is an axiom that fatigue and insufficient nourishment invite all industrial poisoning. It

1 Official Report, House of Commons, March 21st, 1916.

2 House of Commons, April 10th, 1916.

3 In the Woolwich cordite factory women were working alternately a week of 66½ hours by night and a week of 57 hours by day. The cordite gave off vapours producing drowsiness.

was common, they told me, for six or more of the thirty women dope painters to be lying ill on the stones outside the workshop, for half an hour, or three-quarters, before they were able to return to their toil. During a part of this period they were unconscious, and they suffered the agonising sensations of fainting, in losing and regaining consciousness. If the spell outside the workshop were not excessively prolonged, their pay was not stopped for an attack of illness. If, as often happened, they were obliged to absent themselves for a day, they were not allowed to return for a week, and their pay was docked. Illness frequently compelled them to remain at home for a fortnight. Milk being supposed to neutralise somewhat the effects of the dope fumes, the employer provided each worker with a cup of it during the morning and afternoon. No other lunch or tea was permitted.

By dint of agitation I secured some ameliorations, both in wages and conditions ; the women gave thanks very handsomely :

" We, the working women and girls, employed by Messrs. ——, beg to tender our thanks to the Editor of the *Woman's Dreadnought* for agitating on our behalf for better conditions ; and we hereby pledge ourselves to support the paper and bring it to the notice of all working women."

Poor girls, they sorely needed support ! They were working under the grip of the Munitions Act ; they could not change their employment or their employer without permission, and were liable to punishment for absence from their unwholesome toil, unless excused on the ground of illness. Some of the active spirits amongst them were struggling to get their fellow-employees into a Trade Union, the management employing coercion and strategy to prevent them.

From Leeds, came news that women dope painters there, were working from 7 a.m. to 8 p.m., and that fourteen or fifteen of them were often lying unconscious.

The explosive powders, with which shells were filled, were highly injurious to all who handled them. The Press referred humorously to the " yellow girls " who worked with the T.N.T., because their skin soon became a bright mustard yellow. The Medical Inspector of Factories issued a notice :

" High explosives may cause skin irritation ; no danger to life."

The contrary was the case. T.N.T. caused eczema, it is true ; but it was responsible also for mortal ills. Brought into the factory in the form of powder, it was heated and mixed with a nitrate and poured into the shells in liquid form. The powder blowing about the factory, and the fumes from the hot liquid being inhaled by the workers, caused symptoms similar to pneumonia, jaundice, and pitch cancer—a disease contracted in the manufacture of a patent fuel which had long been scheduled as a dangerous trade. As in white lead and other dangerous processes, all the workers in T.N.T. suffered to a greater or lesser extent, though only a minority died from absorption. T.N.T. attacked the red corpuscles of the blood, changing the hæmoglobin into methæmoglobin. It attacked the tissues of the organs, especially of the liver, which shrank under its influence. The workers suffered from headache, giddiness, and nausea. In the early stages of absorption their lips became blue-grey.

Only gradually was the insidious character of Trinitrotoluene poisoning realised. At a certain Welsh shell-filling factory a doctor examined the workers once a month, recording the result of his examination by numerals: 1A—normal; 2A—early signs of T.N.T. absorption; B—absorption affecting general health; C—more serious absorption; D—worker to be suspended from employment in T.N.T. When early absorption, marked 2A, occurred the worker was to be kept under observation by the foreman; and if the foreman—in his lack of medical knowledge—observed no improvement, the worker was to be given work outside the T.N.T. sheds. Wholly unjustifiable responsibility was thus laid upon the foreman. It is amazing that such an arrangement should have been arrived at. A lad of twenty years obtained work at this factory, on February 28th, 1915; he died of T.N.T. poisoning on July 6th, 1916. On March 21st and on April 19th he had been marked 1A. About a week later he visited the factory doctor as a private patient. He said he had had a cold, and thought it might be pneumonia. He had vomited, felt sick, and had a little pain in the stomach. The doctor found the tongue "furred and large and flabby." He advised the lad to remain away from work, and on May 15th certified him fit to return. He "hesitated very much" to give a certificate that the illness had been due to T.N.T. absorption—as the lad asked, in order that compensation might be paid—but eventually did so. The lad went back to the filling and mixing room, and worked 8½ hours a day—but for two days only. At five o'clock on the third day the doctor chanced to examine him on his monthly round, and saw that he was suffering from jaundice and his lips were blue. The boy was surprised to be suspended at once and ordered into hospital; he felt comparatively well and did not know for a month that anything was seriously wrong with him; for though he was kept in hospital he was able to dress and to go out each day. In the doctor's words:

> "He appeared to hold his own for a while. At one time I thought the jaundice was lessening. About three weeks before death a little rambling appeared. The next day he was all right, but the next night there was a little quiet delirium. He got slowly weaker, pulse quicker, until he became drowsy and comatose. On May 18th I thought the liver was of normal size. It remained so for two or three weeks. Then it began to shrink."

The lad died on July 6th. He was then blind. After his death it was found that the liver weighed only 30 oz. as compared with the normal 50 oz. The liver, kidneys, and heart all showed that death was due to absorption by T.N.T. The doctor believed the poison had been absorbed previous to the original illness and had remained latent during the time in which the patient had appeared to improve.

A man employed at the same factory had died showing similar symptoms on the previous March 28th, but when away from work he had been attended by an outside doctor, who knew nothing of T.N.T., and who had not noticed the patient's blue lips, though the factory doctor had observed them. The stages of his illness were diagnosed by the outside doctor as influenza and intestinal colic. It was finally decided that he had died of pneumonia. Though his liver had shrunk there was no mention of T.N.T. The effects of the new poison were not yet clearly recognised. Thus no compensation was paid to the dead man's dependants.

The T.N.T. workers wore caps and overalls, and were instructed to wash their hands before taking a meal; but such precautions were but conscience-smoothers; for it was medically recognised that the main danger to the workers was inhalation through the lungs and absorption by the skin.

At an inquest on Lydia Gibson, an examiner at a munition factory who died from T.N.T. poisoning, in October 1916, the managing-director of the factory stated that so injurious was T.N.T. that some workers could not work an hour with it. A man who cut grass near the T.N.T. shed felt the effects of it. It was revealed that the dead woman wore neither gloves nor respirator. The Home Office Medical Inspector stated that examiners had not been brought under the protective regulations until after this woman's death. It also transpired that no order existed making it compulsory for girls to wear gloves. At an inquest on Annie Nelson, who died from the same cause, Dr. Christine Pillman said that respirators were not used in the factory where she worked, as the medical arguments against them were stronger than those in their favour.

On September 4th an inquest was held on a young married woman who died of T.N.T. jaundice after a month in the infirmary following only about five weeks in a munition factory. The poison had done its work speedily in her case!

Some time later some of our members asked for employment at a Yorkshire munition factory. They were offered work in T.N.T. at a commencing wage of 30s. and a promise of piece-work after three weeks. At their request, they were taken to see the process, and found the strong-smelling fumes intensely nauseating. They saw that the workers wore rubber gloves, mob caps, respirators, and leggings. Their faces were coated with flour and starch, to protect them from T.N.T. dust. Yet in spite of these precautions their skin was yellow. They asked the manager whether the work was dangerous. He answered: "Not so very dangerous." They questioned the women workers, but they whispered they dare not speak of their conditions. Outside they met a woman who told them that one of the workers had given birth to a yellow baby, and that after a couple of months' work in T.N.T. one's bedclothes rotted under one. A few days later the factory was blown up. Thirty-nine people, including the manager, were killed. In April a powder factory had exploded in Kent with 200 casualties—but this is war!

A woman wrote to me that her daughter was working at the No. 11 filling factory at Abbey Wood from 8 a.m. to 8 p.m. To reach there in time she had to leave home at 6 a.m. and did not get back till 10 p.m.[1] The workers had begged leave to start and cease a quarter of an hour earlier, in order that they might catch a more convenient train, but this had been refused. They were searched by men, who were stationed in their dressing-rooms.

I managed to secure the removal of the men searchers and the adjustment of the hours to the train service, but when I urged reduction of the working time, on account of the poisonous nature of the employment, I was met with an extraordinary excuse. The Ministry of Munitions replied that though Abbey Wood filling factory was a national factory under the Ministry's own control, it was managed by the King's Norton Metal Company, which had its own private factory next door. Therefore :

" It would of course be extremely difficult to have two factories, each run by the same firm, and adjoining each other, yet varying in the number of hours worked per week."

A frivolous excuse this, considering that the health, and even the lives of the women were at stake ! Those who made it were indeed unfit to exercise the great power over others given by the Munitions Act. How strong was that power was evidenced by the case of Mrs. Skipper and Miss Brown of Hounslow, who refused to work on C.E. Brown was only 17 and had a certificate from her doctor that she was unfit for this poisonous work. The two women were brought before the Caxton Tribunal and fined 15s. Their plea for leaving certificates was refused. They remained unemployed five weeks, and were then brought up again and fined £3. Equally striking was the case of Martha Wilkinson of Fairburn, who was summoned before the Tribunal by the great firm Armstrong-Whitworth for leaving their munition works in York. She had been absent owing to an injury to her eye received in the works, and instead of returning sent a doctor's certificate that she was suffering from inflamed knees, a complaint not remarkable, since she had to stand 10½ hours a day at her work. She was then seen by the factory doctor, who declared her fit for work. Since the doctors disagreed, the Tribunal sent the woman back to work for a month, to test whether she were physically fit or not—a rigorous decision indeed. Mary Dewison was summoned before the Tees and Darlington Tribunal for refusing to carry frames weighing a hundred-weight, which she pleaded were too heavy for her. A youth was fined by the London Munitions Tribunal for refusal to transfer to a dangerous machine at which a girl lost her fingers a few days later.

A deputation of women munitioners went to the House of Commons to plead against the twelve-hour shifts. They instanced the case of a worker, in a hand-grenade factory, working five days a week from 6 a.m. to 8 p.m. Saturday 6 a.m. to 5 p.m., Sunday 6 a.m. to 6 p.m. Her pay was 2¼d. per hour. These hours were worked under the compulsion of the

[1] The same thing happened at the national munition factory, Queen's Ferry, near Chester. Trains brought the workers from Chester in 20 minutes, but they had to waste 40 to 45 minutes both at the beginning and end of the day, because the factory hours and the trains did not accord. Yet the Government controlled the railways !

Munitions Act. The worker, man, woman, boy, or girl, had no option but to submit. Sir W. Clegg, chairman of the Sheffield Munitions Tribunal, observed that it was " very disappointing " to find the women becoming guilty of bad time-keeping like the men. It would have been convenient had every woman been a female Hercules, but the strength and energy of Hercules could scarcely be maintained at 2¼d. per hour. The enthusiasm with which thousands of women had flocked to the factories, appealing to be allowed to help the men at the Front, was not wholly proof against the conditions prevailing there.

. . . . . . .

The stoicism with which the average working woman endures her hard lot largely prevailed amongst the munitioners. I heard a rough, homely munition worker talking of her experiences with a soldier in the train. Writing in my corner, I took down their words in my note-book :

SHE (jocular) : The only ones as 'ad a soft job in t' factory was t' men ! We used ter find 'em behind t' barrers sleepin'. Aye, but there was one woman as was strong ! She used ter pick up one of them forty lb. shells, like this 'ere—catch ! catch !

HE : I should have liked to be there at supper-time to hear you telling your experiences !

SHE : Aye ! We 'ad some experiences ! I've been pumice-stoning me 'ands for a fortnight since I left, to bring 'em back to the usual. I was frightened w'en I first went yeller ! Yer face goes khaki—like that ! (pointing to his coat). If I'd 'ave been there longer—why ! I was goin' green ! There was one girl there, she 'ad green ribbon in 'er 'air ; yer couldn't tell which was t' ribbon and which was 'er 'air !

HE : Did you stay in hostels ?

SHE : No, in proper lodgin's.

HE : You had fine times, I expect.

SHE : First week we was there we was on night duty ; we was that tired we use-ter go ter bed soon as we got in, and never get up till we 'ad ter go back ter work.

HE : Did you hear anything of the explosions ?

SHE : Didn't we ! We 'eard one every day, an' there was accidents every day we was there ! I never want ter see any more as long as I live ! An' that 'orrible fume ! Yer eyes 'ud start running', and yer nose 'ud start bleedin', and yer 'adn't time even ter take out yer 'andkerchief. . . . I wouldn't 'ave stopped there if they'd give me sixteen pound a week.

Their talk dropped into whispers ; for some time I could not gather its meaning. Then she said aloud : " There'll be more rows after the War." He rejoined emphatically : " I'll bet there is ! "

## CHAPTER XLV

### LLOYD GEORGE FIXES WOMEN'S WAGES

*March 26th*, 1915.

"DEAR MISS PANKHURST,

"The words which you quote would guarantee that women undertaking the work of men would get the same piece rates as men were receiving before the date of this agreement. That of course means that if the women turn out the same quantity of work as men employed on the same job, they will receive exactly the same pay.

"Yours sincerely,

"D. LLOYD GEORGE."

"With regard to wages, I will only say that so far as piece-work is concerned we agree that women shall be paid exactly the same price as men for any piece of work they turn out. . . . All these establishments are going to be under Government control. It is quite impossible for us to do other than assume control of the great establishments for turning out munitions of war. *The Government will see there is no sweated labour*. For some time women will be unskilled, and they will not be able to turn out as much work as men. Therefore we cannot give the same time rate, but a piece rate we can give. . . . Whatever the rate of wages should be it should be a fair rate of wages and a fixed minimum, which will guarantee that we shall not utilise the services of women merely to get cheap labour."

Lloyd George in reply to W.S.P.U. deputation, July 17th, 1915.

"The Government wants to get the women on to piece rates and to arrange a fair minimum wage. When it is fixed it will surprise *some people*, but everything takes time and there are 700 munition factories."

Dr. Addison, assistant to Mr. Lloyd George, in reply to the Workers' Suffrage Federation deputation, September 27th, 1915.

The pledges reiterated in the above quotations deserve recapitulation. They had been broken continuously and invariably, throughout the whole field of munition work. The Munitions Act of 1915 had put an end to the right of individual workers to sell their labour in the dearest market by preventing them from changing their employment except by permission of their employers. It had prevented the munition workers from raising their rates of wages through combined pressure, by making strikes illegal, and providing that the wages of munition workers might not be raised except by consent of the Minister of Munitions. By the Munitions of War Amendment Act, 1916, Lloyd George had secured for himself and any Munitions Minister who might succeed him a still more extensive power over women's labour, as distinct from men's, the power to fix the "rates of wages," "hours of labour," and "conditions of employment" of all women workers in the trades brought under the Munitions Act. This power was taken on the plea that women might thus be protected from exploitation.

The exploitation was obvious enough. A case in point was that of the British Insulated and Helsby Cable Company which in 1915 had paid a dividend of 17½ per cent., and was paying adult women on hand-drilling machines from 7s. to 9s. per week! Lloyd George's first Order fixing women's wages under the new Act was issued on June 26th, 1916. It directed:

"Women of 18 years and over employed on work customarily done by men shall be rated at £1 per week, reckoned at the usual hours of the district for men in engineering establishments."

The unskilled men in these factories were getting 25s. or 26s. a week when war began. Their wages had been raised to 31s. when this Order was issued. In some districts factory hours varied from a 48 to 58-hour working week. The men got the fixed minimum in each case, but the women working a 48-hour week got forty-eight fifty-thirds of £1.

Even so, the rate only applied to a minority of the women. Hans Reynold, one of the largest munition makers in the Manchester area, stated that owing to rearrangement of processes only 12 per cent. of its women employees were entitled to claim the £1 a week minimum.

In relation to piece rates the Order made a show of redeeming the old pledges; it stated that women replacing fully-skilled men should be paid the men's piece rates, with the overtime, night shift, Sunday and holiday allowances payable to these men.

In most cases this Order was completely disregarded by the employers without a protest from the Ministry, though some of the women at Woolwich Arsenal, the Government's own factory, which was not a profit-making concern, got skilled men's piece rates. Ladies of title, and others with political influence and tendencies towards Suffragettism, were employed there. It was a show place, so far as women were concerned. Yet even at Woolwich Arsenal, and amongst women doing the most highly skilled work, the overtime bonus was calculated on a day-work rating of £1 a week for women, though on 31s. or more in the case of men. In most other factories there was no pretence of obeying the Order. The following table, showing the wages paid to men and women for precisely the same operations on 4·4-inch shells, by two Glasgow firms, was supplied to me by one of the local Trade Union organisers.

| | Firm A. *employing men.* | | Firm B. *employing women.* | |
|---|---|---|---|---|
| | Piece-work. Price. | No. done in 10 hrs. | Piece-work. Price. | No. done in 10 hrs. |
| Rough part (open end) . | 2d. | 150 | ¾d. | 150 |
| Boring . . . | 11¾d. | 36 | 3½d. | 34 |
| Cutting to weight . | 4d. | 90 | 1d. | 72 |
| Grooving and waving . | 3d. | 100 | 1½d. | 80 |
| Recessing base . . | 4d. | 65 | 2¼d. | 40 |
| Turning band . . | 4½d. | 65 | 1½d. | 50 |
| Finishing turning . | 6d. | 90 | 1½d. | 50 |

Thus whilst the piece-rate pay of the women, on most operations, varied from a half to a quarter that of the men, their output was not much less. For the masses of women who could not claim to be doing precisely the work hitherto done by men, no standard was yet fixed. At last, on July 6th, when leaving the Munitions Office to succeed Kitchener at the War Office, Lloyd George issued an Order fixing the wages of such women. If over 18 years and employed by time, they were to get 4½d. per hour. Girls of 17 were to get 4d. per hour; girls of 16, 3½d., and girls under 16, 3d. Piece rates were to yield 4d. per hour over 18 years; 3½d. at 17 years; 3d. at 16, and 2½d. under 16 years. It was, of course, highly unusual to fix piece rates below time rates; they were ordinarily fixed to yield at least time and a quarter. *Broken utterly was the vaunted promise of equal pay for piece rates!*

These rates were not minima but fixed wages. Dr. Addison plainly stated in the House of Commons[1] that the women would not be permitted to apply to the arbitrators appointed under the Munitions Acts to secure increased wages.

Only ½d. per hour was to be added to the wage of women employed in the so-called "danger zones," where accidents were a common feature of their employment.

In respect of girls under 18 years, employed on work customarily done by men over 18 years, a further Lloyd George Order was issued. These youngsters were to get 18s. a week at 17 years; 16s. at 16; and 14s. a week under 16 years. The piece rates were to be 10 per cent. less than those of men, for girls of 17 years; 20 per cent. less for girls of 16 years; and 30 per cent. less for girls under 16. These proposals to handicap the girls in setting them to compete with experienced men, would have been Gilbertian in their absurdity had they not been so tragically rapacious in the employers' interest. In numbers of sad cases the girl was at her father's bench, doing his old work at a lower rate, whilst he had returned from the War a broken man, pensionless, or getting perhaps the broken man's pittance of 4s. 8d. a week!

On July 27th the Women's Industrial Council called a conference

[1] August 1st, 1916.

*Workers' Dreadnought*

THE AUTHOR WITH A DEPUTATION OF OLD AGE PENSIONERS

*Daily Mirror*

AN EAST END FOOD QUEUE

which protested against the Lloyd George Orders; but the protest was vitiated by the failure to state what wage the conference desired. The leaders could not bring themselves to demand equal pay for men and women.

Disgusted by the failure on the part of those whose province it was to speak for the organised women workers, I circulated a memorial demanding for women munitioners not less than 30s. a week, or whatever may be the current day rates of the industry for men, as well as the same piece rates as those paid to men. The names of those who signed it might well be written in letters of gold; for it was difficult then to bring people in positions of influence to that point. They included amongst Trade Unionists Robert Smillie, George Dallas, of the Workers' Union, and W. A. Appleton, the reactionary secretary of the General Federation of Trade Unions, who was influenced thereto by Margaret Macmillan. Olive Schreiner, of course, was with us; that old warrior in women's interests, Clementina Black; many prominent Suffragists, Emmeline Pethick Lawrence, Margaret Ashton of Manchester, Lillah McCarthy, Arnold Bennett, Laurence Housman, Emily Hobhouse, Isabella Ford, Mrs. Despard, Hertha Ayrton the scientist, Eleanor Barton of the Women's Co-operative Guild, Barbara Drake of the Fabian Society, Lansbury, Nevinson, Lewis Donaldson of Leicester, not yet made Canon, E. C. Fairchild, and A. A. Watts of the British Socialist Party, Katharine Bruce Glasier, and many others.

It must be emphasised that though we were thus protesting against the scales of wages fixed by the Lloyd George Orders as altogether too low, even these low scales were not enforced.

Legal provisions were now slipped through Parliament, in a composite measure, the "Police, etc. (Miscellaneous Provisions) Act," whereby deductions could be made from the women's small wages in the shape of weekly levies to pay for such matters as canteens, the supply of drinking water, lavatory accommodation, seats for the workrooms, ambulance, and first-aid requisites. The Factory Acts had long before provided powers to compel the employer to provide such necessities, and the Truck Act had protected the workers against deductions from their wages on such account. This new legislation invited the employers to compel their workers to pay for the hygienic equipment of the factories. More extraordinary still, this Act of composite provisions gave power to levy the workers in respect of "arrangements for the supervision of the workers." The sweated women were thus made to provide the salaries of supervisors paid at much higher rates than they could hope to earn. All this was an amazing evidence of reaction.

Should war remain continuous the workers would be reduced to a condition of serfdom from which only the trump of revolution could raise them.

Time soon revealed that there was to be no attempt by the Ministry of Munitions to enforce the Lloyd George Orders against employers who were paying women munitioners less than the low rates the Orders directed. In October 1916 three women were tried for bad time-keeping before the

Cardiff Tribunal. They protested that they were ill. It was revealed that their wages were 8s. a week for working eight hours a day. No action was taken against the firm !

In January 1917 Mary Macarthur was complaining that a Government award had decreed that women over 18 years might begin work in a certain factory at 2d. an hour, their wage rising to 2¾d. per hour after a year, *provided their work was satisfactory to the employer*. Another Southampton firm was paying women munitioners 8s. 9d. to 13s. 3d. a week.

The Ministry of Munitions was by that time advertising for 8,000 women to work in its own shell-filling factories at 27s. a week. The wage was little enough for such dangerous and poisonous employment. Even so such advertisements were often misleading. Women who volunteered for war work often found, when they had left their homes to undertake it, that the conditions were quite other than those represented. This was even more notoriously the case in land work than on munitions.

In opposition to the constant talk of the " big shilling," came the complaint of the chairman of the Glasgow Munitions Tribunal that he had protested fifty times against paying men only 27s. a week for 56 hours a week in the munition factories.

# CHAPTER XLVI

## LITTLE TRAGEDIES

AT the end of March 1916, Hayes Fisher had officially informed the Commons that 45,000 soldiers had been invalided out of the Army. 15,105 of these men had received no pension whatever; only 5,470 had received "final" pensions, which they could rely on as being permanent; the others had merely temporary pensions for short periods, and subject to frequent review. 3,818 soldiers had suffered amputation of limbs, and only 932 had been fitted with artificial limbs, while 300 new cases were requiring artificial limbs each month. Of the 41,000 soldiers' widows, only 23,106 were in receipt of pension. 800 had been refused, and the claims of the remainder were undecided. Where men discharged on account of illness were refused full pension, it was promised that the Statutory Committee should make up what had been granted them to four-fifths of the official pension scale. In the vast majority of cases this was not done; indeed, the Statutory Committee lacked the means to do it.

At last the Government had promised to end the scandalous practice of sending home to a starving family poor broken men, penniless and incapable of working, to wait indefinitely for a pension, which might or might not come. £1 was now to be given to the soldier on discharge, and a temporary grant of £1 a week for married men and 10s. for single men until Chelsea Hospital had decided what pension it would grant. The temporary pension was to come from Baker Street—another office to prove another centre of confusion and delay. Presently this temporary pension was levelled to 14s. a week for both married and single men, a mean and miserable dole indeed on which to support a family!

My old experience had been that the vast majority of the men had to wait weeks and often months for their pension. My present experience showed no great improvement. In October my view was confirmed by Sir Frederick Milner, who sent to the Press a letter he had received from a Brigadier-General in charge of time-expired men, who stated:

"I have a daily average of 50 cases discharged unfit for military duty. . . . I find that about 70 per cent. after being discharged from hospital, and receiving the gratuity of 20s.[1] have to wait some considerable time

[1] On August 16th, 1916, G. N. Barnes moved the adjournment of the House, complaining that the men were not getting the promised £1 a week. J. M. Hogge urged that the men should be given on discharge a book of drafts entitling them to £1 a week. The suggestion was ignored.

before they are settled with by the Pay Office. . . . These men get nothing until I write to S. and S. help, or the minister of the parish to look into the matter. Were it not for the action I am able to take, many of these men would be left utterly destitute."

This helpful action by this particular official was done purely on his own initiative, and formed no part of his official duties. His experience, and that of Sir Frederick Milner, was my own. The question glared at me: was this the grossest inefficiency conceivable, or was it the deliberate policy of the Government to leave the broken men to sink or swim without aid, so that they might be forced into the labour market, and the power of their shattered frames to toil might be tested, under the stern urge of hunger, before their pensions were assessed?

In every case the Medical Board insisted upon knowing the man's earnings when determining pension, and the man must answer truthfully under pain of being punished for a lie. Their earnings, if they could earn at all, were reckoned in reduction of pension, however feeble and broken might be their condition. This done, men with the wounds of battle and operation unhealed, with eyes newly extracted, limbs newly amputated, crippled by rheumatism and "trench foot," had their pensions determined, not on their present state of health and capacity, but on the condition the medical assessors believed would be theirs after a period of recovery. Even then the pension was still only conditional, and subject to reduction or stoppage should their condition improve.

"That disabled men shall not be discharged until arrangements for the payment of pension are complete; that there shall be no interim between the cessation of Army pay and separation allowance, and the commencement of pension."

This was the resolution of our League of Rights often emphasised.

. . . . . . .

" Ask the lady to come upstairs," I said. It was only one short flight, but Nurse Hebbes answered : " Oh no ; she is not fit to walk upstairs ! "

I went down to the visitor. She sat panting for breath. I knew her well. A tidy woman, not yet forty years of age. Nature had given her a clear skin and bright hair ; there was a grey ghastliness over her now. I saw with concern the change hardship had wrought in her. She was eight months pregnant, suffering from heart strain and general debility. She spoke to me painfully, in a slow hoarse voice. Her case had been coming back and back to me since December 1914. When war broke out she had six children, the eldest a girl of seventeen afflicted by hip disease, who would never be able to earn her living, the youngest a two-months-old baby. Her husband was a chief scaffolder, a steady, hard-working man, earning a regular wage of 42s. 6d. a week, never ill, never idle. He had been a soldier years before and had fought through the Boer War. He enlisted when the Great War broke out. From sleeping in tents on marshy ground, without proper protection in wet, cold weather, he had been stricken with rheumatoid arthritis in the arms and legs. His hands were so drawn that he could scarcely open them. He was discharged on December 16th, 1914. His pay and his wife's separation allowance ceased. He had come back to his old life, a broken man, racked with pain, scarcely able to hobble with the aid of a stick. The wife got £2 from the local S.S.F.A., but was told that the Association could do no more. The family had only the earnings of the eldest boy, a child of fourteen, to depend on. Nurse Hebbes brought their unhappy plight to my knowledge, and with Keir Hardie's help, I secured a temporary grant of 17s. 6d. a week. We protested, without success, that this was too small a pittance for the maintenance of eight people. The home was in fact steadily dismantled, everything possible being pawned and sold to keep the rent paid and the children from crying for food.

On April 5th, 1915, " the Lords and other Commissioners " of Chelsea Hospital were " pleased to grant the soldier a pension of eighteenpence a day for twelve months conditional, with arrears from December 17th, 1914. The S.S.F.A. grant of 17s. 6d. a week ceased ; the family must henceforth exist on a mere 10s. 6d. weekly. But the unfortunate people were nevertheless, for the time being, overjoyed ; because the accumulated arrears enabled them to satisfy their chronic hunger, and to get some necessaries out of pawn.

Their future would be grim. Determined to avert the blow, if I could, I claimed 25s. a week for the man and 2s. 6d. each for his five dependent children on the strength of the then recent recommendations of the Select Committee appointed in response to widespread complaint to deal with the pensions scandal.

Chelsea Hospital replied that the Select Committee's recommendations, though men were being recruited on the promise of them, were not yet in force. In May 1915 the man succeeded in doing three weeks' light work ; but from pain and illness was compelled to desist.

The Committee's recommendations were at last embodied in a Royal Warrant. Again I appealed for increased pension, and on our doctor's advice, asked beside that the suffering man should receive radiant heat and massage at a military hospital. The latter request was ignored, but the pension was increased to 18s. 9d. per week for the man and 10s. for his five dependent children. I still demanded full pension, and at last, on September 11th, 1915, nine months after the man's discharge, full pension was conceded; but only for six months conditional. What misery the intervening privations had caused the unfortunate family! The baby born, bonny and healthy, on June 1st, 1914, had flagged as she grew older, especially after being weaned; for often there was neither food nor money in the house, and the unhappy mother could not buy the milk she required. In September 1915 the infant became gravely ill and died in the sick asylum in November. The two children next in age were in poor health; it was on account of one of them the mother had come to me to-day.

The 37s. 6d. a week I had secured after long effort was soon cut down to 28s. 9d. without my knowledge, for the husband and wife were tired of complaining. The man had never been free from pain since his discharge from the Army; but with an invalid's invincible confidence, he was still hoping soon to be well and at work again. On April 5th, 1916, he secured a labourer's job, and held it, with some intervening periods of illness, till July 26th, when he broke down completely. When he appeared before the Medical Board for his half-yearly examination—that ordeal of terrible portent—on July 19th, 1916, a hideous mistake was made. Whoever took down particulars of his pre-war and present earnings transposed them. Since it was written down that he was earning 42s. 6d. a week, and had earned this amount regularly for the past twelve months, his pension was reduced to fifteenpence a day, and his children's allowances were stopped. Again I explained and protested, protested and explained to all the authorities. The local pensions committee agreed to make up the 8s. 9d. pension to £1 a week. The eldest boy was now earning 10s. a week; the eldest girl, as soon as she could leave school, had got work in a biscuit factory and received 6s. a week. At least a part of the children's earnings must be devoted to their individual expenses for fares, food, and clothing. The mother was worn out with anxiety and denying herself to leave more for husband and children.

Unconsciously as we spoke together my eyes fell to her broken boots. She drew her feet back, embarrassed, and explained nervously that she had been obliged to pawn a better pair; and, covering her left hand, that she had pawned her wedding-ring.

. . . . . . .

Nurse Hebbes came anxiously to report the plight of a family living close by us. The mother, a soldier's wife, had been taken ill with rheumatism and neurasthenia before her sixth confinement. Her mother came in to care for her and the children as often as she could; but two little boys, aged five and three, strayed away from the doorstep, and were taken by a well-meaning policeman to Bethnal Green Workhouse. When the mother learnt the children were missing her condition grew rapidly worse; she became delirious and was removed to the nearest Poor Law hospital, the Poplar and Stepney Asylum. Her husband now returned from the Front with shattered nerves, and though he was booked for hospital, was sent home to wait until a bed was available.

Miserably ill, he arrived home to find his wife and two of his children in Poor Law institutions. He procured their discharge; but the military authorities, so lax and dilatory where the interests of the soldiers and their families were concerned, displayed their usual lynx-eyed co-ordinating efficiency where payments might be stopped. They had learnt that his wife and two children had been chargeable to the Poor Law! Separation allowance ceased immediately. The family lacked food. The wife had given birth to a small and feeble infant.

Despite my urgent applications it was three weeks before I could get military payments started again; and even then, the arrears were withheld for several weeks longer, while investigations were made; though I had supplied a doctor's certificate in the mother's case and all other particulars from those concerned.

. . . . . . .

A "Gallipoli hero" had been bombed in the face; his nerves were shattered, his hearing gone, one eye was destroyed and the other advancing rapidly to complete, incurable blindness. He was discharged one Saturday in April, with 17s. "to buy himself a suit of civilian clothes." Men's ready-made suits of the poorest quality cost in his neighbourhood at the time from £1 10s. to £2. Two days later his wife drew her weekly separation allowance as usual, considering herself entitled to it till the pension began. Next day she received a letter telling her to send it back. She replied that she would do so when her husband's pension came. A threat to prosecute followed. A mettlesome little woman, she replied: "Prosecute me if you like; it will show you up!" Then came a milder epistle offering, as a concession, to receive the money back at the rate of 5s. a week. Still the woman persisted that the refund must be made out of the pension. Indeed, she could do nothing other; because, save for the 5s. a week she earned by box-making, the family had no income, and there were several little children beside her broken man to be fed. The regimental authorities now demanded the return of her husband's suit of khaki. She replied that the 17s. given him for that purpose was insufficient to buy him a suit of civilian clothes. Moreover, she had spent it to get him food. The authorities peremptorily demanded that the man should present himself to deliver up the khaki. The wife replied: "Do you want him to come naked?" The authorities retorted that if the man did not bring the khaki clothes he would be imprisoned. Believing that they would be vindictive enough to do this to her poor invalid, she brought forth one of his old suits, and sent back the khaki. Eventually the temporary allowance of £1 a week came through; but four months after discharge the man had not yet been examined by the Medical Board which was to determine his pension.

. . . . . . .

A neighbour asked me to help a "clean, hard-working woman," a soldier's wife, who was refused separation allowance, because some years before the War her husband had gone to live apart from her, in the desperate mood of a workless, penniless man. Enlistment opened to him a chance, as he thought, to re-establish his home. He wrote to her, affectionate and persuasive; yet anxious for a definite decision from her, before taking this step, which no doubt was a desperate plunge to him, for no man in those days could be ignorant of its risks.

"DEAR POLLY,

" . . . I am sending you as much as I can, hoping you will be satisfied, and I have got two rooms, and if you will be suited with them until I can get a house to myself, I will get them furnished, and you can come; but, Polly, if you cannot trust me, I don't wish to force you, but I will keep my promise, if we get together again, to be a good husband to you and to make you happy and comfortable. I should have come over, but I am upset after seeing the children, to have to come away and leave them behind. So if you will write and let me know what you will do I shall be very pleased, and I have sent you a stamped envelope with the address on. So give my love to the children and accept the same yourself from your husband,

CHARLIE."

The wife assented, the man enlisted, and made his allotment in the usual way; but, alas, no separation allowance was forthcoming, because the husband had not supported his wife before enlistment. Again the pitiless, mysterious efficiency in discovering loopholes for refusing payment displayed itself. The soldier wrote to his wife in astonished dismay:

" . . . I don't know what the devil is the matter! I am sick of writing and getting no answer. . . . I only wish I could get a leave, and then they would hear the length of my tongue. . . . I am very much upset . . . but keep your heart up, and there shall be better times for you. . . . I have sent three cards for the children. They are made by the French kiddies. . . . "

Again he wrote anxiously:

" . . . I have written to them and explained till I am sick of writing. . . . I may be getting a leave after Christmas. . . . I will go and play Hell with them, but that is a long time for you to wait. I hope they will let you have it before then. . . . Dear wife, I am pleased to hear that the kiddies are going on well, and I should only like to be with them and you. And you know, Polly, they ought to be bonny, for you were the bonniest lass in —— when I married you, and I still think you are the bonniest yet. . . ."

Still the harsh refusal of officialdom remained firm; he wrote now hopelessly:

" . . . I have seen the pay sergeant and he is going to write to Woolwich for me. . . . I have received orders that I am not to write to the Paymaster any more, as it is not allowed, so you see, Polly, I am in a fix. . . . I only wish I could have my time over again, things would be very different. . . . Well, dear wife, the weather keeps very bad out here, very miserable, and we have to live underground, or else take the risk of being blown to bits by German shells. It gets on one's nerves. The same life day after day, and no sign of change. . . . "

I sent to the War Office a batch of such letters from the soldier to his wife, written, so obviously, for her alone. Two months later I received the cold official reply :

" It is regretted that the evidence of reconciliation produced is not considered sufficient to warrant the issue of separation allowance for the wife."

Thus the man suffering the risk of being " blown to bits," and the " clean, hard-working woman " struggling to maintain her little family, were weighed and found wanting by the officials safely ensconced in the War Office " dug-out ! "

In another case the War Office discovered, quite accidentally, that a husband and wife were not living under the same roof when he enlisted. The man had been drinking, and had taken to quarrelling with his eldest son. On this account it had been agreed that he should go into lodgings for a time, but he came to take his wife out each evening, and gave her all he could from his earnings. The trouble had really arisen because the man was on short time, and his son was bringing home more money than he. This was why he had enlisted, though above the Conscripts' age. Then the son was called up, his contribution to the home ceased, and whilst the War Office was enquiring to its own satisfaction into her relations with her husband, the woman got no separation allowance for herself and children on account of either husband or son. Finally she was awarded 12s. a week, the maximum permitted to dependent mothers, from which a deduction was made each week to pay off the extra she had when receiving the wife's separation allowance.

. . . . . . .

A dipsomaniac subject to periodical drinking bouts, in order not to distress his children, at such times returned to his mother, who best knew how to control him. He enlisted at the close of one such unhappy period, during which he had paid 25s. a week to his wife. Noticing that the husband and wife had not been living at the same address, the War Office refused separation allowance. The man did what he could to get the decision reversed. Three months later the wife wrote to me in despair :

" I think I am lost. I should not mind so much if I were able to work. My health is completely broken."

Just then another woman in like case, for whom I was striving, received information that her husband had been killed, and a printed notice, signed " H. H. Asquith," assuring her of the " true sympathy of the King and Queen." For this woman, and for all in like case, there would be no pension !

. . . . . . .

Occasionally the destitute plight of poor soldiers' mothers obtruded itself. At Bray Petty Sessions in Ireland Marie Kerins was summoned for failing to send her children to school. She said she had no clothes for them. Two of her sons had been killed at the Front. For another son she had an allowance of 4s. 11d. a week, but this for some unexplained reason had been stopped.

. . . . . . .

A soldier's wife of Sutton-in-Ashfield with several young children wrote me that her husband, who had become insane whilst serving in the Army, was in the Radcliff County Asylum, and had been discharged from the Army without pension ten months before. She had been given a small allowance from the Prince of Wales's Fund. It had been gradually reduced, and now she was told that if she required further help she must apply to the Poor Law. The man had been a collier, and prior to enlistment had worked six years for the same employer. A local school teacher, who was secretary of the County Association of the National Union of Teachers, and had known the man ten years, vouched for his intelligence. Eventually, a year and a half after the man's discharge, I secured his pension!

. . . . . . .

Cases of soldiers' wives deprived of allowances for husbands' faults were still cropping up. One who complained to me, in July 1916, that 5s. a week was being deducted from her allowance, because her husband had been an absentee, was still suffering this deduction in November, though her husband at the Front had been promoted to the rank of corporal. Evidently he had expiated his fault to the satisfaction of his superior officers; his wife and children were still paying for it!

. . . . . . .

I was often most grieved and indignant at the treatment of the poor fellows whose cases I had in hand, yet when reading the Parliamentary reports as I did each week it was brought home to me that many men, for lack of an energetic advocate, fared very much worse.

On May 25th, 1916, a Member of Parliament, Crumley, complained that Private Peter O'Neil was granted only 12s. 6d. a week and 1s. 3d. for each of his two children. At the time two pieces of shell were still in his side, one part of his shoulder-blade had been removed, one rib had been cut away, two others remained fractured near the spine, and one lung was torn.

. . . . . . .

A poor fellow stumbled into my room. Only twenty-one years of age, he had been shot through the lungs and had lost his speech. Full pension being refused, he had taken work at Gray's chemical factory, and after two months suffering had collapsed. I sent him round to Dr. Alice Johnson, at the "Mothers' Arms." She reported that his condition was so critical that she feared complete paralysis. She got him electrical treatment at the London Hospital, but unfortunately her prediction was presently realised. In the meantime, with the grim absurdity of pensions administration, the youth was offered a post of book-keeper at 30s. a week. To punish him for not taking this work, his pension was further reduced. My protest to the Chelsea Hospital authorities evoked the reply that the man had refused work on the ground that the pay was below the Trade Union scale! As a fact, the poor fellow had never considered the question of pay; he was incapable of working at any price. He appealed to the local war pensions committee for a grant to raise his dole of 12s. 6d. nearer the 25s. promised for complete disablement. The secretary objected that he had married since his discharge, and that his wife could "not expect to be kept"! Yet the Press was then appealing to chivalrous girls to marry war-broken men!

. . . . . . . .

A widow earning 11s. a week, from which 1s. 3d. had to be deducted for fares, had four little children to support, with the aid of a daughter of fifteen, who earned but 6s. a week. A son of nineteen had come back from the War with his right arm gone, ill and pensionless. Another son, aged sixteen years, in some mysterious freak of youthful madness, had enlisted in a London regiment, and a fortnight later in the Rifle Brigade. He was released from the latter regiment, as his mother thought, through her pleading, only to be arrested as a deserter from the former. His discharge was refused, on the ground that his "official age" was nineteen years and four months. He had given his mother fourteen shillings a week before enlistment. Unable to get him home again, she wrote to the boy and his commanding officer asking for an allotment from his pay. She was told this could not be done then, as the lad was under punishment as a deserter. When the punishment was ended, and the boy made her the usual allotment she was told she could not have separation allowance, because her application was now too late. Even the allotment did not come through. She came to me then, and, though the arrears were never paid, I managed to get the boy out of the Army.

It had always been difficult to get back the boys who enlisted under age. On February 14th, 1917, Macpherson stated, for the War Office, that the discharging of such boys was no longer authorised except under very special circumstances.

. . . . . . . .

Only in July 1916 was the principle conceded that a soldier's wife who had a son at the Front might draw separation allowance on account of both husband and son if she had dependent children whom she could prove to the satisfaction of the authorities had benefited by the soldier brother's contributions before his enlistment.

. . . . . . . .

An eviction order was granted at West London Police Court against the wife of a soldier, who had also a son at the Front, and who for some reason unknown to her had received no separation allowance for three weeks.

## CHAPTER XLVII

### THE AMATEUR WAR STRATEGISTS

THE dreary drawing on of the War, unrelieved by any great glamorous successes of Britain, or even of the Allies, roused the pride of insular patriots to fury. Stay-at-home war enthusiasts clamoured for scapegoats, finding in every reverse evidence of criminal negligence, treachery, pro-Germanism in high places. Lloyd George, as a member of the Cabinet from the outbreak of War, was responsible, with the rest, for all that had happened ; but he assumed the attitude of one who would have put matters right, if only he had known the inner facts of the case, or had been given a free hand. Aloof from the deep sorrows and anxieties of the great populace arose the clamour of rival war strategists, demanding enormous campaigns in the East, great naval adventures, stronger efforts in the West, a more stringent blockade.

The amateur strategists at home outdid the naval and military professionals in vehemence and certitude. Vast theatres of war, huge schemes for recarving the map of Europe seethed in their minds. Westerners, Easterners, more-war-on-the-sea men, intrigued by the would-be management of the World War, entirely forgot that their schemes must all depend on the humble fellows who were being blown, as Lloyd George had it, into " bundles of bloody rags."

The little Welsh lawyer, reared in a country village, untravelled, wholly devoid of military experience, whose pugnacity had made him Secretary of State for War to the largest Empire, in the hugest, ghastliest war of all time, rivalled the ambitious and reckless Churchill in tremendous projects of Eastern conquest. The die-hard Tories, the war-mongers and Conscriptionists of peace time, who had shrieked for more battleships, and denounced him and his Cabinet colleagues as " Little Englanders " in the eight years of Liberal Government before the War, the noisy jingoes of the Boer War, from whom on a once-notorious occasion he had escaped, it was said, disguised as a policeman, were now all in league with Lloyd George. As the instrument and coadjutor of Northcliffe, the jingo of jingoes, he was preparing to oust his old chief in the cause of war ruthlessness, and meanwhile would work with anyone and everyone to that end.

The W.S.P.U. kept pace with his policy—nay, outran it. Lloyd George desired to send an expedition of a million men to attack Germany and Austria in and through the Balkans. *Britannia* described this as " a masterly and victory-bringing plan," deploring that Churchill's Dardanelles adventure had been calamitously preferred to it. " The road to

Berlin passes through the Balkans, Budapest, and Vienna!" *Britannia* headlined, finding great perfidy in Bulgaria, the purest chivalry in her neighbour, Serbia. *Britannia* knew neither scruple nor caution in denouncing as "traitors" the opponents of its policies, however highly-placed. The quick mind of its editor, leaping unhesitant to what seemed to her the point, demanded the fulfilment of the policies she espoused with all the vehemence which had characterised her in Suffragette militancy.

Rumours of treachery and intrigue flew about London. What was whispered elsewhere was printed in the *Britannia* and shouted on the platforms of the W.S.P.U. Some irrational persons conceived the notion that impostors, posing as spiritualists with occult powers, were plotting illicit aid to Germany, by corrupting patriotic minds. Annie Kenny must visit them, to expose them, and get their mouthings published in the *Britannia*. Side by side with such follies, news and documents found their way from official quarters into the columns of *Britannia*. Amongst them were confidential circulars issued to certain politicians and journalists by Brigadier-General Howell, with the alleged approval of General Sir William Robertson, and in harmony, it was said, with the policy of Asquith, Grey, and Haldane. In these circulars Howell discussed the War with great cynicism. He advocated withdrawal from the Dardanelles, and no assistance to Serbia. He suggested that Bulgaria should be "bribed" with territory taken from Greece and Serbia, to induce her "to turn against Germany and cut the communications between the Central Empires and Turkey." He argued that if it were decided to compensate Greece and Serbia for their loss of territory with money, the cost of two or three days of the War divided between them would suffice. He referred to Serbia with disparagement as "our unchosen ally," "a foreign conqueror and bitter oppressor in Macedonia," "moreover, for the time being she does not exist. . . . It is not policy to ourselves . . . to constitute ourselves the champion of all the Serbian ambitions."

Such views accorded ill with the public utterances of British statesmen. They caused *Britannia* to fulminate with rage, denouncing Robertson as "Hindenburg's partner," "the tool and accomplice of the traitors Grey, Asquith, and Cecil." "Robertson spells compromise, peace, and the downfall of the British Empire."

To Haldane, who was made a bogy in many more powerful quarters, *Britannia* attributed the dominant influence in the Foreign Office.

A little crowd of women, led by Jessie Kenney,[1] her pale face working fiercely, mobbed Haldane from the Commons to his residence, shouting: "Traitor Haldane!" Mrs. Annan Bryce, from the W.S.P.U. platform, endeavoured to make the flesh creep, by insisting that nothing was done in the Foreign Office without Haldane's connivance, and that he had actually been to Switzerland to meet Von Buelow. "All these little games have been going on behind your back!" she cried. "You will wake up and find a peace has been made which will be the ruin of our Empire!" Mrs. Annan Bryce was writing to the Liberal and Unionist

[1] An early member of the W.S.P.U., an ex-textile operative from Lees near Oldham. Her sister Annie was a prominent militant before the War.

war committees, fulminating against "Haldanism," urgent in her insistence that "Asquith must go." She was hand in glove with Christabel and also with important jingoes in the Liberal and Tory Parties.

Closer co-operation with the Allies; one diplomatic centre for the Allies in France, where the roar of the guns might spur it to action, not in London among the safe-placed intrigues of pro-German pacifists; an Allied War Council; an Allied General Staff; naval decisions, as well as military, to be taken by the Allies jointly; cotton on the contraband list; fatty oils on the contraband list; a sterner blockade; more extensive internments; the cancellation of naturalisation certificates to all Germans, Austrians, Bulgarians, and Turks; expulsion from the Government service of all people of enemy origin and relationships: these were the demands of Christabel in the *Britannia*. Bitter were her complaints that supplies were reaching Germany from Turkey, through the Balkans, from America, through other neutral nations. "Traitor Grey!" Openly, fiercely she stigmatised him, "pro-Bulgarian Grey"! He had forbidden Serbia to attack Bulgaria until Bulgaria herself had initiated the fight, on the pretence that, if left alone, Bulgaria might remain neutral. That Grey had done this, with the clear and treacherous intent to assist Germany, Christabel amazingly asserted—"Traitor Grey," who refused to guarantee Greek integrity to bring her into the War, who refused to recognise the insurgent Government of "great Venizelos," and to secure from him the munitions collected at Thessaly and an army of 800,000 Greek soldiers to fight on the side of the Allies. More soldiers! More soldiers! More men to maim and mangle; that was the insatiable demand of all the War organs, the *Times*, the *Daily Mail*, the *Morning Post*, the *Globe*, and *Britannia* with the rest. *Britannia* shrieked of "pro-Bulgarianism in the Foreign Office!" "Traitor Grey betrays Venizelos." Mrs. Pankhurst declared on platforms that Grey was weak in mind or corrupt. In Suffragette days her references to opponents had been always couched in temperate terms, though her policy had been extreme. All that was changed.

Now that Lloyd George was at the War Office, the W.S.P.U. came forward with another women's war procession, on July 22nd. It was organised under his patronage, and reviewed by him, this time from a War Office balcony, with Winston Churchill and Herbert Samuel at his elbow.

The *Britannia*, which since November 1915 had existed precariously, printed—and none too clearly—ostensibly by its adherents, now appeared under the open imprint of a commercial firm. It had leaked out that Lloyd George had granted £3,000 of Government money to the W.S.P.U. women's munitions procession of the previous summer. Snowden and Pringle had challenged the expenditure in the Commons. The *Britannia* retorted that the much greater sums paid to newspaper proprietors and advertising agents in connection with the recruiting campaign had not been challenged. The W.S.P.U. procession of 1916 was no less elaborate than its predecessor. There were pageants of Empire, of Allied nations, of war-work and what not. Dominant above all was the demand, enunciated on more than half a hundred banners disposed at intervals throughout the show: "We want Hughes!" "Hughes on the War Council!"

" Hughes the People's choice ! " " Hughes return at once ! " " Come back, Hughes ! " " Hughes . . . ! " " Hughes . . . ! " " Hughes . . . ! " This Hughes was no other than the Labour Prime Minister of Australia, the one-time organiser of the riverside workers there, whom his old Labour colleagues now mostly regarded as a disgraceful renegade. He had climbed to office by the Labour-Socialist Movement to become a mouthpiece of extremest capitalist imperialism. For his drastic way with German commerce he had secured a seat on the British Privy Council, and toured this country making bellicose speeches. The W.S.P.U., and its *Britannia*, hailed Hughes as the destined saviour of the British Empire, if only those pro-German wobblers in the Government could be induced to put him in the War Cabinet. If Hughes had been in the War Cabinet all the strategies the W.S.P.U. and *Britannia* approved would have been carried out ; the blockade would have been intensified ; Bulgaria attacked ; Venizelos recognised ; Constantine and Sophie, " those pro-German spies," consigned to oblivion ; Asquith, Grey, Haldane, " those traitors," altogether dismissed ; and Serbia saved—Serbia ! Serbia ! Serbia ! Roumania would already have come into the War on the side of the Allies, the War would have been won, the Germans utterly vanquished, utterly, utterly—if only Hughes had been in the War Cabinet !

The W.S.P.U. had opened a £10,000 " Victory Fund," " to support the campaign against a compromise peace," and " to get Mr. W. M. Hughes of Australia on to the Inner War Council of the Empire." These objects appeared to be synonymous in W.S.P.U. opinion. What an anti-climax for the Union, which had once placed its faith only in women !

The W.S.P.U. was not alone in demanding the return of Australia's " Billy " Hughes. His name had become the general slogan of extremist jingoism. The *Globe* declared he had greater driving power than any British statesman " since Joe Chamberlain in his prime," and asserted that " pro-German influences " were working to keep him at the Antipodes. The *Financial News* asserted that if a plebiscite were taken of the Stock Exchange there would be a 90 per cent. poll in favour of Hughes ; the *National Review* that " without him we have little chance of winning the War ! " Leo Maxse at the Unionist Party Conference demanded that Bonar Law, as Conservative leader in the Coalition Government, should invite Hughes on to the War Council ; but Law replied that only the Prime Minister could do it. Lord Templetown in the House of Lords raised the same slogan. Ladies Templetown and Leith of Fyvie opened an office in St. James's Place to promote a memorial demanding the appointment of Hughes as " a member of the inner and supreme War council."

Whilst the women munitioners cheered him, striking the bright shell cases they had brought from the factory which rang at their blows with a gong-like sound, Lloyd George applauded the " Come back, Hughes " banner. Yet perhaps, after all, he was not much pleased with this Hughes outcry. Certainly he did not put the Australian in his Cabinet when he seized the Premiership for himself. Munition girls saluted Lloyd George with hands of livid yellow. " Those lasses are making their war sacrifice ! " a soldier said.

## CHAPTER XLVIII

### BERTRAND RUSSELL—ALTERNATIVE SERVICE CAMPS—THE GLASGOW WOMEN'S PEACE CRUSADE

"WHAT was the end of the War ?" asked Shackleton's marooned men when he arrived to free them from thei rice-bound captivity on Elephant Island.[1] They had been in the Far North, removed from all news of civilised communities, since they left England two years before. "It sounds like madness !" was their comment on his forty-hour-long account of the great "war to end war," as men called it then.

Numbers of Conscientious Objectors were being turned adrift, "on furlough," as it was termed, pending the hearing of their appeals to the Tribunals. Unable to secure employment, many found this respite a more difficult ordeal than imprisonment. No doubt it was so intended. Economic pressure oftentimes bends the will which persecution cannot break. Collections were taken to assist those who were destitute, but the aid they received was small.

Some who had passed this stage were concentrated under the Home Office scheme in camps where conditions were often so bad as to cause an excessive rate of illness and even death.

Walter Roberts, a young architect, only twenty years of age when called up, died on September 8th, 1916, at the Dyce Camp near Aberdeen. The Objectors in this camp, as in others, had elected a committee to represent them which was recognised by the Home Office. This "Men's Committee" attributed the death to housing in leaky tents, insufficient and unsuitable food, inadequate and tardy medical attention, above all for men worn by imprisonment and working ten hours a day in the granite quarries, and total lack of equipment for the care of the sick. Such evils were common. At Red Roses Camp, Whiteland, Carmarthenshire, another C.O.'s settlement under the scheme, a severe outbreak of influenza occurred. One of the inmates, Alec Peddieson, was sick nurse to the others. He appealed, in vain, for trained nursing and improved diet for the patients. Peddieson struggled on till himself overcome by the disease. He and two other C.O.'s died during the epidemic. In this camp there were no sanitary facilities and water had to be carried a quarter of a mile. The sleeping cubicles, each of which had bunks for four men, measured only 7½ by 9½ feet.

W. Firth of Norwich accepted alternative service after nine months' imprisonment, owing to ill-health. At Princetown Camp he was treated

[1] August 30th, 1916.

as a malingerer, put to work in the quarry, and told he was "selfish" to complain of the cold. The week before he died he was given cod liver oil, the only medicine he received. His illness was only admitted the day before he died, but even then his comrades' request to telegraph for his wife was refused. An inquest was held and the cause of death disclosed as diabetes. His comrades, seven hundred men, struck work on the day of his funeral. The ringleaders, C. H. Norman and I. P. Hughes, were sent back to prison as a punishment.

The work done in these penal settlements was in the main valueless. E. B. Ludlam, D.Sc., accepted work under the Scheme in 1918 and was sent to Princetown. With fifteen other men he dug a field for oats, three weeks being spent in this work, which he estimated a man with a horse and plough could have done in a day. He and others spent five weeks in digging a huge field. The soil was poor, much manure was applied. He estimated that turnips grown there would cost 9d. each, and that £1,000 had been spent on the work, which a farmer would have done for £60. He volunteered for heaviest labour at the gas works, stoking the retorts, because he had a knowledge of chemistry and experience of gas works. He saw that the ammonia from the gas was all wasted, though sulphate of ammonia cost £20 per ton, and was actually used on the prison farm for manure. He was not permitted to help at the gas works. A grammar school, lacking a science master, applied for his services; but the Home Office refused to sanction such employment. Ludlam refused to remain at Princetown, as he considered the Home Office Scheme "dishonest." He was sent back to Wandsworth Prison and was still there in 1919, after the Armistice had been declared.

The tortures devised for Objectors did not decrease as the War progressed. Long after hostilities had ended their martyrdom continued. At the end of 1918, 3,500 of them were still in penal settlements and 1,500 in prison. Cecil Templeman, a lad who only reached military age in the later part of 1918, was forcibly dressed in khaki at Hounslow Barracks. He tore it off and was then put out in the prison yard in his shirt only. He wrote: ". . . A road a few yards away (public)—and people expressing amazement! I've no boots, so the wet ground won't do me any good." Thereafter he was kept in handcuffs and twice daily the uniform he could no longer remove was stripped off, and he was put out in the yard from 5.30 to 9 a.m. and 4.30 to 6 p.m. Finally he collapsed with pneumonia. His family was sent for, his death being expected. A few days later the crisis of his illness was surmounted; he was sent back to Sittingbourne, where he had been thus exposed, and put to sleep in a guardroom without bed, seat, or fire. Naturally he fell ill again.

The No Conscription Fellowship reported that in March 1917, at 11 p.m., an officer and a corporal came to the bed of Philip Key and three times stabbed him with a bayonet. At Cleethorpes Camp, in June 1917, James Brightmore was put in a pit ten feet deep with water at the bottom. For four days he stood in mud and water, then was given two strips of wood three inches wide and eleven inches apart to stand on. He was told that five of his friends from the same camp had been shot in France, and that he was to go with the next draft. Jack Grey, after serving a sentence in Wormwood Scrubbs Prison, was removed to Hornsea Camp in May 1917. He was beaten and bullied. A live bomb was thrown at his feet. Soft soap was rubbed into his eyes. He was flung into a filthy pond containing sewage, eight or nine times in succession and dragged out by a rope tied tightly round his abdomen. Eight soldiers refused to obey orders to take part in this brutality.

The long-drawn sufferings of the C.O.'s reacted upon their families. Elderly parents lacking their aid and sustenance, tortured by anxiety, cast down by the obliquy heaped upon them, in many cases succumbed. James, Tom, and Peter Allen, after more than two years' imprisonment, were released to attend their mother's funeral in October 1918, and again to attend their sister's funeral in November. When their leave expired they were all too ill to return. Tom and Peter Allen both died within the week. Seven hundred people living near them petitioned for James Allen's release, but he was taken back to prison.

When Percy Brooks had been nearly two and a half years in prison, his father lost his reason, borne down with the sorrow of knowing that Percy, who had contracted serious lung trouble, was hunger-striking in prison, whilst another son had been sent with the Army of Occupation into Germany, and a third had been discharged from the Army suffering from neurasthenia. In 1919 A. A. Tippett was pleading vainly to be released from Princetown Gaol. His young wife had died, leaving a baby, his mother had recently become a widow.

Arthur Butler who was holding a scholarship from Stockport Grammar School was classed A1 physically fit on the highest scale in July 1916. He died of lung trouble in Bristol Gaol in May 1917. Arthur Horton of Manchester, also classed A1 when arrested in 1916, died fourteen months later in Shrewsbury Prison from "natural causes following pneumonia." He had long complained of hunger in prison. A Conscientious Objector in Wormwood Scrubbs wrote to a friend in August 1916: "Food has grown rapidly worse these last few weeks. . . . We cannot rest or sleep for want of food." The men protested that they did not get even the poor ration allowed to prisoners in war time. Sometimes they demanded that the food should be weighed, and received a considerable increase. Some hunger-struck at last, in protest against their treatment. They were forcibly fed and W. E. Burns of Failsworth died of pneumonia caused by cocoa entering the lungs from the stomach tube used during this repulsive proceeding. Poor lads! only those who have endured such loathsome prison experiences can conceive their misery. Towards them greater indignities, harsher brutalities were employed than even towards the poor half-witted criminals for whom such treatment is usually reserved!

There were a few suicides amongst these tortured sufferers. One who had already served a term of imprisonment broke down under the pressure of a subsequent court martial and agreed to become a soldier; then, in remorse, killed himself in the guardroom, by cutting his throat with a razor.

No record was kept by the Tribunals of the men who came before them on conscientious grounds. The Conscientious Objectors' Information Bureau[1] compiled the following estimate of men who refused to take part in the War:

| | |
|---|---|
| Men who resisted the Military Service Acts and were arrested | 6,261 |
| Pelham Committee men | 3,964 |
| Members of Friends' Ambulance Unit | 1,200 |
| Members of War Victims Relief | 200 |
| Objectors who accepted work under Tribunals | 900 |
| Members of Non-Combatant Corps | 3,300 |
| Objectors who joined the Royal Army Medical Corps | 100 |
| Objectors who evaded the Acts | 175[2] |
| | 16,100 |

. . . . . . .

[1] *Conscription and Conscience*, by John W. Graham, M.A. (George Allen and Unwin, London).

[2] Probably an underestimate as many of these men were not in touch with the N.C.F.

Bertrand Russell, the distinguished mathematician and philosopher, was the most notable protagonist of the Conscientious Objectors, and a regular contributor to their weekly organ, *The Tribunal.* In June 1916 he was fined £100 and costs, with the alternative of sixty-one days' imprisonment, for a leaflet on the case of Ernest Everett, a Conscientious Objector whom the military service tribunal had sentenced to two years' hard labour. Six men had been prosecuted for distributing the leaflet, and Russell had written to the *Times*, declaring himself its author.[1]

The neutral world was astonished to learn that Trinity College, Cambridge, had in consequence deprived him of his lectureship there, which to scholars and thinkers all the world over had appeared the glory of the Cambridge of that day. It was recalled, of course, that Edward Carpenter had also been dismissed by Trinity for his lack of orthodoxy, and had been glad to escape to a freer atmosphere. It was remembered that Shelley and Hogge had been expelled from Oxford. In short, the reflection was made that the old British Universities had long been obsequious in their respect for vested interests and constituted authority, and had too often persecuted the spirit of independent enquiry.

The American University of Harvard immediately invited Russell to become a lecturer there ; but on his acceptance, the British Government refused to permit him to leave the country to take up his duties at the University. When Arthur Ponsonby protested in the Commons, Robert Cecil replied that it would not be " in the public interest " to issue a passport to Bertrand Russell. Russell's income was substantially reduced by the loss of his lectureship ; but his announcement that he would now lecture up and down the country to earn a living was doubtless inspired rather by propaganda motives than by financial stress. The Government retorted by serving on him a notice forbidding him to enter any prohibited area, " now or hereafter," except with its written permission. The War Office presently objected to his proposed lecture subjects : " The Sphere of Compulsion in Good Government " and " The Limits of Allegiance to the State." He was refused permission to enter Glasgow to deliver a course of lectures there, on the ground that his propaganda would be prejudicial to the manning of the Army. The Lord Provost of Glasgow presided at a meeting of protest whereat Robert Smillie read the lecture Bertrand Russell had intended to deliver. Later in the War[2] Russell served six months' imprisonment for an article in the *Tribunal.* He gained a meed of adoration from devotees of Science, who saw in him the one Englishman of great academic eminence who had maintained an open stand against the War.

Romain Rolland, the notable French writer and Professor of the History of Art at the Sorbonne, another lonely beacon amongst the eminent men of Europe, was admired by the growing band of pacifists for his war-time articles in the Swiss *Journal de Genève*, his essays " Au dessus de la Melée " and his pre-war novel " Jean-Christophe," to the international spirit of which he had remained true.

. . . . . . . .

[1] His goods were distrained to pay the fine. [2] January 3rd, 1918.

*Alfieri*

FOR THE NAVY

Alfieri

NETTING MINES FOR THE NAVY

A "Women's Peace Crusade" was started in Glasgow during the summer of 1916 and evoked great enthusiasm and zeal. Helen Crawford, a Suffragette, and Agnes Dollan were its most prominent leaders. P. J. Dollan, the husband of the latter, was an I.L.P. City Councillor. For some time past he had sent me weekly "Scottish Notes" for the *Dreadnought*. A tall, lively, enthusiastic Scot, with a great mop of long curls, such as Socialist Scotsmen frequently carried, he was presently clapped into prison as a Conscientious Objector. All the other members of the Corporation of military age were exempted because of their office. Dollan might have accepted the same loophole; he preferred to take an open stand against the war as a Conscientious Objector, knowing that on this account exemption would be refused. Like James Maxton and other Socialist Objectors, he and his wife and boy had much to suffer. He was to be elected to Parliament in recognition of his courage later on.

Anti-war feeling was by no means confined to sophisticated intellectuals. One found it perhaps most firmly rooted amongst the simple, unlettered people of rural areas. In the tiny, small-paned windows of country cottages cards with red crosses indicated that a member of the household was fighting at the Front. On the parlour walls, among the flower-illuminated cards bearing scriptural texts, and the faded pictures of parents and grandparents, were photographs of soldier sons and husbands, and cheap magazine colour-prints of khaki heroes. Yet the talk in the cottages was not of victory, but of grief and bereavement, scarcity and high prices—eggs at 2¾d. each in summer time, bread at 9½d., 10d., 10½d. per quartern. People said that the farmers dare not sell their wheat and hay except to the War Office, that bacon seized by the Government was going mouldy in the docks. Those who had relatives in the Channel seaports told heart-rending tales of the grievous return of vast numbers of wounded.

How Conscription and the D.O.R.A. were used against workers who held anti-war opinions, and how Labour leaders worked to nullify protest, was revealed by two striking cases, unctuously detailed to the Commons[1] by J. H. Thomas, the railwaymen's M.P., with great affectation of patriotism to impress the House—but an eye also to the gallery of popular approbation outside. Thomas already was boasting that he had "friends on the other side," among the railway directors, to wit; though he had not yet departed wholly from the ranks of democracy. He told that at Briton Ferry in South Wales a railway man and a steel smelter were imprisoned under the D.O.R.A. for distributing anti-war leaflets, and thereafter were dismissed by their employers. The steel-smelters immediately struck work, and thus procured the reinstatement of their man. The railwayman's fellow-workers, a more disciplined body, instead of acting on their own account, applied to their Union Executive to provide legal defence for their comrade against the D.O.R.A. charge. The Executive refused to grant their request. When the man was convicted and dismissed, his comrades, instead of striking immediately like the steel workers, applied to their Union Executive for permission to strike. The

[1] August 22nd.

Executive refused this permission, but promised to intercede with the President of the Board of Trade, who was also President of the Railway Executive, established by the Government when the railways were controlled. The dismissed man was induced by the Union Executive to make both a verbal and written apology and expression of contrition, and a pledge that "nothing of the kind" should occur again. After thus abjectly denying his convictions, the man was still refused reinstatement. When J. H. Thomas disclosed these incidents, the Government representative told him that if the man would join the Army and purge his offence by honourable service, his employers might consider taking him back to work for them at the close of the War. It was admitted that the fellow had been a good and efficient servant.

Just then we called a conference of East London Labour organisations to discuss the industrial and political position of women. Delegates came of such varied type as W. C. Anderson, the old pioneer Herbert Burrows, and the young disciple of the Webbs, G. D. H. Cole, then active in the National Guilds movement. Members of the Shop Stewards' and Workers' Committee movement came also, attacking Cole as the exponent of a half-way-house proposal, who had stolen the ideology of De Leon and his S.L.P., and had attempted to wed it to the Fabian State Socialism of the Webbs.

The Trade Union Congress met that year in Birmingham. War opinion still dominated. An invitation was read from old Samuel Gompers, of the American Federation of Labour, to co-operate in holding an International Trade Union Congress at the same time and place as that of the plenipotentiaries who would be arranging the terms of peace. This very innocuous invitation was suspected of a pacifist innuendo and rejected amid a flood of jingo oratory. America was contemned, for, outwardly at least, she stood for peace still, and Gompers and the A.F. of L. with her. They were to show us an example of jingoism we had never reached when Wilson presently carried them into the world conflict, willy-nilly.

# CHAPTER XLIX

## SIDNEY WEBB—THE SERVILE STATE—A FINER BRITAIN?

WHEN Parliament had risen for the autumn recess, the Home Office announced that in compliance with an instrument termed the Convention of Allied States, Russian subjects resident in this country would be conscribed, and given the choice of service in the British or Russian Armies.[1] There was no conscience clause for them, though in the main they were political refugees, and the majority of them Jews, amongst whom objection to war had for long been general, as Herbert Samuel, the Jew-in-Office, who was enforcing this provision, well knew. Already before the issue of the new regulations, he had begun the practice of deporting friendly aliens who were unwilling to enlist in the British Army.

Meanwhile terrible news was coming from Russia of anti-Jewish pogroms incited by police circulars. Tchenkeli had complained in the Duma that half a million Jews had been expelled from their homes by the military authorities, and driven from place to place, men, women, and children, the sick and the aged, trudging along the roads, or carried in the arms of their relatives. The Committee of Delegates of the Russian Socialist groups in London, and Abraham Bezalel of the Russian Jews Protection Society, were active in their protests. Many poor people came to me from Whitechapel and Bethnal Green asking for aid in their trouble.

In September I was in smoky Sheffield to speak at a meeting there. I stayed with Mrs. M——, our branch secretary, a Yorkshire woman married to a Rumanian. She had emigrated to America with a former husband, and been left a widow there, with a baby, in a rough up-country station, among "foreigners," immigrants mainly from Central Europe. M——, who came forward to support her, had been welcomed as a necessity. Her little son of the first marriage was now a man, fending for himself. Another little fellow of three or four years was dependent on her now. It was she who maintained the large house by taking in boarders. M—— had fallen from his position of protector, to a feeble old man, cut off from the hustling Yorkshire folk about them by his deficient English, and the prevailing contempt for foreigners, which in war turned to a smouldering suspicion, ready, without cause, to flame forth in violent hatred. The police harassed him continually, undecided

[1] A similar conscription of Italian and French subjects here took place later. The French Government decided not to interfere with the "friendly aliens" resident in France.

whether to treat him as a friendly alien, or an enemy who should be interned. The little black-eyed boy, with his mother's round red cheeks and pouting lips, seemed the only point of contact between the rest of the household and his father. The old man watched over him tenderly, drying his tears when he fell, wiping away the lavish streams of soup which the child, with his big unwieldy spoon, poured over his clothes. He seemed infinitely nearer to his old father than to his bustling mother. The old man impressed on him continually that he was Rumanian. He had a map of Rumania on the wall, and pointed often to his native place. He laboriously explained to me, with extreme difficulty in finding words to express himself, the need of the people of the Dobrudja, then under Austrian rule, to be united to Old Rumania. Though he called himself an Anarchist and an Internationalist, his hopes appeared to centre mainly upon Rumanian national aspirations. To other visitors he was silent, with a nervous apologetic smile. To me he talked volubly.

Our Federation organiser in Sheffield then was Jessie Stephen. She had been a domestic servant. I had met her in Glasgow and wanted to give her a chance. She later became an I.L.P. organiser under Doctor Salter in Bermondsey, and was on the Borough Council there for a time.

The Shop Stewards' movement was then active in Sheffield. Its most talked-of leader there was J. T. Murphy. I was introduced to him by a little man named Carford, an ex-carpenter who had become almost blind and kept a poor little general shop. Murphy came out of the factory to us in the dinner hour, wearing his blue dungarees. A truculent S.L.P.-er of the argumentative sort, he was affable on that occasion, and talked confidently of large-scale industrial action to bring the people into their own. Dr. Chandler was the financial mainstay of the S.L.P. movement in Sheffield. He provided the wherewithal to pay for a hall for its Sunday weekly meetings, and to advertise them extensively. For a doctor, unusually careless of his appearance, his manner on first acquaintance was truculent and gruff, but his inner man was genial and kindly. His theories were revolutionary in the extreme.

A Zeppelin raid had occurred the night before my arrival. Its explosive missiles had fallen in one of the dingiest quarters of the town. Masses of people were flocking to see the damage, jostling and scrambling for seats on the crowded trams going that way, streaming up and down the steep streets of poor houses, past the great blank factory walls, over the dusty, rubbish-strewn pieces of waste ground. In large blocks of buildings hardly a pane of glass remained. Doors had disappeared, and bits of rough wood were nailed across the aperture. Holes gaped in the roofs. Here and there entire houses had collapsed, nothing remaining of them save heaps of broken bricks. In one short thoroughfare, where fourteen people were said to have lost their lives, most of the houses had fallen. The bricks, shattered in their downfall, had thrown up a bright red dust which had covered the smoke-blackened warehouse opposite, making it appear as though faced with new brick.

Soldiers with fixed bayonets guarded the more conspicuous ruins, and prevented all save inhabitants from passing the heavy wooden barriers placed across certain streets. The people, gloomy and silent, stood behind the barriers gazing on the ruins. Occasionally an awestruck voice whispered of children bereft of parents, of solitary people who had witnessed the death of all their family, of victims who still lived horribly dismembered, of men and women finding themselves in cellars without remembrance of how they came there. Sad-eyed mothers looked out forlornly from near-by doorways, their spirits long since crushed by the drab hopelessness of the slums, stunned by the new fear that even this dreariness would tumble about their ears.

Only the dirty-faced, ragged little children retained their full activity, rushing pell-mell among the sightseers, bobbing under barriers, squeezing through boarded-up doorways.

Half a dozen soldiers were marched up to the barrier. Hastening to overtake them ran a noisy troop of children shouldering long strips of rough wood hacked out to represent guns, with smaller pieces nailed on for bayonets. As the soldiers passed through the narrow space at the end of the barrier, the shouting children pushed through beside them. At their head strutted a tiny waggish girl, eight years old at most, with hair cropped short like a boy's, the leader and bully of the rest. Her stockings, stuffed with rag about the calves, were tied under her small bare knees. For her gun she had no long stake of wood, like the other children, but a brick, precariously balanced against her shoulder. As the soldiers wheeled and stood at attention, grounded arms, and were drilled by the sergeant, she mimicked them, serenely impudent, with exaggerated contortions, bending her knees, as though horribly bandy, crying " rr'ght t'rrn " like the sergeant, swinging out her leg grotesquely far, and bringing her heels together with a bang. By turns she pretended that the brick had cut her, rubbing her cheek with impish grimaces ; caught the brick up in her pinafore like a baby, kissing and petting it ; shouldered it ; feigned to drop it on her toe ; then swung it vigorously as though to hurl it at the soldiers, but let it fall harmlessly behind her. The soldiers scowled at her angrily, and one, a mere lad, rushed out of the ranks with flaming face, angrily kicked the brick away from the small tormentor, and hustled her roughly past the barrier. She dashed away among the other urchins, helter-skelter, with shrieks of laughter. The crowd looked on sombrely. Obviously the soldiers were not popular. The women muttered that when the Zeppelins came the British airmen were drunk.

Crossing the railway bridge by John Brown's munition works one saw huge stacks of great shells with pointed noses, row upon row, beside the line. One end of the factory had been slightly grazed by a falling projectile. The bombs had fallen with devastating force upon a chapel and a slum. The front of the chapel had crashed down, revealing the text, writ large on the wall within :

" A new commandment I give unto you ; that ye love one another."

The slum was piled with the wreckage of its dwellings. Wretched, jerry-built hovels stood half demolished, the remnants of their miserable furniture lying amid the debris. On the window-sills of some houses which still stood, were displayed wreaths of artificial flowers, purchased for the graves of the air-raid victims with pennies collected by the children of the street. Cardboard box-lids were laid beside the wreaths, as receptacles for the pennies being collected to maintain the children bereft of parents, and to procure clothes and furniture for those whose all had been destroyed.

A woman gazing in hopeless sorrow on the ruins, told me she knew all the people killed here. She pointed to a pale, distraught man being led away, almost helpless, by his friends. Whilst he had been saving his children, his wife had been killed.

I reminded her that all over Europe poor people lay under this same terrible menace, that the German workers were suffering with the rest. She assented with a kindling of the eyes, deep wells of patient pain, which seemed to leap at me as though she had waited for that word.

"They always come to poor people's houses!" So often I heard that plaint. The reason was obvious. Only the poor live in the squalid neighbourhood of the docks, the factories, and the great railway termini.

. . . . . . .

When a flaming Zeppelin fell to earth in sight of us in East London loud cheers were heard; but in the buzzing undertone of conversation in the streets, the women were saying: "Poor things; they have to come or they'd be shot—just like our men!"

. . . . . . .

When I was back at Old Ford, Minnie O'Brien told me that a girl she knew, going home in the bus, discovered that her week's wages had disappeared. " Oh, my mother's money ! " she cried, then went home, and lay down and died, without another word. She was the sole support of a widowed mother and younger brothers and sisters. A doctor certified that her death was due to shock.

. . . . . . .

A Crimean veteran drowned himself in the Thames on his way to the workhouse. He had lived with his niece, but she had lost four sons in the War, and lacking their support, could no longer keep him. He could not live on the 5s. old age pension, at war prices !

. . . . . . .

A new D.O.R.A. regulation was announced, giving power to prohibit meetings and processions where disorder was apprehended which might make " undue demands " on the police or military forces. The war-mongers and compulsionists could now get any demonstration for peace or civil liberty stopped, by merely threatening disorder.

The newspapers headlined Lloyd George's account of his visit to the Front :

" I stood, as it were, at the door of hell and saw myriads marching into the furnace. I saw some coming out of it scorched and mutilated."

He insisted on " the carnage and suffering " still to come :

" There is neither clock nor calendar in the British Army. Time is the least vital factor ; only the result counts. It took twenty years to defeat Napoleon. . . . It will not take twenty years to win this war ; but whatever time is required, it will be done. . . . There is no disposition on our part to fix the hour of ultimate victory after the first success. We have no delusion that the War is nearing an end."

He dismissed the pacifists of all nations as " pro-Germans," declaring that " any step . . . by the United States, the Vatican, or any other neutral in the direction of peace would be construed by England as a pro-German move."

The annual conference of the Scottish Advisory Council of the Labour Party had urged the Government to commence peace negotiations. A conscientious objector smuggled a letter to me from the barracks where he was incarcerated, telling me that the soldier who acted as his jailer, two non-commissioned officers and six privates had signed the peace memorial, and that the sergeant had taken two petition forms for his civilian friends.

Another objector awaiting court martial at Fovant, wrote that the soldiers, and particularly the officers, were " more liberal-minded than the ' Island Pharisees ' outside," and the soldiers " frankly fed up."

A mother, Rose Rogers, who hated war, served a month in Holloway Prison with her four months baby, David, because she refused to register his birth in a conscript State. I hoped that her act might be the beginning of a great fight which the mothers of the country would make to remove the shackles of Conscription from their sons; but the War wore on without any great protest; the people gripped in the cleft stick of international conflict knew no means of escape.

A Scotch woman, whose son had been killed in the War, was imprisoned for distributing the Conscientious Objectors' organ, *The Tribunal.* W. Stewart, secretary of the Scottish I.L.P., was fined £10 for saying that this woman had been imprisoned for her desire for peace.

The Cecil Rhodes scholarships, to enable German youths to study at Oxford, were abolished by Act of Parliament; no Member of Parliament had the courage to oppose the Bill.

A little later it transpired that Professor Ethé, an old German, had been compiling a catalogue of the Persian manuscripts at the India Office since 1872. He worked thirty years on the first catalogue, and was not paid till its completion. He had been engaged on the present catalogue, without pay, for fifteen years. Sir Frederick Banbury protested: "We are always being told it is wrong to dress extravagantly; but here you are wasting money on a book! This German . . . ought not to be paid at all—he ought to be told not to come any more!"[1]

Judge Neil of Chicago came to England in October, advocating "Mothers' Pensions," which should properly be called children's allowances, and which, largely by his remarkably enterprising propaganda, had already been established in twenty-seven out of the forty-eight United States. He was a type only America produces: a self-made man, of Irish extraction, with long upper lip, square jaw, harsh voice, slang-laden speech. People expected from him a deal in oil, not an appeal to social righteousness. His argument, couched in short stories, highly sentimental, and phrased in plain every-day language, was conveniently available in numerous copies, for publication as required. Practical as his methods were, he made no headway; everyone he approached was concerned with the War. Disappointed, he booked his passage home, and three days before the boat sailed, called on me at Old Ford. Sick at heart as I was at the treatment of mothers and children by the Poor Law, the Pensions Ministry and society at large, I grasped at this American plan, which provided for mothers in need an allowance for each child substantially better than any authority was paying here, and conveyed it decently through the post, without any queueing up at the post office or regretful attendance at the Guardians' offices. I published an account of his scheme in the *Dreadnought*, and hastily organised a meeting and reception for him. Mrs. Pethick Lawrence, who heard him there, at once arranged for him to lecture for the State Children's Aid Society on a return visit. I also arranged a series of meetings for him on his return, but he did not appear till they were over. Instead of chairing for him, I had had to expound his scheme in his stead. When he turned up at last, he told us he had been twice shipwrecked by torpedoes. One was so much accustomed to hearing of strange war-time experiences in those days, and so pressed with the rush of events, that I paid not very much attention to his story.

. . . . . . .

[1] November 2nd, 1916. Official Parliamentary Report

The nights grew darker yet; the 'buses stopped earlier. Often I had to tramp to the East End. The paint-smeared gas lamps glowed but faintly, casting small zones of shadowy radiance on the pavement. Buildings retired into the shade, only their mass discerned, quietly reposeful. The City deserted, showed lovelier in the dignity and mystery of its shadows, than in the old garishness of many lights. My footsteps echoed along silent pavements.

Past Bishopsgate, as I turned off towards Bethnal Green, and the high façades gave place to the low East End sort, short youths appeared, dark-clad, only some hint of dusk-white collar at the throat, and shorter maidens with their rounded forms shrouded in paler hues. Always they were together. I passed them standing in the shadows; he pallid, with hollow cheeks and deep-set eyes; she, with the visage flower-like, its outlines merging into the shadows of her hair. In the vague rosiness of shade, one saw her eyes were dark, and her soft lips red and full. He looked out straight and thoughtful, his fingers playing with hers, as though in wonder, finding them so small. The awe of the silent night and the happiness of love enfolded them. Waves of their pleasure passed from them into the surrounding air.

Windows were shuttered or shrouded, even the glaring lights of the public-houses masked. Fear of police vigilance, and of neighbours' anger, screened off the tiniest ray. Only the fried fishmonger displayed temerity. No actual naked light was seen through his unglazed window, but the aperture was uncovered as of yore, and the interior showed brilliant, a generous glow in the prevailing gloom. The shopman, his shirt-sleeves rolled above the elbow, leaned out with folded arms upon the sill, exchanging a word with the few loungers still abroad. His customers were few. The once busy night-life of the streets had passed away. No longer were the side turnings thronged with groups of neighbours chatting on their thresholds. Cats, arching their backs in stealthy grace, were now more numerous than the human wayfarers.

. . . . . . .

13,649 workers had now been put on trial before the Munitions Act Tribunals, only 193 employers ;[1] yet the employers were systematically violating the wages provisions of the Acts.

Vickers[2] had opened hostels for their munitioners, charging 18s. a week for men, 14s. for women, 30s. for married couples, and 4s. 6d. to 5s. for children. They were getting back from their workers, as vendors of board and lodging, what they paid them in wages and overtime. Dr. John Hill, of the Government-appointed Health of Munition Workers' Committee, issued a report on the diet suitable for munitioners, and recommended for women and girls :

" *Breakfast*—Two eggs, two rashers bacon, two slices bread and butter and jam, sugar, milk. *Dinner*—Roast beef, potatoes, cabbage, syrup roll. *Tea*—Three slices bread and butter and jam, lettuce or radishes, sugar, milk. *Supper*—Two slices bread and butter, ham, cheese."

" How are such rations to be procured on Mr. Lloyd George's fixed wage scale, which ranges from 2½d. to 4½d. an hour ? " commented Dr. Tchaykovsky. She might well have enquired how women could obtain such a dietary on 8s. a week.

He smugly replied through the *Times :*

" I gave these diets as satisfying the tastes and appetite of a well-to-do munition worker. A far cheaper diet can be formulated."

In war time people were employed on such fooling !

The Ministry of Munitions was issuing notices calling for from 800 to 1,000 new women munition workers each week. A man-power board was in being ; a woman-power board was added. Industrial compulsion was made more complete. Men not medically fit for the Army were to be enrolled at the Labour Exchange, where, though passed as physically unfit for the Army, they were nevertheless given the alternative of munition work or the Army. It was assumed that of course they would choose the former alternative. As a condition of getting the work which would thus save him from the trenches, each unfit man must " voluntarily " sign a form binding him to work wherever the Ministry of Munitions might direct at 7d. per hour,[3] and an additional 2s. 6d. a week if he had four or five children, or 5s. if he had six or more. A subsistence allowance of 2s. 6d. a day was added, if the work obliged him to live away from his home. He remained liable to recall to the Army at any time. Military representatives assured employers that if there were any " hanky panky " on the part of any man thus supplied to them, the man could be taken for the Army and another man sent to work in his place.[4]

The Orient steamship line threatened to hand over to the military

[1] House of Commons Official Report, October 18th, 1916.

[2] Reported in *The Times*.

[3] Or the current rate for the job ; in practice 7d. per hour was the rate almost always paid.

[4] Parliamentary Report, October 17th, 1916. The *Daily Telegraph*, February 9th, 1917, reported that the military representative at Harrow Tribunal had notified coal merchants to report incivility of exempted carmen, and had promised to review the exemption of such men without delay.

authorities any employee who refused to accept a wage reduction of £1 8s. a month.[1] Few men could resist such pressure. Remember that for the unfit man taken into the Army there was no pension if his health broke down under training; no pension for his family if he died. Overtime was exacted, and accepted with avidity under pressure of rising prices which the low wage could not meet without grievous privations.

So the War spread its huge tentacles to all sections of the people, breaking them at the Front, bleeding them of energy and the joy of life in the munition factories. Larger and larger numbers were subjected to the poisonous dust and fumes of the high explosives. The "yellow girls" working in T.N.T. were a common sight. They were kept out of view as far as might be. Restaurant proprietors issued orders to their managers not to serve munition workers. Olive Beamish, a Suffragette hunger-striker, and one of our East End organisers, went to lunch at Fleming's, in Oxford Street. The manageress came to her sternly: "You know you cannot be served!" Beamish retired indignant and wrote a letter of protest to the firm. She received a courteous reply, regretting that she had been mistaken for a munition worker. She had been wearing a khaki-coloured raincoat.

In the general relaxation of the Factory Acts the protection of children was being swept away. It was made permissable to work children of 14 years a 60-hour week, exclusive of meal intervals, and since they might be employed up to 13½ hours in a single day, it was virtually impossible for inspectors to detect violations of the regulations. Girls under 16 years were employed on night shifts even in Woolwich Arsenal.

There were now 60,000 fewer children in the schools, the number of infants under five had been reduced from 55,000 to 25,000, and the number of children of 13 and 14 years was nearly 20,000 less than in 1914. 13,750 children of school age were employed by farmers, 516 of them under 12 years of age. 20,000 teachers had enlisted. W. C. Anderson complained that 100,000 children had been disturbed in their schooling on account of military arrangements, and that such alternative accommodation as had been provided was often overcrowded and unsuitable.

Yet many of diverse views believed that war-time conditions were preparing a more efficient civilisation after the War. Conservatives of militarist mind cherished the hope that the employers were rising to what they considered their proper position as generals of industry, and the masses becoming more disciplined to their essential function: the supply of such labour as cannot be provided by machinery, for reasons either of economy or capacity. State Socialists, and foremost amongst them Beatrice and Sidney Webb, saw in this era the coming of the system they had long looked for. Already Sidney Webb and Arnold Freeman had published a text-book[2] of the desired developments to follow from this beginning. They declared that whilst "a century ago the servile

[1] Reported by Tyson Wilson, Labour M.P., to House of Commons November 1st, 1916. Admitted by Dr. Macnamara for Government.

[2] *Great Britain after the War*, Sidney Webb and Arnold Freeman. George Allen and Unwin, 1/–.

State was no comic figment, but a reality, it is no longer true that the mass of the people are at the mercy of Capitalism." The question was amazingly put:

"Will Great Britain in 1936 be a finer country to live in than it would have been had not the sharp prick of war aroused us from our slothful acquiescence in the social iniquities that persist around us?"

This read as a grim joke to those of us who toiled amongst the miseries of the people ground in the mills of warfare.

Conferences on industrial organisation and the demands the workers should make, both during and after the War, were held by numerous organisations in the hope of influencing the Trade Unions. Our W.S.F. probably started this fashion in London.

Arriving early for one such conference, organised by the Fabian Research Department, in Tothill Street, I found Bernard Shaw in lively discussion with a group of his Fabian colleagues, declaring, in his challenging, jaunty way: "I have not the slightest objection to the servile State, provided I can get my oar in."

Beatrice Webb took the chair, black-gowned and circumscribed, a carefully reared indoor nineteenth-century product who had missed the enlargement of motherhood. She defended the unequal payment of men and women on the trivial ground that women were more costly than men to their employers, who must provide separate lavatories and other amenities for them. It was with difficulty I compelled her to permit my entry into the discussion to put the opposing view. I was not the desired Trade Union official, with mind open for indoctrination by Fabian argument, but a competing theorist, eager to convert him to other policies. I should probably have failed to overcome her determination to wave me into silence, save that a cue was given which enabled me to strike in with: "When Lloyd George wrote me the letter on women's wages which Mr. Cole has mentioned . . ."

Miles Malleson, who had been invalided out of the Army in January 1915, now published, through Henderson's at the "Bomb Shop" in Charing Cross Road, two anti-war plays entitled "D Company" and "Black 'Ell." These plays were banned and Malleson obtained on this account a popularity which remained with him after the War. He came down to us at Old Ford with his mother to rehearse his children's play, "Paddly Pools," which Patricia Lynch was teaching some of our children.

With the official admission that food prices had risen 65 per cent. and the total cost of living 45 per cent.,[1] the Government agreed to grant a war bonus to all its full-time employees, except those who had already received war increases, or had been newly engaged during the War. This tardily granted privilege amounted to 4s. a week for those whose wages were less than 40s. a week, 3s. for those paid 40s. to 60s. a week. Women and persons under eighteen years were to get half the bonus.

[1] Parliamentary Report, October 10th, 1916.

The old-age pensioners still vainly awaited the 2s. 6d. a week increase promised for those who suffered exceptional hardship.

Stanton, the victor of Merthyr, cried out in Parliament: "Why do you not choke these Pacifists down?"[1] Colonel Norton Griffiths demanded African labour for this country, declaring that France was already importing thousands of Kaffirs and Chinese, to make good the shortage of "white labour," and that the "fight to a finish" would demand more of this. Black troops had long been used at the Front. Outhwaite replied that those who supported the "fight to a finish" should carry it out, as they declared they would, "to the last shilling," but not by lending it to the Government at 6 per cent. interest. Prophetically he declared that after the War the forces of revolution would sweep over Europe to determine who should pay for "this wild debauch of blood." No one in this country believed him, but in Russia the Conservative Party was already asking for peace with Germany, because the continuance of warfare would mean the collapse of the monarchical systems of Europe.

[1] Official Report, October 12th.

## CHAPTER L

### A CRY FROM THE INTERNMENT CAMPS—EMILY HOBHOUSE—ELLA SCARLETT SYNGE

EARLY in 1916 Dr. Ella Scarlett Synge[1], M.D., D.P.H., sister of Evelina Haverfield, called on me. Early in the War she had gone from Canada, where she lived, to give medical aid in Serbia. She had been appointed medical officer of Batochina and ten surrounding villages, and remained there ten months after the Germans occupied that part of the country. She was of opinion that the German troops had behaved well, having seen something of the South African War and knowing what to anticipate. She worked on amicable terms with the German doctors. They placed their medical requisites at her disposal, for her own were nearly exhausted when they came, whilst she invited them to place their patients beside hers in the school-house she had converted into a war hospital. Later she asked permission to inspect the camps for prisoners of war in Germany, saying she had done this in South Africa for the British Government, and had taken a degree in sanitation and public health. The German medicos readily gave her a paper, which proved a passport across the frontiers, from one Red Cross doctor to another. She wrote me a report of what she had seen, which I published in the *Dreadnought*, in February 1916. She saw things from the standpoint of the medical officer and sanitary inspector. At Göttingen, where 10,000 men were incarcerated, she approved the new barracks, built on solid brick foundations, suitably ventilated and well trenched, the efficient water supply and sanitary system, the hospital, with isolation of tubercular patients, the new operating room, the anæsthetising room and dispensary. Especially did she admire the disinfecting building and laundry: " Although everything else is as it should be, and far better than it would have been right to expect, these two installations are absolute models." She noticed well-laid-out gardens, a theatre, home-made musical instruments providing a fair orchestra, a library, a school under the direction of Professor Stanger of Göttingen University, where a celebrated French painter and a successful French advocate were amongst the instructors. At Ruhleben she noticed football, a cinema showing three times a day, a school of 1,400 students, where prizes were given for proficiency, and many languages, including Chinese, were taught. In the Wittenberg camp conditions had been bad at the beginning of the War. Improvements made there since had cost over 1,500,000 marks. She saw in her three-hours' visit " no radical improvement it would be reasonable to suggest."

[1] A daughter of the 3rd Baron Abinger.

With the weariness of prisoners congregated in great masses within narrow limits, away from their homes and families and chosen habitual pursuits, with the drab, stale sameness of the barrack life, however sanitary, she did not deal.

She advocated a scientific sanitary commission, to go from each belligerent country for the mutual inspection of camps, with a view to improving the tone of the Press, and the general feeling of the soldiers towards those in the opposite ranks.

Her testimony was important, as a sane counterpoise to the atrocity-mongering of the daily Press, the hectic speeches of politicians, the fabulous stories of German " corpse factories " for converting human bodies into materials for German food and warfare, the gross charges contained in the report of the Bryce Commission on alleged outrages in Belgium and France. It was a needed answer to the persistent assertion that prisoners of war were systematically ill-treated in Germany. I was glad to publish an unbiased report from a witness so efficient and trustworthy. Yet I was not disposed to raise a great hue and cry upon the matter ; I realised too well, that effective sanitation does not compensate to the prisoner for loss of liberty. I was no wise disposed to minimise the sufferings of the war prisoners on either side, which were every day becoming more intolerable.

. . . . . . .

A typewritten slip came to me, worded mysteriously—an invitation to Mrs. Pethick Lawrence's flat in Clements Inn, to meet "a special visitor."

I found there some members of the Women's International League executive, and facing them a frail, elderly woman—Emily Hobhouse, known for her Pacifist zeal during the South African War and her work of alleviation amongst the women and children herded into Concentration Camps when the Boer farms were systematically burned to destroy all cover for their men. I had seen her but once—a decade since. To-day she seemed aged and saddened, and was obviously labouring under a painful agitation. Catherine Marshall explained that Mrs. Lawrence had provided this opportunity for us to meet Miss Hobhouse and hear her story, as it would be impolitic for the executive to invite her to its offices. Marshall's tone was deprecatory in the extreme.

In a silence which breathed hostility and dismay, Emily Hobhouse briefly reported on the work attempted by the headquarter's committee of the Women's International League at The Hague which had called our British section into being, and on which she had worked from its inception. She told us then, that she had come from Germany and Belgium, having obtained from Bethmann Hollweg permission to visit the internment camps in Germany, and to investigate conditions in Belgium. She gave us a plain and, I felt, meticulously accurate story of what she had seen, unlike the lurid versions then current here, but agreeing with what Dr. Scarlett Synge had written for me of the internment camps several months before. On her way here she had gone to the British authorities in Paris, telling them where she had been and what she had seen. On reaching England she was treated with the utmost ignominy, stripped and searched, as though she had been a spy. This had obviously wounded her to the quick. She had written Sir Edward Grey, whom she knew, her desire to lay before him the information she had obtained, but he had refused to see her.

It seemed as she spoke that we were in a Court for the trial of crimes, and she the prisoner in the dock. When she ceased no one questiond her; no one commented on her experience; Catherine Marshall, as secretary, indicated to her that our committee did not accept her as representing the British section of the Women's International League on the international executive at The Hague. She assumed that she expressed our united view, though the question had never been debated on the executive.

A voice at my elbow broke clumsily across the emotional tension, with the observation that Miss Hobhouse might join the British section as an ordinary member, like anyone else, if she chose. She answered that she did not ask credentials to pursue her work at The Hague from the British section of the League. "I do not wish to be a member of the body!" she concluded in trembling indignation.

Shocked by so churlish a reception of this woman with her long record of fearless integrity in the cause of peace, and by her evident distress, I blurted, a grip at my heart making speech difficult: "I have heard what Miss Hobhouse has said with extreme pain! I hope she will join us."

"No! No!" she murmured, and hurried impetuously from the room.

Mrs. Lawrence contributed the only touch of human warmth, with genial words, following her guest to the outer door.

I voiced some brief expressions of respect for the work of Emily Hobhouse, and my opinion that we ought to feel honoured to work with her. My words fell responseless as from a wall of ice.

"When the Government really trusts you, they don't treat you like that!" the foolish phrase jarred on me. I learnt from the others where Hobhouse was staying; hastened there, and telephoned at the entrance to know if she would see me. She refused to come to the instrument, sending a message that she could see no one.

"She classes me with the Philistines, regards me as an emissary of the committee, trying to gloss the matter over!" I thought, my heart on fire.

I hurried home and wrote to her on my way in the 'bus, telling her what I thought of it: "I felt we were like Peter denying Christ!"

"Take this letter to her," I urged Smyth. "Tell her! Explain to her! She thinks I am in the crowd against her. She would not see me. Unless she is really ill she will see you!"

As usual, amiably acquiescent in such turbulent distresses, Smyth smilingly accepted my mission, and sending up my letter as her passport, was warmly received.

Later I saw Emily Hobhouse at the home of Mrs. Hubbard Ellis. She told me that the secretary and chairman of our W.I.L. committee had seen her, and told her categorically that she must not come to their office, and that they repudiated her as representing our section at The Hague. I protested on the executive that our officers had not been authorised to take such action, and that I, at least, was wounded by association with it. As usually happens in such cases, the matter was glossed over. I was outmanœuvred, as often happened, in dealing with the officials; for I had no heart for a wire-pulling contest with co-workers.

Again I heard that phrase: "When the Government really trusts you, they don't treat you like that." These women had had their political training under Millicent Garrett Fawcett. They believed, probably, that she, and not Emily Hobhouse, had given the true version of the South African concentration camps,[1] the hideous death-roll of women and children in the camps notwithstanding. Emily Hobhouse had been anathematised in the Boer War. They shrank from drawing upon themselves the new odium now heaped upon her. As constitutional Suffragists they had prided themselves as being "law-abiding"; they had not learnt yet that obedience to authority is of smaller value than obedience to conscience. Catherine Marshall had the opportunity to learn that when she joined the No Conscription Fellowship committee. When the men were taken to prison she became its honorary secretary. She did not go to prison, but many of her colleagues did.

Emily Hobhouse wrote for the *Dreadnought* an account of her visit

[1] Mrs. Fawcett was one of a number of ladies sent by the British Government of the time to produce a white-washing report on the concentration camps into which the women and children were herded when the Boer farms were systematically burned to the ground.

to Belgium. She computed that 15,000 houses had been burnt out of a total of 2,000,000, which she compared with the destruction wrought in the South African War, when 30,000 Boer farms were burnt and many towns and villages entirely levelled to the ground. She reported the widely advertised destruction of Louvain a fiction, though the world-famous library had been burnt to the ground, and some damage done to the cathedral. Few people can endure such truths in war time. A tremendous outcry was raised against her. Butcher and others in Parliament called upon the Government to punish her.

Thereafter she made a point of seeing me when she came to London. She was in feeble health, and suffered from heart complaint. I have often found those who are least physically able in body most courageous in spirit. I remember going to her when she was staying in the Buckingham Palace Hotel. She was lying on the top of the bed to rest and urged me to lie and rest too. I assented to satisfy her, but felt very restless, anxious to be up and stride about; there was so much to do; I never wanted to be still unless I were absolutely prostrate with illness. I had lost a glove and dismissed the matter carelessly: "Oh, we in the East End seldom put them on!" I saw that I had cut across her prejudices—she was essentially precise and ladylike in the rather finicking manner of those days. She rejoined rather stiffly: "I should have thought they would have been worn for cleanliness." "Why not a mask on one's face?" it was on the tip of my tongue to ask her, flippantly; but I reflected that, after all, there was something in her remark. I remember Keir Hardie once snatching off my gloves, half impatient, half playful, and asking almost in anger: "Aren't your hands clean?" So differently people regard dress and its conventions. He was essentially a child of nature, she a little old maid moulded by the conventions in which her life had been cast. All the greater was the courage she needed to defy, as she did, the full force of conventional opinion at its most rigid point; all the greater was the cost to her.

Hostility now turned also upon Dr. Synge. She published that autumn, through the National Labour Press, a pamphlet, embodying her own report on the internment camps in Germany. She was assailed in the Press as a pro-German. On this account the Birmingham Health Committee refused to sanction her appointment as assistant medical officer to the Little Bromwich fever hospital. As an anti-climax to all the uproar, Bishop Bury went, with Government approval, to report on conditions at the Ruhleben internment camp, and confirmed the reports of Emily Hobhouse and Ella Scarlett Synge.

Very aptly the English wife of a German schoolmaster interned in the Isle of Man wrote to me:

"Everyone here believes that prisoners of war in Germany are deliberately ill-treated. No one believes that prisoners of war in England are anything but luxuriously treated. Yet I hear from my husband in Knockaloe that the poorest of the poor men in his compound have been driven by hunger to killing a stray cat and eating it. In Germany, I take it, the papers extol the excellencies of their camps and the villainies of the English camps. My husband was struck on the head with a bayonet by a drunken soldier, and the commandant refused to hold an enquiry. . . . I do not see what can be done ; no paper would publish an account of a camp from an insider's point of view ! "[1]

In October 1916 an appeal addressed to Asquith from the Head Captains of the men interned in Knockaloe Camp, Isle of Man, came to me, with a request for publication. Its phrases were poignant with despair :

" You have created untold misery for thousands and thousands of families, ruined many of us financially and morally. . . .

" Our records show how reasonable and extraordinarily patient we have been. . . . But everything has its limit. . . . A third winter cannot be tolerated unless you want to turn men into maniacs. We have appealed often . . . all in vain. We now demand : let us free to go . . . to our own countries, or any neutral country. . . . 40,000 men (in the whole of Great Britain) are on your conscience. Yours is the responsibility for all the misery caused to the unhappy wives, children, and relations, for all their sufferings and heart-burning. . . ."

I learnt soon after that one of the prisoners at the Alexandra Palace Aliens Internment Camp had been imprisoned in the guardroom for writing to members of the Government about the hardships there.

There came to me also a letter from Alan MacDougal, a supporter of Suffragettes in pre-War days, protesting against " the horror to which, not only the conscript, but the soldier, and above all the young soldier, of whatever category, is condemned by a few weeks of Army life. . . ."

I put the two protests together under the title : " The Trail of the War." A few days later I received a letter from a reader in Derby, telling me that his house had been raided and the *Dreadnought* seized, on account of these letters.

Boards of Guardians, under instruction of the Local Government Board, were everywhere cutting down the miserable allowances of the British wives of alien enemies, and insisting that they must get work, though, as everyone knew, popular prejudice and jingo intimidation made this well-nigh impossible. Many who were not themselves prejudiced against these unfortunates, were afraid to employ them. One poor British wife, who obtained work under her maiden name, was punished by imprisonment for this newly-fabricated offence.

Some time before Grace Jungk, an unfortunate English woman married to a German, had lost her employment on account of her German name.

[1] The American Ambassador in Germany was instructed by his Government not to visit the prisoners of war camps. Wilson perhaps desired to avoid being drawn into the controversy. Meanwhile the British were distributing within the enemy lines illustrated booklets showing German prisoners regaled upon capture with food and chocolate from British " Tommies," and living under happy conditions in British internment camps.

She went to live with her parents in Gravesend, and was fined £5 or a month's imprisonment, because Gravesend was an area prohibited to enemy subjects. Jessie Klose, another poor Englishwoman who had not seen her German husband for ten years, also lost her work, because of her name, and broke a police station window to call attention to her case.

. . . . . . .

In November 1916, three Irishwomen interned in Holloway managed to smuggle a letter out to me. They disclosed that Miss Howsin, the country squire's daughter about whose official kidnapping there had been so much mystery, had been interned, not at all for German associations but for sympathy with the Indian liberation movement. Mrs. Elzie was interned for the same cause. Her son, only seventeen years of age, was on active service in the British Army. All news of him was withheld from her. The women internees were imprisoned in the ordinary cells, under conditions differing little from those of ordinary prisoners. They complained that a prostitute, suffering from venereal disease, had been put on the same landing as the politicals, and was using the same bath, etc.

Many times I received messages asking me to visit interned women, but permission was invariably refused. In fact there was a black list, and I was on it.

. . . . . . .

"Miss Ahlers." A slight lovely girl of twenty-two stepped into my room; her hair, the clear golden which rarely lasts beyond childhood; her beauty so sensitive, so delicate, and flowerlike, that one felt oneself suddenly of coarser fibre. She gazed at me fixedly, her large, dark blue eyes sad and appealing. Then in low tones, she told me her story. Her father, Adolphus Ahlers, a naturalised Englishman of German birth, had been German consul in Sunderland. When war became imminent people flocked back to their respective countries, and Ahlers, in conformity with his consular duties, assisted many persons to return to Germany. Then came the proclamation which forbade Germans to leave this country. Ahlers did not see it for three hours after its publication, and during those three hours, continued, as before, doing what previously had been a duty, but now had become a crime. For this he was charged with treason and sentenced to death.

The shock of it shattered the nerve of his wife. Though he appealed against the sentence, and was aquitted on the evidence he was able to produce, she did not recover. Always frail and sensitive, she was overwhelmed by horror of the War and by the social ostracism and persecution which now befell the family. She suffered acutely from sleeplessness, and began taking veronal.

In the summer of 1915, when the jingo Press was demanding the internment of all Germans, Ahlers, though legally a British subject, was interned at Islington, no reason for the step being given. His wife was terribly distressed. She grew more and more worried and nervous.

In February 1916 she almost died from an overdose of veronal, and was seriously ill for some time. Her mental balance was destroyed. Her children were obliged to hold her down in bed. The girl broke down as she spoke of it. Her brother, a boy of twenty-one, was in the British Army. He had written to the Home Secretary begging that his father might be liberated to settle his mother in a nursing home.

Ahlers, who had heard of his wife's condition from his children, on the fortnightly visits they were permitted to pay him, wrote many times to the Home Office making the same plea but received no reply of any sort. When Herbert Samuel, the Home Secretary, visited the internment camp, Ahlers asked him why his letters were not answered, and pleaded to be allowed out on leave, to attend to his wife. Samuel said he knew nothing of the letters, but promised to see what could be done.

The result of all this pleading at last came sternly: on February 25th, 1916, detectives removed Mrs. Ahlers from her house at Surbiton, for internment at Aylesbury. The authorities gave no reason for this step, but afterwards stated it was for her own protection. Now that the unfortunate woman was interned, she could no longer visit her husband, and their letters to each other were heavily censored. The children were permitted to see their parents, but were only able to speak to their mother in the presence of a wardress. The condition of the interned women differed little from that of ordinary imprisonment. It was more rigorous than that of men. Many times she attempted to tell her daughter of her life within those walls, but always the wardress intervened to prevent her.

On October 26th, 1916, she was removed from Aylesbury to Holloway Prison, where she was placed in the remand hospital. Her husband was informed that she would only be entitled to a visit once in three months, on condition of good behaviour; but the visit could not be from him. Though the authorities gave no reason for her removal to Holloway Prison, and though he could not learn that she had been tried for any offence, he thought she was under punishment. He wrote to the Home Office begging to know whether this were the case, promising to ask her not to do anything insubordinate. As before there was no reply. The husband and wife were now interned within twenty minutes' walk of each other; for months they begged in vain to be allowed to meet. The woman was ceaseless in her appeals. She addressed many petitions to the Home Office, and in her letters to husband and children emphasised her yearning to see him.

After nearly five months, on Thursday, March 15th, 1917, Ahlers was notified that his wife was dangerously ill. On two consecutive days he was taken to her cell and found her unconscious. On the morning of the third day he was told that she was dead. The long-desired visit had come too late. On Tuesday an inquest was held in the prison, whereat it was declared that Mrs. Ahlers had died of veronal poisoning. A letter had been found under her pillow, telling her husband that she could endure her life no longer, begging him to forgive her, and saying she knew her daughter would keep the home going for her father and brothers. Poor girl, she and the younger boy, a child of fourteen, were alone together. The girl believed, and she had said it at the inquest, that if only her mother might sometimes have seen her father, this tragic thing would not have happened. Her soldier brother said the same, protesting that his father was naturalised, and he and his brother and sister were British subjects born in England. He had chanced to get leave that week, and though the regimental authorities had recalled him when they heard of the inquest, he had disregarded their order, and remained to attend it nevertheless.

Dr. Forward, the prison medical officer and deputy-governor, a quiet pale man (I knew him well), had stated in evidence that he had found Mrs. Ahlers unconscious, and as she complained of pains in the head, he though she might be suffering from a cerebral tumour or epilepsy. Not for some hours did he take a stomach washing and send it to the Home Office analyst, who discovered traces of veronal. The usual methods for combating the drug were not taken until valuable time had been lost. The question of how Mrs. Ahlers obtained the drug was never cleared up. There was no evidence from Aylesbury. Her daughter was passionate to know more; what had happened to her poor mother inside those prisons? I was stricken by the futile cruelty of it all.

## CHAPTER LI

### VOTES FOR WOMEN

THE cry of " Votes for the fighting men ! " was a better stick with which to beat the Government, than talk of remote lands, unknown to the multitude, and the squabbles of war strategists. It was now the slogan of Northcliffe, Carson, and a crowd of Tory extremists, and of Labour jingoes like Will Thorne, who cried : " One gun one vote ! " coupled with a clamour for the disfranchisement of Conscientious Objectors, which was eventually obtained. Already in the spring of 1916 *The Times* had been threatening the Government with " strong and natural hostility," unless a special soldiers' and sailors' franchise were introduced. The first Act, to extend the time of the Parliament of which Conscription had been the price, was nearing the end of its term. Unless it were extended, the Parliament must expire in September. The residential changes brought about by enlistment, and the movement of workers to munition areas, would produce wholesale disfranchisement, if the election were to be taken on the old register, and the old qualifications. Adult suffrage, with continuous registration, was the only practical solution. Before Conscription became law, I had seen Lord Northcliffe. I had sought him, because I knew his power, much as I disliked it. I had urged on him that the tremendous cataclysm of the War, and the huge sacrifices it was forcing on the people, should sweep away the old cheeseparing ideas of the franchise, and extend complete adult suffrage to men and women alike. He declared himself impressed by my argument, and with the air of a super-premier promised to take the matter into consideration.

As already explained, our Federation had been demanding a vote for every woman over 21 since before the War. In December, 1915, I put before the women's suffrage societies the plea I had made to Northcliffe. I got our Federation to call an informal conference in the little room behind Miss Thring's suffrage shop in the Adelphi. With the exception of the W.S.P.U. and Mrs. Fawcett's N.U.W.S.S., most of the societies sent delegates. They all, without exception, gave assent. A management committee was appointed, with myself as hon. secretary, to convene a larger conference. I was greatly rejoiced by this cordial acceptance of the wider demand ; but, alas, when the delegates reported the proposal to their executives, the old guard took alarm. The conference which met in the Essex Hall was a stormy one. It was well attended, all the societies were present ; but almost all were bitterly hostile to our project, and not one was prepared, yet, to go all the way with us, in demanding either a vote for every woman over 21, or adult suffrage for all men and women.

Our East End speakers were received with a running fire of disparaging gibes and interruptions.

Mrs. Pascoe, for all her poverty, a matron of sternest virtue, of iron self-respect, was shouted down by the crowd of well-dressed women. Indignantly she faced them, her little black bonnet gone awry in her distress, her worn hands tightly clasped. " I cannot go on," she protested, " till the *ladies* will let me speak ! "

The W.S.P.U. members led the fray against us, declaring that any talk of a wider franchise would be disastrous to the votes for women cause. I was sore-hearted for our East End mothers and young factory girls, assailed thus rudely. I was bruised in spirit by this littleness and myopia of view. I had not expected this hostility, above all not this bitterness. In the *Dreadnought* that week I had published reports of their work, contributed by themselves from most of the suffrage societies ; all had been thus invited and I had given the addresses of those which had not sent reports. Our members took the strife at once more philosophically and more furiously than I. Our " Poplar girls," the Lagsdings and the Watts's, who worked at Morton's biscuit factory in Millwall, surveyed the interrupters with curling lips and scornful eyes, jeering : " It is a pity we are not well educated like them ! "

When the resolution was put only Emmeline Pethick Lawrence and the Women's International League voted with us. Our proposal was hopelessly defeated. Yet the time-spirit was with our demand, the old proposals to enfranchise a million or so of widows and spinsters would never carry. We had stirred the other societies to feel some need for combined action. It was decided to elect a committee, call another conference, send a deputation to the Government. I resigned the secretaryship, and got our Federation to appoint another delegate, feeling it wise to let the representatives of the other societies go their way without me for a while. Our organisation had a work to do in the country no other would undertake : Manhood Suffrage must and would come ; opinion must be prepared to accept Womanhood Suffrage. We must get as broad a measure as we could.

We had a woman workers' petition going the round of the munition factories, declaring that if a woman could cast a shell she could cast a vote. Katie Manicom, organising for the Workers' Union in the Southern Counties, whom we had trained as an organiser in our Federation, Alice MacLennan[1] in the Manchester district, Mrs. Leigh Rothwell, organising for the National Union of Women Workers, the Labour Councillors, Taylor and Dollan in Glasgow, and numbers of others up and down the country, as well as our own W.S.F. branches in Scotland, the North of

[1] Alice MacLennan was the first woman in the Manchester area to be a party to an agreement in the engineering trade between employers and employed. Her great activities were suddenly cut short by a terrible accident. A fire broke out in the Lime Street Hotel, where she was staying. In attempting to escape, she fell through a glass roof, and was terribly hurt. With one leg gone, and other serious disabilities, she bravely returned to her work when she emerged from the hospital.

England, the Midlands, and the South, were getting these forms into the factories. We had a resolution calling on the Government to enfranchise every adult woman and man steadily circulating amongst the Trade Unions. It was passed by hundreds of branches each week, and sent to the Government.

In the spring of 1916 rumours that the Government would shortly deal with the franchise became more insistent. Mrs. Fawcett emerged from her war silence, with a letter to Asquith, suggesting that women might be included in any forthcoming Franchise Bill. Asquith replied that "if and when" it might be necessary to undertake franchise legislation, the considerations in support of women's enfranchisement would be "fully and impartially weighed without any prejudgment from the controversies of the past." Those words were vague; but they might indicate an advance. One could not be sure of it, yet I had regarded our old opponent, Asquith, as preparing to capitulate since our East End deputation had interviewed him in the weeks before the War.

*The Times* predicted the introduction of a measure to enfranchise the soldiers and sailors after Whitsuntide. I got W. C. Anderson to ask whether women would be included. Bonar Law, on the Government's behalf, refused to answer. I wrote to all the suffrage societies and many prominent suffragists appealing to them to concentrate their energy and attention on the situation. In the Federation we redoubled our activities, in meetings and demonstrations, in inducing the Labour organisations to demand, not a mere Registration Bill, but a Franchise Bill to include the whole people. The United Suffragists and others joined in the pressure for women, if not specifically for all women.

I felt that the moment had come for new action. One morning I woke with the thought: "Call another conference, and invite industrial and co-operative organisations, as well as the suffrage societies to counterbalance the stubborn Old Guard." It was clear to my mind that another effort must be made to create a representative Adult Suffrage Council, and that it could be done with success if the basis of representation were enlarged. I broached the matter to Smyth. To my surprise she opposed me: "Why should we always have the labour and expense of every new move which is made? See how we are burdened: Peace, anti-Conscription, Tribunals, Wages, Suffrage—distress work, political work—always something new—we have scarcely finished with one conference, demonstration, exhibition before another is on our hands; often we are preparing for several big functions at once! Get one of the other societies to call it! We can't afford it!"

I could have overcome her objections; but my heart smote me in regard to finance. She was often coming to the rescue, paying this debt or that for the Federation, making a loan to round the week's expense, and then writing it off, as something which never could be repaid. We were raising at headquarters about £7,000 a year apart from donations in kind, which were substantial, and the incomes of the branches; but the sum was too small for our numerous activities. I reflected that there might be wisdom in getting another society to move. I was on the executive of the Women's

International League ; I would propose the conference there. I did so. The idea was accepted. The conference met in June. Several societies, which had opposed Adult Suffrage in January, now supported it. An executive was formed. The initiators of the Women's International League, trained in the compromise school of Mrs. Fawcett's society, assumed the official positions on this committee also ; it was natural, as they had been conveners ; that is the way of politics. I knew them to be but timid converts, and presently, seeing their disposition to compromise, I endeavoured to strengthen the position by calling a conference of industrial organisations in August, which formed an Adult Suffrage Joint Committee with Fred Bramley as chairman and Dr. Salter (afterwards Labour M.P. for Bermondsey) as treasurer. Smyth raised no objection this time. She was as apprehensive as I, that the new Adult Suffrage Council I had taken the initiative in creating, would abandon the adult suffrage pass. "If only I had not stopped you calling the conference !" she repined. I told her it was probably best as it was.

We pressed on with our work, a conference of Labour organisations in Leicester, public demonstrations in Newcastle, Leeds, Bradford, Birmingham, Sheffield, Portsmouth ; we had branches in these, and other towns now. Mrs. Boyce was pioneering for us in Glasgow, and had all the Labour organisations there supporting an adult suffrage demonstration on Glasgow Green. Lansbury and I went up to speak at it. There was a tremendous crowd.

On July 13th, 1916, Asquith announced a Select Committee to consider franchise and registration. Carson protested against such delay in granting the vote to soldiers and sailors, declaring it a "perfect scandal." Six days later the Government motion for a Select Committee was introduced. Its reception was so hostile that it was withdrawn. Herbert Samuel, who moved it on the Government's behalf, deprecated raising the franchise issue in this, or any form, because women's suffrage and other difficult matters would be involved. Carson responded with a gibe :

"What is a munition worker, what is a woman, who is a woman, and should a woman have a vote, and all the rest of it."

Women's chance of enfranchisement seemed precarious indeed ! To make matters worse, Mrs. Fawcett, on behalf of her National Union of Suffrage Societies, issued a manifesto :

"If the proposed new register is limited to reinstating on the roll of voters those men now serving their country in the Navy or Army, or who have lost their qualifications through not fulfilling the conditions of residence which the present electoral law enforces, we should not raise, or attempt to raise, the consideration of our claims."

In our view this was folly of the most egregious sort. We protested :

"If there is time to make changes in franchise or registration, there is time to give votes to all."

The foremost Liberal organ, the *Manchester Guardian*, was advocating Manhood Suffrage, and assuming the postponement of women's suffrage until after the War. I wrote to object ; the Editor answered :

"It is a question between urging the Government to do something they may conceivably be persuaded to do, and something it is impossible to believe this Government, at this juncture, would think of doing."

Margaret Ashton, a veteran suffragist and pillar of Liberalism in Manchester, declared the *Guardian's* attitude "astounding." Its attitude was but too common, however, in Party political circles.

On August 16th Asquith announced that a General Election would again be avoided by a Bill to prolong the Parliament; and that a Registration Bill would be introduced, to prevent the disfranchisement of those who had been voters before the War through change of residence for munition work or service in the Army or Navy. The military authorities objected to men voting at the Front, so voting in the trenches would not be allowed. As to women, Asquith declared they had an unanswerable claim to be included in the extension of the franchise. He could not think that the House would deny this. For himself he added: "I say frankly I cannot deny their claim."

It was a striking *volte face*, though I had expected it. More amazing was the reply of Commander Bellairs, an anti-suffragist of old standing, who averred that Mrs. Pankhurst and her W.S.P.U. had called him out of the House to repudiate Asquith's statement about the women's claim, and to insist that votes for soldiers and sailors must take precedence of votes for women.

"They express the utmost anxiety that the soldiers and sailors shall be given the vote . . . they authorise me to say that they will not allow themselves to be used to prevent the soldiers and sailors from being given the vote."[1]

I read these words in the Official Parliamentary Report with consternation that so complete an abandonment of convictions which had appeared so passionate had been possible. Many people refused to believe the statement authorised; but, in due course, it was reproduced in the *Britannia*, with solemn confirmation.

The answer to those who were deserting the votes-for-women cause for that of enfranchising the men in the trenches, was: *Votes for All.* We raised that challenge a week later at the Euston Theatre, under the auspices of our Adult Suffrage Joint Committee, with a crowd of speakers, representing working-class interests. Shortly afterwards the spectacle was witnessed of Mrs. Pankhurst, supported by life-long anti-suffragists like Leo Maxse, holding a Queen's Hall meeting to demand votes for the fighting men. She protested that Asquith had "used the men to dish the women," and now was trying to "use the women to dish the men." She declared "in the name of women" that they were ready to make any sacrifice in order that the sacrifices already made should not be in vain.[2]

On August 21st Lord Crewe, moving the Bill to postpone all elections for eight months longer, observed that if the franchise were to be extended on the score of war service, women's claims must be considered. Lord Cromer, as usual, raised the anti-suffrage standard, and demanded a definite pledge that the Government would not put votes for women into

[1] Official Parliamentary Report.
[2] *Britannia*, October 6th, 1916.

its Registration Bill. Crewe obligingly furnished the promise, but added, with a view to pleasing everyone, that the Government desired representative people to be considering how to get "a real representative Parliament" after the War. Lord Salisbury replied that nothing of that sort could be considered in war time; but votes for soldiers and sailors was a very different matter, and he was going to table a Bill next day to give votes to them forthwith. Lord Curzon, a member of the Government, addressed a circular to Members of Parliament declaring that the reasons against votes for women were as strong as before the War.

The next stage in this comedy of errors was opened by a question of Sir John Simon whether it would be in order to move women's franchise Amendments to the Government's proposed Registration Bill. Speaker Lowther replied that neither women, nor soldiers and sailors could be brought in by Amendment, unless included in the original Bill—a farcical declaration which reduced Parliamentary debate to absurdity. This was the ruling Lowther had given in 1913, to extricate Asquith from his inconvenient promise to allow a free vote on women's suffrage under the then Reform Bill. Undoubtedly Lowther had followed the Government's behest on that occasion. In order to avoid for the Government a passage at arms with the Tory militarists he now indicated a loophole of escape from his ruling: if an "Instruction" to the House to include such classes of voters were carried, then the amendments would be in order after all! What a happy expedient! How strange that it had not occurred to him in 1913.

By the time the Registration Bill reached Committee, on November 11th, no fewer than ten Instructions had been placed on the Order Paper: to enfranchise soldiers and sailors, to disfranchise Conscientious Objectors, to give votes to all men over twenty-one years, to hold all elections on one day, and so on and so forth. Strange to relate, not a hint of Votes for Women appeared in any one of them!

How came it that the "Parliamentary friends," in whom Mrs. Fawcett and her colleagues placed so much faith, had been thus remiss? How came it that the omission had not been repaired by the recently formed Parliamentary Adult Suffrage Committee, under Sir John Simon, of which Miss Marshall and Mrs. Swanwick, those accomplished Lobbyists, were so confident? How was it that Sir John Simon had made no move to implement the resolution he had tabled for a "wide and simple franchise exercised by both men and women," which had roused my ire by the words "after the War"? Indignantly I read the ten Instructions; indignantly I scanned every line of the Official Report of the debate—not a word about women appeared, from start to finish.

It mattered not—all the Instructions were swept away—not one of them could be moved! Speaker Lowther again reversed his ruling. "On further consideration" he had discovered that, Instruction or no Instruction, no classes of voters other than those originally included by the Government, could be introduced into the Bill!

All this reads like the veriest gibberish to-day, but so the Parliamentary machine revolved in the days of Asquithian rule!

It has been stated elsewhere that following Asquith's famous declaration of inability to deny the women's claim, on August 14th, 1916, a conference of women's suffrage friends met in the House of Commons, under the auspices of Mrs. Fawcett, and devised Votes for Women Amendments to the Registration Bill, which Amendments were "moved the next day in the House and accepted by the Government." This is history as it might have been! Alas for the faith of "Parliamentary friends"! As recorded above, nothing of the sort happened.

The Government had meanwhile secured the Act it needed to avoid a General Election. The Service Franchise agitation abated. The Special Register Bill was withdrawn. A new franchise project was now gradually gaining prominence. When heavily beset by the Service Franchise protagonists, the Government had announced a "Conference," under the chairmanship of the Speaker, to consider the franchise. The scheme had hung fire until after the withdrawal of the Registration Bill; Carson had jeeringly enquired whether the Conference would report before the end of the War, and Asquith had replied, in his old slippery fashion: "The question should be addressed to Mr. Speaker." But now the Speaker's Conference was beginning to assume a new importance. It was announced that the Government would make no further franchise or registration proposals until after the Speaker's Conference had reported. All suffrage attention therefore centred on that Conference. We memorialised it, other societies memorialised it. The anti-suffragists, including Lords Curzon and Cromer, and Rudyard Kipling, and Mrs. Humphrey Ward of course, announced their intention to offer "strenuous opposition" to the extension of electoral rights to women. Rumour followed rumour: women would be included in the recommendations of the Conference; women would not be included. Again and again the Press published professedly authentic information to the latter effect.[1] All was uncertainty; we could only work on.

Robert Cecil was often named as the most reliable supporter of Votes for Women in the Cabinet. A narrow upholder of caste, as it flourishes in this country, I knew he had been an opponent of Adult Suffrage and judged it important to interview him. He agreed to see a deputation from our Federation; but, to my annoyance, stipulated that the proceedings must be private. After this space of time one may disclose that he thought women might get some sort of vote when the next Reform Bill came along, but expressed a rooted objection to Adult Suffrage, and favoured enfranchising merely the million or so women who possessed a separate household, or property qualification of their own. He spoke gently to Mrs. Drake, as though he were touched by her tense earnestness, her innate

[1] So late as mid-January, 1917, the *Daily Chronicle* stated explicitly that the Conference had decided to make no recommendation whatsoever respecting women. On January 13th, 1917, Arthur Henderson, questioned by a naval officer at a Croydon meeting, replied that after Peace was declared, when the Government would be less fully occupied, it would consider the question of votes for women.

refinement and clarity of mind, and the too patent fact that she was overstrained with labour and under-nourished. Towards me he was harsh and hostile, regarding me, it seemed, as one who was leading my unsophisticated companions to dangerous freedom of thought, and to aspirations beyond their station.

It was inevitable, with the War dominating all else, that apathy should be our greatest enemy. Bernard Shaw wrote flippantly :

" It is not worth fussing about the suffrage until we are sure that there are ever to be any more elections. . . . There is nothing more fatal to democracy than elections . . . what is wanted for women is an iron law that Parliament shall consist of a certain proportion of men and women. . . . M.P.s should be *un*selected like jurors."[1]

Does Shaw ever collate and endeavour to reconcile his political utterances ?

The officials of the suffrage societies, including, to my chagrin, the lobbyist of the Adult Suffrage Council I had created, were at the House of Commons enquiring of Members of Parliament what sort of franchise it would be wise to ask for. There was talk of giving women the vote at a later age than men. This insulting proposition was complacently received by many women eager to snatch at whatever franchise they could secure, in fear that they might get no franchise at all. The hateful atmosphere of Parliamentary intrigue was still maintained in face of the great sorrows of the War, the common humanity of all men and women still obscured by prejudices selfish and absurd.

Sir John Simon was deprecating agitation for the Vote, as he had deprecated agitation against Conscription. We scouted such advice and continued working with all the force we could muster. I was convinced that the question whether we should get the franchise, and the scope of the franchise we should get, depended on the women themselves—the more we demanded, and the more insistent our demand, the more we should secure.

Relays of our working women were daily in the Lobby. As they stood there, pleading for their franchise, they saw a party of French munitionettes, brought over by the W.S.P.U., ushered into the inner citadel, with much ceremony. These French women were liberally fêted and entertained. The Lord Mayor gave them lunch at the Mansion House, with Mrs. Pankhurst and a crowd of war enthusiasts. The patriotism of French women was lauded to the skies ; but they are still without the Vote ! So much for the story that it was their war work which secured the franchise for British women.

[1] *Workers' Dreadnought,* September 16th, 1916.

## CHAPTER LII

### "ON THE RUN"

THE war resisters who refused to appear before the tribunals were of two sorts. Some went about their ordinary avocations until arrested; others attempted to escape altogether from the net the Military Service Acts had drawn. Mrs. ——, one of our Bow members who had been in prison as a Suffragette, with the help of another member, a dressmaker living alone, succeeded in hiding her husband and brother-in-law until the War was over. Up and down the country friendly homes were provided for the fugitives, whose position grew daily more precarious, for the authorities stopped men at random, on the chance that they might be absentees. In those days every man out of khaki carried his exemption or discharge papers on his person—if he possessed them. One poor lad fled to Epping Forest, and led there a spare existence feeding on the bark of trees and on forest roots and fruits not usually employed for human consumption, eked out by occasional gifts of food, obtained on nocturnal visits to friends. Mrs. Payne made up a bed for him on her sofa when he ventured to Old Ford. He told her he was "beginning to see green." She feared his mind was unhinged, and lavished on him her tender sympathy. Her heart warmed always to the feeble in mind, for the sake of her own poor Jessie.

. . . . . . .

On November 16th we were at the *Daily Herald* League's annual reunion in the Holborn Hall. Two military officers suddenly appeared on the platform, with half a dozen soldiers to "round up" absentees. A great shouting arose from the "Heraldites." Lansbury was in the midst of a speech. The officers ordered him to cease talking, and procure order for them. He stood silent and frowning with folded arms. Uproar continued until the officers left the platform and a large force of police filed in to hold the doors and examine the papers of every man who attempted to leave. We dragged out the evening to the latest possible time for closing the hall; then the four youths who were war resisters went down to meet their fate. They had been active in propaganda for peace, speaking out boldly at open-air meetings until this night. One woman fainted as she saw them go. Another, in passionate misery, flung herself desperately upon the police advancing to seize them. They hustled her away with them, under arrest. A youth who was found to possess exemption papers, was flung headforemost down the steps.

A crowd of us tramped back to the East End, for the 'buses had ceased running for the night. Mrs. Payne and Minnie O'Brien were crying. We all were sad.

Next day the youths were fined forty shillings, and handed over to the military. The woman who had been arrested was also fined. Such events became common.

. . . . . . .

Alfieri

"MOTHERS' ARMS" TODDLERS TAUGHT BY THE MONTESSORI METHOD

*Wcrkers' Dreadnought*

THE "MOTHERS' ARMS" MONTESSORI CLASS AT LUNCH

Measles had broken out amongst the troops. It was thought infection had been imparted by the garments made by poor women out-workers. Such matters are disregarded when every man fends for himself; but to the military authorities, anxious to keep every man fit for the fight, this was serious. Orders were issued forbidding all sub-contracting and out-work on Army clothing work. Sub-contracting continued extensively, despite the prohibition, but out-work was largely stopped. Large numbers of mothers who toiled at the sewing-machine to keep their little ones were driven into the factories.

Old Mrs. Savoy could get no brushes to make at home. She would not leave her old mate, who would have been helpless without her. Her existence became more precarious than of yore. Sometimes she presided over Mrs X's little shop fixed up in a coal shed. I went to seek her there, and found its black exterior enlivened by many-coloured advertisements. Within, coal was relegated to one small compartment; the rest of the shed was painted white. A counter, draped in white, was decorated with symmetrical tiers of sweets, soap, matches, and blacklead. A little boy, proudly "minding shop," was carefully putting the final touches to the display, whilst eagerly waiting a chance to serve. Two other children stood by the door, hoping that fate would presently deliver to them his post of honour.

In the inner room I could see the broad back of Mrs. Savoy ladling steaming potatoes on to her old man's plate. Turning, she descried me, and came forward with a cheery welcome, explaining the children's presence with a nod: "They all come round to help me."

A neighbour stopped for a moment's chat, and ordered half a hundredweight of coal. Mrs. Savoy dragged a small heavy sack from the coal compartment. The boy pranced from behind the counter, seized the little truck from behind the door, tilted it to the angle easiest for the old woman to place the sack on it, and prepared to take the coal to the neighbour's home. "Don't let him carry it upstairs; he isn't strong enough!" Mrs. Savoy admonished, offering to send her old man round for the job. The neighbour reassured her. A little girl had triumphantly slipped into the boy's place behind the counter, and was serving another child, who gravely considered everything available before spending her halfpenny on a bar of pink sticky stuff, whereof she politely broke off a third, and presented it to the little saleswoman.

This shopkeeping was a labour of love, established by Mrs. X to enable her to take a house out at Woodford as a haven for C.O.'s "on the run." Her own boy was a fugitive war resister, and she was doing for other lads what she trusted others would do for her own.

Another neighbour came in to talk. A man who was passing rallied Mrs. Savoy on her growing trade. She answered with a joke. Despite the dingy surroundings, the poverty harshly apparent, the joyous spirit of William Morris's *News From Nowhere* was alive here.

Our world was aglow with merry-hearted laughter. I shattered the brightness by a clumsy question: "Prices?" Prices! Laughter departed from all their faces. The grim struggle to make ends meet peered with its questioning terror, even from out the children's eyes.

I left my old friend to call on a soldier's wife who had sent for me; the mother of six children, the eldest twelve years old. Her separation allowance was £1 14s. 6d. She paid 5s. 6d. for two miserably tiny rooms; bread, a sparing modicum, cost 9s.; coals 2s., gas 1s. 2d., insurance 10d. Already 18s. was spent, and only 14s. left for the rest! She could not buy all that was required. Therefore in the crowded little kitchen, hung with clothes-lines on which her children's garments were drying, and with the fretful, delicate baby pulling at her skirts, she was sewing away at khaki suits; not for soldiers, but so-called "children's" khaki for boys to play at war. She was paid 8d. to 10d. each for them, and there was actually more work in them than in the soldiers' coats she used to make for 1s. 2d. Her net earnings varied from 2s. to 6s. per week; but even this seemed worth while for her, for every penny counted, and now that her husband had gone to the Front she had to send him food parcels—above all socks, for the Government did not supply enough changes.

It was growing dusk. The fair-haired children outside were tapping on the window with tiny red-cold fingers, impatient for their tea. Their mother looked at them, loving and indulgent, and one by one, the six of them crept in, and nestled round her. "Poor things!" she said. "When they're little's the only joy they get!" She took the youngest in her arms. A seventh chubby little creature ran in and clasped her round the knees. She stroked the toddler's silky head and murmured: "Old Mim, old Mim," and explained to me that this was the child of the box-maker upstairs who, with her mother, plied that trade from four o'clock each morning, the two women working together earning less than twopence an hour between them. I went up for a word with them. The elder told me that she had worked all her life for the same employer. When she began, as a child, she had been paid 3¼d. per gross for making match-boxes; then the rate fell to 2¼d.; it was 3¼d. again to-day, but the sum had lost much in purchasing power during the interim. So much for progress! Her employer then conducted his business in a small room over a stable, and his children played in the gutter with his young employees. To-day he had a big modern factory, whilst she remained just the poor creature she had always been.

. . . . . . .

Mrs. Payne was crying. "Young Fred! They've took him. He can't stand up to it—not like some of them. There's many can't."

He was a Socialist lad, brought up in the tail of the movement which hung about George Lansbury in Bow, taking quite literally the speeches he heard from platforms, holding opinions deeply, in his dumb, slow way; no hero, only one of the poor, who thought he saw the light of a better day.

He would not be a soldier, a murderer of his fellow-workers, his brother-men. He stuck to his last more closely than before, they were shoemakers, working at home; he scarcely left the house. The fatal yellow paper came summoning him to the colours. No! no! they should not take him! He would not wear the khaki! The soldiers came. No, no; he would not go! "They'll shoot you down!" his mother cried, feeble and old. His trembling father bade him go. . . . The soldiers dragged him forth. . . .

They drilled him, and taught him how he should drive the bayonet into other men. Half crazed with fear and horror, he broke away, and sped back to his home. He slunk in like a thief, and sat by the fire, dejected, with idle hands, quaking with fear at the sound of every footstep in the street, afraid of his own thoughts, and his quaking heart. Hating the War no less than he, the old father in terror, bade him go back to camp. The old mother wailed: "They'll give your father time!"[1]

When darkness fell, they coaxed him to go out walking with them. He went with them undeceived, knowing too well where they would have him go. Many a mile they led him, shuffling their old weary feet. His strength, sapped by cold fear, was less than theirs. They took his arms and dragged him on between them. They plied him with intoxicating liquor, though always, until now, they had charged him never to let it touch his lips. So on the threshold of the camp they left him—seeing him enter with his manhood crushed.

. . . . . . . .

When the No Conscription Fellowship committeemen went to prison they exhorted their members to justify war resistance by earnest peace work. Many objectors needed no urging to this end; they were active till the hour of their arrest, and resumed activities, if released pending their appeals, or to alternative service. Presently came a Government notification that should the objectors engage in public propaganda of any sort, even as rank and file demonstrators at meetings, they would be sent back to prison, or recalled to the Army. The N.C.F. had considered holding a meeting in Hyde Park, but counsels of caution now induced abandonment of the project. Some members of the Fellowship now argued that since Conscientious Objectors did not admit the right of the majority to coerce them into the Army they must not even attempt to impose their views on others by speeches on the public platform. So liberty dwindled, courage sank often faint-hearted by the way.

I met Catherine Marshall in Victoria Street. She had grown more

[1] A sentence of imprisonment.

genial since she became Hon. Sec. of the No Conscription Fellowship, as people do in a big, fervent movement. She told me that they had been discussing in the N.C.F. whether it would be right any longer for Conscientious Objectors to take part in strikes, since these were a means of coercing others. To me such inhibitions appeared sad confusionism in face of Capitalism rampant.

My heart was with the War resisters. Those who would change the current of public thought should never fight a rearguard action, but always lead the assault on the citadels of prejudice.

# CHAPTER LIII

## AUSTRALIA REFUSES CONSCRIPTION—THE AMERICAN ELECTORS REJECT WAR —NEUTRALS AND THE BLOCKADE

HUGHES had gone back to Australia to enforce Conscription there. In August his Government ordered the registration of men of military age; but under the Australian Constitution, Conscription could not become law unless it were ratified by a referendum vote of the men and women of the Dominion. The vote was taken in October. Of course it was preceeded by a raging, tearing campaign, in which the Women's party headed by Vida Goldstein, Celia John, and my sister Adela, was in the forefront of the opposition.

Mrs. Pankhurst publicly repudiated Adela, and Hughes at a public meeting, urged his supporters to throw themselves "like Bengal tigers" upon Adela and her companions. Australians visiting here told me that Adela was at that time the most popular woman in Australia. She wrote a book against the War: *Put Up the Sword.* I remembered that when she was working as a W.S.P.U. organiser in Sheffield with Mrs. —— Adela had told me with consternation that Captain —— was in Germany "spying" on account of the expected European war. At the time her story seemed fantastic.

Lynch and Outhwaite in the House of Commons,[1] alleged that a certain General had appealed to Australian soldiers in Belgium to vote for Conscription; that when it was found they were voting seven to one against it, their voting papers were torn up and a new vote instituted, and that eventually the voting was stopped. These allegations were not denied.

The Australians were the only people permitted to vote on Conscription.

. . . . . . . .

In the American presidential election "Peace, eight hours, and a full dinner pail!" were the slogans used to attract voters to the standard of Woodrow Wilson, whose supporters recommended him as the "President who kept America out of the War!" "I am for Wilson because my boys are alive and not dead," became a rallying call to the women, and ten of the twelves States in which they had obtained the franchise gave a majority for Wilson. I was sorry to learn that Alice Paul, who had been to prison with us here, and her militant colleagues in America, should be supporting the nominee of the war faction. They were doing it because Wilson's Government had not given nation-wide suffrage to women in its previous

[1] Official Report, November 1st.

term of office, though they had no guarantee that his rival would do so. Their policy was intelligible; but under the circumstances it gave me another pang of disgust of the tortuosities of politics and the Party system.

Wilson's re-election was received with great joy by Pacifists here. A people had voted on the issue of peace or war, and had declared for peace! Moreover the legend of Wilson, as the high sponsor of a League of Nations which would guarantee a peace without rancour, wherein all nations would have equal justice, had taken firm hold. I had no illusions about him. I knew that if his policies had been markedly in advance of the American majority, and had defied the great moneyed interests, he would not have been acceptable to his party; for, to say the least, American politics were not more ethical than our own. Yet I hoped there might be a peace movement strong enough to keep America out of the War, and to make her, though not wholly disinterested, yet a comparatively impartial mediator between the rival European belligerents.

Had the story of the dreary peregrinations among the diplomats of Europe of Colonel House (Wilson's confidential mentor and factotum) then been known, the bright edifice of Pacifist hope erected upon the orations of Wilson, which was soon to crash down in sorrowful disillusion, would never have been built. The diary[1] kept by House in those years reveals the illusory foundations on which this hope rested. While the war clouds gathered House set forth from Washington to win "everlasting glory" for Wilson and for American civilisation, by gaining an agreement between Britain, France,[2] Germany, and the United States for the "development" or in the Marxist phrase the exploitation of the "waste places" of the earth. That this development might bring spoliation, enslavement, and stultification to the native populations concerned was a matter he ignored.

In return for a share for American enterprise in the exploitation of the backward areas of other continents, it was his plan that Wilson should permit opportunities of exploitation in South America to the European Great Powers. That the United States had no title to dispose of these opportunities mattered not. It was the accepted custom of Great Powers to allow each other "compensation" for their own deeds of plunder against defenceless peoples, by shutting their eyes to similar deeds by their rivals. House made no pretence of being a peace envoy; indeed he disclaimed the title. His project was not to urge ethical considerations, but to negotiate on the basis of the material advantages America had to offer. Both before and after the War broke out, he regretted that America lacked the naval and military power to enforce her wishes.[3] He saw that the European Great Powers were in chronic dispute with each other over the exploitation of backward and defenceless countries. He believed that their quarrels might be ended by an agreement of mutual self-interest, which would obviate war, and lead to a limitation of armaments. He

[1] *Intimate Papers of Colonel House.* Ernest Benn, Ltd.

[2] At first he mentioned Japan instead of France.

[3] Even before the European War he had urged Conscription on the Swiss model for America.

undertook to convince the Governments that such an arrangement would be materially advantageous to them. From the first he made friendship with Britain, as the greatest naval and colonial Power, the core of his diplomacy.

This scheme of House did not fully materialise, but it may be resurrected at some future time.

Already before the War, he had established what passed with him for intimate relations with Sir Edward Grey and his secretary Sir William Tyrrell; and soon believed himself entirely in Grey's confidence. He was delighted with the courtesies of British diplomatic society, yet on the eve of the World War he found "everything cluttered up with social engagements." Played with by Ministers and officials, who did not want to disclose to him the facts of the case, he attributed the evasions which met him to "the slowness of the British mind." He had seen the Kaiser on June 1st, 1914, without having obtained anything tangible from him, save an expression of general desire to co-operate with Britain and America. It had been agreed that House should open conversations to this end with the British Government and keep the Kaiser in touch with developments. House opened negotiations in London on June 10th, saw Grey and Tyrrell, and thereafter Asquith, Lloyd George, Haldane, Crewe. He found them cordial, interested, sympathetic; but only on July 3rd, when the events which finally precipitated the War were in motion, did he get a verbal message, through Tyrrell, that he might convey to the Kaiser his impression that the British Government favoured a better understanding between the nations of Europe. Grey would put nothing in writing, lest by so doing, if it were discovered, he might offend the susceptibilities of France and Russia. House acceded to Tyrrell's proposal that together they should elaborate a plan acceptable to the British Government which Wilson should submit to the other Powers. The leisurely pace of these placid conversations was powerless to meet the hideous emergency confronting humanity. The brief days in which the world might have been saved from Armageddon were running by. Apparently ignorant of this, House prepared to sail for America on July 21st, 1914, happy in Wilson's comment on his reports: "You have, I hope and believe, begun a great thing." In those supposedly frank discussions with the diplomatists, he had failed (if his Intimate Papers are truly intimate) to pierce beneath the surface. He had accepted, without question, Grey's statement that "there was no written agreement between England, France, and Russia; their understanding was one merely of sympathy, and determination to conserve the interests of one another." A message from Grey, before he sailed, that the Austro-Serbian situation was causing him grave concern, may possibly have been a hint that intervention by the United States might be tried, as a last expedient, to stave off the catastrophe. Who can tell? When hostilities were joined, House planned to assist the Entente to gain the advantage. The war terrors of Europe did not fail to influence him. He feared that Germany, if successful, might expand in Central and South America, seizing what she chose there without regard to the international bargain he desired. He wished America armed, urged Wilson to send the American General Wood to the war zone, to get experience of handling large bodies of troops, endeavoured in November 1914 to induce Wilson to create a reserve Army.

Yet he still kept in mind his view of Wilson as the world mediator. Again and again he proposed to Grey that Wilson, with professions of neutrality, should intervene to propose a settlement, on the basis desired by the Entente, on the understanding that should Germany be unwilling to accept this basis, America would enter into the War on the side of the Entente. According to his own diary, House was at pains to make the Germans believe that he and the President were wholly neutral.

Grey, whom House regarded "with affection," made a show of approving Wilson's mediation, in principle, but opposed every suggestion to carry it into effect. Ever cordial in the abstract, he receded coldly when anything concrete was proposed; to the impressions he had deliberately given, never constant. In December 1914 he had intimated through the British Ambassador in Washington, that he "did not think it would be a good thing" for the Entente to stand out against peace proposals embracing an indemnity to Belgium and a satisfactory plan for disarmament. He negatived the value of his utterance by adding that it was merely his personal attitude—a polite politician's manner of indicating that his words merely express a pious utopian aspiration. In February 1915, when Grey was actually negotiating the secret treaties with their large projects for territorial annexations, both East and West, he told House that he was "extremely anxious" for Britain not to claim anything save evacuation and indemnity for Belgium but unfortunately the Dominions of South Africa and Australia objected to surrendering the German colonies they had taken. So late as February 1915, Grey assured House that he desired the so-called "freedom of the seas," the immunity of merchant shipping during war; but when House proposed that food ships should be immune, in order to induce Germany to abandon submarine warfare on merchant ships, Grey refused to come to terms. In the autumn of 1915 and the spring of 1916 House repeatedly urged Grey to agree that Wilson should offer peace parleys and intervene on the side of the Entente, should Germany refuse to assent; but Grey in each case rejected the offer. At that time House stipulated that the peace conference must formulate a rule to limit armaments on land and sea, make warfare more humane towards neutrals, and bind the signatory Powers to side against any nation refusing to adopt other methods than that of war. Such projects were being denounced in the loudest key by British jingoes; Grey refused to consult either his colleagues or allies about them. The Entente Governments desired no negotiations with Germany; they wanted to vanquish her utterly. Until America were prepared to come into the War for a victory of the knock-out blow she could stay outside.

. . . . . . . . .

The British blockade was steadily being developed. From striving to induce neutral nations contiguous to Germany to prohibit the export there of articles declared contraband in London, the British Government passed to making direct agreement with neutral traders not to sell goods to Germany. Then followed rationing of neutral imports and placing of an embargo on all goods regarded as not essential for the neutral countries' own needs, a system which led to hunger and misery in the small countries, which submitted perforce, because they knew that Britain could stop all their imports if she chose.

The horrors of the blockade, above sea and under sea, were realised only by the men who took part in it. A veil was drawn over the ruthless murdering by submarine torpedoes, ramming, camouflaged war-boats with masked guns, depth charges, decoy boats with submarines in tow, and other hideous inventions of the period. The shooting, drowning, and hanging of men by their captors amid the vastness of mid-ocean, went for the most part unchronicled. When occasionally some ugly deed came to light, the nation of its perpetrators extolled it as an act of heroism or of justified reprisal; their opponents bitterly condemned its inhumanity. Though the ruthless submarine warfare against merchant ships had been abandoned, and attacks on merchant shipping on accepted lines had been reduced for a time, the submarine menace was again growing.[1]

To the small neutral nations the losses by submarine warfare were very terrible. Norway lost in the War which was not hers 831 ships and 1,200 men. She was grievously troubled by food panics and scarcity. Switzerland subsisted sparely; her import of raw materials was thrust down from four million metric tons in 1914 to two millions in 1918; her import of foodstuffs from 1,300,000 to 700,000 tons. Sweden imported an average of 284,000 tons of grain in 1911–13, only 89,000 tons in 1917–18. Her Government was obliged to ration both food and clothing. Danish imports fell, on a quantitative index, from 100 in 1913 to 33 in 1918. So terrible was the food shortage in Holland that it is estimated that the Dutch people were consuming less per head of bread, meat, fat, and sugar at the close of the War than the Germans themselves.

American commerce was profiting enormously by the War. The total value of United States exports had risen from 2,466 million dollars in 1913 to 4,333 million dollars in 1916, the excess of exports over imports having risen from 653 million dollars in 1913 to 2,136 million dollars in 1916. There were unprecedented imports of gold. In 1916 alone the gold import of the United States exceeded the export by $403,760,000. To redress the adverse balance against this country regulations were issued for the mobilising of foreign securities and there were huge shipments to America of gold, securities, and foreign bonds. America was growing richer at the expense of Europe; a fact which aroused fear and detestation in British trade and financial circles.

In America Wilson's policy was denounced as spineless and slothful.

[1] *Vessels sunk by Submarines.*

| | 1914–5 | 1916 |
|---|---|---|
| British merchant vessels | 231 | 288 |
| British fishing vessels | 168 | 134 |
| Allied merchant vessels | 76 | 344 |
| Neutral merchant vessels | 93 | 332 |
| Total | 568 | 1,098 |

The " cotton men " were complaining, for the weight of cotton export had fallen since the War, though the price had increased to more than cover the reduction. Even the exporters of munitions, wheat, bacon, oil, metals, motor-cars, and others, who were reaping huge profits from supplying the Entente, and as much of the rest of the world as the British blockade would permit, complained of the delays and hindrances of the blockade, the permits for dealing with neutrals, the blacklisting of certain firms. Yet the sympathies of American Big Business lay on the whole on the side of those whom Fate and the British Navy made its customers. And the submarine menace raised much greater indignation than the exactions of the British blockade. American super-patriots required the importance of their country to be asserted. Like Colonel House they considered the President of America, by reason of his office, as " the most influential man in the world " and desired the present occupant of the White House to take a strong line. Colonel House considered the Entente statesmen should be grateful to Wilson, that instead of maintaining a strict neutrality and refusing to permit the export of arms to the belligerents, he had allowed an unlimited supply of what House patriotically believed were the only reliable shells at the service of the Entente. He was nettled that the British did not forget that these had been supplied at a handsome profit. President Wilson himself was fully seized of the fact that the great interests controlling America would by no means tolerate the sort of neutrality which would prevent them making dollars out of the European War. He did not press Britain very seriously in relation to the blockade, even when it violated his own and the generally accepted conceptions of international law. He recognised that Britain was able to prevent America doing effective trade with Germany, and that American commerce was securing very ample compensation through the increased trade with the Entente at greatly inflated prices. He saw to it that the loans which his Government permitted Britain to raise in the United States were mainly spent there. The more orders for goods the Entente poured into America, the more the great interests were disposed to look with favour on the cause of their customers. The more American money was lent to the Entente, the more important it was to Americans who lent it that the Entente should be victorious. Many were chafing against neutrality. Re-elected as the " Peace President," Wilson awaited only the appropriate moment to bring America into the War.

## CHAPTER LIV

### THE MINISTRY OF PENSIONS—SOUTH WALES COALFIELD PASSES INTO POSSESSION OF THE BOARD OF TRADE

IN November 1916 the *Daily News* asserted that in London alone 2,000 disabled soldiers had been discharged either without pensions or with no more than a dole of 4s. 8d. per week. The same month the Government so far bowed to the widespread outcry against the cruel maladministration of pensions, as to introduce a Bill to co-ordinate the work, by setting up a sort of joint Board of those already dealing with it. The rank and file Members of Parliament had formed their own pensions committee, in view of the hideous scandal which the question had become, and led by its energetic secretary, J. M. Hogge, it was able to force the Government to establish a Ministry of Pensions, for both Army and Navy, with a Pensions Minister at its head. This was the first substantial act of independence by a much-dragooned House of Commons since war broke out. It was the outcome of an acute evil.

The Statutory Committee, established after so much controversy, was now swept away. Arthur Henderson became the first Minister of Pensions. I wish I could report a great revolution in the administration of pensions. Alas! it remained miserly and truculent. The instruction given by the assistant manager of an Irish employment exchange to a new member of his staff about that time embodied the spirit equally to be found in the Pensions administration:

"I suppose you understand that our main object here is to save the fund, and we never pay benefit if we can possibly avoid it."

The supplementary grants of the Statutory Committee, of which the promise had been very much greater than the performance, disappeared with the old machinery, without any pledges to improve the official scale. I asked whether such pensions were to continue as 10s. 9d. a week for a man and wife and seven children, the man having a shattered leg, which was causing him great pain, and would prevent him ever returning to his trade; or 7s. a week for a man, wife, and five children, the man, an old soldier with India and Boer War medals, suffering from an internal complaint.

Always new efforts were made to renew enthusiasm for the War. Mothers' Day was inaugurated and linked with the War panoply. A woman wrote to me expressing her rage and sorrow that mothers should be "put upon the same basis as 'flags of all nations.'":

"To represent them as mostly desiring tickets for cinemas and 1s. teas with a drive out on top of a 'bus for a great treat, a few peppermints thrown in perhaps, is really the very height and depth of mistaken philanthropy, or desire for notoriety. What mothers want is their husbands and sons intact. . . . How I hate this taking from us of our able-bodied, to whom we have a right to look for sympathy and love! And what is offered to those who are bereaved and cannot be comforted? A few coins, certificates, buttons, badges, rubbish of all sorts! What is there for those who return crippled, insane, nervous wrecks? A beautiful hospital in which to live out their days, chocolates, cigarettes, parts of the alphabet sewn on their coats, visits from duchesses. . . . All sense of values seems lost. . . . I am every day freshly disappointed in my sex—they are too meek and swallow everything imposed upon them as their duty. The men, I believe, would be thankful if we had the courage to make known in high places our scorn, detestation, and silent heartbreak over their barbarism."

That woman had a glimpse of the horror and waste of the War. She was right; the women were too meek. Only one in all those years importuned me with determination to get her husband out of the Army. The only son of Austrian parents, whom he supported by watchmaking, he was himself a British subject by reason of his birth here. His father, a feeble old man, had been cruelly and needlessly interned. The very day his father was incarcerated, the young man was taken for the Army. Previously exempted as medically unfit, he was the victim of the latest "comb out." From France he wrote to his wife repeatedly that his reason would be overthrown were he compelled to remain in the trenches. She was pregnant with their first child. Torn by a grief overwhelming at this separation from her husband, she was plunged with her old mother-in-law into unaccustomed poverty by the removal of their breadwinner, on whose behalf came only the wife's allowance of 12s. 6d. a week! Their home had been given up. They were living in one room in a slum. Even so they went short of food. These were the elements of the case. I had small hope of achievement when I commenced, but by sheer persistence I managed to get him released. She came frequently to spur me, white and tragic, beautiful and passionate. I was stirred to the depths by her torrents of grief. I gave her tea each time she came and was pained by her ravenous hunger.

. . . . . . . .

The Welsh miners had adopted a resolution threatening to strike on November 27th if the Government had not taken control of the food supplies by that date, as well as to secure the increased wage to which they were entitled by the rules of the coalfield, in accordance with the rise in the selling price of coal. The strike was averted by a Government promise to appoint a Food Controller; by a temporary increment of 15 per cent. in wages whilst an audit of coal prices was being made; and a D.O.R.A. order that the South Wales mines "should pass into the possession of the Board of Trade." The ownership was merely nominal, but the miners were jubilant at this sign of their power.

I was often among them and saw them flushed with triumph. The South Wales Socialist Society, which led the Left Wing in the mines, met in the Aberystwith Café, a modest little tea-shop at Tonypandy, in the Rhondda. The advent of the social revolution was confidently discussed there. By demanding higher wages and lower hours, getting all mine workers into the Miners' Federation, and gaining control of the Federation by the Left Wing, it was thought that, in some crisis, Socialism would be secured. Dai Davis, the secretary, assured me that because of the Navy's dependence on South Wales coal the miners held the fate of the British Empire in their hand. When the right time came, they would lead the rest of the proletariat into the promised land, where all should be "better than well." He brushed aside my warning that the Navy would soon be run by oil. "Impossible!" he declared. "Impossible! It cannot be done!"

I stayed in his house, a poor place. His wife, tired and careworn, was sewing for their living, for his wage-earning was interrupted by his outside activities. His colleagues were mainly better read and more thoughtful than he. Charlie Gibbons, whose eyesight was compelling him to leave the mines, aspired to a lectureship at the Central Labour College. W. M. Hay, jolly and portly, in the War aftermath of unemployment and disillusion, became a lecturer in the brewers' interests against temperance legislation, a dismal denial of his old faith and work. Will Mainwaring, the learned Marxian and real leader of the group, with his caustic tongue, was feared and respected by all the rest. His thesis was ever that the long era of Capitalism was preparing for the sure and inevitable advent of Socialism. Most excitable, most active and talkative, least theoretical and visionary, was A. J. Cook. They all made game of him. Yet he had the ear of the crowd, for he had been to prison for the cause. He cried his convictions to the four winds, whilst others expressed their most revolutionary sentiments at the Aberystwith. He was a lean, gawky fellow, poorly and carelessly dressed, his red hair dishevelled, always hoarse and shaken with a cough from too much oration, limping from an injury to his leg, rushing from meeting to meeting, with scant time or patience to talk in cafés.

. . . . . . . .

The committees appointed to regulate food prices in the early months of war had been forgotten. Coal had risen in price since the Coal Act, which was passed ostensibly to keep the price stationary.

In November 1916 the *Statist* estimated that since the War the price of vegetables had risen 129 per cent.; sugar, tea, and coffee 74 per cent.; textiles 70 per cent.; sundries 67 per cent.; minerals 63 per cent.; animal food 58 per cent. "Standard Bread," much lauded by the *Daily Mail*, produced by milling a higher proportion of the wheat, was now compulsory; but the cost was not thereby lowered. The quartern loaf reached 10½d. on November 6th and the waste available for animal food rose steeply in price. Potatoes had more than trebled in price. The supply was restricted and a potato crop failure in Ireland occasioned acute distress, but the usual relief was not forthcoming. The distress committees under the Unemployed Workman Act and the Mayors' committees had all been closed down. Since 1914 sugar had been controlled by a Government Commission which limited its issue. The 1916 issue had been only 65 per cent. of that permitted in 1915, and was still to be further reduced. Shopkeepers persistently refused to sell sugar, except to purchasers of other commodities, often insisting that at least 4s. worth of other groceries must be bought. Poor mothers were often compelled to buy things they did not want or could not afford in order to get sugar.

Threatenings of industrial unrest now induced some slight measures of food control. Only the price of milk was to be fixed, and at the existing high rate, without guarantee that further increases might not be permitted. The price of other commodities might be regulated, if there were widespread popular clamour. In all schemes for price-fixing, the Government assumed that the profit of manufacturers, importers, and traders must be greater than before the War. The increased cost was therefore passed on from stage to stage, the whole burden falling on the poor working-class mother, anxiously clutching her slender and shabby purse in the market-place ; for she alone had no one on whom she might deposit the load. The Chancellor of the Exchequer had by this time received more than a hundred million pounds in excess profits tax, more than the entire revenue of the State at the beginning of the last decade of last century, and though nominally this was 60 per cent. of the vast profits being made, everyone knew it was far from being the case.

Colonel House summed up the situation aptly enough at the beginning of the War for all the belligerents, though his strictures were only applied to Germany :

"The big industrialists are making big money (Krupps, etc.) and making the War last by insisting on keeping Belgium (in order to control the European steel, iron, and coal trade), and the Yunkers (Prussian country squires) are also in favour of continuing the War, as they get three or four times the former price for their products and are getting work done by prisoners at 6 cents a day."[1]

The danger of permitting the food supply of the people to be at the mercy of private trading was again revealed when Runciman told the Commons[2] that private dealers were refusing to accumulate the stocks of grain it was wise to have ready to meet emergencies. The traders feared the large stocks accumulated in certain grain-exporting countries might be freed by the military occupations, and thus coming on to the market might reduce prices. Private enterprise would not take the risk of losing money even to avert the possibility of famine. He further disclosed incidentally that stores of wheat, which the Australian Government had bought up to benefit the British people, had remained unused in the granaries. It had been pretended that it was not worth while using British ships to fetch it. Only now when wheat prices had risen to record height,

[1] *Intimate Papers of Colonel House*, Vol. I, p. 104. Benn.
[2] October 10th, 1916.

and the corn merchants had reaped a rich harvest therefrom, would this Australian wheat be fetched from store.

Towns' meetings to complain of prices were held in Poplar and other places. Runciman replied that the Government had safeguarded the people by purchasing the whole export of frozen meat from New Zealand and Australia, as well as much of the South American output, and had requisitioned nearly all the ships plying to those countries which were fitted with refrigerated storage. It was made known, however, that whilst the Governments of Australia and New Zealand had fixed the rate at which their farmers must sell, in order that the British Government might purchase cheaply, the British Government had sold the meat it did not require for the Army at high prices, in the interests of the meat rings, which were exploiting the public.

High freight charges still remained one of the principal causes of high food prices. Universally condemned, this exploitation continued. Yet Runciman told the Commons that out of 10,000 ocean-going steamers by October 1916 only 1,000 were left free to conduct their own operations, and some of these were trading on behalf of the Allies or the Dominions.

The price of ships had risen to enormous heights. Any old hulk afloat was worth a fortune. The *Scottish Field* recorded some of the phenomenal prices paid for these arks of prosperity. The *Scottish Glen*, sold in February 1910 for £3,000, after six years' wear and tear, now fetched £47,250. The *Alcides*, sold in January 1912 for £6,100, fetched £66,750 in 1916. The *Cossack*, after eight years' seafaring, increased in price from £7,250 in March 1908 to £83,500 in 1916. The *Scarpino*, sold for £33,250 in October 1915, a year later was sold again for £78,000!

A Departmental Committee on prices was appointed, but it recommended only some vague minor reforms. Runciman's policy, the policy in fact of the three war governments, was to stimulate production and trading by permitting large profits and to use the scourge of high prices to limit popular consumption. All was organised on the basis of a soulless utilitarianism, in which the individual was nothing, Art was nothing, Science nothing except in so far as it might minister to war. That is, and must be, warfare, as modern nations make it; for more and more the entire nation becomes involved.

## CHAPTER LV

### PEACE TALK IN THE CABINET—LLOYD GEORGE OUSTS ASQUITH

THOUGH the Secret Treaties[1] between the Entente Powers were secret still, vast annexationist war aims were gradually being disclosed.

Asquith at the Lord Mayor's Banquet declared the War must continue till Turkey was expelled from Europe, an objective remote indeed from the vindication of "poor little Belgium" and the protection of "the sacred soil of our ally France!" of which we had heard so much when war began! Since the time of Disraeli the Great Powers had intended the despoliation of Turkey. Only their mutual rivalries had deferred the matter so long.

The German Chancellor now alleged that in 1915 England, France, and Russia had entered into a secret agreement, guaranteeing to Russia territorial rule over Constantinople, the Bosphorus, the western shores of the Dardenelles and its hinterland, whilst Asia Minor was to be divided between Britain, France, and Russia, and France was to have Alsace-Lorraine; the International Peace Union now talked of in Britain and the United States was not for international justice but to guarantee the annexations to be made by the Entente in the present war—a grim charge the future was to justify but too well.

David Mason[2] asked the Prime Minster for time to discuss a motion that in view of von Bethmann Hollweg's repeated statements that Germany was prepared to negotiate for the termination of the War, a commission should be appointed with that object. Bonar Law contemptuously refused. The Commons cheered. If Members experienced regret that the slaughter should continue, they did not show it. Next day Mason raised the same question on the Adjournment, but Members declined to listen: the House was counted out. Philip Snowden posed the direct question whether the secret agreement alleged by the German Chancellor had actually been concluded. The British Government refused a reply; but the Russian Minister, Trepoff, presently confirmed a substantial part of the German allegation, by announcing that the Allies had "established in most definite fashion the right of Russia to the Straits and to Constantinople." He blurted out that it was Russia's intention to hold the Allies to fight with her until German and Austrian Poland had been

[1] Later published by the Russian Bolshevists when they seized power.

[2] For his championship of the Suffragettes before the War the Liberal Association which had sponsored him had warned Mason it would seek another candidate at the next election.

wrested from the Central Empires and "united in inseparable union with Russia."[1]

People might wonder whether the tyranny of the Russian Czardom might, or might not, be less terrible than that of the Sultan of Turkey. All the world knew the sufferings of Poland in the autocratic grip of Russia. The Socialists in the Russian Duma rose in their places to protest and impeded the proceedings till a dozen of them had been removed. Philip Snowden declared that henceforth he would vote against the war credits, as Karl Liebknecht and his group had done in Germany; but he did not carry out the intention. He explained to the I.L.P. conference that his Parliamentary colleagues considered the step inadvisable.

The selling by auction of the German properties seized in Nigeria was discussed in Parliament. Carson, the Tory, Josiah Wedgwood, the future Labour man, demanded the exclusion of neutral bidders. The Government spokesman, probably in deference to powerful America, answered that it was desired to throw the bidding open to all save enemy subjects, because, since the Germans had been ousted, the British companies had formed a ring, and had driven prices up threefold, whilst paying the native producer less than before. Sir Alfred Moritz Mond, son of a German chemist, whose home would assuredly have been raided had he chanced to be poor, replied with the fervour of a true patriot: "I should have thought it was the British Empire first, the British trader second, and all other considerations afterwards; and the native (an after-thought) in his right place."

Like many another, I was stung to wrathful misery by knowledge that the acquisitive aims of the vast struggle for power were steadily enlarging. One preached, one knew, that the War was being fought for materialistic ends; yet one could scarcely endure the concrete realisation of the fact. Peace, and the popular government of the world to end this capitalist system of ruthless materialism, stood out for me as the two great needs of the hour.

It was announced that certain members of the Government would tour the country to revivify the flagging fires of war enthusiasm. I wrote to the Ministers and to the Press that every week at great provincial meetings, attended by thousands of people, I was putting, and carrying with few dissentients, two resolutions:

"This meeting calls on the Government to introduce a Bill to enfranchise every man and woman of adult age."

"This meeting calls on the Government to stop the War."

I asserted that the campaign of the Ministers must fail to arouse enthusiasm, unless the Government would publish its terms of peace, and give definite assurances that aims of conquest and secret agreements would be abandoned, the War brought to a speedy end, and the whole people enabled, as voters, to pronounce their judgment upon the War at the next General Election.

[1] If the Czardom had not been overthrown, there is no doubt the victorious Entente would have given Russia a free hand to effect the conquests her government desired.

Though still we were a minority, in large measure it was true that enthusiasm was passing to the side of the Pacifists. Yet though our numbers grew, the country still lay under the hypnotism of the War propaganda thundered from Parliament, platform, Press, and pulpit, and the compulsion of the D.O.R.A., Conscription and the Munitions Acts. Whoever might so desire, had freedom to break up the meetings of Pacifists. The office of the Peace Society was sacked. A conference advocating peace negotiations held by the National Council for Civil Liberties in Cardiff, and attended by 415 delegates, was raided with great violence by a mob organised by the jingo, Stanton, Member for Merthyr, and the notorious Captain Tupper, at that time associated with Havelock Wilson, the renegade leader of the Seamen's Union. J. H. Thomas, the railwaymen's M.P., complained of the affair in Parliament. Stanton retorted that he would do the same for the adjourned conference to be attempted in Merthyr. The Welsh miners threatened a one-day strike if the conference were disturbed. The Home Secretary induced Stanton to "ignore" the conference.

A bye-election occurred in North Ayrshire, a Conservative seat. The Coalition Government put forward a Conservative, Colonel Hunter-Weston, who was fighting at the Front, and thus had all the glamour of war service, and might escape the stigma of war profiteering and callousness towards the soldiers which could be cast upon home-staying politicians. Humphrey Chalmers, without influence, organisation, or party backing, came forward as Peace candidate. Aided only by a few Socialists, he held meetings of tremendous enthusiasm. He polled only 1,300 votes against his opponent's 7,000 ; yet the Labour Party had scored only 1,800 votes in the previous election, with all the backing of its leaders and machinery.

The German Chancellor, his seat in the Reichstag decorated with flowers to lend a glamour to the event, introduced the Compulsory Civilian Service Bill, recommending it with a call to sacrifice :

"Extreme necessity demands an iron will. . . . The German people is faced with a great trial. . . . Every sacrifice is consecrated by the thought that we are all carrying forward stones for the building of a better future for the fatherland."

The Minister of the Interior declared :

"This Bill will become the life of the people and the highest freedom in the highest moral sense. Away with the word compulsion !"

Such utterances are ever the stock-in-trade of war-mongering : "The comradeship of the trenches !" "All classes standing together !" "A better Britain !" Lloyd George had told Colonel House of the good the war would bring to Britain :

"Life will be lengthened, because of better habits and the training of youth. The productive power will be strengthened, because the drones have all been put to work, and will probably continue there. . . . Untold millions will be saved, because of the simple lives people will live from now."[1]

How grimly those words read in the long-drawn years of post-war depression, with the unemployed in Britain and the United States counted by the million, Germany bankrupt and a panic " National Government " formed in Britain to save the £, by an all-round lowering of the standard of life and culture of the middle and working classes !

. . . . . . . .

Heart-rending stories came through to us from Belgium, of men snatched from their homes to work in Germany, of Belgian women struggling with the soldiers to retain their husbands and sons, and flinging themselves in front of the trains which bore their dear ones away. Lord Newton demanded in the House of Lords that the German war prisoners and internees here[2] should also do their part in winning the " War for Freedom," with the black, brown, and yellow men imported to fight willy-nilly, from all the territories under dominance of the Allies.

George Chicherin, who later was to become the Commissar for Foreign Affairs in revolutionary Russia, was writing to the little proletarian papers to protest that the Communist club in Soho had been raided and looted by police and soldiers. The wine had been drunk, watches, rings, and other belongings confiscated. An officer had excused all irregularities by the phrase : " It is war time ! "

" One wonders why war against Germany justifies looting in Soho ! " protested Chicherin. A little earlier he had been complaining that the British authorities had been aiding the Tsarist in suppressing the Russian Seamen's Union. Liberty, poor Liberty ! she leads a precarious life in time of War !

. . . . . . . .

When Friedrich Adler killed Count Stürgkh, the Austrian Prime Minister, a shock thrilled us ; for Stürgkh was one of the five Ministers in Austria who had signed the declaration of war ! Adler's action was remarkable, because his father, Viktor Adler, for more than a quarter of a century the leader of the Austrian Socialist Party, had asserted it the duty of Socialists to " spill their last drop of blood " in defence of their country " in this war : and had declared it " natural " for them to send representatives into the Coalition War Cabinets.

It was said that Friedrich Adler hoped his deed would be the signal for the rising of the workers against the War. He risked his life on the throw. It failed of immediate result ; but the temper of the people was such that the death penalty could not be imposed, and in two years he was free.

. . . . . . . .

[1] January 14th, 1916. *Intimate Papers of Colonel House.* Benn.

[2] They were employed in agriculture and we have it on the authority of the *Encyclopædia Britannica* that they proved docile and efficient, and were more popular with the farmers than the C.O.'s. !

Peace talk was everywhere growing. In public hotly repudiated by the British Government, it was actually going on in the War Committee of the Cabinet itself.

As Asquith revealed later there was disquiet and disunion in the inner circle. General Sir William Robertson[1] on August 31st, 1916, confidentially informed the Cabinet that in his opinion negotiations for peace might come from the enemy Powers any day. He urged that the British should decide upon their terms and secure the assent of their Allies before meeting their enemies in conference. In October the Cabinet received reports from the Navy that the submarine difficulty was acute and British destroyers insufficient to cope with it. The Board of Trade notified the Cabinet that the losses from submarine warfare outpaced replacements by shipbuilding; the President of the Board of Agriculture that the potato crop had failed, breadstuffs were short, and the supply of fish below the normal. Food, which had long been made costly by the machinations of speculators, was now actually growing short. From the Army came complaint that "man power" was reaching its inevitable limit, that British war casualties had reached 1,100,000 men and 15,000 officers.

In face of these gloomy findings Asquith invited the members of the Cabinet War Committee to express their opinions. Lord Lansdowne, the aged leader of the Conservatives in the Lords, responded on November 13th with a paper in which he reviewed the situation gloomily, deprecated prolongation of hostilities and affirmed that the Government ought not to discourage any movement in favour of an exchange of views between the belligerent Powers on the possibility of a peace settlement. To this declaration of Lansdowne, Asquith attributed the destruction of his Government.

The old Peer was replied to by another Tory aristocrat, Lord Robert Cecil, cadaverous and gloomy, a monk, one would say, who had mistaken his calling. He had opposed, in his time, old-age pensions, the miners' eight-hour day, every effort towards social solidarity and kindliness—with the exception of votes for women, and even that he would have with a class bias. Confident in his ghoulish work of operating the hunger blockade, he declared peace at that time "could only be disastrous"; the War must go on. To this end "drastic changes" must be made in civilian life; imports must be further restricted to limit the food consumption of the people.

. . . . . . . .

Rumania was in the War at last!

Tempted by promises of territory which would double the size of the country, on condition of immediate entry into the War, her Government joined the Entente in August, under a treaty signed by Britain, France, Italy, and Russia. The "Easterners" were delighted. The noisiest of them, the *Britannia*, declared "joy inexpressible" on learning the news. Alas! poor Rumania! So soon she was overwhelmed by superior

[1] Chief of the Imperial General Staff at the War Office and anathematised by certain extreme militarists as pro-German.

forces. The cry went up from the "Easterners," as it had done when Serbia lay in like case, for more men to be sent from Britain, Italy, Russia, anywhere, to die in that far-off land, for honour and glory and to strike a blow, if a vain one, in the struggle to prevent food supplies reaching the hungry people of Austria and Germany. The forces demanded by the "Easterners" to relieve Rumania, to attack the enemy Powers on their Eastern flank, were not sent. Lloyd George sprang to his favourite rôle of the defender of small nations: "Is it necessary that a little nation be laid on the altar of the War every Christmas?" he fulminated—an impertinence, truly, from one whose policy was to drag the small nations into the conflict, as pieces in a ghastly game of chess!

Cabinet discord came to a head at last. The extreme militarists, spurred by the whips and scorpions of the Northcliffe Press, had decided that Asquith must go. The reverses to British arms in the Dardanelles and Mesopotamia; the surrender to the Turks of 9,000 British and Indian troops at the fall of Kut, and the 24,000 casualties incurred in vain efforts to relieve the besieged; the stalemate in the West, the meagre results of the costly fighting on the Somme—these demanded a scapegoat.

Supported by Northcliffe and the Tories, Lloyd George's passage to the Premiership was easy. His proposal that Asquith, whilst remaining nominally Prime Minister, should be permitted to attend the War Council, but debarred from a vote in its decisions, was humiliating in the extreme. No Prime Minister could accept it. His position, had he done so, would have been tantamount to that of a bankrupt who must submit to the administration of his estate by the Official Receiver. The scheme was acclaimed by the Tory Press because it must obviously mean Asquith's resignation. The *Times* declared that Lloyd George would lose his backing if he flinched from his insistence. Even that pillar of Liberalism, the *Manchester Guardian*, assented, maintaining a change of Government was necessary, on the ground that the Asquith administration had mismanaged the War. Asquith attempted to form a new coalition, but neither the Tories nor Lloyd George would serve under him now upon any footing.

So Asquith fell. I had no regret for his political demise. He had always been a calculating politician, with an arid lawyer's brain, knowing little of human sympathy, the result in part, perhaps, of the repression in childhood so common in his day. His main merit, a well-bred loyalty to colleagues (which was so conspicuously absent in Lloyd George), had too often proved a political vice, making a close corporation of government, blanketing the truth from emergence. His departures from his promises were so gross in their frequency and callousness as to have become a by-word.

The daily jottings he made during the War and afterwards published,[1] have revealed an abyss of petty rivalry and reckless incompetence in his Government which will astonish posterity. From cover to cover of that amazing volume, no word appears of sorrow or solicitude for the dead, the wounded, the bereaved. Asquith's aloofness from the populace is not

[1] *Memoirs and Reflections* (Cassell).

the militant hatred of a Northcliffe, but a cold, contemptuous dislike. "I am anxious now . . . to bring the multitude of idle, able-bodied loafers into the recruiting net." His regrets are not for the victims of Gallipoli, Kut, Festubert, but for the "cruel luck" of "poor Winston" "pouring out his woes" over the loss of one of the best and newest of the super-dreadnoughts; for the German Ambassador and his wife, "the poor Lichnowskys." "She spends her days in tears." They had suffered a rude awakening indeed from the genial confidence of the days when they gave sumptuous dinners to London Society.

I did not believe the change of Government would make any great difference to the conduct of the War. Asquith had been harried along by the hideous exigencies of the contest, the demands of the military and naval experts, the cries of the jingo "bitter-enders." The pace of surrender to war rapacities might be hastened under the new Government—yet, I thought, not much. Given the will to a peace of conquest, all else must ultimately be subordinated to war necessities.

Asquith and Grey had followed a tortuous course of greedy secret diplomacy; if any genuine effort toward international concord were to come, it must be from another source.

How absolutely Lloyd George would soon be cut off from the Liberal Party, and left a party of one—a head without a tail—was not yet obvious. The Liberal War Committee in the House promised its support to his Government—even Asquith gave it a verbal support. At the bidding of his backers, Lloyd George appointed high Tories to his Government. On his small War Council Curzon and Milner ensured the imperialist tradition, Bonar Law, who was Leader of the House of Commons and therefore his mouthpiece, as well as Chancellor of the Exchequer, guarded the interest of Big Business. Arthur Henderson was retained to keep the workers to the bench. How largely he was a mere outsider in the Cabinet appeared, in full clarity, somewhat later. Representatives of Big Business headed several Government departments. Sir Albert Stanley, director of the underground railway combine, was at the Board of Trade; Lord Devonport, the grocer of Kearley & Tonge's, was Minister of Food; Sir Joseph Maclay, a Glasgow shipowner, who disdained a seat in Parliament, was made Controller of Shipping; Lord Cowdray, the head of Pearson's, the big contractors, became president of the newly-created Air Board; Lord Rhondda, the Welsh coalowner, was President of the Local Government Board. In short, it was a Big Business Government.

Lansdowne, the old Tory leader who had had the temerity to express a desire for peace, had been eliminated; Grey was ousted from the Foreign Office wherein he had taken up the threads laid by his predecessors, and followed them to their inevitable climax in the World War. Balfour succeeded him as Foreign Secretary with Robert Cecil as Minister of Blockade. It was said that Asquith had stipulated these two should control foreign affairs, as a condition of giving his support to the new Government. The ruthless school was not satisfied. The *Morning Post* roundly declared Cecil unfit for his post; the *Times* complained that Balfour was "tired and ill-placed," *Britannia* fulminated enraged, crying out that two governments and not one now held sway in Britain; that of Lloyd George, and that of Balfour and Cecil at the Foreign Office, wherein, it was alleged, the dominance of Asquith, Grey, and Haldane was yet maintained. Now that Lloyd George was Prime Minister he did not protect *Britannia* from the consequences of these outbursts. Again and again it was raided, and found greater difficulty than ever in appearing; two or three of its weekly issues were often missed. Its little band of devoted adherents printed it somehow—sometimes on the roofs of houses, it was said.

The *Times* had mainly based its demand for the supercession of Asquith upon the question of "man power"; more men must be found for the spring offensive. Henderson having accepted office in the extreme war Government, declared[1] that to win the War the service of every man and woman should be placed at the disposal of the State. There was a new "comb-out"—a hateful term—of the men who had been exempted on account of physical unfitness, or because they were employed on essential work. A small shop-stewards' organ, the *Trade Unionist*, was suppressed for an article, "Forty Millions—Mostly Fools," wherein the poor fellows "combed out" of industry for the Army were likened to lice eradicated by a fine-tooth comb, for thus it was claimed they were regarded by their masters and rulers. The author of the screed was "Billie" Watson, a crude, unshaven fellow, a working engineer at the bench, who secured a following amongst the men in the engineering shops because he was voicing their passionate indignation at the soulless conditions capitalist society in war time thrust upon them.

Though Lloyd George had become the instrument of the extreme Tory conscriptionists, the legend that he was a liberty-loving democrat still in certain quarters survived tenuously from his land-tax days, and was industriously propagated. Press paragraphs asserted that he was about to democratise the Government of the country by setting up Parliamentary Committees after the French model, for dealing with finance, foreign affairs, and so on; that he was pledged to the conscription of wealth, in order that the rich, and not the poor, should pay for the War; to the nationalisation of shipping, mines, railways, and the food supply in the interests of the masses. In actual fact some measure of Government control was now exercised over railways, mines, and shipping. There was a 50 per cent. increase in railway fares, trains were fewer and slower, but the workers discovered no improvement in their lot. Despite the appointment of a Food Controller food difficulties increased. Women stood in queues for potatoes, sugar, meat, butter and other fats, cheese, jam, etc. In February 1918, when rationing was at long last introduced, the police[2] estimated that 1,300,000 people were standing in the food queues in the Metropolitan area, and this was doubtless an underestimate. The *Times* dubbed him "wizard" for his power of carrying the rival factions along with him. To me it seemed, rather, that he was a madman compelling his slaves to build a rude barrack on marshy and fever-infected land, insisting that it was a marble palace with pillars of alabaster and rarest

[1] Speech at Southampton.
[2] *Encyclopædia Britannica*, 12th Edition.

carving; flinging to the ground some litter of coloured paper, and declaring it a blossoming garden of lovely flowers; riveting shackles upon the people, and proclaiming that he was crowning them with liberty.

The Labour Party had decided to support Lloyd George's Government. Brace and Roberts again got subordinate posts; James Parker was made a Junior Lord of the Treasury. It was the end of his connection with the I.L.P., which had sponsored him. Stephen Walsh was appointed to serve under Neville Chamberlain in the Ministry of National Service, which the working Trade Unionist was apt to regard as a ministry of national slavery. Stout John Hodge, of the Steelsmelters' Union, was made Minister of Labour. A shrewd, efficient administrator of his Union, he was one of the team whose lack of idealism had crucified the spirit of Keir Hardie. Little was to be expected of him. George Barnes was at the Pensions Office. I went to him, as I had been to other Ministers, in the effort to get injustices redressed. He received me alone and cordially, repeatedly protesting anxiety to better the sad plight of the discharged men. There seemed about him an almost eager friendliness, and the wistfulness of one who has severed connection with old friends and old endeavours and finds himself a stranger in his new office, its pomps unreal, unsatisfying, its barriers overwhelming, himself a weak man, his possibilities of achievement very small.

He spoke of my mother, assuring me she was right in her war attitude; in justifying her, I thought, striving to justify himself. At moments he seemed to me a phantom, blotted out by the memory of his earlier self, as I saw him when first the "Labour Representation Committee" got its "Labour Group" into Parliament, and he was wont to speak affectionately of Keir Hardie as "our honoured chief." Often on the Terrace beside the Thames I had talked with those two so different men—friends as it seemed. Deep was the rift between them when Keir Hardie died, despised and rejected by the Party he had formed!

## CHAPTER LVI

### TRAINING THE CHILD

"ALL these little children have lost their fathers in the War!" Annie Ferne at the Mothers' Arms told me sadly, with a sweep of her hand which comprehended two-thirds of the babies on the flat roof.

I was worried about the toddlers. They grew chubby and rosy; they acquired cleanly habits; voluntary workers came to pet and play with them; toys poured into the Mothers' Arms without stint, but as soon as they came, they were broken and thrown away. Sybil Smith sent a big rocking-horse, as large as a Shetland pony, used for years by her children, but in perfect condition still. Within a month of its arrival, it was no more. Every hair of the tail and mane had gone; the eyes were gouged out, every joint in the wood severed; the remnants had been torn from their stand. To me it was amazing that young children under five years of age could have done it. To the busy staff at the nursery it was all a matter of course; one could not even get the horse repaired, for half the almost unrecognisable pieces of battered wood had been thrown in the fire or the dustbin before I knew. To me this meant more than the wrecking of a costly toy. It impressed on me that the toddlers had learnt only one sort of game: to pound and break, to tear and destroy. That must be altered. As I rushed through the day's papers, marking the news items, my eye caught a tiny paragraph: Muriel Matters had returned from studying under Maria Montessori in Barcelona. I telephoned here and there until I got in touch with her. She responded with zealous understanding. She had herself experienced the same need when she helped Larkin and Connolly in the Dublin lock-out of 1912. She had tried to procure a Montessori teacher then, and having discovered such teachers unobtainable, she had gone to Barcelona to fit herself to supply the lack. Of course, I would have it that she must come to the Mothers' Arms to initiate the Montessori Method.

Within a fortnight we had everything in readiness. Willie Lansbury had got the low shelves and little tables made for us at Lansbury's yard. A partition had been removed on the second floor at the Mothers' Arms to throw two rooms into one. The Montessori apparatus had been procured. Mrs. Savoy had made at cost price the small hair, nail, and sweeping brushes. Muriel Matters and her coadjutor, Hildegarde Gunn, with admirable good taste, economy, and expedition, had run about procuring all else that was appropriate.

Seven little children between three and five years were selected as the first subjects for THE METHOD. The commencement was slyly reported to me as utter chaos. Nurse Hebbes, who won children's affection by romping with them, wore the enigmatic smile of the sphinx, Lucy Burgis, who had been Norland trained, talked fast with ardent approval of the intention, Nurse Clarke was aloof in manner, and obviously sceptical. The devotees of Montessori, with Pleasance Napier as musician and pupil, held on bravely. Muriel Matters would have no compromise; there must be no physical compulsion, no "violence," as she termed it, even of the mildest; yet there must be ordered activity. Any child who was "disorderly" was banished from the sanctuary, condemned to be returned to the babies, if only for an hour or two, as "not yet old enough" to remain. At a certain stage there was one child only in the Montessori room, many times but two; yet in some brief days the children had been completely won. Now with what grave delight they handled the apparatus, swept, and dusted their room, washed hands and faces, changed bibs and pinafores, waited on each other at meals. With care they handled dainty china—Muriel Matters would permit no coarse unbreakable stuff. Instead of the old clump, clump, clump on the flat of stamping little feet, they went lightly on their toes, acquiring grace and balance by stepping to music on a white line painted on the floor. They learnt the magic of quiet in the silence game.

My hope was fulfilled. Yet always there was the sorrowful thought: "We are building only a little oasis here." Around us was the vast misery and lack of far-extending slums.

. . . . . . .

A little later I was speaking in Luton. A girl who had been victimised as the leader of a strike in a hosiery factory, came to me, flushed and eager, begging me to let her come to the Mothers' Arms to learn the Montessori Method. Her friend, who had also been victimised, had written to Margaret Macmillan, and had been received as a student at her Deptford Camp School. She, too, was eager to be an "educationist" and the Montessori Method, she was certain, embodied her own desires. She was ardently importunate. I arranged for her to come to us.

Then, almost immediately, came a plea from her friend. She was not happy in Deptford; her brother was a Conscientious Objector, and she also was against the War. The staff at the camp school was hostile to her on that account. Margaret Macmillan herself was for the War; indeed, somewhat vehemently so, it appeared. That was a saddening disappointment to me; to the girl a most poignant disillusionment and grief. Our finances were heavily burdened; here was another young woman desirous of flinging herself on our pay-roll, for penniless girls must have the wherewithal to live! Yet the wherewithal was found as usual, on this occasion by the help of Mrs. Bernard Shaw.

Muriel Matters tackled the instruction of these pupils conscientiously, prescribing for them courses of reading and study, both to reinforce their general education, and to supply their theoretical equipment as teachers.

Their time was divided between practice with the children, attendance at lectures and reading at the British Museum. The girl who had been at Deptford appeared intensely delicate ; excessively round-shouldered, and with painfully prominent teeth, one scarcely anticipated from her the joyousness one would desire for the leader of little children. Yet her gentleness and perseverance redeemed her physical disabilities, the legacy of a feeble childhood in a crowded working-class home. When she left us, she continued her studies, graduated as B.A., and obtained a post in a Luton elementary school. Her companion, robust, dark-eyed and straight-featured, was less amenable to the Method. She could not win the children as her friend did without effort ; she sought to impose her will on them, and they rebelled against her. Her horrified instructor found her, hot and desperate, forcibly holding down a little boy who would not sleep—the very antithesis this of the Montessori scheme ! With the grown-ups also the girl from Luton was apt to be tempestuous. She wrote to me a scathing condemnation of an elder member of the staff, which troubled me ; I grieved that there should be friction in the nursery and felt that somehow I must spare more time to influence and unite the workers there, to breathe into them the enthusiasm which would transmute emotional unrestfulness into fruitful works. In such cases it was generally my way to call them to the planning of some new function. The Luton girl wept out her emotions in my room. It became obvious to me that she was too eager in the quest after her own development to be able to give herself to the children. I suggested to her at last that instead of continuing as a teacher she might prefer to be a Trade Union organiser. She seemed pleased by the prospect. I introduced her to one of the East End Unions, where she was gladly received, as coming from us. Her young blood remained unsatisfied. This was not yet the *milieu* she desired. She was panting to escape from the drab tedium of industrialism, and could not find satisfaction in the East End. Eventually she secured a studentship to the working women's section of Ruskin College, and later she became a teacher of juvenile adults under a scheme started in connection with the Employment Exchanges.

. . . . . . .

Already before the Montessori work was started we had planned another " Women's Exhibition " in the Caxton Hall to be held on three December days. Dr. Tchaykovsky was determined it should be a success. She had the maternity group from the Gladstone memorial in the Strand reproduced as a poster to advertise it, and the underground railways actually displayed it for us free of charge. We agreed that we must have a special exhibition secretary, freed from other work to attend to it. I happened to come across Sonia Rodker, who had been a reader of Dora Marsden's *Freewoman*. She came on to our staff as Exhibition secretary. She was in her element, fixing up portrait sketches by Amy Browning and John Collard, dancers from the Margaret Morris school, and concerts with famous artistes arranged by lovely Maria Levinskaya. It was her idea to organise an amateur photographic competition. She induced that very fine photographic artist, Hoppé, to be the judge, and to take my photograph without charge, to be raffled for the funds.

As before, old Mrs. Savoy gathered from the East End a little group of women engaged in sweated industries. Charlotte Drake prepared a food prices exhibit, demonstrating in actual commodities that the food procured for a typical working-class household before the War for 16s. 10½d. now cost 32s. 4½d. Official estimates of the rise in the cost of living always fell short of hard experience. Emily Dyce Sharp had made charts showing that for 1s. now one got less fish than one got before the War for 4¾d., little more egg than for a pre-War 5d., less potato and chilled breast of mutton than used to be procured for 5½d. and little more flank of beef than before the War for 6d. Of sugar one could get less for a shilling than used to be had for 4½d., and we in the East End usually had to content ourselves with black Manilla sugar which cost as much as they paid in the West End for white loaf sugar.

These and the Montessori demonstrations were the essentials of the show. The last was a veritable *tour de force*. Of the seven children who had been initiated at the Mothers' Arms five weeks before, five had succumbed to some childish illness. Their places were filled by newcomers, two of them twin girls aged barely three. Muriel Matters declared that her class ought not to be on exhibition for at least another six months, but she cheerfully persevered, and the children rewarded her by calmly working away at their apparatus, and when tea time came, laying and eating their meal, waiting upon each other, and sweeping up the crumbs when they had finished, without heed to the visitors crowding in to watch them.

Among the speakers were George Lansbury, R. L. Outhwaite, Emmeline Pethick Lawrence, J. M. Hogge, chairman of the House of Commons Pensions Committee, and Susan Lawrence. No one anticipated then that she would hold Government office in less than eight years' time. She was never a suffragist, but she was one of the first to receive the fruits of the struggle when women received the Parliamentary vote.

Humphreys of the Proportional Representation Society organised a mock Parliamentary election on P.R. lines. There were men and women candidates, and every visitor to the exhibition might nominate a candidate and cast a vote. It was natural enough, since our organisation had arranged the show, that I should head the poll. George Lansbury and Philip Snowden followed. Who could imagine Viscount Snowden then!

The hall looked charming; everything draped in soft grey, a foil to the brilliant bunting of the Suffrage and Women's Labour organisations which had accepted our invitation to take stalls. There was a crowd which presaged success. I saw Olive Schreiner, Nevinson, and Annie Cobden Sanderson in the throng. Evelyn Sharp was at the United Suffragists' stall, Miss Halford at the exhibit of the National Association for Infant Welfare, Mrs. Lamartine Yates at the Suffragettes of the W.S.P.U. formed as a protest against the jingo policy of the original Union. I heard for the first time the silvery singing of the boys of the Westminster

Choristers Dr. Harry Schütze had procured for us. My thoughts were transported by their enchantment to the golden age of eternal youth.

Zangwill was the opener. His snaky locks grown grey and sober, he was worn and saddened by the War, as though his soul had striven with its tempests. He spoke genially, yet on the whole mournfully, and though he made many quips they had not the magic gaiety of the past. I remembered in pre-War days, which seemed so far off now, wandering into a sparsely-peopled theatre to see his peace play put on for a brief run of *matinées*. Its theme appeared unreal, even fantastic then. I had discounted its value because it ignored economic motives. Seen now in the heat of the world conflict it would grip the heart. . . .

He spoke of us kindly, too kindly :

" In the Workers' Suffrage Federation and its manifold activities there is fortunately more organising ability, a more humane ideal than is likely to be discovered in the most up-to-date Cabinet. What the country wants is not so much man power as brain power and soul power. It is because Miss Sylvia Pankhurst in the East End is a greater centre of sweetness and light than anything or anybody in Whitehall that I feel it such a privilege to support her. When she founded a paper with the clumsy title of the *Women's Dreadnought* I must say my literary sense shuddered ; but now it has so lived up to its name that my only anxiety is lest it be torpedoed by the submarine censorship. . . . The hope of the world lies in changing the ' Gunmakers' Arms ' into the ' Mothers' Arms ' ! I trust that our Sylvia's action will be symbolic of the whole future course of history ; for we will not pretend here that we are saving these babies merely that they may grow up to be food for cannon."

They were generous compliments, pointed for propaganda ; but compliments, after all, rip people and their doings from their environment, exposing them to a glamour of unreality ; the task so huge, the need so great, and we, with all our eagerness, so few.

## CHAPTER LVII

### THE GERMAN PEACE NOTE—PRESIDENT WILSON'S APPEAL

BEFORE Wilson's re-election to the Presidency in October the Germans had urged him to initiate peace negotiations, warning him that unless negotiations were opened they would revert to unrestricted submarine warfare. Bethmann Hollweg, the Chancellor, was opposed to it, but the extremer militarists demanded it, for Germany was suffering seriously by the blockade, and must eventually be conquered by it should the War continue at stalemate.

House, whose chosen mission had been to stir the President to this rôle, now strove to deter him, declaring Germany unwilling to accede to any terms the United States could propose, and the Entente Powers averse to peace of any sort because they were just beginning to gain substantial successes—as he mistakenly believed—after two years of War.

On December 12th, 1916, long-gathering rumour received sudden justification : the Central Powers proposed peace negotiations.

" Being at the same time inspired by a desire to prevent further bloodshed and to put an end to the cruelties of war, the four Allied Powers have proposed to enter forthwith into peace negotiations."

A peace offer at last ! The news brought a thrill of hope to thousands, though the Press, in the act of announcing it, repudiated the overture, howled it out of court with a roar of hatred and ridicule, insisting there must be war ruthlessly to the bitter end, no negotiations, no compromise, no question of a draw, that Germany and her confederates must be utterly beaten, totally disarmed.

In the pause before the Allied Governments gave their official answer, House cabled from America, urging the British Foreign Office to postpone its reply until he had ascertained, through confidential sources, the nature of Germany's intended terms. His plea was swept aside, the German proposal rejected without parley. The Entente Governments knew well enough the terms were not those of a vanquished suppliant ; and none other would they consider in their present temper. Balfour, the mild-mannered elegant, Grey and Asquith who so often had discussed with House a negotiated Peace of general concord, even though now they were freed of the inhibitions of office, uttered no welcome to this first showing of the olive branch.

" Will John Burns speak ? Will John Morley speak ? " I wrote the question. Their knowledge of the inner history of foreign affairs had led them to quit the Government on the eve of war ; if they came forward now with a big appeal for settlement there would be a great rallying to them from many quarters. They still were dumb.

In the evil illusion, war, it is the huge apparent unanimity of its support which stays the agonised protest burning for utterance in the breast of the silent multitude. What one could do to break the spell of that unanimity I did, demanding that the offer to negotiate be accepted, and the terms demanded by our Government and its Allies be published, in order that the peoples on both sides might know them. If the Government would not take the initiative in action towards peace—then let it submit the question to a referendum vote of the people.

I endeavoured to secure a joint demonstration for Peace at the Dock Gates the following Sunday, refusing to feel the chill which greeted me, the aloof indifference even of those who spoke on platforms for a negotiated peace. Lansbury had engagements in the provinces. The Poplar Trades and Labour Council refused to co-operate; like the official Labour movement as a whole, it was unready for such a step.

Time admitted of no delay. We rushed our posters on to the walls, announcing simply a peace meeting at the East India Dock Gates, without waiting for the names of organisations and speakers who might join us. On Saturday fell a dense black fog. Our posters could not be seen. On Sunday the fog was only a little less. A fairly large crowd gathered nevertheless; though not the multitude I had hoped. All the East London Socialist organisations had been communicated with, but they were slow to move, and the fear of violence from the jingoes was still a substantial deterrent; indeed many people thought it folly to offer oneself to their onslaughts. Only the Poplar I.L.P. had responded by sending a speaker, T. S. Attlee, whose brother became Under-Secretary for War in the Labour Government of 1924. Old Miss Bennett mounted the chair to call the crowd together, in words simple as a child's, yet voicing clearly and poignantly the facts of war most obvious to the poor. The "Poplar girls," the mothers who had been with us on deputations, Mrs. Crabbe, panting for breath, Mrs. Nuess, whose home had been wrecked in the anti-German raids, gathered nearest. Edgar and Minnie Lansbury were in the crowd, she with her black sparkling eyes, and jaunty smile which always pleased me, hanging to his arm, her Puck-like glance seeming to convey to me, as she caught my eye, that she was here at his side to stir up, in kindly affectionate spirit, her big, good-natured lazy-bones. I loved her for her forthright gaiety and clear brain, her staunch faithfulness in regarding herself always as the advocate of the distressed applicant.

A bare half-dozen elderly well-dressed men had come to make mischief. With vindictive faces, reddened by exertion, they yelled at us, backed by a gang of irresponsible lads barely above school age. A Canadian soldier demanded a hearing for us, hotly declaring that only those who had never been to the trenches and believed themselves absolutely safe from the danger of being sent there, were opposed to peace negotiations. Others in the crowd reinforced him, taking our part so vigorously that the hubbub was immense. Mrs. Drake and Mrs. Walker in turn subdued the turmoil, the one by her terse common sense, the other by pathos and Celtic fire.

When Attlee mounted the chair which was all our platform, the opponents leapt at him and threw him down. I sprang to take his place. Quiet was restored. I spoke till the disturbers made a concerted rush and old Miss Bennett, resisting the pressure of the opponents, slipped and fell to the ground. I jumped down to aid her. Again we righted the chair. I easily secured order. The opponents, outnumbered, retired to the rear. The police, a substantial force of them, had watched the scrimmage aloof; now it was over, they dashed into the crowd, laying about them with knees and fists, shouting that this was a disorderly meeting and must be dispersed. Having pushed us all round the corner into the East India Dock Road, amid cries of protest, and groans of people thrown to the ground, they left us. The wide road here was bordered by iron railings with a broad stone base about eighteen inches high—a sufficiently good platform. I mounted it and began to speak. In a moment the police came running back and the sergeant said: "If you will get down from here you can go back to speak in the proper place." I agreed very willingly, but as soon as I moved towards the Dock Gates the police pushed me roughly in the opposite direction with laughter and jeers. Powerless against this buffeting I turned away. The police were soon out of sight, but the crowd remained. Again I returned to the railings, and spoke to a quiet, attentive crowd, till the police were informed and returned to arrest me. As they dragged me away Mrs. Drake clung to me. They took her also and Mrs. Walker, whom they noticed speaking at the Dock Gates to an orderly crowd. Edgar Lansbury was arrested for no particular reason, and Minnie for running beside him as he was hauled along.

Official word had been given that our meeting must not be held. If no one else would break it up, then the police must do it.

In court next morning the police alleged that they had taken me into custody for my own protection as a disorderly crowd was threatening to throw me in the dock—an absurd invention, but the authorities must have it that we had no support. The magistrates discharged Edgar and Minnie Lansbury and assured Mrs. Drake and me that he recognised the sincerity of our convictions. He urged us to be bound over to go away when the police asked us. Of course we declined, and were ordered to pay £2. If we refused we were not to be taken to prison: our possessions must be distrained. Mrs. Walker was accused of "insulting language and behaviour." Though she denied the charge and the magistrate declared her "perfectly respectable and truthful," he awarded her a fine of £2! Friends paid our fines. The affair fizzled out quietly.

The Government did not want us to be going to prison then. They remembered too well the growth of the Suffragette movement under the stimulous of imprisonment. Some little time later Saklatvala, the Indian Communist, was interviewed by Sir Basil Thompson who took him to task for sitting on a committee with me. He said, so Saklatvala reported:

"She is a dreadful woman. We could have had her in prison dozens

*General Photographic Agency*

"ZERO HOUR"

Norah Smyth

THE HOMES THEY FOUGHT FOR

East End children come out to play with my dog "Jim."

of times during the War. But the family has a weakness ; they like going to prison."

I was to serve another term in Holloway ; but not yet.

. . . . . . .

The Entente Governments had indicated their contemptuous rejection of the Peace Note, though the official Allied answer had not yet been given. Lloyd George had refused Parliament an opportunity to discuss it.

Bonar Law, the new Chancellor of the Exchequer, secured another war credit of four hundred millions and disclosed that the War was now costing £5,710,000 a day ; enough, complained the poor old Liberal, Sir William Byles, to provide every family in the British Isles with a comfortable cottage and two acres of land.

On December 20th President Wilson, acting at last without the procrastinating Colonel House, issued his long-belated summons to the belligerent nations to make peace. The Press here received it with a howl of fury, denouncing especially his statement that the concrete objects for which the War was being waged had not been defined by either side, and that, as stated in general terms by their leaders, the objects of the belligerent governments on both sides appeared the same.

Despite the chorus of newspaper repudiation directed by the Government Press Bureau, great hopes were raised. The I.L.P. sent President Wilson a letter of gratitude, which appeared fulsome when read later on, after Wilson had become the war leader of America, at the head of a government which was persecuting American Conscientious Objectors, and had flung into jail the old Socialist, Eugene Debs.

The Central Powers replied to Wilson's Note, by proposing "an immediate meeting of delegates of the belligerent States at some neutral place" and expressed their willingness to collaborate with America in the prevention of future war.

The House-Wilson plan to join the Entente in the War, on the plea of Germany's refusal to accept America's call to peace, had miscarried—for Germany had accepted ; the Entente had rejected the call. It is true her Government had not openly made an avowal of her terms as Wilson had demanded, but the terms were conveyed to the President confidentially. Wilson declared them inadmissible. The best that can be said of them is that they were a bluff to ascertain how much Germany could obtain by bartering and manœuvre. In the confidential negotiations then taking place between the Entente Powers, the Tsar's Government offered to France and Britain "perfect freedom in drawing up the Western frontiers of Germany" in the expectation that they would allow the Russians "equal freedom in drawing up" their "frontiers between Germany and Austria."[1] The German Emperor's Government regarded frontiers and peoples in the same light as the Tsarist. Could it be otherwise ? Do my readers desire to believe that the Kaiser's Government was more enlight-

[1] Telegram of Sazonoff. Petrograd, February 24th, 1917.

ened than those of Britain, France, Italy, and Russia? All, in fact, were animated by the same spirit. Thus it was not surprising that the German terms[1] conveyed by Bernstorff to Wilson, indicated clearly enough, though with diplomatic reserve, a desire to extend Germany's boundaries as far as possible—both east and west, to add to her colonies, to secure improved trading agreements, and any war indemnities she might be able to obtain from her adversaries. Nevertheless the terms contained phrases which indicated that the Germans were prepared to be reasonable, if necessary, and to treat with their adversaries at the Peace Conference, if not as brother-angels, at least as fellow-plunderers. Despite decided hints of aggression contained in the terms, had they been countered by opposing claims from Powers of not inferior strength, as would have been the case had negotiations then been opened, a settlement could have been arrived at less heavily fraught with suffering to both sides than has been brought about by the treaties the victors ultimately imposed.

In conveying their terms, the Germans thanked Wilson for his peace effort and begged him to continue it, announcing at the same time that they were recommencing their ruthless submarine blockade.

The answer of the Entente Powers could be inferred from their Press. The Russian Prime Minister was the first of their official spokesmen to utter a public reply. He delivered a brusque rebuff. The War must continue until a decisive victory had been won. To Wilson's assumption that all nations now deprecated sectional alliances and desired a League of

[1] Restitution of German Upper Alsace occupied by the French.

Gaining of a frontier protecting Germany and Poland economically and strategically against Russia—a polite method of inferring a piece of Russia should be sliced off.

Restitution of German Colonies in form of agreement giving Germany colonies "adequate to her population and economic interest"—a delicate manner of saying that these should be added to.

Restitution of the parts of France occupied by Germany under reservation of strategical frontiers and financial compensation—annexation and indemnity is suggested here if Germany can compass it.

Restitution of Belgium under special guarantee for safety of Germany which would have to be decided on by negotiations with Belgium—a proposal which suggests negotiation between the lion and the lamb.

Economic and financial compensation on the basis of exchange of territories conquered and to be restituted at conclusion of peace. This shows Germany in reasonable mien. As realists her statesmen see that they are not dealing with conquered foes or defenceless small nations; they will give and take in the effort to get the best terms they can without further sacrifice.

Compensation for German business concerns and private persons who suffered by the War—an effort to get as much as possible and off-set claims coming from the other side.

Adjustment of economic agreements and measures which would form an obstacle to normal commerce and intercourse after the conclusion of peace and instead reasonable treaties of commerce—All this, whether for good or evil, would depend on the negotiators; were they far-sighted and reasonable, and the power equally matched on either side, the situation might be bettered considerably.

The Freedom of the Seas.

Agreement to enter a second international congress after the Peace Conference on the basis of Wilson's proposals for a League of Peace.

Nations, he replied, that so far from this being the case, the military alliance between Britain, France, and Russia would be cemented after the War and reinforced by a close economic union. The joint reply of the Entente was a definite refusal to entertain peace negotiations, and an indication that the War must continue till the whole of Europe had been "reorganised." Reorganisation by the tank and the machine-gun in the interests of big business! Alas, how great a mockery!

So died the Wilson peace effort. Capitalist civilisation was too deeply impregnated by its never-ceasing contest for wealth and power to find emergence from the strife through an appeal to reason and righteousness. Till crowns were overthrown and empires disintegrated, it persisted in the ignoble contest. Wilson himself, in the high arc of his oratory, was uttering ideals of international righteousness he would fail to implement when his professions were put to the test. Indeed, they were only half real to him.

Its ill-reception by the Allied Governments notwithstanding, the Peace Talk had stimulated and emboldened the pacifist movement. On Christmas Eve the Peace Negotiations Committee held a service of prayer in Trafalgar Square for the coming peace. It was a strange, sad scene. Men and women pacifists fervently sang the hymns. A crowd of colonial soldiers, marshalled and prompted by those same middle-aged civilians we had recognised for years at such work, broke in with strident yells and ribald songs. Dr. Orchard, a slight figure in black cassock, led the prayers, his low voice reaching surprisingly through the din. After the service people lingered for hours in the Square, discussing the hope of peace. The story that the event was paid for by Germany had been industriously circulated amongst the soldiers, but many of them came to the literature sellers to express their longing that the peace talk might bear fruit.

"I think you are going to make me sad, girlie," an Australian soldier said to me when I offered him a paper. "I came ten thousand miles to do my bit. I'd rather not be discouraged; but I'll read it."

## CHAPTER LVIII

### "IF THIS HAD BEEN FOR LIFE AND NOT FOR DEATH!"

WE at Old Ford worked strenuously at our Peace Campaign. Street after street was visited, pavements chalked with announcements of the meetings, leaflets distributed from door to door. Then those who could speak took turns to be on the chair, dispersing themselves as each one had said her say, to further chalking, bill distribution, speaking. I kept at it, spurred by anxiety, which could find respite only in effort. Old Mrs. Boyce toiled slowly after with her sore feet. I read in her face disapproval of this notion that speakers should undertake these additional labours; nor would she. She was old and battered by Life, the hard life of a working-class widow toiling to bring up her children. She presently had one of them sent back to her from the War, an incurable cripple. I was seething with energy. Racked with pain, prostrate with headache, at times I might be, yet within me was a rage at this merciless War, this squalor of poverty! Oh! that all the wealth and effort the nation was squandering might be to rebuild these slums, to restore these faded women, these starved and stunted children.

. . . . . . . .

In the dusk childish figures were gathering on the doorsteps. Frail little arms reached up to knock at the doors, still silent, responseless. Mother was not yet returned from the gun factory! Little ones whimpered and crouched on the cold stone doorsteps.

. . . . . . . .

Before Christmas a woman dying of phthisis sent for me to say good-bye. I went to her in her little home: two rooms and a scullery on the ground floor of a workman's cottage. She was in the small back parlour, propped up in bed, her wan face moist with exhaustion, working some table mats for the factory with bloodless, emaciated fingers. Her bed was placed as well as it could be in that small space, to give her light for the sewing. Even though dying she must persevere with it, for there were eight of them to feed. It pained me that in her last days she should see only these drab, discoloured walls and poor forlorn sticks of furniture. Outside all was grey and cheerless. The rain drizzled down on the trodden earth of the little yard, where grew no single blade. One could scarcely see the sky, shut away by surrounding buildings. A patch of brown paper blocked out a broken pane, but even the window she could not see; all the free great pageantry of the skies was cut off from her. I was stung with raging sorrow that she should be toiling thus in the last ebb of her being; it was a shame and a scandal to humanity, an outrage against the public health that these things should be.

The light was waning. She lay in the shadow recounting to me her struggles and privations, telling her bitter regret that she must die so soon and leave her little children; that all her hard toil and ceaseless striving had led only to this.

I knew her story. She had come to me first in the early weeks of the War, a bonny woman then, though full of trouble, for her husband had received the order: "Enlist or go!" She had been left with six little children, the eldest twelve years, the youngest less than one. He had been a steady man, who never lost a day's work or suffered a day's illness. He had given her 22s. for housekeeping, and bought and mended the children's boots; and she, despite her large family, had earned a further 15s. a week by tailoring. She had to work without cease, but her children grew strong and rosy, and she had been happy in her contented way.

When her man was taken away for military training his wages stopped, no separation allowance was paid. The factory for which she herself worked had shut down in those first days of War panic. She went to the Soldiers and Sailors Families Association, and there waited in a long queue of women, until the office door was shut in the evening. Many days this happened before she had a chance even to utter her plea for help. Meanwhile the children were hungry, and day by day she pawned something to buy a little food. At last she got speech with the young woman secretary with the peremptory manner; but there were more applicants than the young lady could attend to, and she simply told her to call again. This happened twice. At the third interview particulars of her case were taken down, and she was told to go home and await a visitor.

Three weeks passed; the visitor did not come. Everything in the house she could pawn had gone by then and she had not a scrap of food to give to the children.

Other women were going to the Suffragettes in the Old Ford Road. A neighbour persuaded her, though she was shy, to come too. She and the children had a meal in the restaurant there. At once I had telephoned to the S.S.F.A. and persuaded them to make her an immediate grant, and then had written further to the S.S.F.A. and the War Office and pestered them till they made further grants. She reminded me of it with a catch in her voice. The grants were paid, but not regularly; and the income was a good deal less than she had before the War, though it cost much more to live. After a time the factories began to reopen. She got a little sewing machining, but trade was still slack, and she could not earn more than 10s. a week. After three months the separation allowance began to be paid. She did not get all the arrears due to her, but she thought she had given me and the others at Old Ford trouble enough already; and as the authorities paid no attention to her own letters, she let the arrears go.

She and the children had food to eat now, but before the separation allowance came she began to have a little hacking cough. As the winter advanced it grew worse. She made light of it, but it remained. Then followed a severe attack of bronchitis and pleurisy. The doctor told her she had a tendency to consumption and should go to a sanatorium; but there was no one to leave with the children, and she let the months drift by, hoping that either the War would end, or something else would happen to make it easier for her to go. Then suddenly she was taken so ill that the doctor sent her away at once. Her eldest girl was fourteen now and able to stay at home.

She remained at the sanatorium from May to July 1916, and was brought home worse than she went. In the same month her husband was discharged from the Army with gastric ulcers. He had already been in and out of hospital for five months. His Army pay and her separation allowance immediately stopped. Pension was refused him. The family was again destitute. Neighbours, hard pressed to find food for their own children, generously spared a meal or a shilling for these unfortunate ones when they could; but the children often cried for hunger. "We had to manage the best way we could," said the mother—stern words, so often heard in working-class homes.

After five weeks the husband was well enough to go to work. If he felt ill he hid it from his wife. The eldest girl had now learnt to take the care of the home and children upon her shoulders. The acuteness of the crisis passed, but the mother, a young woman of thirty-six, had been broken in the struggle. The doctor ordered brandy every hour for her; but his order was never executed unless he left 2s. on the table for it. He ordered milk, and she got that from the Mothers' Arms; for though she would not "trouble" us again, we had heard, too tardily, of her need. A lady from the Insurance Commissioners had recently called to ask if she were working; but though the seal of death was on the woman's face, no benefit was paid. She was working still!

Fearing that she had grown to be a burden on her children, she had asked to be taken to the infirmary, but the doctor had said she was too ill to be moved. She was doing what she could to ease the burden she would not be, with those frail hands.

The eldest girl and the youngest sat huddled together for warmth, both listening to their mother's tale. For them, as for her, it was part of the history of the Great War. She saw her life shipwrecked in the whirlpool of the immense tragedy wherein millions had lost their all; and asked, with wistful pity for those who would live on after her, when this cruel War would end.

. . . . . . . .

In the highways and byways we rang a loud muffin bell to call the people to the Peace meetings; we gave out handbills announcing a Victoria Park demonstration on the last Sunday of the year to call for immediate peace negotiations. Poorly-clad women, with pinched white faces and backs bent by excessive toil, their eyes flashing and fists clenched, rushed out from their hovels screaming: "No peace without victory! We want peace on *our* terms!" They roused in me profound pity and sorrow. No longer I flinched from opening their eyes to the sordid ugliness of the War. I pleaded with them for their sons; I wrestled for the mastery of their hearts, trying to reveal to them the ultimate meaning, to such as them, of war "to a knock out," of the long struggle of attrition, for markets and spheres of influence, for coal and oil and rubber, for wealth and power. I recalled to them the Boer War, which I so vividly remembered, the development of the gold-fields, the exploitation of the natives, the importation of Chinese indentured labourers which followed in South Africa, the unemployment and depression here. I warned them of the enormously greater unemployment and depression which must follow this immense War, with its load of debt which the producers of wealth must ultimately pay.

Some left me shouting: "We want our sons to have their revenge!" but the many stood on, cleaving together with upturned faces. I strove to reveal to them that they and theirs were the poor unregarded pawns in the great Capitalist struggle. I spoke of the huge aggregate of soldiers of all the warring countries already dead; of the hapless fate of the poor fellows discharged to drag out their broken lives in direst need; of the young lads still under military age, whose turn would come for the slaughter, if War dragged on. The faces of many changed as I spoke. I saw waves of emotion passing over them, eyes brightening with the tension of interest, dimmed and softening to tears.

Yet some turned away in despair. "Our sons are dead; your talk of peace can never bring them back!" Alas, poor mothers, my heart cried to them: what shall it profit your dear dead that other sons shall die?

Saddest of all were the degraded, the starved and shabby, who rushed intoxicated from the public-houses, shrieking with hideous epithets: "Fight on to victory!" demanding that the entire German population should be "wiped out"! Sometimes they would attempt a tipsy war dance in the midst of our crowd, till the sober elements thrust them out. Always the sober and thoughtful rallied to us.

On the Saturday before the demonstration I spoke with Mrs. Drake at a corner in Chrisp Street, Poplar, thronged with its market stalls. The audience shifted; occupied with their marketing, folk could not stay long to listen. The opposition was noisier than hitherto; we were both too tired, after a strenuous week, to cope with it well. A crowd of lads from ten to fifteen years of age, incited by a little knot of men from one of the public-houses, took to throwing paper soaked in the gutter, orange peel, bits of bone, and other refuse from the stalls. A man with a huge stentorian voice poured forth a stream of lurid oratory. Our voices already were failing before he came; we could not compete with his huge roars. I closed the meeting. As we left the pitch the crowd of children followed us shouting and laughing, their numbers growing fast. We had worked so long and amicably in the East End, that we had no other thought than to go directly to our Poplar headquarters at 20 Railway Street, an ex-public-house, deprived of its license, which we rented from a clergyman. Old Suffragette experience would have warned me against going there with that rabble of unruly children had it been anywhere than the East End. In any other district I should have boarded a 'bus to shake off their pursuit. We entered by the swing doors. Bang! Bang! Huge reports, and some startled screams.

As luck would have it, the road-menders had left a heap of stones in the road just by. A few of the youngsters had hurled stones through every one of the great windows.

I went out to an awestruck silence. "I am sorry you have done it, children. How can we afford to go on buying babies' milk when you put us to such unnecessary expense?" They departed quietly, and very shamefaced.

Victoria Park was thronged next day as it had not been since the War. The mass of the crowd was friendly, but there were some noisy opponents; and approving comments were punctuated by hostile retorts. A man in the front kept gnashing great yellow teeth at me as I spoke, declaring that he would like to bite off a German's nose. Several police reporters were present and many Pressmen. One of the latter, a new hand perhaps, commended us with enthusiasm. "They are women of ability! Remarkable! What courage!" As I stepped from the platform he rushed forward to take my hand, profuse in congratulations. . . .

In the pause whilst a speaker descended from our little rostrum, a mere step with a high front of lightly-erected match-boarding, and another took her place, the opponents made a rush at us. It was successfully resisted. Melvina Walker silenced the crowd with her poignant tales of woe. . . . A man with a Union Jack made a sudden dash for the platform. An organised gang behind him, thrusting forward unitedly in a compact wedge. The rostrum was overturned and smashed to pieces. A park-keeper, Mrs. Drake, and Mrs. Cressall were thrown to the ground. . . .

They were helped to their feet. The disturbance was over. People were standing about discussing the brief affray.

The disturbers had achieved their object. The report could now go out that the Peace meeting was broken up.

The vast crowd remained. Mrs. Boyce, not to be baulked from getting her say, began to speak from the ground a dozen yards away. The people were attentive, but the park-keepers, fearing another disturbance, ordered her to desist. People clamoured about me for another speech. Our women hoisted me. I spoke but briefly—I would not long burden my kind upholders. Clara Cole, Mrs. Bouvier, and others followed. I left them speaking and went home alone, tired out, and a little pensive, that after all these years, we should have our platform broken in Victoria Park.

Mrs. Payne was on the doorstep waiting for me; two anxious women beside her. They had come over unexpectedly from West Ham and found their sister in sore straits. Her husband was discharged from the War, unable to work, and without pension, and she had given birth to twins fourteen days before. A new-comer to the street, she knew no one here to help her. They had found her in this plight and having done what they could—not much, for they had brought with them only a few pence—they must hasten away now and begged that I would aid. It was a sad sequel to a broken up Peace meeting!

I went immediately to the address they had given. The mother lay pallid as parchment, almost unconscious; the babies, blue and flaccid, wellnigh moribund. Their father, with bowed head, ill and dejected, sat by a fireless grate; five little children crouched in a corner.

I ran back to Old Ford and got a bucket of coal and some sticks to make a fire and called to Mrs. Payne to send her Jim for Nurse Hebbes and a doctor, and to parcel up food to keep the family for some days.

Later the man told me his story. He was a Royal Marine, a "Gallipoli hero," as the men sent out on the hapless Dardanelles expedition were termed then. Having contracted enteritis in Egypt, after leaving the

Dardanelles, he had been discharged with a certificate of good character and £1 gratuity in February. In April he was granted a pension of 11s. 3d. a week. Many months later he was notified, first by his approved society, then by the Panel Committee for the County of London, that he was entitled to medical benefit. There had evidently been a muddle, for the panel committee had written that they were " endeavouring to establish the claim to medical benefit of some of the cases of Dr. Paynton," his panel doctor. Nevertheless, up to the day when I found the family in this plight, neither sickness nor unemployment benefit had been received. Weak and suffering as he was, sheer necessity drove him to seek employment. In July he was engaged for shell boring at the National Projectile Factory, Hackney Marshes. A Government pledge had now been given that pensions should be based on the disability of the soldier, not on the wages he might happen to be earning at the time. Nevertheless his pension was cut off altogether as soon as the authorities became aware that he was employed. Soon after his pension had been stopped, his work at the factory was changed. He was set to feed six machines with 95-lb. shells. Strain as he might, he could not maintain this exertion. He explained that the work was too hard for him, and was told that he must go. He received his discharge certificate on November 4th. He was now too ill to work at all, and he and his family wholly without income, save what they could raise by pawning their furniture and clothing. His wife was in poor health and expecting shortly to be confined. On December 14th she gave birth to twins, after a difficult labour, in which the midwife was obliged to summon medical aid. The maternity benefit fortunately came through before Christmas; but little of it remained when doctor and midwife had been paid. The midwife ceased her visits at the end of the prescribed ten days, though the mother was still too ill to do anything for herself. The midwife had induced the organisation for providing invalid dinners, recently started in our district, to send in a daily meal for the mother; but after she had partaken of it four days, this boon was discontinued " for the holidays "—of those who superintended the service! Alas, the needs of the human body are not conveniently suspended at such times!

The poor " hero," one of those for whom Lloyd George averred he would make Britain a " land worth fighting for," applied to the Local War Pensions Committee in his desperate situation. In response to his appeal the S.S.F.A. official had called. (That lady official again! Would she ever grow less callous, I wondered.) She had seen the poor mother lying there with her puny babies, the fireless grate, the hungry children; she asked only to see the rent book. When the sick woman murmured that there was no use in looking at it, for no rent was owing, the lady enquired the address of the landlord and went away.

For four days the mother had been too ill to wash the babies, the father too ill to attempt the unaccustomed task. Her sisters had found them thus, with no food or fuel in the penniless home. They washed the babes and put the room in order. With the few pence in their pockets they procured such nourishment as they could to sustain their sister.

Mrs. Wakefield, whose little shop in the Old Ford Road was open on Sundays sent them round to me.

The doctor certified that the Marine was "absolutely unfit for any heavy work whatsoever." His heart, after resting, gave a rate of 102 per minute, which increased rapidly under exertion. The mother made a slow, painful recovery. By doctor's instruction, Nurse Hebbes massaged the twin babies daily, to recover them from inanition. All her devotion and resource were needed to save them. The boy especially was at first despaired of.

Presently I obtained the naval pension—but for how long? Nothing in this regard was permanent, nothing secure.

. . . . . . .

So the old year went out. Israel Zangwill wrote for it a bitter Quatrain :

" 1916 "

" The world bloodily-minded,
The Church dead or polluted,
The blind leading the blinded,
And the deaf dragging the muted."

The evils we had fought throughout the War continued still. In the *Times* of December 20th, 1916, Mary Macarthur complained that cases were appearing before the Scottish munitions tribunals in which women munition workers were paid only 8s. 9d., 10s., and 11s. a week. A girl of nineteen years who had five brothers at the Front was paid 9s. 9d. for 52½ hours' work and was refused a leaving certificate.

Miss Hattrell, a Portsmouth elementary school teacher, was fined £10 under D.O.R.A. and dismissed by the education authorities for having in her possession a leaflet entitled : " 1000 Conscientious Objectors." The elementary school places of 186,277 children were now occupied for military purposes, though the Vice-Chancellor of Sheffield University was Minister of Education.

Sad letters came to me by every post. The relatives of an officer, never before this a pacifist, who enlisted in August 1914, sent me a note from him " opened and passed by the censor."

" You cannot think what the Army is like out here ; it is ' peace at any price ' almost ; we are so desperately fed up."

A private wrote to me from the Front :

" It's a tragic pity that people at home don't understand conditions out here. . . . It is a life absolutely opposed to every concept of life you have. . . . The fools and dolts who prate about fighting to a finish ought to come out here."

That was the smouldering thought in many a soldier's brain, uttered only to such as me, for whom the War held no glamour, no illusions of righteousness or worth.

A man ordered to the Front sent me his wife's letter in sorrow and anxiety ; her confinement was near.

" Dear Husband George,

" I feel broken-hearted. I know if I worry much more it will bring my illness on. If anything happens to me and our children are left, you will have Government to thank. Life is very hard. They have taken you from me, and now are leaving me to starve. It was a struggle to live and pay my way on 17s. 6d., so how do they expect me to manage on less ? I had a letter from Hounslow saying forty-three days' pay was to be deducted from my allowance at the rate of 6d. a day. And if my book has not come back to the Post Office I shall not be able to draw any at all. People won't lend you money if you cannot pay back, and the soldiers and sailors fund won't help me, as they have done that already. So the best thing I can do, my darling, is to take my life out of it, or else go to the

Workhouse. But what a thing for our child to be born in the Workhouse! No, I will not do that!

"I have been very queer, and my head so bad since I had the letter to tell me. I suppose they will be sending you away to France soon—oh God help me!

"From your broken-hearted wife,

"NELL."

So it rolled on, the War of iniquity, falsely extolled as "the War to end war." It continued till it had piled up a total expenditure of £11,076,600,000 by this country, the total cost to the British Empire and its Allies being £40,963,600,000, the total cost to Germany and her Allies £15,122,900,000.[1] The figures seem to suggest amazing extravagance on the part of the Entente, yet war itself is the paramount extravagance.

In 1917, America came into the War; the high and dearly cherished hopes of President Wilson's exalted mediation, as the great neutral, "too proud to fight," his promises of a peace without victory and without rancour came tumbling down, like a mere house of cards, amid the disillusion and sorrow of a multitude. Then Russia, her people oppressed by intolerable burdens, burst into revolution, whereof the reverberations, huge and far-reaching, were to influence the whole course of the War and its aftermath. Slogans she flung forth which hastened the World War to its close, and turned the military force of nations from international strife to internal conflict. The story of what I know of that pregnant struggle and its influence here must be told in another volume.

. . . . . . .

Though the Great War already dims to a waning memory, the world still wearies under its burdens. The British Budget of 1930–1931[2] amounted for all services to £822,000,000; of this sum no less than £523,000,000 was allocated to War Debts, War Pensions and preparation for further war: 63.6 per cent. being spent on war, 36.6 per cent. only being left for all the manifold needs of the country. In 1931–1932[2] out of a Budget of £793,000,000, despite all the talk of disarmament and the dwindling of War Pensions, a sum of £477,000,000 was spent on War Debts, War Pensions and War preparation: 60.4 per cent. of the revenue, as compared with 39.6 per cent. on the Peace services. For the year 1932–1933 the National Government estimated that its "Economy" Budget would amount to £789,000,000, of which £461,000,000 will go for War Debts, War Pensions and War preparations: 58.7 per cent. for war, 41.6 per cent. for all other needs.

A large proportion of the sums allocated in each Budget to the War charges is absorbed by the immense burden of debt. In 1930, £53,500,000 went for War Pensions, £113,000,000 for the Army, Navy and

[1] Adapted from *Inter-Ally Debts*, by H. E. Fisk, Bankers' Trust Company, New York, 1924.

[2] Calculated from the Finance Accounts.

Air Services, and £378,000,000 for debts—so much for usury! It is not generally realised that the Internal War Debt to British subjects who lent their money to the Government during the War far surpassed the External War Debt. In 1931 the nominal value of the Internal War Debt amounted to £6,463,000,000, the nominal value of the External Debt to £1066,700,000. The Conversion scheme by which £2,080,000,000 of 5 per cent. War Loan was converted to 3½ per cent. stock, with a tax free bonus of £1 per cent., to be spent or to be re-invested at will, applied to one-third of the National Debt. It was estimated that this Conversion plan would lighten the Budget by £23,000,000, the greater part of the load of debt still remaining!

Even so militarism remains unsatisfied and calls for increased expenditure for war preparedness. Mimic air battles and films supported by the Navy League, depicting attempted invasions are now employed to prepare the popular mind for the next conflict. As I pen these last words comes the letter from a, to me, unknown soldier, "one of the youngest warrant officers in the Canadian Army":

"In 1916 a bursting shell struck me directly over the eye, eliminating me from the greatest drama of all time. Since then many operations and a fading vision have forced me to forego all the best things in life—just another of these so-called glories of war!"

Must these things be? Can we not free humanity from the enslaving burden of war preparedness which leads to war? Must the world see yet another blood bath, yet more slaughter and sacrifice for vain, ignoble objects? Shall we not take the way of human solidarity and mutual aid at this long last? I believe that humanity is advancing towards the establishment of the United States of the World, consolidated in a free Socialism, wherein all shall co-operate gladly in giving to the common stock according to their abilities and in receiving from its abundance according to their needs.

To me it is as certain as the coming of day after night that humanity will rise above the present competitive struggle for existence, assuring the necessities of life to every one of its members as a matter of course, creating a world polity to cater co-operatively for the needs of a world people. In that day the sad East End shall be joyous and beautiful as the Elysium of the Greeks and wars shall be no more.

# INDEX

# A NOTE TO READERS

We hope you have enjoyed this Cresset Library edition and would like to take this opportunity to invite you to put forward your suggestions about books that might be included in the series.

The Cresset Library was conceived as a forum for bringing back books that we felt should be widely available in attractively designed and priced paperback editions. The series themes can be loosely described as social, cultural, and intellectual history though, as you can see from the list of published titles at the front of this book, these themes cover a broad range of interest areas.

If you have read or know of books that fall into this category which are no longer available or not available in paperback, please write and tell us about them. Should we publish a book that you have suggested we will send you a free copy upon publication together with three other Cresset Library titles of your choice.

Please address your letter to Claire L'Enfant at:-

Century Hutchinson
FREEPOST
London
WC2N 4BR

There is no need to stamp your envelope.

We look forward to hearing from you.

THE CRESSET LIBRARY